THE ILLUSTRATED BOOK
of
WORLD RANKINGS

THE ILLUSTRATED BOOK

of

WORLD RANKINGS

George Thomas Kurian

1997 Library Reference Edition published by Sharpe Reference
Sharpe Reference is an imprint of M.E. Sharpe INC.

M.E. Sharpe INC.
80 Business Park Drive
Armonk, NY 10504

Library of Congress Cataloging-in-Publication Data

Kurian, George Thomas.
The illustrated book of world rankings / George Thomas Kurian.—4th ed.
p.   cm.
Rev. ed. of: The new book of world rankings. 3rd ed. c1991.
Includes index.
ISBN 1-56324-892-1 (alk. paper)
1. Statistics.
2. Social indicators.
3. Economic indicators.
4. Quality of life—Statistics.
I. Kurian, George Thomas. New book of world rankings.
II. Title.
HA155.K87   1997
310—DC20
96-46086
CIP

Printed and bound in the United States of America

The paper used in this publication meets the minimum requirements of American National Standard for Information Sciences—Permanence of Paper for Printed Library Materials
ANSI Z 39.48-1984

EB (c) 10 9 8 7 6 5 4 3 2 1

Les chiffres sont les signes de Dieu
(Statistics are signs from God)

Prior Roger Schultz of Taize

TABLE OF CONTENTS

SECTION XI. INDUSTRY & MINING

SECTION XII. ENERGY

SECTION XIII. LABOR

SECTION XIV. TRANSPORTATION & COMMUNICATIONS

SECTION XX. CRIME & LAW ENFORCEMENT

SECTION XXI. MEDIA

SECTION XXII. THE WORLD'S CITIES

PREFACE

THE ILLUSTRATED BOOK OF WORLD RANKINGS is designed as an international scorecard that compares and ranks over 190 nations of the world according to their performance in more than 300 key areas.

The output and refinement of international statistics have reached a level where it now seems possible, timely and logical to convert this raw data into indicators of comparative performance. Such rankings are widely used in business and industry—the *Fortune 500* list is perhaps the most familiar American example. Nation-states function within an environment as competitive as corporations, and an evaluation of their track records is vastly more significant.

THE ILLUSTRATED BOOK OF WORLD RANKINGS includes over 50,000 variables that measure national achievement by using no less than 300 specific performance yardsticks, making it one of the most comprehensive data bases ever attempted in the field of international affairs. Interpreted sensibly, the data in these rankings will help not only to explain and evaluate national behavior but sometimes even to predict it.

Numbers may be used to terrify as well as to comfort, to inform as well as to amuse, to encourage as well as to edify, to accuse as well as to honor, and the numbers in this book do all of these. Perhaps one of the most important contributions of these rankings is to test popular perceptions of national performance and environments. Most of us hold on to perceived notions of alien cultures, notions that are often stereotyped and embedded in prejudice. We may believe that Icelanders are the best read, Americans the most productive, Germans the most ingenious, Indians the poorest and so on. While the rankings bear out these perceptions in a number of cases, they disprove them even more often. Some of these rankings can also tell us what makes the nations tick; why some of them are rich while others are powerless and dependent; why some are cauldrons of change, while others are mired in inertia. An effort has been made in each ranking to briefly analyze and interpret the data, but the analyses hew closely to the framework of facts; there has been no attempt to predict trends or force conclusions, although the temptation to do so has frequently been very great.

THE ILLUSTRATED BOOK OF WORLD RANKINGS is not simply concerned with bestowing superlatives (although it indirectly measures excellence) but with establishing the proper rung on which each nation stands. All nations for which comparable data are available are represented in the rank-lists, even those that are not currently independent. Only in the rhetoric of the United Nations General Assembly are all nations equal, but in the real world of nations inequality is the rule, and this work underscores just how unequal the nations are in each area of performance.

The selection of data to be included was based on five concepts: availability, comparability, usability, reliability and rankability. Much of the available data was derived from the publications of the United Nations, the World Bank, the International Monetary Fund and the U.S. Agency for International Development, the four principal agencies engaged in the collection of international statistics. Despite the efforts of these agencies, there are a number of subjects on which there are no data for any country and others for which available data are fragmentary. In the *UN Statistical Yearbook* there is only one complete table—"Population"—which provides data for each country. Even in this table the figures for many countries represent estimates and conjectures based on sample surveys.

From this pool of available data my first task was to select comparable data, i.e., series that have information on at least 20 countries. The problems of comparability are discussed in detail below.

The third element is usability. Do the figures really tell us something? Does the ranking add to our knowledge or give us some new insight? Does it provide a backdrop to some emerging trend, or a clue to some problem or solution?

The fourth element is reliability. Have the statistics been collected by an international organization without any revealed bias? If they were collected by national organizations, have they been checked for reliability and verified through independent sources?

The fifth element is rankability. Not all valid data are rankable; the spread between the highest and the lowest units may be too small in some cases to be statistically significant. For example, the age of suffrage varies only by a few years among countries. As emphasized earlier we are treating inequalities, and where there are no discernible inequalities, ranking becomes pointless.

One significant feature of the work is that the geographical coverage is as complete as the sources permit. Another is the broad-spectrum characteristic of the indicators themselves. With so many rankings, every important segment of national activity has been included. Some crucial subjects, such as defense spending, have been examined from different angles: per capita, as percentage of GNP and so on. The comprehensiveness of the list of rankings is essential since what may be considered of minor importance in large industrialized countries may be critical for small countries. The production of phosphates, for example, is more important for Nauru than even GNP or population. Indeed, with the growing web of interdependence, some apparently trivial indicators can affect the economies of superpowers.

One source of unending despair in international statistics is the comparability of data. Strictly, data used in rankings should be based on identical definitions, relate to the same calendar year or other base period, use the same techniques of collection, and be presented in the same form. Few, if any, of these conditions are ideally met in the rankings in this book. First of all, definitions vary from country to country even for terms that one might imagine could be defined only in one way, such as birth, death, marriage, household etc. Secondly, the year or base period varies even more widely. Agricultural or housing censuses are held once in every 20 or 30 years, and sometimes censuses are begun but never completed because of lack of funds or because of a change of government in the intervening period. There are also discontinuities in the publication of collected data resulting from political instability or civil war. Thirdly, the methodology and techniques of data collection vary from country to country.

Only a few countries have the necessary personnel skilled in data-gathering and data analysis procedures. Small countries, faced with the constant demand for statistics beyond the resources of their trained personnel to collect, may find ingenious ways of reporting fabricated data. Given these circumstances, I have invariably taken *the best available data for the latest available year* for each country. In practice this means that data for varying years have been used together and some of the information may go back to the 1960s. If some readers feel this method offends scientific requirements, they should remember that these rankings can only reflect the state of the art in international statistics; the rankings are no better and no worse than the sources from which they are derived.

A further caveat must be entered here about the quality and reliability of data on developing countries. In general there is a direct relationship between the quality and availability of data and the level of economic development. This is attributable not only to the lack of resources and expertise in developing countries but also to deliberate distortions of facts. Many of the developing countries manipulate data to suit their self-image. Because the appearance of economic might or of rapid development or of a literate and healthy population are important national assets, data in these areas may be modified to back up the official claims. (In one recent case with an ironic twist, Singapore which has had phenomenal economic growth in recent years, has been accused of doctoring or at the very least misinterpreting various economic indicators to prove that it is poorer than it is in order to continue to qualify for the special concessions granted developing countries by the international financial agencies.) In addition, there is a prohibition against collection and publication of data in some developing countries. There are many more countries that consider dissemination of data about their failing economies undesirable for political reasons. Data on developing countries are therefore subject to more serious qualifications and should be used with greater caution.

It must be pointed out here that in most cases only the aggregate or total figures have been derived from the sources cited and that per capita figures or share of total figures are based on my own calculations. In general an effort has been made to present the rankings in their most meaningful form, particularly by minimizing the impact of sheer physical size on national performance. Because the book is aimed at a general rather than specialized audience, I have also tried to avoid, perhaps not always successfully, the scholarly trappings and buzzwords that may turn off the lay reader. Technical notes are limited to the bare minimum. Scholars who need more information on the vintage and quality of the data and the methodology used for collecting data in each case are advised to consult the source or sources cited at the end of each ranking.

I wish to acknowledge that this book, like many others before it, could not have been written without the support and encouragement of my wife, Annie Kurian.

Every effort has been made to make the work as comprehensive, up to date and accurate as possible. However, errors and inadequacies (for which the author assumes full responsibility) are inevitable in a work of such a large scope, and the author welcomes criticisms, corrections and suggestions for inclusion in future editions.

GEORGE THOMAS KURIAN

NOTES ON FORMAT AND ENTRY ORDER

Each ranking (in some cases a group of related rankings) is preceded by an introduction highlighting the salient features and peculiarities of the topic covered in the ranking. In all but a few cases the ranked nations are divided into Top 10, Upper Middle, Lower Middle and Bottom 10. Where countries have the same values, they are ranked alphabetically.

Coverage. Unless otherwise noted, all data in this edition refer to the years 1994 or 1995. There is usually a time lag of a year or two between collection of data by the major international organizations and their publication in book or electronic format. Rankings which are derived from published statistics suffer additional delays. However, careful students and observers who are interested in monitoring or analyzing trends will find that the rankings remain valid over a period of time.

Because the rankings hew as closely as possible to the original sources, the deficiencies of these sources are sometimes reflected in the rank order. Even standard sources such as the *UN Statistical Yearbook,* do not provide data for nonreporting countries. Users sometimes wonder why countries like the United States do not appear in certain rankings. They have to remember that the international statistical reporting systems are far from perfect, and that there is a long way to go before all countries are represented in every ranking.

PROLOGUE

THE USE OF STATISTICS

A reader confronted with the over 50,000 pieces of data in this book might well ask the questions: What do they tell us? How do they add to our knowledge of the world?

Justice Louis Brandeis once remarked that nothing so clearly proved the finiteness of human intelligence as its inability to truly comprehend the number billion. For example, if *every minute* had been counted since the day Christ was born, the number would have reached 1 billion, in 1902. There are large numbers that one can grasp only in the gross, without understanding their true significance. Yet, this book is full of millions and billions and some figures that are in the trillions.

The learning process starts, as Paul Lazarsfeld said, only when one attaches a number to an idea. Numbers must therefore be looked upon as stages and as tools in the learning process, not as ends in themselves. Pythagoras contended that number is the sole inner reality of each thing. According to the *New Catholic Encyclopedia*:

> Number is a way of knowing the quantity, intensity, order and structure of material reality. With the aid of statistics and probability, number affords scientists the opportunity of predicting and controlling countable or measurable things or events with varying degrees of success.

A number thus relates to the discreteness, the individuality and what German philosophers, especially Immanuel Kant, described as *das Ding an sich* of each material object. A total subsumes all numbers within its sets but does not destroy or cancel any of them, for without each of them, the total would be materially different.

Thus, numbers have a philosophical basis, but they have a strong practical application as well. It has been estimated that a person of average intelligence can have a personal, caring and meaningful relationship with not more than 15 or 20 people; he or she could sustain and manage face-to-face, first-name-basis relationships with not more than 60 to 70 people; and he or she could be familiar with, keep track of or remember the names of not more than 500 to 600 people. With all others he or she can have only what is best described as a *statistical relationship*. Therefore, in a world of 5.6 billion people, it is important that we evolve statistical systems which will enable us to establish such a relationship with the masses of people living outside our own little "puddle." These people are the amorphous "they" who constitute the rest of the world for each one of us.

Statistics is a science of indicators by which to judge the total environment of man, or as the American Statistical Association defines it, "to illustrate the conditions and prospects of society." Quantification is thus an important preliminary step leading to "qualitification," to coin a word. It is a diagnostic tool enabling us not only to present large sets of data and describe activities, events and phenomena to those without direct, first-hand knowledge but also to assess growth, determine excellence, detect flaws and recognize dangers.

Viewed thus, numbers are important in themselves and in the trends and directions to which they point. Many of the policies and decisions that affect the lives of millions are taken on the basis of what Plato called the idols of the cave: opinions, prejudices, semantic distinctions, conventional wisdom and so on. Facts are the best cure for opinions, and statistical systems provide the bast antidote for biased and ill-informed judgments. Such statistics need not always be based on actual enumeration; they can be the assessments and guesstimates of knowledgeable people. And the statistics do not have to be exact figures, which may be rarely available and even where available may soon become out of date. Thus, when it is noted that the earth's population is 5.6 billion, the figure could be off the mark by several millions or by just a few hundreds. Nobody knows for sure and nobody ever will. (In any case, it changed while you were reading this sentence.) But what is important is the general order of magnitude. For the same reason, rounded figures are used in most rankings of this book, because they serve our purposes as well as exact figures.

The threefold purpose of the vast array of number in this book is, to present the totality of the human situation on the eve of the 21st century; to describe this totality in terms of the component national groups, i.e., to determine how the earth's total resource pie is cut into unequal shares and how each national share is multiplied or depleted; and to interpret the data in the wider context of national growth or decline and, where possible, to suggest solutions or alternative avenues of development.

Throughout this book nations and territories are treated as homogeneous units, whereas, in actuality, they are not. Nations are mosaics of differing racial linguistic, religious and social segments as well as occupational and age groups, each of them subdivided into still smaller units. Sometimes these groups share a common heritage, common economic interests or political experiences, and sometimes they do not. Even nations, such as South Korea or Japan, that rank high on the Ethnic and Linguistic Homogeneity Index, are homogeneous only in a cultural and ethnic sense and exhibit deep social fissures and divisions. Just as global aggregates mask variations within the component national groups, so do national aggregates presented in this book mask smaller variations within domestic groups. A statement such as "Only 10% of the Afghans are literate" might be true of a whole nation but could be inaccurate in reference to particular groups within a country. Similarly, there are immensely rich persons in statistically poor countries and extremely well-fed persons in statistically starving countries. While we invariably have to break up larger units into smaller ones to gain new insights into national behavior and performance, there are limits on such an effort because there are very little data available on groups or units smaller than nation-states or cities. Nations and cities are therefore the lowest levels at which we can attempt to construct a system of rankings such as this one.

Statistics can be presented in a number of meaningful ways (gross total, percentage, growth rate, per capita rate, ratio and so on), and in at least four primary modes: rhetorical, gross, comparative and interpretative. The rhetorical is the non-numerical or symbolic expression of a fact, such as when God tells Abraham his children will one day be more numerous than the sands of the seashore. The gross presentation simply establishes the broad order of magnitude, for example the statement: "There are 16 million Jews in the world today." The comparative presents the data in the context of the whole as well as in relation to others, for example, the statement: "Arabs outnumber Jews by 20 to 1." The interpretative tries to derive factual conclusions from the data, such as the statement: "The fact that the Jewish population is dispersed over 80 countries is a cause of their strength rather than a weakness, although the reverse is true of other peoples whose strengths lie in their concentration."

The statistics presented in this volume have three areas of use:

—*To understand the past.* Each datum in this book is the sum of historical experiences, resources, successes and failures and it cannot be understood without some reference to the past. The present is the legacy of the past and it will always remain a riddle to those who do not understand the past. For example, Senegal's prosperity today can be understood only in light of the French colonial policies of the 19th century. Furthermore, the international borders of almost all nations are the results of a series of historical accidents, and these borders, in turn, determine the size of a country, the level of population, the extent of natural resources and so on.

—*To analyze the present.* The rankings calibrate and audit national performance, compare such performances with other nation-states and territories, highlight successes and failures and assess national development strategies and ideologies.

—*To plan for the future.* Each datum is not merely a statement of fact but also a call to some sort of action, remedy or correction or at least concern. The statement, for example, that "75% of Chadians live in absolute poverty" is a direct pointer to a tragic situation and should be looked upon as a cry of agony rather than simple fact. Further, these numbers indicate where each country is heading, how fast and what efforts will be needed to get there.

For most people, statistics are dry bones. Yet, their very dry nature makes them valuable in a study of nations where our judgments must be grounded in fact. At the same time, it must be remembered that each "dry bone" in this book refers to human beings with flesh and blood or some situation relating to human beings. In the final analysis, therefore, this book is about people. But it requires intelligence, imagination and, even more than these, compassion to see beyond numbers and to grasp the vast and imponderable human predicament with which these numbers deal.

PROFILE OF THE PLANET

Rankings essentially show how the global pie is divided and what the national shares are. But at the same time, it is important to know how large the global pie is in each of the major sectors. The following section provides the key numbers that, when pieced together, provide a profile of the planet. The section also serves as a sort of instrument panel with the appropriate gauges showing how well spaceship earth is functioning.

GEOGRAPHY

Total area	510.072 million sq km
Total land area:	148.94 million sq km (29.2%)
Total water area:	361.132 million sq km (70.8%)
Total land boundaries:	250,883.64 km
Total coastlines:	356,000 km
Percentage of arable land:	10%
Percentage of permanent cropland:	1%
Percentage of meadows and pastures:	24%
Percentage of forests and woodland:	31%
Other	34%
Number of administrative divisions (Nations, Territories):	265

GEOLOGY

Mass of the Earth:	6,585,000,000,000,000,000,000 tons
Volume:	259,875,300,000 cubic miles
Polar circumference:	24,859.73 miles
Equatorial circumference:	24,901.46 miles
Equatorial diameter:	7,296.677 miles
Polar diameter:	7899.99 miles
Tilt of axis:	66.5 degrees
Revolutionary orbit:	1120 miles per minute, 67000 miles per hour, 590 million miles a year around the sun.
Active volcanoes:	600
Largest island:	Greenland
Largest continent:	Asia
Longest river:	Nile (4,145 miles)
Largest lake:	Caspian Sea (143,550 sq miles)
Deepest lake:	Lake Baykal in Siberia (5,715 feet)
Median temperature:	60°F
Glaciation:	10.5% of the land surface
Oceans:	4
Seas:	32

GLOBAL POPULATION

World	5,759 million
Males	2,900 million
Females	2,859 million
Ratio males to females	1.014
Population density, per sq. km.	42
Age distribution, as % of world:	
Infants, ages 0–4	11.5
Children, ages 5–14	20.4
Children under 15	31.9
Youths, ages 15–24	17.9
Seniors, ages 60 or over	9.5
Elderly, ages 65 or over	6.5
Aged, ages 80 or over	1.0
School-age children (6–11)	12.4
School-age children (12–14)	5.8
School-age children (15–17)	5.4
School-age youths (18–23)	10.8
Median age, years	25.1
Population average annual growth rate:	1.6%

VITAL STATISTICS

Population increase p.a.	93.3 million
Births p.a.	144.8 million
Deaths p.a.	51.5 million
Natural increase, % p.a.	1.63
Birth rate:	25/1000
Death rate:	6/1000

Infant mortality rate:	66/1000 live births
Under–5 mortality rate:	75/1000 live births
Life expectancy combined:	62
Life expectancy (Males)	60
Life expectancy (Females)	64
Total fertility rate:	3.2 children

CITIES WORLDWIDE

Metropolises (over 100,000 population)	3,780
Megacities (over 1 million population)	380
Urbanites (urban dwellers)	2,603 million
Ruralities (rural dwellers)	3,156 million
Urbanites, % of world	45.2
Ruralities, % of world	54.8
Urban poor	1,640 million
Urban slum dwellers	810 million
Population in urban agglomerations of 1 million or more as % of total population:	18
Average annual growth rate of urban population 1980–93	2.6%

FAMILIES

Families/homes/households	1,339 million
Household size, persons	4.3
Households headed by women, %	33
New families each year	34 million
% women 15–19 already married	23
Dependency ratio, %	62.6
Marriage rate per 1000 population p.a.	4
Divorce rate per 1000 population p.a.	0.4
Battered women	200 million
Women raped p.a.	15 million
Child-abuse incidents p.a.	90 million

MOTHERHOOD

Women of childbearing age (15–49)	1,341 million
Women of childbearing age % of world population	25.3
Fertility rate (births per woman)	3.17
Gross reproduction rate, per woman	1.55
Net reproduction rate, per woman	1.36
Contraceptive prevalence rate, %	56
Birth rate, % p.a. (males, females)	2.51
Birth p.a. (males, females)	144.8 million
Induced abortions, p.a.	60 million
Maternal mortality, p.a., total	500,000
Maternal mortality, due to abortion	200,000

CHILDREN

Infants (0–4 years)	662 million
Children (5–14)	1,175 million
School-age children (6–14)	1,048 million
Babies born malnourished, p.a.	10 million
Sick/ill children	600 million
Exploited child labor	50 million
Orphans	450 million
Abandoned children and infants	60 million
Homeless/familyless children	300 million
Magacity street children	100 million
Infant mortality (under 1), % p.a.	5.9
Toddler mortality (1–4 years), % p.a.	1.0

HUMAN RIGHTS AND ABUSES

The poor (living in poverty)	2.4 billion
Absolutely poor (in absolute poverty)	960 million
Undernourished	1.8 billion
Hungry	950 million
Severely malnourished	550 million
On verge of starvation	400 million
Starvation-related deaths p.a.	20 million
Without safe drinking water	1.3 billion
With unsafe water and bad sanitation	3.0 billion
Killed by dirty water, per day	25,000
With no access to electricity, %	41
With no access to radio or TV, %	67
Without adequate shelter	1.1 billion
With no shelter whatsoever	100 million
No access to schools	1 billion
Without money to buy food	1.1 billion
With no access to medical care	1.5 billion
Cave-dwellers	50 million
Stateless (with no nationality)	10 million
Prisoners	100 million
Prisoners being tortured	100,000
Disenfranchised (no control by vote)	2.1 billion
Non-readers (orate, illiterate adults)	1,392 million
Permanently unsettled refugees	14 million
Persons abused in childhood	300 million
Persons with human rights violated	2,590 million

RELIGION

Christians	1,923,812,000
Muslims	1,047,616,000
Nonreligious	931,409,000
Hindus	772,896,000
Buddhists	336,742,000
Atheists	231,150,000
Chinese folk-religionists	195,156,000
New-religionists	151,209,000
Tribal religionists	99,460,000
Sikhs	19,811,000
Jews	16,986,000
Shamanists	11,057,000
Confucians	6,357,000
Baha'is	5,892,000
Jains	4,003,000
Shintoists	3,399,000
Other religionists	19,541,000

ECONOMY

Gross Global Product:	$25.6 trillion
Gross Global Product average annual growth rate: 1990–95:	0.5%
Gross Global Product per capita:	$4600
Inflation rate: 1980–93:	19.6%
Developed nations:	5%
Developing nations:	50%
External debt:	$1.0 trillion
Gross International Reserves: 1994:	$1.4666 trillion
Growth rate of gross government consumption, 1980–93:	2.3%
Growth rate of private consumption, 1980–93:	3.1%
Growth rate of gross domestic investment, 1980–93:	3.2%
Industrial production average annual growth rate, 1994:	–1.1%
Production of automobiles:	32,222,375
Production of commercial vehicles:	12,369,371

FINANCE AND TRADE

Balance of trade, $	100 billion
Gold reserves, kg	32 million
Foreign economic aid, $ p.a.	60 billion
Average family income, $ p.a.	13,440
Transnationals (TNCs, multinationals)	10,800
Nongovernmental organizations (NGOs)	3,500
Millionaires (each worth over $1 million)	2.5 million
Billionaires (each worth over $1 billion)	400
Cost of advertising, $ p.a.	120 billion
Betting and gambling, $ p.a.	700 billion
Business failures (bankruptcies) p.a.	250,000

INDUSTRIALIZATION

Economically active persons	2.4 billion
Unemployed	100 million
Underemployed	600 million
Beggars	80 million
Scientists and engineers	38 million
Pure scientists	1 million
Scientific research, $ p.a.	125 billion
Industrial robots	14 million
Known chemicals	7 million
New chemicals created p.a.	10,000
Police officers	5.1 million
Professional firefighters	2 million
Lawyers	6 million
Labor migrants	150 million

AGRICULTURE AND LIVESTOCK

Agricultural land, sq. km.	46.5 million
Agricultural land, as % all land	34
Forest land, sq. km.	40.1 million
Harvested land as % all arable land	77
Global agricultural research, $ p.a.	9 billion
Chickens	9.0 billion
Rats	20 billion
Food/property destroyed by rats, $ p.a.	350 billion
Domestic pets	1 billion
Nomads and pastoralists	220 million
Cereal imports:	227,178,000 tons
Fertilizer consumption:	87,400 grams per hectare of arable land
Fish consumption:	7.2% of total daily protein supply
Tractors:	26.544 million
Fish catch:	27,245 million tons
World cattle population	12.946 billion
World sheep population	1.202 billion
World pig population	857.099 million
World horse population	61.620 million
World roundwood production:	3.450 billion cubic meters

TRANSPORTATION

Roads, length in miles	17 million
Bicycles	850 million
Rail passenger-miles p.a.	1,100 million
Air traffic, passenger-miles p.a.	950 billion
Airport and airfields	67,000
Sea freight, tons p.a.	3.6 billion
Seamen (merchant seafarers)	10 million
Merchant Marine:	21943 ships
Merchant Marine total DWT:	652,025,000
Rail Trackage:	1,201,337 km

ENERGY PRODUCTION

Primary energy, quads BTU p.a.	3.2 quadrillion
Coal, known reserves, metric tons	7,600 billion
Coal, kg mined per capita p.a.	1,870
Petroleum, known reserves, metric tons	91 billion
Oil, total recoverable reserves, barrels	1,635 billion
Oil, output in barrels p.a.	19.8 billion
Nuclear power produced, kilowatt hours p.a.	630 billion
Natural gas, known reserves, cubic meters	86 trillion
Total energy use:	8,035,058,000 metric tons
Energy use per capita:	1,434 kg
Energy use average annual growth rate: 1990–94	0.3%
GDP output per kg of energy:	$33
Commercial energy production average annual growth rate: 1980–92:	4%
Commercial energy consumption average annual growth rate: 1980–92:	4%
Electricity: Capacity:	2,864,000,000 kW
Production:	11,450,000 kWh
Per Capita:	2150 kWh

TRADE

Exports:	$3.63 trillion
Imports:	$3.82 trillion
Average annual growth rate of exports, 1990–94:	5.7%
Average annual growth rate of imports, 1990–94:	5.7%
Terms of trade (1987 = 100):	103

ENVIRONMENT

CO_2 emissions	18,821.8 million metric tons
CO_2 emissions per capita:	3.46 metric tons
Protected natural areas: Number	9849
Protected natural areas:	9315.5 (000 sq km)
Protected natural areas (as % of total area):	7.1%
Internal renewable water reserves per capita:	7.6 (000 m^3 per year)
Annual freshwater resources as % of total freshwater resources:	8%
Annual freshwater resources per capita:	(m^3) 638

LABOR

Total labor force:	2.667 billion
Labor force average annual growth rate, 1990–94:	1.7%
Percentage of labor force in agriculture:	48
Percentage of labor force in industry:	18
Percentage of labor force in services:	34

EDUCATION

Primary schools	3.2 million
Pupils in school	980 million
Adults, primary-educated	1.2 billion
Adults without primary education	2.7 billion
School teachers	39 million
University campuses	20,000
College students	65 million
Foreign students	3 million
Literacy (age 15+)	
Combined:	74%
Males:	81%
Females:	67%
Ratio of Females to Males in Secondary Schools:	81%
Female enrollment rate/secondary schools:	57
Male enrollment rate/secondary schools:	65
Tertiary enrollment combined ratio:	18
World expenditures on education:	$1.19 trillion

MILITARIZATION

Paramilitary troops	280 million
Military supply personnel	52 million
Combat aircraft	60,000
Nuclear warheads	65,000
Submarine-borne SLBMs	9,200
Chemical weapons, tons	300,000
Handguns (personal firearms)	600 million
Military expenditures:	$1 trillion
Total strength of armed forces:	208,201,000
Defense expenditures as % of GDP:	3.8%
Defense expenditures per capita:	$105
Arms exports:	$45.320 billion

HEALTH CARE

Persons in good health	1.1 billion
Physicians	5.2 million
Nurses and midwives	7.7 million
Dentists	500,000
Pharmacists	520,000
World pharmaceutical market, $ p.a.	130 billion
Hospitals	240,000
Hospital beds	18.2 million
Mental institutions	150,000
Health care costs, $ p.a.	2,500 billion
Population per doctor	3,780

ILLNESS AND DISEASE

Sufferers from disease or illness	1,152 million
Sufferers experiencing chronic pain	900 million
Nonsighted (totally blind)	28 million
Hearing-impaired (deaf)	320 million
Leprosy sufferers (lepers)	13 million
New malaria cases p.a.	400 million
Psychotics	51 million
Schizophrenics	10 million
Psychoneurotics	950 million
Suicides per year	410,000
Disables (handicapped)	1.6 billion
Handicapped children	340 million

Severely mentally-retarded	130 million
Arthritics	300 million
Persons not immunized	4 billion
Diarrheal deaths of under-5-year olds, p.a.	5 million
AIDS carriers	70 million
AIDS-related deaths p.a.	500,000
Tobacco smokers	650 million
Tobacco-related deaths p.a.	2.6 million
Drug addicts (illicit drug users)	65 million

TOURISM

Foreign tourists p.a.	350 million
Domestic tourists p.a.	3.7 billion
Registered hotel beds	15.0 million
Religious pilgrims p.a.	350 million

COMMUNICATION

Languages	9,500
Trade languages	700
Official state languages	95
Countries with own radio services	270
Countries with own TV services	150
Radio sets in use	1.8 billion
Radio hours broadcast p.a.	24 million
Television sets	850 million
TV hours broadcast	21 million
Ham radio operators	1.2 million
Daily newspapers	8,300
Newspaper circulation	590 million
Newsprint per global inhabitant, pounds p.a.	12
Mail, pieces p.a.	280 billion
Electronic mail messages p.a.	6 billion
Telephones	750 million
Direct-dial telephones	710 million
Telephone calls made, p.a.	120 billion
Fax machines	35 million
Videocassette recorders (VCRs)	500 million
Cinemas	250,000
Cinema seats	75 million
Cinema attendees p.a.	15 billion
General-purpose computers	150 million
Computer sales p.a.	35 million
Computer power, MIPS (world total)	29 million
Electronic bulletin boards	100,000
Internet computer users	18 million
Paper consumption:	70.2 million metric tons
Long films produced:	4,615

CRIME

Crimes (registered) p.a.	500 million
Property crimes p.a.	100 million
Violent crimes p.a.	27 million
Criminals	550 million
Murders p.a.	950,000
Terrorist incidents p.a.	4,000
Cost of all varieties of crime, $ p.a.	3,300 billion
White-collar crime, $ p.a.	1,000 billion
Financial fraud, $ p.a.	900 billion
Organized crime, $ p.a.	600 billion
Credit card fraud, $ p.a.	550 million
Alcohol/liquor expenditures, $ p.a.	380 billion
World purchases of cigarettes, $ p.a.	290 billion
Illegal drug traffic, $ p.a.	150 billion
Shoplifting, $ p.a.	95 billion
Computer crime, $ p.a.	60 billion
Major art thefts, $ p.a.	25 billion
Pornography, $ p.a.	20 billion
Automobile thefts, $ p.a.	20 billion

STATUS OF WOMEN

Global female population	2,859 million
% literate among women	56
Female life expectancy, years	64.0
Women denied full rights or equality	2,500 million
% world income received by women	10
% world property owned by women	1
Women as % of all poor	70

Women as % of all illiterates	66
Women as % of all refugees	80
Women as % of all ill/sick	75
Female urban poor	700 million
Female urban slum dwellers	320 million

LITERATURE

Adult population (over 15)	3,937 million
Literate	2,545 million
Nonliterate	1,392 million
Literate, % of adults	54.7
Nonliterate, % of adults	45.3
New book titles yearly	880,000
Books printed yearly	30 billion
Scientific journals	350,000
Scientific articles published yearly	2 million
Periodicals	130,000
Magazines	500,000
Encyclopedias	500
General encyclopedias	70
Subject encyclopedias	430
Bookshops	600,000
Public libraries	270,000
Library volumes (books)	3.7 billion

GEOPOLITICAL WORLDS

Group I (UN terminology)	*1,126 million*
Europe	516 million
Northern America	292 million
Oceania	29 million
Eurasia (former U.S.S.R.)	289 million
Group II	*4,633 million*
Africa	744 million
Latin America	482 million
China	1,238 million
India	931 million
Other Asia	1,238 million
GLOBE	*5,759 million*

Source: David B. Barrett in George Kurian and Graham T.T. Molitor (ed): *Encyclopedia of the Future* (Macmillan)

THE ILLUSTRATED BOOK
of
WORLD RANKINGS

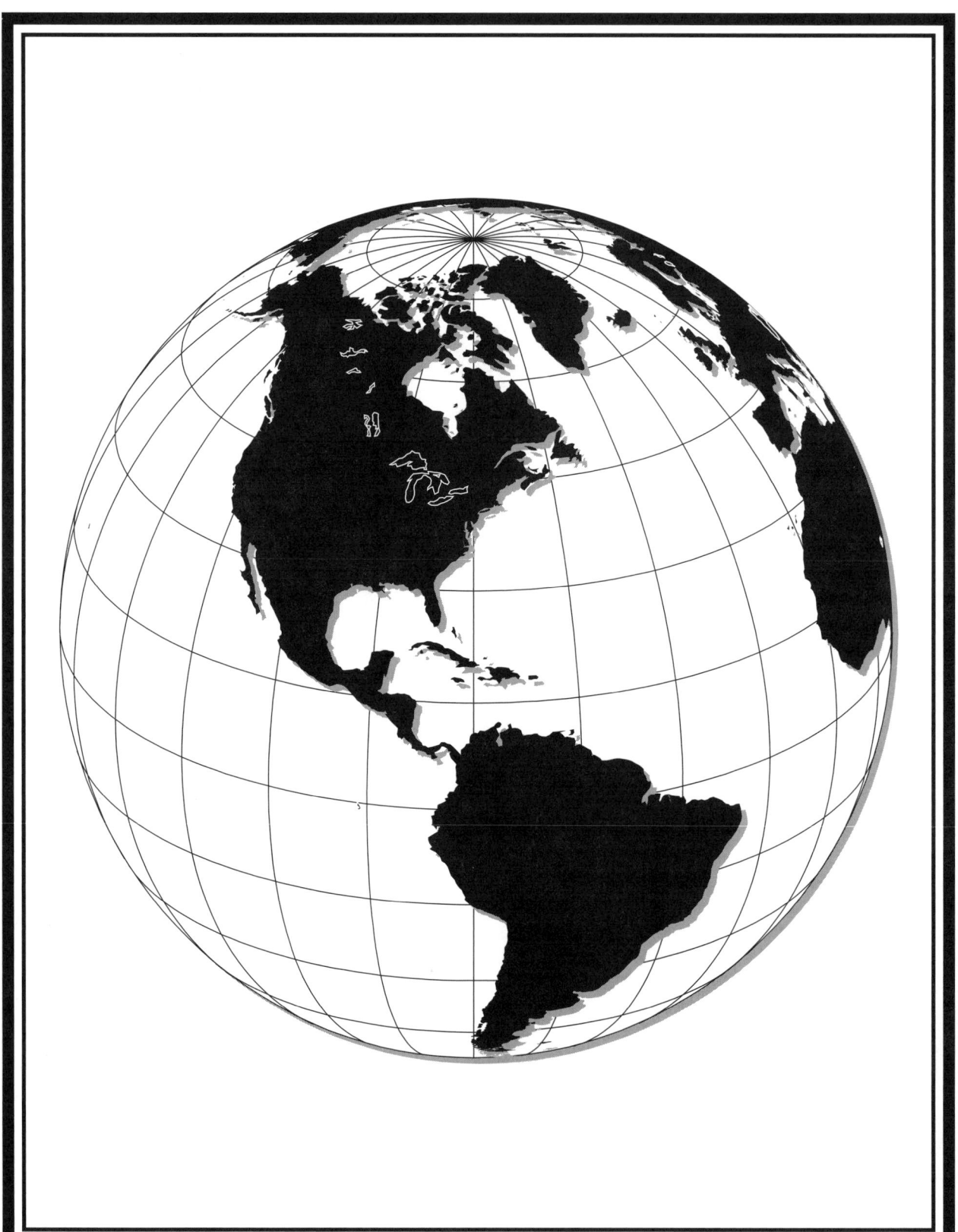

Section

I

GEOGRAPHY
& CLIMATE

Geography is the gateway to the study of nations. The earth's 135 million sq km (52 million sq mi), excluding Antarctica's 16 million sq km (6 million sq mi), are divided so unevenly among nations that it could be described as the original inequality, as theologians might describe original sin. Geographers, historians, politicians and military strategists group these countries differently according to the conceptual bases or biases of their respective disciplines. The United Nations has adopted a scheme described in World *Population Prospects, 1970–2000* that refers to eight macro regions on the basis of demographic characteristics. Six of these macro regions are further subdivided into 22 regions. Using a broader approach that takes into account geographic and political features as well as demographic ones, we can discern at least 10 zones. In descending order of size they are:

Rank	Country	Million sq km
1	Russia, CIS, Eastern Europe & Mongolia	24.8
2	North America	24.0
3	Middle East & North Africa	18.1
4	South America	17.6
5	Africa South of the Sahara	17.0
6	East Asia	10.8
7	Oceania	7.7
8	South Asia	6.1
9	Europe	3.9
10	South East Asia	3.9

Physical size is the most important equation in the calculus of power. Not only does size determine living space but it also affects our perceptions of national strength. It is true that many small nations because of their strategic location or financial clout (Israel, Singapore and Switzerland are obvious examples) have a disproportionately large impact, but by and large the so-called superpowers hog the stage of world affairs.

This chapter also deals with five other areas that are purely geographical in character and content: the coldest, the warmest, the wettest and the highest, as well as coastline. The first ranks countries by the length of their international borders. A long coastline and a long border may confer some advantages, but, as the United States is discovering, they also pose problems of surveillance against smugglers and illegal migrants.

1. INTERNATIONAL BORDERS

Among the principal responsibilities of a sovereign nation is the defense of its frontiers. Because most national boundaries were determined by historical accidents or were settled through warfare or by colonization, many borders appear as arbitrary lines drawn across maps. The length of the borders, the number of neighbors, the political compatibility of these neighbors and the pressures of irredentist claims or territorial ambitions are among the more crucial determinants of foreign policy. Although a long border may require more customs and immigration checkpoints and surveillance, some of the longest borders are among the most peaceful in the world; the U.S.-Canadian border is a case in point. On the other hand, the sensitivity of the frontier is often inversely related to the homogeneity of the neighbors. The most heavily armed border, however, is that which divides South and North Korea. Also, frontiers are more important for landlocked nations than for those with access to the sea.

Rank	Country	Land Boundaries (km)	Rank	Country	Land Boundaries (km)	Rank	Country	Land Boundaries (km)
TOP 10			51	Germany	3,621	102	Georgia	1,461
1	China	22,143	52	Kenya	3,446	103	Tunisia	1,424
2	Russia	20,139	53	Tanzania	3,402	104	Moldova	1,389
3	Brazil	14,691	54	Guinea	3,399	105	Belgium	1,385
4	India	14,103	55	Burkina	3,192	106	Oman	1,374
5	United States	12,248	56	Poland	3,114	107	Bosnia & Herzegovina	1,369
6	Kazakhstan	12,012	57	Cote d'Ivoire	3,110	108	Slovakia	1,355
7	Zaire	10,271	58	Belarus	3,098	109	Lithuania	1,273
8	Argentina	9,665	59	Zimbabwe	3,066	110	Armenia	1,254
9	Canada	8,893	60	Nepal	2,926	111	Nicaragua	1,231
10	Mongolia	8,114	61	France	2,892	112	Portugal	1,214
			62	Malawi	2,881	113	Greece	1,210
UPPER MIDDLE			63	Uganda	2,698	114	Latvia	1,078
11	Sudan	7,697	64	Egypt	2,689	115	Bhutan	1,075
12	Colombia	7,408	65	Malaysia	2,669	116	Netherlands	1,027
13	Mali	7,243	66	Senegal	2,640	117	Israel	1,006
14	Peru	6,940	67	Finland	2,628	118	Slovenia	999
15	Pakistan	6,774	68	Turkey	2,627	119	Burundi	974
16	Bolivia	6,743	69	Indonesia	2,602	120	Sierra Leone	958
17	Algeria	6,343	70	Cambodia	2,572	121	Lesotho	909
18	Uzbekistan	6,221	71	Gabon	2,551	122	Rwanda	893
19	Chile	6,171	72	Norway	2,515	123	United Arab Emirates	867
20	Chad	5,968	73	Romania	2,508	124	Macedonia	748
21	Myanmar (Burma)	5,876	74	Austria	2,496	125	Gambia	740
22	Niger	5,697	75	Guyana	2,462	126	Guinea-Bissau	724
23	Zambia	5,664	76	Somalia	2,366	127	Albania	720
24	Afghanistan	5,529				128	Costa Rica	639
25	Congo	5,504	**LOWER MIDDLE**			129	Estonia	557
26	Iran	5,440	77	Syria	2,253	130	Panama	555
27	Ethiopia	5,311	78	Yugoslavia	2,234	131	El Salvador	545
28	Central African Republic	5,203	79	Sweden	2,205	132	Equatorial Guinea	539
29	Angola	5,198	80	Ghana	2,093	133	Swaziland	535
30	Laos	5,083	81	Azerbaijan	2,013	134	Belize	516
31	Mauritania	5,074	82	Ecuador	2,010	135	Djibouti	508
32	Venezuela	4,993	83	Morocco	2,002	136	Kuwait	464
33	South Africa	4,973	84	Benin	1,989	137	Lebanon	454
34	Thailand	4,863	85	Hungary	1,952	138	Brunei	381
35	Cameroon	4,591	86	Spain	1,903	139	Ireland	360
36	Mozambique	4,571	87	Italy	1,899	140	United Kingdom	360
37	Ukraine	4,558	88	Czech Republic	1,880	141	Luxembourg	359
38	Mexico	4,538	89	Switzerland	1,852			
39	Saudi Arabia	4,415	90	Croatia	1,843	**BOTTOM 10**		
40	Libya	4,383	91	Bulgaria	1,808	142	Dominican Republic	275
41	Bangladesh	4,246	92	Yemen	1,746	143	Haiti	275
42	Nigeria	4,047	93	Suriname	1,707	144	Korea, South	238
43	Botswana	4,013	94	Guatemala	1,687	145	Andorra	125
44	Namibia	3,935	95	Korea, North	1,673	146	Liechtenstein	78
45	Paraguay	3,920	96	Togo	1,647	147	Denmark	68
46	Kyrgyzstan	3,878	97	Eritrea	1,630	148	Qatar	60
47	Vietnam	3,818	98	Jordan	1,619	149	San Marino	39
48	Turkmenistan	3,736	99	Liberia	1,585	150	Cuba	29
49	Tajikistan	3,651	100	Uruguay	1,564	151	Monaco	4.4
50	Iraq	3,631	101	Honduras	1,520			

Source: *World Data*

2. NATIONAL COASTLINES

A coastline is one of the most strategic advantages and natural resources of a nation. It ensures free and unfettered participation in world commerce, provides access to coastal fishing grounds and extends territorial sovereignty over offshore mineral deposits. It may also promote the development of a strong navy and the creation of urban settlements and free trade zones around ports and harbors.

Attractive beaches often bring in additional tourist revenues.

The problem of nations without coastlines has engaged the attention of the United Nations and has been the subject of many international conferences, There are 42 such landlocked nations in the world, 14 in Europe, two in Latin America, 11 in Asia and 15 in Africa. They are: Bolivia and Paraguay in Latin

America; Czech Republic, Slovakia, Macedonia, Hungary, Switzerland, Austria, Liechtenstein, San Marino, Andorra, Luxembourg, Moldova, Belarus, Armenia and the Vatican in Europe; Afghanistan, Bhutan, Nepal, Laos, Turkmenistan, Kyrgyzstan, Tajikistan, Uzbekistan, Azerbaijan, Kazakhstan and Mongolia in Asia; and Malawi, Zimbabwe, Botswana, Zambia, Swaziland, Lesotho, Central African Republic, Mali, Niger, Ethiopia, Chad, Burkina, Uganda, Rwanda and Burundi in Africa.

Rank	Country	Coastline (km)	Rank	Country	Coastline (km)	Rank	Country	Coastline (km)
TOP 10			51	Oman	2,092	102	Tonga	419
1	Canada	243,791	52	Myanmar (Burma)	1,930	103	Western Samoa	403
2	Indonesia	54,716	53	Yemen	1,906	104	Cameroon	402
3	Russia	37,653	54	Morocco	1,835	105	Sierra Leone	402
4	Philippines	36,289	55	Portugal	1,793	106	Guyana	400
5	Japan	29,751	56	Haiti	1,771	107	Belize	386
6	Australia	25,760	57	Libya	1,770	108	Suriname	386
7	Norway	21,925	58	Turkmenistan	1,768	109	Albania	362
8	United States	19,924	59	Angola	1,600	110	Trinidad and Tobago	362
9	New Zealand	15,134	60	Namibia	1,489	111	Bulgaria	354
10	China	14,500	61	Ireland	1,448	112	Guinea-Bissau	350
			62	Tanzania	1,424	113	Comoros	340
UPPER MIDDLE			63	Estonia	1,393	114	Guinea	320
11	Greece	13,676	64	Sri Lanka	1,340	115	Djibouti	314
12	United Kingdom	12,429	65	United Arab Emirates	1,318	116	Georgia	310
13	Mexico	9,330	66	Costa Rica	1,290	117	El Salvador	307
14	Brazil	7,491	67	Dominican Republic	1,288	118	Guatemala	306
15	Turkey	7,200	68	Eritrea	1,151	119	Equatorial Guinea	296
16	India	7,000	69	Tunisia	1,148	120	Israel	273
17	Chile	6,435	70	Kiribati	1,143	121	Lebanon	225
18	Croatia	5,790	71	Fiji	1,129	122	Romania	225
19	Solomon Islands	5,313	72	Finland	1,126	123	Sao Tome e Principe	209
20	Papua New Guinea	5,152	73	Pakistan	1,046	124	Yugoslavia	199
21	Italy	4,996	74	Jamaica	1,022	125	Singapore	193
22	Argentina	4,989	75	Algeria	998	126	Syria	193
23	Iceland	4,988	76	Cape Verde	965	127	Mauritius	177
24	Spain	4,964				128	Congo	169
25	Madagascar	4,828	**LOWER MIDDLE**			129	Bahrain	161
26	Malaysia	4,675	77	Nicaragua	910	130	Brunei	161
27	Cuba	3,738	78	Gabon	885	131	St. Lucia	158
28	Bahamas	3,542	79	Nigeria	853	132	Antigua and Barbuda	153
29	Vietnam	3,444	80	Sudan	853	133	Dominica	148
30	France	3,427	81	Honduras	820	134	Malta	140
31	Denmark	3,379	82	Azerbaijan	800	135	St. Kitts and Nevis	135
32	Colombia	3,280	83	Mauritania	754	136	Benin	121
33	Thailand	3,219	84	Uruguay	680	137	Grenada	121
34	Sweden	3,218	85	Cyprus	648	138	Lithuania	108
35	Somalia	3,025	86	Maldives	644	139	Bermuda	103
36	Kazakhstan	2,909	87	Bangladesh	580	140	Barbados	97
37	South Africa	2,881	88	Liberia	579	141	St. Vincent	84
38	Venezuela	2,800	89	Qatar	563	142	Gambia	80
39	Ukraine	2,782	90	Ghana	539			
40	Saudi Arabia	2,640	91	Kenya	536	**BOTTOM 10**		
41	Vanuatu	2,528	92	Latvia	531	143	Belgium	64
42	Korea, North	2,495	93	Senegal	531	144	Iraq	58
43	Panama	2,490	94	Cote d'Ivoire	515	145	Togo	56
44	Mozambique	2,470	95	Puerto Rico	501	146	Zaire	37
45	Egypt	2,450	96	Kuwait	499	147	Slovakia	32
46	Iran	2,440	97	Poland	491	148	Nauru	30
47	Peru	2,414	98	Seychelles	491	149	Jordan	26
48	Korea, South	2,413	99	Netherlands	451	150	Tuvalu	24
49	Germany	2,389	100	Cambodia	443	151	Bosnia & Herzegovina	20
50	Ecuador	2,237	101	Uzbekistan	420	152	Monaco	4.1

Source: *World Data*

3. TOTAL LAND AREA

There are approximately 135 million sq km (52.5 million sq mi) of land surface in the world divided among 188 nations. Of these, the top 17 nations occupy nearly two-thirds of the total land mass and the top 71 occupy nearly 80%. But many of the biggest countries have enormous areas of desert and wasteland; only about 26% of Russia is arable, cultivated or natural pastureland and much of the rest is permafrost. Canada has much less arable or cultivated land (6%) and China a little more (11%). This factor scales these giants down in size considerably so that they roughly match the United States, which has 45% of its territory in arable land or cultivated pasture. Farther down the scale, Australia, India and Argentina have almost half or more of their land cultivated or arable. Perceptions of territorial extent must therefore be qualified by the determining factor of usable or inhabitable land area.

Territorial extent is based on de facto political sovereignty and does not reflect border disputes or border claims. But following UN and U.S. State Department usage, territories under Turkish occupation in Cyprus, under Israeli occupation in the West Bank, and under Moroccan occupation in the former Western Sahara have been excluded from the national territories of Turkey, Israel and Morocco respectively.

TOP 10*
Total Land Area in Square Miles

Kazakhstan 1,049,200
Sudan 966,757
Argentina 1,073,518
Russia 6,592,800
India 1,222,243
Australia 2,986,200
Brazil 3,286,500
Canada 3,849,674
United States 3,679,192
China 3,696,100

*The Top 10 makes up 55% of the total land area of the world.

Country	Area sq mi	Country	Area sq mi	Country	Area sq mi
UPPER MIDDLE		36 Turkey	300,948	62 Congo	132,047
11 Algeria	919,595	37 Chile	292,135	63 Finland	130,559
12 Zaire	905,446	38 Zambia	290,586	64 Malaysia	127,584
13 Saudi Arabia	865,000	39 Myanmar (Burma)	261,228	65 Vietnam	127,246
14 Mexico	756,066	40 Afghanistan	251,825	66 Norway	125,050
15 Indonesia	741,052	41 Somalia	246,000	67 Cote d'Ivoire	123,847
16 Libya	678,400	42 Central African Republic	240,324	68 Poland	120,728
17 Iran	632,457	43 Madagascar	226,658	69 Oman	118,150
18 Mongolia	604,800	44 Kenya	224,961	70 Italy	116,334
19 Niger	496,900	45 Botswana	224,607	71 Philippines	115,860
20 Peru	496,225	46 France	210,026	72 Burkina	105,946
21 Chad	495,755	47 Yemen	205,356	73 Ecuador	105,037
22 Mali	482,077	48 Ukraine	203,100	74 New Zealand	104,454
23 Agola	481,354	49 Thailand	198,115	75 Gabon	103,347
24 South Africa	472,281	50 Spain	194,898	76 Guinea	94,926
25 Colombia	440,831	51 Turkmenistan	188,500	77 United Kingdom	94,251
26 Ethiopia	437,794	52 Cameroon	183,569	78 Uganda	93,070
27 Bolivia	424,164	53 Papua New Guinea	178,704	79 Ghana	92,098
28 Mauritania	398,000	54 Morocco	177,117	80 Romania	91,699
29 Egypt	385,229	55 Sweden	173,732	81 Laos	91,429
30 Tanzania	364,017	56 Uzbekistan	172,700	82 Guyana	83,044
31 Nigeria	356,669	57 Iraq	167,975	83 Belarus	80,153
32 Venezuela	352,144	58 Paraguay	157,048	84 Kyrgyzstan	78,600
33 Pakistan	339,697	59 Zimbabwe	150,872	85 Senegal	75,951
34 Namibia	318,580	60 Japan	145,850	86 Syria	71,498
35 Mozambique	313,661	61 Germany	137,823	87 Cambodia	70,238

Rank	Country	Area sq mi		Rank	Country	Area sq mi		Rank	Country	Area sq mi
88	Uruguay	68,037		122	Togo	21,925		158	Gambia	4,127
89	Tunisia	63,378		123	Croatia	21,829		159	Lebanon	3,950
90	Suriname	63,251		124	Bosnia & Herzegovina	19,741		160	Cyprus	3,572
91	Bangladesh	57,295		125	Costa Rica	19,730		161	Puerto Rico	3,515
92	Nepal	56,827		126	Slovakia	18,933		162	Brunei	2,226
93	Tajikistan	55,300		127	Dominican Republic	18,704		163	Trinidad and Tobago	1,980
94	Greece	50,949		128	Bhutan	18,150		164	Cape Verde	1,557
95	Nicaragua	50,838		129	Estonia	17,462		165	Western Samoa	1,093
				130	Denmark	16,639		166	Luxembourg	999
LOWER MIDDLE				131	Netherlands	16,033		167	Mauritius	788
96	Korea, North	47,399		132	Switzerland	15,940		168	Comoros	719
97	Malawi	45,747		133	Taiwan	13,969		169	Sao Tome e Principe	386
98	Eritrea	45,300		134	Guinea-Bissau	13,948		170	Kiribati	313
99	Benin	43,500		135	Moldova	13,000		171	Dominica	290
100	Honduras	43,277		136	Belgium	11,787		172	Tonga	290
101	Bulgaria	42,855		137	Lesotho	11,720		173	Bahrain	268
102	Cuba	42,804		138	Armenia	11,500		174	Singapore	247
103	Guatemala	42,042		139	Albania	11,100		175	St. Lucia	238
104	Iceland	39,699		140	Solomon Islands	10,954		176	Andorra	181
105	Yugoslavia	39,449		141	Equatorial Guinea	10,831		177	Seychelles	176
106	Korea, South	38,330		142	Burundi	10,740		178	Antigua and Barbuda	171
107	Liberia	38,250		143	Haiti	10,695		179	Barbados	166
108	Hungary	35,920		144	Rwanda	10,169		180	St. Vincent	150
109	Portugal	35,574		145	Macedonia	9,928				
110	Jordan	34,342		146	Djibouti	8,950		**BOTTOM 10**		
111	Azerbaijan	33,400		147	Belize	8,867		181	Grenada	133
112	Austria	32,378		148	El Salvador	8,124		182	Malta	122
113	Czech Republic	30,450		149	Israel	7,992		183	Maldives	115
114	United Arab Emirates	30,000		150	Slovenia	7,821		185	St. Kitts and Nevis	104
115	Panama	29,157		151	Fiji	7,056		186	Liechtenstein	62
116	Sierra Leone	27,699		152	Kuwait	6,880		187	San Marino	24
117	Ireland	27,137		153	Swaziland	6,704		188	Bermuda	21
118	Georgia	26,900		154	Bahamas	5,382		189	Tuvalu	9.4
119	Sri Lanka	25,332		155	Vanuatu	4,707		190	Nauru	8.2
120	Lithuania	25,213		156	Qatar	4,412		191	Monaco	0.75
121	Latvia	24,946		157	Jamaica	4,244				

Source: *World Data*

4. HIGHEST ELEVATION

This ranking rates countries by the elevation of their highest point, often the highest national peak. Although the percentage of mountainous terrain in each country's land area would have been more meaningful, such statistics have never been compiled. Elevation might, however, give us a clue in this direction because the countries with the highest elevations are also very often the most mountainous.

Rank	Country	Elevation of Highest Point meters	ft		Rank	Country	Elevation of Highest Point meters	ft		Rank	Country	Elevation of Highest Point meters	ft
TOP 10					14	Myanmar (Burma)	6,096	20,000		30	Rwanda	4,532	14,870
1	China	8,848	29,028		15	Canada	5,950	19,520		31	Papua New Guinea	4,509	14,793
2	Nepal	8,848	29,028		16	Tanzania	5,894	19,340		32	Mongolia	4,362	14,311
3	Pakistan	8,611	28,250		17	Colombia	5,775	18,947		33	Guatemala	4,220	13,845
4	India	7,817	25,645		18	Iran	5,771	18,934		34	Morocco	4,165	13,665
5	Bhutan	7,541	24,740		19	Mexico	5,700	18,701		35	Malaysia	4,101	13,455
6	Russia	7,495	24,590		20	Kenya	5,199	17,058		36	Taiwan	3,997	13,113
7	Afghanistan	7,485	24,557		21	Turkey	5,185	17,011		37	Costa Rica	3,819	12,530
8	Argentina	7,485	24,557		22	Zaire	5,109	16,762		38	Austria	3,797	12,457
9	Chile	6,880	22,572		23	Indonesia	5,030	16,503		39	Japan	3,776	12,388
10	Peru	6,768	22,205		24	Venezuela	5,002	16,411		40	New Zeland	3,764	12,349
					25	Uganda	4,876	16,000		41	Yemen	3,760	12,336
UPPER MIDDLE					26	France	4,807	15,771		42	Greenland	3,700	12,139
11	Bolivia	6,400	21,000		27	Italy	4,731	15,521		43	Iraq	3,609	11,840
12	Ecuador	6,267	20,561		28	Switzerland	4,634	15,203		44	Lesotho	3,482	11,425
13	United States	6,194	20,320		29	Ethiopia	4,618	15,153		45	Spain	3,478	11,411

Rank	Country	Elevation of Highest Point meters	ft	Rank	Country	Elevation of Highest Point meters	ft	Rank	Country	Elevation of Highest Point meters	ft
46	Panama	3,477	11,410	80	Yemen	2,513	8,245	116	Suriname	1,286	4,218
47	South Africa	3,377	11,081	81	Poland	2,499	8,199	117	Central African Republic	1,280	4,200
48	Dominican Republic	3,175	10,417	82	Norway	2,470	8,104	118	Bangladesh	1,229	4,034
49	Libya	3,150	10,335	83	Cameroon	2,438	8,000	119	Botswana	1,219	4,000
50	Chad	3,145	10,318	84	Nicaragua	2,438	8,000	120	Israel	1,208	3,963
51	Vietnam	3,143	10,312	85	Mozambique	2,436	7,992	121	Equatorial Guinea	1,200	3,937
52	Saudi Arabia	3,133	10,279	86	El Salvador	2,417	7,933	122	Ireland	1,041	3,414
53	Lebanon	3,083	10,115	87	Somalia	2,406	7,894	123	Tonga	1,030	3,380
54	Malawi	3,048	10,000	88	Comoros	2,361	7,746	124	Hungary	1,015	3,330
55	Brazil	3,014	9,888	89	Jamaica	2,256	7,402	125	Togo	986	3,235
56	Algeria	3,003	9,852	90	Australia	2,228	7,310	126	Trinidad & Tobago	940	3,085
57	Germany	2,963	9,721	91	Sudan	2,133	7,000	127	Belize	914	3,000
58	Philippines	2,954	9,690	92	Zambia	2,133	7,000	128	Seychelles	912	2,993
59	Andorra	2,946	9,665	93	Iceland	2,119	6,952	129	Ghana	884	2,900
60	Bulgaria	2,925	9,596	94	Sweden	2,111	6,926	130	Grenada	840	2,757
61	Greece	2,917	9,570	95	Nigeria	2,042	6,699	131	Mauritius	826	2,711
62	Madagascar	2,880	9,450	96	Sao Tome & Principe	2,024	6,640	132	Cambodia	762	2,500
63	Honduras	2,870	9,400	97	Cuba	1,994	6,552	133	Burkina	717	2,352
64	Yugoslavia	2,863	9,393	98	Portugal	1,993	6,539	134	Mali	701	2,300
65	Guyana	2,835	9,304	99	Cyprus	1,952	6,406	135	Belgium	694	2,277
66	Cape Verde	2,829	9,281	100	Korea, South	1,950	6,398	136	Benin	610	2,001
67	Laos	2,816	9,242	101	Sierra Leore	1,947	6,390	137	Paraguay	609	1,998
68	Syria	2,814	9,232	102	Swaziland	1,862	6,109				
69	Albania	2,750	9,023	103	Guinea	1,828	6,000		**BOTTOM 10**		
70	Korea, North	2,744	9,003	104	Niger	1,798	5,900	138	Uruguay	609	1,998
71	Haiti	2,677	8,783	105	Jordan	1,754	5,755	139	Luxembourg	559	1,835
72	Czech Republic	2,654	8,707	106	Cote d'Ivoire	1,752	5,748	140	Senegal	487	1,600
73	Egypt	2,642	8,668	107	Burundi	1,706	5,600	141	Mauritania	457	1,500
74	Angola	2,620	8,595	108	Gabon	1,574	5,165	142	Netherlands	322	1,051
				109	Tunisia	1,544	5,065	143	Guinea-Bissau	300	1,000
	LOWER MIDDLE			110	United Arab Emirates	1,527	5,010	144	Denmark	173	568
75	Liechtenstein	2,599	8,527	111	Congo	1,500	4,921	145	Bahrain	135	443
76	Zimbabwe	2,595	8,517	112	Liberia	1,380	4,528	146	Bahamas	63	206
77	Thailand	2,595	8,514	113	United Kingdom	1,343	4,406	147	Maldives	24	80
78	Rumania	2,543	8,343	114	Finland	1,324	4,344				
79	Sri Lanka	2,524	8,281	115	Fiji	1,323	4,341				

Source: *World Book Encyclopedia*

5.WETTEST PLACES

Total annual world precipitation is estimated by the U.S. Geological Survey at 420,000 cubic km (102,000 cubic mi), of which 320,000 cubic km (78,000 cubic mi) falls on the oceans and is not of much use to man and 110,303 cubic km (24,000 cubic mi) falls on the land surface. By continents, Asia receives the most precipitation (32,690 cu km) and is followed by South America (29,335 cu km), Africa (20,780 cu km), North America (13,910 cu km), Europe (7,165 cu km) and Oceania (6,405 cu km). As with other natural resources, there is wide disparity in the distribution of rainfall. There are places in the Sahara region that receive rain only once in several years and even then only a few millimeters, while Cherrapunji in India receives on the average 2.95 cm (1.2 in.) every day of the year. Because precipitation ultimately determines the groundwater table, the volume of river runoff and the water balance, its absence or paucity can be critical. Nothing can be more damaging to human settlements, agriculture, livestock and indeed every form of human activity as the lack of rain, as was demonstrated so tragically in the Sahel in Africa in the early 1970s.

Rank	Country	TOP 10* Wettest Places	cm	in.
1	Cherrapunji, India		1,079.50	425.1
2	Andagoya, Colombia		713.74	281.1
3	Pago Pago, Samoa		492.76	193.6
4	Moulmein, Myanmar (Burma)		482.60	190.2
5	Tabing, Indonesia		444.50	175.4
6	Monrovia, Liberia		441.96	174.9
7	Conakry, Guinea		429.26	169.0
8	Kuching, Malaysia		391.16	153.7
9	Guadeloupe		355.60	140.4
10	Freetown, Sierra Leone		350.52	137.6

Each ⬤ represents 100 cm/39.4 in. of rainfall

*The Top 10 makes up 22% of the total highest recorded rainfall.

Rank	Country	Highest Recorded Rainfall cm	in.
UPPER MIDDLE			
11	Madang, Papua NewGuinea	347.98	137.2
12	Yakutat, United States	335.28	132.0
13	Brunei	332.74	131.0
14	Cayenne, French Guyana	320.04	126.1
15	Tulagi, Solomon Islands	312.42	123.4
16	Los Evangelistas, Chile	302.26	119.4
17	Suva, Fiji	297.18	117.1
18	Iquitos, Peru	274.32	107.7
19	Vaupes, Brazil	266.70	105.4
20	Libreville, Gabon	248.92	98.8
21	Tela, Honduras	243.84	96.1
22	Prince Rupert, Canada	241.30	95.3
23	Singapore	241.30	95.0
24	Seychelles	233.68	92.5
25	Colombo, Sri Lanka	233.68	92.3
26	Paramaribo, Suriname	231.14	91.0
27	Reunion	228.60	90.5
28	Georgetown, Guyana	226.06	88.7
29	Bolama, Guinea-Bissau	218.44	85.9
30	Hong Kong	215.90	85.1
31	Manila, Philippines	208.28	82.0
32	Martinique	203.20	80.4
33	Bergen, Nonway	200.66	78.8
34	Cocos (Keeling) Islands	198.12	78.2
35	Ho Chi Minh City, Vietnam	198.12	78.1
36	Abidjan, Cote d'Ivoire	195.58	77.1
37	Nagasaki, Japan	190.50	75.5
38	Santa Isabel, Equatorial Guinea	190.50	74.9
39	Belize	187.96	74.4
40	Dacca, Bangladesh	187.96	73.9
41	Taipei, Taiwan	185.42	72.7
42	Lagos, Nigeria	182.88	72.3
43	San Jose, CostaRica	180.34	70.8
44	Santa Elena, Venezuela	180.34	70.7
45	San Salvador, El Salvador	177.80	70.0
46	Thursday Island, Australia	170.18	67.5
47	Vientiane, Laos	170.18	67.5
48	Kisangani, Zaire	170.18	67.1
49	Vera Cruz, Mexico	167.64	65.7
50	San Juan, Puerto Rico	162.56	64.2
51	St. Clair, Trinidad & Tobago	162.56	64.2
52	Canton, China	162.56	63.6
53	Yaounde, Cameroon	154.94	61.2
54	Bangui, Central African Empire	154.94	60.8
55	Kampala, Uganda	154.94	60.7
56	Sofala, Mozambique	152.40	59.9
57	Oursso, Congo	149.86	58.6
58	Bangkok, Thailand	147.32	57.8
59	Hamilton, Bermuda	147.32	57.6
60	Nova Lisboa, Angola	144.78	57.0
61	Faeroe Islands	142.24	56.2
62	Katmandu, Nepal	142.24	56.2
63	Santo Domingo, Dominican Rep.	142.24	55.8
64	Kumasi, Ghana	139.70	55.2
65	Phnom Penh, Cambodia	139.70	54.8
66	Braganca, Portugal	137.16	53.8
67	Antananarive, Madagascar	134.62	53.4
68	Port au Prince, Haiti	134.62	53.3
69	Zomba, Malawi	134.62	52.9
70	Cotonou, Benin	132.08	52.4
71	Asuncion, Paraguay	132.08	51.8
72	Guatemala City, Guatemala	129.54	51.8
73	Bathurst, Gambia	129.54	51.0
74	La Guerite, St. Christopher Nevis	129.54	50.9
75	Mauritius	129.54	50.6
76	Barbados	127.00	50.3
77	Seoul, South Korea	124.46	49.2
78	Auckland, New Zealand	124.46	49.1
79	Gambela,Ethiopia	124.46	48.8
LOWER MIDDLE			
80	Artigas, Uruguay	124.46	48.6
81	Havana, Cuba	121.92	48.2
82	Mombasa, Kenya	119.38	47.3
83	Genoa, Italy	119.38	46.6
84	Djibouti	116.84	46.0
85	Corrientes, Argentina	116.84	46.4
86	Nassau, Bahamas	116.84	46.4
87	Babo Dioulasso, Burkina	116.84	46.4
88	Bamako, Mali	111.76	44.1
89	Quito, Ecuador	111.76	43.9
90	Noumea, New Caledonia	109.22	43.5
91	Wau, Sudan	109.22	43.3
92	Durres, Albania	109.22	42.9
93	Dar es Salaam,Tanzania	106.68	41.9
94	Cardiff United Kingdom	106.68	41.9
95	Cork, Ireland	104.14	41.3
96	Zurich, Switzerland	104.14	40.9
97	Durban, South Africa	101.60	39.7
98	Concepcion, Bolivia	99.06	38.6
99	Balovale, Zambia	96.52	38.3
100	Sao Tome, Sao Tome & Principe	96.52	38.0
101	Cherbourg, France	93.98	37.3
102	Am Timan, Chad	93.98	37.2
103	Rawalpindi, Pakistan	91.44	36.5
104	Pyongyang, North Korea	91.44	36.4
105	Petropavlovsk, Russia	91.44	35.9
106	Tangier, Morocco	88.90	35.3
107	Beirul, Lebanon	88.90	35.1
108	Split, Yugoslavia	88.90	35.1
109	Les Escaldes, Andorra	88.90	34.3
110	Munich, Germany	86.36	34.1
111	Reykjavik, Iceland	86.36	33.9
112	Innsbruck, Austria	86.36	33.8
113	Salisbury, Zimbabwe	83.82	32.6
114	St. Helena	81.28	32.1
115	Kingston, Jamaica	78.74	31.5
116	Istanbul Turkey	78.74	31.5
117	Bone, Algeria	78.74	31.0
118	Lome, Togo	78.74	31.0
119	Goteberg, Sweden	76.20	30.5
120	Kaolack, Senegal	76.20	30.3
121	Monaco	76.20	30.1
122	Gibraltar	76.20	29.7
123	Luxembourg	73.66	29.2
124	Krakow, Poland	73.66	28.6
125	Rhodes,Greece	71.12	28.5
126	Helsinki, Finland	71.12	27.6
127	Falkland Islands	68.58	26.8
128	Aarhus, Denmark	68.58	26.6
129	Haifa, Israel	66.04	26.2
130	Amsterdam, Netherlands	66.04	25.6
131	Sofia, Bulgaria	63.50	25.0
132	Prerov, Czech Republic	63.50	24.8
133	Budapest, Hungary	60.96	24.2
134	Cluj, Rumania	60.96	24.0
135	Barcelona, Spain	58.42	23.5
136	Niamey, Niger	55.88	21.6
137	Valetta, Malta	50.80	20.3
138	Maun, Botswana	45.72	18.2
139	Mogadiscio, Somalia	43.18	16.9
140	Tunis, Tunisia	40.64	16.5
141	Kermanshah, Iran	40.64	16.4
142	Aleppo, Syria	38.10	15.5
143	Mosul, Iraq	38.10	15.2
144	Tripoli, Libya	38.10	15.1
145	Nicosia, Cyprus	38.10	14.6
146	Windhoek, Namibia	35.56	14.3
147	Kabul, Afghanistan	33.02	12.6
148	Nema, Mauritania	29.52	11.6
BOTTOM 10			
149	Amman, Jordan	27.46	10.9
150	Porto da Praia, CapeVerde	26.03	10.2
151	Ulan Bator, Mongolia	19.05	7.7
152	Alexandria, Egypt	17.78	7.0
153	Kuwait	12.85	5.1
154	Sharjah, United Arab Emirates	10.47	4.2
155	Muscat, Oman	10.00	3.9
156	Dhahran, Saudi Arabia	8.89	3.5
157	Kamaran, Yemen	8.25	3.4

Source: Library of Congress

6. COLDEST PLACES

Outside of Antarctica and the Arctic regions, there are very few cold regions where some form of human activity cannot be carried on. Yet, human settlements do not thrive in places where the temperatures are consistently below zero in winter because of the extra burdens imposed on the economy in terms of heating, warm clothing, snow removal, etc. The following ranking rates countries by the lowest temperatures recorded in each. Winters are notably erratic, with cycles of warm winters alternating with cycles of cold ones. The figures therefore represent outer limits recorded over a period of time rather than regular temperatures. They are also for cities; therefore lower temperatures have undoubtedly been reached in more remote or mountainous regions in most of the countries included in this ranking.

Rank	Country	°C	°F
TOP 10			
1	Eismitte, Greenland	−64.8	−85
2	Yakutsk, Russia	−64.3	−84
3	Fairbanks, U.S.	−54.4	−66
4	Aklavik, Canada	−52.2	−62
5	Ulan Bator, Mongolia	−44.4	−48
6	Harbin, China	−41.7	−43
7	Kuusamo, Finland	−40.0	−40
8	Haparanda, Sweden	−36.7	−34
9	Krakow, Poland	−33.3	−28
10	Cluj, Rumania	−32.2	−26
UPPER MIDDLE			
11	Prerov, Czech Republic	−30.6	−26
12	Debrecen, Hungary	−30.0	−22
13	Trondheim, Norway	−30.0	−22
14	Erzurum, Turkey	−30.0	−22
15	Kushiro, Japan	−28.3	−19
16	Pyongyang, North Korea	−28.3	−19
17	Nurnberg, Germany	−27.8	−18
18	Sofia, Bulgaria	−27.2	−17
19	Innsbruck, Austria	−26.7	−16
20	Belgrade, Yugoslavia	−25.6	−14
21	Lyon, France	−25.0	−13
22	Kermanshah, Iran	−25.0	−13
23	Aarhus, Denmark	−24.4	−12
24	Seoul, South Korea	−24.4	−12
25	Zurich, Switzerland	−24.4	−12
26	Luxembourg	−23.3	−10
27	Akureyi, Iceland	−22.2	−8
28	Kabul, Afghanistan	−22.2	−6
29	Ushuaia, Argentina	−21.1	−6
30	Srinagar, India	−20.0	−4
31	Les Escaldes, Andorra	−17.8	0
32	Burgos, Spain	−17.8	0
33	Perth, United Kingdom	−17.8	0
34	Amsterdam Netherlands	−16.1	3
35	Thorshavn, Faroe Islands	−13.3	8
36	Dublin, Ireland	−13.3	8
37	Aleppo, Syria	−12.8	9
38	Braganca, Portugal	−12.2	10
39	Punta Arenas, Chile	−11.7	11
40	Stanley, Falkland Islands	−11.1	12
41	Mosul, Iraq	−11.1	12
42	Chihuahua, Mexico	−11.1	12
43	Canberra, Australia	−10.0	14
44	Venice, Italy	−10.0	14
45	Tsabong, Botswana	−9.4	15
46	Thessaloniki, Greece	−9.4	15
47	Cusco, Peru	−8.9	16
48	Fort Flatters, Algeria	−7.2	19
49	Riyadh, Saudi Arabia	−7.2	19
50	Cangamba, Angola	−6.7	20
51	Bela Vista, Brazil	−6.7	20
52	Kimberley, South Africa	−6.7	20
53	Durres, Albania	−6.1	21
54	Amman, Jordan	−6.1	21
55	Christchurch, New Zealand	−6.1	21

Rank	Country	°C	°F
56	Nicosia, Cyprus	−5.0	23
57	Sabhah, Libya	−4.4	24
58	Artigas, Uruguay	−4.4	24
59	Sucre, Bolivia	−3.9	25
60	Quito, Ecuador	−3.9	25
61	Windhoek, Namibia	−3.9	25
62	Rawalpindi, Pakistan	−3.9	25
63	Jerusalem, Israel	−3.3	26
64	Monaco	−2.8	27
65	Marrakech, Morocco	−2.8	27
66	Katmandu, Nepal	−2.8	27
67	Gabes, Tunisia	−2.8	27
68	Bulawayo, Zimbabwe	−2.2	28
69	Wadi Halfa, Sudan	−2.2	28
70	Bilma, Niger	−1.7	29
71	Asuncion, Paraguay	−1.7	29
72	Bogota, Colombia	−1.1	30
73	Beirut, Lebanon	−1.1	30
74	Asmara, Ethiopia	−0.6	31
75	Hong Kong	0.0	32
76	Chicoa, Mozambique	0.0	32
77	Taipei, Taiwan	0.0	32
78	Vientiane, Laos	0.0	32
79	Kuwait	0.6	33
80	Cairo, Egypt	1.1	34
LOWER MIDDLE			
81	Antananrive, Madagascar	1.1	34
82	Valetta, Malta	1.1	34
83	Gibraltar	1.7	35
84	Faya, Chad	2.8	37
85	Araouane, Mali	2.8	37
86	Sharjah, United Arab Emirates	2.8	37
87	Balovale, Zambia	3.3	38
88	Kouroussa, Guinea	3.9	39
89	Atar, Mauritania	3.9	39
90	Hamilton, Bermuda	4.4	40
91	Reunion	4.4	40
92	Nassau, Bahamas	5.0	41
93	Guatemala City, Guatemala	5.0	41
94	Nairobi, Kenya	5.0	41
95	Zomba, Malawi	5.0	41
96	Hanoi, Vietnam	5.0	41
97	Iringa, Tanzania	5.6	42
98	Havana, Cuba	6.1	43
99	Dacca, Bangladesh	6.1	43
100	Maiduguri, Nigeria	6.1	43
101	Mandalay, Myanmar	6.7	44
102	San Salvador, El Salvador	7.2	45
103	Bathurst, Gambia	7.2	45
104	Ngaoundere, Cameroon	7.8	46
105	Bobo Dioulasso, Burkina	7.8	46
106	Kaolack, Senegal	8.9	48
107	Merida, Venezuela	8.9	48
108	Belize	9.4	49
109	San Jose, Costa Rica	9.4	49
110	Mauritius	10.0	50
111	St. Helena	10.0	50

Rank	Country	°C	°F
112	Bangkok, Thailand	10.0	50
113	Lira, Uganda	10.0	50
114	Kalemi Zaire	10.0	50
115	Kumasi, Ghana	10.6	51
116	Muscat, Oman	10.6	51
117	Noumea, New Caledonia	11.1	52
118	St. Clair, Trinidad & Tobago	11.1	52
119	Brazzaville, Congo	12.2	54
120	Camp Jacob, Guadeloupe	12.2	54
121	Phnom Penh, Cambodia	12.8	55
122	Suva, Fiji	12.8	55
123	Porto de Praia, Cape Verde	13.3	56
124	Kingston, Jamaica	13.3	56
125	Martinique	13.3	56
126	Sao Tome, Sao Tome & Principe	13.3	56
127	Bangui, Central African Republic	13.9	57
128	Bouake, Cote d'Ivoire	13.9	57
129	Aden, Yemen	13.9	57
130	Port-au-Prince, Haiti	14.4	58
131	Tela Honduras	14.4	58
132	Penfui, Indonesia	14.4	58
133	Manila, Philippines	14.4	58
134	Berbera, Somalia	14.4	58
135	Lome, Togo	14.4	58
136	Santo Domingo, Dominican Rep.	15.0	59
137	Bolama, Guinea-Bissau	15.0	59
138	Colombo, Sri Lanka	15.0	59
139	Mayoumba, Gabon	15.6	60
140	San Juan, Puerto Rico	15.6	60
141	Barbados	16.1	61
142	Santa Isabel, Equatorial Guinea	16.1	61
143	St. Kitts-Nevis	16.1	61
144	Monrovia, Liberia	16.7	62
145	Madang, Papua New Guinea	16.7	62
146	Freetown, Sierra Leone	16.7	62
147	Paramaribo, Suriname	16.7	62
148	Lethem, Guyana	17.2	63
149	Djibouti	17.2	63
150			
BOTTOM 10			
151	Kuala Lumpur, Malaysia	17.8	64
152	Benin	18.3	65
153	Cayenne, French Guyana	18.3	65
154	Kamaran, Yemen	18.9	66
155	Singapore	18.9	66
156	Pago Pago, Samoa	19.4	67
157	Seychelles	19.4	67
158	Cocos (Keeling) Islands	20.0	68
159	Tulagi, Solomon Islands	20.0	68
160	Brunei	21.1	70

Source: Library of Congress

7. WARMEST PLACES

One of summer's worst ordeals is to watch the mercury climbing inexorably past the 100s until the air crackles with the heat and the earth becomes a scorching hot plate. In 43 countries of the world temperatures over 43.3°C (110°F) have been recorded, and these places are considered as among the most inhospitable to man. Scientists have concluded that the human body can withstand cold better than heat, and it is difficult to imagine that humans can survive in these places for any length of time. The ranking is by no means conclusive because it is limited to places with meteorological stations. It is conceivable that in the forbidding Rub al-Khali in Saudi Arabia, the kavirs of the Central Plateau in Iran and in the Sahara where there are no recording stations, temperatures soar above 60°C (140°F) in the summer. Desert winds such as the harmattan in the Sahara also tend to intensify the heat and shrivel all living things.

Rank	Country	Highest Recorded Temperature °C	°F
TOP 10			
1	Arouane, Mali	54.4	130
2	Cloncurry, Australia	52.8	127
3	Abadan, Iran	52.8	127
4	Wadi Halfa, Sudan	52.8	127
5	Fort Flatters, Algeria	51.1	124
6	Aswan, Egypt	51.1	124
7	Mosul, Iraq	51.1	124
8	Cufra, Libya	50.0	122
9	Multan, Pakistan	50.0	122
10	Gabes, Tunisia	50.0	122
UPPER MIDDLE			
11	Faya, Chad	49.4	121
12	Nema, Mauritania	48.9	120
13	Marrakech, Morocco	48.8	120
14	Dhahran, Saudi Arabia	48.9	120
15	Lucknow, India	48.3	119
16	Kuwait	48.3	119
17	Sharjah, United Arab Emirates	47.8	118
18	Phoenix, United States	47.8	118
19	Ouagadougou, Burkina	47.8	118
20	Djibouli	47.2	117
21	Guaymas, Mexico	47.2	117
22	Chicao, Mozambique	47.2	117
23	Berbera, Somalia	47.2	117
24	Seville, Spain	47.2	117
25	Aleppo, Syria	47.2	117
26	Santiago del Estero, Argentina	46.7	116
27	Nicosia, Cyprus	46.7	116
28	Bilma, Niger	46.7	116
29	Muscat, Oman	46.7	116
30	Iraklion, Crete, Greece	45.6	114
31	Kaolack, Senegal	45.6	114
32	Palermo, Italy	45.0	113
33	Urumchi, China	44.4	112
34	Haifa, Israel	44.4	112
35	Maiduguri, Nigeria	44.4	112
36	Kandahar, Afghanistan	43.9	111
37	Mandalay, Myanmar	43.9	111
38	Gambela, Ethiopia	43.9	111
39	Toulouse, France	43.9	111
40	Aden, Yemen	43.9	111
41	Regina, Canada	43.3	110
42	Asuncion, Paraguay	43.3	110
43	Maun, Botswana	43.3	110
44	Cangamba, Angola	42.8	109
45	Ndele, Central African Republic	42.8	109
46	Kouroussa, Guinea	42.8	109
47	Amman, Jordan	42.8	109
48	Adana, Turkey	42.8	109
49	Montevideo, Uruguay	42.8	109
50	Dacca, Bangladesh	42.2	108
51	Uruguaiana, Brazil	42.2	108
52	Vientiane, Laos	42.2	108
53	Tulear, Madagascar	42.2	108

Rank	Country	Highest Recorded Temperature °C	°F
54	Keetmanshoop, Namibia	42.2	108
55	Kazalinsk, Russia	42.2	108
56	Hanoi, Vietnam	42.2	108
57	Balovale, Zambia	42.2	108
58	Varna, Bulgaria	41.7	107
59	Beirut, Lebanon	41.7	107
60	Lagos, Portugal	41.7	107
61	Durban, South Africa	41.7	107
62	Belgrade, Yugoslavia	41.7	107
63	Oursso, Congo	41.1	106
64	Bathurst, Gambia	41.1	106
65	Bolama, Guinea-Bissau	41.1	106
66	Phnom Penh, Cambodia	40.6	105
67	San Salvador, El Salvador	40.6	105
68	Veletta, Malta	40.6	105
69	Bucharest, Rumania	40.6	105
70	Kamaran, Yemen	40.6	105
71	Havana, Cuba	40.0	104
72	Bouake, Cote d'Ivoire	40.0	104
73	Bangkok, Thailand	40.0	104
74	Budapest, Hungary	39.4	103
75	Ngaoundere, Cameroon	38.9	102
76	Santa Isabel, Equatorial Guinea	38.9	102
77	Osaka, Japan	38.9	102
78	Maracaibo, Venezuela	38.9	102
79	Concepcion, Bolivia	38.2	101
80	Taipei, Taiwan	38.3	101
LOWER MIDDLE			
81	Port-au-Prince, Haiti	38.3	101
82	Penfui, Indonesia	38.3	101
83	Manila, Philippines	38.3	101
84	Geneva, Switzerland	38.3	101
85	St. Clair, Trinidad & Tobago	38.3	101
86	Prerov, Czech Republic	37.8	100
87	Frankfurt, Germany	37.8	100
88	Accra, Ghana	37.8	100
89	Pyongyang, North Korea	37.8	100
90	Rabaul, Papua New Guinea	37.8	100
91	Iquitos, Peru	37.8	100
92	Kigoma, Tanzania	37.8	100
93	Lira, Uganda	37.8	100
94	Hamilton, Bermuda	37.2	99
95	Brunei	37.2	99
96	Santiago, Chile	37.2	99
97	Libreville, Gabon	37.2	99
98	Seoul, South Korea	37.2	99
99	Luxembourg	37.2	99
100	Karonga, Malawi	37.2	99
101	Kuala Lumpur, Malaysia	37.2	99
102	Katmandu, Nepal	37.2	99
103	Noumea, New Caledonia	37.2	99
104	Bulawayo, Zimbabwe	37.2	99
105	Colombo, Sri Lanka	37.2	99
106	Paramaribo, Suriname	37.2	99
107	London, United Kingdom	37.2	99

Rank	Country	Highest Recorded Temperature °C	°F
108	Vienna, Austria	36.7	98
109	Cartagena, Colombia	36.7	98
110	Santo Domingo, Dominican Rep.	36.7	98
111	Guayquil, Ecuador	36.7	98
112	Suva, Fiji	36.7	98
113	Warsaw, Poland	36.7	98
114	Pago Pago, Samoa	36.7	98
115	Freetown, Sierra Leone	36.7	98
116	Belize	38.1	97
117	Cayenne, French Guyana	36.1	97
118	Gibraltar	36.1	97
119	Lethem, Guyana	36.1	97
120	Hong Kong	36.1	97
121	Kingston, Jamaica	36.1	97
122	Monrovia, Liberia	36.1	97
123	Ulan Bator, Mongolia	36.1	97
124	Singapore	36.1	97
125	Stockholm, Sweden	36.1	97
126	Kinshasa, Zaire	36.1	97
127	Tela, Honduras	35.6	96
128	Mombasa, Kenya	35.6	96
129	Fort-de-France, Martinique	35.6	96
130	Christchurch, New Zealand	35.6	96
131	Tulagi, Solomon Islands	35.6	96
132	Durres, Albania	35.0	95
133	Bridgetown, Barbados	35.0	95
134	Cotonou, Benin	35.0	95
135	Mauritius	35.0	95
136	Amsterdam, Netherlands	35.0	95
137	Trondheim, Norway	35.0	95
138	Nassau, Bahamas	34.4	94
139	Cape Verde	34.4	94
140	Cocos (Keeling) Islands	34.4	94
141	San Juan, Puerto Rico	34.4	94
142	Lome, Togo	34.4	94
143	Monaco	33.9	93
144	San Jose, Costa Rica	33.3	92
145	Camp Jacob, Guadeloupe	33.3	92
146	Seychelles	33.3	92
147	Les Escaldes, Andorra	32.8	91
148	Copenhagen, Denmark	32.8	91
149	St. Kitts-Nevis	32.8	91
BOTTOM 10			
150	Sao Tome, Sao Tome & Principe	32.8	91
151	Kuusamo, Finland	32.2	90
152	Guatemala City, Guatemala	32.2	90
153	Ivigtut, Greenland	30.0	86
154	Dublin, Ireland	30.0	86
155	Reunion	28.9	84
156	Akureyri, Iceland	28.3	83
157	St. Helena	27.8	82
158	Stanley, Falkland Islands	24.4	76
159	Thorshavn, Faroe Islands	21.1	70

Source: Library of Congress

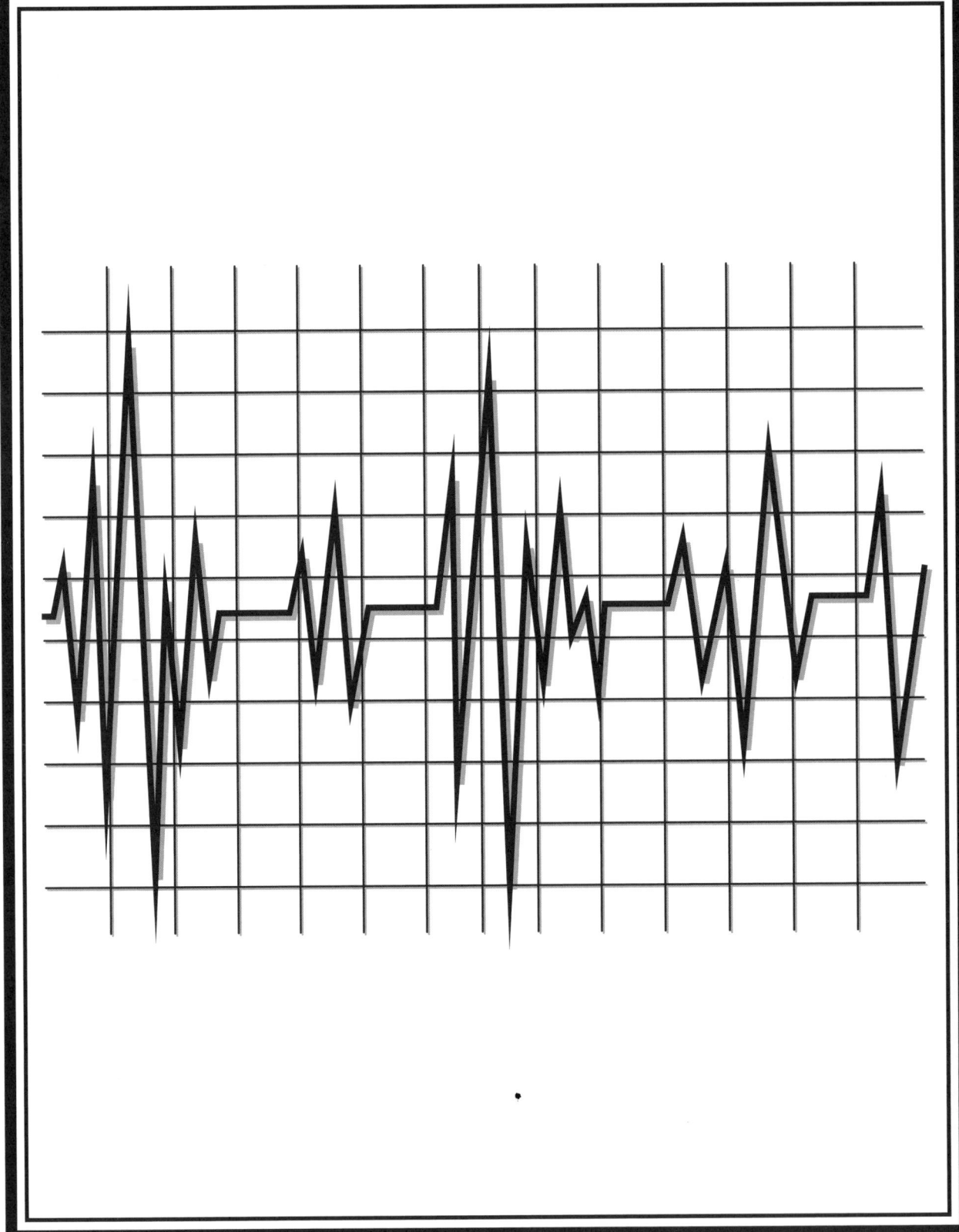

Section

II

VITAL
STATISTICS

Population is the key indicator in this book, determining all other indicators. (Because population data are available for all countries, these rankings are also the most comprehensive.) Although national censuses are still uneven in quality and sporadic in occurrence, the United Nations has refined its techniques for collecting population data to such a degree that the error range is only 1.0% in censuses taken at least decennially. In countries where no censuses have been held regularly, the United Nations estimates the outer limits of the size of population through sample surveys and even unconventional counts and conjectures. The error range in the case of sample surveys is 5.0%, in the case of unconventional counts 10.0% and in the case of conjectures 20.0%. Size of population is presented for two periods, Current and 2000, the latter representing an estimate.

Demographers are concerned not only with the size of population but also with growth rates or trends. Growth rates are determined on the basis of three indicators, all of which are presented here: Crude Birth Rates, Crude Death Rates and Fertility Rates. The reverse correlation between population growth and economic development is generally acknowledged, and in many of the poorer countries a rising birth rate is watched with the same alarm as a rising crime rate. It is interesting to recall that in Indira Gandhi's India people were jailed and their ration cards confiscated for begetting more than the legally permitted quota of children. It is conceivable that in a *regimented* society procreation itself could become the ultimate crime.

8. CURRENT POPULATION

The total population of the globe was estimated by the U.N. in 1995 at 5.601 billion. Nearly 90% of this total live in countries with populations of 15 million or more. Approximately one-half of the population resides in the four largest countries: China, India, the United States and Indonesia. Altogether, the 42 most populated states have within their borders more than nine-tenths of the world's inhabitants. Although a large population is a mixed blessing in countries like Bangladesh, the size of population remains an important–if far from the exclusive–determinant of national power and economic development.

Population figures for each country are based partly on national censuses and partly on U.N. estimates. Both are subject to wide margins of error. A serious source of inaccuracy is the practice in some countries of excluding jungle tribes, aborigines, nomadic peoples, displaced persons and refugees. In some undeveloped countries censuses are hampered by opposition to the enumeration of women and children. In other countries, including Saudi Arabia and Afghanistan, an official census has never been conducted.

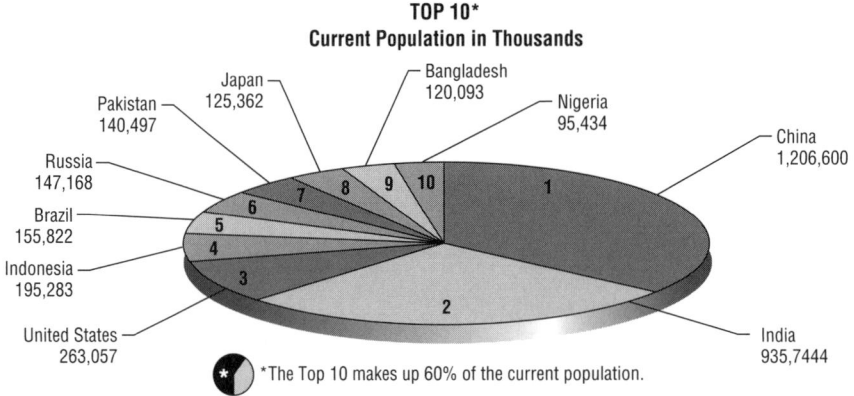

TOP 10*
Current Population in Thousands

Japan 125,362
Pakistan 140,497
Russia 147,168
Brazil 155,822
Indonesia 195,283
United States 263,057
Bangladesh 120,093
Nigeria 95,434
China 1,206,600
India 935,7444

*The Top 10 makes up 60% of the current population.

Rank	Country	Current Population (thousands)
UPPER MIDDLE		
11	Mexico	91,145
12	Germany	81,912
13	Vietnam	74,545
14	Philippines	70,011
15	Turkey	62,526
16	Iran	61,271
17	Egypt	59,695
18	Thailand	58,791
19	United Kingdom	58,586
20	France	58,172
21	Italy	57,386
22	Ethiopia	55,053
23	Ukraine	52,003
24	Myanmar (Burma)	46,527
25	Korea, South	44,834
26	Zaire	43,901
27	South Africa	41,465
28	Spain	39,188
29	Poland	38,641
30	Colombia	35,099
31	Argentina	34,587
32	Canada	29,463
33	Kenya	28,626
34	Sudan	28,098
35	Tanzania	28,072
36	Algeria	27,939
37	Morocco	26,980
38	Peru	23,489
39	Korea, North	23,487
40	Uzbekistan	22,866
41	Romania	22,693
42	Venezuela	21,844
43	Taiwan	21,268
44	Iraq	20,413
45	Nepal	20,093
46	Malaysia	19,948
47	Uganda	18,659
48	Afghanistan	18,129
49	Sri Lanka	18,090
50	Australia	18,025
51	Mozambique	17,889
52	Saudi Arabia	17,880
53	Kazakhstan	16,869
54	Ghana	16,472
55	Netherlands	15,487
56	Madagascar	14,763
57	Syria	14,313
58	Cote d'Ivoire	14,253
59	Chile	14,210
60	Cameroon	13,233
61	Yemen	13,058
62	Angola	11,558
63	Ecuador	11,460
64	Zimbabwe	11,261
65	Cuba	11,068
66	Guatemala	10,621
67	Yugoslavia	10,555
68	Greece	10,493
69	Czech Republic	10,346
70	Belarus	10,332
71	Burkina	10,324

Rank	Country	Current Population (thousands)
72	Hungary	10,231
73	Belgium	10,064
74	Malawi	9,939
75	Portugal	9,906
76	Cambodia	9,608
77	Zambia	9,456
78	Niger	9,151
79	Mali	9,008
80	Tunisia	8,896
81	Sweden	8,826
82	Bulgaria	8,406
83	Senegal	8,312
84	Austria	8,063
85	Rwanda	7,855
86	Dominican Republic	7,823
87	Azerbaijan	7,525
88	Bolivia	7,414
89	Switzerland	7,039
90	Somalia	6,734
91	Guinea	6,700
92	Haiti	6,589
93	Chad	6,361
94	Burundi	5,936
95	Tajikistan	5,832
LOWER MIDDLE		
96	El Salvador	5,768
97	Georgia	5,514
98	Honduras	5,512
99	Benin	5,409
100	Libya	5,407
101	Israel	5,386
102	Slovakia	5,355
103	Denmark	5,223
104	Finland	5,101
105	Laos	4,882
106	Paraguay	4,828
107	Sierra Leone	4,509
108	Croatia	4,495
109	Kyrgyzstan	4,463
110	Norway	4,355
111	Moldova	4,346
112	Nicaragua	4,340
113	Papua New Guinea	4,302
114	Jordan	4,187
115	Togo	4,138
116	Turkmenistan	4,081
117	Puerto Rico	3,725
118	Lithuania	3,700
119	Ireland	3,590
120	New Zealand	3,568
121	Armenia	3,548
122	Eritrea	3,531
123	Bosnia & Herzegovina	3,459
124	Albania	3,412
125	Costa Rica	3,344
126	Uruguay	3,186
127	Central African Republic	3,141
128	Lebanon	3,009
129	Singapore	2,989
130	Panama	2,631
131	Congo	2,590

Rank	Country	Current Population (thousands)
132	Jamaica	2,520
133	Latvia	2,515
134	Liberia	2,380
135	Mongolia	2,307
136	Mauritania	2,274
137	United Arab Emirates	2,195
138	Oman	2,163
139	Macedonia	2,104
140	Lesotho	2,050
141	Slovenia	1,971
142	Kuwait	1,691
143	Namibia	1,651
144	Botswana	1,549
145	Estonia	1,487
146	Trinidad and Tobago	1,265
147	Gabon	1,156
148	Mauritius	1,128
149	Gambia	1,115
150	Guinea-Bissau	1,073
151	Swaziland	913
152	Bhutan	816
153	Cyprus	806
154	Fiji	791
155	Guyana	770
156	Djibouti	586
157	Bahrain	579
158	Qatar	579
159	Comoros	545
160	Suriname	430
161	Luxembourg	409
162	Equatorial Guinea	396
163	Cape Verde	392
164	Solomon Islands	382
165	Malta	370
166	Brunei	291
167	Bahamas	276
168	Iceland	269
169	Barbados	265
170	Maldives	253
171	Belize	216
172	Vanuatu	168
173	Western Samoa	166
174	St. Lucia	143
175	Sao Tome e Principe	131
176	St. Vincent	112
177	Tonga	100
178	Grenada	92
179	Kiribati	80.4
180	Seychelles	75.5
BOTTOM 10		
181	Dominica	72.1
182	Antigua and Barbuda	63.9
183	Andorra	62.9
184	Bermuda	61
185	St. Kitts and Nevis	39.4
186	Liechtenstein	30.9
187	Monaco	30.4
188	San Marino	24.9
189	Nauru	10.4
190	Tuvalu	9.4

Source: UN Population Division

9. ANNUAL POPULATION GROWTH RATE

The annual growth rate of population has become one of the most critical factors influencing a nation's strategy for achieving economic prosperity and in some cases for staving off disaster. Although population experts in industrialized countries have been talking of zero population growth as the ideal for a stable society, developing countries have been experiencing uncontrolled growth rates as high as 6% annually. Another way of looking at the problem is to determine in how many years a national population will double itself. With a 4% growth rate a population could easily double itself in 20 years. Percentages are, however, deceptive and may not reveal the full enormity of the problems some countries face. In India, for example, each 0.1% growth rate means another 600,000 additional mouths to feed. At the same time, all growth is not undesirable. A country like Kuwait may find a higher population growth rate necessary to effectively use its vast economic resources and to allow its native population to outnumber aliens.

Rank	Country	Population Growth Rate 1985–1994 (%)
TOP 10		
1	Jordan	5.2
2	Malawi	4.5
3	Qatar	4.5
4	Oman	4.4
5	Andorra	4.2
6	Djibouti	4.1
7	Gambia	4.1
8	Cote d'Ivoire	3.6
9	Libya	3.6
10	Saudi Arabia	3.6
UPPER MIDDLE		
11	Syria	3.5
12	Solomon Islands	3.4
13	Swaziland	3.4
14	Botswana	3.3
15	Iran	3.3
16	United Arab Emirates	3.3
17	Zaire	3.3
18	Zambia	3.3
19	Angola	3.2
20	Liberia	3.2
21	Maldives	3.2
22	Niger	3.2
23	Bahrain	3.1
24	Cambodia	3.1
25	Ghana	3.1
26	Laos	3.1
27	Nicaragua	3.1
28	Tanzania	3.1
29	Togo	3.1
30	Benin	3.0
31	Burundi	3.0
32	Congo	3.0
33	Honduras	3.0
34	Madagascar	3.0
35	Paraguay	3.0
36	Zimbabwe	3.0
37	Afghanistan	2.9
38	Ethiopia	2.9
39	Guatemala	2.9
40	Guinea	2.9
41	Iraq	2.9
42	Kenya	2.9
43	Nigeria	2.9
44	Tajikistan	2.9
45	Cameroon	2.8
46	Mali	2.8
47	Pakistan	2.8
48	Burkina	2.7
49	Comoros	2.7
50	Israel	2.7
51	Lebanon	2.7
52	Lesotho	2.7

Rank	Country	Population Growth Rate 1985–1994 (%)
53	Namibia	2.7
54	Rwanda	2.7
55	Senegal	2.7
56	Sudan	2.7
57	Belize	2.6
58	Nepal	2.6
59	Algeria	2.5
60	Costa Rica	2.5
61	Equatorial Guinea	2.5
62	Malaysia	2.5
63	Mauritania	2.5
64	Sierra Leone	2.5
65	Uganda	2.5
66	Vanuatu	2.5
67	Venezuela	2.5
68	Central African Republic	2.4
69	Mongolia	2.4
70	South Africa	2.4
71	Turkmenistan	2.4
72	Brunei	2.3
73	Cape Verde	2.3
74	Chad	2.3
75	Ecuador	2.3
76	Tunisia	2.3
77	Uzbekistan	2.3
78	Bolivia	2.2
79	Colombia	2.2
80	Mexico	2.2
81	Morocco	2.2
82	Papua New Guinea	2.2
83	Dominican Republic	2.1
84	Guinea-Bissau	2.1
85	Myanmar (Burma)	2.1
86	Philippines	2.1
87	Sao Tome e Principe	2.1
88	Turkey	2.1
89	Vietnam	2.1
90	Bangladesh	2.0
91	Egypt	2.0
92	Haiti	2.0
93	India	2.0
LOWER MIDDLE		
94	Mozambique	2.0
95	Panama	2.0
96	Peru	2.0
97	El Salvador	1.9
98	Brazil	1.8
99	Gabon	1.8
100	Korea, North	1.8
101	St. Lucia	1.7
102	Bahamas	1.7
103	Chile	1.7
104	Kyrgyzstan	1.7
105	Albania	1.6

Rank	Country	Population Growth Rate 1985–1994 (%)
106	Indonesia	1.6
107	Somalia	1.6
108	Thailand	1.6
109	Armenia	1.5
110	Australia	1.5
111	Kiribati	1.5
112	Argentina	1.4
113	China	1.4
114	Fiji	1.4
115	Liechtenstein	1.4
116	Azerbaijan	1.3
117	Canada	1.3
118	Monaco	1.3
119	Seychelles	1.3
120	Sri Lanka	1.3
121	Bermuda	1.2
122	Trinidad and Tobago	1.2
123	Cyprus	1.1
124	Iceland	1.1
125	Macedonia	1.1
126	Singapore	1.1
127	Suriname	1.1
128	Yemen	1.1
129	Korea, South	1.0
130	Luxembourg	1.0
131	Switzerland	1.0
132	Taiwan	1.0
133	United States	1.0
134	St. Vincent	0.9
135	Cuba	0.9
136	Jamaica	0.9
137	Mauritius	0.9
138	New Zealand	0.9
139	Puerto Rico	0.9
140	Yugoslavia	0.9
141	Kazakhstan	0.8
142	Tonga	0.8
143	Croatia	0.7
144	Netherlands	0.7
145	Slovenia	0.7
146	Malta	0.6
147	Uruguay	0.6
148	Antigua and Barbuda	0.5
149	Austria	0.5
150	France	0.5
151	Germany	0.5
152	Greece	0.5
153	Guyana	0.5
154	Moldova	0.5
155	Russia	0.5
156	Sweden	0.5
157	Finland	0.4
158	Georgia	0.4
159	Hungary	0.4
160	Japan	0.4

Rank	Country	Population Growth Rate 1985–1994 (%)
161	Lithuania	0.4
162	Norway	0.4
163	Slovakia	0.4
164	Barbados	0.3
165	Poland	0.3
166	Spain	0.3
167	United Kingdom	0.3
168	Belarus	0.2
169	Belgium	0.2
170	Dominica	0.2
171	Grenada	0.2
172	Romania	0.2
173	Denmark	0.1
LOWER MIDDLE		
174	Italy	0.1
175	Latvia	0.1
176	Portugal	0.1
177	Ukraine	0.1
178	Czech Republic	0.0
179	Estonia	0.0
180	Ireland	0.0
181	Bulgaria	−0.2
182	St. Kitts and Nevis	−0.5
183	Kuwait	−0.5

Source: *Demographic Yearbook*

10. ESTIMATED POPULATION IN 2000

World population grew by nearly 2 billion between 1983 and 1995 and is estimated to reach 5.916 billion by 2000. This means that more people will be born in these 17 years than were born during all the millennia up to around the year 1920. Assumptions about future growth are based on analyses of recent fertility and mortality trends in each country. It is assumed that the life expectancy rate will continue to rise for both males and females, while fertility rates will decline until a stationary population is reached. These are highly speculative assumptions and should not be regarded as predictions. Through extrapolation of these same assumptions, it is estimated that world population will reach an ultimate size of about 10 billion in about 200 years, when dwindling natural resources will force it to decline until the net replacement level reaches 1:1.

Rank	Country	Population Projection 2000 (000)
TOP 10		
1	China	1,260,154
2	India	1,018,105
3	United States	275,327
4	Indonesia	219,496
5	Brazil	169,543
6	Pakistan	148,540
7	Bangladesh	143,548
8	Russia	141,460
9	Japan	127,554
10	Nigeria	118,620
UPPER MIDDLE		
11	Mexico	102,912
12	Germany	82,239
13	Vietnam	80,533
14	Iran	78,347
15	Philippines	77,747
16	Ethiopia	70,340
17	Turkey	69,624
18	Egypt	67,542
19	Thailand	63,620
20	France	59,354
21	United Kingdom	58,951
22	Italy	58,865
23	Ukraine	51,931
24	Zaire	51,413
25	South Africa	51,334
26	Myanmar (Burma)	49,300
27	Korea, South	47,861
28	Spain	39,972
29	Poland	39,531
30	Colombia	39,172
31	Argentina	36,202
32	Kenya	32,479
33	Tanzania	32,254
34	Morocco	32,189
35	Algeria	31,473
36	Canada	29,867
37	Peru	26,258
38	Afghanistan	25,725
39	Korea, North	25,491
40	Uzbekistan	25,467
41	Iraq	24,731
42	Nepal	24,364
43	Romania	23,383
44	Venezuela	23,196
45	Uganda	22,748
46	Taiwan	22,448
47	Saudi Arabia	22,070
48	Malaysia	21,953
49	Mozambique	20,868
50	Ghana	20,608
51	Australia	19,386
52	Sri Lanka	19,146
53	Syria	18,519
54	Kazakhstan	17,886
55	Cote d'Ivoire	17,371
56	Madagascar	16,232
57	Netherlands	15,801
58	Cameroon	15,677
59	Chile	15,207
60	Yemen	13,603
61	Guatemala	12,408
62	Cambodia	12,098
63	Zimbabwe	12,013
64	Ecuador	11,945
65	Burkina	11,871
66	Cuba	11,617
67	Angola	11,513
68	Yugoslavia	11,121
69	Malawi	11,045
70	Mali	10,911
71	Greece	10,878
72	Portugal	10,744
73	Niger	10,651
74	Zambia	10,625
75	Czech Republic	10,607
76	Belarus	10,576
77	Senegal	10,533
78	Hungary	10,372
79	Belgium	10,144
80	Rwanda	9,715
81	Tunisia	9,599
82	Somalia	9,176
83	Sweden	8,994
84	Bolivia	8,801
85	Bulgaria	8,742
86	Dominican Republic	8,644
87	Azerbaijan	8,243
88	Austria	8,108
89	Guinea	7,372
90	Switzerland	7,268
91	Haiti	7,102
92	Tajikistan	6,956
93	Burundi	6,939
94	Benin	6,517
95	El Salvador	6,459
LOWER MIDDLE		
96	Libya	6,294
97	Chad	6,221
98	Honduras	6,192
99	Paraguay	6,104
100	Georgia	5,925
101	Slovakia	5,585
102	Laos	5,557
103	Israel	5,507
104	Sierra Leone	5,421
105	Togo	5,263
106	Denmark	5,255

Rank	Country	Population Projection 2000 (000)	Rank	Country	Population Projection 2000 (000)	Rank	Country	Population Projection 2000 (000)
107	Finland	5,153	135	Estonia	2,670	163	Malta	382
108	Kyrgyzstan	5,119	136	Mauritania	2,653	164	Brunei	331
109	Bosnia & Herzegovina	4,828	137	Kuwait	2,494	165	Maldives	310
110	Jordan	4,814	138	Macedonia	2,324	166	Bahamas	298
111	Papua New Guinea	4,812	139	Lesotho	2,242	167	Iceland	277
112	Nicaragua	4,759	140	Oman	2,098	168	Barbados	260
113	Croatia	4,717	141	Slovenia	1,998	169	Belize	242
114	Moldova	4,565	142	Bhutan	1,996	170	Vanuatu	193
115	Turkmenistan	4,474	143	Namibia	1,957	171	Sao Tome e Principe	159
116	Norway	4,387	144	Botswana	1,554	172	St. Lucia	151
117	Lebanon	4,115	145	Trinidad and Tobago	1,420	173	St. Vincent	122
118	Lithuania	4,007	146	Guinea-Bissau	1,263	174	Tonga	110
119	Puerto Rico	3,838	147	Gabon	1,244	175	Grenada	98
120	Costa Rica	3,797	148	Mauritius	1,194	176	Dominica	95
121	Armenia	3,685	149	Gambia	1,154	177	Kiribati	87
122	Ireland	3,672	150	Swaziland	1,137			
123	Liberia	3,620	151	Fiji	823		**BOTTOM 10**	
124	Albania	3,610	152	Cyprus	768	178	Seychelles	75
125	United Arab Emirates	3,582	153	Guyana	710	179	Andorra	73
126	Central African Republic	3,511	154	Bahrain	687	180	Antigua and Barbuda	68
127	New Zealand	3,476	155	Comoros	656	181	Bermuda	64
128	Uruguay	3,344	156	Qatar	572	182	St. Kitts and Nevis	43
129	Singapore	3,025	157	Cape Verde	503	183	Monaco	32
130	Panama	2,934	158	Equatorial Guinea	478	184	Liechtenstein	32
131	Latvia	2,833	159	Solomon Islands	470	185	San Marino	25
132	Mongolia	2,826	160	Suriname	465	186	Tuvalu	11
133	Congo	2,784	161	Djibouti	454	187	Nauru	11
134	Jamaica	2,746	162	Luxembourg	415			

Source: UN Population Division

11. TEEN PREGNANCIES

Despite official measures in almost all countries to discourage teen pregnancies and promote abstinence, teen pregnancy rates have soared since 1990. Teen pregnancies represent a setback to girls trying to continue educational careers and achieve a reasonable degree of economic independence. They also tend to increase abortion rates correspondingly and to create welfare problems in communities where social expenditures on teen mothers have come under attack from fiscal conservatives. What is behind the higher rates? Some blame poor sex education, while others point to the fading stigma of adolescent sex and motherhood. Pregnant teens are more prone to complications and their babies face a higher risk of prematurity, low birth weight and death.

Pregnancies in Women Ages 19 and Under in 1988

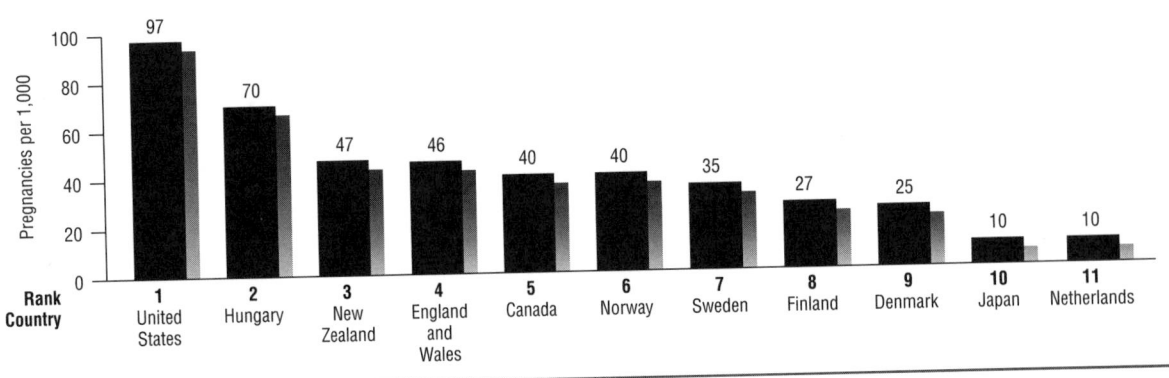

Source: *US News and World Report*

12. FEMALE LIFE EXPECTANCY

Why do women live longer than men? The usual answer is that men and women have slightly different life cycles. Women tend to mature early. Men have a more active midlife and their physiological functions peak between 45 and 55.

Rank	Country	Life Expectancy for Women (years)	Rank	Country	Life Expectancy for Women (years)	Rank	Country	Life Expectancy for Women (years)
TOP 10			63	Antigua and Barbuda	74.95	126	Botswana	65.65
1	San Marino	85.27	64	Qatar	74.68	127	Bolivia	65.33
2	France	82.16	65	Argentina	74.65	128	Maldives	65.28
3	Japan	82.15	66	Ukraine	74.65	129	Sao Tome e Principe	64.9
4	Canada	81.6	67	Azerbaijan	74.63	130	Cape Verde	64.15
5	Switzerland	81.54	68	Paraguay	74.62	131	Namibia	63.91
6	Monaco	81.49	69	Tunisia	74.62	132	Ethiopia	63.88
7	Andorra	81.34	70	Latvia	74.55	133	Tuvalu	63.82
8	Iceland	81.04	71	Colombia	74.53	134	Lesotho	63.6
9	Spain	81.04	72	Romania	74.34	135	Egypt	62.41
10	Sweden	81.02	73	Mauritius	74.3	136	Indonesia	62.34
			74	Sri Lanka	74.21	137	Myanmar (Burma)	61.63
UPPER MIDDLE			75	United Arab Emirates	74.2	138	Vanuatu	60.58
11	Liechtenstein	80.9	76	Russia	74.04	139	Swaziland	60.03
12	Italy	80.85	77	Korea, South	73.68	140	Liberia	59.76
13	Netherlands	80.78	78	Jordan	73.51	141	Comoros	59.55
14	Norway	80.73	79	St. Vincent	73.28	142	Togo	58.83
15	Australia	80.63	80	Trinidad and Tobago	73.22	143	Cameroon	58.74
16	Luxembourg	80.3	81	Seychelles	73.07	144	India	58.59
17	Belgium	80.21	82	Turkey	72.82	145	Pakistan	57.52
18	Greece	80.12	83	Korea, North	72.75	146	Senegal	57.48
19	New Zealand	79.95	84	Kazakhstan	72.73	147	Ghana	57.17
20	Israel	79.93	85	Brunei	72.65	148	Gabon	57.01
21	Austria	79.8	86	Solomon Islands	72.65	149	Papua New Guinea	56.88
22	Dominica	79.71	87	Grenada	72.54	150	Kenya	55.92
23	Finland	79.62	88	Ecuador	72.25	151	Nigeria	55.88
24	Costa Rica	79.52	89	Kyrgyzstan	72.15	152	Kiribati	55.78
25	United Kingdom	79.43	90	Uzbekistan	71.84	153	Madagascar	55.45
26	United States	79.29	91	Malaysia	71.81	154	Sudan	54.73
27	Germany	79.0	92	Suriname	71.76	155	Bangladesh	54.38
28	Cuba	78.99	93	St. Lucia	71.69	156	Equatorial Guinea	53.76
29	Malta	78.9	94	Thailand	71.66	157	Benin	53.16
30	Singapore	78.63				158	Laos	52.77
31	Denmark	78.56	**LOWER MIDDLE**			159	Nepal	52.12
32	Portugal	78.56	95	Moldova	71.53	160	Yemen	52.11
33	Taiwan	78.39	96	Lebanon	71.52	161	Gambia	51.87
34	Ireland	78.36	97	Tajikistan	71.48	162	Cote d'Ivoire	51.03
35	Cyprus	78.31	98	Tonga	70.24	163	Cambodia	50.6
36	Slovenia	78.13	99	Dominican Republic	70.21	164	Djibouti	50.59
37	Bosnia & Herzegovina	77.67	100	Western Samoa	70.08	165	Mauritania	50.48
38	Puerto Rico	77.61	101	Belize	69.88	166	Mozambique	49.9
39	Chile	77.29	102	Honduras	69.62	167	Congo	49.84
40	Panama	77.27	103	Morocco	69.4	168	Bhutan	49.58
41	Uruguay	77.11	104	Oman	69.27	169	Zaire	49.12
42	Bermuda	76.97	105	El Salvador	69.2	170	Guinea-Bissau	48.73
43	Croatia	76.89	106	Nauru	69.18	171	Sierra Leone	48.71
44	Kuwait	76.87	107	Saudi Arabia	69.01	172	Burkina	48.3
45	Slovakia	76.85	108	St. Kitts and Nevis	68.85	173	Angola	47.35
46	Czech Republic	76.58	109	China	68.8	174	Haiti	47.11
47	Poland	76.51	110	Turkmenistan	68.62	175	Mali	47.06
48	Barbados	76.46	111	Algeria	68.41	176	Zambia	46.16
49	Georgia	76.46	112	Mongolia	68.13	177	Guinea	45.93
50	Jamaica	76.36	113	Guyana	68.1	178	Tanzania	45.87
51	Mexico	76.3	114	Philippines	67.69			
52	Bulgaria	76.26	115	South Africa	67.63	**BOTTOM 10**		
53	Albania	76.21	116	Peru	67.44	179	Niger	45.75
54	Lithuania	76.08	117	Brazil	67.33	180	Zimbabwe	44.49
55	Bahamas	75.96	118	Vietnam	67.25	181	Central African Republic	44.45
56	Venezuela	75.77	119	Syria	67.22	182	Afghanistan	43.71
57	Belarus	75.66	120	Fiji	67.21	183	Burundi	42.76
58	Bahrain	75.63	121	Guatemala	66.55	184	Rwanda	42.28
59	Macedonia	75.41	122	Nicaragua	66.41	185	Chad	41.5
60	Armenia	75.36	123	Iran	66.19	186	Malawi	41.37
61	Hungary	75.12	124	Iraq	65.86	187	Uganda	38.71
62	Estonia	74.99	125	Libya	65.7	188	Somalia	32.95

Source: *Demographic Yearbook*

13. MALE LIFE EXPECTANCY

Expectation of life is defined as the average number of years that males and females could hope to live on the basis of the mortality rates prevailing during the period 1994–95. However, in many cases this understates the expectation of life because mortality rates are decreasing almost universally. This limitation apart, the figures are considered to be very reliable because of the ability of actuaries to build computerized model life tables. Expectation of life is presented for males and females separately. A comparison of the two rankings proves the traditional assumption that females have a greater expectation of life than males in most countries of the world.

Rank	Country	Life Expectancy for Men (years)	Rank	Country	Life Expectancy for Men (years)	Rank	Country	Life Expectancy for Men (years)
TOP 10			59	Bulgaria	69.55	118	Philippines	62.59
1	San Marino	77.09	60	Brunei	69.27	119	Maldives	62.5
2	Costa Rica	76.56	61	Colombia	68.99	120	Guatemala	61.46
3	Iceland	76.45	62	Mexico	68.99	121	Guyana	61.46
4	Japan	76.35	63	Sri Lanka	68.94	122	Turkmenistan	61.4
5	Israel	75.72	64	Czech Republic	68.9	123	Libya	61.35
6	Andorra	75.35	65	Georgia	68.89	124	Tuvalu	61.27
7	Sweden	75.3	66	Armenia	68.36	125	Sao Tome e Principe	61.19
8	Greece	75.02	67	Romania	68.32	126	Nicaragua	60.7
9	Switzerland	74.6	68	Bahamas	68.19	127	Bolivia	60.34
10	Cuba	74.59	69	Slovakia	68.18	128	Cape Verde	60.3
			70	Turkey	68.11	129	Lesotho	59.91
UPPER MIDDLE			71	Argentina	67.91	130	Botswana	59.52
11	Canada	74.54	72	Trinidad and Tobago	67.91	131	Egypt	58.61
12	Netherlands	74.48	73	Grenada	67.79	132	Namibia	58.57
13	Malta	74.32	74	Solomon Islands	67.73	133	Brazil	58.28
14	Australia	74.24	75	Korea, South	67.1	134	Indonesia	58.28
15	Italy	74.22	76	Ecuador	67.09	135	Poland	58.14
16	Spain	74.22	77	St. Lucia	66.98	136	India	57.69
17	France	74.04	78	Hungary	66.81	137	Myanmar (Burma)	57.5
18	Dominica	73.89	79	China	66.78	138	Vanuatu	57.11
19	Norway	73.79	80	Azerbaijan	66.77	139	Pakistan	56.54
20	Cyprus	73.75	81	Suriname	66.65	140	Comoros	55.23
21	Monaco	73.7	82	Lebanon	66.63	141	Papua New Guinea	55.19
22	Liechtenstein	73.65	83	Korea, North	66.42	142	Bangladesh	55.0
23	Belgium	73.41	84	Lithuania	66.39	143	Liberia	54.88
24	Bermuda	73.36	85	Mauritius	66.34	144	Cameroon	54.65
25	United Kingdom	73.31	86	Algeria	66.32	145	Senegal	54.59
26	Austria	73.18	87	Belarus	66.04	146	Togo	54.45
27	Singapore	73.07	88	Malaysia	65.96	147	Nigeria	53.54
28	Germany	73.0	89	Belize	65.91	148	Ghana	53.27
29	St. Kitts and Nevis	72.78	90	Dominican Republic	65.87	149	Sudan	53.0
30	Luxembourg	72.71	91	Saudi Arabia	65.71	150	Kiribati	52.56
31	Denmark	72.63	92	Morocco	65.7	151	Kenya	52.27
32	Ireland	72.56	93	Seychelles	65.66	152	Swaziland	51.97
33	United States	72.49	94	Tajikistan	65.66	153	Nepal	51.84
34	Kuwait	72.47				154	Madagascar	51.65
35	New Zealand	72.46	**LOWER MIDDLE**			155	Gabon	51.46
36	Bosnia & Herzegovina	72.11	95	Tonga	65.5	156	Bhutan	50.74
37	Panama	71.99	96	Oman	65.47	157	Ethiopia	50.6
38	Jamaica	71.92	97	Ukraine	65.32	158	Yemen	49.83
39	Finland	71.85	98	Western Samoa	65.19	159	Laos	49.67
40	Taiwan	71.84	99	Syria	65.07	160	Equatorial Guinea	49.56
41	Portugal	71.43	100	Thailand	65.05	161	Benin	49.51
42	Paraguay	71.42	101	Uzbekistan	65.05	162	Cambodia	47.6
43	Chile	71.16	102	Honduras	64.82	163	Gambia	47.41
44	Macedonia	71.15	103	Estonia	64.75	164	Djibouti	47.01
45	Antigua and Barbuda	70.81	104	Moldova	64.49	165	Cote d'Ivoire	46.98
46	Barbados	70.75	105	Iran	64.37	166	Burkina	46.66
47	Bahrain	70.72	106	Nauru	64.3	167	Congo	46.3
48	Tunisia	70.55	107	Iraq	64.2	168	Mozambique	46.22
49	Uruguay	70.52	108	Latvia	64.15	169	Zaire	45.45
50	Puerto Rico	70.25	109	El Salvador	63.93	170	Guinea-Bissau	45.38
51	St. Vincent	70.21	110	Russia	63.59	171	Afghanistan	45.09
52	Slovenia	70.08	111	Mongolia	63.53	172	Zambia	44.97
53	Albania	70.01	112	Kyrgyzstan	63.47	173	Mauritania	44.81
54	United Arab Emirates	69.91	113	Kazakhstan	63.17	174	Mali	43.89
55	Jordan	69.83	114	Vietnam	63.08	175	Haiti	43.68
56	Venezuela	69.76	115	Peru	63.02	176	Angola	43.20
57	Qatar	69.73	116	South Africa	62.67	177	Sierra Leone	43.1
58	Croatia	69.7	117	Fiji	62.62	178	Niger	42.6

Rank	Country	Life Expectancy for Men (years)	Rank	Country	Life Expectancy for Men (years)	Rank	Country	Life Expectancy for Men (years)
BOTTOM 10			182	Zimbabwe	41.2	186	Uganda	39.09
179	Tanzania	42.19	183	Rwanda	40.2	187	Burundi	38.79
180	Guinea	41.49	184	Malawi	39.61	188	Somalia	32.86
181	Central African Republic	41.46	185	Chad	39.36			

Source: *Demographic Yearbook*

14. BIRTH RATE

Birth rates measure gross additions to the population and, when used in combination with death rates, provide some estimate of population growth. Statistics on live birth rates are subject to the same errors as other vital statistics. Most of the rates are based on civil registers, which in many cases are incomplete or unreliable. In other cases there is a prolonged lag between birth and registration. Some countries do not include in the statistics infants who are born alive but who die within the first 24 hours of life. The rates are also affected by the problems of underenumeration or overenumeration of the total population.

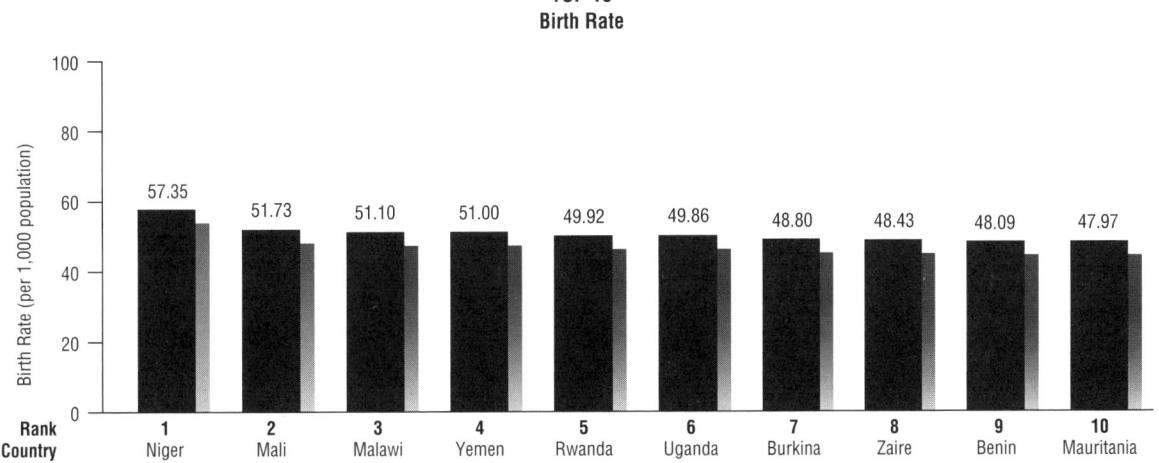

TOP 10
Birth Rate

Rank	1	2	3	4	5	6	7	8	9	10
Birth Rate	57.35	51.73	51.10	51.00	49.92	49.86	48.80	48.43	48.09	47.97
Country	Niger	Mali	Malawi	Yemen	Rwanda	Uganda	Burkina	Zaire	Benin	Mauritania

Rank	Country	Birth Rate (per 1,000 population)	Rank	Country	Birth Rate (per 1,000 population)	Rank	Country	Birth Rate (per 1,000 population)
UPPER MIDDLE			33	Laos	43.82	56	Zimbabwe	38.16
11	Togo	47.87	34	Nigeria	43.8	57	Nepal	37.99
12	Cape Verde	47.02	35	Namibia	43.77	58	Guatemala	36.19
13	Gambia	46.95	36	Senegal	43.32	59	Honduras	35.82
14	Cote d'Ivoire	46.88	37	Swaziland	43.22	60	Belize	35.75
15	Comoros	46.75	38	Kenya	43.18	61	Nicaragua	35.61
16	Zambia	46.53	39	Djibouti	43.05	62	Tajikistan	35.52
17	Angola	45.8	40	Iran	43.0	63	Bangladesh	35.41
18	Libya	45.66	41	Central African Republic	42.77	64	Sao Tome e Principe	35.39
19	Madagascar	45.66	42	Sudan	42.65	65	Lesotho	34.64
20	Tanzania	45.66	43	Pakistan	42.59	66	Papua New Guinea	33.77
21	Cambodia	45.52	44	Chad	42.21	67	South Africa	33.77
22	Sierra Leone	45.47	45	Somalia	41.95	68	Mongolia	33.41
23	Ethiopia	45.37	46	Guinea-Bissau	41.26	69	Botswana	33.39
24	Mozambique	45.35	47	Equatorial Guinea	41.1	70	Vanuatu	33.16
25	Guinea	44.76	48	Congo	40.68	71	El Salvador	33.12
26	Ghana	44.66	49	Cameroon	40.66	72	Egypt	33.0
27	Burundi	44.59	50	Oman	40.56	73	Western Samoa	33.0
28	Iraq	44.57	51	Haiti	40.47	74	Bolivia	32.83
29	Maldives	44.34	52	Bhutan	39.59	75	Paraguay	32.61
30	Syria	44.08	53	Jordan	39.48	76	Kiribati	32.03
31	Liberia	43.9	54	Solomon Islands	39.37	77	Turkmenistan	30.91
32	Afghanistan	43.83	55	Saudi Arabia	38.59	78	Grenada	30.85

Rank	Country	Birth Rate (per 1,000 population)	Rank	Country	Birth Rate (per 1,000 population)	Rank	Country	Birth Rate (per 1,000 population)
79	Uzbekistan	30.57	115	Seychelles	22.35	153	Ireland	14.39
80	Algeria	30.38	116	Jamaica	22.24	154	Estonia	14.05
81	Kuwait	30.29	117	Brazil	21.77	155	Latvia	13.99
82	Morocco	29.23	118	Chile	20.9	156	Malta	13.9
83	India	29.11	119	St. Vincent	20.86	157	Andorra	13.78
84	Malaysia	28.93	120	Dominica	20.82	158	Sweden	13.78
85	Myanmar (Burma)	28.88	121	Israel	20.72	159	Norway	13.75
86	Gabon	28.63	122	Guyana	20.47	160	Romania	13.66
87	United Arab Emirates	28.4	123	Trinidad and Tobago	20.08	161	Poland	13.59
88	Vietnam	27.99	124	Thailand	19.97	162	United Kingdom	13.58
89	Philippines	27.9	125	Argentina	19.75	163	Bosnia & Herzegovina	13.54
90	Lebanon	27.86	126	Mauritius	19.67	164	Belarus	13.28
91	Mexico	27.67	127	Qatar	19.61	165	France	13.24
92	Bahrain	26.89	128	Kazakhstan	19.55	166	Liechtenstein	13.15
93	Tuvalu	26.79	129	Bahamas	18.97	167	Czech Republic	13.0
94	Kyrgyzstan	26.69	130	Nauru	18.92	168	Luxembourg	12.96
			131	Sri Lanka	18.71	169	Netherlands	12.81
LOWER MIDDLE			132	China	18.29	170	Russia	12.73
95	Turkey	26.62	133	Uruguay	17.82	171	Finland	12.61
96	Brunei	26.55	134	Antigua and Barbuda	17.51	172	Denmark	12.5
97	Ecuador	26.54	135	Cyprus	17.14	173	Ukraine	12.38
98	Venezuela	26.37	136	Singapore	17.12	174	Switzerland	12.37
99	Peru	26.19	137	Cuba	17.08	175	Hungary	12.33
100	Costa Rica	26.07	138	Iceland	16.99	176	Belgium	11.94
101	Suriname	25.85	139	Puerto Rico	16.93	177	Slovenia	11.93
102	Armenia	25.79	140	Georgia	16.48	178	Bulgaria	11.69
103	Dominican Republic	25.68	141	Moldova	16.15			
104	Tonga	25.16	142	New Zealand	15.93	**BOTTOM 10**		
105	Panama	25.08	143	Macedonia	15.91	179	Portugal	11.59
106	Indonesia	24.84	144	Taiwan	15.88	180	Austria	11.54
107	Fiji	24.74	145	Barbados	15.78	181	Croatia	11.38
108	Tunisia	24.24	146	Korea, South	15.72	182	San Marino	11.32
109	Azerbaijan	24.09	147	United States	15.48	183	Germany	11.0
110	Korea, North	24.09	148	Bermuda	15.21	184	Spain	10.88
111	St. Lucia	23.97	149	Lithuania	14.95	185	Monaco	10.8
112	St. Kitts and Nevis	23.93	150	Slovakia	14.59	186	Italy	10.65
113	Colombia	23.4	151	Canada	14.48	187	Greece	10.42
114	Albania	23.24	152	Australia	14.43	188	Japan	10.31

Source: *Demographic Yearbook*

15. FERTILITY RATE

Fertility rates are the number of live births reported in a calendar year per 1,000 females aged 15 to 49. When used together with birth rates, they provide a useful tool for the measurement of population growth rates.

Rank	Country	Total Fertility Rate	Rank	Country	Total Fertility Rate	Rank	Country	Total Fertility Rate
TOP 10			18	Togo	6.5	38	Guinea-Bissau	5.7
1	Yemen	7.5	19	Burkina	6.4	39	Cameroon	5.6
2	Cote d'Ivoire	7.3	20	Mozambique	6.4	40	Central African Republic	5.6
3	Niger	7.3	21	Nigeria	6.4	41	Iraq	5.6
4	Uganda	7.2	22	Rwanda	6.4	42	Gambia	5.5
5	Malawi	7.1	23	Sierra Leone	6.4	43	Gabon	5.4
6	Oman	7.1	24	Libya	6.3	44	Guatemala	5.3
7	Benin	7.0	25	Saudi Arabia	6.3	45	Nepal	5.3
8	Mali	7.0	26	Congo	6.2	46	Solomon Islands	5.3
9	Ethiopia	6.9	27	Pakistan	6.1	47	Cambodia	5.2
10	Guinea	6.9	28	Comoros	6.0	48	Kenya	5.2
			29	Madagascar	6.0	49	Mauritania	5.2
UPPER MIDDLE			30	Senegal	6.0	50	Namibia	5.2
11	Somalia	6.9	31	Ghana	5.9	51	Jordan	5.1
12	Afghanistan	6.8	32	Zambia	5.9	52	Lesotho	5.1
13	Burundi	6.7	33	Chile	5.8	53	Papua New Guinea	5.0
14	Liberia	6.7	34	Equatorial Guinea	5.8	54	Iran	4.9
15	Maldives	6.7	35	Syria	5.8	55	Nicaragua	4.9
16	Laos	6.6	36	Tanzania	5.8	56	Zimbabwe	4.9
17	Zaire	6.6	37	Djibouti	5.7	57	Botswana	4.8

Rank	Country	Total Fertility Rate
58	Haiti	4.8
59	Honduras	4.8
60	Swaziland	4.8
61	Tajikistan	4.8
62	Bolivia	4.7
63	Vanuatu	4.6
64	Bangladesh	4.3
65	Qatar	4.3
66	Cape Verde	4.2
67	Paraguay	4.2
68	United Arab Emirates	4.2
69	Belize	4.1
70	Myanmar (Burma)	4.1
71	El Salvador	4.0
72	South Africa	4.0
73	Philippines	3.9
74	Turkmenistan	3.9
75	Algeria	3.8
76	Egypt	3.8
77	Uzbekistan	3.8
78	Vietnam	3.8
79	Bahrain	3.7
80	India	3.7
81	Kyrgyzstan	3.6
82	Morocco	3.6
83	Malaysia	3.5
84	Mongolia	3.5
85	Ecuador	3.4
86	Peru	3.3
87	Turkey	3.3
88	Venezuela	3.2
89	Costa Rica	3.1
90	Kuwait	3.1
91	Mexico	3.1
92	Tunisia	3.1
93	Brunei	3.0
LOWER MIDDLE		
94	Dominican Republic	3.0

Rank	Country	Total Fertility Rate
95	Lebanon	3.0
96	Fiji	2.9
97	Albania	2.8
98	Brazil	2.8
99	Indonesia	2.8
100	Israel	2.8
101	Panama	2.8
102	Argentina	2.7
103	Armenia	2.6
104	Colombia	2.6
105	Suriname	2.6
106	Azerbaijan	2.5
107	Chad	2.5
108	Cyprus	2.5
109	Guyana	2.5
110	Kazakhstan	2.5
111	Sri Lanka	2.4
112	Trinidad and Tobago	2.4
113	Jamaica	2.3
114	Korea, North	2.3
115	Mauritius	2.3
116	Uruguay	2.3
117	Iceland	2.2
118	New Zealand	2.2
119	Puerto Rico	2.2
120	Angola	2.1
121	Georgia	2.1
122	Ireland	2.1
123	Malta	2.1
124	Moldova	2.1
125	Sweden	2.1
126	Thailand	2.1
127	United States	2.1
128	Bahamas	2.0
129	China	2.0
130	Macedonia	2.0
131	Yugoslavia	2.0
132	Australia	1.9
133	Canada	1.9

Rank	Country	Total Fertility Rate
134	Finland	1.9
135	Norway	1.9
136	Poland	1.9
137	Slovakia	1.9
138	Barbados	1.8
139	Cuba	1.8
140	Czech Republic	1.8
141	Lithuania	1.8
142	Taiwan	1.8
143	United Kingdom	1.8
144	Belarus	1.7
145	Belgium	1.7
146	Croatia	1.7
147	Denmark	1.7
148	France	1.7
149	Hungary	1.7
150	Korea, South	1.7
151	Luxembourg	1.7
152	Singapore	1.7
153	Sudan	1.7
154	Estonia	1.6
155	Latvia	1.6
156	Netherlands	1.6
157	Portugal	1.6
158	Switzerland	1.6
159	Ukraine	1.6
BOTTOM 10		
160	Austria	1.5
161	Bulgaria	1.5
162	Japan	1.5
163	Romania	1.5
164	Russia	1.5
165	Slovenia	1.5
166	Greece	1.4
167	Germany	1.3
168	Italy	1.3
169	Spain	1.2

Source: UN Population Division

16. INFANT MORTALITY RATE

Infant mortality, or the number of deaths of infants under one year of age per 1,000 live births, is a direct measure of the physical quality of life. Infant mortality rates are sensitive to even small improvements in national health care, and rates have been declining in all parts of the world. The problem, however is still severe in many countries of Asia and Africa as the spread between the highest and lowest rates indicates. The reliability of the figures is affected by the requirements and means provided for registration. Even the definition of an infant varies from country to country. Some countries require breathing to establish a live birth but others recognize any signs of life. Some countries do not register as a live birth any infant dying within 24 hours or before registration. A few countries report births and deaths not by year of occurrence but by year of registration. A few others do not report infant deaths. However, none of these limitations is serious enough to significantly distort the data or make them incomparable.

Rank	Country	Infant Mortality Rate (per 1,000)
TOP 10		
1	Somalia	162.7
2	Afghanistan	158.9
3	Angola	148.6
4	Sierra Leone	145.0
5	Malawi	141.9

Rank	Country	Infant Mortality Rate (per 1,000)
6	Guinea	141.7
7	Central African Republic	138.7
8	Chad	134.0
9	Mozambique	131.4
10	Gambia	126.3

Rank	Country	Infant Mortality (per 1,000)
UPPER MIDDLE		
11	Bhutan	123.3
12	Guinea-Bissau	122.1
13	Burkina	119.8
14	Rwanda	119.4
15	Liberia	115.9

Rank	Country	Infant Mortality Rate (per 1,000)	Rank	Country	Infant Mortality Rate (per 1,000)	Rank	Country	Infant Mortality Rate (per 1,000)
16	Burundi	115.6	75	Morocco	53.4	132	St. Lucia	18.7
17	Yemen	115.6	76	China	52.1	133	Fiji	18.4
18	Djibouti	113.2	77	Turkey	52.0	134	St. Vincent	18.3
19	Zaire	113.2	78	Philippines	51.9	135	Uruguay	18.0
20	Niger	112.8	79	Guyana	49.3	136	Jamaica	17.5
21	Benin	112.7	80	South Africa	48.3	137	Panama	17.2
22	Congo	112.7	81	Kyrgyzstan	47.8	138	Lithuania	16.9
23	Uganda	112.1	82	Honduras	47.2	139	Trinidad and Tobago	16.9
24	Cambodia	111.5	83	Vietnam	46.4	140	Chile	15.9
25	Tanzania	110.4	84	Mongolia	44.9	141	Puerto Rico	14.0
26	Haiti	109.5	85	Syria	43.9	142	Poland	13.8
27	Bangladesh	109.2	86	El Salvador	42.8	143	Bosnia & Herzegovina	13.2
28	Ethiopia	108.8	87	Kazakhstan	41.8	144	Bermuda	13.1
29	Mali	108.0	88	Lebanon	41.0	145	Hungary	13.1
30	Equatorial Guinea	104.9	89	Ecuador	40.8	146	Kuwait	13.1
31	Laos	104.4	90	Botswana	40.6	147	Grenada	12.7
32	Pakistan	103.6	91	Nauru	40.6	148	Bulgaria	12.6
33	Kiribati	98.4	92	Western Samoa	38.6	149	Seychelles	12.1
34	Gabon	97.3	93	Thailand	38.5	150	Costa Rica	11.6
35	Cote d'Ivoire	97.0				151	Slovakia	10.8
36	Swaziland	95.7	**LOWER MIDDLE**			152	Dominica	10.7
37	Togo	91.3	94	Oman	38.4	153	Cuba	10.5
38	Madagascar	91.0	95	Belize	36.5	154	Portugal	9.8
39	Mauritania	87.0	96	Tunisia	35.9	155	Czech Republic	9.7
40	Nepal	85.8	97	Azerbaijan	35.7	156	Cyprus	9.3
41	Ghana	84.5	98	Jordan	33.3	157	New Zealand	9.1
42	Zambia	83.9	99	Suriname	32.4	158	Croatia	9.0
43	Comoros	81.8	100	Albania	31.8	159	Greece	8.9
44	Sudan	81.3	101	Bahamas	31.6	160	Israel	8.9
45	India	80.5	102	Moldova	30.8	161	Slovenia	8.3
46	Cameroon	78.8	103	Argentina	30.0	162	United States	8.3
47	Egypt	78.3	104	Colombia	29.7	163	Malta	8.2
48	Senegal	77.8	105	Macedonia	29.7	164	Andorra	8.1
49	Nigeria	77.3	106	Solomon Islands	29.0	165	Italy	7.8
50	Bolivia	76.7	107	Venezuela	28.9	166	Ireland	7.6
51	Zimbabwe	75.3	108	Mexico	28.8	167	Australia	7.4
52	Kenya	74.7	109	Korea, North	28.6	168	Belgium	7.4
53	Iraq	71.8	110	Armenia	28.2	169	United Kingdom	7.4
54	Lesotho	71.5	111	Russia	27.6	170	Austria	7.3
55	Turkmenistan	71.2	112	Tuvalu	26.8	171	Monaco	7.3
56	Vanuatu	69.9	113	Malaysia	26.5	172	Denmark	7.1
57	Indonesia	69.6	114	Paraguay	26.4	173	Canada	7.0
58	Myanmar (Burma)	65.7	115	Brunei	25.7	174	Germany	7.0
59	Libya	65.5	116	Georgia	24.2	175	Spain	7.0
60	Papua New Guinea	64.9	117	Sri Lanka	22.8	176	Luxembourg	6.9
61	Sao Tome e Principe	64.9	118	Qatar	22.7	177	France	6.8
62	Namibia	63.8	119	Korea, South	22.5			
63	Tajikistan	63.6	120	United Arab Emirates	22.5	**BOTTOM 10**		
64	Iran	62.1	121	Latvia	22.0	178	Switzerland	6.6
65	Brazil	61.7	122	Barbados	21.3	179	Norway	6.4
66	Cape Verde	59.6	123	Tonga	21.3	180	Netherlands	6.2
67	Maldives	57.6	124	Romania	21.2	181	Singapore	5.8
68	Peru	56.4	125	Ukraine	21.0	182	Sweden	5.8
69	Guatemala	55.6	126	St. Kitts and Nevis	20.5	183	San Marino	5.7
70	Saudi Arabia	55.3	127	Bahrain	20.1	184	Finland	5.4
71	Nicaragua	54.8	128	Estonia	19.5	185	Liechtenstein	5.3
72	Uzbekistan	54.4	129	Antigua and Barbuda	19.2	186	Japan	4.3
73	Algeria	54.0	130	Belarus	19.2	187	Iceland	4.0
74	Dominican Republic	53.6	131	Mauritius	19.0			

Source: UN Population Division

17. DEATH RATE

Death is defined as the permanent disappearance of all evidence of life at any time after live birth has taken place. Death statistics are subject to the same qualifications as other vital statistics and are obtained mostly from civil registers, the reliability of which varies from country to country.

Rank	Country	Death Rate (per 1,000 population)
TOP 10		
1	Djibouti	76.06
2	Somalia	28.41
3	Uganda	22.98
4	Malawi	22.87
5	Niger	22.44
6	Burundi	21.25
7	Chad	20.93
8	Rwanda	20.87
9	Mali	20.81
10	Central African Republic	20.49
UPPER MIDDLE		
11	Guinea	20.13
12	Sierra Leone	19.39
13	Afghanistan	19.33
14	Tanzania	19.02
15	Angola	18.96
16	Haiti	18.88
17	Burkina	18.19
18	Zimbabwe	17.68
19	Guinea-Bissau	17.45
20	Zaire	16.91
21	Zambia	16.88
22	Mozambique	16.71
23	Cambodia	16.57
24	Myanmar (Burma)	16.57
25	Mauritania	16.54
26	Congo	16.28
27	Bhutan	16.26
28	Gambia	16.1
29	Yemen	15.37
30	Laos	15.22
31	Equatorial Guinea	15.11
32	Cote d'Ivoire	15.07
33	Benin	14.8
34	Ethiopia	14.23
35	Gabon	14.08
36	Madagascar	13.71
37	Nepal	13.66
38	Hungary	13.02
39	Nigeria	12.85
40	Latvia	12.73
41	Pakistan	12.6
42	Ukraine	12.53
43	Ghana	12.52
44	Sudan	12.45
45	Liberia	12.38
46	Senegal	12.38
47	Monaco	12.32
48	Kiribati	12.31
49	Estonia	12.13
50	Bangladesh	11.94
51	Togo	11.8
52	Cameroon	11.63
53	Bulgaria	11.54
54	Czech Republic	11.44
55	Denmark	11.42
56	Kenya	11.41
57	Swaziland	11.41
58	Russia	11.32
59	Comoros	11.31
60	Belarus	11.1
61	Germany	11.0

Rank	Country	Death Rate (per 1,000 population)
62	Sweden	10.96
63	Lithuania	10.94
64	United Kingdom	10.87
65	Croatia	10.73
66	Papua New Guinea	10.57
67	Norway	10.54
68	India	10.52
69	Austria	10.42
70	St. Kitts and Nevis	10.39
71	Belgium	10.32
72	Romania	10.17
73	Moldova	10.01
74	Finland	9.91
75	Portugal	9.77
76	Italy	9.66
77	Slovenia	9.6
78	Poland	9.59
79	Vanuatu	9.57
80	Uruguay	9.52
81	Slovakia	9.47
82	Lesotho	9.44
83	Cape Verde	9.43
84	Tuvalu	9.41
85	Greece	9.36
86	France	9.3
87	Switzerland	9.24
88	Namibia	9.13
89	Sao Tome e Principe	9.06
90	Egypt	9.0
91	Spain	8.76
92	Indonesia	8.73
LOWER MIDDLE		
93	Ireland	8.71
94	Georgia	8.68
95	Argentina	8.64
96	Bolivia	8.63
97	Barbados	8.53
98	Netherlands	8.53
99	Libya	8.37
100	Brazil	8.3
101	New Zealand	8.11
102	Botswana	8.06
103	Iran	8.06
104	Kazakhstan	7.95
105	Vietnam	7.92
106	Maldives	7.91
107	Puerto Rico	7.88
108	Cyprus	7.74
109	Guatemala	7.74
110	Iraq	7.71
111	South Africa	7.65
112	Turkmenistan	7.6
113	Malta	7.52
114	Kyrgyzstan	7.45
115	Guyana	7.39
116	Australia	7.38
117	China	7.34
118	San Marino	7.25
119	Japan	7.17
120	Mongolia	7.16
121	Peru	7.15
122	Seychelles	7.12
123	Philippines	7.03

Rank	Country	Death Rate (per 1,000 population)
124	Andorra	6.99
125	Nicaragua	6.94
126	Tajikistan	6.87
127	Macedonia	6.79
128	Armenia	6.77
129	Tonga	6.75
130	Iceland	6.74
131	Lebanon	6.66
132	Uzbekistan	6.63
133	Liechtenstein	6.62
134	Azerbaijan	6.61
135	Fiji	6.59
136	Luxembourg	6.56
137	Morocco	6.56
138	El Salvador	6.53
139	Cuba	6.5
140	Grenada	6.46
141	Israel	6.45
142	Honduras	6.44
143	Mauritius	6.44
144	Syria	6.44
145	Algeria	6.41
146	Bosnia & Herzegovina	6.38
147	Dominican Republic	6.38
148	Thailand	6.33
149	Trinidad and Tobago	6.31
150	Western Samoa	6.17
151	Korea, South	6.16
152	Belize	6.15
153	Suriname	6.1
154	Saudi Arabia	6.05
155	Turkey	5.97
156	Oman	5.94
157	St. Lucia	5.91
158	Sri Lanka	5.84
159	Ecuador	5.8
160	Malaysia	5.77
161	Jamaica	5.72
162	Chile	5.55
163	Taiwan	5.54
164	Korea, North	5.52
165	Antigua and Barbuda	5.5
166	Albania	5.45
167	St. Vincent	5.39
168	Singapore	5.25
169	Bahamas	5.15
170	Nauru	5.1
171	Dominica	5.06
172	Tunisia	5.04
173	Brunei	5.02
174	Panama	4.94
175	Colombia	4.82
BOTTOM 10		
176	Mexico	4.82
177	Solomon Islands	4.76
178	Venezuela	4.69
179	Paraguay	4.58
180	Jordan	4.32
181	Bahrain	3.87
182	Costa Rica	3.57
183	Qatar	3.53
184	United Arab Emirates	3.07
185	Kuwait	2.39

Source: *Demographic Yearbook*

Section

III

POPULATION DYNAMICS & THE FAMILY

This section deals with four key areas of population dynamics: density, urbanization, marriage and divorce, and family planning. The density rankings reflect dispersion and concentration of population within national borders. Of the two rankings, the density per sq km/sq mi of agricultural land is the more reliable because it is the effective density measured against usable land area. Urban rankings appear under Section XXII (Cities) but a new ranking on rural population appears here. The rise of megalopolises is making the traditional dichotomy between rural and urban less viable. A person could live within 100 miles of New York City or London and still lead an urban and unrural existence because of the availability of fast transport, electronic media and other conveniences.

The central themes of the marriage and divorce rankings are those that concern every sociologist. They may not answer the question: Will the family survive as an institution? But they point to some significant trends. Two related rankings are provided here: Illegitimate Births and the Average Size of Household. Another ranking is presented on family planning. Although family planning has been accepted as official policy in 33 countries, statistics are available only on the developing countries, but it is difficult to determine how much these resemble Potemkin Villages, facades created not to inform but to mislead.

The quality of the data in these rankings is among the most deficient in the book. The reasons are obvious. There is a lack of comparability even in definitions of such terms as marriage or household. Many countries do not have the capability to collect such specialized data, and even where such capability exists, there is no national provision for registration of events such as marriage or divorce but only municipal or state ordinances, which vary in force and sanction. The comparability of the data is further undermined by the differing periods or time frames to which they refer. Thus, considerable caution should be exercised in interpreting the data in the rankings or in attempting analysis or comparisons.

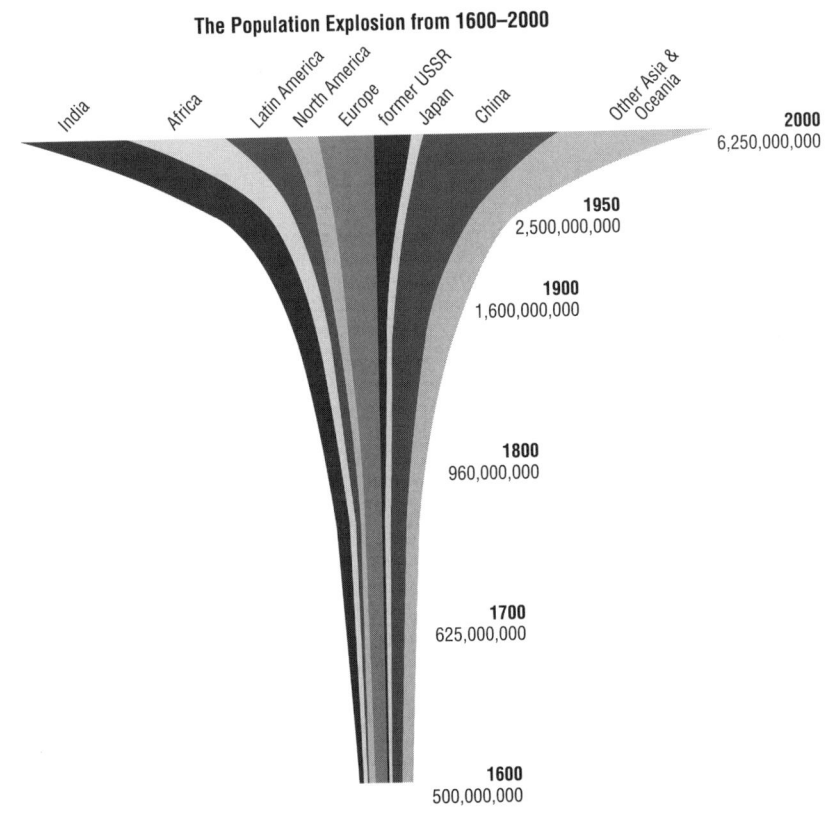

The Population Explosion from 1600–2000

India   Africa   Latin America   North America   Europe   former USSR   Japan   China   Other Asia & Oceania

2000
6,250,000,000

1950
2,500,000,000

1900
1,600,000,000

1800
960,000,000

1700
625,000,000

1600
500,000,000

18. POPULATION DENSITY

Population density is the most common indicator of the relation of population to available land. However, since overall density figures obscure unequal distribution within countries, this ranking should be read in light of the ranking for density in agricultural areas. In many countries with a moderate overall density (Egypt is a good example), virtually the entire population is concentrated along rivers or other productive areas. Density of population is both a cause and a result of economic development. A thinly spread population, for example, often requires greater investment in transportation and infrastructure.

Rank	Country	Density (per sq mi)	Rank	Country	Density (per sq mi)	Rank	Country	Density (per sq mi)
TOP 10			57	Dominica	298	114	Senegal	114
1	Monaco	40,155	58	Thailand	297	115	Cote d'Ivoire	112
2	Singapore	11,731	59	Portugal	296	116	Latvia	110
3	Bermuda	3,208	60	Yugoslavia	294	117	Jordan	108
4	Malta	2,935	61	St. Kitts and Nevis	291	118	Fiji	107
5	Bahrain	2,379	62	Hungary	290	119	Tajikistan	106
6	Bangladesh	2,365	63	Slovakia	284	120	Iran	100
7	Maldives	2,099	64	Indonesia	280	121	Guinea-Bissau	99
8	Taiwan	1,693	65	Kiribati	276	122	Ecuador	98
9	Mauritius	1,550	66	France	273	123	Bhutan	94
10	Barbados	1,538	67	Malawi	271	124	Burkina	93
			68	Nigeria	270	125	Estonia	92
UPPER MIDDLE			69	Cape Verde	264	126	South Africa	91
11	Nauru	1,219	70	Romania	261	127	Panama	88
12	Korea, South	1,177	71	Cuba	256	128	Colombia	87
13	Netherlands	1,166	72	Slovenia	252	129	Nicaragua	86
14	Puerto Rico	1,098	73	Uganda	251	130	United Arab Emirates	82
15	San Marino	1,030	74	Guatemala	250	131	Tanzania	80
16	Tuvalu	963	75	Austria	248	132	Liberia	77
17	Lebanon	899	76	Kuwait	247	133	United States	73
18	St. Vincent	875	77	Gambia	241	134	Zimbabwe	73
19	Belgium	860	78	Bosnia & Herzegovina	234	135	Cameroon	70
20	Rwanda	845	79	Azerbaijan	227	136	Bahamas	69
21	Japan	818	80	Ukraine	222	137	Afghanistan	66
22	India	787	81	Macedonia	221	138	Guinea	66
23	Grenada	717	82	Croatia	215	139	Kyrgyzstan	60
24	Sri Lanka	714	83	Georgia	209	140	Venezuela	59
25	El Salvador	705	84	Bulgaria	207	141	Madagascar	58
26	Trinidad and Tobago	663	85	Greece	207	142	Sweden	55
27	Israel	627	86	Turkey	205	143	Mozambique	54
28	United Kingdom	621	87	Cyprus	203	144	Yemen	53
29	St. Lucia	612	88	Spain	203	145	Laos	51
30	Comoros	611	89	Syria	202	146	Brazil	48
31	Jamaica	605	90	Togo	195	147	Chile	48
32	Burundi	604	91	Myanmar (Burma)	171	148	Djibouti	47
33	Haiti	600	92	Costa Rica	167	149	Peru	47
34	Germany	597	93	Sierra Leone	163	150	Uruguay	47
35	Philippines	595	94	Lesotho	162	151	Zaire	47
36	Vietnam	571				152	Finland	43
37	Italy	511	**LOWER MIDDLE**			153	Equatorial Guinea	37
38	Korea, North	487	95	Morocco	162	154	Norway	36
39	Liechtenstein	481	96	Lithuania	152	155	Solomon Islands	35
40	Switzerland	455	97	Egypt	151	156	Paraguay	33
41	Pakistan	416	98	Western Samoa	150	157	Argentina	32
42	Dominican Republic	411	99	Malaysia	149	158	New Zealand	32
43	Seychelles	406	100	Cambodia	145	159	Zambia	31
44	Luxembourg	399	101	Tunisia	143	160	Algeria	30
45	Nepal	389	102	Swaziland	137	161	Vanuatu	29
46	Antigua and Barbuda	379	103	Brunei	136	162	Somalia	27
47	Tonga	375	104	Ethiopia	133	163	Sudan	27
48	Sao Tome e Principe	359	105	Ireland	133	164	Papua New Guinea	24
49	Andorra	356	106	Belarus	129	165	Belize	23
50	Moldova	342	107	Uzbekistan	128	166	Russia	23
51	Czech Republic	341	108	Kenya	125	167	Saudi Arabia	21
52	Poland	328	109	Mexico	122	168	Turkmenistan	21
53	China	327	110	Benin	121	169	Angola	20
54	Denmark	316	111	Honduras	120	170	Oman	20
55	Albania	315	112	Qatar	118	171	Mali	19
56	Armenia	303	113	Iraq	114	172	Bolivia	18

Rank	Country	Density (per sq mi)	Rank	Country	Density (per sq mi)	Rank	Country	Density (per sq mi)
173	Congo	18		**BOTTOM 10**		184	Australia	6
174	Niger	17	179	Guyana	10	185	Botswana	6
175	Kazakhstan	16	180	Canada	8	186	Mauritania	5
176	Central African Republic	13	181	Iceland	7	187	Namibia	5
177	Chad	11	182	Libya	7	188	Mongolia	4
178	Gabon	11	183	Suriname	7			

Source: *Demographic Yearbook*

19. POPULATION DENSITY IN AGRICULTURAL AREAS

The old demographic concept of living space perhaps may be expressed best through a ranking of population density in agricultural areas. By restricting consideration to areas that are capable of supporting human life, we can devise a more accurate ratio of human beings to land. Agricultural land is defined by the Food and Agriculture Organization as covering arable land, land under permanent crops, and permanent meadows and pastures. It also includes lands temporarily fallow, land under markets and kitchen gardens, plantations, and land under trees, vines and shrubs. Potentially productive land is sometimes excluded, and in any case, it is difficult to determine accurately what land is potentially productive and what is not.

Rank	Country	People per Acre of Cropland	Rank	Country	People per Acre of Cropland	Rank	Country	People per Acre of Cropland
	TOP 10		38	Yemen	3.00	76	Madagascar	1.48
1	Kuwait	194.15	39	Haiti	2.80	77	Nigeria	1.42
2	Bahrain	92.59	40	El Salvador	2.79	78	Malaysia	1.40
3	Qatar	28.33	41	New Zealand	2.66	79	Malawi	1.38
4	U. Arab Emirates	15.57	42	Liberia	2.61	80	Mexico	1.37
5	Iceland	12.60	43	Suriname	2.55	81	Ethiopia	1.34
6	Oman	11.82	44	Germany	2.50	82	Zimbabwe	1.33
7	Malta	10.74	45	Rwanda	2.34	83	Iran, Islamic Rep	1.33
8	Japan	10.58	46	Somalia	2.29	84	Belize	1.31
9	Korea, Rep	8.06	47	Colombia	2.27	85	Iraq	1.31
10	Egypt	8.06	48	Peru	2.25	86	Cote d'Ivoire	1.28
			49	Solomon Islands	2.16	87	Algeria	1.28
	UPPER MIDDLE		50	Lesotho	2.12	88	Cuba	1.26
11	Switzerland	6.43	51	Costa Rica	2.05	89	Fiji	1.23
12	Netherlands	6.42	52	Pakistan	2.05	90	Czechoslovakia	1.23
13	Congo	5.06	53	Austria	2.03	91	Yugoslavia	1.23
14	Belgium	4.87	54	Ghana	1.98	92	Chile	1.18
15	Saudi Arabia	4.79	55	Norway	1.97	93	Sweden	1.18
16	Bangladesh	4.75	56	Mozambique	1.95	94	France	1.17
17	China	4.58	57	Venezuela	1.95	95	Nicaragua	1.16
18	Bhutan	4.27	58	India	1.94	96	Guinea-Bissau	1.14
19	Jordan	4.26	59	Italy	1.91	97	Morocco	1.10
20	Trinidad & Tobago	4.19	60	Tanzania	1.91	98	Honduras	1.10
21	Israel	4.15	61	The Gambia	1.90	99	Thailand	1.09
22	Vietnam	4.11	62	Guatemala	1.89	100	Portugal	1.09
23	Mauritius	4.00	63	Dominican Rep	1.88	101	Angola	1.06
24	Papua New Guinea	3.97	64	Swaziland	1.82	102	South Africa	1.04
25	Mauritania	3.88	65	Comoros	1.81	103	Kampuchea, Dem	1.04
26	Kenya	3.84	66	Albania	1.78	104	Poland	1.04
27	Guinea	3.70	67	Cyprus	1.77	105	Greece	1.03
28	Korea, North	3.69	68	Laos	1.74	106	Uganda	0.98
29	Jamaica	3.65	69	Zaire	1.73	107	Afghanistan	0.98
30	Lebanon	3.58	70	Panama	1.67	108	Burkina Faso	0.97
31	Cape Verde	3.57	71	Myanmar	1.62	109	Benin	0.97
32	Sri Lanka	3.53	72	Burundi	1.56	110	Gabon	0.96
33	Indonesia	3.33				111	Togo	0.95
34	United Kingdom	3.30		**LOWER MIDDLE**		112	Uruguay	0.92
35	Barbados	3.12	73	Mali	1.54	113	Sierra Leone	0.88
36	Nepal	3.10	74	Ecuador	1.54	114	Bulgaria	0.88
37	Philippines	3.03	75	Ireland	1.50	115	Romania	0.87

Rank	Country	People per Acre of Cropland	Rank	Country	People per Acre of Cropland	Rank	Country	People per Acre of Cropland
116	Syrian Arab Rep	0.85	127	Brazil	0.74	136	Central African Rep	0.56
117	Finland	0.82	128	Paraguay	0.74	137	Senegal	0.55
118	Hungary	0.8	129	Equatorial Guinea	0.70	138	United States	0.52
119	Bolivia	0.8	130	Chad	0.68	139	U.S.S.R.	0.50
120	Denmark	0.8	131	Tunisia	0.65	140	Argentina	0.36
121	Libya	0.80	132	Guyana	0.65	141	Botswana	0.34
122	Niger	0.79	133	Cameroon	0.65	142	Canada	0.23
123	Turkey	0.78		**BOTTOM 10**		143	Australia	0.4
124	Spain	0.77	134	Mongolia	0.62			
125	Namibia	0.77	135	Zambia	0.58			
126	Sudan	0.77						

Source: United Nations Food and Agriculture Organization

20. AVERAGE HOUSEHOLD SIZE

The concept of household is based on the arrangements made by persons, either individually or in groups, for providing themselves with food or other essentials of living. When it consists of more than one person, members of a household may pool their incomes and have a common budget and may occupy a whole, a part of, or more than one housing unit. The members of a household may be related or unrelated, or may consist of extended families with a common head. Unmarried couples living in consensual unions are also regarded as households. Although the United Nations defines a household on the basis of common housekeeping arrangements, some countries simply define a household as the entire group of persons jointly occupying a housing unit or as a person living alone in a separate unit. Such differing definitions of households limit the international comparability of data. Aside from the definition of a household, national practices in collecting and compiling statistics of households also differ according to certain differences in enumeration practices. In some countries persons are counted only where physically present, but in other physical presence is not required for enumeration.

TOP 10
Average Household Size

Rank	Country	Household and Family Size	Rank	Country	Household and Family Size
1	Iraq	8.9	6	Kuwait	7.4
2	Senegal	8.8	7	Maldives	7.1
3	Gambia	8.3	8	Algeria	6.9
4	Nauru	8.0	9	Nicaragua	6.9
5	Western Samoa	7.8	10	United Arab Emirates	6.8

1 person = 1 person

Rank	Country	Household & Family Size	Rank	Country	Household & Family Size	Rank	Country	Household & Family Size
UPPER MIDDLE			71	Nigeria	5.0	130	Bolivia	3.8
11	Kiribati	6.6	72	Belize	4.9	131	Korea, South	3.8
12	Saudi Arabia	6.6	73	Egypt	4.9	132	Portugal	3.8
13	Bahrain	6.5	74	El Salvador	4.9	133	Taiwan	3.8
14	Niger	6.4	75	Ghana	4.9	134	Barbados	3.7
15	Qatar	6.4	76	Malaysia	4.9	135	Cuba	3.7
16	Tuvalu	6.4	77	Somalia	4.9	136	Grenada	3.7
17	Pakistan	6.3	78	Angola	4.8	137	Israel	3.7
18	Afghanistan	6.2	79	Azerbaijan	4.8	138	Oman	3.7
19	Burkina	6.2	80	Korea, North	4.8	139	St. Kitts and Nevis	3.7
20	Kenya	6.2	81	Lesotho	4.8	140	Bosnia & Herzegovina	3.6
21	Syria	6.2	82	Mongolia	4.8	141	Malta	3.6
22	Tajikistan	6.1	83	Namibia	4.8	142	Poland	3.6
23	Tonga	6.1	84	Seychelles	4.8	143	Puerto Rico	3.6
24	Fiji	6.0	85	Uganda	4.8	144	Yugoslavia	3.6
25	Jordan	6.0	86	Vietnam	4.8	145	Antigua and Barbuda	3.5
26	Laos	6.0	87	Zimbabwe	4.8	146	Cyprus	3.5
27	Zaire	6.0	88	Albania	4.7	147	Spain	3.5
28	Brunei	5.8	89	Armenia	4.7	148	Moldova	3.4
29	Morocco	5.8	90	Central African Republic	4.7	149	Bulgaria	3.3
30	Botswana	5.7	91	Congo	4.7	150	Greece	3.3
31	Honduras	5.7	92	Guinea	4.7	151	Uruguay	3.3
32	Philippines	5.7	93	Madagascar	4.7	152	Argentina	3.2
33	Swaziland	5.7				153	Belarus	3.2
34	Cambodia	5.6	**LOWER MIDDLE**			154	Lithuania	3.2
35	Comoros	5.6	94	Paraguay	4.7	155	Russia	3.2
36	Djibouti	5.6	95	Rwanda	4.7	156	Ukraine	3.2
37	India	5.6	96	Sierra Leone	4.7	157	Croatia	3.1
38	Mali	5.6	97	Burundi	4.6	158	Estonia	3.1
39	Solomon Islands	5.6	98	Papua New Guinea	4.6	159	Latvia	3.1
40	Togo	5.6	99	South Africa	4.6	160	Romania	3.1
41	Turkmenistan	5.6	100	St. Lucia	4.6	161	Slovenia	3.1
42	Yemen	5.6	101	Equatorial Guinea	4.5	162	Australia	3.0
43	Nepal	5.5	102	Ethiopia	4.5	163	Japan	3.0
44	Uzbekistan	5.5	103	Indonesia	4.5	164	Liechtenstein	3.0
45	Benin	5.4	104	Turkey	4.5	165	Slovakia	3.0
46	Bhutan	5.4	105	Haiti	4.4	166	Hungary	2.9
47	Colombia	5.4	106	Macedonia	4.4	167	Iceland	2.9
48	Cote d'Ivoire	5.4	107	Mozambique	4.4	168	New Zealand	2.9
49	Guatemala	5.4	108	Panama	4.4	169	Italy	2.8
50	Libya	5.4	109	Zambia	4.4	170	Luxembourg	2.8
51	Bangladesh	5.3	110	Dominica	4.3	171	Belgium	2.7
52	Lebanon	5.3	111	Malawi	4.3	172	Canada	2.7
53	Mauritius	5.3	112	Brazil	4.2	173	Czech Republic	2.7
54	Sudan	5.3	113	Costa Rica	4.2	174	San Marino	2.7
55	Thailand	5.3	114	Jamaica	4.2	175	United Kingdom	2.7
56	Venezuela	5.3	115	Kyrgyzstan	4.2	176	Austria	2.6
57	Cameroon	5.2	116	Chile	4.1	177	Bermuda	2.6
58	Myanmar (Burma)	5.2	117	China	4.1			
59	Sri Lanka	5.2	118	Ecuador	4.1	**BOTTOM 10**		
60	Cape Verde	5.1	119	Georgia	4.1	178	France	2.6
61	Dominican Republic	5.1	120	Guinea-Bissau	4.1	179	United States	2.6
62	Guyana	5.1	121	Trinidad and Tobago	4.1	180	Netherlands	2.4
63	Iran	5.1	122	Gabon	4.0	181	Finland	2.3
64	Mexico	5.1	123	Kazakhstan	4.0	182	Germany	2.3
65	Peru	5.1	124	Chad	3.9	183	Denmark	2.2
66	Tanzania	5.1	125	Ireland	3.9	184	Monaco	2.2
67	Tunisia	5.1	126	Singapore	3.9	185	Norway	2.2
68	Vanuatu	5.1	127	St. Vincent	3.9	186	Sweden	2.2
69	Liberia	5.0	128	Suriname	3.9	187	Switzerland	2.2
70	Mauritania	5.0	129	Bahamas	3.8			

Source: UN Population Division

21. SENIOR CITIZENS (65 AND OVER) IN THE POPULATION

Every solution, it has been said, has a problem. Developed countries that congratulate themselves on reducing birth and death rates are soon confronted with a problem of a different, if equally serious, dimension: the growing proportion of senior citizens in the population. The economic costs of this phenomenon are enormous, especially in countries with social security, medicare and other support systems. Eventually, fewer and fewer people who are economically productive are supporting more and more retirees. In addition, there are social and psychological costs of aging that are paid by the elderly alone, such as victimization, loneliness, dependence, etc.

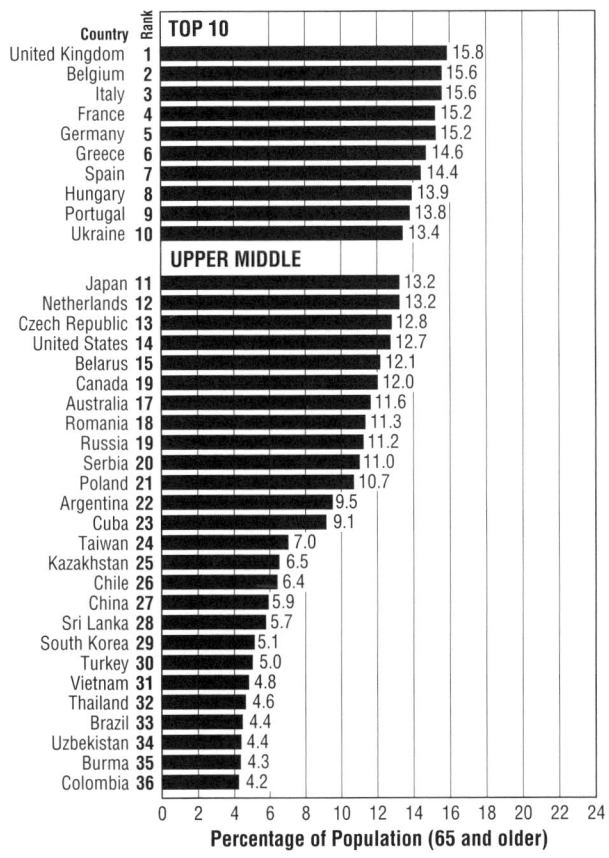

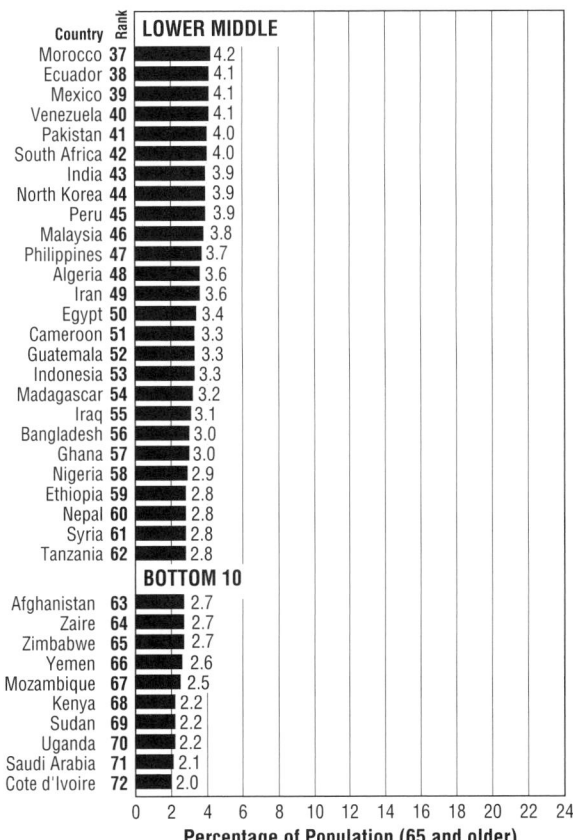

Source: *Statistical Abstract of the Untied States on CD-ROM*

22. SENIORS (65 AND OVER) IN THE POPULATION 2000

As life expectancy rates rise in virtually all countries, one indirect result is the corresponding rise in the percentage of seniors in the general population. In turn, this leads to pressures on social welfare and Social Security systems and, ironically, places additional stresses on geriatric care services, nursing homes, and hospitals. In 1975 the percentage of seniors in highest ranking Austria was only 14.2; in this ranking Italy has the highest at 17.5%. The less developed countries, however, have not shown much change in the relative percentage.

Rank	Country	Percentage of Seniors in Population	Rank	Country	Percentage of Seniors in Population	Rank	Country	Percentage of Seniors in Population
TOP 10			25	Chile	7.3	50	Pakistan	3.9
1	Italy	17.5	26	Kazakhstan	7.3	51	Guatemala	3.7
2	Belgium	17.2	27	China	6.8	52	Egypt	3.5
3	Greece	17.1	28	Sri Lanka	6.6	53	Cameroon	3.4
4	Germany	16.5	29	South Korea	6.5	54	Bangladesh	3.1
5	Japan	16.5	30	Turkey	5.8	55	Ghana	3.0
6	France	16.4	31	Thailand	5.7	56	Madagascar	3.0
7	Spain	16.4	32	Brazil	5.2	57	Nepal	3.0
8	United Kingdom	15.9	33	Vietnam	5.2	58	Iraq	2.9
9	Portugal	15.1	34	Colombia	5.0	59	Nigeria	2.9
10	Hungary	14.9	35	Uzbekistan	4.9	60	Ethiopia	2.8
			36	Mexico	4.8	61	Saudi Arabia	2.8
UPPER MIDDLE						62	Syria	2.8
11	Belarus	14.5						
12	Ukraine	14.5	**LOWER MIDDLE**			**BOTTOM 10**		
13	Netherlands	14.1	37	North Korea	4.7	63	Tanzania	2.8
14	Serbia1	14.0	38	Venezuela	4.7	64	Afghanistan	2.7
15	Romania	13.6	39	Burma	4.6	65	Zimbabwe	2.7
16	Czech Republic	13.4	40	Morocco	4.6	66	Mozambique	2.6
17	Canada	12.8	41	Ecuador	4.5	67	Yemen	2.6
18	United States	12.7	42	Peru	4.5	68	Zaire	2.6
19	Russia	12.6	43	India	4.4	69	Kenya	2.4
20	Poland	12.3	44	Indonesia	4.3	70	Cote d'Ivoire	2.3
21	Australia	12.0	45	South Africa	4.1	71	Sudan	2.3
22	Argentina	10.0	46	Malaysia	4.0	72	Uganda	2.2
23	Cuba	9.9	47	Philippines	4.0			
24	Taiwan	8.4	48	Algeria	3.9			
			49	Iran	3.9			

Source: *Demographic Yearbook*

23. PERCENTAGE OF CHILDREN IN THE POPULATION

In pre-modern societies, children formed between one-third and one-half of the population. It was only in this century that this percentage began to shift in favor of the older age groups. Nevertheless, in less developed societies, especially those with high birth rates, the percentage is closer to 40 and even 50%. It means that these countries have a permanent baby boom whose ripple effects will be felt well beyond this century.

Rank	Country	Percentage of Population Age 1–14	Rank	Country	Percentage of Population Age 1–14	Rank	Country	Percentage of Population Age 1–14
TOP 10			14	Swaziland	47.3	30	Mali	46.1
1	Jordan	51.6	15	Comoros	47.2	31	Yemen	45.7
2	Zimbabwe	51.0	16	Tanzania	47.2	32	Madagascar	45.6
3	Togo	49.8	17	Maldives	46.9	33	Rwanda	45.6
4	Kenya	49.1	18	Cote d'Ivoire	46.8	34	Somalia	45.6
5	Niger	48.7	19	Oman	46.7	35	Vanuatu	45.5
6	Syria	48.5	20	Benin	46.6	36	Djibouti	45.2
7	Zambia	48.4	21	Ethiopia	46.6	37	Iraq	45.2
8	Burkina	48.3	22	Burundi	46.4	38	Sudan	45.2
9	Uganda	48.3	23	Cameroon	46.4	39	Zaire	45.2
10	Nicaragua	48.1	24	Libya	46.4	40	Ghana	45.0
			25	Guinea	46.3	41	Guatemala	44.9
UPPER MIDDLE			26	Sao Tome e Principe	46.3	42	Cape Verde	44.8
11	Senegal	47.5	27	Botswana	46.1	43	Congo	44.7
12	Nigeria	47.4	28	Eritrea	46.1	44	Honduras	44.6
13	Solomon Islands	47.3	29	Malawi	46.1	45	Afghanistan	44.5

Rank	Country	Percentage of Population Age 1–14
46	Pakistan	44.5
47	El Salvador	44.4
48	Mozambique	44.4
49	Namibia	44.4
50	Guinea-Bissau	44.3
51	Iran	44.3
52	Cambodia	44.2
53	Laos	44.2
54	Mauritania	44.1
55	Algeria	43.9
56	Belize	43.9
57	Sierra Leone	43.9
58	Chad	43.3
59	Central African Republic	43.2
60	Liberia	43.2
61	Saudi Arabia	42.9
62	Tajikistan	42.9
63	Lebanon	42.6
64	Nepal	42.3
65	Morocco	42.2
66	Mongolia	41.9
67	Angola	41.7
68	Equatorial Guinea	41.7
69	Bangladesh	41.4
70	Bolivia	41.2
71	Peru	41.2
72	Western Samoa	41.1
73	Gambia	40.8
74	Guyana	40.8
75	Uzbekistan	40.8
76	Lesotho	40.7
77	Myanmar (Burma)	40.7
78	Bhutan	40.6
79	Dominican Republic	40.6
80	Tonga	40.6
81	Turkmenistan	40.5
82	Papua New Guinea	40.4
83	Kiribati	40.3
84	Paraguay	40.1
85	Tunisia	39.7
86	Philippines	39.6
87	Egypt	39.5
88	Suriname	39.3
89	Haiti	39.2
90	Vietnam	39.0
91	Ecuador	38.8
92	Mexico	38.3
93	Venezuela	38.3
94	Fiji	38.2

Rank	Country	Percentage of Population Age 1–14
LOWER MIDDLE		
95	Malaysia	38.1
96	Costa Rica	37.9
97	Kyrgyzstan	37.5
98	St. Vincent	37.4
99	Antigua and Barbuda	37.2
100	Kuwait	36.8
101	St. Lucia	36.8
102	Indonesia	36.6
103	Colombia	36.1
104	India	36.0
105	Grenada	35.9
106	Sri Lanka	35.3
107	Dominica	35.1
108	Turkey	35.0
109	Panama	34.8
110	Brazil	34.7
111	Brunei	34.5
112	Seychelles	33.6
113	Albania	33.0
114	Gabon	33.0
115	Azerbaijan	32.8
116	Israel	32.6
117	Jamaica	32.5
118	St. Kitts and Nevis	32.5
119	Bahamas	32.2
120	South Africa	32.1
121	Kazakhstan	31.9
122	United Arab Emirates	31.9
123	Tuvalu	31.8
124	Bahrain	31.7
125	Trinidad and Tobago	31.3
126	Argentina	30.6
127	Chile	30.6
128	Armenia	30.3
129	Cuba	30.3
130	Mauritius	29.7
131	Australia	29.1
132	Macedonia	29.1
133	Thailand	28.8
134	Korea, North	28.6
135	Moldova	27.9
136	Qatar	27.8
137	China	27.7
138	Bosnia & Herzegovina	27.5
139	Puerto Rico	27.2
140	Taiwan	27.1
141	Ireland	26.7
142	Uruguay	26.6
143	Cyprus	26.1

Rank	Country	Percentage of Population Age 1–14
144	Korea, South	25.7
145	Portugal	25.5
146	Poland	25.4
147	Slovakia	25.0
148	Georgia	24.8
149	Iceland	24.8
150	San Marino	24.4
151	Barbados	24.1
152	Malta	24.1
153	Romania	23.9
154	New Zealand	23.2
155	Singapore	23.2
156	Russia	23.1
157	Belarus	23.0
158	Liechtenstein	23.0
159	Yugoslavia	22.8
160	Lithuania	22.6
161	Estonia	22.2
162	Ukraine	21.5
163	United States	21.5
164	Latvia	21.4
165	Hungary	21.3
166	Czech Republic	21.0
167	Canada	20.9
168	Bulgaria	20.2
169	Slovenia	20.0
170	Bermuda	19.5
171	Croatia	19.4
172	Finland	19.3
173	France	19.1
174	United Kingdom	19.1
175	Norway	18.8
176	Switzerland	18.8
177	Sweden	18.7
178	Greece	18.4
179	Spain	18.4
BOTTOM 10		
180	Netherlands	18.3
181	Belgium	18.2
182	Japan	18.2
183	Austria	17.4
184	Italy	17.3
185	Luxembourg	17.3
186	Denmark	17.0
187	Andorra	16.3
188	Germany	14.6
189	Monaco	12.3

Source: UN Population Division

24. RURAL POPULATION

Worldwide, the historical dominance of rural areas will end by 2000 when for the first time the urban populations will be in the majority. But in over 78 developing countries, the rural populations will continue to be more numerous for many decades to come. There is a strong correlation between the size of the rural population and the strength of the agricultural sector. Industrialization always heralds urbanization.

Rank	Country	Rural Population (as % of total)
TOP 10		
1	Bhutan	94
2	Rwanda	94
3	Burundi	93
4	Malawi	88

Rank	Country	Rural Population (as % of total)
5	Nepal	88
6	Oman	88
7	Uganda	88
8	Ethiopia	87
9	Papua New Guinea	85

Rank	Country	Rural Population (as % of total)
10	Niger	84
UPPER MIDDLE		
11	Solomon Islands	84
12	Bangladesh	83

Rank	Country	Rural Population (as % of total)	Rank	Country	Rural Population (as % of total)	Rank	Country	Rural Population (as % of total)
13	Cambodia	81	52	Ghana	65	89	Algeria	47
14	Thailand	81	53	Guyana	65	90	Cyprus	47
15	Vanuatu	81	54	Antigua and Barbuda	64	91	Congo	44
16	Afghanistan	80	55	Nigeria	63	92	Ecuador	44
17	Laos	80	56	Central African Republic	62	93	Tunisia	44
18	Vietnam	80	57	Equatorial Guinea	61	94	Iran	43
19	Chad	79	58	Fiji	60	95	Bolivia	42
20	Guinea-Bissau	79	59	Guatemala	60	96	Brunei	42
21	Lesotho	79	60	Mauritius	59	97	Mongolia	41
22	Western Samoa	79	61	Saint Kitts and Nevis	59	98	Korea, South	40
23	Burkina	78	62	Senegal	59	99	Dominican Republic	38
24	Sri Lanka	78				100	Nicaragua	38
25	Tanzania	78	**LOWER MIDDLE**			101	Turkey	36
26	Sudan	77	63	Cameroon	58	102	Jordan	30
27	Gambia	76	64	Cote d'Ivoire	58	103	Trinidad and Tobago	30
28	Botswana	75	65	Honduras	58	104	Colombia	29
29	Kenya	75	66	Zambia	58	105	Peru	29
30	Madagascar	75	67	Saint Vincent	57	106	Iraq	27
31	Mali	75	68	Egypt	56	107	Mexico	26
32	Myanmar (Burma)	75	69	El Salvador	56	108	Cuba	25
33	Somalia	75	70	Liberia	56	109	Brazil	24
34	India	74	71	Sao Tome e Principe	56	110	Korea, North	23
35	Maldives	74	72	Barbados	54	111	Saudi Arabia	22
36	China	72	73	Belize	53	112	Djibouti	19
37	Guinea	72	74	Morocco	53	113	United Arab Emirates	18
38	Comoros	71	75	Saint Lucia	53	114	Chile	16
39	Swaziland	71	76	Costa Rica	52	115	Libya	16
40	Zaire	71	77	Gabon	52			
41	Angola	70	78	Cape Verde	51	**BOTTOM 10**		
42	Benin	70	79	Suriname	51	116	Bahamas	15
43	Haiti	70	80	Mauritania	50	117	Lebanon	14
44	Mozambique	70	81	South Africa	50	118	Argentina	13
45	Togo	70	82	Malaysia	49	119	Bahrain	11
46	Zimbabwe	70	83	Paraguay	49	120	Qatar	10
47	Yemen	69	84	Philippines	49	121	Uruguay	10
48	Indonesia	67	85	Syria	49	122	Venezuela	9
49	Pakistan	67	86	Jamaica	48	123	Hong Kong	6
50	Namibia	66	87	Panama	48	124	Kuwait	5
51	Sierra Leone	66	88	Seychelle	48	125	Singapore	0

Source: *World Development Report*

25. MARRIAGE RATE

Marriage is defined in most countries of the world as the legal union of husband and wife through civil, religious or other means. Because marriage is a legal event, unlike birth and death, which are biological events, it is affected by the laws of the individual countries. In some countries statistics are compiled only for civil marriages and in others only for religious marriages as recorded in church registers. Although the legal requirements vary, some form of registration is required in all countries, and therefore marriage statistics tend to be more reliable than those on births and deaths. However, customary unions and consensual unions (where unmarried couples live together) are universally excluded from these statistics, and the recent decline in marriage rates may in some cases only reflect a rise in such de facto unions. Marriage rates are also seriously affected by the age and sex structure of the populations to which they relate.

Rank	Country	Marriage Rate (per 1,000)	Rank	Country	Marriage Rate (per 1,000)	Rank	Country	Marriage Rate (per 1,000)
TOP 10			8	Puerto Rico	12.6	14	Cyprus	9.6
1	Vanuatu	34.0	9	Maldives	11.7	15	Fiji	9.6
2	Bermuda	15.1	10	Bangladesh	10.7	16	Tajikistan	9.6
3	Cuba	15.0				17	Korea, North	9.3
4	Philippines	14.0	**UPPER MIDDLE**			18	Bahamas	9.1
5	Liechtenstein	13.1	11	Turkmenistan	10.7	19	Moldova	9.1
6	Benin	12.8	12	Mauritius	10.3	20	Korea, South	9.0
7	Seychelles	12.7	13	Uzbekistan	10.3	21	United States	9.0

Rank	Country	Marriage Rate (per 1,000)	Rank	Country	Marriage Rate (per 1,000)	Rank	Country	Marriage Rate (per 1,000)
22	Costa Rica	8.8	56	Kazakhstan	6.6	92	Brazil	4.9
23	Sri Lanka	8.7	57	Czech Republic	6.4	93	Estonia	4.9
24	Barbados	8.5	58	Ecuador	6.4	94	Georgia	4.9
25	Singapore	8.4	59	Japan	6.4	95	Honduras	4.9
26	Azerbaijan	8.3	60	Lithuania	6.4	96	Bolivia	4.8
27	Egypt	8.3	61	Luxembourg	6.4	97	Italy	4.8
28	Thailand	8.3	62	Slovakia	6.4	98	Finland	4.7
29	Tonga	8.2	63	Belize	6.2	99	France	4.7
30	Ukraine	8.2	64	Israel	6.2	100	Greece	4.7
31	Iran	8.1	65	Netherlands	6.2	101	Western Samoa	4.7
32	Iraq	8.1	66	New Zealand	6.2	102	Armenia	4.6
33	Jordan	8.1	67	Switzerland	6.2	103	Croatia	4.6
34	Turkey	8.0	68	Uruguay	6.2	104	Iceland	4.6
35	Belarus	7.9	69	Denmark	6.1	105	Suriname	4.6
36	Indonesia	7.9	70	Jamaica	6.1	106	Latvia	4.5
37	Kuwait	7.8	71	Nauru	6.1	107	Norway	4.5
38	Mongolia	7.8	72	Poland	6.1	108	Paraguay	4.5
39	China	7.7	73	United Kingdom	6.1	109	Slovenia	4.5
40	Tunisia	7.7	74	Argentina	6.0	110	Ireland	4.4
41	Albania	7.6	75	Algeria	5.9	111	Mali	4.4
42	Mexico	7.6	76	Bahrain	5.9	112	Peru	4.4
43	Monaco	7.5	77	Yugoslavia	5.9	113	El Salvador	4.3
44	Syria	7.5	78	Kyrgyzstan	5.8	114	Sweden	4.3
45	Russia	7.4	79	Austria	5.6	115	St. Vincent	3.7
46	San Marino	7.4	80	Trinidad and Tobago	5.6			
47	Macedonia	7.3	81	Canada	5.5	**BOTTOM 10**		
48	Romania	7.1	82	Hungary	5.5	116	Dominica	3.3
49	Taiwan	7.1	83	Belgium	5.4	117	Nicaragua	3.3
50	Bosnia & Herzegovina	7.0	84	Germany	5.4	118	Cape Verde	3.2
51	Portugal	6.9	85	Guatemala	5.4	119	St. Lucia	3.2
52	Malta	6.8	86	Venezuela	5.4	120	Qatar	3.0
53	Brunei	6.7	87	Kiribati	5.2	121	South Africa	3.0
			88	Panama	5.2	122	Colombia	2.3
LOWER MIDDLE			89	Bulgaria	5.0	123	Dominican Republic	2.3
54	Chile	6.7	90	Spain	5.0	124	Andorra	2.2
55	Australia	6.6	91	Antigua and Barbuda	4.9	125	Botswana	1.5

Source: *Demographic Yearbook*

26. DIVORCE RATE

Divorce is defined as the final legal dissolution of a marriage conferring on the parties the right to remarry in accordance with the laws of each country. Divorce is a legal event and the laws pertaining to divorce vary from one country to another. The incidence of divorce is affected by the relative ease or difficulty in obtaining a divorce and by the ability of individuals to meet the financial and other costs of court procedures. Another influential factor is the authority of the prevailing religious system. In most Catholic countries, such as Chile, Argentina, Brazil, Malta, Paraguay, the Philippines, St. Lucia and Spain, divorce is still illegal, and it became legal in Italy and Colombia only in the 1970s. For these reasons divorce statistics are not strictly comparable, particularly when there are other legal means of family dissolution, such as separation. Divorce statistics are obtained from court records and civil registers. These registers refer to the number of divorces granted and not to the persons obtaining them. Divorce rates—like birth, death and marriage rates—are also affected by the age-sex structure of the population to which they relate.

Rank	Country	Divorce Rate (per 1,000)	Rank	Country	Divorce Rate (per 1,000)	Rank	Country	Divorce Rate (per 1,000)
TOP 10			36	Jordan	1.5	72	Qatar	0.8
1	Barbados	16.7	37	Kuwait	1.5	73	St. Vincent	0.8
2	Maldives	6.8	38	Slovakia	1.5	74	Syria	0.8
3	Latvia	5.6	39	Tunisia	1.5	75	Thailand	0.8
4	United States	4.7	40	Italy	1.4	76	Fiji	0.7
5	Russia	4.5	41	Kazakhstan	1.4	77	Georgia	0.7
6	Belarus	4.3	42	Malawi	1.4	78	Mauritius	0.7
7	Cuba	4.2	43	Romania	1.4	79	Poland	0.7
8	Ukraine	4.2	44	Singapore	1.4	80	Vanuatu	0.7
9	Puerto Rico	4.0	45	Turkmenistan	1.4	81	Yugoslavia	0.7
10	Estonia	3.8	46	Bahrain	1.3	82	Belize	0.6
			47	Liechtenstein	1.3	83	Ecuador	0.6
UPPER MIDDLE			48	Bahamas	1.2	84	Greece	0.6
11	Lithuania	3.7	49	Kyrgyzstan	1.2	85	Japan	0.6
12	Bangladesh	3.6	50	Portugal	1.2	86	Libya	0.6
13	Moldova	3.3	51	Uzbekistan	1.2	87	Spain	0.6
14	Uruguay	3.1	52	Costa Rica	1.1	88	Brazil	0.5
15	United Kingdom	3.0	53	Korea, South	1.1	89	El Salvador	0.5
16	Czech Republic	2.9				90	Jamaica	0.5
17	Australia	2.7	**LOWER MIDDLE**			91	Mongolia	0.5
18	Kenya	2.7	54	Seychelles	1.1	92	Turkey	0.5
19	New Zealand	2.7	55	Tonga	1.1	93	Chile	0.4
20	Denmark	2.5	56	Croatia	1.0	94	Dominica	0.4
21	Norway	2.5	57	Slovenia	1.0	95	Honduras	0.4
22	Suriname	2.5	58	Armenia	0.9	96	Mexico	0.4
23	Sweden	2.5	59	Azerbaijan	0.9	97	Nicaragua	0.4
24	Finland	2.4	60	Bulgaria	0.9			
25	Belgium	2.2	61	San Marino	0.9	**BOTTOM 10**		
26	Hungary	2.2	62	Tajikistan	0.9	98	Bosnia & Herzegovina	0.3
27	Algeria	2.1	63	Trinidad and Tobago	0.9	99	Macedonia	0.3
28	Austria	2.0	64	United Arab Emirates	0.9	100	Pakistan	0.3
29	Iceland	2.0	65	Venezuela	0.9	101	St. Lucia	0.3
30	Netherlands	2.0	66	Albania	0.8	102	Antigua and Barbuda	0.2
31	Djibouti	1.9	67	Benin	0.8	103	Guatemala	0.2
32	France	1.9	68	Brunei	0.8	104	Korea, North	0.2
33	Germany	1.9	69	China	0.8	105	Sri Lanka	0.2
34	Luxembourg	1.9	70	Indonesia	0.8	106	Western Samoa	0.2
35	Canada	1.7	71	Panama	0.8	107	Mozambique	0.01

Source: *Demographic Yearbook*

27. LEGAL INDUCED ABORTIONS

Abortion is defined in most countries of the world as an interruption of pregnancy before 28 weeks of gestation causing the death of the fetus. Abortions are either spontaneous or induced, and the latter are subject to government regulations in almost all countries of the world. These regulations vary from complete prohibition to abortion on request by or under the supervision of authorized medical professionals. Abortion is currently legal in only 51 countries of the world. The following ranking is restricted to these countries. Abortion is permitted on request in 41 countries, but in 55 coun-

tries they are permitted for economic or social reasons, in 78 countries for fetal impairment, in 81 countries for rape or incest, in 95 countries to preserve the mental health of the mother, in 95 countries to preserve the physical health of the mother, and in 173 countries to save the mother's life. The data suffer from serious limitations because in almost all countries of the world, including countries where abortion is legal, many abortions are performed illegally or are not reported at all due to fear of social consequences.

Rank	Country	Induced Abortions (per 100 live births)	Rank	Country	Induced Abortions (per 100 live births)	Rank	Country	Induced Abortions (per 100 live births)
TOP 10			18	China	47.7	36	New Zealand	20.4
1	Russia	339.0	19	Kyrgyzstan	44.8	37	Barbados	19.6
2	Romania	265.7	20	United States	35.5	38	Finland	18.7
3	Ukraine	159.5	21	Armenia	34.9	39	Iceland	16.1
4	Estonia	139.5	22	Singapore	34.5	40	Israel	14.9
5	Bulgaria	137.5	23	Japan	34.2	41	Germany	14.7
6	Laos	110.5	24	Uzbekistan	33.8			
7	Czech Republic	96.2	25	Turkmenistan	31.3	**BOTTOM 10**		
8	Lithuania	90.3	26	Denmark	30.7	42	Belize	12.1
9	Kazakhstan	87.6				43	Bermuda	11.0
10	Cuba	79.0	**LOWER MIDDLE**			44	Tunisia	10.9
			27	Sweden	28.4	45	Greece	10.8
UPPER MIDDLE			28	Tajikistan	27.2	46	Netherlands	9.3
11	Belarus	76.6	29	Italy	26.1	47	Poland	5.7
12	Georgia	75.6	30	Canada	25.7	48	India	2.4
13	Moldova	74.7	31	Norway	25.2	49	Vanuatu	2.4
14	Hungary	71.5	32	Azerbaijan	23.2	50	Dominican Republic	0.5
15	Slovenia	66.4	33	Seychelles	22.8	51	Botswana	0.1
16	Slovakia	61.5	34	United Kingdom	21.9			
17	Macedonia	57.9	35	France	21.2			

Source: UN Population Division

28. ILLEGITIMATE BIRTHS

Illegitimacy is almost as old as the human family. Despite the many contributions that bastards have made to civilization (Leonardo da Vinci and Willy Brandt are two of the more familiar names), social stigma, religious anathema and legal sanctions have combined to give illegitimacy a sinister reputation. Under English common law an illegitimate child is an outlaw with no legal rights to his or her father's prop-erty except by specific designation, as in a will. Recently the condition of illegitimate offsprings has been somewhat improved. In about half the states of the United States, the union of the parents in marriage after the birth of a child makes that child legitimate. The figures are, of course, significantly distorted by the informality of marriage rituals and legal registra-tion in many countries.

Rank	Country	Percentage of Illegitimate Births
TOP 10		
1	Sao Tome e Principe	90.2
2	Guinea-Bissau	88.7
3	St. Lucia	85.8
4	Jamaica	85.1
5	St. Kitts and Nevis	80.8
6	Antigua and Barbuda	76.6
7	Panama	74.5
8	Barbados	73.1
9	Seychelles	72.8
10	Botswana	71.2
UPPER MIDDLE		
11	El Salvador	69.4
12	Dominican Republic	67.2
13	Guatemala	65.2
14	Bahamas	58.8
15	Iceland	58.3
16	Belize	57.5
17	Western Samoa	56.5
18	Venezuela	53.0
19	Sweden	49.5
20	Denmark	46.8
21	Cape Verde	44.8
22	Norway	44.4
23	Peru	42.2
24	Costa Rica	37.2
25	Puerto Rico	36.8
26	New Zealand	36.7
27	Bermuda	36.1
28	Chile	34.3
29	Estonia	33.9
30	Argentina	32.5
31	Ecuador	32.1
32	France	31.9

Rank	Country	Percentage of Illegitimate Births
33	Paraguay	31.3
34	United Kingdom	30.9
35	United States	29.5
36	Mozambique	26.9
37	Austria	24.8
38	Colombia	24.8
39	South Africa	24.1
40	Australia	23.0
41	Ireland	19.5
42	Tonga	19.4
43	Bolivia	19.1
44	Finland	18.9
45	Hungary	18.5
46	Latvia	18.4
47	Tuvalu	17.8
48	Georgia	17.7
LOWER MIDDLE		
49	Mexico	17.5
50	Fiji	17.3
51	Mauritius	17.2
52	Kyrgyzstan	16.8
53	Canada	16.2
54	Uruguay	16.2
55	Germany	14.9
56	Liechtenstein	14.7
57	Russia	14.6
58	Portugal	14.5
59	Luxembourg	12.7
60	Netherlands	12.5
61	Kazakhstan	12.4
62	Armenia	12.3
63	Bulgaria	12.0
64	Ukraine	10.8
65	Moldova	10.4

Rank	Country	Percentage of Illegitimate Births
66	Singapore	9.8
67	Slovakia	9.8
68	Czech Republic	9.7
69	Belgium	9.2
70	Belarus	9.0
71	Spain	8.0
72	Tajikistan	7.0
73	Lithuania	6.7
74	Italy	6.3
75	Switzerland	6.3
76	Philippines	6.1
77	Sri Lanka	5.4
78	Poland	5.0
79	San Marino	4.8
80	Uzbekistan	4.2
81	Greece	3.9
82	Turkmenistan	3.5
83	Djibouti	3.2
84	Monaco	3.2
85	Zimbabwe	3.2
86	Azerbaijan	2.5
BOTTOM 10		
87	Malta	2.3
88	Taiwan	2.3
89	Israel	1.5
90	Egypt	1.0
91	Japan	1.0
92	Kuwait	1.0
93	Korea, South	0.5
94	Brunei	0.4
95	Cyprus	0.4
96	Tunisia	0.2

Source: UN Population Division

29. USERS OF CONTRACEPTIVES

Estimates of contraceptive users come from what are known as KAP (Knowledge, Attitude and Practice) surveys. Because intercourse may occur more than once, duplications in count can easily arise and therefore the number of users is often an educated estimate made by program administrators and evaluators. The main family planning methods covered are intrauterine devices, oral contraceptives, sterilization and abortion.

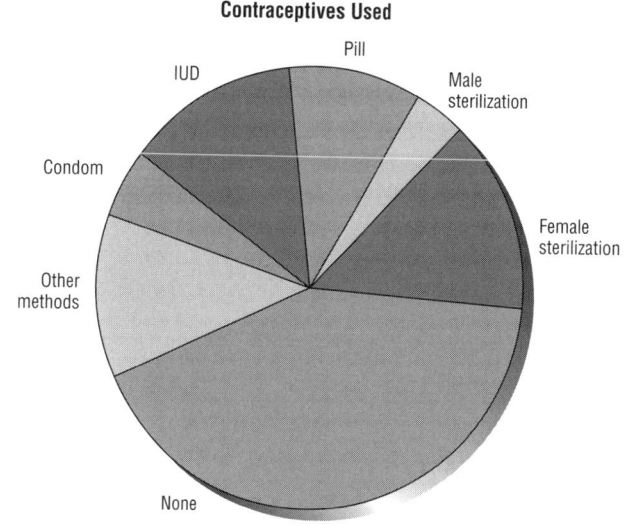

Contraceptives Used

IUD · Pill · Male sterilization · Condom · Female sterilization · Other methods · None

Rank	Country	Percentage of Contraceptive Use (All Methods) Married Women of Childbearing Age
TOP 10		
1	China	83
2	France	81
3	United Kingdom	81
4	Finland	80
5	Belgium	79
6	Korea, South	79
7	Puerto Rico	79
8	Denmark	78
9	Italy	78
10	Sweden	78
UPPER MIDDLE		
11	Australia	76
12	Bulgaria	76
13	Netherlands	76
14	Norway	76
15	Costa Rica	75
16	Germany	75
17	Mauritius	75
18	Poland	75
19	Singapore	74
20	Slovakia	74
21	United States	74
22	Canada	73
23	Hungary	73
24	Austria	71
25	Taiwan	71
26	Cuba	70
27	New Zealand	70
28	Czech Republic	69
29	Jamaica	67
30	Brazil	66
31	Colombia	66
32	Portugal	66
33	Thailand	66
34	Iran	65
35	Japan	64
36	Turkey	63
37	Bahamas	62
38	Sri Lanka	62

Rank	Country	Percentage of Contraceptive Use (All Methods) Married Women of Childbearing Age
39	Peru	59
40	Spain	59
41	Panama	58
42	St. Vincent	58
43	Romania	57
44	Dominican Republic	56
45	Barbados	55
46	Yugoslavia	55
47	Grenada	54
48	Antigua and Barbuda	53
49	Bahrain	53
50	Ecuador	53
51	El Salvador	53
52	Mexico	53
53	Trinidad and Tobago	53
54	Vietnam	53
55	Dominica	50
56	Indonesia	50
57	South Africa	50
LOWER MIDDLE		
58	Tunisia	50
59	Nicaragua	49
60	Venezuela	49
61	Malaysia	48
62	Paraguay	48
63	Algeria	47
64	Belize	47
65	Honduras	47
66	St. Lucia	47
67	Egypt	46
68	India	43
69	Zimbabwe	43
70	Morocco	42
71	St. Kitts and Nevis	41
72	Bangladesh	40
73	Philippines	40
74	Jordan	35
75	Kuwait	35
76	Botswana	33
77	Kenya	33

Rank	Country	Percentage of Contraceptive Use (All Methods) Married Women of Childbearing Age
78	Qatar	32
79	Guyana	31
80	Bolivia	30
81	Namibia	29
82	Guatemala	23
83	Lesotho	23
84	Nepal	23
85	Rwanda	21
86	Swaziland	20
87	Syria	20
88	Madagascar	17
89	Cameroon	16
90	Zambia	15
91	Iraq	14
92	Ghana	13
93	Malawi	13
94	Gambia	12
95	Pakistan	12
96	Togo	12
97	Haiti	10
98	Tanzania	10
99	Benin	9
100	Burundi	9
101	Oman	9
102	Sudan	9
103	Burkina	8
104	Zaire	8
BOTTOM 10		
105	Senegal	7
106	Yemen	7
107	Liberia	6
108	Nigeria	6
109	Mali	5
110	Uganda	5
111	Ethiopia	4
112	Niger	4
113	Cote d'Ivoire	3
114	Mauritania	3

Source: *World Development Report*

Section
IV

RACE
& RELIGION

This chapter deals with race and religion, both of which are not susceptible to statistical analysis or quantification but which, nevertheless, constitute important dimensions of every society.

Historically, ethnic homogeneity has been one of the great strengths of a nation, although its contribution to social cohesiveness has also been greatly exaggerated. Ethnic diversity is more often than not a source of conflict; when coupled with language and religion, it can become a powerful and explosive force in national life. One has only to think of Cyprus, India, South Africa, Belgium, Ireland and Lebanon to perceive the destructiveness of racial, religious and linguistic rivalries as well as the tenacity of ethnic affiliations. The trend, therefore, has been to suppress ethnicity, to make it irrelevant and even to obliterate its manifestations in speech, conduct and dress.

Censuses throughout the world now deliberately omit references to ethnic origin. The result, unfortunately, has been not only enforced uniformity and homogeneity but also the assimilation of the small minorities into the dominant majority. The process may be slower but the end result is the same as that which Hitler's Germany and Turkey achieved through their respective "Final Solutions." The dangers inherent in such a policy are best illustrated by the experience of the plant geneticists who, during the Green Revolution, attempted to eliminate weaker strains of rice and wheat in favor of the high-yielding ones. They discovered that such homogenization increased the vulnerability of the chosen strain to diseases and ultimate extinction. In plants as well as races there is safety in variety. Current thinking thus favors ethnic diversity. In countries such as the United States, Canada and Australia the melting pot is being transformed into the mixing pot.

Religion is the subject of the next five rankings. The quality and intensity of religious beliefs vary so greatly from individual to individual that a head count becomes a futile exercise. Nevertheless, if we adopt the usual precautions, the rankings can give some insights into the composition of the religious mosaic. The lead ranking is on Christianity, which is not only the world's largest religion but the one that had the greatest impact on the course of human history. The only other religion whose adherents constitute a majority in at least 33 countries is Islam. The medieval and even draconian character of Muslim ethics and jurisprudence (stoning for adultery, amputation for stealing and prohibition of music) has not prevented it from growing in Asia and Africa, and its propagation has been helped by the grace of both Allah and petrodollars. Judaism is included not so much because of but in spite of the size of its membership; there are few countries in the world that the Jews have not enriched with their contributions and fewer countries where they have escaped persecution and prejudice.

Hinduism is included for valid reasons. Hindus form the majority in only two countries (India and Nepal), although they command a plurality in a number of small countries, such as Guyana, Fiji and Mauritius. In addition to these organized religions, the world is full of cults ranging from Scientology to Jim Jones-type suicide squads, but statistics on these cults are as unreliable as their doctrines.

30. FOREIGN POPULATION IN WESTERN EUROPE

Until the end of World War II, Europe was ethnically homogeneous. Even the large colonial powers like United Kingdom, France and Netherlands, had only a sprinkling of non-Caucasians in their midst. However, the end of Western dominance also signaled a rush of non-Western peoples to European countries. Worker shortages in Germany, France, Switzerland and Netherlands after World War II also helped to flood the labor market with legal and illegal migrants, known as *Gastarbeiter* or guest workers. By the time the wave of immigration had been stanched, aliens had become a sizable part of the population requiring many cultural and social readjustments for the national populations. Because migrants have higher birthrates, while in many cases native Europeans have below replacement birthrates, it is expected that aliens will become numerically even more prominent in these countries.

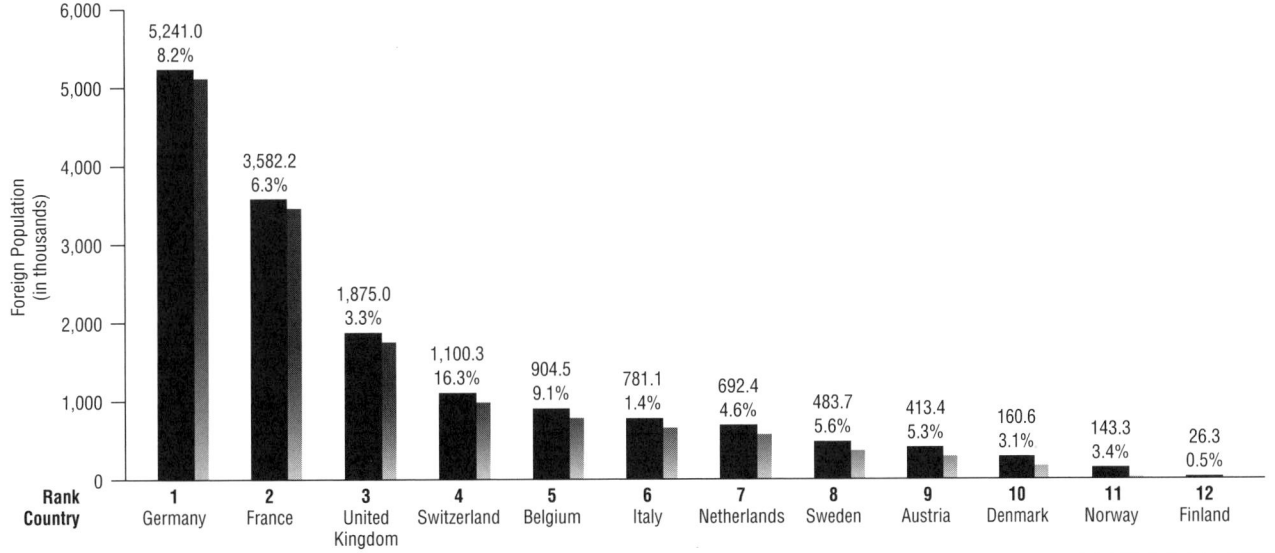

Source: "Foreign Population in 13 OECD Countries, 1980–1990." *OECD Observer* 176 (June/July 1990), p. 19.

31. INDIGENOUS PEOPLES

Indigenous people, also called aborigines or autochthons, are the original inhabitants of a country displaced by more "civilized" peoples or driven out of their homes into more primitive environments. American Indians are typical in the popular imagination of such indigenous peoples, although it is not certain they are the original inhabitants of the land or later arrivals themselves. But in many Asian and European countries there are tribal pockets outside the pale of society. The Maoris of New Zealand, the Australian aborigines, the Ainu of Japan and the scheduled tribes of India are good examples of endangered primitive peoples. Their numbers are diminishing and their cultures are becoming anthropological curiosities.

Country	Population[1] (million)	Share of National Population	Country	Population[1] (million)	Share of National Population	Country	Population[1] (million)	Share of National Population
Papua New Guinea	3.0	77	Mexico	10.9	12	Australia	0.4	2
Bolivia	5.6	70	New Zealand	0.4	12	Brazil	1.5	1
Guatemala	4.6	47	Chile	1.2	9	Bangladesh	1.2	1
Peru	9.0	40	Philippines	6.0	9	Thailand	.5	1
Ecuador	3.8	38	India	63.0	7	United States	2.0	1
Myanmar (Burma)	14.0	33	Malaysia	0.8	4	Russia	1.4	<1
Laos	1.3	30	Canada	0.9	4			

[1]Generally excludes those of mixed ancestry. *Source:* Worldwatch Institute

32. AMERICANS ABROAD

There is an American diaspora consisting of permanent U.S. residents in foreign countries engaged in business, missionary work, education and other activities. France, United Kingdom, Canada and Mexico have long been favorite destinations for a group of people loosely known as American expatriates. Such expatriates made significant cultural contributions in the interwar years to France and Italy. After the war the phenomenon became universal, with American citizens being found in out-of the way countries like Nepal as well as in newer nations like Israel. While some countries have asked the Yankees to go home, many others have asked them to come and stay.

Rank	Country	Residents U.S. Citizens (000)	Rank	Country	Residents U.S. Citizens (000)	Rank	Country	Residents U.S. Citizens (000)
TOP 10			9	Australia	62	16	South Korea	30
1	Mexico	539	10	France	59	17	Switzerland	27
2	Germany	354				18	Portugal	26
3	Canada	296	**MIDDLE**			19	Hong Kong	24
4	United Kingdom	255	11	Ireland	46	20	Venezuela	24
5	Israel	112	12	Jerusalem	43	21	Costa Rica	23
6	Italy	104	13	Saudi Arabia	40	22	Netherlands	19
7	Dominican Republic	97	14	Panama	36	23	Egypt	17
8	Spain	79	15	Greece	32	24	Argentina	13

Source: *1993 Statistical Abstract of the United States on CD-ROM*

33. CHRISTIANS

Christianity is perhaps the only true world religion in the sense of having adherents and churches in virtually every country in the world. Out of 205 countries there are only 10 countries—Afghanistan, Maldives, Yemen, Somalia, Comoros, Mauritania, Morocco, Tunisia, Turkey and Algeria—where there are fewer than 1% native or permanent Christian congregations. Christians form the majority of the population in 109 countries.

Religious statistics are available only for 2.5 billion of the earth's total population of 4.5 billion. Of this, close to 1 billion are Christians, although Protestants and Catholics employ different methods for counting members. The Roman Catholic Church claims a membership of 794 million, which makes it the largest single religious organization in the world. Nearly 29% of the world's Christian population lives in Europe, 16% in North America, 27% in South America, 10% in Asia and 16% in Africa.

Rank	Country	Christians (%)
TOP 10		
1	Moldova	98.5
2	Paraguay	97.75
3	Norway	97.41
4	St. Lucia	97.30
5	Costa Rica	97.23
6	Colombia	97.22
7	Honduras	97.14
8	Tonga	96.97
9	Greece	96.72
10	Iceland	96.21
UPPER MIDDLE		
11	Puerto Rico	96.12
12	Slovenia	96.0
13	Monaco	95.95
14	Liechtenstein	95.67
15	Spain	95.59
16	Grenada	95.44
17	Bolivia	95.06
18	Tuvalu	95.01
19	Western Samoa	94.81
20	Malta	94.77
21	Dominica	94.66
22	Ireland	94.61
23	Andorra	94.57
24	Cape Verde	94.57
25	Seychelles	94.48
26	El Salvador	94.46
27	Venezuela	94.42
28	Haiti	94.39
29	San Marino	94.37
30	Denmark	94.23
31	Portugal	94.16
32	Nicaragua	94.09
33	Armenia	94.0
34	Brazil	93.91
35	Mexico	93.15
36	Austria	93.12
37	Argentina	92.79
38	Kiribati	92.02
39	Lithuania	92.0
40	Gabon	90.68
41	Poland	90.12
42	Estonia	90.0
43	Belgium	89.90
44	Bermuda	89.24
45	Equatorial Guinea	89.0
46	Yugoslavia	89.0
47	Sao Tome e Principe	88.77
48	Latvia	88.0
49	Finland	87.93
50	Panama	87.65
51	Croatia	87.6

Rank	Country	Christians (%)
52	Chile	87.42
53	Guatemala	87.34
54	Luxembourg	87.01
55	Switzerland	86.92
56	Namibia	85.92
57	Dominican Republic	85.74
58	Philippines	85.03
59	St. Kitts and Nevis	84.87
60	Italy	83.55
61	Romania	83.34
62	Bahamas	83.22
63	Georgia	83.0
64	Hungary	82.88
65	Ukraine	82.5
66	Germany	82.0
67	France	81.73
68	Solomon Islands	81.48
69	Belize	81.36
70	Lesotho	80.69
71	Zaire	79.83
72	Russia	79.76
73	Burundi	79.13
74	Cyprus	78.03
75	Vanuatu	76.87
76	Papua New Guinea	76.10
77	New Zealand	75.46
78	United Kingdom	74.62
79	Canada	73.88
80	Slovakia	72.8
81	Ecuador	72.53
82	Netherlands	72.04
83	United States	71.47
84	Antigua and Barbuda	71.45
85	St. Vincent	71.14
86	Sweden	70.92
87	Peru	69.76
88	Rwanda	69.47
89	Australia	66.42
90	Uganda	65.75
91	Angola	65.54
92	Trinidad and Tobago	65.36
93	Bulgaria	64.93
94	Uruguay	64.90
LOWER MIDDLE		
95	Macedonia	64.0
96	Zambia	63.39
97	Barbados	62.39
98	South Africa	61.39
99	Suriname	60.88
100	Kenya	60.29
101	Lebanon	59.78
102	Congo	58.57
103	Malawi	56.88

Rank	Country	Christians (%)
104	Central African Republic	55.58
105	Ethiopia	54.40
106	Swaziland	54.34
107	Cameroon	50.63
108	Bosnia & Herzegovina	50
109	Eritrea	50.0
110	Jamaica	48.67
111	Fiji	47.72
112	Czech Republic	46.8
113	Mauritius	46.29
114	Zimbabwe	46.12
115	Madagascar	44.47
116	Guyana	44.01
117	Ghana	43.87
118	Nauru	43.54
119	Cuba	42.37
120	Tanzania	36.43
121	Mozambique	33.02
122	Togo	33.0
123	Botswana	28.83
124	Nigeria	28.42
125	Cote d'Ivoire	27.76
126	Liberia	27.73
127	Korea, South	27.06
128	Benin	22.80
129	Chad	21.75
130	Egypt	17.88
131	Kazakhstan	17.0
132	United Arab Emirates	12.37
133	Burkina	12.16
134	Qatar	11.94
135	Brunei	11.75
136	Azerbaijan	11.2
137	Djibouti	11.02
138	Turkmenistan	11.0
139	Sierra Leone	10.78
140	Indonesia	10.42
141	Singapore	10.14
142	Sudan	9.96
143	Syria	9.57
144	Guinea-Bissau	9.35
145	Uzbekistan	9.0
146	Vietnam	8.14
147	Sri Lanka	7.83
148	Taiwan	7.20
149	Kuwait	6.88
150	Malaysia	6.81
151	Myanmar (Burma)	6.60
152	Albania	6.02
153	China	6.0
154	Senegal	5.83
155	Jordan	4.89
156	Gambia	3.95
157	Bahrain	3.78

Rank	Country	Christians (%)	Rank	Country	Christians (%)	Rank	Country	Christians (%)
158	Iraq	3.77	169	Iran	1.35	**BOTTOM 10**		
159	Laos	3.73	170	Thailand	1.19	179	Bangladesh	0.57
160	India	3.64	171	Saudi Arabia	1.18	180	Mauritania	0.56
161	Tajikstan	3.5	172	Korea, North	0.92	181	Nepal	0.50
162	Libya	3.23	173	Morocco	0.90	182	Bhutan	0.41
163	Mali	3.15	174	Oman	0.84	183	Turkey	0.40
164	Guinea	2.20	175	Cambodia	0.83	184	Comoros	0.39
165	Israel	2.15	176	Algeria	0.81	185	Afghanistan	0.25
166	Mongolia	1.97	177	Tunisia	0.80	186	Yemen	0.2
167	Japan	1.87	178	Niger	0.58	187	Maldives	0.17
168	Pakistan	1.54				188	Somalia	0.10

Source: *World Christian Encyclopedia*

34. MUSLIMS

Islam is the second largest religion in the world, both in the number of adherents and in the number of countries where it is professed by the majority of the population. Islam is an expansionary religion and, backed by petrodollars, it has been making gains in Africa, Europe and North America. Islam's appeal is enhanced by a number of factors, particularly its approval of polygamy (Muhammad himself had 13 wives), its easy divorce laws and its simple theology.

Rank	Country	Muslims (millions)	Rank	Country	Muslims (millions)	Rank	Country	Muslims (millions)
TOP 10			33	Tajikstan	4.940	66	Madagascar	0.690
1	Indonesia	169.840	34	Ghana	4.820	67	Benin	0.630
2	Pakistan	127.230	35	Jordan	3.930	68	Georgia	0.610
3	Bangladesh	101.730	36	Turkmenistan	3.520	69	Zaire	0.610
4	India	100.00	37	France	3.190	70	Macedonia	0.540
5	Turkey	60.690	38	Kyrgyzstan	3.140	71	Djibouti	0.535
6	Iran	59.140	39	Burkina	3.080	72	Comoros	0.523
7	Egypt	52.600	40	Philippines	2.940	73	Qatar	0.510
8	Nigeria	42.060	41	Chad	2.860	74	Netherlands	0.490
9	Algeria	27.680	42	Cameroon	2.810	75	Bahrain	0.470
10	Morocco	26.240	43	Sierra Leone	2.770	76	Togo	0.470
			44	Thailand	2.270	77	Central African Republic	0.460
UPPER MIDDLE			45	Mozambique	2.250	78	Singapore	0.451
11	Uzbekistan	19.700	46	Albania	2.190	79	Spain	0.450
12	Iraq	19.120	47	Mauritania	2.060	80	South Africa	0.380
13	Sudan	18.760	48	United Arab Emirates	2.040	81	Liberia	0.330
14	Saudi Arabia	17.730				82	Guinea-Bissau	0.320
15	China	17.00	**LOWER MIDDLE**			83	Maldives	0.244
16	Afghanistan	16.740	49	Yugoslavia	2.000	84	Cambodia	0.200
17	Ethiopia	16.060	50	Malawi	1.950	85	Brunei	0.188
18	Yemen	12.940	51	Eritrea	1.900	86	Mauritius	0.180
19	Malaysia	10.320	52	Bosnia & Herzegovina	1.780	87	Greece	0.160
20	Syria	10.250	53	Lebanon	1.770			
21	Tanzania	9.550	54	Oman	1.760	**BOTTOM 10**		
22	Tunisia	8.710	55	Germany	1.750	88	Cyprus	0.150
23	Niger	8.690	56	Myanmar (Burma)	1.750	89	Mongolia	0.140
24	Kazakhstan	7.970	57	Kenya	1.650	90	Canada	0.120
25	Mali	7.940	58	Sri Lanka	1.350	91	Suriname	0.083
26	Senegal	7.630	59	Kuwait	1.330	92	Rwanda	0.080
27	Somalia	6.650	60	Uganda	1.200	93	Trinidad and Tobago	0.074
28	Azerbaijan	6.460	61	Gambia	1.010	94	Guyana	0.066
29	Guinea	5.530	62	United Kingdom	0.820	95	Congo	0.060
30	Cote d'Ivoire	5.400	63	Bulgaria	0.800	96	Croatia	0.060
31	Libya	5.070	64	Israel	0.760	97	Fiji	0.060
32	United States	5.060	65	Nepal	0.740			

Source: *World Factbook*

35. JEWS

Jews are among the most widely dispersed communities in the world, and the word *diaspora* has been applied most properly to their dispersion. They are also among the few communities in the world that have succeeded in maintaining their nationhood without a nation. The Jewish diaspora began in A.D. 70, following the destruction of the Temple by Emperor Titus, and in succeeding waves, known as *galut* in Hebrew, first reached North Africa and Spain, then Russia and Northern Europe and finally the New World, where the first Sephardic Jews are believed to have arrived soon after the Spaniards. Isolated groups of Jews are also believed to have migrated to Cochin in India and even as far as China, where their presence was recorded by medieval travelers. Their present concentration in North America and Israel is a much later phenomenon and is the product of what might be described as remigration. The impact of the Jewish presence in a country cannot be measured adequately by numbers alone, because the drive and intellectual vigor of this people have left a vastly disproportionate imprint in almost every country where they have resided. Their remarkable resilience is attested by many instances, such as a Jew becoming the chancellor of Catholic Austria within a few decades of the virtual extermination of the Jews in the Holocaust.

Rank	Country	Percent of Jews	Rank	Country	Percent of Jews	Rank	Country	Percent of Jews
TOP 10			7	Uruguay	2	12	Bulgaria	0.8
1	Israel	82	8	Moldova	1.5	13	Gaza Strip	0.3
2	West Bank	12	9	Algeria	1	14	Turkey	0.2
3	Luxembourg	3	10	France	1	15	Morocco	0.2
4	Argentina	2						
5	Gibraltar	2	**BOTTOM 5**					
6	United States	2	11	Tunisia	1			

Source: U.S. Central Intelligence Agency; *The World Factbook*

36. HINDUS

Until the end of the last century, Hindus were restricted almost entirely to the Indian subcontinent. Upper class Hindus were barred by Vedic injunctions from crossing the sea and migrating to any other country. The British who ruled India until 1947 had other ideas. They found that Indians were hard workers and did not cause much political trouble. As a result, they began to export Indians to many of their possessions, including Fiji, Guyana, Mauritius, and Trinidad and Tobago. Most of these immigrants were lower class Hindus. After World War II, a second wave of immigration brought Hindus to the shores of Great Britain, the United States and Canada. Most of them were educated professionals. The percentage of people of Western origin practicing any form of Hinduism is minuscule.

Rank	Country	Percent of Hindus	Rank	Country	Percent of Hindus	Rank	Country	Percent of Hindus
TOP 10			7	Bhutan	25	13	Martinique	5
1	Nepal	90	8	Trinidad and Tobago	24.3	14	Indonesia	2
2	India	82.6	9	Bangladesh	16	15	Thailand	0.1
3	Mauritius	52	10	Sri Lanka	15			
4	Fiji	38						
5	Guyana	33	**BOTTOM 5**					
6	Suriname	27.4	12	Guadeloupe	5			

Source: *World Data*

37. CATHOLICS

Although Christians are ranked elsewhere, Catholics deserve special consideration. The Catholic Church is the largest single religious body in the world and it is also the most organized. Historically, Catholics are baptized just after birth, and confirmed after childhood. Once their names are entered in the parish register, they remain listed as Catholics until death.

This practice varies from that of Protestants, who count only those who are formally accepted as members. Virtually all of Latin America is Catholic and Catholicism is entrenched in many countries of Europe. The Catholic Church also is an efficient collector of statistical data and its *Annuario* is an outstanding publication.

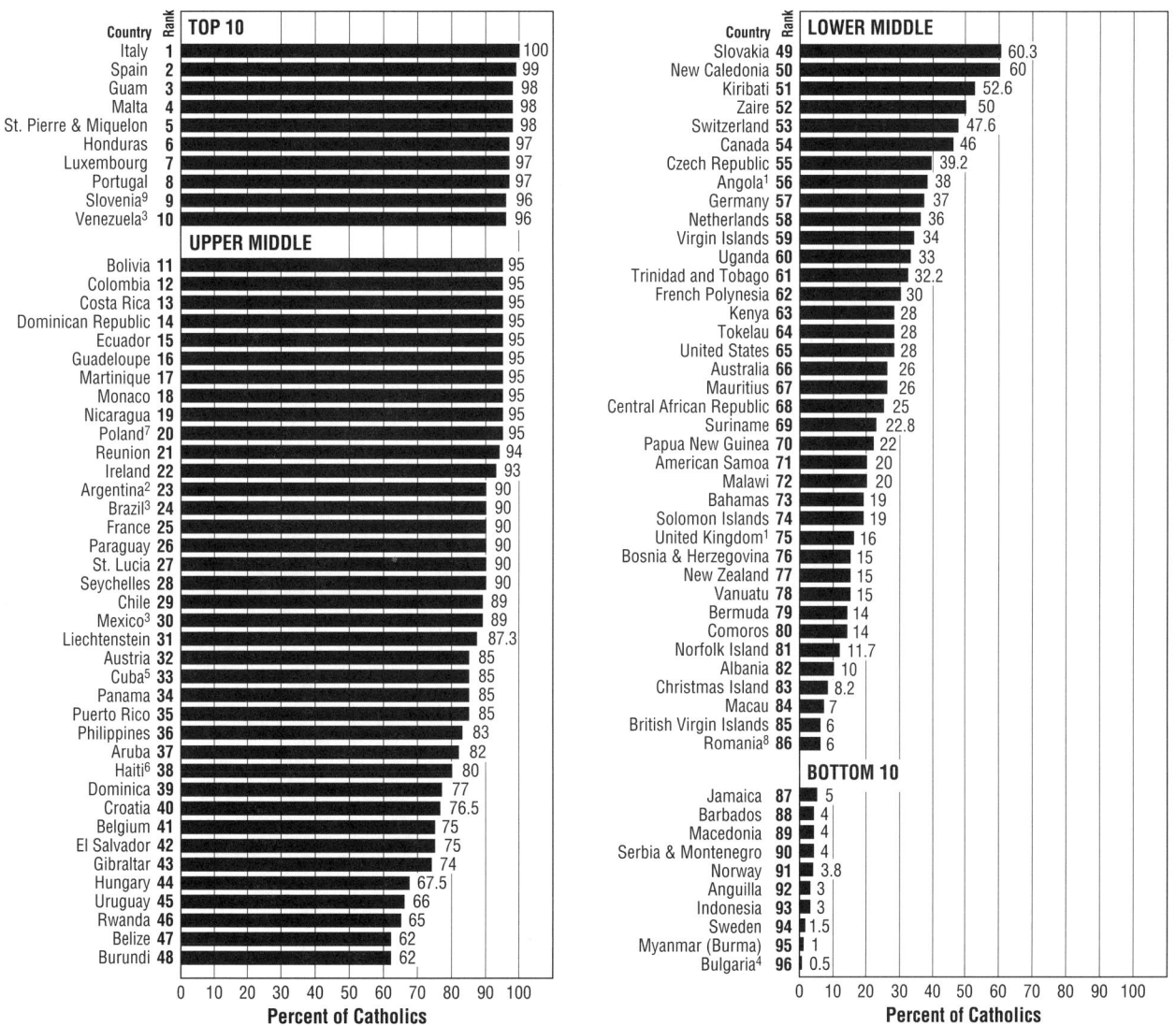

Country	Rank	TOP 10	Percent of Catholics
Italy	1		100
Spain	2		99
Guam	3		98
Malta	4		98
St. Pierre & Miquelon	5		98
Honduras	6		97
Luxembourg	7		97
Portugal	8		97
Slovenia[9]	9		96
Venezuela[3]	10		96

UPPER MIDDLE

Country	Rank		Percent of Catholics
Bolivia	11		95
Colombia	12		95
Costa Rica	13		95
Dominican Republic	14		95
Ecuador	15		95
Guadeloupe	16		95
Martinique	17		95
Monaco	18		95
Nicaragua	19		95
Poland[7]	20		95
Reunion	21		94
Ireland	22		93
Argentina[2]	23		90
Brazil[3]	24		90
France	25		90
Paraguay	26		90
St. Lucia	27		90
Seychelles	28		90
Chile	29		89
Mexico[3]	30		89
Liechtenstein	31		87.3
Austria	32		85
Cuba[5]	33		85
Panama	34		85
Puerto Rico	35		85
Philippines	36		83
Aruba	37		82
Haiti[6]	38		80
Dominica	39		77
Croatia	40		76.5
Belgium	41		75
El Salvador	42		75
Gibraltar	43		74
Hungary	44		67.5
Uruguay	45		66
Rwanda	46		65
Belize	47		62
Burundi	48		62

Country	Rank	LOWER MIDDLE	Percent of Catholics
Slovakia	49		60.3
New Caledonia	50		60
Kiribati	51		52.6
Zaire	52		50
Switzerland	53		47.6
Canada	54		46
Czech Republic	55		39.2
Angola[1]	56		38
Germany	57		37
Netherlands	58		36
Virgin Islands	59		34
Uganda	60		33
Trinidad and Tobago	61		32.2
French Polynesia	62		30
Kenya	63		28
Tokelau	64		28
United States	65		28
Australia	66		26
Mauritius	67		26
Central African Republic	68		25
Suriname	69		22.8
Papua New Guinea	70		22
American Samoa	71		20
Malawi	72		20
Bahamas	73		19
Solomon Islands	74		19
United Kingdom[1]	75		16
Bosnia & Herzegovina	76		15
New Zealand	77		15
Vanuatu	78		15
Bermuda	79		14
Comoros	80		14
Norfolk Island	81		11.7
Albania	82		10
Christmas Island	83		8.2
Macau	84		7
British Virgin Islands	85		6
Romania[8]	86		6

BOTTOM 10

Country	Rank		Percent of Catholics
Jamaica	87		5
Barbados	88		4
Macedonia	89		4
Serbia & Montenegro	90		4
Norway	91		3.8
Anguilla	92		3
Indonesia	93		3
Sweden	94		1.5
Myanmar (Burma)	95		1
Bulgaria[4]	96		0.5

Notes: 1. Estimated. 2. Less than 20 percent practicing. 3. Nominal. 4. 0.2 percent are Uniate Catholic. 5. Nominally; prior to Castro assuming power. 6. Majority also practice Voodoo. 7. About 75 percent practicing. 8. 3 percent are Uniate Catholic. 9. 2 percent are Uniate.

Source: *Annuario Statistico*

38. ETHNIC HOMOGENEITY INDEX

While developed societies in the West are moving toward pluralism and multiculturalism, traditional societies in Asia and Africa are moving toward mono-cultures. Many governments are striving to create nations from heterogeneous populations and finding the task difficult. Because the primary loyalty of an individual in traditional societies is to his race, language and religion, ethnicity becomes the basis for factional and separatist tendencies. More civil wars have been fought in Asia and Africa in modern times on the issue of race, language or religion than on that of political ideology. Unfortunately, in the process of achieving ethnic cohesiveness minorities are brutally suppressed and even—as in Turkey in the aftermath of World War I—exterminated or driven into exile.

Rank	Country	Ethnic Homogeneity Index (%)
TOP 10		
1	Algeria	99
2	Bangladesh	99
3	Comoros	99
4	Egypt	99
5	Japan	99
6	Jordan	99
7	Korea, North	99
8	Korea, South	99
9	Madagascar	99
10	Maldives	99
UPPER MIDDLE		
11	Portugal	99
12	Poland	98
13	Somalia	98
14	Tunisia	98
15	Vanuatu	98
16	Yemen	98
17	Ireland	97
18	Kiribati	97
19	Denmark	96
20	Iceland	96
21	Norway	96
22	Australia	95
23	Cyprus	95
24	Greece	95
25	Haiti	95
26	Netherlands	95
27	St. Kitts and Nevis	95
28	Tonga	95
29	France	94
30	Italy	94
31	Solomon Islands	94
32	United Kingdom	94
33	Armenia	93
34	Austria	93
35	Finland	93
36	Germany	93
37	China	92
38	Hungary	92
39	Turkey	92
40	Antigua and Barbuda	91
41	Belgium	91
42	Paraguay	91
43	Tuvalu	91
44	Albania	90
45	Honduras	90
46	St. Lucia	90
47	Sweden	90
48	Chile	89

Rank	Country	Ethnic Homogeneity Index (%)
49	Dominica	89
50	El Salvador	89
51	Libya	89
52	Romania	89
53	Seychelles	89
54	Cambodia	88
55	Slovenia	88
56	Syria	88
57	Western Samoa	88
58	Costa Rica	87
59	Laos	87
60	Vietnam	87
61	Bulgaria	86
62	Uruguay	86
63	Argentina	85
64	Bahamas	85
65	Grenada	85
66	Lesotho	85
67	Russia	85
68	Rwanda	85
69	Slovakia	85
70	Papua New Guinea	84
71	Swaziland	84
72	Taiwan	84
73	Azerbaijan	83
74	Equatorial Guinea	83
75	Burundi	82
76	Saudi Arabia	82
77	Sri Lanka	82
78	Czech Republic	81
79	Israel	81
80	Lithuania	81
81	Barbados	80
82	Lebanon	80
83	Puerto Rico	80
84	Mongolia	79
85	Thailand	79
86	Croatia	78
87	Belarus	77
88	Iraq	77
89	San Marino	77
90	Singapore	77
91	Botswana	75
92	Jamaica	74
93	New Zealand	74
LOWER MIDDLE		
94	United States	74
95	Oman	73
96	Turkmenistan	73
97	Uzbekistan	73

Rank	Country	Ethnic Homogeneity Index (%)
98	Spain	72
99	Ukraine	72
100	Cape Verde	71
101	Dominican Republic	70
102	Georgia	70
103	Morocco	70
104	Zimbabwe	70
105	Luxembourg	69
106	Myanmar (Burma)	69
107	Nicaragua	69
108	Mauritius	68
109	Brunei	67
110	Venezuela	67
111	Macedonia	66
112	St. Vincent	65
113	Moldova	64
114	Panama	64
115	Tajikistan	64
116	Bahrain	63
117	Switzerland	63
118	Yugoslavia	62
119	Andorra	61
120	Djibouti	61
121	Estonia	61
122	Liechtenstein	61
123	Malaysia	60
124	Mexico	60
125	Colombia	58
126	Latvia	58
127	Malawi	58
128	Nauru	58
129	Brazil	54
130	Nepal	53
131	Niger	53
132	Ghana	52
133	Kyrgyzstan	52
134	Congo	51
135	Cuba	51
136	Bhutan	50
137	Fiji	50
138	Mali	50
139	Bosnia & Herzegovina	49
140	Guyana	49
141	Sudan	49
142	Burkina	48
143	Eritrea	48
144	Pakistan	48
145	Mozambique	47
146	Namibia	47
147	Peru	47
148	Guatemala	45

Rank	Country	Ethnic Homogeneity Index (%)	Rank	Country	Ethnic Homogeneity Index (%)	Rank	Country	Ethnic Homogeneity Index (%)
149	Iran	45	163	Ethiopia	37	177	South Africa	22
150	Belize	43	164	Zambia	36			
151	Senegal	43	165	Gabon	35		**BOTTOM 10**	
152	Togo	43	166	Suriname	35	178	Nigeria	21
153	Cote d'Ivoire	42	167	Gambia	34	179	Qatar	20
154	Kazakhstan	41	168	Sierra Leone	34	180	Cameroon	19
155	Kuwait	41	169	Bolivia	31	181	Liberia	19
156	Ecuador	40	170	Philippines	28	182	Zaire	18
157	Guinea	40	171	Chad	27	183	Kenya	17
158	Mauritania	40	172	Guinea-Bissau	27	184	Uganda	17
159	Trinidad and Tobago	40	173	Tanzania	26	185	United Arab Emirates	12
160	Indonesia	39	174	Benin	25	186	India	11
161	Afghanistan	38	175	Canada	23	187	Malta	05
162	Angola	37	176	Central African Republic	23			

Source: *World Factbook*

Section
V

POLITICS & INTERNATIONAL RELATIONS

It us unfortunate that politics, although one of the critical areas of national life, has been subjected to so little statistical study and analysis. The central theme of politics is power; power gained, power used, power transferred and power opposed. While power is the universal given in politics, the power structure and the political behavior of the masses vary sharply from nation to nation. It is possible, therefore, only to rank countries on the basis of the relative capabilities and stabilities of political systems. The resulting profile would enable us to discern patterns in what would otherwise appear to be a mere concatenation of political events. Professor Ray Cline has attempted to scale the world's nations on the basis of perceived power, combining economic, military and geopolitical factors.

39. AGE OF NATIONS

It was Henry Kissinger who in the early 1970s raised the interesting question of the legitimacy of nations. One determinant of legitimacy is of course age. A nation-state that has been around for a long time acquires the patina of legitimacy and becomes accepted more easily into the community of nations. Pursuing this line of argument, it becomes obvious that not many nations have been around for longer than a century. (We are considering nations here and not countries.) The relative youth of nations is a major factor in the conduct of international affairs. It might explain their immaturity, sibling rivalries and frequent alternations between assertiveness and dependence. This raises the question: how do we determine the age of nations. It is easy in the case of countries that were under colonial rule until the mid-20th century and therefore can point to a particular year as the year of independence. It becomes more difficult in the case of nations that have no such clearly demarcated watershed. In their case it is necessary to establish a point in time when they became accepted political entities within their present borders and in their present form. Using this formula, countries such as Egypt, China and India with a long history behind them must be regarded as comparatively young nations. In other words, the age of nations has been determined on the basis of unbroken independence and systemic continuity.

Rank	Country	Age of Nations
TOP 10		
1	China	1523 B.C.
2	Ethiopia	1000 B.C.
3	Japan	660 B.C.
4	Denmark	800
5	Sweden	836
6	France	Aug. 843
7	San Marino	855
8	Uganda	Oct. 9, 1062
9	United Kingdom	Oct. 14, 1066
10	Portugal	1140
UPPER MIDDLE		
11	Andorra	Dec. 6, 1288
12	Thailand	1350
13	Spain	1492
14	Switzerland	Sept. 22, 1499
15	Nepal	Nov. 13, 1769
16	United States	July 4, 1776
17	Haiti	Jan. 1, 1804
18	Liechtenstein	July 12, 1806
19	Colombia	July 20, 1810
20	Mexico	Sept. 16, 1810
21	Chile	Sept. 18, 1810
22	Paraguay	May 14, 1811
23	Venezuela	July 5, 1811
24	Netherlands	Mar. 30, 1814
25	Peru	July 28, 1821
26	Costa Rica	Sept. 15, 1821
27	Guatemala	Sept. 15, 1821
28	Ecuador	May 24, 1822
29	Brazil	Sept. 7, 1822
30	Bolivia	Aug. 6, 1825
31	Uruguay	Aug. 25, 1828
32	Greece	Feb. 3, 1830
33	Belgium	Oct. 4,1830
34	Nicaragua	April 30, 1838
35	Honduras	Nov. 5, 1838
36	El Salvador	Jan. 30, 1841
37	Dominican Republic	Feb. 27, 1844
38	Liberia	July 26, 1847
39	Monaco	Feb. 2, 1861
40	Italy	March 17, 1861
41	Luxembourg	May 10, 1867
42	Canada	July 1, 1867
43	Romania	May 21, 1877
44	Australia	Jan. 1, 1901
45	Cuba	May 20, 1902

Rank	Country	Age of Nations
46	Panama	Nov. 3, 1903
47	Norway	June 7, 1905
48	Iran	Oct. 7, 1906
49	New Zealand	Sept. 26, 1907
50	Bulgaria	Oct. 5, 1908
51	Bhutan	Mar. 24, 1910
52	South Africa	May 31, 1910
53	Albania	Nov. 28, 1912
54	Argentina	July 9, 1916
55	Finland	Dec. 6, 1917
56	Austria	Oct. 13, 1918
57	Poland	Nov. 10, 1918
58	Hungary	Nov. 16, 1918
59	Yemen	Dec. 1918
60	Yugoslavia	Dec. 1, 1918
61	Afghanistan	Aug. 19, 1919
62	Ireland	Dec. 6, 1921
63	Egypt	Feb. 28, 1922
64	Turkey	Oct. 29, 1923
65	Mongolia	Mar. 13, 1931
66	Saudi Arabia	Sept. 23, 1932
67	Iraq	Oct. 3, 1932
68	Lebanon	Nov. 26, 1941
69	Iceland	June 17, 1944
70	Indonesia	Aug. 17, 1945
71	Vietnam	Sept. 2, 1945
72	Taiwan	Oct. 25, 1945
73	Syria	April 17, 1946
74	Jordan	May 25, 1946
75	Philippines	July 4, 1946
76	Pakistan	Aug. 14, 1947
77	India	Aug. 15, 1947
78	Myanmar (Burma)	Jan. 4, 1948
79	Sri Lanka	Feb. 4, 1948
80	Israel	May 14, 1948
81	Korea, South	Aug. 15, 1948
82	Korea, North	Sept. 9, 1948
83	Oman	Dec. 20, 1951
84	Libya	Dec. 24, 1951
85	Laos	Oct. 23, 1953
86	Cambodia	Nov. 9, 1953
87	Germany	May 5, 1955
88	Sudan	Jan. 1956
89	Morocco	Mar. 2, 1956
90	Tunisia	March 20, 1956
91	Ghana	March 6, 1957
92	Malaysia	Aug. 31, 1957
93	Guinea	Oct. 2, 1958

Rank	Country	Age of Nations
LOWER MIDDLE		
94	Cameroon	Jan. 1, 1960
95	Zimbabwe	April 18, 1960
96	Togo	April 27, 1960
97	Madagascar	Jun 26, 1960
98	Zaire	June 30, 1960
99	Somalia	July 1, 1960
100	Benin	Aug 1, 1960
101	Niger	Aug. 3, 1960
102	Burkina	Aug. 5, 1960
103	Cote d'Ivoire	Aug. 7, 1960
104	Chad	Aug. 11, 1960
105	Central African Republic	Aug. 13, 1960
106	Congo	Aug. 15, 1960
107	Cyprus	Aug. 16, 1960
108	Gabon	Aug. 17, 1960
109	Senegal	Aug. 20, 1960
110	Malta	Sept. 21, 1960
111	Mali	Sept. 22, 1960
112	Nigeria	Oct. 1, 1960
113	Mauritania	Nov. 28, 1960
114	Sierra Leone	April 27, 1961
115	Kuwait	June 19, 1961
116	Tanzania	Dec. 9, 1961
117	Western Samoa	Jan. 1962
118	Burundi	July 1, 1962
119	Rwanda	July 1, 1962
120	Algeria	July 5, 1962
121	Jamaica	Aug. 6, 1962
122	Trinidad and Tobago	Aug. 31, 1962
123	Kenya	Dec. 12, 1963
124	Malawi	July 6, 1964
125	Zambia	Oct. 24, 1964
126	Gambia	Feb. 18, 1965
126	Maldives	July 26, 1965
127	Singapore	Aug. 9, 1965
128	Guyana	May 26, 1966
129	Botswana	Sept. 30, 1966
130	Lesotho	Oct. 4, 1966
131	Barbados	Nov. 30, 1966
132	Nauru	Jan. 31, 1968
133	Mauritius	March 12, 1968
134	Swaziland	Sept. 6, 1968
135	Equatorial Guinea	Oct. 12, 1968
136	Tonga	June 4, 1970
137	Fiji	Oct. 10, 1970
138	Bangladesh	Mar. 26, 1971
139	Bahrain	Aug. 15, 1971

Rank	Country	Age of Nations	Rank	Country	Age of Nations	Rank	Country	Age of Nations
140	Qatar	Sept. 3, 1971	157	St. Lucia	Feb. 2, 1979	174	Azerbaijan	Aug. 30, 1991
141	United Arab Emirates	Dec. 2, 1971	158	Kiribati	July 12, 1979	175	Kyrgyzstan	Aug. 31, 1991
142	Bahamas	July 10, 1973	159	St. Vincent	Oct. 27, 1979	176	Uzbekistan	Aug. 31, 1991
143	Grenada	Feb. 7, 1974	160	Vanuatu	July 30, 1980	177	Lithuania	Sept. 6, 1991
144	Guinea-Bissau	Sept. 10, 1974	161	Belize	Sept. 21, 1981		**BOTTOM 10**	
145	Mozambique	June 25, 1975	162	Antigua and Barbuda	Nov. 1, 1981	178	Tajikistan	Sept. 9, 1991
146	Cape Verde	July 5, 1975	163	St. Kitts and Nevis	Sept. 19, 1983	179	Armenia	Sept. 23, 1991
147	Comoros	July 6, 1975	164	Brunei	Jan. 1, 1984	180	Turkmenistan	Oct. 27, 1991
148	Sao Tome e Principe	July 12, 1975	165	Namibia	Mar. 21, 1990	181	Russia	Dec. 8, 1991
149	Papua New Guinea	Sept. 16, 1975	166	Georgia	April 9, 1991	182	Kazakhstan	Dec. 16, 1991
150	Angola	Nov. 11, 1975	167	Croatia	June 15, 1991	183	Bosnia & Herzegovina	Mar. 3, 1992
151	Suriname	Nov. 25, 1975	168	Slovenia	June 25, 1991	184	Macedonia	April 1992
152	Seychelles	June 29, 1976	169	Estonia	Aug. 20, 1991	185	Czech Republic	Jan. 1, 1993
153	Djibouti	June 27, 1977	170	Latvia	Aug. 21, 1991	186	Slovakia	Jan. 1, 1993
154	Solomon Islands	July 7, 1978	171	Ukraine	Aug. 24, 1991	187	Eritrea	May 24, 1993
155	Tuvalu	Oct. 1, 1978	172	Belarus	Aug. 25, 1991			
156	Dominica	Nov. 3, 1978	173	Moldova	Aug. 27, 1991			

Source: *Encyclopedia Britanica*

40. OFFICIAL DEVELOPMENT ASSISTANCE RECEIVED

Development assistance is defined by the United Nations as financial and technical aid from developed market economic (or donor countries) to developing countries expressly intended for the economic and social development of the latter when the financial terms are concessional in character. At least 25% of the assistance must be in the form of grants. Only 17 nations are officially classified as donor countries and all of them are members of the Development Assistance Committee of the Organization for Economic Cooperation and Development.

Rank	Country	Total Official Development Assistance Received, 1993 (net disbursements) per Capita (US$)	Rank	Country	Total Official Development Assistance Received, 1993 (net disbursements) per Capita (US$)	Rank	Country	Total Official Development Assistance Received, 1993 (net disbursements) per Capita (US$)
	TOP 10		30	Mozambique	76.5	60	Chad	38.3
1	Sao Tome e Principe	378.0	31	El Salvador	69.2	61	Ghana	37.9
2	Cape Verde	313.5	32	Swaziland	69.2	62	Egypt	37.4
3	Saint Kitts and Nevis	261.9	33	Lesotho	67.9	63	Mali	35.7
4	Djibouti	235.2	34	Guinea	66.6	64	Mauritius	35.7
5	Vanuatu	198.8	35	Jordan	64.2	65	Uganda	35.5
6	Suriname	198.1	36	Cote d'Ivoire	63.1	66	Kenya	35.2
7	Saint Lucia	194.2	37	Senegal	62.8	67	Tanzania	34.9
8	Solomon Islands	180.8	38	Honduras	58.9	68	Cambodia	32.3
9	Mauritania	153.2	39	Central African Republic	57.0	69	Togo	32.2
10	Dominica	140.8	40	Congo	54.4	70	Panama	31.1
			41	Rwanda	52.2	71	Sri Lanka	30.9
	UPPER MIDDLE		42	Cameroon	51.3	72	Costa Rica	30.0
11	Seychelles	138.9	43	Benin	50.7	73	Angola	29.2
12	Belize	137.3	44	Mongolia	48.3	74	Paraguay	28.3
13	Equatorial Guinea	134.6	45	Cyprus	48.2	75	Tunisia	27.5
14	Maldives	130.3	46	Malawi	47.9	76	Madagascar	26.6
15	Saint Vincent	127.3	47	Lebanon	47.0	77	Yemen	25.5
16	Namibia	113.6	48	Antigua and Barbuda	46.2	78	Peru	24.5
17	Guyana	104.2	49	Jamaica	46.0	79	Ethiopia	23.3
18	Somalia	98.4	50	Burundi	45.8	80	Morocco	23.3
19	Grenada	97.8	51	Sierra Leone	44.7	81	Philippines	22.9
20	Guinea-Bissau	95.3	52	Burkina	43.6	82	Ecuador	21.6
21	Gambia	92.1				83	Guatemala	20.1
22	Zambia	90.8		**LOWER MIDDLE**		84	Haiti	18.6
23	Papua New Guinea	87.3	53	Laos	43.0	85	Brunei	18.2
24	Comoros	84.0	54	Liberia	42.5	86	Sudan	18.2
25	Nicaragua	81.9	55	Bhutan	42.0	87	Nepal	17.3
26	Gabon	81.7	56	Zimbabwe	39.9	88	Chile	12.8
27	Bolivia	80.7	57	Niger	39.1	89	Afghanistan	12.7
28	Botswana	79.9	58	Oman	38.7	90	Algeria	12.4
29	Fiji	77.8	59	Uruguay	38.4	91	Syria	12.3

Rank	Country	Total Official Development Assistance Received, 1993 (net disbursements) per Capita (US$)	Rank	Country	Total Official Development Assistance Received, 1993 (net disbursements) per Capita (US$)	Rank	Country	Total Official Development Assistance Received, 1993 (net disbursements) per Capita (US$)
92	Bangladesh	11.8	105	Malaysia	5.2	116	Iran	2.2
93	Thailand	10.7	106	South Africa	4.9	117	Nigeria	2.0
94	Indonesia	10.6	107	Zaire	4.6	118	Saudi Arabia	1.8
95	Iraq	8.7	108	Vietnam	4.5	119	Kuwait	1.7
96	Argentina	8.3	109	Mexico	4.4	120	India	1.7
97	Singapore	8.2	110	Barbados	3.8	121	Brazil	1.5
98	Pakistan	8.0	111	Colombia	3.0	122	Libya	1.2
99	Turkey	7.7	112	Cuba	2.9	123	Korea, North	0.8
100	Bahamas	7.5	113	China	2.7	124	Korea, South	0.7
101	Bahrain	7.5	114	Myanmar (Burma)	2.3			
102	Hong Kong	5.7	**BOTTOM 10**					
103	Qatar	5.7	115	Venezuela	2.3			
104	Trinidad and Tobago	5.5						

Source: OECD

41. REFUGEES

It was not until recently that the problem of refugees has engaged the attention of demographers and politicians. The right of asylum was not considered as a human right in international law until the 1980s. Since then, there has been a massive flow of national populations across borders and in some cases across the seas, both legally and illegally. In some cases the refugee situations reflect genocide in neighboring countries; in other cases, famine and economic distress are regarded as legitimate reasons for fleeing one country and seeking asylum in another. The destinations of most refugees are safe havens in neighboring countries. In modern times, massive transfers of populations have taken place in the Indian subcontinent, central Africa, the former Yugoslavia and Lebanon.

Rank	Country	Refugees by Country of Asylum (thousands) 1992	Rank	Country	Refugees by Country of Asylum (thousands) 1992	Rank	Country	Refugees by Country of Asylum (thousands) 1992
TOP 10			27	Senegal	72	54	Burkina	6
1	Iran	4,151	28	Thailand	64	55	Egypt	6
2	Pakistan	1,629	29	Afghanistan	60	56	Lebanon	6
3	Malawi	1,059				57	Sierra Leone	6
4	Sudan	726	**LOWER MIDDLE**			58	Syria	6
5	Guinea	479	30	Yemen	60	59	Brazil	5
6	Ethiopia	432	31	Swaziland	56	60	Cuba	5
7	Kenya	402	32	Hong Kong	45	61	Nigeria	5
8	Zaire	391	33	Cameroon	42	62	Gambia	4
9	Mexico	361	34	Mauritania	38	63	Niger	4
10	Tanzania	292	35	Saudi Arabia	29	64	Togo	3
			36	Turkey	29	65	Venezuela	2
UPPER MIDDLE			37	Djibouti	28	66	Bolivia	1
11	China	288	38	Rwanda	25	67	Botswana	1
12	Burundi	272	39	Belize	20	68	Colombia	1
13	India	258	40	El Salvador	20			
14	Bangladesh	245	41	Central African Republic	19	**BOTTOM 10**		
15	Guatemala	223	42	Indonesia	16	69	Dominican Republic	1
16	Algeria	219	43	Vietnam	16	70	Panama	1
17	Uganda	196	44	Nicaragua	15	71	Peru	1
18	Cote d'Ivoire	174	45	Mali	13	72	Somalia	1
19	Zambia	142	46	Argentina	12	73	Cambodia	0
20	Zimbabwe	137	47	Ghana	12	74	Laos	0
21	Kuwait	125	48	Guinea-Bissau	12	75	Libya	0
22	Costa Rica	114	49	Angola	11	76	Qatar	0
23	Honduras	100	50	Congo	10	77	South Africa	0
24	Liberia	100	51	Malaysia	10	78	United Arab Emirates	0
25	Iraq	95	52	Papua New Guinea	7			
26	Nepal	76	53	Philippines	7			

Source: UN High Commissioner for Refugees

42. FOREIGN AID PER CAPITA

Foreign aid is broadly defined as the flow of financial resources from developed market economies to developing countries expressly intended for the economic and social development of the latter. Developing countries include all countries and territories in Africa except South Africa; in the Western Hemisphere, all except the United States, Canada, Greenland and Puerto Rico; in Asia, all except China, North Korea, Vietnam, Japan, Mongolia and Turkey; and in Oceania, all except Australia, New Zealand and U.S. possessions. Developed market economies comprise the 17 members of the Development Assistance Committee of the Organization for Economic Cooperation and Development: Australia, Austria, Belgium, Canada, Denmark, Finland, Germany, France, Italy, Japan, the Netherlands, New Zealand, Norway, Sweden, Switzerland, the United Kingdom and the United States and also Iceland, Ireland, Luxembourg, Portugal and South Africa. Multilateral institutions extending aid to developing countries include the World Bank, regional banks and financial institutions of the European Community and a number of U.N. agencies and funds.

Rank	Country	Foreign Aid per Capita $	Rank	Country	Foreign Aid per Capita $	Rank	Country	Foreign Aid per Capita $
TOP 10			29	Burkina	46.8	58	Guatemala	21.1
1	Oman	538.8	30	Jamaica	45.0	59	Ethiopia	21.0
2	Sierra Leone	269.4	31	Cameroon	43.7	60	Nepal	17.5
3	Israel	242.5	32	Laos	43.2	61	Algeria	13.4
4	Mauritania	153.2				62	Chile	13.3
5	Namibia	105.6	**LOWER MIDDLE**			63	Bangladesh	12.0
6	Gabon	100.9	33	Zimbabwe	42.8	64	Indonesia	10.8
7	Zambia	97.3	34	Egypt	40.8	65	Thailand	10.6
8	Guinea-Bissau	94.6	35	Burundi	40.6	66	Pakistan	8.7
9	Botswana	90.4	36	Niger	40.5	67	Argentina	8.4
10	Gambia	88.0	37	Ghana	38.5	68	Turkey	7.7
			38	Uruguay	38.5	69	Malaysia	5.2
UPPER MIDDLE			39	Chad	38.1	70	Mexico	4.5
11	Bolivia	80.6	40	Mali	35.5	71	Vietnam	4.5
12	Nicaragua	78.5	41	Kenya	35.3	72	Grenada	4.2
13	Mozambique	77	42	Uganda	34.2	73	Colombia	3.0
14	Papua New Guinea	73.7	43	Tanzania	33.9	74	China	2.8
15	El Salvador	73.4	44	Panama	31.3	75	Nigeria	2.7
16	Lesotho	65.7	45	Sri Lanka	30.8			
17	Guinea	65.6	46	Costa Rica	30.1	**BOTTOM 10**		
18	Senegal	64.3	47	Paraguay	29.1	76	Venezuela	2.4
19	Honduras	60.7	48	Morocco	29.0	77	Myanmar (Burma)	2.3
20	Jordan	59.7	49	Tunisia	28.9	78	Iran	2.2
21	Cote d'Ivoire	57.5	50	Madagascar	26.7	79	Saudi Arabia	2.0
22	Albania	57.3	51	Togo	25.9	80	Trinidad and Tobago	2.0
23	Central African Republic	55.0	52	Peru	24.5	81	India	1.7
24	Congo	52.9	53	Mauritius	24.3	82	Brazil	1.5
25	Benin	52.4	54	Yemen	23.4	83	Kuwait	1.5
26	Mongolia	48.6	55	Philippines	23.0	84	Dominican Republic	0.2
27	Malawi	47.8	56	Ecuador	21.9	85	United Arab Emirates	−4.8
28	Rwanda	47.7	57	Korea, South	21.9			

Source: *World Development Report*

43. DEVELOPMENT ASSISTANCE

In the 19th century the German general Karl von Clausewitz defined war as diplomacy by other means. Foreign aid in the 20th century might be similarly defined. Large-scale aid to poorer nations in a comparatively recent phenomenon that exists on three fronts:
- From Western nations, especially the United States, to developing nations that are within their sphere of influence;
- From oil-rich Arab nations to poorer Muslim nations as well as to nations that extend moral support to the Arabs in their struggle with Israel;

- From the United Nations and other international agencies, such as the World Bank, to all developing countries.

In addition there are specific bodies, such as the Development Assistance Committee of the OECD that meet regularly and determine the amount and nature of aid and monitor repayment schedules. Currently much of foreign aid is nonconcessional in nature and the grant element has been decreasing for years. (On the other hand, Sweden set a remarkable example to other developed nations by writing off all loans to developing nations in 1977.)

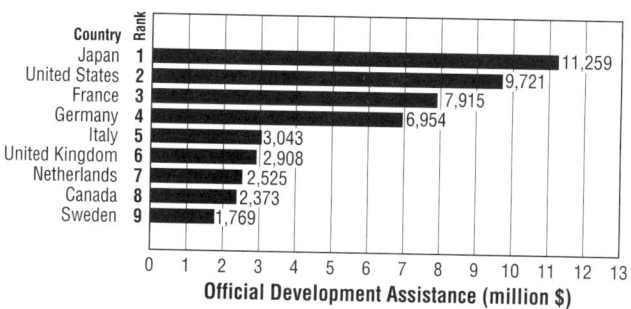

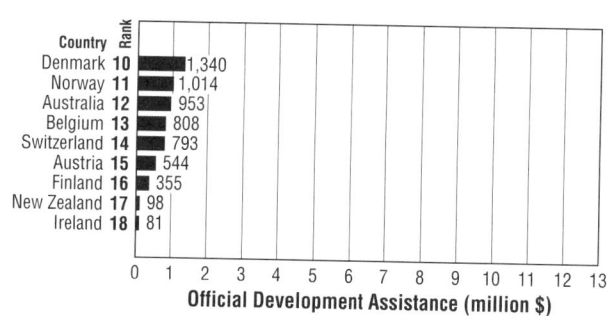

Source: OECD

44. MOST POWERFUL NATIONS

Power is an intriguing subject. Decisions affecting foreign policy and international conflicts are usually made by national leaders on the basis of projections of what they perceive their own power or the power of others to be. Although the perceptions of power are thus often blurred or diffuse, they contain concrete elements and ingredients that can be identified and even measured broadly. One of the most successful attempts to do so is that by Professor Ray Cline in *World Power Assessment,* in which he presents an overall conceptual methodology that incorporates military, economic, geopolitical and psychological factors. He has also devised a calibrated scale of perceived power on which the rank of each nation can be determined. There are five basic elements in Dr. Cline's scale of perceived power: (1) Critical Mass (Population plus Territory), (2) Economic Capability, (3) Military Capability, (4) Strategic Purpose and (5) Will to Pursue National Strategy. National power is a mix of all these factors. It is determined by its potential for the deterrence of war, and even more so by the size and strategic location of territory, the nature of its frontiers, population size, political and economic alliances, technological development, raw material resources, economic structure, financial strength, ethnic mix, social cohesiveness, political stability and, above all, that intangible quality generally described as national will. The index numbers used by Dr. Cline easily convey estimates of comparative strengths and weaknesses among nations. Because these elements are being measured in a broad context, precise details may not significantly vary the rank order.

Rank	Country	1 Critical Mass	2 Economic Capability	3 Military Capability	Total	4 & 5 x Strategy & Will	Total
TOP 10							
1	United States	100	146	188	434	0.7	304
2	Russia	90	30	121	241	1.0	241
3	Brazil	80	50	3	98	1.4	137
4	Germany	30	34	13	77	1.5	116
5	Japan	44	28	5	77	1,4	108
6	Australia	50	22	1	73	1,2	88
7	China	75	23	41	139	0.6	83
8	France	28	33	21	82	0.9	74
9	United Kingdom	29	21	18	68	1.0	68
10	Canada	56	30	1	87	0.7	61
UPPER MIDDLE							
11	Indonesia	56	4	1	61	0.9	55
12	Taiwan	14	3	12	29	1.7	49
13	South Korea	20	5	8	33	1.4	46
14	Egypt	25	n.a.	13	38	1.2	46
15	South Africa	23	9	4	36	1.1	40
16	Vietnam	28	n.a.	11	39	1.0	39
17	Saudi Arabia	12	18	n.a.	30	1.3	39
18	Israel	n.a.	1	22	23	1.7	39
19	Spain	25	9	5	39	1.0	39
20	India	52	11	8	71	0.5	36
21	Italy	29	14	5	48	0.7	34
22	Argentina	31	7	2	40	0.8	32
23	Chile	15	4	n.a.	19	1.3	25
24	Philippines	27	3	n.a.	30	0.8	24
25	Netherlands	n.a.	17	2	19	1.2	23
26	Pakistan	25	2	1	28	0.8	22
27	Nigeria	26	2	n.a.	28	0.8	22
28	Mexico	27	5	n.a.	32	0.7	22
LOWER MIDDLE							
29	Norway	15	5	1	21	1.0	21
30	Zaire	19	2	n.a.	21	1.0	21
31	North Korea	5	n.a.	10	15	1.4	21
32	Algeria	17	3	n.a.	20	1.0	20
33	Poland	14	10	4	28	0.7	20
34	Thailand	17	2	1	20	1.0	20
35	Turkey	26	3	7	36	0.5	38
36	Libya	10	5	n.a.	15	1.2	18
37	New Zealand	15	1	n.a.	16	1.1	18
38	Denmark	10	4	1	15	1.1	17

Rank	Country	1 Critical Mass	2 Economic Capability	3 Military Capability	Total	4 & 5 x Strategy & Will	Total
39	Iran	18	12	2	32	0.5	16
40	Syria	5	n.a.	10	15	1.0	15
41	Sweden	5	8	1	14	1.1	15
42	Rumania	10	4	1	15	1.0	15
43	Iraq	5	5	7	17	0.8	14
44	Peru	11	2	n.a.	13	1.0	13
45	Yugoslavia	10	3	3	16	0.8	13
46	Sudan	18	n.a.	n.a.	18	0.7	13
47	Columbia	11	1	n.a.	12	1.0	12
48	Bangladesh	27	1	n.a.	28	0.4	11
49	Czech Republic	4	6	4	14	0.8	11
50	Switzerland	n.a.	7	n.a.	7	1.6	11
51	Morocco	10	n.a.	n.a.	10	1.0	10
52	Belgium-Luxembourg	n.a.	6	2	8	1.1	9
53	Tanzania	9	n.a.	n.a.	9	1.0	9
54	Venezuela	5	6	n.a.	11	0.8	9
55	Kenya	9	n.a.	n.a.	9	1.0	9
56	Zimbabwe	5	1	n.a.	6	1.2	7
57	Ethiopia	14	n.a.	n.a.	14	0.5	7
58	Greece	5	1	2	8	0.8	6
59	Finland	5	3	n.a.	8	0.8	6
60	Zambia	5	2	n.a.	7	0.7	5
61	Guinea	5	1	n.a.	6	0.9	5
62	Austria	n.a.	4	n.a.	4	1.3	5
63	Bulgaria	na.a	3	2	5	0.9	5
64	Malaysia	5	2	n.a.	7	0.7	5
65	Kuwait	n.a.	6	n.a.	6	0.8	5
66	Burma	13	n.a.	n.a.	13	0.3	4
BOTTOM 10							
67	Suriname	5	1	n.a.	6	0.6	4
68	Hungary	n.a	3	1	4	0.8	3
69	Cuba	n.a.	n.a.	2	2	1.2	2
70	Mongolia	8	n.a	n.a.	8	0.3	2
71	United Arab Emirates	n.a.	4	n.a.	4	0.5	2
72	Liberia	n.a.	2	n.a.	2	0.8	2
73	Singapore	n.a.	2	n.a.	2	1.1	2
74	Jamaica	n.a.	1	n.a.	1	1.0	1
75	Albania	n.a.	1	n.a.	1	1.0	1
76	Portugal	n.a.	n.a.	1	1	0.9	1

Source: Ray Cline, *World Power Assessment.* Reprinted by permission.

45. CORRUPTION

Corruption is a clandestine "industry" estimated to net about $1.5 billion annually worldwide. This industry extends into politics, the judicial system, transportation, the police, and other public services. In parts of Asia and Africa corruption is so prevalent that an ordinary citizen bribes on average over 32 public officials in the course of a year. In many countries bribes are an accepted cost of business, much of it passed onto the consumer. There are illegal commissions that are openly demanded before any project is approved or before any sale is completed. In some countries rates are "published" for each transaction and for each level of public servant. The list extends from heads of state and heads of government to the lowest customs clerk. A bribe is one of the modern variants of the ancient practice of paying tribute. It is a tribute that the powerless pay to the powerful.

Some years ago, Peter Eigen, formerly of the World Bank, brought together business leaders, politicians and academics to study the ways in which corruption stunts national development. Out of that initiative was born Transparency International, a watchdog organization, that compiles an annual international corruption index. Their first index, published in 1995, ranked 41 countries on a scale of 1–10 in which 0 is the highest rate of corruption and 10 is the lowest. As can be imagined, no country merited a 10. But New Zealand came closest with 9.55. The United States and United Kingdom are in the lower middle with 7.79 and 8.57 respectively. Lee Kuan Yew's Singapore does better, showing that his draconian laws serve their purpose. Six of the worst eight countries are in Asia. The worst European country is Italy where public servants are not held in great respect in any case. If African countries had been included many of them would have been close to zero, but Transparency International's archives at this time do not include data on Africa.

TOP 10 Corruption

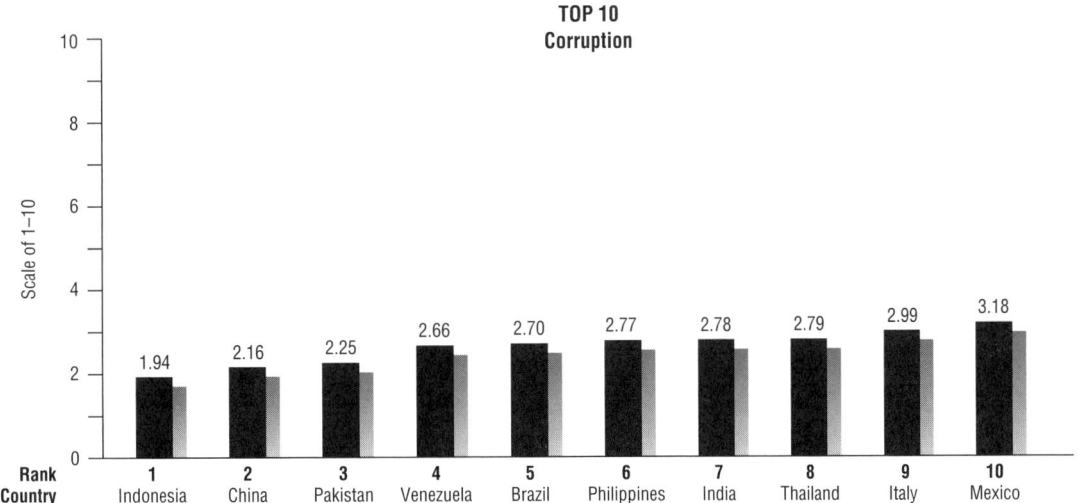

Rank	1	2	3	4	5	6	7	8	9	10
Country	Indonesia	China	Pakistan	Venezuela	Brazil	Philippines	India	Thailand	Italy	Mexico
	1.94	2.16	2.25	2.66	2.70	2.77	2.78	2.79	2.99	3.18

Rank	Country	Scale of 1–10	Rank	Country	Scale of 1–10	Rank	Country	Scale of 1–10
THE MIDDLE 21			21	South Africa	5.62	**THE LEAST CORRUPT 10**		
11	Colombia	3.44	22	Japan	7.62	32	Norway	8.61
12	Greece	4.04	23	Belgium/Luxembourg	6.85	33	Netherlands	8.69
13	Turkey	4.10	24	France	7.00	34	Switzerland	8.76
14	Hungary	4.12	25	Hong Kong	7.12	35	Australia	8.80
15	South Korea	4.29	26	Austria	7.13	36	Canada	8.87
16	Spain	4.35	27	United States	7.79	37	Sweden	8.87
17	Taiwan	5.08	28	Chile	7.94	38	Finland	9.12
18	Argentina	5.24	29	Germany	8.14	39	Singapore	9.26
19	Malaysia	5.28	30	United Kingdom	8.57	40	Denmark	9.32
20	Portugal	5.56	31	Ireland	8.57	41	New Zealand	9.55

Source: Transparency International

Section
VI

MILITARY
POWER

"How many divisions has the Pope?" Stalin's probably apocryphal question illustrates one aspect of military power: its easy measurability. It seems pertinent to mention here that military strength ideally should be measured not on a general scale but only against that of neighboring countries. Except for Russia and the United States, no nation today has the reach or capacity to wage intercontinental warfare or for that matter any type of warfare against nations other than its neighbors. One cannot conceive of Bolivia being attacked by Ethiopia; the relative military rankings of these two nations are irrelevant because one is not a threat to the other. On the other hand, the military power of Ethiopia is best evaluated against those of say Somalia or Sudan, its hostile neighbors. This brings us to the concept of usable military power, which is vastly different from actual military power. Usable military power may be defined in terms of its effectiveness against hostile neighbors, its credibility and its state of readiness. The United States discovered in the 1960s that the very awesome military power at its command inhibited it from taking appropriate measures in certain situations, thus making its power useless in short-of-war confrontations.

A second disturbing element on the world military scene is the indiscriminate arms transfers from developed countries to smaller and more irresponsible nations. The smaller the country and the less responsible its leadership, the greater and the more credible its military posture becomes. The proliferation of arms is in itself an invitation to promiscuous use of weapons. In this sense there is considerable logic behind the efforts to limit the size of the nuclear club. The moral is that the powerful may be trusted with power but the powerless may not be. To rephrase Lord Acton, power corrupts, but powerlessness corrupts absolutely.

The third element is the folly of alliances and treaties. With U.S. withdrawal from Vietnam, we may have reached the end of the age of alliances. The dynamics of international affairs are such that there is no longer any guarantee that one nation will rush to the aid of the other for fear of enlarging the area of conflict. The old theory that the military strength of a nation is in its alliances no longer holds true.

46. MILITARY MANPOWER PER CAPITA

Since the collapse of the Soviet Union and the end of the Cold War military establishments in virtually every country have been downsized. This has led to largescale demobilization. The only exceptions are in small countries, such as Israel, Bosnia and North Korea, where peace is still unstable and hostilities can-not be ruled out. Some countries, like Japan, are constitutionally barred from engaging in external hostilities; some like Swaziland, do not maintain a standing army, and some neutral countries like Switzerland maintain only a token force.

Rank	Country	Military Manpower per 1,000 Inhabitants	Rank	Country	Military Manpower per 1,000 Inhabitants	Rank	Country	Military Manpower per 1,000 Inhabitants
TOP 10			52	France	7.1	104	Sierra Leone	2.9
1	Korea, North	48.9	53	Sri Lanka	7.1	105	New Zealand	2.8
2	Israel	32.3	54	Chile	6.7	106	Canada	2.7
3	Taiwan	30.7	55	Austria	6.4	107	Kyrgyzstan	2.7
4	Syria	29.5	56	Myanmar (Burma)	6.3	108	Latvia	2.7
5	United Arab Emirates	28.9	57	United States	6.3	109	Uganda	2.7
6	Bosnia & Herzegovina	24.7	58	Belgium	6.2	110	Zambia	2.6
7	Jordan	23.3	59	Finland	6.1	111	Burundi	2.5
8	Croatia	21.9	60	Malaysia	5.9	112	China	2.5
9	Albania	21.0	61	Saudi Arabia	5.8	113	Moldova	2.5
10	Oman	20.9	62	Italy	5.6	114	Lithuania	2.4
			63	El Salvador	5.4	115	Costa Rica	2.3
UPPER MIDDLE			64	Spain	5.3	116	Guyana	2.3
11	Iraq	19.2	65	Botswana	5.2	117	Argentina	2.1
12	Singapore	18.4	66	Denmark	5.2	118	Brazil	2.1
13	Qatar	18.3	67	Portugal	5.2	119	Luxembourg	2.0
14	Cyprus	16.3				120	Trinidad and Tobago	2.0
15	Brunei	15.5	**LOWER MIDDLE**			121	Uzbekistan	2.0
16	Greece	15.4	68	Ecuador	5.1	122	Japan	1.9
17	Lebanon	14.9	69	Fiji	5.1	123	Mexico	1.9
18	Djibouti	14.8	70	Namibia	5.1	124	South Africa	1.9
19	Bahrain	14.7	71	Yemen	5.1	125	Nepal	1.8
20	Korea, South	14.2	72	Macedonia	5.0	126	Tanzania	1.8
21	Libya	13.4	73	Malta	5.0	127	Togo	1.8
22	Bulgaria	12.1	74	Peru	4.9	128	Estonia	1.7
23	Yugoslavia	12.0	75	Chad	4.7	129	Central African Republic	1.6
24	Russia	11.7	76	Netherlands	4.6	130	Philippines	1.6
25	Kuwait	11.3	77	Sudan	4.6	131	Senegal	1.6
26	Seychelles	11.1	78	Germany	4.5	132	Madagascar	1.5
27	Romania	10.1	79	Pakistan	4.5	133	India	1.4
28	Ukraine	9.9	80	Panama	4.5	134	Indonesia	1.4
29	Cuba	9.6	81	Algeria	4.4	135	Jamaica	1.3
30	Bahamas	9.4	82	Thailand	4.4	136	Cameroon	1.1
31	Mongolia	9.4	83	United Kingdom	4.4	137	Guinea	1.1
32	Cambodia	9.3	84	Belize	4.3	138	Haiti	1.1
33	Armenia	9.2	85	Guatemala	4.3	139	Malawi	1.1
34	Czech Republic	9.0	86	Suriname	4.3	140	Zaire	1.1
35	Belarus	8.9	87	Zimbabwe	4.3	141	Bangladesh	1.0
36	Guinea-Bissau	8.8	88	Bolivia	4.2	142	Burkina	1.0
37	Slovakia	8.8	89	Colombia	4.2	143	Lesotho	1.0
38	Iran	8.6	90	Tunisia	4.1	144	Benin	0.9
39	Turkey	8.2	91	Slovenia	4.0			
40	Uruguay	8.1	92	Ireland	3.7	**BOTTOM 10**		
41	Vietnam	7.9	93	Venezuela	3.7	145	Kenya	0.9
42	Laos	7.8	94	Gabon	3.6	146	Papua New Guinea	0.9
43	Mauritania	7.8	95	Nicaragua	3.6	147	Gambia	0.8
44	Norway	7.7	96	Congo	3.5	148	Mali	0.8
45	Azerbaijan	7.5	97	Paraguay	3.5	149	Nigeria	0.8
46	Egypt	7.5	98	Australia	3.4	150	Cote d'Ivoire	0.6
47	Angola	7.3	99	Equatorial Guinea	3.4	151	Niger	0.6
48	Hungary	7.3	100	Honduras	3.2	152	Rwanda	0.6
49	Poland	7.3	101	Bhutan	3.1	153	Ghana	0.4
50	Sweden	7.3	102	Cape Verde	3.1	154	Switzerland	0.3
51	Morocco	7.2	103	Dominican Republic	3.1			

Source: *World Military Expenditures and Arms Transfers*

47. ARMS IMPORTS

In a military sense, the world is divided into patron states and client states. One of the characteristics of client states is that they are dependent on the patron states not only for products and goods but also for military hardware and armaments. Arms supply is an extremely lucrative trade conducted for the most part surreptitiously and with significant political overtones. Some of these arms fall into the hands of terrorists and some of them are so sophisticated that they remain unused for years; See the ranking on Arms Exports to discover the top suppliers of arms.

TOP 10*
Arms Imports

Rank	Country	million $	Rank	Country	million $
1	Saudi Arabia	6,900	6	Turkey	800
2	Afghanistan	1,900	7	Japan	775
3	United States	1,900	8	South Korea	775
4	Iran	1,600	9	Syria	650
5	India	800	10	Portugal	550

1 tank = 1,000,000,000 $

*The Top 10 makes up 65% of the arms imports.

Rank	Country	Arms Imports (million $)		Rank	Country	Arms Imports (million $)		Rank	Country	Arms Imports (million $)
UPPER MIDDLE				39	Korea, North	90		66	Qatar	20
11	Cuba	525		40	South Africa	90		67	Tunisia	20
12	Egypt	525						68	Argentina	10
13	United Kingdom	525		**LOWER MIDDLE**				69	Austria	10
14	Germany	520		41	Sudan	90		70	Bolivia	10
15	Israel	460		42	Ethiopia	80		71	Chad	10
16	Taiwan	450		43	Philippines	80		72	Ecuador	10
17	Thailand	430		44	Chile	70		73	Kenya	10
18	Libya	370		45	Indonesia	70		74	Laos	10
19	Myanmar (Burma)	370		46	Colombia	60		75	Mozambique	10
20	Netherlands	360		47	Jordan	60		76	Peru	10
21	China	240		48	Bahrain	50		77	Tanzania	10
22	Australia	210		49	Czech Republic	50		78	Uganda	10
23	Belarus	210		50	Denmark	50		79	Zambia	10
24	Canada	200		51	El Salvador	50		80	Botswana	5
25	Norway	200		52	Kuwait	50				
26	Vietnam	200		53	Sri Lanka	50		**BOTTOM 10**		
27	Yemen	200		54	Bangladesh	40		81	Burundi	5
28	Italy	180		55	Cambodia	40		82	Finland	5
29	Romania	170		56	Mexico	40		83	Guinea	5
30	Spain	150		57	New Zealand	40		84	Guinea-Bissau	5
31	United Arab Emirates	150		58	Oman	40		85	Jamaica	5
32	Venezuela	140		59	Sweden	40		86	Lebanon	5
33	France	130		60	Angola	30		87	Nigeria	5
34	Greece	130		61	Malaysia	30		88	Panama	5
35	Pakistan	120		62	Morocco	30		89	Uruguay	5
36	Singapore	120		63	Brazil	20		90	Zimbabwe	5
37	Switzerland	110		64	Honduras	20				
38	Algeria	100		65	Luxembourg	20				

Source: *World Military Expenditures and Arms Transfers*

48. MILITARY EXPENDITURES AS PERCENTAGE OF GNP

In terms of global gross product, military expenditures not only constitute a relatively small element but have actually decreased from 7.06% in 1960 to 4.5% in 1995. Although this might seem to belie reports of an escalating arms race, the decrease is restricted to the heavily industrialized nations (which are overmilitarized in any case). Defense expenditures as percentage of GNP have increased 250% from 1.78% to 4.6% during the same period for developing countries and may permanently inhibit their economic potential. Because of their ripple effects, the long-term adverse consequences of large military expenditures may exert a significant drag not only on the economy but also on the political structure, environment, education and infrastructure. The military competes with the civilian sector for scarce scientific and management talents, raw materials and transportation facilities. Ultimately, military expenditures intensify existing economic problems, while diluting the efforts to solve them.

Rank	Country	Military Expenditures as Percentage of GNP	Rank	Country	Military Expenditures as Percentage of GNP	Rank	Country	Military Expenditures as Percentage of GNP
TOP 10			48	Albania	4.1	96	Belize	2.0
1	Kuwait	102.2	49	Bulgaria	4.0	97	Benin	2.0
2	Iraq	74.9	50	Romania	4.0	98	Canada	2.0
3	Angola	23.9	51	Yugoslavia	4.0	99	Finland	2.0
4	Ethiopia	21.9	52	Korea, South	3.8	100	Haiti	2.0
5	Korea, North	20.0	53	Suriname	3.8	101	Mali	2.0
6	Syria	17.9	54	Malaysia	3.7	102	Argentina	1.9
7	Nicaragua	17.2	55	South Africa	3.7	103	Senegal	1.9
8	Saudi Arabia	16.5	56	Burkina	3.6	104	Switzerland	1.9
9	Oman	15.8	57	France	3.6	105	Algeria	1.8
10	United Arab Emirates	15.6	58	Gabon	3.6	106	Central African Republic	1.7
			59	Venezuela	3.6	107	Honduras	1.7
UPPER MIDDLE			60	Lebanon	3.5	108	Paraguay	1.7
11	Yemen	14.4	61	Chile	3.4	109	Spain	1.7
12	Mozambique	13.0	62	Egypt	3.4	110	Cameroon	1.6
13	Cape Verde	11.8				111	Indonesia	1.6
14	Jordan	11.2	**LOWER MIDDLE**			112	Panama	1.6
15	Laos	10.5	63	Tunisia	3.4	113	Sao Tome e Principe	1.6
16	Qatar	9.3	64	China	3.3	114	Zimbabwe	1.5
17	Libya	8.7	65	Portugal	3.3	115	Bangladesh	1.4
18	Brunei	8.1	66	Norway	3.2	116	New Zealand	1.4
19	Djibouti	8.1	67	Somalia	3.2	117	Swaziland	1.4
20	Israel	8.1	68	Papua New Guinea	3.0	118	Brazil	1.3
21	Afghanistan	7.7	69	Togo	3.0	119	Guinea	1.3
22	Bahrain	7.7	70	El Salvador	2.9	120	Ireland	1.3
23	Sudan	7.7	71	Kenya	2.8	121	Niger	1.3
24	Rwanda	7.5	72	Sweden	2.8	122	Madagascar	1.2
25	Cyprus	7.1	73	India	2.7	123	Malawi	1.1
26	Pakistan	6.1	74	Thailand	2.7	124	Nepal	1.1
27	Iran	5.7	75	Australia	2.6	125	Peru	1.1
28	Seychelles	5.6	76	Colombia	2.6	126	Austria	1.0
29	Greece	5.5	77	Czech Republic	2.6	127	Guatemala	1.0
30	Lesotho	5.4	78	Uganda	2.6	128	Guyana	1.0
31	Turkey	5.4	79	Germany	2.5	129	Japan	1.0
32	Tanzania	5.3	80	Netherlands	2.5	130	Dominican Republic	0.8
33	Chad	5.2	81	Belgium	2.4	131	Luxembourg	0.8
34	Singapore	5.2	82	Bolivia	2.4	132	Malta	0.8
35	Taiwan	5.2	83	Burundi	2.4	133	Nigeria	0.8
36	Congo	5.1	84	Guinea-Bissau	2.4			
37	Botswana	4.9	85	Myanmar (Burma)	2.4	**BOTTOM 10**		
38	Mongolia	4.9	86	Zambia	2.4	134	Zaire	0.8
39	United States	4.9	87	Sierra Leone	2.3	135	Gambia	0.7
40	Liberia	4.8	88	Fiji	2.2	136	Jamaica	0.7
41	Sri Lanka	4.8	89	Cote d'Ivoire	2.1	137	Barbados	0.6
42	Vietnam	4.8	90	Denmark	2.1	138	Ghana	0.6
43	Poland	4.6	91	Ecuador	2.1	139	Trinidad and Tobago	0.6
44	Mauritania	4.3	92	Hungary	2.1	140	Bahamas	0.5
45	Morocco	4.3	93	Italy	2.1	141	Costa Rica	0.4
46	United Kingdom	4.3	94	Philippines	2.1	143	Mauritius	0.4
47	Cuba	4.2	95	Uruguay	2.1	144	Mexico	0.4

Source: *World Military Expenditures and Arms Transfers*

49. MEN AND WOMEN UNDER ARMS

Historically, a standing army is one of the most visible expressions of national sovereignty. This explains why one of the first acts of a newly independent nation almost always is to create its own military establishment, even when there is no external threat to its existence.

Rank	Country	Total Military Manpower (000)
TOP 10		
1	China	2,930.0
2	Russia	1,714.0
3	United States	1,650.5
4	India	1,265.0
5	Korea, North	1,128.0
6	Korea, South	633.0
7	Pakistan	587.0
8	Venezuela	572.0
9	Ukraine	517.0
10	Iran	513.0
UPPER MIDDLE		
11	Turkey	502.8
12	Egypt	440.0
13	Taiwan	425.0
14	France	409.6
15	Syria	408.0
16	Iraq	382.0
17	Germany	367.3
18	Brazil	336.8
19	Italy	322.3
20	Myanmar (Burma)	286.0
21	Poland	283.6
22	Indonesia	276.0
23	Thailand	256.0
24	United Kingdom	254.3
25	Japan	237.7
26	Romania	230.5
27	Spain	206.5
28	Morocco	195.5
29	Mexico	175.0
30	Israel	172.0
31	Greece	159.3
32	Colombia	146.4
33	Sri Lanka	128.0
34	Yugoslavia	126.5
35	Algeria	121.7
36	Sudan	118.5
37	Bangladesh	115.5
38	Peru	115.0
39	Malaysia	114.5
40	Bosnia & Herzegovina	110.0
41	Philippines	106.5
42	Cuba	106.0
43	Croatia	105.0
44	Saudi Arabia	104.0
45	Bulgaria	101.9
46	Qatar	101
47	Jordan	98.6
48	Chile	93.0
49	Czech Republic	92.9
50	Belarus	92.5
51	Cambodia	88.5

Rank	Country	Total Military Manpower (000)
52	Angola	82
53	Vanuatu	79.0
54	South Africa	78.5
55	Canada	78.1
56	Nigeria	76.5
57	Hungary	74.5
58	Albania	73
59	Netherlands	70.9
60	Libya	70.0
61	Argentina	69.8
62	Yemen	66.0
63	Sweden	64.0
64	Belgium	62.0
65	Australia	61.6
66	United Arab Emirates	61.5
LOWER MIDDLE		
67	Ecuador	57.5
68	Azerbaijan	56.0
69	Singapore	54.0
70	Austria	51.3
71	Portugal	50.7
72	Uganda	50.0
73	Tanzania	49.6
74	Zaire	49.1
75	Slovakia	47.0
76	Zimbabwe	46.9
77	Uzbekistan	45.0
78	Lebanon	44.3
79	Guatemala	44.2
80	Oman	42.9
81	Laos	37.0
82	Tunisia	35.5
83	Nepal	35.0
84	Bolivia	33.5
85	Norway	33.5
86	Armenia	32.7
87	Finland	31.2
88	El Salvador	30.7
89	Chad	30.4
90	Denmark	27.0
91	Uruguay	25.6
92	Dominican Republic	24.5
93	Kenya	24.2
94	Zambia	24.0
95	Mongolia	21.3
96	Madagascar	21.0
97	Honduras	16.8
98	Kuwait	16.6
99	Paraguay	16.5
100	Mauritania	15.7
101	Nicaragua	15.2
102	Burundi	14.6
103	Cameroon	14.6

Rank	Country	Total Military Manpower (000)
104	Senegal	13.4
105	Sierra Leone	13.4
106	Ireland	13.0
107	Kyrgyzstan	12.0
108	Panama	11.7
109	Moldova	11.1
110	Macedonia	10.4
111	Malawi	10.4
112	Burkina	10.0
113	Congo	10.0
114	Cyprus	10.0
115	New Zealand	10.0
116	Guinea-Bissau	9.3
117	Lithuania	8.9
118	Cote d'Ivoire	8.4
119	Djibouti	8.4
120	Bahrain	8.1
121	Namibia	8.1
122	Slovenia	8.1
123	Botswana	7.5
124	Costa Rica	7.5
125	Mali	7.4
126	Haiti	7.3
127	Togo	7.0
128	Ghana	6.9
129	Guinea	6.9
130	Latvia	6.9
131	Niger	5.3
132	Central African Republic	5.0
133	Rwanda	5.0
134	Gabon	4.7
135	Benin	4.5
136	Brunei	4.4
137	Bhutan	4.0
138	Fiji	3.9
139	Papua New Guinea	3.8
140	Jamaica	3.3
141	Bahamas	2.6
142	Trinidad and Tobago	2.6
143	Estonia	2.5
144	Lesotho	2.0
BOTTOM 10		
145	Malta	1.9
146	Suriname	1.8
147	Switzerland	1.8
148	Guyana	1.7
149	Equatorial Guinea	1.3
150	Cape Verde	1.1
141	Belize	0.9
152	Gambia	0.8
153	Luxembourg	0.8
154	Seychelles	0.8

Source: *World Military Expenditures and Arms Transfers*

50. MILITARY EXPENDITURES AS PERCENTAGE OF EDUCATION AND HEALTH EXPENDITURES COMBINED

The Peace Dividend was one of the much anticipated benefits of the end of the Cold War. This meant that resources formerly devoted to arms buildup could be devoted to development, particularly the two most critical areas of development: health and education.

The military still have a powerful influence on national budgets and their clout is used to maintain substantial war establishments. Even so, both the education and health sectors have gained as a result of the redistribution of national priorities.

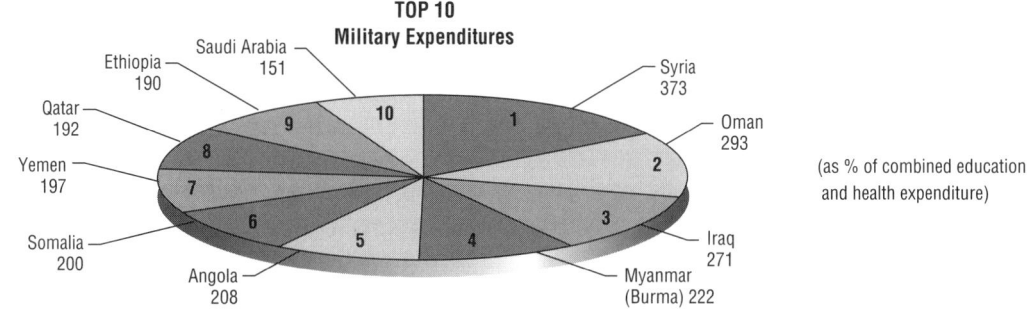

TOP 10
Military Expenditures

Saudi Arabia 151
Ethiopia 190
Qatar 192
Yemen 197
Somalia 200
Angola 208
Syria 373
Oman 293
Iraq 271
Myanmar (Burma) 222

(as % of combined education and health expenditure)

Rank	Country	Military Expenditure (as % of combined education and health expenditures) 1990–1991
	UPPER MIDDLE	
11	Jorda	138
12	Russia	132
13	Singapore	129
14	Brunei	125
15	Cuba	125
16	Pakistan	125
17	Mozambique	121
18	China	114
19	Sri Lanka	107
20	Israel	106
21	Nicaragua	97
22	Honduras	92
23	Kuwait	88
24	Turkey	87
25	Tanzania	77
26	Chad	74
27	Morocco	72
28	Greece	71
29	Libya	71
30	Thailand	71
31	Zaire	71
32	Chile	68
33	El Salvador	66
34	Zimbabwe	66
35	India	65
36	Zambia	63
37	Korea, North	60
38	Bolivia	57
39	Colombia	57
40	Mali	53
41	Egypt	52
42	Albania	51
43	Argentina	51
44	Gabon	51
45	Indonesia	49
46	Cameroon	48
47	Lesotho	48
48	Liberia	47
49	United States	46
50	United Arab Emirates	44
51	Sudan	44

Rank	Country	Military Expenditure (as % of combined education and health expenditures) 1990–1991
52	Burundi	42
53	Paraguay	42
54	Bahrain	41
55	Bangladesh	41
	LOWER MIDDLE	
56	Papua New Guinea	41
57	Philippines	41
58	South Africa	41
59	United Kingdom	40
60	Mauritania	40
61	Peru	39
62	Togo	39
63	Iran	38
64	Malaysia	38
65	Uruguay	38
66	Congo	37
67	Fiji	37
68	Guinea	37
69	Madagascar	37
70	Nepal	35
71	Panama	34
72	Central African Republic	33
73	Nigeria	33
74	Senegal	33
75	Venezuela	33
76	Portugal	32
77	Guatemala	31
78	Tunisia	31
79	Poland	30
80	Burkina	30
81	Haiti	30
82	France	29
83	Germany	29
84	Bulgaria	29
85	Suriname	27
86	Ecuador	26
87	Romania	25
88	Rwanda	25
89	Australia	24
90	Kenya	24
91	Malawi	24

Rank	Country	Military Expenditure (as % of combined education and health expenditures) 1990–1991
92	Brazil	23
93	Namibia	23
94	Sierra Leone	23
95	Netherlands	22
96	Norway	22
97	Botswana	22
98	Dominican Republic	22
99	Italy	21
100	Guyana	21
101	Belgium	20
102	Spain	18
103	Denmark	18
104	Hungary	18
105	Uganda	18
106	Czech Republic	17
107	Cyprus	17
108	Sweden	16
109	New Zealand	16
110	Canada	15
111	Finland	15
112	Switzerland	14
113	Cote d'Ivoire	14
114	Japan	12
115	Ireland	12
116	Ghana	12
117	Algeria	11
118	Gambia	11
119	Niger	11
120	Swaziland	11
	BOTTOM 10	
121	Luxembourg	10
122	Malta	10
123	Hong Kong	10
124	Austria	9
125	Trinidad and Tobago	9
126	Jamaica	8
127	Barbados	5
128	Costa Rica	5
129	Mexico	5
130	Mauritius	4

Source: *Human Development Report*

51. ARMS EXPORTS

It has been said that war is good business, and the saying applies not merely to the actual conduct of it but also to the preparations and rumors of wars. In fact, since the end of the Cold War removed the last remaining rationale for unlimited military buildups, the arms trade has grown to a multibillion dollar industry with global reach and international lobbies.

Much of the industry is directly patronized and promoted by governments, both to improve their balance of trade and to play their rivals and enemies against one another. The merchants of death, as these arms traders are called, specialize in inflaming hostilities and sabotaging peace moves in order to find additional markets for their armaments.

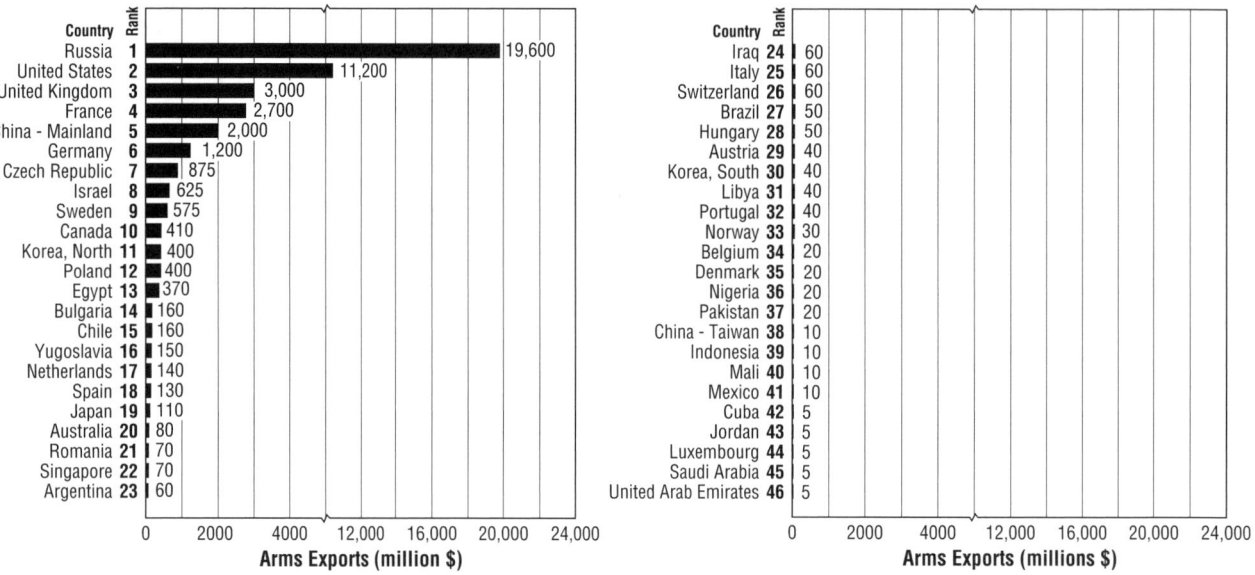

Country	Rank	Arms Exports (million $)
Russia	1	19,600
United States	2	11,200
United Kingdom	3	3,000
France	4	2,700
China - Mainland	5	2,000
Germany	6	1,200
Czech Republic	7	875
Israel	8	625
Sweden	9	575
Canada	10	410
Korea, North	11	400
Poland	12	400
Egypt	13	370
Bulgaria	14	160
Chile	15	160
Yugoslavia	16	150
Netherlands	17	140
Spain	18	130
Japan	19	110
Australia	20	80
Romania	21	70
Singapore	22	70
Argentina	23	60

Country	Rank	Arms Exports (millions $)
Iraq	24	60
Italy	25	60
Switzerland	26	60
Brazil	27	50
Hungary	28	50
Austria	29	40
Korea, South	30	40
Libya	31	40
Portugal	32	40
Norway	33	30
Belgium	34	20
Denmark	35	20
Nigeria	36	20
Pakistan	37	20
China - Taiwan	38	10
Indonesia	39	10
Mali	40	10
Mexico	41	10
Cuba	42	5
Jordan	43	5
Luxembourg	44	5
Saudi Arabia	45	5
United Arab Emirates	46	5

Source: *World Military Expenditures and Arms Transfers*

52. MILITARY RULE

The Greeks called it stratocracy, or rule by the generals, and they dreaded it as one of the worst evils that can befall a country. Some of history's most hated tyrants have been professional soldiers. In the modern age, 82 countries have been under the military heel, sometimes for more than a generation, but the military regimes were invariably brought down, either by the power of the people they misruled or by the pressure of other nations. Almost all the countries in Africa and Latin America have had their military interregna, and some countries seem to be prone to militant takeovers. In Europe, the Iberian peninsula and Greece are found in this list, but few countries where democracy is well established ever had problems with overambitious generals.

Rank	Country	Years Under Military Rule 1960–92
TOP 10		
1	El Salvador	33
2	Iran	33
3	Iraq	33
4	Korea, North	33
5	Nicaragua	33
6	Paraguay	33
7	Syria	33

Rank	Country	Years Under Military Rule 1960–92
8	Thailand	33
9	Vietnam	33
10	Albania	32
UPPER MIDDLE		
11	Haiti	32
12	Korea, South	32
13	Mongolia	31

Rank	Country	Years Under Military Rule 1960–92
14	Myanmar (Burma)	31
15	Pakistan	31
16	Taiwan	31
17	Algeria	30
18	Honduras	30
19	Laos	30
20	Togo	30
21	Yemen	30

Rank	Country	Years Under Military Rule 1960–92	Rank	Country	Years Under Military Rule 1960–92	Rank	Country	Years Under Military Rule 1960–92
22	Congo	29	42	Nigeria	23	64	Ecuador	14
23	Chad	28	43	Portugal	23	65	Liberia	14
24	Zaire	28	44	Somalia	23	66	Mauritania	14
25	Burkina	27	45	Guinea	22	67	Zimbabwe	13
26	Guatemala	27	46	Panama	22	68	Singapore	12
27	Indonesia	27	47	Madagascar	21	69	Uruguay	12
28	Zambia	27	48	Peru	21	70	Egypt	11
29	Brazil	26	49	Philippines	20	71	Colombia	9
30	Burundi	26	50	Afghanistan	19	72	Ghana	9
31	Turkey	26	51	Chile	19			
			52	Bolivia	18		**BOTTOM 10**	
	LOWER MIDDLE		53	Cyprus	18	73	Brunei	8
32	Uganda	26	54	Lesotho	18	74	Greece	6
33	Argentina	25	55	Niger	18	75	Dominican Republic	5
34	Central African Republic	25	56	Bangladesh	17	76	Fiji	5
35	Jordan	25	57	Cuba	17	77	Morocco	5
36	Sudan	25	58	Ethiopia	17	78	Tanzania	5
37	Benin	24	59	Lebanon	17	79	China	4
38	Equatorial Guinea	24	60	South Africa	17	80	Gambia	4
39	Libya	24	61	Sri Lanka	17	81	Papua New Guinea	4
40	Mali	24	62	Angola	16	82	Seychelles	1
41	Cambodia	23	63	Mozambique	16			

Source: *World Military and Social Expenditures*

53. WARS & WAR-RELATED DEATHS

In his classic and seminal study entitled *Study of War* Quincy Wright distinguished four types of wars: (1) balance of power wars between nations, (2) civil wars within nations, (3) defensive wars against alien nations, and (4) imperial wars, or wars of conquest. To this list we may add world wars which differ from these four both in their magnitude or scale of operations and in their severity and destructiveness.

Wright's taxonomy of wars suffers from many ambiguities, not the least of which is the fact that it is not always possible to define a "defensive" war, especially when both sides are claiming to be defending themselves. In fact, the distinction between defenders and initiators could be invidious and indefensible on most occasions. Further, many civil wars take on, in course of time, an international character and involve nations outside national borders whether in open combat or in a state of undeclared war.

In the following ranking an effort is made to rank nations on the basis of wars experienced from 1945 through 1995. Of a number of possible indicators, only two have been selected: intensity or the number of battle deaths, and extent of the wars, measured in months. Both these indicators suffer from many inadequacies. Casualties in themselves tell us nothing about the overall destructiveness of wars. Sometimes many lives may be lost through a commander's blunders, while a superior strategy may enable an army to win without suffering too many battle losses. Similarly, battle months may sometimes be misleading because some wars may drag on for years, as the Iraqi-Iranian war, while others may be short, swift, and bloody.

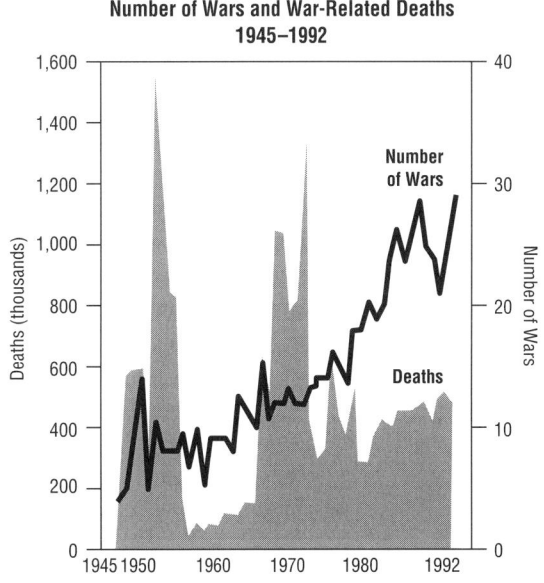

Number of Wars and War-Related Deaths 1945–1992

Rank	Country	War-Related Deaths 1945–1995	Rank	Country	War-Related Deaths 1945–1995	Rank	Country	War-Related Deaths 1945–1995
TOP 10			24	Kuwait	200,000	48	Kenya	16,000
1	Vietnam	2,994,000	25	Greece	160,000	49	South Africa	16,000
2	China	2,610,000				50	Zimbabwe	16,000
3	Nigeria	2,011,000	**LOWER MIDDLE**			51	Guinea-Bissau	15,000
4	Afghanistan	1,505,000	26	Yugoslavia	145,000	52	Madagascar	15,000
5	Korea, North	1,505,000	27	Guatemala	141,000	53	Malaysia	13,000
6	Korea, South	1,505,000	28	Algeria	104,000	54	Jordan	10,000
7	Cambodia	1,221,000	29	Zaire	100,000	55	Pakistan	9,000
8	Sudan	1,106,000	30	Philippines	84,000	56	Chad	7,000
9	Mozambique	1,080,000	31	Nicaragua	80,000	57	Cuba	5,000
10	Bangladesh	1,000,000	32	Egypt	79,000	58	Cyprus	5,000
			33	El Salvador	75,000	59	Honduras	5,000
UPPER MIDDLE			34	Turkey	70,000	60	Dominican Republic	3,000
11	Rwanda	1,000,000	35	Sri Lanka	42,000			
12	India	856,000	36	Russia	41,000	**BOTTOM 10**		
13	Indonesia	691,000	37	Cameroon	32,000	61	Morocco	3,000
14	Ethiopia	614,000	38	Laos	30,000	62	Tunisia	3,000
15	Uganda	613,000	39	Yemen	30,000	63	Costa Rica	2,000
16	Iran	588,000	40	Chile	28,000	64	Bolivia	1,000
17	Somalia	550,000	41	Peru	26,000	65	Ghana	1,000
18	Angola	355,000	42	Taiwan	26,000	66	Jamaica	1,000
19	Colombia	323,000	43	Israel	24,000	67	Panama	1,000
20	Lebanon	246,000	44	Argentina	20,000	68	Paraguay	1,000
21	Iraq	227,000	45	Hungary	20,000	69	Romania	1,000
22	Liberia	227,000	46	Myanmar (Burma)	20,000	70	Zambia	1,000
23	Burundi	218,000	47	Syria	20,000			

Source: Melvin Small and David Singer: *Resort to Arms* (Sage)

54. MILITARY EXPENDITURES

National military expenditures include current and capital expenditures on the armed forces, military assistance to foreign countries, and military components of military, space, and research and development programs. Standard definitions of military expenditures do not include expenditures on veterans' benefits, interest on war debts, civil defense and outlays for strategic stockpiling. There are also substantial social costs that are not reflected in defense budgets, such as tax exemptions extended to military properties and cheap manpower made available through conscription.

World military expenditures have been climbing steadily since the end of World War II. One result of this explosive advance in military technology has been the manufacture, stockpiling, and sale of sophisticated arms and weaponry on an unprecedented scale. With a procurement budget of $120 billion, the armament industry is one of the largest and richest in the world, and its power and influence is felt on political power structures as well as on economic systems. Although military spending accounts for only 5% of global GNP, its real burden on the world economy is much greater. In many limited national budgets, military spending competes with civilian expenditures on education and on health and social services. In other countries it feeds the inflationary spiral and damages prospects for long-term economic development.

There are a number of countries that do not maintain standing armies and hence do not have a defense budget. These include Iceland, Papua New Guinea, Swaziland, Lesotho, the Gambia and Botswana.

Rank	Country	Military Expenditures (million $)
TOP 10		
1	Russia	311,000
2	United States	304,100
3	France	35,260
4	United Kingdom	34,630
5	Germany, West	33,600
6	Japan	28,410
7	China	22,330
8	Italy	20,720
9	Iraq	NA
10	Poland	15,480
UPPER MIDDLE		
11	Saudi Arabia	14,690
12	Germany, East	13,970
13	Canada	10,840
14	Korea, South	9,100
15	Czech Republic	8,361
16	India	8,174
17	Taiwan	8,060
18	Spain	7,775
19	Romania	6,916
20	Netherlands	6,399
21	Brazil	NA
22	Australia	6,153
23	Korea, North	6,000
24	Bulgaria	5,885
25	Israel	5,745
26	Sweden	4,872
27	Hungary	4,064
28	Belgium	3,881
29	Switzerland	3,806
30	South Africa	3,786
31	Egypt	3,499
32	Libya	3,309
33	Turkey	3,150
34	Greece	3,097
35	Norway	2,925
36	Pakistan	2,488
37	Iran	NA
38	Algeria	2,313
39	Syria	2,234
40	Denmark	2,184
41	Yugoslavia	2,126
42	Kuwait	1,964
43	Argentina	1,858
44	Thailand	1,843
45	Finland	1,788
46	Qatar	NA
47	Oman	1,552
48	Indonesia	1,510

Rank	Country	Military Expenditures (million $)
49	Singapore	1,475
50	United. Arab Emirates	1,471
51	Portugal	1,457
52	Austria	1,402
53	Vietnam	NA
54	Cuba	1,377
55	Morocco	1,203
56	Malaysia	1,039
57	Philippines	960
58	Mexico	875
59	New Zealand	847
60	Chile	790
61	Ethiopia	763
62	Colombia	758
LOWER MIDDLE		
63	Angola	NA
64	Yemen (Sanaa)	618
65	Burma	611
66	Jordan	548
67	Peru	NA
68	Ireland	449
69	Venezuela	407
70	Zimbabwe	386
71	Sudan	339
72	Bangladesh	323
73	Tunisia	273
74	Lebanon	NA
75	Mongolia	259
76	El Salvador	252
77	Sri Lanka	223
78	Yemen (Aden)	NA
79	Afghanistan	NA
80	Zaire	NA
81	Kenya	210
82	Bahrain	196
83	Bolivia	182
84	Uruguay	NA
85	Ecuador	163
86	Albania	157
87	Honduras	150
88	Cameroon	148
89	Panama	141
90	Gabon	140
91	Guatemala	131
92	Nigeria	130
93	Cote d'Ivoire	130
94	Tanzania	110
95	Mozambique	107
96	Cambodia	NA
97	Senegal	90

Rank	Country	Military Expenditures (million $)
98	Nicaragua	NA
99	Congo	NA
100	Luxembourg	76
101	Zambia	65
102	Laos	NA
103	Botswana	62
104	Uganda	NA
105	Paraguay	61
106	Trinidad & Tobago	59
107	Liberia	58
108	Burkina	NA
109	Dominican Republic	52
110	Papua New Guinea	48
111	Haiti	45
112	Togo	43
113	Mali	41
114	Cyprus	41
115	Mauritania	40
116	Suriname	39
117	Rwanda	NA
118	Jamaica	36
119	Madagascar	35
120	Malawi	35
121	Nepal	33
122	Benin	33
123	Chad	NA
124	Ghana	30
125	Guinea	NA
126	Burundi	28
127	Niger	27
128	Fiji	26
129	Costa Rica	22
130	Malta	22
131	Lesotho	NA
132	Central African Republic	18
133	Cape Verde	NA
134	Somalia	NA
BOTTOM 10		
135	Swaziland	11
136	Barbados	10
137	Guyana	6
138	Sierra Leone	NA
139	Mauritius	5
140	Guinea-Bissau	NA
141	Equatorial Guinea	NA
142	Gambia	1
143	Sao Tome e Principe	NA
144	Iceland	0

Source: *World Military Expenditures and Arms Transfers*

Section
VII

ECONOMY

Rankings in this section deal with economic performance—not resources. Here—unlike in politics—the statistician is at home, and there is such a wealth of data that it becomes positively embarrassing. But considering the many levels of economic activity, the abundance of data is more apparent than real. The section kicks off with a close look at GNP. GNP (gross national product) is perhaps the world's best known and widely used economic indicator; it is also the most overrated. Although presented in three rankings below (total, per capita and annual growth rate), it fails to reflect the disparities in income within a nation. Its usefulness is further reduced by the need to convert national currencies into dollars—a conversion that may actually serve to introduce new distortions into the calculation.

55. GROSS NATIONAL PRODUCT (GNP)

The most frequently employed measure of the production and total wealth and resources of a country is the gross national product. The GNP is the measure of total domestic and foreign output claimed by residents of a country. The gross domestic product measures the total final output of a country's economy—that is, all goods produced and services rendered within its territory by residents and nonresidents—without regard to its allocation among domestic and foreign claims. GDP and GNP are commonly valued either at factor cost or at market prices. At factor cost they comprise compensation of employees, operating surplus and provision for the consumption of fixed capital. At market prices they include indirect taxes less subsidies to producers. The difference between GNP and GDP consists in the addition or subtraction of the value of return on foreign investment. GDP equals GNP plus income earned in the country but sent abroad, minus income earned abroad but sent into the country. GDP thus tends to exceed GNP in debtor countries, while the reverse is true in creditor countries.

GNP does not reflect income disparities in a country and is frequently unreliable when employed as a measure of comfort or well-being. Variations in accuracy are related to the extent of income disparities, which exist not merely in developing countries, as is commonly supposed, but also in developed countries.

TOP 10
Gross National Product (million $)

Country	GNP	Rank
United States	6,137,367	1
Japan	4,321,136	2
Germany	2,075,452	3
France	1,355,039	4
Italy	1,101,258	5
United Kingdom	1,069,457	6
China	630,202	7
Canada	569,949	8
Brazil	536,309	9
Spain	525,334	10

Rank	Country	GNP (millions $)	Rank	Country	GNP (millions $)	Rank	Country	GNP (millions $)
UPPER MIDDLE			61	Ecuador	14,703	110	Armenia	2,532
11	Russia	392,496	62	Slovenia	14,246	111	Mali	2,421
12	Mexico	368,679	63	Guatemala	12,237	112	Tajikistan	2,075
13	Korea, South	366,484	64	Croatia	12,093	113	Niger	2,040
14	Netherlands	328,144	65	Slovakia	11,914	114	Benin	1,954
15	Australia	320,705	66	Vietnam	11,775	115	Fiji	1,785
16	India	278,739	67	Sri Lanka	11,634	116	Barbados	1,704
17	Argentina	275,657	68	Oman	10,779	117	Macedonia	1,653
18	Switzerland	264,974				118	Congo	1,607
19	Belgium	231,051	**LOWER MIDDLE**			119	Malawi	1,560
20	Sweden	206,419	69	Bulgaria	10,255	120	Haiti	1,542
21	Taiwan	200,000	70	Dominican Republic	10,109	121	Laos	1,496
22	Austria	197,475	71	Cameroon	8,735	122	Lesotho	1,398
23	Indonesia	167,632	72	El Salvador	8,365	123	Nicaragua	1,395
24	Turkey	149,002	73	Costa Rica	7,856	124	Mozambique	1,328
25	Denmark	145,384	74	Qatar	7,810	125	Togo	1,267
26	Thailand	129,864	75	Paraguay	7,606	126	Albania	1,229
27	Saudi Arabia	126,597	76	Ghana	7,311	127	Central African Republic	1,191
28	South Africa	125,225	77	Cote d'Ivoire	7,070	128	Chad	1,153
29	Norway	114,328	78	Ethiopia	6,947	129	Mauritania	1,063
30	Finland	95,817	79	Panama	6,905	130	Swaziland	1,048
31	Poland	94,613	80	Kenya	6,643	131	Burundi	904
32	Portugal	92,124	81	Iceland	6,545	132	Mongolia	801
33	Ukraine	80,921	82	Latvia	5,920	133	Sierra Leone	698
34	Greece	80,194	83	Jordan	5,849	134	Belize	535
35	Israel	78,113	84	Bolivia	5,601	135	St. Lucia	501
36	Malaysia	68,674	85	Zimbabwe	5,424	136	Guyana	454
37	Singapore	65,842	86	Lithuania	4,992	137	Antigua and Barbuda	453
38	Philippines	63,311	87	Senegal	4,952	138	Seychelles	453
39	Venezuela	59,025	88	Papua New Guinea	4,857	139	Gambia	384
40	Colombia	58,935	89	Trinidad and Tobago	4,838	140	Suriname	364
41	Pakistan	55,565	90	Estonia	4,351	141	Cape Verde	346
42	Chile	50,051	91	Nepal	4,174	142	Solomon Islands	291
43	Ireland	48,275	92	Bahrain	4,114	143	Bhutan	272
44	New Zealand	46,578	93	Botswana	4,037	144	Guinea-Bissau	253
45	Algeria	46,115	94	Brunei	3,975	145	Comoros	249
46	Peru	44,110	95	Yemen	3,884	146	Grenada	241
47	Egypt	40,950	96	Moldova	3,853			
48	Hungary	39,009	97	Azerbaijan	3,730	**BOTTOM 10**		
49	Czech Republic	33,051	98	Uganda	3,718	147	St. Vincent	235
50	Kuwait	31,433	99	Gabon	3,669	148	Maldives	221
51	Morocco	30,330	100	Jamaica	3,553	149	Dominica	201
52	Nigeria	29,995	101	Mauritius	3,514	150	St. Kitts and Nevis	195
53	Romania	27,921	102	Guinea	3,310	151	Vanuatu	189
54	Bangladesh	26,636	103	Bahamas	3,207	152	Equatorial Guinea	167
55	Belarus	21,937	104	Zambia	3,206	153	Western Samoa	163
56	Uzbekistan	21,142	105	Honduras	3,162	154	Tonga	160
57	Kazakhstan	18,896	106	Madagascar	3,058	155	Kiribati	56
58	Luxembourg	15,973	107	Namibia	3,045	156	Sao Tome e Principe	31
59	Tunisia	15,873	108	Burkina	2,982			
60	Uruguay	14,725	109	Kyrgyzstan	2,825			

Source: *World Development Report*

56. GNP PER CAPITA

The inadequacies of GNP as an economic indictor are pointed out in the introduction to GNP ranking. It has been humorously suggested that what is wrong with GNP is that it is gross. As a derived indicator, per capita GNP suffers from all these inadequacies; in addition, it has deficiencies of its own. It fails to reflect the distributional inequalities of income and it is easily affected by differences in population estimates. However, despite all these shortcomings, it is still the best known and most widely used indicator in the world. Furthermore, in dealing with macroeconomics, it is questionable whether any indicator can ever be devised that does not have some kind of bias. In fact, in the context in which per capita GNP is generally used, the trends and patterns are more important than details, and this indicator can reveal them more satisfactorily than any other known indicator.

Rank	Country	GNP per Capita ($)	Rank	Country	GNP per Capita ($)	Rank	Country	GNP per Capita ($)
TOP 10			53	Estonia	2,820	106	Egypt	710
1	Luxembourg	39,850	54	Botswana	2,800	107	Lesotho	700
2	Switzerland	37,180	55	Dominica	2,760	108	Cameroon	680
3	Japan	34,630	56	Venezuela	2,760	109	Armenia	670
4	Denmark	26,580	57	Panama	2,670	110	Congo	640
5	Norway	26,480	58	Russia	2,650	111	Sri Lanka	640
6	United States	25,860	59	Grenada	2,620	112	Kyrgyzstan	610
7	Germany	25,580	60	Costa Rica	2,580	113	Senegal	610
8	Austria	24,950	61	Belize	2,550	114	Honduras	580
9	Iceland	24,590	62	Croatia	2,530	115	China	530
10	France	23,470	63	Poland	2,470	116	Guyana	530
			64	Turkey	2,450	117	Comoros	510
UPPER MIDDLE			65	Fiji	2,320	118	Cote d'Ivoire	510
11	Singapore	23,360	66	Latvia	2,290	119	Guinea	510
12	Belgium	22,920	67	Slovakia	2,230	120	Azerbaijan	500
13	Netherlands	21,970	68	Thailand	2,210	121	Zimbabwe	490
14	Canada	19,570				122	Mauritania	480
15	Italy	19,270	**LOWER MIDDLE**			123	Pakistan	440
16	Kuwait	19,040	69	Belarus	2,160	124	Equatorial Guinea	430
17	Finland	18,850	70	St. Vincent	2,120	125	Ghana	430
18	United Kingdom	18,410	71	Namibia	2,030	126	Bhutan	400
19	Australia	17,980	72	Peru	1,890	127	Benin	370
20	Qatar	14,540	73	Tunisia	1,800	128	Central African Republic	370
21	Israel	14,410	74	Algeria	1,690	129	Albania	360
22	Brunei	14,240	75	Colombia	1,620	130	Gambia	360
23	Ireland	13,630	76	Paraguay	1,570	131	Tajikistan	350
24	Sweden	13,630	77	Ukraine	1,570	132	Zambia	350
25	Spain	13,280	78	El Salvador	1,480	133	Mongolia	340
26	New Zealand	13,190	79	Jamaica	1,420	134	Nicaragua	330
27	Bahamas	11,790	80	Jordan	1,390	135	Togo	320
28	Taiwan	10,000	81	Lithuania	1,350	136	India	310
29	Portugal	9,370	82	Dominican Republic	1,320	137	Burkina	300
30	Korea, South	8,220	83	Ecuador	1,310	138	Nigeria	280
31	Argentina	8,060	84	Romania	1,230	139	Yemen	280
32	Bahrain	7,900	85	Guatemala	1,190	140	Kenya	266
33	Greece	7,710	86	Bulgaria	1,166	141	Mali	250
34	Saudi Arabia	7,240	87	Papua New Guinea	1,160	142	Sao Tome e Principe	250
35	Slovenia	7,140	88	Swaziland	1,160	143	Guinea-Bissau	240
36	Antigua and Barbuda	6,970	89	Morocco	1,150	144	Bangladesh	230
37	Barbados	6,330	90	Vanuatu	1,150	145	Madagascar	230
38	Seychelles	6,210	91	Kazakhstan	1,110	146	Niger	230
39	Oman	5,200	92	Tonga	1,040	147	Haiti	220
40	St. Kitts and Nevis	4,760	93	Western Samoa	970			
41	Uruguay	4,650	94	Philippines	960	**BOTTOM 10**		
42	Mexico	4,010	95	Uzbekistan	950	148	Nepal	200
43	Hungary	3,840	96	Cape Verde	910	149	Uganda	200
44	Trinidad and Tobago	3,740	97	Maldives	900	150	Vietnam	190
45	Chile	3,560	98	Indonesia	880	151	Burundi	150
46	Gabon	3,550	99	Moldova	870	152	Sierra Leone	150
47	Malaysia	3,520	100	Suriname	870	153	Malawi	140
48	St. Lucia	3,450	101	Solomon Islands	800	154	Ethiopia	130
49	Brazil	3,370	102	Macedonia	790	155	Laos	120
50	Czech Republic	3,210	103	Djibouti	780	156	Chad	100
51	Mauritius	3,180	104	Bolivia	770	157	Mozambique	80
52	South Africa	3,010	105	Kiribati	730			

Source: *World Bank Atlas*

57. PER CAPITA GNP ANNUAL GROWTH RATE 1994

The principal indicator of economic change is the annual growth rate of per capita GNP. The pace of growth in GNP per capita must be positive if a nation is not to suffer a decrease in its absolute level of income. Unfortunately, GNP per capita growth rates do not reflect inequalities inherent in the economy, particularly inequalities among sectors and among income groups. In some cases, growth in absolute or per capita terms may accentuate and even perpetuate these inequalities. If wealth is concentrated in the hands of a small minority, a higher average income reflects only the greater welfare of this minority. What is important, therefore, is balanced growth, although no indicator has yet been devised to measure such a balanced growth.

Rank	Country	GNP per Capita Real Growth Rate 1994	Rank	Country	GNP per Capita Real Growth Rate 1994	Rank	Country	GNP per Capita Real Growth Rate 1994
TOP 10			55	Guinea-Bissau	3.7	110	Iceland	1.3
1	Thailand	10.0	56	Luxembourg	3.7	111	Panama	1.3
2	Bostowana	9.1	57	Malawi	3.7	112	Ethiopia	1.2
3	Koarea, South	9.1	58	United Arab Emirates	3.7	113	Syria	1.2
4	Belize	8.3	59	Honduras	3.6	114	Tonga	1.2
5	Taiwan	8.3	60	Uruguay	3.6	115	Niger	1.1
6	Malaysia	8.1	61	Burundi	3.5	116	Gabon	1.0
7	Singapore	8.0	62	Saudi Arabia	3.5	117	New Zealand	1.0
8	China	7.9	63	Venezuela	3.5	118	Norway	1.0
9	Chile	7.7	64	Fiji	3.4	119	South Africa	0.9
10	Swaziland	7.6	65	Lesotho	3.4	120	Turkmenistan	0.9
			66	Papua New Guinea	3.4	121	Somalia	0.8
UPPER MIDDLE			67	Kenya	3.3	122	Uzbekistan	0.8
11	Vietnam	7.2	68	Morocco	3.3	123	Kiribati	0.7
12	Mauritius	6.9	69	Spain	3.3	124	Sweden	0.7
13	Bhutan	6.7	70	Ecuador	3.2	125	Sao Tome e Principe	0.6
14	Indonesia	6.6	71	Antigua and Barbuda	3.1	126	Algeria	0.4
15	Cyprus	6.3				127	Western Samoa	0.4
16	Nigeria	6.1	**LOWER MIDDLE**			128	Guyana	0.3
17	St. Lucia	6.1	72	Chad	3.0	129	Belarus	0.2
18	St. Vincent	5.5	73	Egypt	3.0	130	Togo	0.2
19	Solomon Islands	5.4	74	El Salvador	3.0	131	Finland	0.1
20	Costa Rica	5.3	75	Vanuatu	3.0	132	Jordan	0.0
21	Namibia	5.3	76	Austria	2.8	133	Barbados	−0.1
22	Israel	5.2	77	Burkina	2.8	134	Central African Republic	−0.3
23	India	5.1	78	Belgium	2.7	135	Hungary	−0.5
24	Oman	5.1	79	Mexico	2.7	136	Kyrgyzstan	−0.5
25	Turkey	5.1	80	Netherlands	2.7	137	Rwanda	−0.6
26	Uganda	5.1	81	Senegal	2.7	138	Cote d'Ivoire	−1.4
27	Laos	5.0	82	Argentina	2.6	139	Peru	−1.4
28	Seychelles	4.9	83	Australia	2.6	140	Poland	−1.4
29	Zambia	4.9	84	Mauritania	2.6	141	Trinidad and Tobago	−1.4
30	Ireland	4.8	85	Puerto Rico	2.6	142	Haiti	−1.5
31	St. Kitts and Nevis	4.8	86	Sudan	2.6	143	Mali	−1.5
32	Cape Verde	4.7	87	Germany	2.5	144	Czech Republic	−2.0
33	Gambia	4.7	88	Mongolia	2.5	145	Kuwait	−2.1
34	Pakistan	4.6	89	Zaire	2.5	146	Slovakia	−2.2
35	Qatar	4.6	90	France	2.4	147	Bulgaria	−3.6
36	Dominica	4.5	91	Dominican Republic	2.2	148	Kazakhstan	−3.6
37	Ghana	4.5	92	Suriname	2.2	149	Nicaragua	−3.6
38	Mozambique	4.5	93	Bahrain	2.1	150	Ukraine	−3.6
39	Nepal	4.4	94	Benin	2.1	151	Cameroon	−4.3
40	Tanzania	4.4	95	Italy	2.1	152	Latvia	−4.6
41	Tunisia	4.3	96	United States	2.1			
42	Guinea	4.2	97	Angola	2.0	**BOTTOM 10**		
43	Paraguay	4.2	98	Sierra Leone	2.0	153	Russia	−4.6
44	Portugal	4.1	99	Zimbabwe	2.0	154	Moldova	−4.9
45	Bangladesh	4.0	100	Greece	1.8	155	Tajikistan	−5.0
46	Grenada	4.0	101	Canada	1.7	156	Estonia	−5.1
47	Japan	4.0	102	Switzerland	1.7	157	Albania	−5.2
48	Colombia	3.9	103	Bahamas	1.6	158	Lithuania	−5.7
49	Jamaica	3.9	104	United Kingdom	1.6	159	Romania	−6.5
50	Philippines	3.9	105	Comoros	1.5	160	Azerbaijan	−8.0
51	Sri Lanka	3.9	106	Congo	1.4	161	Armenia	−10.3
52	Equatorial Guinea	3.8	107	Madagascar	1.4	162	Georgia	−16.0
53	Bolivia	3.7	108	Brazil	1.3			
54	Guatemala	3.7	109	Denmark	1.3			

Source: *World Bank Atlas*

58. INCOME DISPARITIES

Estimates of national income have been under fire for a number of years because they conceal rather then reveal income disparities among sectors, especially between the poorest and the richest. A number of efforts, therefore, have been made to measure these disparities; the most widely adopted one is the percentage of national income received by the lowest and poorest 20%. These rankings should be read together to determine the patterns of income distribution within a country.

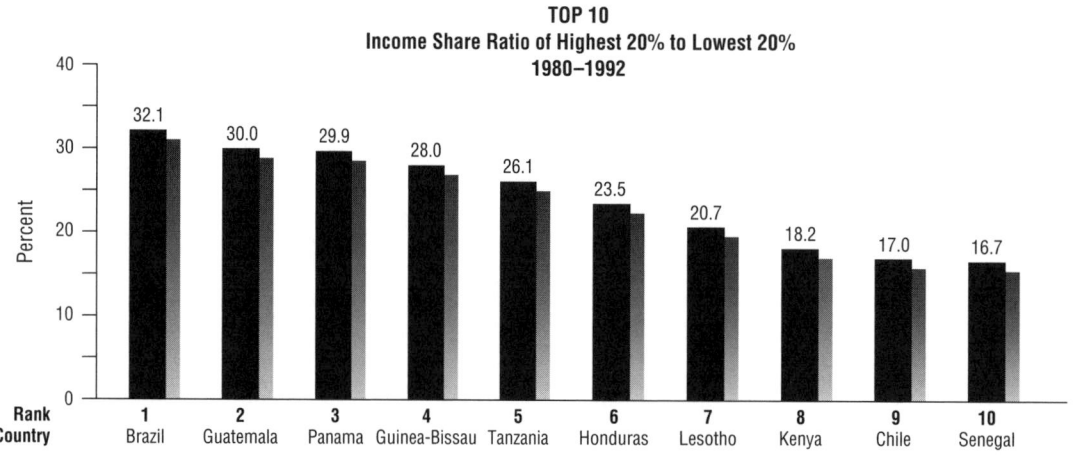

TOP 10
Income Share Ratio of Highest 20% to Lowest 20%
1980–1992

Rank	Country	Income Share Ratio of Highest 20% to Lowest 20% (%) 1980–1992	Rank	Country	Income Share Ratio of Highest 20% to Lowest 20% (%) 1980–1992	Rank	Country	Income Share Ratio of Highest 20% to Lowest 20% (%) 1980–1992
UPPER MIDDLE			29	Switzerland	8.6	50	Uganda	4.9
11	Botswana	16.4	30	Thailand	8.3	51	Ethiopia	4.8
12	Zimbabwe	15.6	31	Jamaica	8.1	52	India	4.7
13	Colombia	15.5	32	Tunisia	7.8	53	Pakistan	4.7
14	Mexico	13.6	33	France	7.5	54	Belgium	4.6
15	Dominican Republic	13.2	34	Philippines	7.4	55	Sweden	4.6
16	Mauritania	13.2	35	Jordan	7.3			
17	Costa Rica	12.7	36	Canada	7.1	**BOTTOM 10**		
18	Malaysia	11.7	37	Denmark	7.1	56	Netherlands	4.5
19	Peru	10.5	38	Morocco	7.0	57	Spain	4.4
20	Venezuela	10.3	39	Algeria	6.7	58	Sri Lanka	4.4
21	Australia	9.6	40	Israel	6.6	59	Japan	4.3
22	United Kingdom	9.6	41	China	6.5	60	Nepal	4.3
23	Singapore	9.6	42	Ghana	6.3	61	Bangladesh	4.1
24	United States	8.9	43	Finland	6.0	62	Rwanda	4.0
25	Zambia	8.9	44	Italy	6.0	63	Poland	3.9
26	New Zealand	8.8	45	Norway	5.9	64	Bulgaria	3.5
27	Hong Kong	8.7	46	Cote d'Ivoire	5.8	65	Hungary	3.2
			47	Germany	5.8			
LOWER MIDDLE			48	Korea, North	5.7			
28	Bolivia	8.6	49	Indonesia	4.9			

Source: *World Development Report*

Rank	Country	Income Share Lowest 40% of Households (%) 1980–1992	Rank	Country	Income Share Lowest 40% of Households (%) 1980–1992	Rank	Country	Income Share Lowest 40% of Households (%) 1980–1992
TOP 10			8	Sri Lanka	22.0	14	Pakistan	21.3
1	Hungary	25.7	9	Japan	21.9	15	Sweden	21.2
2	Bulgaria	24.3	10	Belgium	21.6	16	Indonesia	20.8
3	Poland	23.0				17	Uganda	20.6
4	Bangladesh	22.9	**UPPER MIDDLE**			18	Korea, North	19.7
5	Rwanda	22.8	11	Ethiopia	21.3	19	Cote d'Ivoire	19.2
6	Nepal	22.0	12	India	21.3	20	Norway	19.0
7	Spain	22.0	13	Netherlands	21.3	21	Germany	18.8

Rank	Country	Income Share Lowest 40% of Households (%) 1980–1992
22	Italy	18.8
23	Finland	18.4
LOWER MIDDLE		
24	Ghana	18.3
25	Israel	18.1
26	Algeria	17.9
27	Canada	17.5
28	China	17.4
29	Denmark	17.4
30	France	17.4
31	Morocco	17.1
32	Switzerland	16.9
33	Jordan	16.8
34	Philippines	16.6
35	Tunisia	16.3
36	Hong Kong	16.2
37	Jamaica	15.9
38	New Zealand	15.9
39	United States	15.7
40	Australia	15.5
41	Thailand	15.5
42	Bolivia	15.3
43	Zambia	15.2
44	Singapore	15.0
45	United Kingdom	14.6
46	Venezuela	14.3
47	Mauritania	14.2
48	Peru	14.1
49	Costa Rica	13.1
50	Malaysia	12.9
51	Dominican Republic	12.1
52	Mexico	11.9
53	Colombia	11.2
54	Botswana	10.5
55	Chile	10.5
BOTTOM 10		
56	Senegal	10.5
57	Zimbabwe	10.3
58	Kenya	10.1
59	Lesotho	9.3
60	Honduras	8.7
61	Guinea-Bissau	8.6
62	Panama	8.3
63	Tanzania	8.1
64	Guatemala	7.9
65	Brazil	7.0

Source: *World Development Report*

59. POPULATION IN ABSOLUTE POVERTY

Poverty is relative and therefore defies definition; yet, everyone knows it when he sees it, as U.S. Justice Byron White said of another social evil. One-fourth of the planet's population—some one billion human beings—live in poverty so stark and dehumanizing that is inconceivable for most people living in Western societies. The upper limits of absolute poverty, so described to distinguish it from the kind of poverty with which we are familiar, are lower than the poverty levels fixed by governments in the developed world. By thus excluding the developed world, the characteristics and extent of poverty in the developing world emerge into startling focus.

Rank	Country	People in Poverty (%) Urban 1990
TOP 10		
1	Honduras	74
2	Haiti	65
3	Guatemala	60
4	Ghana	59
5	Bangladesh	56
6	Peru	52
7	Colombia	40
8	Mozambique	40
9	Philippines	40
10	Brazil	38
11	India	38
12	Panama	36
13	Egypt	34
14	Botswana	30
15	Venezuela	30
16	Morocco	28
17	Uganda	25
18	Costa Rica	24
19	Mexico	23
20	Madagascar	21
BOTTOM 10		
21	Indonesia	20
22	Pakistan	20
23	Nepal	19
24	Tunisia	16
25	Argentina	15
26	Sri Lanka	15
27	Uruguay	10
28	Malaysia	8
29	Thailand	7
30	Korea, North	5

Rank	Country	People in Poverty (%) Rural 1990
TOP 10		
1	Bolivia	86
2	Guatemala	80
3	Haiti	80
4	Honduras	80
5	Peru	72
6	Mozambique	70
7	Brazil	66
8	Botswana	64
9	Ghana	54
10	Philippines	54
11	Syria	54
12	Panama	52
13	Bangladesh	51
14	India	49
15	Colombia	45
16	Mexico	43
17	Nepal	43
18	Venezuela	42
19	Trinidad and Tobago	40
20	Madagascar	37
21	Sri Lanka	36
22	Egypt	34
23	Uganda	33
24	Morocco	32
25	Pakistan	31
26	Tunisia	31
BOTTOM 10		
27	Costa Rica	30
28	Yemen	30
29	Thailand	29
30	Algeria	25
31	Malaysia	23
32	Uruguay	23
33	Argentina	20
34	Indonesia	16
35	China	12
36	Korea, North	4

Source: *Human Development Report*

60. AVERAGE ANNUAL RATE OF INFLATION

Inflation may be the single most important fact of life in the latter part of the 20th century and therefore bears watching. Even normal and healthy economic systems experience a slow but constant escalation in prices given the push of population growth and the pull of finite and depleting resources. But this process is accelerated in times of internal and external stress.

Economists sometimes distinguish between creeping inflation and galloping inflation and have introduced various terms such as stagflation to characterize peculiar types of inflation. But these distinctions are purely academic because every form of inflation represents a threat to the stability of economic and, ultimately, political systems.

Rank	Country	Average Inflation Rate 1985–1994 (%)	Rank	Country	Average Inflation Rate 1985–1994 (%)	Rank	Country	Average Inflation Rate 1985–1994 (%)
TOP 10			55	Hungary	19.5	110	Luxembourg	5.0
1	Nicaragua	1,314.9	56	Malawi	18.8	111	New Zealand	4.7
2	Brazil	913.0	57	Chile	18.5	112	Grenada	4.5
3	Peru	495.3	58	Guinea	18.5	113	Antigua and Barbuda	4.4
4	Argentina	317.2	59	Costa Rica	18.2	114	Djibouti	4.4
5	Georgia	233.9	60	Israel	18.0	115	Dominica	4.4
6	Ukraine	160.2	61	Egypt	16.4	116	Taiwan	4.4
7	Kazakhstan	150.2	62	El Salvador	16.2	117	Finland	4.2
8	Belarus	137.8	63	Madagascar	15.7	118	Australia	4.1
9	Russia	134.0	64	Greece	15.5	119	Cyprus	4.1
10	Armenia	133.7	65	South Africa	14.2	120	Papua New Guinea	4.1
			66	Lesotho	14.1	121	Singapore	3.9
UPPER MIDDLE			67	Haiti	13.4	122	Rwanda	3.7
11	Azerbaijan	122.8	68	Iceland	13.2	123	Switzerland	3.7
12	Tajikistan	104.3	69	Swaziland	12.8	124	Belize	3.5
13	Vietnam	102.6	70	Honduras	12.4	125	Central African Republic	3.5
14	Lithuania	102.3	71	Nepal	12.0	126	Comoros	3.5
15	Poland	101.7	72	Portugal	11.9	127	Mali	3.4
16	Kyrgyzstan	100.9				128	St. Vincent	3.4
17	Uzbekistan	92.8	**LOWER MIDDLE**			129	Bahamas	3.3
18	Zambia	92.0	73	Botswana	11.8	130	St. Lucia	3.3
19	Estonia	78.1	74	Czech Republic	11.8	131	United States	3.3
20	Somalia	75.4	75	Kenya	11.7	132	Austria	3.2
21	Uganda	75.2	76	Solomon Islands	11.2	133	Belgium	3.2
22	Uruguay	73.9	77	Sri Lanka	11.0	134	Gabon	3.2
23	Latvia	69.9	78	Gambia	10.9	135	Canada	3.1
24	Sierra Leone	67.8	79	Maldives	10.7	136	Malaysia	3.1
25	Guinea-Bissau	66.0	80	Namibia	10.7	137	Norway	3.0
26	Turkey	65.8	81	Western Samoa	10.6	138	Benin	2.9
27	Romania	63.5	82	Philippines	9.9	139	Denmark	2.9
28	Guyana	56.4	83	India	9.7	140	France	2.9
29	Sudan	55.3	84	Slovakia	9.7	141	Germany	2.9
30	Mozambique	53.2	85	China	9.6	142	Malta	2.9
31	Ecuador	47.5	86	Mauritius	9.0	143	Puerto Rico	2.9
32	Turkmenistan	46.0	87	Indonesia	8.9	144	Senegal	2.9
33	Mongolia	45.7	88	Pakistan	8.8	145	Barbados	2.8
34	Bulgaria	41.7	89	Tonga	8.6	146	Saudi Arabia	2.7
35	Mexico	39.9	90	Bhutan	8.2	147	Seychelles	2.7
36	Sao Tome e Principe	37.2	91	Cape Verde	7.2	148	Togo	2.5
37	Venezuela	36.6	92	Mauritania	7.2	149	Equatorial Guinea	2.1
38	Albania	32.7	93	Korea, South	6.8	150	Ireland	2.0
39	Suriname	31.7	94	Bangladesh	6.6	151	Chad	1.8
40	Nigeria	29.6	95	Trinidad and Tobago	6.5	152	Burkina	1.7
41	Dominican Republic	28.8	96	Tunisia	6.3	153	Netherlands	1.6
42	Ghana	28.4	97	Italy	6.2	154	Panama	1.5
43	Jamaica	28.3	98	Angola	5.9			
44	Paraguay	26.1	99	St. Kitts and Nevis	5.8	**BOTTOM 10**		
45	Colombia	25.1	100	Sweden	5.8	155	Japan	1.3
46	Myanmar (Burma)	25.1	101	Ethiopia	5.6	156	Cameroon	1.1
47	Laos	24.2	102	Vanuatu	5.5	157	Jordan	1.1
48	Tanzania	23.4	103	United Kingdom	5.4	158	Spain	0.6
49	Algeria	22.3	104	Bermuda	5.3	159	Bahrain	0.3
50	Syria	22.1	105	Fiji	5.3	160	Brunei	0.2
51	Iran	22.0	106	Burundi	5.2	161	Cote d'Ivoire	0.2
52	Bolivia	20.1	107	Kiribati	5.1	162	Niger	0.2
53	Zimbabwe	19.7	108	Morocco	5.1	163	Oman	0.1
54	Guatemala	19.5	109	Thailand	5.1	164	Congo	−0.3

Source: *World Development Report*

61. RURAL-URBAN DISPARITIES

The following three rankings show rural-urban disparities in the Third World in three major areas affecting quality of life: safe water, health and sanitation. The rankings confirm that the rural folks in almost all countries are shortchanged in terms of essential life-support services. Even so, conditions of life are better in rural areas than in urban areas because of the availability of living space and the absence of overcrowding.

Rank	Country	Rural-Urban Disparity in Services (100 = rural-urban parity) Safe Water 1988–93
TOP 10		
1	Burkina	141
2	Central African Republic	137
3	Cote d'Ivoire	116
4	Guinea	112
5	Sierra Leone	112
6	Bangladesh	104
7	Jamaica	100
8	Venezuela	100
9	Tunisia	99
10	Mauritius	98
UPPER MIDDLE		
11	Niger	98
12	Jordan	97
13	Mauritania	97
14	Hong Kong	96
15	Colombia	94
16	Philippines	93
17	India	92
18	Trinidad and Tobago	92
19	Cuba	91
20	Egypt	91
21	Lebanon	89
22	Costa Rica	86
23	Oman	85
24	Zimbabwe	84
25	Chad	83
26	Rwanda	83
27	Thailand	83
28	Libya	80
29	Sudan	78
30	Botswana	77

Rank	Country	Rural-Urban Disparity in Services (100 = rural-urban parity) Safe Water 1988–93
31	Chile	77
32	Korea, North	76
33	Lesotho	76
34	Cameroon	75
35	Iran	75
36	Saudi Arabia	74
LOWER MIDDLE		
37	Mali	72
38	Benin	70
39	Mexico	70
40	Malaysia	69
41	Sri Lanka	69
42	Tanzania	69
43	Togo	69
44	Ecuador	68
45	Panama	66
46	Turkey	66
47	Algeria	65
48	Brazil	64
49	Syria	64
50	Guinea-Bissau	63
51	Indonesia	63
52	China	61
53	Laos	61
54	Haiti	60
55	Pakistan	59
56	Kenya	58
57	Mongolia	58
58	Nepal	58
59	Somalia	58
60	Honduras	57
61	Gabon	56

Rank	Country	Rural-Urban Disparity in Services (100 = rural-urban parity) Safe Water 1988–93
62	Burundi	55
63	Vietnam	54
64	Malawi	52
65	Cambodia	51
66	Bhutan	50
67	Yemen	49
68	Afghanistan	48
69	Paraguay	48
70	Uganda	48
71	Dominican Republic	47
72	Iraq	44
73	Zambia	40
74	Mozambique	39
75	Argentina	38
76	Ghana	38
77	Nigeria	37
78	Namibia	36
79	Zaire	35
80	Senegal	31
81	Angola	28
82	Nicaragua	28
BOTTOM 10		
83	Liberia	24
84	Peru	24
85	Bolivia	23
86	El Salvador	22
87	Ethiopia	21
88	Papua New Guinea	21
89	Madagascar	16
90	Morocco	15
91	Uruguay	6
92	Congo	2

Source: *Human Development Report*

Rank	Country	Rural-Urban Disparity in Services (100 = rural-urban parity) Health 1985–93
TOP 10		
1	Korea, North	100
2	Madagascar	100
3	Mauritius	100
4	Thailand	100
5	Egypt	99
6	Trinidad and Tobago	99
7	Cuba	97
8	Jordan	97
9	Philippines	96
10	Burkina	94
UPPER MIDDLE		
11	Oman	94
12	Cameroon	89
13	China	88
14	Saudi Arabia	88
15	Syria	88
16	Lebanon	87
17	Botswana	85
18	Zimbabwe	83
19	Algeria	80

Rank	Country	Rural-Urban Disparity in Services (100 = rural-urban parity) Health 1985–93
20	India	80
21	Iraq	80
22	Tunisia	80
23	Vietnam	80
24	Burundi	79
25	Mexico	75
26	Nigeria	73
27	Tanzania	73
28	Congo	72
LOWER MIDDLE		
29	Guinea	70
30	Honduras	70
31	Bolivia	68
32	Iran	68
33	Panama	67
34	Namibia	65
35	Cambodia	63
36	Costa Rica	63
37	Liberia	60
38	Nicaragua	60
39	El Salvador	50

Rank	Country	Rural-Urban Disparity in Services (100 = rural-urban parity) Health 1985–93
40	Morocco	50
41	Zambia	50
42	Ghana	49
43	Mauritania	46
44	Sudan	44
45	Zaire	43
46	Paraguay	42
47	Uganda	42
BOTTOM 10		
48	Yemen	40
49	Pakistan	35
50	Mozambique	30
51	Niger	30
52	Somalia	30
53	Ecuador	29
54	Argentina	26
55	Sierra Leone	22
56	Afghanistan	21
57	Cote d'Ivoire	18

Source: *Human Development Report*

Rural-Urban Disparity in Services
(100 = rural-urban parity)

Rank	Country	Sanitation 1988–93
TOP 10		
1	Malawi	270
2	Lesotho	164
3	Paraguay	120
4	Guinea-Bissau	119
5	Uruguay	108
6	Cote d'Ivoire	105
7	Central African Republic	102
8	Jordan	100
9	Korea, North	100
10	Mauritius	100
UPPER MIDDLE		
11	Trinidad and Tobago	99
12	Syria	98
13	Tunisia	96
14	Costa Rica	94
15	Myanmar (Burma)	90
16	Thailand	90
17	Libya	85
18	Tanzania	84
19	Jamaica	80
20	Dominican Republic	79
21	Philippines	78
22	Nigeria	75
23	Benin	74
24	Rwanda	73
25	Sudan	73
26	Venezuela	72
27	Yemen	69
28	Cuba	68
29	Ecuador	68
30	Panama	68
31	Burundi	66
LOWER MIDDLE		
32	Sri Lanka	66
33	Cameroon	64
34	Algeria	63
35	Honduras	63
36	Angola	60
37	Hong Kong	56
38	Indonesia	56
39	Uganda	55
40	Oman	53
41	Sierra Leone	53
42	Argentina	51
43	Kenya	51
44	Ghana	50
45	Mongolia	47
46	Namibia	46
47	Botswana	45
48	Peru	43
49	El Salvador	42
50	Senegal	42
51	Bangladesh	41
52	Morocco	40
53	Brazil	38
54	Vietnam	38
55	Iran	35
56	Egypt	33
57	Saudi Arabia	30
58	Haiti	29
59	Pakistan	28
60	Bolivia	27
61	Madagascar	25
62	Mexico	24
63	United Arab Emirates	24
64	Zaire	24
65	Nicaragua	23
66	Zimbabwe	23
67	Colombia	21
68	India	19
69	Lebanon	19
70	Mozambique	18
71	Papua New Guinea	18
72	Togo	18
73	Burkina	17
74	Zambia	16
75	Bhutan	14
BOTTOM 10		
76	Guinea	12
77	Mali	12
78	Somalia	11
79	Cambodia	10
80	Laos	8
81	Ethiopia	7
82	Chile	6
83	Nepal	6
84	Niger	6
85	China	5

Source: *Human Development Report*

62. BALANCE OF PAYMENTS

Balance of Payments is the summary of all external transactions of a current nature between one country and the rest of the world. The account shows a country's net overseas receipts and obligations, including not only the trade of goods and merchandise (the balance of trade) but also invisible items such as services, interest and dividends, investments, tourism, workers' remittances, etc. Any international transaction automatically creates a deficit in the balance of payments of one country and a surplus in that of another.

Rank	Country	Balance of Payments 1993 (million $)
TOP 10		
1	Japan	131,510
2	Switzerland	16,696
3	Belgium	12,588
4	Italy	11,062
5	France	10,201
6	Netherlands	9,371
7	Taiwan	6,714
8	Denmark	4,711
9	Ireland	3,646
10	Norway	2,453
UPPER MIDDLE		
11	Kuwait	2,412
12	Egypt	2,299
13	Nigeria	2,268
14	Libya	2,201
15	Singapore	2,039
16	Indonesia	2,016
17	South Africa	1,805
18	Cote d'Ivoire	1,229
19	Portugal	947
20	Colombia	912
21	Papua New Guinea	554
22	Korea, South	384
23	Algeria	361
24	Ecuador	360
25	Lithuania	311
26	Bangladesh	197
27	Turkmenistan	195
28	Slovenia	193
29	Kenya	153
30	Namibia	142
31	Botswana	130
32	Trinidad and Tobago	102
33	Guinea	70
34	Barbados	64
35	Uzbekistan	57
36	Estonia	38
37	Gambia	37
38	Lesotho	22
39	Bhutan	12
40	Suriname	11
41	Sierra Leone	10
42	Bermuda	6
43	Tonga	4
44	Panama	2
45	Vanuatu	−1
46	Seychelles	−2
47	Solomon Islands	−2
48	Iceland	−5
49	Sao Tome e Principe	−8

Rank	Country	Balance of Payments 1993 (million $)
50	Cape Verde	−10
51	Fiji	−13
52	Antigua and Barbuda	−20
53	St. Kitts and Nevis	−21
54	Dominica	−23
55	Equatorial Guinea	−25
56	Burundi	−26
57	Guinea–Bissau	−29
58	Niger	−29
59	Moldova	−35
60	Swaziland	−37
61	Grenada	−38
62	Comoros	−39
63	Western Samoa	−39
64	St. Lucia	−42
LOWER MIDDLE		
65	St. Vincent	−42
66	Maldives	−48
67	Belize	−49
68	Benin	−52
69	Ethiopia	−54
70	Central African Republic	−57
71	Malta	−68
72	Bahamas	−73
73	Haiti	−78
74	Chad	−84
75	Rwanda	−85
76	Djibouti	−88
77	Mauritius	−94
78	Malawi	−96
79	Togo	−98
80	Mali	−103
81	Uganda	−107
82	Mongolia	−111
83	Zimbabwe	−116
84	Mauritania	−117
85	Burkina	−118
86	El Salvador	−118
87	Madagascar	−136
88	Dominican Republic	−161
89	Nepal	−223
90	Jamaica	−226
91	Uruguay	−227
92	Cyprus	−242
93	Honduras	−256
94	Gabon	−269
95	Senegal	−305
96	Zambia	−307
97	Ghana	−378
98	Mozambique	−381
99	Sri Lanka	−381

Rank	Country	Balance of Payments 1993 (million $)
100	Tanzania	−409
101	Kazakhstan	−438
102	Costa Rica	−470
103	Sudan	−506
104	Congo	−508
105	Morocco	−525
106	Bolivia	−533
107	Paraguay	−603
108	Syria	−607
109	Jordan	−629
110	Brazil	−637
111	Zaire	−643
112	Nicaragua	−644
113	Guatemala	−702
114	Cameroon	−742
115	Greece	−747
116	Austria	−875
117	Tunisia	−912
118	New Zealand	−932
119	Finland	−980
120	Bahrain	−993
121	Oman	−1,069
122	Romania	−1,162
123	Israel	−1,373
124	Peru	−1,800
125	Chile	−2,096
126	Venezuela	−2,223
127	Malaysia	−2,466
128	Pakistan	−2,936
129	Philippines	−3,289
130	Puerto Rico	−3,401
131	Sweden	−4,057
132	Hungary	−4,262
133	Russia	−4,300
134	Spain	−4,640
135	Poland	−5,365
136	Turkey	−6,380
137	Iran	−6,504
138	India	−6,826
BOTTOM 10		
139	Thailand	−6,928
140	Argentina	−7,452
141	Australia	−10,369
142	China	−11,609
143	United Kingdom	−12,776
144	Saudi Arabia	−14,218
145	Germany	−14,760
146	Mexico	−23,391
147	Canada	−23,869
148	United States	−103,930

Source: *Balance of Payments Yearbook*

63. PER CAPITA GNP ANNUAL GROWTH RATE 1985–1994

In the Bible, Joseph's Egypt experienced seven years of prosperity followed by seven years of famine, known as the Locust Years. Many modern nations also experience this form of economic cycle, although perhaps in less drastic form. In the modern version, per capita income of certain nations may stagnate for many years or slide down, and, then when the exports of certain commodities pick up and their prices improve on world markets, the per capita income receives a corresponding boost. It does not necessarily mean that a growth in per capita income generally translates into an improvement in national welfare.

The trickle down theory does not always operate, especially if the channels of wealth distribution within a country are clogged. But that is a problem of equity which does not concern economists as much as it does sociologists.

TOP 10
Per Capita GNP Annual Growth Rate 1985–1994

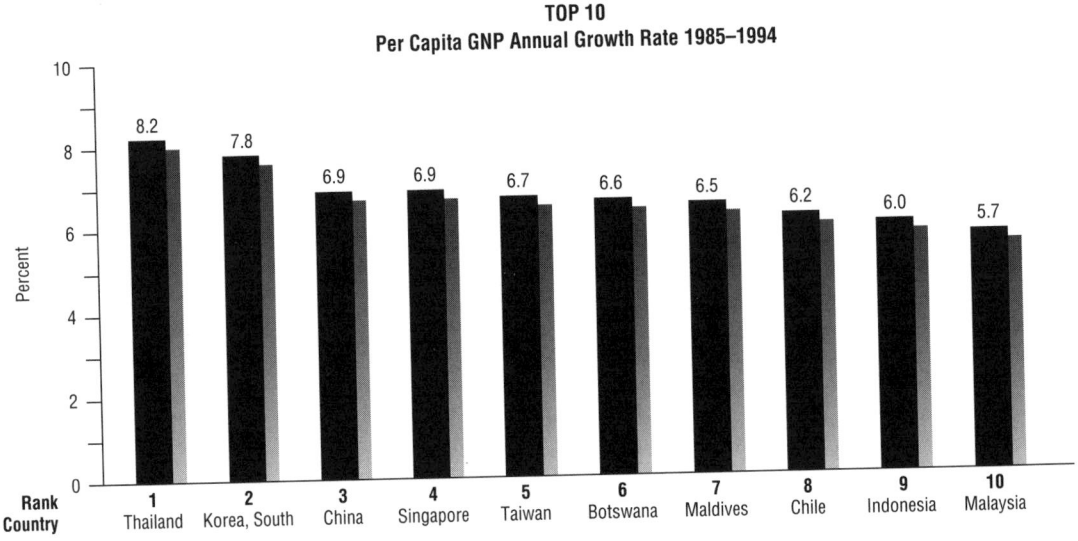

Rank	Country	GNP Annual Growth Rate 1985–94
UPPER MIDDLE		
11	Mauritius	5.6
12	Belize	5.3
13	Malta	5.3
14	Cyprus	5.2
15	Ireland	5.2
16	Portugal	4.9
17	St. Kitts and Nevis	4.7
18	Seychelles	4.5
19	St. Vincent	4.4
20	Dominica	4.2
21	St. Lucia	4.0
22	Grenada	3.9
23	Mozambique	3.5
24	Namibia	3.4
25	Japan	3.2
26	Uganda	3.0
27	Uruguay	3.0
28	India	2.9
29	Costa Rica	2.8
30	Sri Lanka	2.8
31	Antigua and Barbuda	2.7
32	Spain	2.7
33	Israel	2.5
34	Sao Tome e Principe	2.5
35	Austria	2.3
36	Belgium	2.3
37	Nauru	2.2
38	Bangladesh	2.1
39	Czech Republic	2.1
40	Dominican Republic	2.1
41	Laos	2.1
42	Papua New Guinea	2.1
43	Fiji	2.0
44	Argentina	1.9
45	Bolivia	1.9
46	Colombia	1.9
47	Germany	1.9
48	Guinea-Bissau	1.9
49	Netherlands	1.9
50	Cape Verde	1.8
51	Italy	1.8
52	Philippines	1.8
53	Tunisia	1.8
54	France	1.7
55	Jamaica	1.7
56	Puerto Rico	1.7
57	Egypt	1.6
58	El Salvador	1.6
59	Equatorial Guinea	1.6
60	Pakistan	1.6
61	Turkey	1.5
62	Ghana	1.4
63	Norway	1.4
64	United Kingdom	1.4
65	Denmark	1.3
66	Greece	1.3
67	Luxembourg	1.3
68	United States	1.3
69	Australia	1.2
70	Guinea	1.2
LOWER MIDDLE		
71	Nigeria	1.2
72	Somalia	1.2
73	Morocco	1.1
74	Tanzania	1.1
75	Ecuador	1.0
76	Paraguay	1.0
77	Chad	0.9
78	Guatemala	0.9
79	Mali	0.9
80	Poland	0.9
81	Qatar	0.8
82	Mexico	0.6
83	Oman	0.6
84	Suriname	0.6
85	Venezuela	0.6
86	Gambia	0.5
87	Lesotho	0.5
88	New Zealand	0.5
89	Switzerland	0.5
90	Canada	0.4
91	Guyana	0.3
92	Iceland	0.3
93	Mauritania	0.2
94	United Arab Emirates	0.2
95	Tonga	0.1
96	Kenya	0.0
97	Panama	0.0
98	Sweden	0.0
99	Barbados	−0.1
100	Honduras	−0.1
101	Burkina	−0.2
102	Sudan	−0.2
103	Finland	−0.3
104	Brazil	−0.4
105	Senegal	−0.5
106	Ethiopia	−0.6
107	Zimbabwe	−0.6
108	Bahamas	−0.7
109	Benin	−0.8
110	Zaire	−0.8
111	Angola	−0.9
112	Bahrain	−0.9
113	Hungary	−0.9
114	Vanuatu	−0.9
115	Burundi	−1.0
116	Iran	−1.0
117	Kiribati	−1.0
118	Bermuda	−1.2
119	Saudi Arabia	−1.2
120	Comoros	−1.3
121	Kuwait	−1.3
122	Swaziland	−1.3
123	Zambia	−1.3
124	Brunei	−1.5
125	Turkmenistan	−1.5
126	South Africa	−1.6
127	Belarus	−1.7
128	Madagascar	−1.7
129	Solomon Islands	−1.8
130	Sierra Leone	−1.9
131	Malawi	−2.0
132	Niger	−2.2
133	Rwanda	−2.2
134	Gabon	−2.3
135	Trinidad and Tobago	−2.3
136	Algeria	−2.4
137	Syria	−2.4
138	Uzbekistan	−2.4
139	Peru	−2.5
140	Congo	−2.7
141	Togo	−2.7
142	Central African Republic	−2.8
143	Bulgaria	−3.2
144	Mongolia	−3.3
145	Slovakia	−3.3
146	Russia	−4.4
147	Haiti	−5.0
148	Ukraine	−5.1
149	Cote d'Ivoire	−5.2
150	Kyrgyzstan	−5.4
151	Albania	−6.0
152	Latvia	−6.2
153	Romania	−6.2
BOTTOM 10		
154	Jordan	−6.3
155	Estonia	−6.4
156	Nicaragua	−6.4
157	Kazakhstan	−6.5
158	Cameroon	−6.6
159	Lithuania	−7.8
160	Tajikistan	−11.7
161	Azerbaijan	−12.2
162	Armenia	−12.9
163	Georgia	−18.6

Source: *United Nations Statistical Yearbook*

GNP ORIGINS

GNP allows broad comparisons of the relative size of national economies but its strengths and weaknesses are revealed when the aggregates are analyzed according to the industrial sectors of origin and component expenditures and costs. Generally GNP is distributed among 10 industrial sectors (grouped into three mega sectors: agriculture, industry and services). The three major domestic components of GNP expenditure are private consumption, government spending and gross domestic investment. The nondomestic component is net foreign trade, both exports (a positive value) and imports (a negative value).

64. GNP ORIGINS—INVESTMENTS

Rank	Country	Investments as Percentage of GNP	Rank	Country	Investments as Percentage of GNP	Rank	Country	Investments as Percentage of GNP
TOP 10			53	Seychelles	24	106	Slovakia	17
1	Lesotho	86	54	Tunisia	24	107	Tonga	17
2	Mozambique	60	55	Uzbekistan	24	108	Brazil	16
3	Sao Tome e Principe	51	56	Vietnam	24	109	Congo	16
4	Tanzania	51	57	Azerbaijan	23	110	Ghana	16
5	Cape Verde	45	58	India	23	111	Iceland	16
6	Maldives	45	59	Iran	23	112	Malawi	16
7	China	43	60	Israel	23	113	Senegal	16
8	Western Samoa	42	61	Suriname	23	114	United States	16
9	Botswana	41	62	Burkina	22	115	Uruguay	16
10	Thailand	40	63	Germany	22	116	Bolivia	15
			64	Hungary	22	117	Papua New Guinea	15
UPPER MIDDLE			65	Peru	22	118	Poland	15
11	Malaysia	39	66	Switzerland	22	119	Rwanda	15
12	St. Kitts and Nevis	39	67	Turkey	22	120	United Kingdom	15
13	Korea, South	38	68	Zimbabwe	22	121	Bangladesh	14
14	Belarus	35				122	Cameroon	14
15	Algeria	33	**LOWER MIDDLE**			123	Croatia	14
16	Estonia	32	69	Comoros	21	124	Denmark	14
17	Mauritius	32	70	Ecuador	21	125	Ethiopia	14
18	Singapore	32	71	Mongolia	21	126	Finland	14
19	Belize	31	72	Morocco	21	127	Guinea	14
20	Jamaica	31	73	Nepal	21	128	Ireland	14
21	Japan	30	74	New Zealand	21	129	Trinidad and Tobago	14
22	Kyrgyzstan	30	75	Slovenia	21	130	Uganda	14
23	Grenada	29	76	Argentina	20	131	Albania	13
24	Indonesia	29	77	Australia	20	132	Barbados	13
25	Malta	29	78	Benin	20	133	Central African Republic	13
26	Bahrain	28	79	Bulgaria	20	134	Cote d'Ivoire	13
27	Bhutan	28	80	Dominican Republic	20	135	Djibouti	13
28	Costa Rica	28	81	Guinea-Bissau	20	136	Fiji	13
29	Lebanon	28	82	Namibia	20	137	Sweden	13
30	Russia	28	83	Nicaragua	20	138	Madagascar	12
31	Chile	27	84	Norway	20	139	Myanmar (Burma)	12
32	Mali	27	85	Pakistan	20	140	Togo	12
33	Romania	27	86	Spain	20	141	Yemen	12
34	Sri Lanka	27	87	Guyana	19	142	Burundi	11
35	Dominica	26	88	Netherlands	19	143	Kuwait	11
36	Honduras	26	89	Belgium	18	144	Armenia	10
37	Jordan	26	90	Canada	18	145	Nigeria	10
38	Luxembourg	26	91	Czech Republic	18	146	Chad	9
39	Portugal	26	92	Egypt	18			
40	Austria	25	93	El Salvador	18	**BOTTOM 10**		
41	Gabon	25	94	France	18	147	Latvia	9
42	Philippines	25	95	Gambia	18	148	Sierra Leone	9
43	St. Lucia	25	96	Greece	18	149	Venezuela	9
44	United Arab Emirates	25	97	Lithuania	18	150	Zambia	9
45	Colombia	24	98	Macedonia	18	151	Moldova	8
46	Cyprus	24	99	South Africa	18	152	Niger	6
47	Equatorial Guinea	24	100	Swaziland	18	153	Ukraine	5
48	Kazakhstan	24	101	Guatemala	17	154	Georgia	4
49	Mexico	24	102	Italy	17	155	Haiti	2
50	Panama	24	103	Mauritania	17	156	Kenya	2
51	Paraguay	24	104	Oman	17			
52	Saudi Arabia	24	105	Puerto Rico	17			

Source: *World Development Report*

65. GNP ORIGINS—PRIVATE CONSUMPTION

Rank	Country	Share of Private Consumption in GNP (%)
TOP 10		
1	Lesotho	131
2	Guinea-Bissau	111
3	Lebanon	110
4	Cuba	95
5	Nicaragua	95
6	Comoros	92
7	Armenia	91
8	Cape Verde	89
9	Central African Republic	89
10	El Salvador	89
UPPER MIDDLE		
11	Georgia	89
12	Madagascar	89
13	Uganda	89
14	Chad	88
15	Ethiopia	87
16	Togo	86
17	Benin	85
18	Ghana	85
19	Guatemala	85
20	Tanzania	85
21	Sierra Leone	84
22	Burkina	83
23	Burundi	83
24	Mali	83
25	Vanuatu	83
26	Niger	82
27	Bolivia	81
28	Dominican Republic	81
29	Nepal	81
30	Djibouti	80
31	Malawi	80
32	Peru	80
33	Senegal	80
34	Ukraine	80
35	Bangladesh	79
36	Paraguay	79
37	Swaziland	79
38	Bulgaria	78
39	Guinea	78
40	Rwanda	77
41	Equatorial Guinea	76
42	Jordan	76
43	Philippines	75
44	Sao Tome e Principe	75
45	Somalia	75
46	Sri Lanka	75
47	Bahamas	74
48	Gambia	74
49	Nigeria	74
50	Zambia	74
51	Congo	73
52	Egypt	73
53	Venezuela	73
54	Greece	72
55	Mexico	72

Rank	Country	Share of Private Consumption in GNP (%)
56	St. Lucia	72
57	Syria	72
58	Uruguay	72
59	Bermuda	71
60	Romania	71
61	Sudan	71
62	Colombia	70
63	Kiribati	70
64	Pakistan	70
65	Cameroon	69
66	Hungary	69
67	Solomon Islands	69
68	United States	69
69	Zaire	69
70	Dominica	68
71	Ecuador	68
72	Lithuania	68
73	Mozambique	68
74	St. Vincent	68
75	Yemen	68
76	Barbados	67
77	Honduras	67
78	Poland	67
79	Cote d'Ivoire	66
80	Cyprus	66
81	Fiji	66
82	Grenada	66
LOWER MIDDLE		
83	Kenya	66
84	Mongolia	66
85	Portugal	66
86	Morocco	65
87	Chile	64
88	Turkey	64
89	United Kingdom	64
90	Zimbabwe	64
91	Australia	63
92	Belgium	63
93	Iceland	63
94	Italy	63
95	Mauritius	63
96	Namibia	63
97	Puerto Rico	63
98	Spain	63
99	Kazakhstan	62
100	Tunisia	62
101	Angola	61
102	Canada	61
103	India	61
104	Israel	61
105	Malta	61
106	New Zealand	61
107	Belize	60
108	Brazil	60
109	Costa Rica	60
110	France	60
111	Iran	60

Rank	Country	Share of Private Consumption in GNP (%)
112	Jamaica	60
113	Netherlands	60
114	Panama	60
115	South Africa	60
116	Bhutan	59
117	Estonia	59
118	Ireland	59
119	Trinidad and Tobago	59
120	Liberia	58
121	Papua New Guinea	58
122	Switzerland	58
123	Taiwan	58
124	Finland	57
125	Japan	57
126	Luxembourg	56
127	Slovenia	56
128	St. Kitts and Nevis	56
129	Austria	55
130	Czech Republic	55
131	Kuwait	55
132	Thailand	55
133	Azerbaijan	54
134	Germany	54
135	Korea, South	54
136	Mauritania	54
137	Slovakia	54
138	Sweden	54
139	Algeria	53
140	Denmark	52
141	Indonesia	52
142	Norway	52
143	Russia	52
144	Suriname	52
145	Belarus	51
146	China	51
147	Guyana	51
148	Kyrgyzstan	51
149	Malaysia	51
150	Seychelles	51
151	Maldives	49
152	Antigua and Barbuda	48
153	Iraq	48
154	Gabon	47
155	Botswana	46
BOTTOM 10		
156	United Arab Emirates	45
157	Turkmenistan	44
158	Uzbekistan	44
159	Singapore	43
160	Saudi Arabia	40
161	Latvia	39
162	Bahrain	36
163	Libya	34
164	Oman	33
165	Qatar	31

Source: *World Development Report*

66. GNP ORIGINS—TRADE

Rank	Country	Share of Trade in GNP
TOP 10		
1	Djibouti	35
2	El Salvador	35
3	Yugoslavia	33
4	Chad	31
5	Vanuatu	31
6	Eritrea	30
7	Guinea	29
8	Cape Verde	28
9	Ireland	28
10	Lebanon	28
UPPER MIDDLE		
11	Central African Republic	27
12	Guinea-Bissau	27
13	Sao Tome e Principe	27
14	Senegal	27
15	Barbados	26
16	Comoros	26
17	Mexico	26
18	Russia	26
19	Cameroon	25
20	Jamaica	25
21	St. Lucia	25
22	Tunisia	25
23	Guatemala	24
24	Antigua and Barbuda	23
25	Bahamas	23
26	St. Kitts and Nevis	23
27	Suriname	23
28	Syria	23
29	Myanmar (Burma)	22
30	Costa Rica	21
31	Cyprus	21
32	Ecuador	21
33	Grenada	21
34	Morocco	21
35	Sri Lanka	21
36	Croatia	20
37	Cuba	20
38	Iraq	20
39	Sierra Leone	20
40	Benin	19
41	Fiji	19
42	Gambia	19
43	Belize	18
44	Egypt	18
45	Ghana	18
46	Italy	18
47	Maldives	18
48	Nicaragua	18
49	Niger	18
50	Switzerland	18
51	Turkey	18
52	Zaire	18
53	Australia	17
54	Indonesia	17
55	Iran	17
56	Mali	17
57	Mauritius	17
58	Peru	17

Rank	Country	Share of Trade in GNP
59	Portugal	17
60	Rwanda	17
61	Seychelles	17
62	Singapore	17
63	Thailand	17
64	Togo	17
65	Austria	16
66	Chile	16
67	Haiti	16
68	Hungary	16
69	Luxembourg	16
70	Netherlands	16
71	New Zealand	16
72	Taiwan	16
73	United States	16
74	Argentina	15
75	Botswana	15
76	Burkina	15
77	Dominican Republic	15
LOWER MIDDLE		
78	France	15
79	Mongolia	15
80	Puerto Rico	15
81	St. Vincent	15
82	Tanzania	15
83	Trinidad and Tobago	15
84	Tuvalu	15
85	Belgium	14
86	Bosnia & Herzegovina	14
87	Denmark	14
88	Dominica	14
89	Estonia	14
90	Iceland	14
91	Japan	14
92	Kenya	14
93	Kiribati	14
94	Latvia	14
95	Lithuania	14
96	Malta	14
97	Mauritania	14
98	Oman	14
99	Pakistan	14
100	Philippines	14
101	Poland	14
102	South Africa	14
103	United Kingdom	14
104	Venezuela	14
105	Congo	13
106	Greece	13
107	India	13
108	Malawi	13
109	Nigeria	13
110	Paraguay	13
111	Romania	13
112	Slovenia	13
113	Solomon Islands	13
114	Uruguay	13
115	Yemen	13
116	Brunei	12
117	Canada	12

Rank	Country	Share of Trade in GNP
118	Finland	12
119	Malaysia	12
120	Panama	12
121	Uganda	12
122	Vietnam	12
123	Bahrain	11
124	Burundi	11
125	Colombia	11
126	Honduras	11
127	Macedonia	11
128	Madagascar	11
129	Namibia	11
130	Norway	11
131	Sweden	11
132	Zambia	11
133	Bolivia	10
134	Czech Republic	10
135	Ethiopia	10
136	Gabon	10
137	Israel	10
138	Jordan	10
139	Korea, South	10
140	Papua New Guinea	10
141	Slovakia	10
142	United Arab Emirates	10
143	Afghanistan	9
144	Lesotho	9
145	Libya	9
146	Moldova	9
147	Somalia	9
148	Swaziland	9
149	Bangladesh	8
150	Bulgaria	8
151	Germany	8
152	Kuwait	8
153	Western Samoa	8
154	Zimbabwe	8
155	Bhutan	7
156	Brazil	7
157	Cote d'Ivoire	7
158	Equatorial Guinea	7
159	Laos	7
160	Qatar	7
161	Saudi Arabia	7
162	Tajikistan	7
163	Angola	6
164	Armenia	6
165	Belarus	6
BOTTOM 10		
166	China	6
167	Nepal	6
168	Ukraine	6
169	Guyana	5
170	Kyrgyzstan	5
171	Liberia	5
172	Mozambique	5
173	Kazakhstan	4
174	Georgia	3
175	Azerbaijan	1

Source: *World Development Report*

67. GNP ORIGINS—IMPORTS

Rank	Country	Share of Imports in GNP (all minus %)
TOP 10		
1	Myanmar (Burma)	−2
2	Iraq	−5
3	Somalia	−5
4	Brazil	−7
5	Argentina	−8
6	Japan	−8
7	Sudan	−10
8	Ethiopia	−11
9	United States	−11
10	Haiti	−12
UPPER MIDDLE		
11	Peru	−13
12	Suriname	−13
13	Cameroon	−14
14	Colombia	−16
15	Bangladesh	−17
16	Iran	−18
17	Italy	−18
18	Mexico	−18
19	Niger	−18
20	Turkey	−18
21	Ukraine	−18
22	Australia	−19
23	South Africa	−19
24	Zaire	−19
25	Pakistan	−20
26	Poland	−20
27	Spain	−20
28	France	−21
29	Mauritania	−22
30	Uruguay	−22
31	Central African Republic	−23
32	Liberia	−23
33	Lithuania	−23
34	Uganda	−23
35	Nigeria	−24
36	Rwanda	−24
37	China	−25
38	Madagascar	−25
39	United Kingdom	−25
40	Angola	−26
41	Bolivia	−26
42	Finland	−26
43	Nepal	−26
44	Sierra Leone	−26
45	Sweden	−26
46	Canada	−27
47	Cote d'Ivoire	−27
48	Ghana	−27
49	Guatemala	−27
50	Indonesia	−27
51	Kenya	−27
52	Mali	−27
53	Venezuela	−27

Rank	Country	Share of Imports in GNP (all minus %)
54	Algeria	−28
55	Ecuador	−28
56	El Salvador	−28
57	Gabon	−28
58	Libya	−28
59	Morocco	−28
60	Senegal	−28
61	Burundi	−29
62	Chile	−29
63	Denmark	−29
64	New Zealand	−29
65	Guinea	−30
66	Korea, South	−30
67	Paraguay	−30
68	Trinidad and Tobago	−30
69	Burkina	−31
70	Dominican Republic	−31
LOWER MIDDLE		
71	Germany	−31
72	Iceland	−31
73	Egypt	−32
74	Russia	−32
75	Togo	−32
76	Yemen	−32
77	Benin	−33
78	Chad	−33
79	Greece	−33
80	Switzerland	−33
81	Vietnam	−33
82	Comoros	−34
83	Hungary	−34
84	Philippines	−34
85	Qatar	−34
86	Equatorial Guinea	−35
87	Romania	−35
88	Zambia	−35
89	Honduras	−36
90	Norway	−36
91	Portugal	−37
92	Austria	−38
93	Oman	−38
94	Panama	−38
95	Syria	−38
96	Malawi	−39
97	Zimbabwe	−39
98	Saudi Arabia	−40
99	Sri Lanka	−41
100	Taiwan	−41
101	Thailand	−41
102	Congo	−42
103	Moldova	−42
104	Costa Rica	−43
105	Israel	−45
106	Kyrgyzstan	−46
107	Tunisia	−46

Rank	Country	Share of Imports in GNP (all minus %)
108	Botswana	−47
109	Netherlands	−48
110	Nicaragua	−48
111	Seychelles	−48
112	Papua New Guinea	−49
113	Barbados	−50
114	Ireland	−52
115	Czech Republic	−53
116	Fiji	−53
117	Maldives	−53
118	Cape Verde	−54
119	Estonia	−54
120	Sao Tome e Principe	−54
121	Bahamas	−55
122	Bermuda	−56
123	Cyprus	−56
124	Guinea–Bissau	−56
125	Kuwait	−57
126	United Arab Emirates	−57
127	Belarus	−58
128	Grenada	−59
129	Tanzania	−59
130	Slovenia	−62
131	Puerto Rico	−63
132	Gambia	−65
133	Mauritius	−65
134	Solomon Islands	−65
135	Georgia	−66
136	Mongolia	−66
137	Belgium	−67
138	Djibouti	−67
139	Belize	−68
140	Dominica	−68
141	Jamaica	−68
142	St. Vincent	−68
143	Namibia	−69
144	Kiribati	−70
145	Latvia	−73
146	Mozambique	−75
147	Malaysia	−76
148	St. Kitts and Nevis	−76
149	St. Lucia	−77
150	Vanuatu	−77
151	Swaziland	−78
BOTTOM 10		
152	Jordan	−85
153	Slovakia	−87
154	Albania	−92
155	Antigua and Barbuda	−92
156	Luxembourg	−93
157	Lebanon	−96
158	Malta	−99
159	Bahrain	−102
160	Guyana	−107
161	Lesotho	−139

Source: *World Development Report*

68. ANNUAL GDP GROWTH RATE

The principal formula of developmental experts is one which compares annual population growth rate with annual GDP growth rate. If the former is more than latter for any significant period of time, the nation has two choices: to reduce its population growth or to increase its GDP growth. Both are difficult. Although it seems easier to manipulate or man-age GDP growth, it will be difficult to do so for nations that have reached a developmental plateau. Fortunately, one law of development is that for every notch up the GDP ladder, there is a downward pressure on population growth. Economic growth by itself seems to act as a brake on population growth.

Rank	Country	GDP Annual Growth Rate 1980–93 (%)	Rank	Country	GDP Annual Growth Rate 1980–93 (%)	Rank	Country	GDP Annual Growth Rate 1980–93 (%)
TOP 10			42	Portugal	3.0	84	Greece	1.3
1	Botswana	9.6	43	Belarus	2.9	85	Namibia	1.3
2	China	9.6	44	Honduras	2.9	86	Panama	1.3
3	Korea, South	9.1	45	Dominican Republic	2.8	87	Uruguay	1.3
4	Thailand	8.2	46	Paraguay	2.8	88	Gabon	1.2
5	Oman	7.6	47	Senegal	2.8	89	Jordan	1.2
6	Singapore	6.9	48	Benin	2.7	90	Bolivia	1.1
7	Malaysia	6.2	49	Congo	2.7	91	Rwanda	1.1
8	Mauritius	6.0	50	Nigeria	2.7	92	Sierra Leone	1.1
9	Pakistan	6.0	51	United States	2.7	93	Central African Republic	1.0
10	Indonesia	5.8	52	Zimbabwe	2.7	94	Mozambique	1.0
						95	Bulgaria	0.9
UPPER MIDDLE			**LOWER MIDDLE**			96	Madagascar	0.9
11	Lesotho	5.5	53	Canada	2.6	97	South Africa	0.9
12	India	5.2	54	Germany	2.6	98	Zambia	0.9
13	Chile	5.1	55	Iran	2.6	99	Argentina	0.8
14	Nepal	5.0	56	Norway	2.6	100	Myanmar (Burma)	0.8
15	Chad	4.8	57	Turkmenistan	2.6	101	Poland	0.7
16	Guinea-Bissau	4.8	58	United Kingdom	2.5	102	Togo	0.7
17	Laos	4.8	59	Ecuador	2.4	103	Ukraine	0.5
18	Turkey	4.6	60	Gambia	2.4	104	Saudi Arabia	0.4
19	Egypt	4.3	61	Austria	2.3	105	United Arab Emirates	0.3
20	Bangladesh	4.2	62	Jamaica	2.3	106	Cote d'Ivoire	0.1
21	Israel	4.1	63	Netherlands	2.3	107	Cameroon	0.0
22	Puerto Rico	4.1	64	Italy	2.2	108	Hungary	−0.1
23	Japan	4.0	65	Uzbekistan	2.2	109	Latvia	−0.3
24	Sri Lanka	4.0	66	Algeria	2.1	110	Peru	−0.5
25	Ireland	3.8	67	Belgium	2.1	111	Russia	−0.5
26	Kenya	3.8	68	Brazil	2.1	112	Kazakhstan	−0.6
27	Mongolia	3.8	69	France	2.1	113	Niger	−0.6
28	Uganda	3.8	70	Venezuela	2.1	114	Tajikistan	−0.8
29	Burkina	3.7	71	Denmark	2.0			
30	Colombia	3.7	72	Finland	2.0	**BOTTOM 10**		
31	Guinea	3.7	73	Mauritania	2.0	115	Moldova	−1.3
32	Morocco	3.7	74	Kyrgyzstan	1.9	116	Albania	−1.8
33	Tunisia	3.7	75	Mali	1.9	117	Nicaragua	−1.8
34	Burundi	3.6	76	Switzerland	1.9	118	Azerbaijan	−2.2
35	Costa Rica	3.6	77	Ethiopia	1.8	119	Lithuania	−2.2
36	Tanzania	3.6	78	Guatemala	1.7	120	Romania	−2.5
37	Ghana	3.5	79	Sweden	1.7	121	Estonia	−2.6
38	Australia	3.1	80	El Salvador	1.6	122	Armenia	−2.8
39	Papua New Guinea	3.1	81	Mexico	1.6	123	Trinidad and Tobago	−3.6
40	Spain	3.1	82	New Zealand	1.5	124	Georgia	−6.1
41	Malawi	3.0	83	Philippines	1.4			

Source: *World Development Report*

69. PURCHASING POWER PARITY ESTIMATES OF GNP PER CAPITA

The UN International Comparison Programme (ICP) has developed measures of GNP on an internationally comparable scale, using purchasing power parities rather than the less reliabile exchange rates or conversion factors. Called Purchasing Power Parity (PPP) it is related to the number of units of a country's currency required to buy the same amount of goods and services in the United States. ICP collects average domestic prices of representative products included in each participating country's national accounts through special price surveys and derives its PPP in relation to the average international prices that are implicitly derived from the prices of all participating countries.

Rank	Country	Purchasing Power Parity Estimates of GNP per Capita (US = 100) 1994	Rank	Country	Purchasing Power Parity Estimates of GNP per Capita (US = 100) 1994	Rank	Country	Purchasing Power Parity Estimates of GNP per Capita (US = 100) 1994
TOP 10			39	Hungary	23.5	78	Zimbabwe	7.9
1	United States	100.0	40	Panama	22.1	79	Cameroon	7.5
2	Switzerland	97.2	41	Poland	21.2	80	Honduras	7.5
3	Kuwait	95.6	42	Brazil	20.9	81	Congo	7.3
4	Singapore	84.6	43	Colombia	20.6	82	Nicaragua	7
5	Japan	81.7	44	Botswana	20.1	83	Kyrgyzstan	6.7
6	Belgium	78.3	45	South Africa	19.8	84	Lesotho	6.7
7	Norway	78.1	46	Tunisia	19.4	85	Benin	6.3
8	Canada	77.1	47	Turkey	18.2	86	Mauritania	6.1
9	Denmark	76.8				87	Senegal	6.1
10	France	76.0	**LOWER MIDDLE**			88	Azerbaijan	5.8
			48	Russia	17.8	89	Uganda	5.4
UPPER MIDDLE			49	Estonia	17.4	90	Cote d'Ivoire	5.3
11	Austria	75.6	50	Bulgaria	16.9	91	Bangladesh	5.1
12	Germany	75.3	51	Belarus	16.7	92	Kenya	5.1
13	Netherlands	72.4	52	Namibia	16.7	93	India	4.9
14	Italy	71.3	53	Ecuador	16.2	94	Nepal	4.8
15	Australia	70.0	54	Jordan	15.8	95	Nigeria	4.6
16	United Kingdom	69.4	55	Romania	15.8	96	Central African Republic	4.5
17	Sweden	66.2	56	Dominican Republic	14.5	97	Togo	4.4
18	Finland	62.4	57	Egypt	14.4	98	Gambia	4.3
19	New Zealand	61.3	58	Indonesia	13.9	99	Tajikistan	3.7
20	Israel	59.1	59	Peru	13.9	100	Haiti	3.6
21	Spain	53.1	60	Paraguay	13.7	101	Mozambique	3.3
22	Ireland	52.4	61	Morocco	13.4	102	Zambia	3.3
23	Mauritius	49.1	62	Guatemala	13.3	103	Guinea-Bissau	3.2
24	Portugal	46.3	63	Jamaica	13.1	104	Burkina	3.1
25	Greece	42.2	64	Lithuania	12.7			
26	Korea, South	39.9	65	Latvia	12.4	**BOTTOM 10**		
27	Saudi Arabia	36.6	66	Sri Lanka	12.2	105	Niger	3.0
28	Chile	34.4	67	Kazakhstan	10.9	106	Chad	2.8
29	Czech Republic	34.4	68	Philippines	10.6	107	Burundi	2.7
30	Argentina	33.7	69	Papua New Guinea	10.4	108	Sierra Leone	2.7
31	Trinidad and Tobago	33.5	70	Ukraine	10.1	109	Madagascar	2.5
32	Oman	33.2	71	China	9.7	110	Malawi	2.5
33	Malaysia	32.6	72	Bolivia	9.3	111	Tanzania	2.4
34	Venezuela	30.0	73	El Salvador	9.3	112	Mali	2.0
35	Uruguay	29.8	74	Uzbekistan	9.2	113	Ethiopia	1.7
36	Mexico	27.2	75	Armenia	8.3	114	Rwanda	1.3
37	Thailand	26.9	76	Pakistan	8.2			
38	Slovenia	24.1	77	Ghana	7.9			

Source: *Human Development Report*

Section

VIII

FINANCE
& BANKING

There is a strange, mysterious quality about financial rankings that brings to mind the smoke-filled boardrooms of high finance peopled by the gnomes of Zurich. The fact is that finance is not merely another facet of economic activity; it is the pilot of the economy determining its direction, speed, and thrust and manipulating its controls. If the economy tends to pitch and roll or if it goes into a nosedive, it must be maneuvered back into safety with a few simple and crude mechanisms, such as higher interest rates, devaluation or large-scale borrowing. In no sector is there such a heavy concentration of power as in finance. The economy of the free world is probably controlled by fewer than 500 men who guide the surging flow of money through the invisible financial pipelines.

70. EXTERNAL PUBLIC DEBT

The debt bomb—the external public debt burden of the Third World—has been ticking away more and more ominously for the past decade. Already, localized detonations of this bomb in Mexico, Brazil, Ghana and other countries have sent bankers and financiers scurrying from their paneled offices into conferences and emergency summits. The result has been a reduction in the rate of flow of money into developing countries; nevertheless, the bomb continues to tick and will pose a major threat to international economic stability.

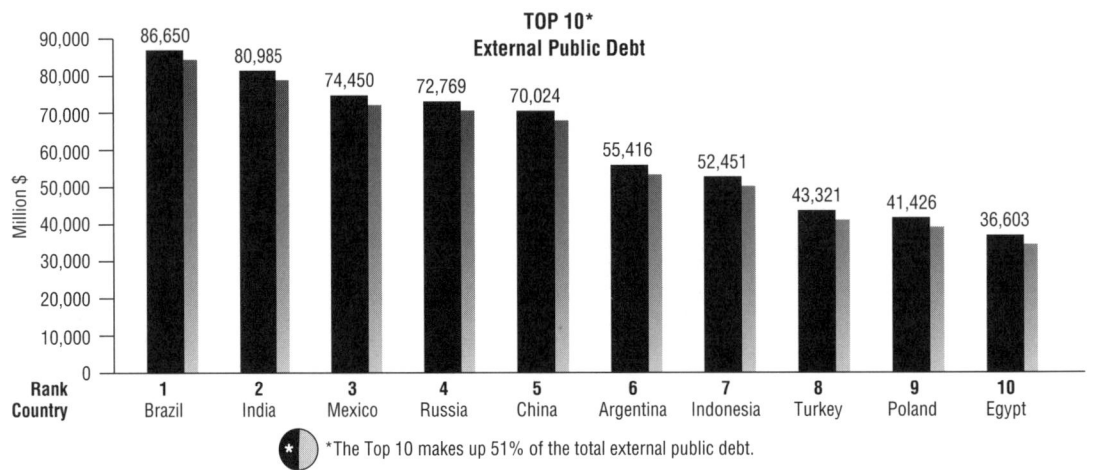

*The Top 10 makes up 51% of the total external public debt.

Rank	Country	External Public Debt (million $)	Rank	Country	External Public Debt (million $)	Rank	Country	External Public Debt (million $)
	UPPER MIDDLE		24	Malaysia	13,863	38	Jordan	6,825
11	Nigeria	28,237	25	Bangladesh	13,048	39	Tanzania	6,734
12	Venezuela	26,856	26	Colombia	12,861	40	Sri Lanka	5,936
13	Portugal	25,173	27	Cote d'Ivoire	10,551	41	Cameroon	5,436
14	Algeria	24,587	28	Ecuador	9,935	42	Czech Republic	5,392
15	Korea, South	24,567	29	Bulgaria	9,746	43	Yemen	5,341
16	Philippines	24,471	30	Sudan	8,994	44	Myanmar (Burma)	5,135
17	Vietnam	21,554	31	Iran	8,880	45	Kenya	5,121
18	Hungary	20,357	32	Chile	8,868	46	Zambia	4,666
19	Morocco	20,310	33	Nicaragua	8,773	47	Mozambique	4,650
20	Pakistan	20,306	34	Zaire	8,769	48	Uruguay	4,629
21	Syria	16,234	35	Yugoslavia	8,199	49	Ethiopia	4,530
22	Peru	16,123	36	Angola	7,727	50	Congo	4,097
23	Thailand	14,562	37	Tunisia	7,424	51	Madagascar	3,920

Rank	Country	External Public Debt (million $)	Rank	Country	External Public Debt (million $)	Rank	Country	External Public Debt (million $)
52	Dominican Republic	3,763	80	Benin	1,409	110	Swaziland	217.8
53	Panama	3,709	81	Niger	1,354	111	Moldova	201.6
54	Bolivia	3,687	82	Paraguay	1,283	112	Fiji	199.4
55	Jamaica	3,604	83	Slovenia	1,256	113	Djibouti	192.6
56	Honduras	3,479	84	Togo	1,128	114	Albania	173.9
57	Ukraine	3,456.7	85	Burkina	1,093	115	Comoros	169.4
58	Ghana	3,341	86	Liberia	1,070	116	Lithuania	163.5
59	Costa Rica	3,139	87	Burundi	999	117	Belize	162.2
60	Zimbabwe	3,021	88	Croatia	870	118	Cape Verde	148.7
61	Senegal	3,011	89	Belarus	864.4	119	Armenia	140
62	Gabon	2,889	90	Rwanda	835.8	120	Western Samoa	139.2
63	Guinea	2,675	91	Central African Republic	797.2	121	Seychelles	138.1
			92	Uzbekistan	735.9	122	Malta	127.9
LOWER MIDDLE			93	Sierra Leone	728	123	Latvia	118.8
64	Uganda	2,617	94	Mauritius	717	124	Maldives	111.6
65	Mali	2,506	95	Chad	704.6	125	St. Lucia	96.8
66	Oman	2,319	96	Botswana	665.8	126	Grenada	96.2
67	Guatemala	2,301	97	Guinea-Bissau	633.6	127	Solomon Islands	95
68	Romania	2,080	98	Haiti	617.6			
69	Slovakia	2,058	99	Georgia	568.0	**BOTTOM 10**		
70	Mauritania	1,960	100	Macedonia	528	128	Estonia	85.8
71	Laos	1,948	101	Lesotho	471.9	129	Dominica	85.5
72	Nepal	1,938	102	Lebanon	375	130	Bhutan	83.3
73	El Salvador	1,897	103	Gambia	348.8	131	St. Vincent	62.4
74	Somalia	1,897	104	Barbados	346.5	132	Tonga	43.7
75	Guyana	1,727	105	Mongolia	344.4	133	Tajikistan	41.2
76	Malawi	1,724	106	Kyrgyzstan	248.1	134	St. Kitts and Nevis	39.5
77	Trinidad and Tobago	1,704	107	Cambodia	239.4	135	Vanuatu	39.4
78	Kazakhstan	1,552.2	108	Sao Tome e Principe	225.8	136	Azerbaijan	35.5
79	Papua New Guinea	1,516	109	Equatorial Guinea	218.7	137	Turkmenistan	9.0

Source: *World Debt Tables*

71. EXTERNAL PUBLIC DEBT AS PERCENTAGE OF GNP

External public debt represents outstanding publicly guaranteed loans that have been disbursed less canceled loan commitments and repayments of principal. Because disbursements of loans and grants are made on differing financial terms, the burden of the external public debt may vary from country to country. Concessional loans are those with an interest rate of 3% or less usually extended by governments or international organizations.

Rank	Country	External Debt as Percentage of GNP	Rank	Country	External Debt as Percentage of GNP	Rank	Country	External Debt as Percentage of GNP
TOP 10			18	Honduras	101.2	38	Macedonia	52.5
1	Nicaragua	695.4	19	Ecuador	98.8			
2	Mozambique	339.4	20	Gabon	77.7	**LOWER MIDDLE**		
3	Tanzania	248.7	21	Morocco	72.8	39	Niger	52.1
4	Cote d'Ivoire	224.0	22	Egypt	70.5	40	Algeria	51.3
5	Congo	215.0	23	Hungary	66.9	41	Poland	49.7
6	Guinea-Bissau	192.1	24	Togo	66.2	42	Burundi	49.6
7	Mauritania	177.9	25	Zimbabwe	64.6	43	Costa Rica	48.1
8	Sierra Leone	177.3	26	Venezuela	62.6	44	Ghana	47.6
9	Vietnam	161.8	27	Bolivia	61.9	45	Trinidad and Tobago	47.6
10	Zambia	160.8	28	Guinea	60.9	46	Senegal	46.7
			29	Papua New Guinea	60.0	47	Peru	46.1
UPPER MIDDLE			30	Philippines	59.8	48	Laos	46.0
11	Bulgaria	119.4	31	Mali	58.8	49	Dominican Republic	45.1
12	Jordan	117.1	32	Indonesia	58.5	50	Chile	44.7
13	Nigeria	110.0	33	Cameroon	57.7	51	Malawi	42.6
14	Madagascar	108.7	34	Uganda	55.7	52	Sri Lanka	41.9
15	Jamaica	103.5	35	Tunisia	54.3	53	Portugal	41.5
16	Kenya	103.0	36	Uruguay	54.3	54	Central African Republic	41.4
17	Panama	101.6	37	Gambia	53.2	55	Benin	40.0

Rank	Country	External Debt as Percentage of GNP	Rank	Country	External Debt as Percentage of GNP	Rank	Country	External Debt as Percentage of GNP
56	Pakistan	39.1	71	Mauritius	26.5	86	Kyrgyzstan	7.2
57	Turkey	38.2	72	Brazil	26.3	87	Kazakhstan	6.2
58	Malaysia	37.0	73	Nepal	25.6			
59	Thailand	36.5	74	Russia	25.4		**BOTTOM 10**	
60	Oman	33.3	75	Guatemala	22.4	88	Armenia	5.6
61	Mexico	32.8	76	Lesotho	21.9	89	Moldova	5.6
62	Colombia	32.3	77	Burkina	21.4	90	Lithuania	5.5
63	Chad	31.7	78	El Salvador	21.0	91	Latvia	4.3
64	Bangladesh	31.1	79	Paraguay	20.4	92	Ukraine	3.1
65	India	29.1	80	China	18.0	93	Uzbekistan	3.1
66	Rwanda	28.8	81	Georgia	16.4	94	Belarus	2.6
67	Argentina	28.6	82	Romania	16.4	95	Estonia	2.6
68	Slovakia	28.5	83	Slovenia	15.7	96	Tajikistan	1.0
69	Czech Republic	26.7	84	Botswana	13.6	97	Azerbaijan	0.7
70	Mongolia	26.6	85	Korea, South	13.0			

Source: *World Debt Tables*

72. GROWTH IN MONEY STOCK

The growth in money stock is a reliable index of a number of economic phenomena, such as inflation, strength of currency and international reserves. It is also one of the most effective fiscal tools in the hands of the treasury for manipulating interest rates and for priming the economy.

Economists distinguish three types of money stock: The sum of currency outside banks and private sector demand deposits constitute M1; M1 plus reserve money and time, savings and foreign currency deposits of residents constitute M2 or "quasi-money"; foreign assets, claims on government and private sector, liquid liabilities and capital accounts constitute M3.

Rank	Country	Money Stock Average Annual Growth Rate (%) 1980–93	Rank	Country	Money Stock Average Annual Growth Rate (%) 1980–93	Rank	Country	Money Stock Average Annual Growth Rate (%) 1980–93
	TOP 10		29	Gambia	19.0	58	Italy	10.5
1	Argentina	356.7	30	Romania	18.8	59	Burkina	9.8
2	Peru	296.6	31	Yemen	18.7	60	Denmark	9.8
3	Bolivia	207.1	32	Malawi	18.6	61	Oman	9.6
4	Israel	78.6	33	El Salvador	18.5	62	Norway	9.5
5	Uruguay	70.1				63	Papua New Guinea	8.7
6	Poland	64.1		**LOWER MIDDLE**		64	Japan	8.2
7	Turkey	60.6	34	Portugal	18.5	65	Canada	8.1
8	Guinea-Bissau	59.8	35	Iran	18.4	66	Rwanda	8.1
9	Mexico	57.8	36	Bangladesh	18.0	67	United Arab Emirates	8.0
10	Sierra Leone	57.2	37	Nigeria	18.0	68	Mali	7.7
			38	Philippines	17.4	69	Ireland	7.4
	UPPER MIDDLE		39	India	16.7	70	Austria	7.3
11	Ghana	42.0	40	South Africa	16.6	71	United States	7.2
12	Ecuador	38.8	41	Kenya	16.4	72	Saudi Arabia	7.1
13	Paraguay	36.9	42	Madagascar	16.4	73	Sweden	6.9
14	Dominican Republic	29.3	43	Lesotho	16.3	74	Germany	6.8
15	Chile	29.1	44	Myanmar (Burma)	15.8	75	Benin	6.3
16	Jamaica	27.3	45	Sri Lanka	15.6	76	Switzerland	6.2
17	Indonesia	26.3	46	Tunisia	15.5			
18	China	25.7	47	Honduras	14.3		**BOTTOM 10**	
19	Costa Rica	25.5	48	Pakistan	14.2	77	Chad	5.6
20	Botswana	25.2	49	Morocco	13.7	78	Trinidad and Tobago	5.5
21	Venezuela	22.7	50	Singapore	13.5	79	Congo	4.9
22	Greece	22.3	51	Ethiopia	13.0	80	Senegal	4.7
23	Korea, South	21.9	52	Malaysia	12.6	81	Niger	3.9
24	Mauritius	21.6	53	Jordan	12.4	82	Central African Republic	3.5
25	Egypt	21.4	54	Spain	11.6	83	Togo	3.2
26	Nepal	19.9	55	Australia	11.5	84	Cameroon	3.1
27	Guatemala	19.3	56	Finland	11.4	85	Gabon	3.1
28	Thailand	19.2	57	Mauritania	10.9	86	Cote d'Ivoire	2.5

Source: *International Financial Statistics Yearbook*

73. BUDGET SURPLUS OR DEFICIT

Budgetary deficit, one of the cardinal sins in Reaganomics, is becoming the norm rather than the exception throughout the world, revealing the impact of Keynesian theories on the postwar era. Most heads of state and their finance ministers still pay lip service to the ideal of a balanced budget but yield to the seductions of the sirens of pet projects, bigger bureau-cracies and expensive social programs when the time comes to prepare the annual budget. High inflation rates; fixed treasury obligations, such as pension payments, interest on bonds, social security and heavy defense expenditures; and a general distaste for austerity add to their problems and make sound and prudent budget management almost impossible.

Rank	Country	Overall Budget Deficit/Surplus as a Percentage of GNP	Rank	Country	Overall Budget Deficit/Surplus as a Percentage of GNP	Rank	Country	Overall Budget Deficit/Surplus as a Percentage of GNP
TOP 10			25	Israel	−1.7	50	Egypt	−4.1
1	Singapore	12.6	26	Gabon	−1.8	51	South Africa	−4.4
2	Botswana	11.2	27	Peru	−1.8	52	Romania	−4.7
3	Jordan	6.0				53	India	−4.8
4	Panama	4.4	**LOWER MIDDLE**			54	Namibia	−4.8
5	Czech Republic	2.6	28	Cameroon	−2.0	55	Sierra Leone	−5.0
6	Chile	2.1	29	Estonia	−2.0	56	United Kingdom	−5.1
7	Thailand	2.1	30	Mongolia	−2.0	57	Madagascar	−5.9
8	Malaysia	1.7	31	Bolivia	−2.1	58	Nepal	−6.3
9	Paraguay	1.2	32	Portugal	−2.2	59	Papua New Guinea	−6.4
10	Indonesia	0.7	33	Australia	−2.3	60	Sri Lanka	−6.4
			34	China	−2.3	61	Belgium	−7.0
UPPER MIDDLE			35	Ireland	−2.3	62	Turkey	−7.0
11	Korea, South	0.6	36	Denmark	−2.4	63	Zimbabwe	−7.0
12	Lithuania	0.6	37	Germany	−2.4	64	Pakistan	−7.4
13	Uruguay	0.6	38	Ghana	−2.5			
14	Ecuador	0.5	39	Tunisia	−2.6	**BOTTOM 10**		
15	Nicaragua	0.5	40	Belarus	−2.9	65	Chad	−7.5
16	New Zealand	0.1	41	Venezuela	−3.0	66	Rwanda	−9.1
17	Costa Rica	−0.2	42	Myanmar (Burma)	−3.1	67	Italy	−10.1
18	United Arab Emirates	−0.2	43	Guinea	−3.3	68	Sweden	−12.2
19	Lesotho	−0.3	44	Spain	−3.7	69	Bulgaria	−12.9
20	El Salvador	−0.8	45	Canada	−3.8	70	Finland	−15.4
21	Netherlands	−0.9	46	France	−3.8	71	Greece	−15.6
22	Brazil	−1.0	47	Kenya	−3.8	72	Oman	−17.4
23	Iran	−1.4	48	Austria	−3.9	73	Yemen	−20.6
24	Philippines	−1.5	49	United States	−4.0	74	Kuwait	−26.1

Source: *World Development Report*

74. INTERNATIONAL RESERVES

One of the principal financial criteria of the relative economic health of a country is the size of its international reserves. International reserves comprise the sum of a country's (1) reserve position in the IMF, a quota subscribed in the country's own currency constituting a level up to which transactions may be effected within the IMF system, (2) holdings of foreign exchange, (3) holdings of gold and (4) holdings of Special Drawing Rights or SDRs, an unconditional credit allocation, within the quota system set up by IMF, of currency needed by a country to maintain stability of foreign exchange transactions or markets. At appropriate accounting intervals these four elements are combined into a single unit of account, the SDR, and summed up. The portion of the total reserves comprised by foreign exchange is very significant as an indicator of the country's international liquidity (ability to pay its debts immediately in hard or convertible currencies). The ratio of external debt to total reserves, however, is less susceptible of interpretation in isolation. A low ratio, for example, may mean either that the country has little need to borrow or that it has substantial debt but also the means to repay it. A high ratio, on the other hand, may not be alarming if a country also has high export earnings.

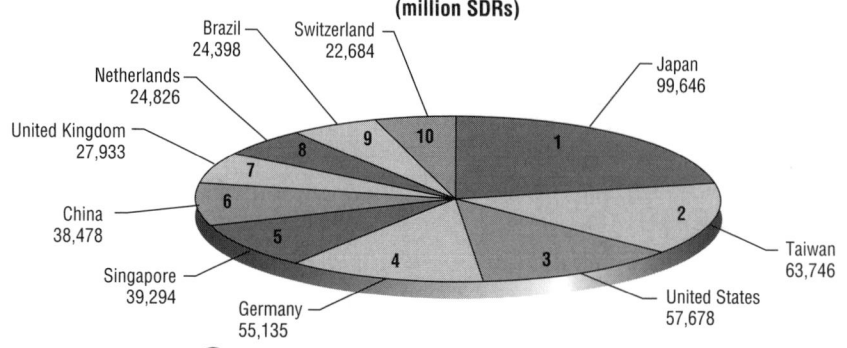

TOP 10*
International Reserves 1995
(million SDRs)

Brazil 24,398
Switzerland 22,684
Netherlands 24,826
United Kingdom 27,933
China 38,478
Singapore 39,294
Germany 55,135
Japan 99,646
Taiwan 63,746
United States 57,678

*The Top 10 makes up 54% of the International Reserves

Rank	Country	International Reserves 1995 (million SDRs)	Rank	Country	International Reserves 1995 (million SDRs)	Rank	Country	International Reserves 1995 (million SDRs)
UPPER MIDDLE			53	Algeria	1,640	94	Guyana	157
11	Spain	21,544	54	Senegal	1,321	95	Burundi	147
12	France	20,677	55	Romania	1,298	96	Mali	146
13	Thailand	19,598	56	Sri Lanka	1,191	97	Central African Republic	144
14	Italy	19,331	57	Malta	1,151	98	Moldova	127
15	Kuwait	17,341	58	Nigeria	1,102	99	Bahamas	125
16	Malaysia	16,108	59	Jordan	1,090	100	Barbados	124
17	Sweden	15,888	60	Ecuador	1,078	101	Honduras	117
18	Norway	14,474	61	Tunisia	991	102	Niger	88
19	Austria	14,004				103	Zaire	79
20	India	13,727	**LOWER MIDDLE**			104	Bhutan	74
21	Belgium	11,308	62	South Africa	946	105	Gambia	62
22	Portugal	10,280	63	Bahrain	894	106	Togo	59
23	Greece	10,191	64	Cyprus	843	107	Chad	58
24	Canada	9,509	65	Paraguay	697	108	Djibouti	50
25	Egypt	9,085	66	Uruguay	697	109	Sudan	50
26	Chile	8,895	67	Oman	664	110	Madagascar	42
27	Australia	8,197	68	Costa Rica	585	111	Gabon	36
28	Indonesia	7,947	69	Jamaica	529	112	Congo	35
29	Argentina	7,747	70	Qatar	481	113	Mauritania	35
30	Turkey	7,440	71	Panama	480	114	Rwanda	35
31	Finland	6,821	72	Nepal	467	115	St. Lucia	32
32	Israel	6,044	73	Mauritius	449	116	Western Samoa	31
33	Denmark	5,986	74	Ghana	428	117	Vanuatu	28
34	Mexico	5,741	75	Guatemala	427	118	Antigua and Barbuda	27
35	Poland	5,661	76	El Salvador	415	119	Sierra Leone	27
36	Venezuela	5,373	77	Ethiopia	407	120	Maldives	26
37	Saudi Arabia	5,350	78	Bolivia	364	121	Malawi	24
38	Czech Republic	5,310	79	Myanmar (Burma)	351	122	Papua New Guinea	23
39	Colombia	5,236	80	Kenya	350	123	Comoros	20
40	Hungary	4,757	81	Zimbabwe	340			
41	United Arab Emirates	4,726	82	Lesotho	268	**BOTTOM 10**		
42	Libya	4,622	83	Cote d'Ivoire	225	124	Seychelles	20
43	Peru	4,545	84	Tanzania	220	125	St. Kitts and Nevis	19
44	Ireland	4,291	85	Trinidad and Tobago	220	126	Grenada	18
45	Philippines	3,674	86	Iceland	218	127	Tonga	18
46	Botswana	3,027	87	Swaziland	210	128	Belize	17
47	New Zealand	2,628	88	Uganda	209	129	St. Vincent	16
48	Lebanon	2,612	89	Dominican Republic	175	130	Solomon Islands	15
49	Morocco	2,514	90	Yemen	173	131	Cameroon	12
50	Bangladesh	2,191	91	Benin	168	132	Dominica	5
51	Kyrgyzstan	2,142	92	Fiji	161	133	Suriname	2
52	Pakistan	1,715	93	Burkina	158			

Source: *International Financial Statistics Yearbook*

75. RATIO OF EXTERNAL DEBT TO INTERNATIONAL RESERVES

Rank	Country	Ratio of External Debt to International Reserves	Rank	Country	Ratio of External Debt to International Reserves	Rank	Country	Ratio of External Debt to International Reserves
TOP 10			33	India	7.5	66	Mexico	3.0
1	Cote d'Ivoire	3,840.6	34	Mali	7.5	67	Nepal	3.0
2	Congo	2,982.7	35	Togo	7.2	68	Burkina	2.9
3	Gabon	2,103.2	36	Central African Republic	7.1	69	Brazil	2.8
4	Senegal	548.0	37	Ecuador	7.1	70	Egypt	2.8
5	Cameroon	329.8	38	Guyana	7.0	71	Venezuela	2.7
6	Sudan	242.5	39	Niger	7.0	72	Western Samoa	2.7
7	Zaire	187.8				73	Guatemala	2.6
8	Guinea-Bissau	46.1	**LOWER MIDDLE**			74	Djibouti	2.5
9	Mauritania	43.2	40	Turkey	6.7	75	Oman	2.5
10	Yemen	36.0	41	Panama	6.2	76	Barbados	2.3
			42	Burundi	6.1	77	Paraguay	2.0
UPPER MIDDLE			43	Comoros	6.1	78	St. Vincent	2.0
11	Honduras	35.7	44	Benin	5.8	79	Lesotho	1.9
12	Tanzania	33.1	45	Dominican Republic	5.8	80	Romania	1.9
13	Malawi	29.9	46	Philippines	5.7	81	Colombia	1.7
14	Sierra Leone	22.1	47	Morocco	5.5	82	St. Lucia	1.6
15	Nigeria	20.1	48	Uruguay	5.5	83	Portugal	1.5
16	Uganda	17.8	49	Bangladesh	5.4	84	Czech Republic	1.4
17	Chad	17.7	50	Indonesia	4.6	85	St. Kitts and Nevis	1.4
18	Rwanda	17.4	51	Peru	4.6	86	Korea, South	1.2
19	Myanmar (Burma)	16.3	52	Solomon Islands	4.6	87	Tonga	1.2
20	Equatorial Guinea	15.9	53	Dominica	4.4	88	Bhutan	1.1
21	Pakistan	15.7	54	Maldives	4.3			
22	Algeria	14.1	55	Belize	4.2	**BOTTOM 10**		
23	Bolivia	13.8	56	Jordan	4.1	89	Chile	0.9
24	Kenya	12.5	57	Argentina	4.0	90	Mauritius	0.9
25	Jamaica	11.4	58	Seychelles	3.9	91	Swaziland	0.8
26	Papua New Guinea	10.5	59	Gambia	3.7	92	Vanuatu	0.8
27	Poland	10.1	60	Sri Lanka	3.6	93	Fiji	0.7
28	Ethiopia	9.8	61	Grenada	3.5	94	Thailand	0.6
29	Tunisia	8.6	62	El Salvador	3.4	95	Malaysia	0.5
30	Zimbabwe	8.6	63	Costa Rica	3.1	96	Botswana	0.2
31	Trinidad and Tobago	8.2	64	China	3.0	97	Lebanon	0.1
32	Ghana	7.9	65	Hungary	3.0	98	Malta	0.1

Source: *World Debt Tables*

76. PUBLIC EXPENDITURES ON SOCIAL WELFARE

Governmental expenditures on social security and welfare provide an important yardstick for measuring social progress. Because social welfare programs must compete with other sectors for funds and for their share of finite national revenues, such expenditures can reveal the extent of a government's commitment to general welfare and the satisfaction of human needs.

Rank	Country	Expenditures on Social Security as Percent of National Budget
TOP 10		
1	Uruguay	53.9
2	Sweden	50.7
3	Switzerland	49.9
4	Germany	48.5
5	Austria	44.8
6	Finland	44.8
7	Luxembourg	44.6
8	France	43.2
9	Estonia	41.9
10	Belgium	41.3
UPPER MIDDLE		
11	Norway	38.0
12	Denmark	37.6
13	Ireland	37.0
14	Spain	36.4
15	Argentina	35.3
16	Netherlands	34.4
17	New Zealand	34.0
18	United Kingdom	33.1
19	Brazil	32.1
20	Chile	31.8
21	Malta	29.8
22	Greece	28.8
23	Canada	28.6
24	Italy	28.5
25	Hungary	27.7
26	Australia	27.5
27	Portugal	27.3
28	Iraq	26.2
29	Romania	25.1
30	Czech Republic	23.0
31	Israel	21.0
32	Panama	20.9
33	United States	20.6
34	Barbados	19.8
35	Colombia	19.6
36	Cyprus	19.6
37	Iceland	18.5
38	Bolivia	17.9
39	Sri Lanka	17.6
40	Bulgaria	16.7
41	Mauritius	14.7
42	Taiwan	13.8

Rank	Country	Expenditures on Social Security as Percent of National Budget
43	Iran	13.7
44	Costa Rica	12.5
45	Mexico	12.3
46	Tunisia	12.2
47	Egypt	12.0
48	Paraguay	11.7
49	Bangladesh	9.8
50	St. Kitts and Nevis	9.4
51	Bahamas	9.3
52	Guinea-Bissau	8.8
53	Benin	8.7
54	Burkina	8.4
LOWER MIDDLE		
55	Korea, South	7.8
56	Jordan	6.9
57	Namibia	6.6
58	Cameroon	6.5
59	Togo	6.5
60	Ghana	6.4
61	Central African Republic	6.2
62	Djibouti	6.2
63	Suriname	6.0
64	Yugoslavia	6.0
65	Morocco	5.4
66	Malawi	5.3
67	Seychelles	5.3
68	Trinidad and Tobago	5.3
69	Guatemala	5.2
70	Haiti	5.1
71	Grenada	5.0
72	Dominican Republic	4.7
73	Honduras	4.5
74	Fiji	4.0
75	Ethiopia	3.9
76	Guyana	3.7
77	Mauritania	3.7
78	Cote d'Ivoire	3.6
79	Gambia	3.5
80	Oman	3.4
81	Thailand	3.4
82	Nicaragua	3.3
83	Jamaica	3.2
84	United Arab Emirates	3.2
85	Belize	3.0

Rank	Country	Expenditures on Social Security as Percent of National Budget
86	Mali	3.0
87	Rwanda	2.9
88	Senegal	2.6
89	Nigeria	2.5
90	Zimbabwe	2.5
91	St. Vincent	2.3
92	El Salvador	2.2
93	Sudan	2.2
94	Bahrain	2.1
95	Uganda	2.1
96	Chad	1.9
97	Ecuador	1.9
98	Sierra Leone	1.9
99	Singapore	1.9
100	Kuwait	1.8
101	Niger	1.7
102	Somalia	1.7
103	Philippines	1.6
104	Syria	1.6
105	Lesotho	1.5
106	Macedonia	1.5
107	Zambia	1.5
108	Dominica	1.4
109	Liberia	1.0
110	Madagascar	1.0
111	Maldives	1.0
112	Vanuatu	0.9
113	Papua New Guinea	0.8
114	Tonga	0.8
115	Turkey	0.8
116	Burundi	0.7
117	Nepal	0.7
118	Botswana	0.6
BOTTOM 10		
119	Solomon Islands	0.6
120	Tanzania	0.6
121	Bhutan	0.5
122	Congo	0.4
123	Swaziland	0.4
124	Zaire	0.4
125	Myanmar (Burma)	0.3
126	Pakistan	0.2
127	Peru	0.2
128	Kenya	0.1

Source: *Government Finance Yearbook*

77. DEBT-SERVICE RATIO

Nations, like individuals, are subject to constant scrutiny by lender organizations and donor countries regarding their creditworthiness. One element of such a scrutiny is the debt-service ratio, which determines the extent of burden that repayment places on a nation's economic resources. The debt-service ratio varies according to various factors, particularly inter-national reserves, export revenues, and the size of the national budget which ultimately bears the responsibility for the repayment of debt. Countries caught in a vicious circle of more borrowing coupled with reduced solvency may find that their debt service ratio is more than they can afford. This is generally the time when the IMF steps in to enforce strict fiscal discipline.

Rank	Country	Debt-Service Ratio (%)
TOP 10		
1	Uganda	115.3
2	Algeria	73.5
3	Bolivia	50.2
4	Peru	39.3
5	Argentina	39.1
6	Uruguay	37.8
7	Hungary	35.8
8	Burundi	35.2
9	Guyana	30.2
10	Nigeria	29.0
UPPER MIDDLE		
11	Honduras	28.8
12	Morocco	27.9
13	Nicaragua	27.8
14	Colombia	25.4
15	Mauritania	25.0
16	Zimbabwe	24.9
17	India	24.7
18	Tanzania	23.3
19	Turkey	22.7
20	Philippines	22.1
21	Ecuador	21.4
22	Zambia	20.4
23	Indonesia	19.9
24	Malawi	19.9
25	Pakistan	19.2
26	Trinidad and Tobago	18.7
27	Kenya	18.4
28	Tunisia	18.2
29	Mozambique	17.2
30	Niger	16.8
31	Mexico	16.2
32	Portugal	15.9
33	Jamaica	15.3
34	Sao Tome e Principe	15.0
35	El Salvador	14.8
36	Costa Rica	14.6
37	Paraguay	14.0
38	Cote d'Ivoire	13.7
39	Ghana	13.7

Rank	Country	Debt-Service Ratio (%)
40	Cameroon	13.6
41	Venezuela	13.3
42	Jordan	13.2
43	Egypt	13.0
44	Chile	12.8
45	Guinea	11.9
46	Brazil	11.3
47	Nepal	11.2
48	Barbados	11.1
49	Myanmar (Burma)	11.0
LOWER MIDDLE		
50	Dominican Republic	10.9
51	Gambia	10.9
52	Guatemala	10.9
53	Bangladesh	10.8
54	Madagascar	10.5
55	China	9.9
56	Papua New Guinea	9.7
57	Laos	9.5
58	Vietnam	9.3
59	Sri Lanka	8.8
60	Oman	8.4
61	Guinea-Bissau	8.3
62	Ethiopia	8.2
63	Poland	8.2
64	Congo	8.0
65	Czech Republic	7.6
66	Slovakia	7.4
67	Bhutan	6.9
68	Panama	6.9
69	Benin	6.6
70	Burkina	6.6
71	Korea, South	6.3
72	Malaysia	6.3
73	Belize	6.2
74	Yemen	6.2
75	Seychelles	6.1
76	Comoros	5.9
77	Chad	5.8
78	Fiji	5.8
79	Grenada	5.6

Rank	Country	Debt-Service Ratio (%)
80	Lesotho	5.5
81	Senegal	5.2
82	Sudan	5.1
83	Mauritius	5.0
84	Solomon Islands	5.0
85	Western Samoa	5.0
86	Rwanda	4.9
87	Bulgaria	4.6
88	Cape Verde	4.6
89	Thailand	4.4
90	Togo	4.3
91	Dominica	4.1
92	Swaziland	3.8
93	Maldives	3.7
94	Botswana	3.6
95	Romania	3.6
96	Mongolia	3.5
97	St. Vincent	3.5
98	St. Lucia	3.4
99	Mali	3.3
100	Syria	3.3
101	Iran	3.2
102	Lebanon	3.2
103	Tonga	3.2
104	Angola	3.0
105	Central African Republic	2.7
106	Georgia	2.7
107	Gabon	2.5
108	Sierra Leone	2.4
109	St. Kitts and Nevis	2.1
BOTTOM 10		
110	Djibouti	2.0
111	Equatorial Guinea	1.8
112	Estonia	1.6
113	Vanuatu	1.4
114	Ukraine	1.0
115	Armenia	0.9
116	Albania	0.8
117	Malta	0.7
118	Belarus	0.6
119	Moldova	0.2

Source: *World Debt Tables*

78. TOTAL NATIONAL BUDGET AS PERCENTAGE OF GNP

The national budget is a marvelous tool for not merely the redistribution of wealth and the achievement of social policy goals, but also for adding to the national wealth through appropriate sectoral allocations. The budget also reveals the interface between policy goals and policy implementation and measures the extent and scope of government consumption, an integral part of GNP. In developed countries where governments are pro-active in tackling national problems and setting priorities, the budgets are a much larger part of the GNP than they are in countries where the governments are more laissez-faire. With the rise of Thatcherism, privatization and post-socialist developments, the trend is toward less government and therefore to a smaller share of the budget in GNP.

Rank	Country	Total National Budget as Percentage of GNP
TOP 10		
1	Pakistan	63.9
2	Kuwait	54.6
3	Netherlands	53.9
4	Sweden	53.9
5	Italy	53.4
6	Belgium	50.9
7	Yemen	50.7
8	Bulgaria	47.8
9	Ireland	47.0
10	Egypt	46.6
UPPER MIDDLE		
11	Denmark	45.5
12	France	45.5
13	Finland	44.5
14	Israel	44.2
15	United Kingdom	43.4
16	Greece	43.1
17	Portugal	42.3
18	Czech Republic	41.7
19	Romania	40.4
20	Botswana	40.2
21	Namibia	40.2
22	Austria	39.7
23	Nicaragua	39.5
24	New Zealand	36.6
25	Zimbabwe	36.2

Rank	Country	Total National Budget as Percentage of GNP
26	Jordan	36.0
27	Papua New Guinea	35.8
LOWER MIDDLE		
28	Spain	35.1
29	Gabon	33.8
30	Germany	33.6
31	Tunisia	33.2
32	Belarus	33.1
33	South Africa	32.6
34	Lesotho	32.1
35	Panama	32.1
36	Chad	32.0
37	Rwanda	31.9
38	Oman	29.2
39	Uruguay	29.2
40	Kenya	28.9
41	Australia	28.2
42	Sri Lanka	26.9
43	Costa Rica	26.7
44	Estonia	26.7
45	Malaysia	26.7
46	Bolivia	26.6
47	Turkey	25.9
48	Canada	25.8
49	Brazil	25.6
50	Mongolia	25.3
51	United States	23.8

Rank	Country	Total National Budget as Percentage of GNP
52	Sierra Leone	23.0
53	Chile	22.6
54	Mauritius	22.2
55	Guinea	21.9
56	Ghana	21.0
57	Lithuania	20.4
58	Iran	20.1
59	Singapore	19.7
60	Venezuela	19.2
61	Indonesia	18.9
62	Nepal	18.7
63	Cameroon	18.3
64	Philippines	18.1
65	Korea, South	17.1
BOTTOM 10		
66	India	16.9
67	Thailand	16.3
68	Madagascar	16.1
69	Ecuador	15.4
70	Peru	14.0
71	Paraguay	13.0
72	Myanmar (Burma)	12.1
73	United Arab Emirates	11.4
74	El Salvador	11.2
75	China	9.2

Source: *World Development Report*

79. CHIEF EXECUTIVE SALARIES

Chief executives in every industrialized country are rewarded handsomely, and the scale of their remuneration (both salary and perquisites) has become scandalously high. With transnational corporations functioning as fiefdoms sometimes only loosely accountable to their shareholders, there are no legal restrictions on the salaries of top echelons. In the United States, one chief executive receives an annual salary (with share options) of $58 million.

Chief Executive Salaries

Rank	Country		Salary (in U.S. dollars)
1	United States	$ $ $ $ $ $ $ $	777,579
2	Argentina	$ $ $ $ $ $	581,097
3	Brazil	$ $ $ $ $	501,349
4	France	$ $ $ $ $	491,273
5	Mexico	$ $ $ $ $	488,488
6	Japan	$ $ $ $ $	451,871
7	Belgium	$ $ $ $ $	449,378
8	Venezuela	$ $ $ $ $	438,766
9	Switzerland	$ $ $ $ $	432,432
10	Germany	$ $ $ $ $	416,791
11	Canada	$ $ $ $	405,101

$ = $100,000

Source: Crawford, Michael. "Peanuts for Elephants." *Canadian Business* (July 1994), p. 16. Primary source: Towers Perrin.

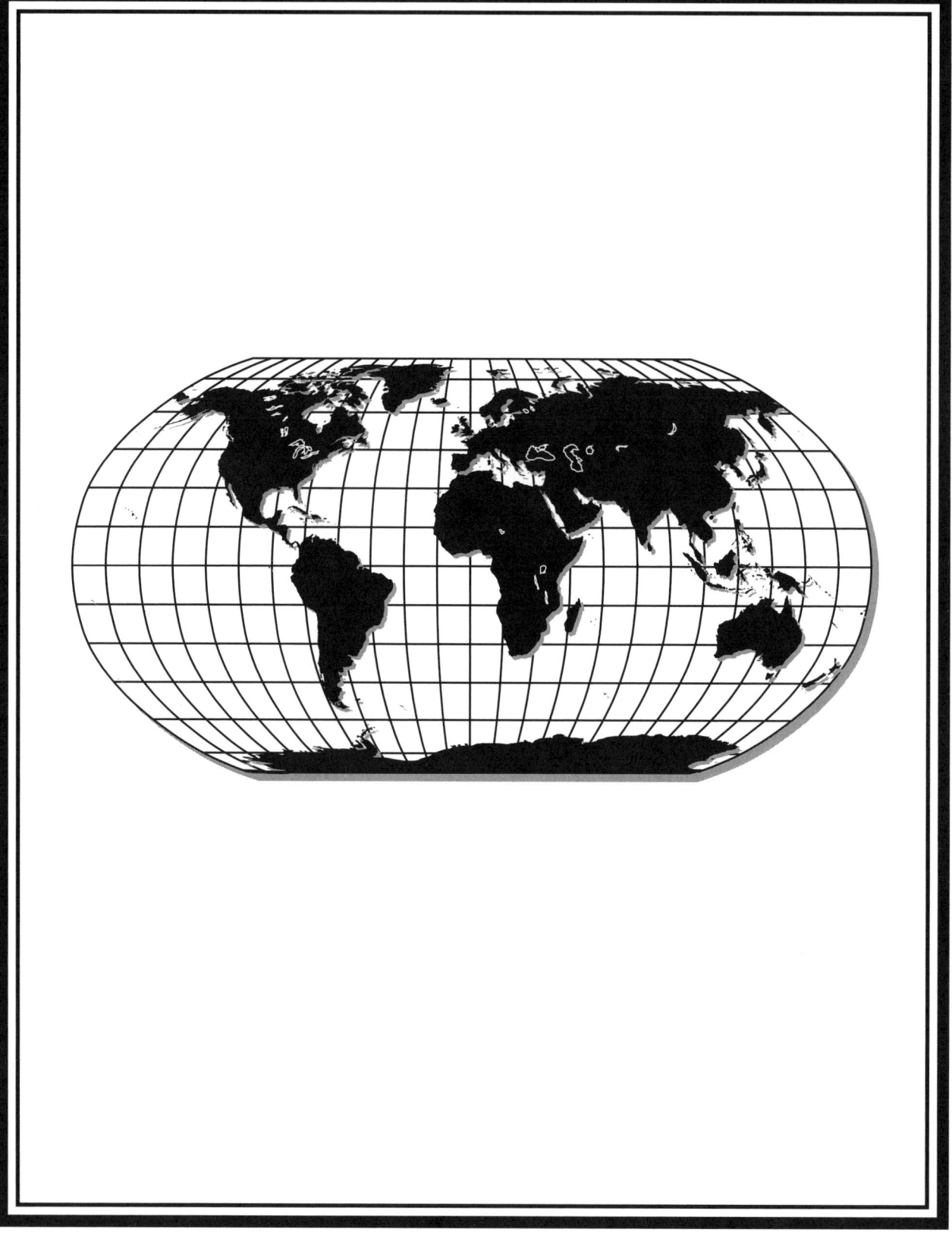

Section

IX

TRADE

The world entered the 1990s with a wave of protectionist sentiment in industrialized countries. These sentiments stemmed primarily from the loss of domestic markets for labor-intensive products based on simple technology (shoes, textiles and radios, for example), to newly industrializing countries and the consequent rash of domestic plant closures, rising unemployment and bankruptcies. It also stemmed from what was perceived as unfair competition from other industrialized countries.

The rise of protectionism led observers to predict a series of brushfire trade wars, such as when Britain established quotas limiting imports of U.S. nylon and polyester yarns, France embargoed lamb from Britain, U.S. steel corporations charged European governments with dumping subsidized steel on U.S. markets and U.S. automakers demanded restrictions on imports of Japanese cars.

An even more insidious form of protectionism is in effect in agriculture, where the United States and the EU have farm policies designed to boost and sustain artificially high prices of food and agricultural commodities without reference to actual production costs.

The barriers to trade are for the most part not generalized tariff increases but sector-specific quotas negotiated bilaterally outside the GATT framework.

Voluntary export restraints are another variety of the new protectionism. They are informal agreements reached by private suppliers rather than by governments, voluntary in name only because there are implicit threats and alternative official sanctions lurking in the background. There are also hidden barriers to trade stemming from variations in customs, laws and government support to local business. Japan, in particular, has been cited for an interpenetration of government and business that has effectively closed its markets to foreigners. Examples of these barriers include exclusive marketing organizations and dealerships, domestic procurement and subsidies, and laws regulating banking and insurance excluding competition from abroad. Other barriers include trigger pricing to establish a minimum import price, countervailing duties to offset foreign export subsidies and antidumping duties. A recent study has suggested that more than 20% of all categories of manufactured imports into the United States were subject to these restrictions.

Because the U.S. economy is the bellwether of the global economy, the course of protectionism is dependent on the wisdom and moderation of U.S. trade policy makers. Although adherents of trade liberalism in the United States are more embattled than ever before, it is encouraging that they still dominate official thinking. There are a few other hopeful signs. The framework of codes negotiated at the "Tokyo Round" will help bring several nontariff barriers under international control. In addition, the Generalized System of Tariff Preferences (GSTP) has reduced trade barriers on many developing country exports.

80. EXPORTS AS PERCENTAGE OF GDP

In a global economy, the economic strength of nations is directly proportional to export-driven trade. Exports may be of primary commodities, as in the case of most developing countries, manufactured commodities, as in the case of most industrialized countries, or in services and invisibles, such as banking and tourism, as in the case of very advanced nations. The mere fact that exports form a larger than average percentage of GDP does not provide a reliable guide to economic health, especially in the case of developing countries where such exports may be at the expense of domestic consumption.

Rank	Country	Exports as Percentage of GDP	Rank	Country	Exports as Percentage of GDP	Rank	Country	Exports as Percentage of GDP
TOP 10			50	Saudi Arabia	40	100	Italy	23
1	Singapore	177	51	Trinidad and Tobago	40	101	Mozambique	23
2	Bahrain	107	52	Armenia	39	102	Vietnam	23
3	Malta	94	53	Thailand	39	103	Central African Republic	22
4	Malaysia	90	54	Zimbabwe	39	104	Egypt	22
5	Luxembourg	86	55	Austria	38	105	Germany	22
6	Guyana	77	56	Kenya	38	106	Greece	22
7	Latvia	72	57	Belize	37	107	Madagascar	22
8	Djibouti	71	58	Georgia	37	108	Mali	22
9	Lithuania	71	59	Panama	37	109	Nigeria	22
10	Slovakia	71	60	Senegal	36	110	United Kingdom	22
			61	Switzerland	36	111	Laos	21
UPPER MIDDLE			62	Bhutan	35	112	Morocco	21
11	Estonia	70	63	Philippines	35	113	Tonga	21
12	Swaziland	70	64	Denmark	34	114	Turkey	21
13	Belgium	69	65	Kyrgyzstan	34	115	Guinea	20
14	Ireland	68				116	Ukraine	20
15	United Arab Emirates	68	**LOWER MIDDLE**			117	Australia	19
16	St. Lucia	66	66	Sri Lanka	34	118	Guatemala	19
17	Seychelles	65	67	Finland	33	119	Guinea-Bissau	19
18	Gabon	62	68	Iceland	33	120	Spain	19
19	Botswana	61	69	Sweden	33	121	Comoros	18
20	Mauritius	61	70	Togo	32	122	Nauru	18
21	Jamaica	58	71	Israel	31	123	Uruguay	18
22	Slovenia	58	72	New Zealand	31	124	Bolivia	17
23	Czech Republic	57	73	Tanzania	31	125	Colombia	17
24	Fiji	57	74	Western Samoa	31	126	Sierra Leone	17
25	Mongolia	56	75	Canada	30	127	Cape Verde	16
26	Azerbaijan	55	76	Iran	30	128	Pakistan	16
27	Equatorial Guinea	55	77	Cameroon	29	129	Lesotho	15
28	Kuwait	55	78	Hungary	29	130	Burundi	13
29	Bulgaria	54	79	Malawi	29	131	Chad	13
30	Gambia	54	80	Venezuela	29	132	El Salvador	13
31	Namibia	53	81	Chile	28	133	Mexico	13
32	Papua New Guinea	53	82	Kazakhstan	28	134	Niger	13
33	Netherlands	51	83	Korea, South	28	135	Albania	12
34	Grenada	50	84	Benin	27	136	Bangladesh	12
35	Barbados	49	85	Paraguay	27	137	Burkina	12
36	Jordan	49	86	Russia	27			
37	Cote d'Ivoire	47	87	China	26	**BOTTOM 10**		
38	Cyprus	47	88	Ecuador	26	138	India	12
39	Dominica	47	89	Portugal	26	139	Ethiopia	11
40	Belarus	46	90	Romania	26	140	Lebanon	10
41	Croatia	45	91	Ghana	25	141	United States	10
42	Tunisia	45	92	Indonesia	25	142	Japan	9
43	Congo	44	93	Dominican Republic	24	143	Peru	9
44	Mauritania	43	94	Nicaragua	24	144	Uganda	8
45	Norway	43	95	Poland	24	145	Argentina	7
46	Sao Tome e Principe	43	96	South Africa	24	146	Brazil	7
47	Honduras	41	97	Zambia	24	147	Rwanda	7
48	Macedonia	41	98	Algeria	23	148	Haiti	4
49	Costa Rica	40	99	France	23	149	Myanmar (Burma)	2

Source: *United Nations Statistical Yearbook*

81. TERMS OF TRADE

Terms of trade indicates change in the level of export prices expressed as a percentage of import price. It is calculated by dividing export prices by import prices × 100. A country's ranking on this scale shows the profitability of its international trade if it were conducted under barter arrangements. The unit values of the index are derived from the *Handbook of International Trade & Development Statistics* compiled by the United Nations Conference on Trade and Development (UNCTAD).

Rank	Country	Terms of Trade (1987 = 100)	Rank	Country	Terms of Trade (1987 = 100)	Rank	Country	Terms of Trade (1987 = 100)
TOP 10			34	China	101	68	Guatemala	93
1	Botswana	152	35	Greece	101	69	Venezuela	93
2	Benin	133	36	Netherlands	101	70	Guinea-Bissau	92
3	Dominican Republic	130	37	United States	101	71	Trinidad and Tobago	92
4	Mozambique	122	38	Belgium	100	72	Central African Republic	91
5	Japan	119	39	Germany	100	73	Finland	91
6	Philippines	117	40	Korea, South	100	74	Papua New Guinea	91
7	Argentina	116				75	Ecuador	90
8	Mauritania	115	**LOWER MIDDLE**			76	Indonesia	90
9	Morocco	114	41	Pakistan	100	77	Peru	90
10	Spain	114	42	Tunisia	100	78	Zimbabwe	89
			43	Egypt	99	79	El Salvador	88
UPPER MIDDLE			44	Israel	99	80	Yemen	88
11	Uruguay	114	45	Malaysia	99	81	Panama	87
12	Paraguay	112	46	Mexico	99	82	Kuwait	86
13	Myanmar (Burma)	111	47	Nigeria	99	83	Malawi	86
14	Romania	111	48	Australia	98	84	Sri Lanka	86
15	Jamaica	109	49	Congo	98	85	Tanzania	85
16	New Zealand	109	50	Saudi Arabia	98	86	Guinea	84
17	Turkey	109	51	United Arab Emirates	98	87	Oman	84
18	Mauritius	108	52	Zambia	98	88	Kenya	81
19	Burkina	106	53	Brazil	97	89	Cote d'Ivoire	79
20	Gabon	106	54	Canada	97	90	Cameroon	77
21	Senegal	106	55	Norway	97			
22	United Kingdom	106	56	Togo	97	**BOTTOM 10**		
23	Niger	105	57	India	96	91	Sierra Leone	76
24	South Africa	105	58	Iran	96	92	Honduras	73
25	Chile	104	59	Algeria	95	93	Rwanda	73
26	Denmark	104	60	Gambia	95	94	Colombia	68
27	Italy	104	61	Ireland	95	95	Madagascar	68
28	Portugal	104	62	Poland	95	96	Ethiopia	67
29	France	103	63	Bangladesh	94	97	Ghana	65
30	Sweden	103	64	Costa Rica	94	98	Burundi	52
31	Thailand	103	65	Nicaragua	94	99	Uganda	49
32	Mali	102	66	Singapore	94	100	Bolivia	18
33	Chad	101	67	Austria	93			

Source: UNCTAD

82. IMPORTS PER CAPITA

Imports measure two factors: the success of import-substitution efforts and the degree of economic self-dependence. Both goals can be pursued only to a limited degree without affecting development efforts adversely. Most nations that impose import controls and high tariffs also classify imports into various classes ranging from essential to prohibited. Others permit imports only through state agencies or through a rigorous system of licenses. The efficiency of such controls and licensing varies from country to country. In many countries they only tend to encourage smuggling, an activity which is not reflected in the statistics presented below.

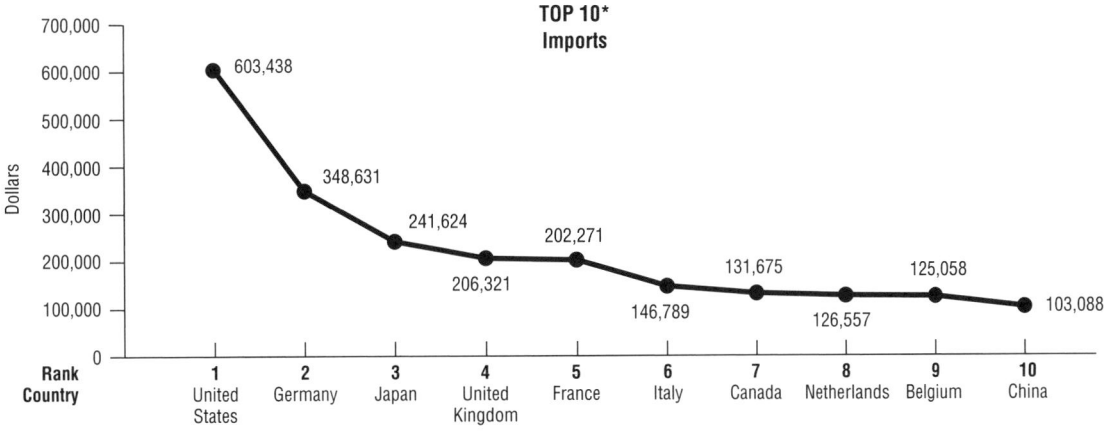

TOP 10*
Imports

Dollars

| 700,000 |
| 600,000 | 603,438 |
| 500,000 |
| 400,000 | 348,631 |
| 300,000 |
| 200,000 | 241,624 | 206,321 | 202,271 | 146,789 | 131,675 | 126,557 | 125,058 | 103,088 |
| 100,000 |
| 0 |

Rank 1 2 3 4 5 6 7 8 9 10
Country United States, Germany, Japan, United Kingdom, France, Italy, Canada, Netherlands, Belgium, China

*The Top 10 makes up 66% of the trade imports.

Rank	Country	Imports per Capita ($)	Rank	Country	Imports per Capita ($)	Rank	Country	Imports per Capita ($)
UPPER MIDDLE			50	Kuwait	7,036	88	Mozambique	955
11	Singapore	85,234	51	Morocco	6,760	89	Lesotho	933
12	Korea, South	83,800	52	Slovenia	6,498	90	Nepal	880
13	Spain	78,626	53	Romania	6,404	91	Zambia	870
14	Switzerland	56,716	54	Slovakia	6,345	92	Gabon	835
15	Mexico	50,147	55	Tunisia	6,214	93	Myanmar (Burma)	814
16	Austria	48,578	56	Ukraine	4,700	94	Ethiopia	787
17	Thailand	46,058	57	Bulgaria	4,239	95	Belarus	777
18	Malaysia	45,657				96	Turkmenistan	749
19	Sweden	42,681	**LOWER MIDDLE**			97	Nicaragua	727
20	Australia	42,259	58	Sri Lanka	4,227	98	Mauritania	670
21	Russia	33,100	59	Oman	4,114	99	Burkina	642
22	Iran	30,662	60	Bangladesh	4,001	100	Estonia	618
23	Denmark	29,521	61	Jordan	3,539	101	Guinea	600
24	Turkey	29,174	62	Peru	3,389	102	Malawi	546
25	Saudi Arabia	28,198	63	Costa Rica	2,907	103	Congo	541
26	Indonesia	28,086	64	Guatemala	2,599	104	Uganda	516
27	Brazil	25,439	65	Ecuador	2,562	105	Lithuania	486
28	Portugal	24,598	66	Yemen	2,400	106	Mali	477
29	Norway	23,956	67	Botswana	2,390	107	Georgia	460
30	India	22,761	68	Uruguay	2,300	108	Madagascar	452
31	Israel	22,621	69	Panama	2,188	109	Togo	418
32	Ireland	21,386	70	Dominican Republic	2,125	110	Tajikistan	374
33	Greece	20,542	71	Jamaica	2,097	111	Benin	360
34	United Arab Emirates	19,520	72	El Salvador	1,919	112	Laos	353
35	Poland	18,834	73	Ghana	1,728	113	Latvia	339
36	South Africa	18,591	74	Mauritius	1,715	114	Niger	331
37	Finland	18,032	75	Kenya	1,711	115	Chad	300
38	Argentina	16,784	76	Paraguay	1,689			
39	Czech Republic	13,487	77	Cote d'Ivoire	1,663	**BOTTOM 10**		
40	Hungary	12,597	78	Tanzania	1,523	116	Rwanda	288
41	Venezuela	10,979	79	Zimbabwe	1,500	117	Azerbaijan	241
42	Chile	10,596	80	Trinidad and Tobago	1,448	118	Gambia	234
43	Colombia	9,841	81	Papua New Guinea	1,299	119	Burundi	212
44	New Zealand	9,636	82	Uzbekistan	1,280	120	Moldova	210
45	Pakistan	9,500	83	Kazakhstan	1,269	121	Armenia	188
46	Phillipines	8,757	84	Senegal	1,262	122	Central African Republic	165
47	Nigeria	8,276	85	Bolivia	1,206	123	Sierra Leone	147
48	Egypt	8,175	86	Cameroon	1,108	124	Kyrgyzstan	112
49	Algeria	7,770	87	Honduras	1,059	125	Guinea-Bissau	62

Source: *United Nations Statistical Yearbook*

83. EXPORTS PER CAPITA

Export or perish is the catch phrase that describes the mercantile strategy of most nations of the world. Suc- cess in this strategy is best measured in terms of exports per capita.

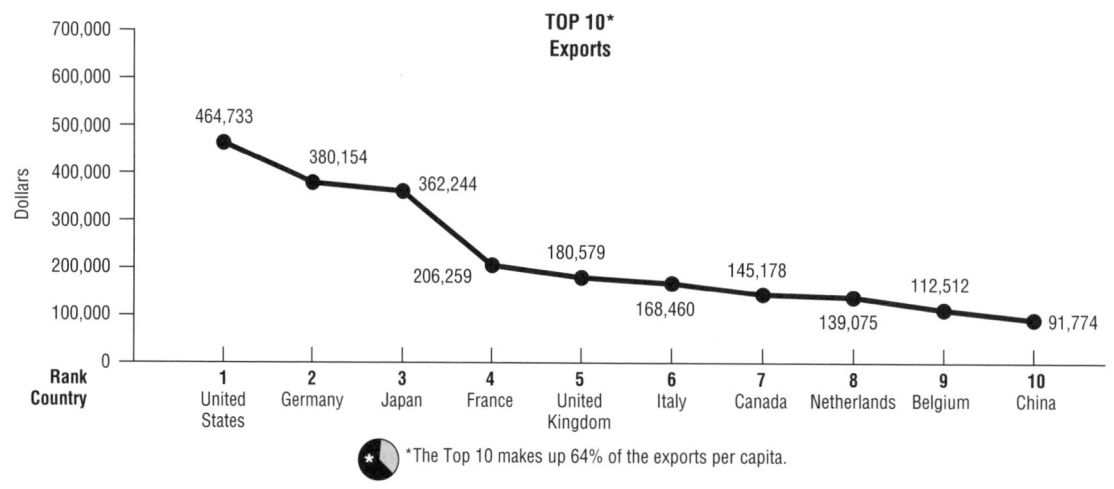

TOP 10* Exports

Rank Country	Dollars
1 United States	464,733
2 Germany	380,154
3 Japan	362,244
4 France	206,259
5 United Kingdom	180,579
6 Italy	168,460
7 Canada	145,178
8 Netherlands	139,075
9 Belgium	112,512
10 China	91,774

*The Top 10 makes up 64% of the exports per capita.

Rank	Country	Exports per Capita ($)	Rank	Country	Exports per Capita ($)	Rank	Country	Exports per Capita ($)
UPPER MIDDLE			51	Ukraine	6,300	90	Tajikistan	663
11	Taiwan	84,678	52	Slovenia	6,088	91	Yemen	650
12	Korea, South	82,236	53	Slovakia	5,451	92	Myanmar (Burma)	583
13	Singapore	74,012	54	Oman	5,428	93	Dominican Republic	555
14	Spain	62,872	55	Romania	4,892	94	El Salvador	555
15	Switzerland	61,403	56	Bulgaria	4,071	95	Panama	553
16	Sweden	49,857	57	Morocco	3,991	96	Estonia	461
17	Malaysia	47,122	58	Tunisia	3,802	97	Latvia	460
18	Russia	43,900				98	Mauritania	450
19	Australia	42,723	**LOWER MIDDLE**			99	Guinea	440
20	Saudi Arabia	40,858	59	Peru	3,463	100	Tanzania	420
21	Austria	40,174	60	Ecuador	2,904	101	Nepal	390
22	Brazil	38,597	61	Sri Lanka	2,896	102	Azerbaijan	351
23	Thailand	36,800	62	Cote d'Ivoire	2,880	103	Mali	342
24	Denmark	35,914	63	Gabon	2,297	104	Togo	322
25	Indonesia	33,612	64	Bangladesh	2,272	105	Malawi	320
26	Norway	31,853	65	Egypt	2,244	106	Niger	283
27	Mexico	30,241	66	Costa Rica	1,999	107	Madagascar	267
28	Ireland	28,611	67	Cameroon	1,815	108	Nicaragua	266
29	Finland	23,446	68	Papua New Guinea	1,790	109	Georgia	222
30	South Africa	22,873	69	Botswana	1,725	110	Ethiopia	199
31	India	21,553	70	Uruguay	1,645	111	Uganda	179
32	United Arab Emirates	20,500	71	Trinidad and Tobago	1,612	112	Chad	176
33	Iran	16,700	72	Kazakhstan	1,529	113	Moldova	174
34	Portugal	15,429	73	Uzbekistan	1,466	114	Burkina	145
35	Turkey	15,343	74	Kenya	1,374	115	Mozambique	132
36	Israel	14,779	75	Guatemala	1,340	116	Central African Republic	124
37	Poland	13,997	76	Mauritius	1,299			
38	Venezuela	13,239	77	Jordan	1,232	**BOTTOM 10**		
39	Argentina	13,118	78	Zimbabwe	1,180	117	Sierra Leone	118
40	Czech Republic	12,929	79	Zambia	1,168	118	Benin	115
41	Nigeria	11,886	80	Turkmenistan	1,156	119	Kyrgyzstan	112
42	Philippines	11,089	81	Congo	1,116	120	Lesotho	109
43	New Zealand	10,537	82	Ghana	1,051	121	Gambia	80
44	Kuwait	10,248	83	Jamaica	1,047	122	Laos	80
45	Algeria	10,230	84	Honduras	814	123	Burundi	68
46	Chile	9,328	85	Senegal	740	124	Rwanda	68
47	Hungary	8,886	86	Belarus	737	125	Armenia	29
48	Greece	7,960	87	Bolivia	728	126	Guinea-Bissau	16
49	Colombia	7,052	88	Lithuania	696			
50	Pakistan	6,636	89	Paraguay	695			

Source: *United Nations Statistical Yearbook*

EXPORTS AND IMPORTS

The following two tables are among the most important in international economics. Merchandise exports and imports determine trade balances and also provide a clue to the economic health of nations. Exports are generally f.o.b. and imports are c.i.f., but there are exceptions. The World Trade Organization and the International Monetary Fund keep tab on the export and import figures, the former to ensure that the trade is conducted according to the many agreements that govern the trade relations of nations and the latter to monitor the international reserves that are affected by the extent and volume of trade. Ideally, the total global exports and total global imports should tally, but in all the years that records have been kept they have not done so. In fact, one of the great mysteries of international trade is that a substantial part of trade goes unreported and unaccounted for. Part of the reason may be poor accounting procedures, and part of it may be simply old fashioned smuggling.

84. EXPORTS

Rank	Country	Exports (million $)	Rank	Country	Exports (million $)	Rank	Country	Exports (million $)
TOP 10			47	Libya	11,211.7	94	Azerbaijan	1,449.8
1	United States	512,337.0	48	Algeria	11,136.8	95	Liechtenstein	1,371.8
2	Germany	423,994.8	49	Hungary	10,700.8	96	Kenya	1,361.7
3	Japan	395,600.0	50	Greece	8,783.7	97	Malta	1,355.4
4	France	234,352.8	51	Ukraine	8,044.7	98	Zambia	1,350.2
5	United Kingdom	205,020.7	52	Colombia	7,454.9	99	Estonia	1,305.9
6	Italy	178,937.3	53	Pakistan	7,370.2	100	Guatemala	1,295.3
7	Canada	165,836.8	54	Iraq	6,659.0	101	Jordan	1,255.7
8	Netherlands	145,825.3	55	Slovenia	6,082.9	102	Zimbabwe	1,248.9
9	China	121,006.3	56	Luxembourg	5,942.4	103	Namibia	1,244.4
10	Belgium	120,686.6	57	Slovakia	5,450.9	104	Ghana	1,072.3
			58	Cuba	5,392.0	105	Macedonia	1,055.3
UPPER MIDDLE			59	Oman	5,299.0	106	Jamaica	1,052.8
11	Singapore	96,375.9	60	Romania	4,892.2	107	Latvia	989.7
12	Taiwan	92,819.8	61	Yugoslavia	4,704.1	108	Congo	977.7
13	Korea, South	82,232.2	62	Morocco	4,033.9	109	Moldova	968.0
14	Spain	75,031.4	63	Croatia	3,903.8	110	Cyprus	961.2
15	Switzerland	68,903.5	64	Tunisia	3,804.5	111	Zaire	853.0
16	Mexico	61,964.3	65	Bahrain	3,710.1	112	Lebanon	825.0
17	Sweden	61,359.6	66	Belarus	3,558.8	113	Bolivia	808.9
18	Russia	54,230.0	67	Peru	3,496.5	114	Paraguay	725.2
19	Australia	47,548.1	68	Kazakhstan	3,449.0	115	El Salvador	716.3
20	Malaysia	47,099.0	69	Angola	3,409.7	116	Guinea	671.2
21	Saudi Arabia	45,630.0	70	Bulgaria	3,369.9	117	Dominican Republic	658.3
22	Austria	44,070.9	71	Qatar	3,245.4	118	Senegal	652.2
23	Indonesia	40,053.4	72	Sri Lanka	3,210.1	119	Swaziland	566.2
24	Denmark	39,834.6	73	Egypt	3,110.0	120	Fiji	544.5
25	Brazil	38,700.9	74	Syria	3,093.1	121	Honduras	515.7
26	Thailand	37,166.9	75	Ecuador	3,020.0	122	Panama	507.6
27	Norway	34,814.2	76	Cote d'Ivoire	2,931.2	123	Yemen	474.4
28	Ireland	28,881.9	77	Cameroon	2,892.5	124	Suriname	472.6
29	Finland	25,457.9	78	Bahamas	2,592.6	125	Myanmar (Burma)	464.3
30	United Arab Emirates	24,436.0	79	Brunei	2,466.5	126	Mauritania	451.4
31	South Africa	24,353.7	80	Gabon	2,463.8	127	Tajikistan	426.7
32	India	22,236.9	81	Turkmenistan	2,149.0	128	Tanzania	416.1
33	Kuwait	19,536.5	82	Bangladesh	2,137.6	129	Liberia	396.3
34	Israel	16,884.0	83	Vietnam	2,087.0	130	Nepal	354.6
35	Portugal	15,417.4	84	Lithuania	2,028.8	131	Mongolia	349.0
36	Turkey	15,348.9				132	Mali	330.3
37	Venezuela	15,208.1	**LOWER MIDDLE**			133	Sudan	319.3
38	Iran	14,619.0	85	Papua New Guinea	1,931.1	134	Madagascar	291.7
39	Poland	14,142.5	86	Uruguay	1,918.2	135	Kyrgyzstan	285.0
40	Puerto Rico	13,952.8	87	Botswana	1,853.5	136	Nicaragua	267.5
41	Argentina	13,090.5	88	Costa Rica	1,833.7	137	Albania	267.4
42	Czech Republic	12,770.6	89	Korea, North	1,703.0	138	Malawi	266.9
43	Nigeria	12,265.0	90	Trinidad and Tobago	1,662.1	139	Guyana	265.9
44	New Zealand	12,185.5	91	Iceland	1,626.7	140	Niger	262.6
45	Philippines	11,374.8	92	Uzbekistan	1,497.0	141	Togo	253.2
46	Chile	11,368.7	93	Mauritius	1,467.1	142	Afghanistan	235.1

Rank	Country	Exports (million $)	Rank	Country	Exports (million $)	Rank	Country	Exports (million $)
143	Cambodia	219.1	159	Solomon Islands	102.9	175	Cape Verde	28.6
144	Laos	203.1	160	Benin	97.5	176	St. Kitts and Nevis	27.7
145	Chad	193.9	161	Somalia	81.0	177	Vanuatu	23.6
146	Ethiopia	188.6	162	St. Vincent	78.1	178	Comoros	21.9
147	Barbados	181.0	163	Haiti	77.7			
148	Uganda	171.4	164	Burundi	74.7	**BOTTOM 10**		
149	Mozambique	162.0	165	Bosnia & Herzegovina	70.3	179	Grenada	20.1
150	Burkina	151.1	166	Bhutan	68.1	180	Antigua and Barbuda	19.4
151	Central African Republic	140.3	167	Gambia	63.7	181	Guinea-Bissau	19.3
152	Rwanda	131.9	168	Equatorial Guinea	61.7	182	Eritrea	17.4
153	Belize	126.6	169	Dominica	54.2	183	Djibouti	17.3
154	Georgia	121.0	170	Seychelles	51.6	184	Tonga	12.8
155	St. Lucia	119.7	171	Andorra	41.1	185	Western Samoa	7.6
156	Sierra Leone	115.8	172	Bermuda	35.3	186	Sao Tome e Principe	5.0
157	Lesotho	109.1	173	Maldives	34.4	187	Kiribati	4.7
158	Armenia	108.0	174	Nauru	28.9	188	Tuvalu	0.2

Source: *World Development Report*

85. IMPORTS

Rank	Country	Imports (million $)
TOP 10		
1	United States	689,030.0
2	Germany	377,992.3
3	Japan	274,742.0
4	France	229,334.2
5	United Kingdom	227,228.6
6	Italy	156,958.7
7	Canada	147,851.0
8	Netherlands	130,511.7
9	China	115,613.6
10	Belgium	111,063.8
UPPER MIDDLE		
11	Singapore	102,286.7
12	Spain	92,057.9
13	Taiwan	85,474.3
14	Korea, South	83,794.0
15	Mexico	80,170.3
16	Switzerland	66,653.1
17	Austria	55,058.5
18	Australia	53,425.0
19	Sweden	51,778.3
20	Thailand	46,239.3
21	Russia	45,840.0
22	Malaysia	45,610.0
23	Denmark	33,937.2
24	Indonesia	31,983.5
25	Turkey	29,429.3
26	Brazil	27,712.3
27	Norway	27,357.4
28	Portugal	24,244.3
29	Israel	24,242.0
30	Saudi Arabia	23,343.5
31	India	23,304.1
32	Finland	23,017.6
33	Greece	22,802.6
34	Ireland	21,677.4
35	South Africa	20,042.6
36	Iran	18,869.3
37	Poland	18,783.2
38	Philippines	18,772.7
39	Argentina	16,772.9
40	Hungary	14,553.7
41	United Arab Emirates	13,921.2
42	Czech Republic	12,566.8
43	New Zealand	11,901.4
44	Puerto Rico	11,859.1
45	Venezuela	11,266.6
46	Chile	11,149.1
47	Colombia	9,840.8
48	Nigeria	9,031.0
49	Pakistan	8,897.0
50	Algeria	8,647.8
51	Egypt	8,187.8
52	Cuba	8,122.1
53	Luxembourg	7,545.0
54	Morocco	7,194.0
55	Ukraine	7,098.9
56	Kuwait	7,042.1
57	Slovakia	6,655.0
58	Iraq	6,525.5
59	Romania	6,521.7
60	Slovenia	6,500.9
61	Tunisia	6,214.2
62	Yugoslavia	5,548.6

Rank	Country	Imports (million $)
63	Libya	5,357.5
64	Lebanon	5,039.0
65	Peru	4,901.3
66	Croatia	4,666.4
67	Sri Lanka	4,483.6
68	Bulgaria	4,233.3
69	Oman	4,114.0
70	Kazakhstan	4,107.0
71	Bahrain	3,858.0
72	Jordan	3,560.7
73	Belarus	3,499.0
74	Syria	3,490.3
75	Cyprus	3,014.1
76	Bahamas	2,919.9
77	Costa Rica	2,789.1
78	Bangladesh	2,708.8
79	Uruguay	2,707.2
80	Yemen	2,589.6
81	Ecuador	2,552.7
82	Guatemala	2,462.8
83	Jamaica	2,353.4
84	Vietnam	2,338.0
LOWER MIDDLE		
85	Cameroon	2,306.2
86	Zimbabwe	2,213.3
87	Panama	2,187.4
88	Cote d'Ivoire	2,185.3
89	Malta	2,173.4
90	Dominican Republic	1,988.1
91	Botswana	1,946.5
92	Mauritius	1,919.2
93	Qatar	1,890.7
94	El Salvador	1,858.3
95	Kenya	1,793.0
96	Uzbekistan	1,756.0
97	Jamaica	1,692.8
98	Paraguay	1,688.0
99	Estonia	1,660.4
100	Papua New Guinea	1,485.0
101	Iceland	1,472.4
102	Trinidad and Tobago	1,462.9
103	Ghana	1,412.3
104	Korea, North	1,407.0
105	Angola	1,347.0
106	Bolivia	1,249.6
107	Latvia	1,241.5
108	Zambia	1,237.7
109	Macedonia	1,199.4
110	Namibia	1,167.1
111	Andorra	1,136.8
112	Brunei	1,111.2
113	Senegal	1,097.0
114	Tanzania	1,021.5
115	Turkmenistan	1,009.0
116	Lesotho	977.0
117	Afghanistan	936.4
118	Azerbaijan	929.9
119	Moldova	905.0
120	Mozambique	899.0
121	Myanmar (Burma)	845.2
122	Fiji	830.5
123	Sudan	820.9
124	Gabon	772.0
125	Nicaragua	755.1

Rank	Country	Imports (million $)
126	Tajikistan	733.8
127	Zaire	711.0
128	Guinea	699.0
129	Nepal	696.0
130	Liechtenstein	678.6
131	Honduras	667.8
132	Swaziland	666.0
133	Mali	601.8
134	Congo	594.5
135	Bermuda	588.9
136	Barbados	574.0
137	Burkina	539.6
138	Uganda	524.4
139	Malawi	508.3
140	Mongolia	488.0
141	Mauritania	486.0
142	Suriname	472.0
143	Ethiopia	471.8
144	Albania	446.5
145	Togo	443.9
146	Bosnia & Herzegovina	422.2
147	Cambodia	403.9
148	Madagascar	402.5
149	Kyrgyzstan	396.0
150	Somalia	394.0
151	Niger	388.8
152	Armenia	310.0
153	Guyana	306.6
154	St. Lucia	300.3
155	Chad	296.6
156	Rwanda	291.1
157	Belize	280.9
158	Haiti	278.0
159	Liberia	272.3
160	Antigua and Barbuda	247.0
161	Seychelles	241.6
162	Gambia	234.2
163	Burundi	229.5
164	Georgia	216.0
165	Djibouti	214.4
166	Benin	207.3
167	Maldives	191.4
168	Central African Republic	159.1
169	Sierra Leone	149.9
170	Eritrea	138.5
171	Cape Verde	136.3
172	Solomon Islands	133.9
173	St. Vincent	132.1
174	Grenada	117.2
175	St. Kitts and Nevis	110.7
176	Dominica	109.6
177	Western Samoa	98.9
178	Guinea-Bissau	85.7
BOTTOM 10		
179	Vanuatu	81.8
180	Bhutan	78.1
181	Tonga	62.6
182	Equatorial Guinea	61.6
183	Comoros	59.4
184	Laos	353.0
185	Kiribati	36.7
186	Sao Tome e Principe	28.1
187	Nauru	17.8
188	Tuvalu	4.8

Source: *World Development Report*

DOMESTIC TRADE

Less attention is focused on domestic trade than on international trade, yet domestic trade is critical for meeting consumer needs for essential goods. Although the channels of mass merchandising have changed in the past few decades, every country has two subsectors of domestic trade: wholesale and retail. The distinction between them is fluid, and the end retailer may be part of a large chain handling wholesale merchandise. However, domestic trade is statistically well served because governments keep close watch on the sector as one of the best sources of sales tax revenues.

86. DOMESTIC TRADE AS PERCENTAGE OF GDP

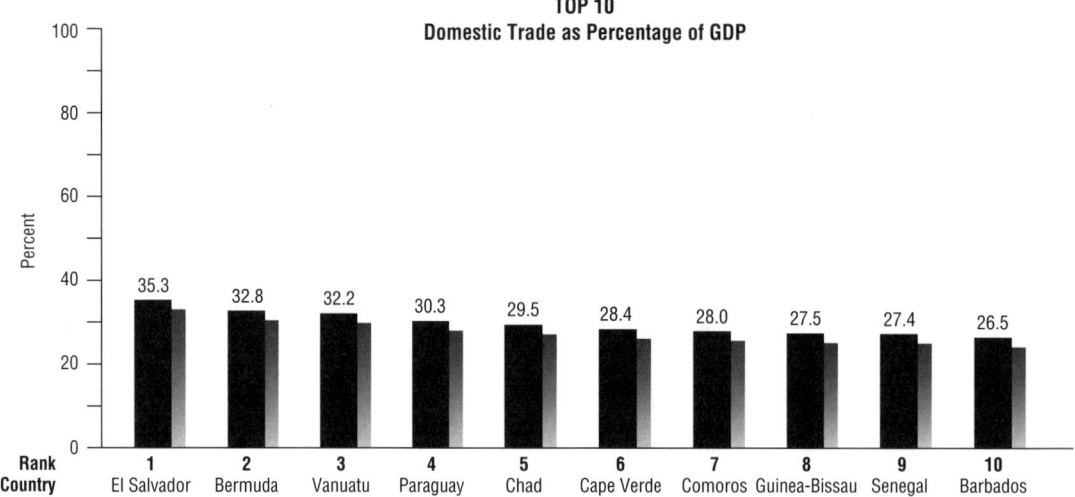

TOP 10
Domestic Trade as Percentage of GDP

Rank	1	2	3	4	5	6	7	8	9	10
Country	El Salvador	Bermuda	Vanuatu	Paraguay	Chad	Cape Verde	Comoros	Guinea-Bissau	Senegal	Barbados
Percent	35.3	32.8	32.2	30.3	29.5	28.4	28.0	27.5	27.4	26.5

Rank	Country	Domestic Trade as Percentage of GDP	Rank	Country	Domestic Trade as Percentage of GDP	Rank	Country	Domestic Trade as Percentage of GDP
UPPER MIDDLE			70	United States	15.8	128	Ireland	11.2
11	Antigua and Barbuda	25.6	71	Chile	15.6	129	Colombia	11.0
12	Mexico	25.6	72	Iraq	15.6	130	Honduras	11.0
13	Tunisia	24.7	73	Mali	15.5	131	Malawi	11.0
14	St. Lucia	24.6	74	Trinidad and Tobago	15.5	132	Norway	11.0
15	Andorra	24.2	75	Argentina	15.4	133	Madagascar	10.9
16	Guatemala	24.0	76	Burkina	15.3	134	Sweden	10.9
17	Guinea	23.8	77	Botswana	15.2	135	Zambia	10.9
18	Jamaica	23.7	78	Dominican Republic	15.2	136	Bahrain	10.6
19	Central African Republic	23.5	79	Russia	15.1	137	Bulgaria	10.5
20	Suriname	23.5	80	France	15.0	138	Western Samoa	10.3
21	Bahamas	23.0	81	Tuvalu	14.9	139	Ethiopia	10.2
22	Syria	22.8	82	Puerto Rico	14.7	140	United Arab Emirates	10.2
23	Vietnam	22.8	83	Tanzania	14.6	141	Bolivia	10.1
24	Myanmar (Burma)	22.5	84	Estonia	14.5	142	Sao Tome e Principe	10.0
25	Yugoslavia	22.5	85	Pakistan	14.5	143	Gabon	9.6
26	St. Kitts and Nevis	22.4	86	Denmark	14.4	144	Papua New Guinea	9.6
27	Mongolia	21.7				145	Solomon Islands	9.6
28	Costa Rica	21.3	**LOWER MIDDLE**			146	Israel	9.4
29	Morocco	20.9	87	Poland	14.4	147	Moldova	9.4
30	Ecuador	20.8	88	Malta	14.3	148	Jordan	9.3
31	Grenada	20.6	89	Venezuela	14.3	149	Somalia	9.3
32	Spain	20.5	90	Belgium	14.1	150	Burundi	9.1
33	Sri Lanka	20.4	91	Kenya	14.1	151	Slovakia	8.9
34	Croatia	20.2	92	Kiribati	14.1	152	Libya	8.8
35	Cuba	20.1	93	Slovenia	14.1	153	Swaziland	8.7
36	Sierra Leone	20.0	94	United Kingdom	14.1	154	Romania	8.5
37	Macedonia	19.8	95	Japan	14.0	155	Zimbabwe	8.3
38	Benin	19.5	96	Bosnia & Herzegovina	13.9	156	Bangladesh	8.1
39	Gambia	19.5	97	Oman	13.9	157	Germany	8.1
40	Cyprus	19.3	98	Iceland	13.7	158	Afghanistan	7.9
41	Mauritania	19.1	99	Philippines	13.7	159	Lebanon	7.7
42	Fiji	19.0	100	South Africa	13.7	160	Lesotho	7.7
43	Nicaragua	18.5	101	Dominica	13.6	161	Bhutan	7.6
44	Egypt	18.4	102	Latvia	13.6	162	Laos	7.2
45	Italy	18.4	103	Lithuania	13.5	163	Equatorial Guinea	7.1
46	Turkey	18.3	104	Niger	13.2	164	Saudi Arabia	6.9
47	Switzerland	18.0	105	St. Vincent	13.2	165	Brazil	6.8
48	Maldives	17.9	106	Greece	13.1	166	Qatar	6.7
49	Singapore	17.9	107	Nigeria	13.1	167	Hungary	6.6
50	Belize	17.7	108	Uruguay	13.0	168	Belarus	6.5
51	Algeria	17.6	109	Yemen	13.0	169	Uzbekistan	6.5
52	Zaire	17.5	110	Cote d'Ivoire	12.9	170	Angola	6.1
53	Australia	17.4	111	Czech Republic	12.9	171	Nepal	6.0
54	Mauritius	17.4	112	Sudan	12.8	172	China	5.9
55	Portugal	17.4	113	India	12.7	173	Armenia	5.7
56	Togo	17.4	114	Korea, South	12.7			
57	Iran	17.1	115	Tonga	12.6	**BOTTOM 10**		
58	Rwanda	17.1	116	Peru	12.4	174	Ukraine	5.7
59	Tajikistan	17.0	117	Brunei	12.3	175	Kuwait	5.5
60	Thailand	17.0	118	Congo	12.3	176	Liberia	5.3
61	Cambodia	16.8	119	Malaysia	12.3	177	Guyana	4.9
62	Indonesia	16.6	120	Uganda	12.3	178	Mozambique	4.9
63	Taiwan	16.5	121	Finland	12.2	179	Albania	4.6
64	Austria	16.4	122	Canada	12.1	180	Georgia	3.3
65	Luxembourg	16.4	123	Panama	11.8	181	Kyrgyzstan	3.0
66	New Zealand	16.4	124	Cameroon	11.7	182	Azerbaijan	2.2
67	Djibouti	16.3	125	Namibia	11.5	183	Kazakhstan	1.4
68	Haiti	16.2	126	Ghana	11.3			
69	Netherlands	16.2	127	Seychelles	11.3			

Source: *World Data*

87. RETAIL TRADE ESTABLISHMENTS

Rank	Country	Retail Trade Establishments	Rank	Country	Retail Trade Establishments	Rank	Country	Retail Trade Establishments
TOP 10			44	Kazakhstan	42,168	88	Barbados	1,911
1	India	3,132,000	45	Bulgaria	41,339	89	Iceland	1,680
2	Japan	1,591,186	46	Denmark	40,733	90	Botswana	1,660
3	United States	1,547,000	47	Norway	40,154	91	Zambia	1,636
4	Korea, South	1,147,734	48	Finland	37,303	92	Tanzania	1,620
5	Italy	1,033,725	49	Jordan	34,086	93	Madagascar	1,570
6	Poland	785,000	50	Austria	33,601	94	Ghana	1,500
7	Mexico	713,315	51	Ireland	31,699	95	El Salvador	1,416
8	Spain	710,865	52	New Zealand	29,961	96	Sri Lanka	1,348
9	Brazil	680,634	53	Angola	29,138	97	Cameroon	1,312
10	Iran	634,084	54	Libya	26,825	98	Namibia	1,248
						99	Fiji	1,188
UPPER MIDDLE			**LOWER MIDDLE**			100	San Marino	1,126
11	Argentina	500,342	55	Oman	25,840	101	Chad	1,125
12	Turkey	445,365	56	Vietnam	25,723	102	China	1,110
13	France	363,701	57	Belarus	22,300	103	Brunei	833
14	Taiwan	355,760	58	Nicaragua	20,610	104	Guinea-Bissau	685
15	Russia	319,500	59	Croatia	17,969	105	Swaziland	656
16	United Kingdom	318,751	60	Singapore	17,798	106	Haiti	653
17	Philippines	279,968	61	Laos	15,000	107	Andorra	592
18	Pakistan	276,701	62	Central African Republic	14,543	108	Ecuador	554
19	Bangladesh	271,000	63	Kuwait	14,521	109	Malawi	500
20	Thailand	260,030	64	United Arab Emirates	13,906	110	Djibouti	431
21	Australia	209,909	65	Suriname	13,000	111	Nigeria	421
22	Hungary	200,049	66	Albania	11,741	112	Solomon Islands	405
23	Greece	184,821	67	Dominican Republic	11,220	113	Trinidad and Tobago	370
24	Germany	147,974	68	Jamaica	10,150	114	Bermuda	310
25	Belgium	135,534	69	Costa Rica	9,713	115	Senegal	289
26	Iraq	108,460	70	Puerto Rico	9,164	116	Vanuatu	256
27	Peru	103,010	71	Cyprus	8,474	117	Bahrain	255
28	Malaysia	95,993	72	Panama	7,561	118	Uganda	251
29	Guatemala	88,200	73	Ethiopia	7,416	119	Liechtenstein	228
30	Romania	82,035	74	Latvia	7,214			
31	Netherlands	81,500	75	Slovenia	6,896	**BOTTOM 10**		
32	Saudi Arabia	80,266	76	Lithuania	6,425	120	Mauritius	207
33	Syria	75,865	77	Slovakia	5,590	121	Antigua and Barbuda	199
34	Chile	74,567	78	Qatar	4,956	122	Togo	181
35	Sweden	70,467	79	Portugal	4,889	123	Benin	170
36	Czech Republic	62,667	80	Mongolia	4,828	124	Guyana	147
37	South Africa	58,100	81	Kenya	4,316	125	Bahamas	132
38	Cuba	56,916	82	Morocco	4,000	126	Seychelles	131
39	Indonesia	54,632	83	Algeria	3,600	127	Mauritania	59
40	Switzerland	53,465	84	Luxembourg	3,438	128	Kiribati	30
41	Uruguay	52,954	85	Zaire	3,036	129	Malta	4
42	Yugoslavia	51,159	86	Egypt	2,545			
43	Israel	43,844	87	Cote d'Ivoire	2,023			

Source: *World Data*

88. RETAIL TRADE SALES

Rank	Country	Retail Trade Sales (million $)	Rank	Country	Retail Trade Sales (million $)	Rank	Country	Retail Trade Sales (million $)
TOP 10			50	Yugoslavia	8,958	100	Iceland	825
1	United States	2,081,600	51	Colombia	8,600	101	Dominica	790
2	Japan	1,043,976	52	Peru	8,500	102	Nicaragua	790
3	Germany	404,296	53	Malaysia	8,200	103	Zambia	768
4	France	320,274	54	Cuba	8,124	104	Nepal	736
5	United Kingdom	242,802	55	Syria	7,330	105	Madagascar	696
6	China	235,910	56	Puerto Rico	7,206	106	Zimbabwe	693
7	Canada	150,200	57	Iraq	7,077	107	Papua New Guinea	669
8	Italy	122,978	58	United Arab Emirates	5,910	108	Senegal	664
9	India	108,300	59	Morocco	5,750	109	Laos	576
10	Australia	107,230	60	Bangladesh	5,500	110	Fiji	558
			61	Uruguay	5,397	111	Haiti	500
UPPER MIDDLE			62	Uganda	5,285	112	Chad	497
11	Korea, South	90,756	63	Philippines	4,836	113	El Salvador	485
12	Turkey	73,834				114	Costa Rica	475
13	Ukraine	70,800	**LOWER MIDDLE**			115	Bahamas	466
14	Netherlands	65,626	64	Luxembourg	4,603	116	Honduras	401
15	Sweden	59250	65	Vietnam	4,414	117	Rwanda	350
16	Spain	54,777	66	Slovenia	4,271	118	Ethiopia	273
17	Poland	53,382	67	Turkmenistan	4,150	119	Barbados	264
18	Austria	40432	68	Tanzania	3,975	120	Namibia	254
19	Mexico	39,810	69	Indonesia	3451	121	Ghana	252
20	Brazil	39,312	70	Zaire	3,300	122	Lithuania	236
21	Croatia	39,231	71	Sudan	3,278	123	Central African Republic	230
22	Iran	37,350	72	Portugal	3,057	124	Burundi	210
23	South Africa	35,592	73	Estonia	2981	125	Sierra Leone	177
24	Finland	35,052	74	Tunisia	2,814	126	Botswana	165
25	Bulgaria	34700	75	Paraguay	2,645	127	Mauritius	164
26	Denmark	32145	76	Oman	2,449	128	Benin	150
27	Norway	31264	77	Saudi Arabia	2,292	129	Kuwait	145
28	Egypt	29,700	78	Nigeria	2,202	130	Solomon Islands	139
29	Switzerland	23620	79	Yemen	2,195	131	Kyrgyzstan	138
30	Hungary	21,400	80	Myanmar (Burma)	2,116	132	Malawi	127
31	Czech Republic	21,235	81	Cote d'Ivoire	1,800	133	Bermuda	116
32	Belgium	20,957	82	Trinidad and Tobago	1,670	134	Liberia	115
33	Latvia	20,425	83	Lebanon	1,662	135	Togo	112
34	Romania	19,926	84	Bahrain	1,601	136	Suriname	110
35	Belarus	19,900	85	Albania	1,570	137	Mauritania	103
36	Russia	18,771	86	Bolivia	1,570			
37	Bosnia & Herzegovina	18,065	87	Dominican Republic	1,529	**BOTTOM 10**		
38	New Zealand	17,055	88	Jamaica	1,457	138	Ecuador	102
39	Algeria	16,200	89	Cameroon	1,430	139	Guyana	93
40	Taiwan	14,291	90	Chile	1,403	140	Guinea-Bissau	44
41	Thailand	13,683	91	Panama	1,334	141	Belize	33
42	Pakistan	12,848	92	Slovakia	1,313	142	Antigua and Barbuda	23
43	Venezuela	12,345	93	Mongolia	1,235	143	Swaziland	23
44	Greece	12,263	94	Guatemala	1,200	144	Grenada	6
45	Singapore	12,058	95	Sri Lanka	1,116	145	Maldives	5
46	Ireland	10,952	96	Cyprus	1,102	146	Kiribati	3.8
47	Israel	10,763	97	Qatar	1,048	147	Malta	2.3
48	Macedonia	9,238	98	Argentina	1,003			
49	Libya	9,205	99	Jordan	1,002			

Source: *World Data*

Section

X

AGRICULTURE

This is the largest section in the book because agriculture is a truly universal economic activity. (There are nations without any industries and without any mines but hardly any without farms and farmers.) Agriculture is also the world's largest economic sector in terms of employment, although its share of the GDP and its budgetary allocations have been declining in most countries of the world. Agricultural data are generally reliable because governments consider the collection of statistics relating to land one of their traditional and prime responsibilities.

Agriculture is characterized by many dichotomies: between modern and traditional, between rain-fed and irrigated, between subsistence and commercial, between owner-operated and rented, between large and small, and between mechanized and labor-intensive. In almost all countries, agriculture is the least efficient and least productive sector of the economy and the sector that receives the smallest share of investment capital and credit. In some countries, such as the United States, inefficiency is perpetuated by government intervention to maintain higher prices for farmers. It is conceded by agricultural experts that few countries of the world have reached their full agricultural potential; with proper land use, soil management, mechanization, use of improved seeds and application of fertilizers, present agricultural production rates can be quadrupled and decupled as was demonstrated by the Green Revolution.

Over 100 countries in the world have what are generally described as agricultural economies. In these countries agriculture employs the bulk of the labor force, contributes most of the GNP and accounts for the lion's share of production. Agricultural economies operate on three levels: a subsistence level consisting of small farms that provide little more than food for their owners; a more advanced level including truck farms that supply surplus crops for domestic markets, and an export level consisting of cash crops for exports. In most countries, the third level is dominated by estates and plantations; as a result of mechanization and scientific application of fertilizers, this sector is generally the most efficient and productive of the three.

Interestingly, agricultural production is or appears to be unrelated to the size of the country; few countries, except perhaps for the United States, have managed to achieve a commanding position in more than one or two crops. Farmers are universally conservative, sticking to their traditional crops, resisting large-scale introduction of new crops (the failure of the peanut plantation scheme in Kenya in the 1940s provides a classic moral for agriculture innovators) and receiving only limited official encouragement in the form of capital, credit and marketing services.

There is no country in the world that is totally self-sufficient in agricultural commodities; many of the developing countries are chronically dependent on imports for their basic food grains. The patterns of agricultural production illustrate not only the state of agriculture in each country but also their global implications. In an interdependent world, if the wheat crop fails in Iowa, the shortage will be felt not only in the United States but also in Russia, India and Saudi Arabia.

As it stands now, the majority of the countries of the world that are not self-sufficient in food have to spend hard-earned foreign currency for food imports. Exporters of agricultural products and foodgrains are bound to acquire considerable leverage in international trade in the coming years as the problem of feeding the world's growing population becomes critical. Called agripower, it was demonstrated most dramatically in 1972, when Russia was forced to purchase millions of tons of grain from the United States to offset its bad harvests.

89. ARABLE LAND

On the map, certain countries are impressive. Russia and Canada, for example, occupy vast areas and appear at the very top in the ranking of nations by physical size. But what is critical is not the gross size, but the percentage of arable land. Only about 26% of Russia is arable and much of the rest is permafrost. Canada and China have less at 6 and 11 percent respectively. This factor scales these giants down in size considerably so that they roughly match the United States, which has 46% of its territory in arable land or cultivated pasture.

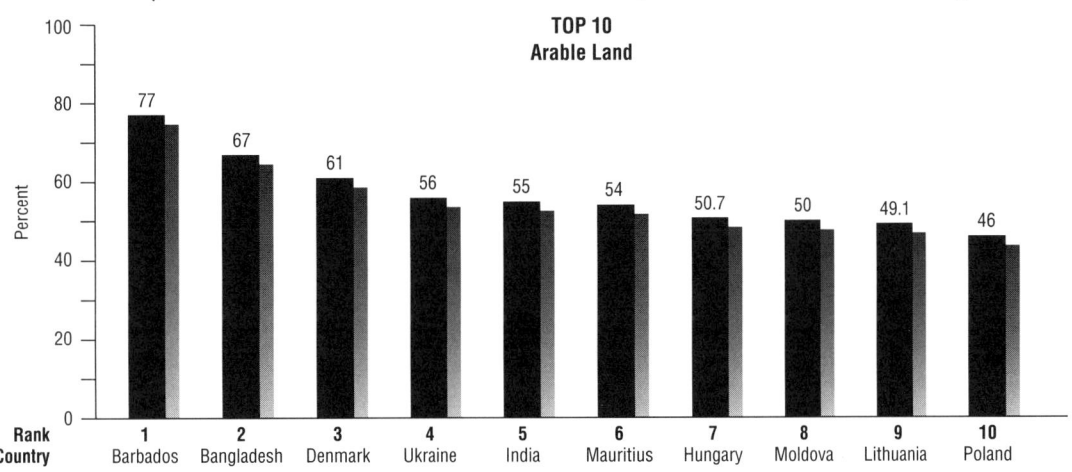

TOP 10
Arable Land

Rank	1	2	3	4	5	6	7	8	9	10
Country	Barbados	Bangladesh	Denmark	Ukraine	India	Mauritius	Hungary	Moldova	Lithuania	Poland
	77	67	61	56	55	54	50.7	50	49.1	46

Rank	Country	Percentage of Arable Land	Rank	Country	Percentage of Arable Land	Rank	Country	Percentage of Arable Land
UPPER MIDDLE			51	St. Kitts and Nevis	22	90	China	10
11	Burundi	43	52	Vietnam	22	91	Lesotho	10
12	Romania	43	53	Albania	21	92	Maldives	10
13	Cyprus	40	54	Korea, South	21	93	Slovenia	10
14	Malta	38	55	Lebanon	21	94	South Africa	10
15	St. Vincent	38	56	Bosnia & Herzegovina	20	95	Switzerland	10
16	Comoros	35	57	Haiti	20	96	Uzbekistan	10
17	Bulgaria	34	58	Paraguay	20	97	Argentina	9
18	Germany	34	59	Tunisia	20	98	Cape Verde	9
19	Thailand	34	60	United States	20	99	Cote d'Ivoire	9
20	Croatia	32	61	Jamaica	19	100	Dominica	9
21	France	32	62	Western Samoa	19	101	Nicaragua	9
22	Italy	32	63	Antigua and Barbuda	18	102	Equatorial Guinea	8
23	Portugal	32	64	Azerbaijan	18	103	Fiji	8
24	Nigeria	31	65	Korea, North	18	104	Finland	8
25	Spain	31	66	Morocco	18	105	Indonesia	8
26	Turkey	30	67	Austria	17	106	Iran	8
27	Yugoslavia	30	68	Israel	17	107	Puerto Rico	8
28	Armenia	29	69	Nepal	17	108	St. Lucia	8
29	Belarus	29	70	San Marino	17	109	Swaziland	8
30	United Kingdom	29	71	Cambodia	16	110	Uruguay	8
31	Syria	28	72	Gambia	16	111	Brazil	7
32	El Salvador	27	73	Sri Lanka	16	112	Chile	7
33	Latvia	27	74	Grenada	15	113	Sweden	7
34	Senegal	27	75	Kazakhstan	15	114	Zambia	7
35	Netherlands	26	76	Myanmar (Burma)	15	115	Zimbabwe	7
36	Pakistan	26	77	Honduras	14	116	Australia	6
37	Philippines	26	78	Ireland	14	117	Costa Rica	6
38	Liechtenstein	25	79	Trinidad and Tobago	14	118	Ecuador	6
39	Malawi	25	80	Cameroon	13	119	Guinea	6
40	Sierra Leone	25	81	Japan	13	120	Panama	6
41	Togo	25				121	Tajikstan	6
42	Tonga	25	**LOWER MIDDLE**			122	Yemen	6
43	Belgium	24	82	Afghanistan	12	123	Canada	5
44	Luxembourg	24	83	Benin	12	124	Ghana	5
45	Taiwan	24	84	Ethiopia	12	125	Macedonia	5
46	Cuba	23	85	Guatemala	12	126	Sudan	5
47	Dominican Republic	23	86	Iraq	12	127	Tanzania	5
48	Greece	23	87	Mexico	12	128	Colombia	4
49	Uganda	23	88	Guinea-Bissau	11	129	Jordan	4
50	Estonia	22	89	Burkina	10	130	Laos	4

Rank	Country	Percentage of Arable Land	Rank	Country	Percentage of Arable Land	Rank	Country	Percentage of Arable Land
131	Madagascar	4	146	Turkmenistan	3	161	Somalia	2
132	Mozambique	4	147	Venezuela	3	162	Bahamas	1
133	Seychelles	4	148	Zaire	3	163	Brunei	1
134	Singapore	4	149	Andorra	2			
135	Algeria	3	150	Angola	2		**BOTTOM 10**	
136	Bolivia	3	151	Bahrain	2	164	Gabon	1
137	Central African Republic	3	152	Belize	2	165	Iceland	1
138	Egypt	3	153	Bhutan	2	166	Liberia	1
139	Eritrea	3	154	Botswana	2	167	Mauritania	1
140	Guyana	3	155	Chad	2	168	Mongolia	1
141	Kenya	3	156	Congo	2	169	Namibia	1
142	Malaysia	3	157	Libya	2	170	Sao Tome e Principe	1
143	Niger	3	158	Mali	2	171	Saudi Arabia	1
144	Norway	3	159	New Zealand	2	172	Solomon Islands	1
145	Peru	3	160	Oman	2	173	Vanuatu	1

Source: *World Data*

90. IRRIGATED LAND

Irrigation is used chiefly in regions receiving an annual rainfall of less than 51 cm (20 in.) and also in areas of great rainfall to supply the high water requirements of certain crops such as rice. Methods of irrigation include free-flooding, check-flooding (in which water is guided over trips or checks of land between levees), the furrow method (in which water is run between rows of crops at distances) and the surface-pipe method (in which water is conducted through movable slip-joint pipes). The use of canals, dams, weirs and reservoirs for distribution, control and storage of water dates back to ancient Egypt. In the 20th century, large-scale irrigation is commonly a part of multipurpose water projects combining irrigation, water supply, flood control and production of hydroelectric power.

Rank	Country	Irrigated Land (sq km)	Rank	Country	Irrigated Land (sq km)	Rank	Country	Irrigated Land (sq km)
	TOP 10		34	Greece	11,900	68	Senegal	1,800
1	China	478,220	35	France	11,600	69	Hungary	1,750
2	India	430,390	36	South Africa	11,280	70	Bolivia	1,650
3	United States	181,020	37	Kyrgyzstan	10,320	71	Ethiopia	1,620
4	Pakistan	162,200	38	Myanmar (Burma)	10,180	72	Somalia	1,600
5	Indonesia	75,500	39	Nepal	9,430	73	United Kingdom	1,570
6	Russia	61,590	40	Madagascar	9,000	74	Tanzania	1,530
7	Iran	57,500	41	Cuba	8,960	75	Belarus	1,490
8	Mexico	51,500	42	Nigeria	8,650	76	Guyana	1,300
9	Thailand	42,300	43	Canada	8,400	77	El Salvador	1,200
10	Uzbekistan	41,550	44	Tajikstan	6,940	78	Laos	1,200
			45	Syria	6,700	79	Costa Rica	1,180
	UPPER MIDDLE		46	Portugal	6,340	80	Mozambique	1,150
11	Romania	34,500	47	Sri Lanka	5,600	81	Sweden	1,120
12	Spain	33,600	48	Ecuador	5,500	82	Uruguay	1,100
13	Italy	31,000	49	Netherlands	5,500	83	Poland	1,000
14	Japan	28,680	50	Colombia	5,150	84	Norway	950
15	Bangladesh	27,380	51	Germany	4,800	85	Cambodia	920
16	Brazil	27,000	52	Georgia	4,660	86	Honduras	900
17	Afghanistan	26,600	53	Saudi Arabia	4,350	87	Lebanon	860
18	Ukraine	26,000	54	Denmark	4,300	88	Nicaragua	850
19	Egypt	25,850	55	Albania	4,230	89	Guatemala	780
20	Iraq	25,500	56	Malaysia	3,420	90	Mongolia	770
21	Kazakhstan	23,080	57	Algeria	3,360	91	Haiti	750
22	Turkey	22,200	58	Yemen	3,100	92	Burundi	720
23	Sudan	18,900	59	Armenia	3,050	93	Paraguay	670
24	Australia	18,800	60	Moldova	2,920	94	Cote d'Ivoire	620
25	Vietnam	18,300	61	New Zealand	2,800	95	Finland	620
26	Argentina	17,600	62	Tunisia	2,750	96	Kenya	620
27	Azerbaijan	14,010				97	Swaziland	620
28	Korea, North	14,000		**LOWER MIDDLE**		98	Suriname	590
29	Korea, South	13,530	63	Venezuela	2,640	99	Jordan	570
30	Chile	12,650	64	Libya	2,420	100	Lithuania	430
31	Morocco	12,650	65	Dominican Republic	2,250	101	Oman	410
32	Peru	12,500	66	Zimbabwe	2,200	102	Puerto Rico	390
33	Turkmenistan	12,450	67	Israel	2,140	103	Cyprus	350

Rank	Country	Irrigated Land (sq km)	Rank	Country	Irrigated Land (sq km)	Rank	Country	Irrigated Land (sq km)
104	Jamaica	350	119	Mauritania	120	134	Botswana	20
105	Bhutan	340	120	Estonia	110	135	Cape Verde	20
106	Sierra Leone	340	121	Chad	100			
107	Niger	320	122	Zaire	100		**BOTTOM 10**	
108	Panama	320	123	Uganda	90	136	Kuwait	20
109	Zambia	320	124	Ghana	80	137	Liberia	20
110	Cameroon	280	125	Togo	70	138	St. Lucia	10
111	Switzerland	250	126	Benin	60	139	St. Vincent	10
112	Guinea	240	127	Mali	50	140	Bahrain	10
113	Trinidad and Tobago	220	128	United Arab Emirates	50	141	Belgium	10
114	Malawi	200	129	Austria	40	142	Brunei	10
115	Mauritius	170	130	Congo	40	143	Bulgaria	10
116	Burkina	160	131	Namibia	40	144	Fiji	10
117	Latvia	160	132	Rwanda	40	145	Malta	10
118	Gambia	120	133	Belize	20			

Source: *World Data*

91. AGRICULTURE'S SHARE OF THE GDP

Despite the importance of food production in a hungry world, agriculture remains labor intensive, agricultural products are subject to price fluctuations and agricultural pursuits are characterized by low productivity. As a result, agriculture's share of the GDP is highest in the least-developed countries, and in most countries of the world it has been declining in relation to other sectors. National policy in almost all countries deliberately favors industry over agriculture and even short-term growth prospects in this sector are depressed by the irreversible migration of manpower to towns and cities, and consequent depletion of the agricultural labor force.

Rank	Country	Percentage of GDP in Agriculture	Rank	Country	Percentage of GDP in Agriculture	Rank	Country	Percentage of GDP in Agriculture
	TOP 10		38	Zambia	31	76	Turkey	16
1	Myanmar (Burma)	63	39	Bangladesh	30	77	Dominican Republic	15
2	Ethiopia	57	40	India	30	78	Latvia	15
3	Tanzania	56	41	Nicaragua	30	79	Tunisia	15
4	Albania	55	42	Kenya	29	80	Zimbabwe	15
5	Burundi	51	43	Gambia	28	81	Lesotho	14
6	Laos	51	44	Papua New Guinea	28	82	Malaysia	14
7	Armenia	50	45	Vietnam	28	83	Namibia	14
8	Central African Republic	50	46	Azerbaijan	27	84	Cape Verde	13
9	Equatorial Guinea	50	47	Mauritania	27	85	Eritrea	13
10	Uganda	49	48	Paraguay	26	86	Grenada	13
			49	Suriname	26	87	Algeria	12
	UPPER MIDDLE		50	Guatemala	25	88	Bulgaria	12
11	Moldova	48	51	Pakistan	25	89	Ecuador	12
12	Ghana	46	52	Guinea	24	90	Swaziland	12
13	Guinea-Bissau	45	53	Kiribati	24	91	Croatia	11
14	Chad	44	54	Sao Tome e Principe	24	92	Iceland	11
15	Kazakhstan	44	55	Sri Lanka	24	93	Peru	11
16	Nepal	43	56	Uzbekistan	23	94	St. Lucia	11
17	Nigeria	43	57	Philippines	22	95	Congo	10
18	Haiti	42	58	Dominica	21	96	Estonia	10
19	Mali	42	59	Iran	21	97	Panama	10
20	Bhutan	41	60	Lithuania	21	98	Thailand	10
21	Cote d'Ivoire	41	61	Mongolia	21	99	El Salvador	9
22	Rwanda	41	62	Morocco	21	100	Mauritius	9
23	Togo	41				101	Uruguay	9
24	Western Samoa	40		**LOWER MIDDLE**		102	Gabon	8
25	Niger	39	63	Egypt	20	103	Ireland	8
26	Ukraine	39	64	Honduras	20	104	Jamaica	8
27	Comoros	37	65	Romania	20	105	Jordan	8
28	Guyana	36	66	Belize	19	106	Mexico	8
29	Tonga	36	67	China	19	107	Hungary	7
30	Kyrgyzstan	35	68	Yemen	19	108	Korea, South	7
31	Madagascar	35	69	Fiji	18	109	New Zealand	7
32	Benin	34	70	Belarus	17	110	Russia	7
33	Georgia	34	71	Indonesia	17	111	Slovakia	7
34	Sudan	34	72	Senegal	17	112	Argentina	6
35	Mozambique	33	73	Colombia	16	113	Cyprus	6
36	Cameroon	32	74	Costa Rica	16	114	Czech Republic	6
37	Malawi	31	75	Greece	16	115	Poland	6

Rank	Country	Percentage of GDP in Agriculture	Rank	Country	Percentage of GDP in Agriculture	Rank	Country	Percentage of GDP in Agriculture
116	St. Kitts and Nevis	6	127	Italy	3		BOTTOM 10	
117	Barbados	5	128	Malta	3	138	United Arab Emirates	2
118	Botswana	5	129	Netherlands	3	139	United Kingdom	2
119	Finland	5	130	Oman	3	140	United States	2
120	Slovenia	5	131	Spain	3	141	Venezuela	2
121	South Africa	5	132	Trinidad and Tobago	3	142	Bahrain	1
122	Antigua and Barbuda	4	133	Austria	2	143	Germany	1
123	Denmark	4	134	Belgium	2	144	Luxembourg	1
124	Seychelles	4	135	France	2	145	Puerto Rico	1
125	Australia	3	136	Japan	2	146	Kuwait	0
126	Djibouti	3	137	Sweden	2	147	Singapore	0

Source: *World Development Report*

92. FISH CATCH

Fishing is not only one of the oldest human occupations but also one of the most universal. According to international law, the fish of the oceans (outside of territorial limits) are the common resources of all peoples, perhaps the only resource for which this claim can be made. In recent years, therefore, developing nations with limited internal resources have turned to the ocean to supplement their revenues. Despite ease of entry, fishing requires substantial long-term investments in refrigeration, vessels and equipment, and marketing facilities.

TOP 10
Fish Catch

Rank	Country	(000 metric tons)	Rank	Country	(000 metric tons)
1	Peru	8,450.6	6	Russia	4,461.4
2	Japan	8,128.1	7	India	4,324.2
3	China	7,567.9	8	Indonesia	3,637.7
4	Chile	6,038.0	9	Thailand	3,348.1
5	United States	5,939.3	10	Korea, South	2,649.0

1 fish = 1,000,000 metric tons

Rank	Country	Fish Catch (000 metric tons)	Rank	Country	Fish Catch (000 metric tons)	Rank	Country	Fish Catch (000 metric tons)
	UPPER MIDDLE		30	South Africa	563.2	50	Sri Lanka	220.9
11	Norway	2,561.8	31	Italy	552.0	51	Uganda	219.8
12	Philippines	2,263.8	32	Turkey	550.6	52	Australia	218.3
13	Korea, North	1,780.0	33	Netherlands	486.9	53	Greece	199.6
14	Iceland	1,718.5	34	New Zealand	470.4	54	Kenya	185.4
15	Denmark	1,534.1	35	Poland	423.0	55	Panama	158.2
16	Taiwan	1,415.8	36	Venezuela	390.3	56	Finland	152.5
17	Spain	1,290.0	37	Senegal	377.7	57	Zaire	147.3
18	Mexico	1,200.7	38	Ukraine	371.3	58	Estonia	146.9
19	Canada	1,171.6	39	Ghana	371.2	59	Colombia	146.4
20	Vietnam	1,100.0	40	Sweden	347.8	60	Latvia	142.2
21	Bangladesh	1,047.2	41	Tanzania	345.0	61	Lithuania	119.9
22	Argentina	930.6	42	Iran	343.9	62	Uruguay	118.8
23	United Kingdom	898.1	43	Ecuador	330.7	63	Oman	116.5
24	Myanmar (Burma)	836.9	44	Namibia	329.8	64	Madagascar	115.0
25	France	830.0	45	Germany	316.4	65	Cambodia	108.9
26	Brazil	780.0	46	Ireland	305.0	66	Tunisia	93.8
27	Malaysia	680.0	47	Egypt	302.8	67	Cuba	93.4
28	Morocco	622.4	48	Portugal	274.2	68	Mauritania	92.8
29	Pakistan	621.7	49	Nigeria	255.5	69	United Arab Emirates	92.5

Rank	Country	Fish Catch (000 metric tons)
70	Algeria	90.5
71	Maldives	90.0
72	Yemen	86.8
73	Angola	80.7
74	Cameroon	80.0
75	Chad	80.0
76	Kazakhstan	75.0
77	Cote d'Ivoire	70.2
78	Zambia	65.3
79	Malawi	65.0
80	Mali	64.4
81	Sierra Leone	62.0
82	Saudi Arabia	49.4
83	Solomon Islands	45.4
84	Congo	41.5
85	Guinea	40.0
LOWER MIDDLE		
86	Guyana	40.0
87	Benin	39.0
88	Georgia	37.0
89	Turkmenistan	37.0
90	Belgium	36.4
91	Azerbaijan	36.0
92	Romania	34.9
93	Sudan	31.7
94	Fiji	31.4
95	Laos	30.5
96	Croatia	30.3
97	Mozambique	30.2
98	Kiribati	29.3
99	Gabon	28.3
100	Papua New Guinea	26.0
101	Czech Republic	24.4
102	Honduras	24.4
103	Iraq	23.5
104	Hungary	23.4
105	Uzbekistan	23.4
106	Burundi	22.0
107	Zimbabwe	21.8

Rank	Country	Fish Catch (000 metric tons)
108	Bulgaria	21.6
109	Mauritius	21.1
110	Gambia	20.5
111	Israel	18.7
112	Costa Rica	17.7
113	Togo	17.0
114	Nepal	16.9
115	Paraguay	16
116	Somalia	14.9
117	Dominican Republic	14.1
118	Belarus	14.0
119	Central African Republic	13.5
120	El Salvador	13.0
121	Singapore	11.7
122	Jamaica	11.0
123	Trinidad and Tobago	10.6
124	Bahamas	10.1
125	Suriname	9.5
126	Bahrain	9.0
127	Libya	8.8
128	Nicaragua	8.8
129	Kuwait	8.6
130	Guatemala	8.1
131	Liberia	7.8
132	Cape Verde	7.1
133	Burkina	7.0
134	Comoros	7.0
135	Qatar	7.0
136	Seychelles	7.0
137	Yugoslavia	6.5
138	Bolivia	6.2
139	Haiti	5.6
140	Malta	5.6
141	Syria	5.6
142	Guinea-Bissau	5.4
143	Moldova	4.7
144	Austria	4.6
145	Armenia	4.3
146	Ethiopia	4.2
147	Equatorial Guinea	3.8

Rank	Country	Fish Catch (000 metric tons)
148	Tajikistan	3.7
149	Rwanda	3.6
150	Albania	3.5
151	Switzerland	3.2
152	Slovenia	3.0
153	Barbados	2.9
154	Cyprus	2.9
155	Vanuatu	2.9
156	Slovakia	2.8
157	Bosnia & Herzegovina	2.5
158	Eritrea	2.5
159	Tonga	2.5
160	Antigua and Barbuda	2.4
161	Lebanon	2.2
162	Niger	2.2
163	Sao Tome e Principe	2.2
164	Belize	2.1
165	Grenada	2.1
166	Botswana	2.0
167	Puerto Rico	1.9
168	Brunei	1.8
169	St. Vincent	1.8
170	St. Kitts and Nevis	1.7
171	Western Samoa	1.6
172	Tuvalu	1.5
173	Macedonia	1.4
174	Afghanistan	1.2
BOTTOM 10		
175	Kyrgyzstan	1.1
176	St. Lucia	1.1
177	Dominica	0.8
178	Nauru	0.5
179	Bermuda	0.4
180	Bhutan	0.4
181	Djibouti	0.3
182	Jordan	0.1
183	Mongolia	0.1
184	Swaziland	0.1

Source: FAO

93. PRODUCTION OF ROUNDWOOD

Production of roundwood (wood felled and stripped of bark but not cut into logs) varies only slightly from year to year.

Rank	Country	Production of Roundwood (000 cubic meters)
TOP 10		
1	United States	495,800
2	China	300,668
3	India	287,449
4	Brazil	272,078
5	Russia	207,452
6	Indonesia	188,118
7	Canada	179,967
8	Nigeria	118,052
9	Sweden	62,954
10	Malaysia	54,332
UPPER MIDDLE		
11	Ethiopia	46,969
12	Zaire	44,532
13	France	44,069
14	Finland	39,644
15	Philippines	39,576
16	Kenya	38,554
17	Thailand	38,039
18	Germany	36,156
19	Tanzania	36,072

Rank	Country	Production of Roundwood (000 cubic meters)
20	Vietnam	33,483
21	Japan	32,570
22	Bangladesh	32,513
23	Chile	32,241
24	Pakistan	27,776
25	Sudan	24,781
26	Mexico	23,285
27	Myanmar (Burma)	22,544
28	Colombia	20,903
29	Australia	20,531
30	Nepal	20,060
31	South Africa	19,811
32	Poland	18,822
33	Ghana	17,192
34	Mozambique	16,013
35	New Zealand	15,948
36	Uganda	15,580
37	Turkey	15,350
38	Spain	14,796
39	Cameroon	14,741
40	Zambia	13,804
41	Cote d'Ivoire	13,694

Rank	Country	Production of Roundwood (000 cubic meters)
42	Austria	12,857
43	Argentina	11,865
44	Portugal	11,584
45	Guatemala	11,263
46	Czech Republic	10,306
47	Norway	10,134
48	Malawi	10,075
49	Belarus	10,031
50	Italy	9,860
51	Romania	9,536
52	Burkina	9,520
53	Sri Lanka	9,374
54	Somalia	9,047
55	Madagascar	8,858
56	Paraguay	8,538
57	Peru	8,329
58	Papua New Guinea	8,188
59	Zimbabwe	8,065
60	Afghanistan	7,817.0
61	Iran	7,647
62	Ecuador	7,499
63	Cambodia	7,025

Rank	Country	Production of Roundwood (000 cubic meters)	Rank	Country	Production of Roundwood (000 cubic meters)	Rank	Country	Production of Roundwood (000 cubic meters)
	LOWER MIDDLE		93	Congo	3,561	123	Guinea-Bissau	574
64	Angola	6,583	94	Tunisia	3,373	124	Lebanon	496
65	El Salvador	6,493	95	Sierra Leone	3,308	125	Jamaica	495
66	Korea, South	6,485	96	Cuba	3,146	126	Solomon Islands	468
67	Honduras	6,454	97	Yugoslavia	3,056	127	Yemen	324
68	United Kingdom	6,195	98	Greece	2,779	128	Fiji	307
69	Liberia	6,183	99	Albania	2,556	129	Brunei	295
70	Haiti	6,171	100	Estonia	2,439	130	Belize	188
71	Mali	6,145	101	Egypt	2,404	131	Guyana	180
72	Rwanda	5,660	102	Algeria	2,367	132	Iraq	155
73	Benin	5,538	103	Swaziland	2,297	133	Suriname	154
74	Niger	5,467	104	Venezuela	2,245	134	Western Samoa	131
75	Bosnia & Herzegovina	5,379	105	Denmark	2,192	135	Singapore	120
76	Slovakia	5,250	106	Croatia	2,131	136	Bahamas	117
77	Senegal	5,022	107	Morocco	2,009	137	Israel	113
78	Laos	4,906	108	Ireland	1,756	138	Vanuatu	63
79	Korea, North	4,830	109	Bolivia	1,555			
80	Hungary	4,660	110	Bhutan	1,497		**BOTTOM 10**	
81	Burundi	4,613	111	Botswana	1,440	139	Taiwan	61
82	Latvia	4,558	112	Netherlands	1,403	140	Syria	55
83	Switzerland	4,553	113	Togo	1,295	141	Cyprus	50
84	Guinea	4,549	114	Slovenia	1,168	142	Trinidad and Tobago	48
85	Gabon	4,346	115	Panama	1,045	143	Mauritius	15
86	Costa Rica	4,315	116	Dominican Republic	982	144	Mauritania	13
87	Chad	4,283	117	Gambia	958	145	Jordan	11
88	Belgium	4,240	118	Mongolia	865	146	Sao Tome e Principe	9
89	Uruguay	4,087	119	Macedonia	756	147	Barbados	5
90	Central African Republic	3,701	120	Lesotho	651	148	Tonga	5
91	Nicaragua	3,697	121	Libya	648			
92	Bulgaria	3,565	122	Equatorial Guinea	638			

Source: FAO

94. MILK PRODUCTION

Milk is one of the most universal drinks, and it is also one of the most important farm products. As a commercial product it is subject to regulations regarding its composition, such as proportion of butterfat and other solids, its nonadulteration and its purity. The following ranking is limited to the milk of the cow, buffalo, sheep and goat, but milk from many other animals is widely consumed, including that of the mare, camel, ass, zebra, reindeer, llama and yak.

Rank	Country	Production of Milk (000 metric tons)	Rank	Country	Production of Milk (000 metric tons)	Rank	Country	Production of Milk (000 metric tons)
	TOP 10		24	Colombia	4,690	50	Bulgaria	1,135
1	United States	69,682	25	Denmark	4,442	51	Israel	1,105
2	Russia	44,000	26	Pakistan	4,100	52	Egypt	995
3	India	30,000	27	Switzerland	3,900	53	Latvia	937
4	Germany	28,200	28	Romania	3,600	54	Moldova	846
5	France	24,935	29	Belgium	3,533	55	Peru	830
6	Ukraine	17,933	30	Sweden	3,357	56	Morocco	820
7	Brazil	15,774	31	Czech Republic	3,231	57	Estonia	812
8	United Kingdom	15,005	32	Austria	3,200	58	Greece	787
9	Poland	12,218	33	Sudan	2,610	59	Bangladesh	774
10	Netherlands	10,755	34	Uzbekistan	2,600	60	Kyrgyzstan	750
			35	Finland	2,512	61	Syria	750
	UPPER MIDDLE		36	Lithuania	2,400	62	Ethiopia	738
11	Italy	10,300	37	South Africa	2,350	63	Cuba	700
12	Turkey	8,950	38	Korea, South	1,986	64	Azerbaijan	650
13	New Zealand	8,379	39	Iran	1,930	65	Croatia	600
14	Japan	8,365	40	Hungary	1,906	66	Algeria	595
15	Australia	8,326	41	Kenya	1,905	67	Somalia	550
16	Argentina	7,868	42	Norway	1,863	68	Albania	520
17	Canada	7,700	43	Ecuador	1,832	69	Zimbabwe	495
18	Mexico	7,547	44	Chile	1,730	70	Costa Rica	482
19	Spain	5,751	45	Venezuela	1,611	71	Madagascar	481
20	China	5,600	46	Portugal	1,500	72	Bosnia & Herzegovina	475
21	Ireland	5,523	47	Yugoslavia	1,500	73	Tanzania	471
22	Belarus	5,300	48	Uruguay	1,188	74	Tajikistan	450
23	Kazakhstan	5,300	49	Slovakia	1,155	75	Tunisia	450

Rank	Country	Production of Milk (000 metric tons)	Rank	Country	Production of Milk (000 metric tons)	Rank	Country	Production of Milk (000 metric tons)
76	Uganda	446	109	Cameroon	122	144	Suriname	17
77	Myanmar (Burma)	441	110	Macedonia	120	145	Benin	16
			111	Senegal	106	146	Barbados	15
LOWER MIDDLE			112	Iceland	101	147	Kuwait	14
78	Indonesia	425	113	Jordan	93	148	Philippines	14
79	Honduras	398	114	Mauritania	91	149	Guinea-Bissau	13
80	Nigeria	389	115	Korea, North	90	150	Laos	12
81	Dominican Republic	385	116	Zambia	89	151	Liechtenstein	12
82	Slovenia	380	117	Botswana	88	152	Trinidad and Tobago	11
83	Puerto Rico	359	118	Fiji	86	153	Togo	10
84	Georgia	350	119	Rwanda	85	154	Zaire	8
85	Saudi Arabia	345	120	Namibia	71	155	Belize	7
86	Afghanistan	300	121	Mozambique	57	156	Djibouti	7
87	Taiwan	289	122	Libya	55	157	Gambia	7
88	El Salvador	280	123	Jamaica	54	158	Antigua and Barbuda	6
89	Nepal	278	124	Central African Republic	50	159	United Arab Emirates	6
90	Guatemala	273	125	Guinea	48	160	Dominica	5
91	Thailand	265	126	Swaziland	43	161	Comoros	4
92	Mongolia	251	127	Malawi	42	162	Qatar	4
93	Paraguay	250	128	Vietnam	42	163	Vanuatu	3
94	Sri Lanka	227	129	Eritrea	36	164	Bahamas	2
95	Turkmenistan	204	130	Malaysia	34			
96	Armenia	200	131	Bhutan	29	**BOTTOM 10**		
97	Iraq	200	132	Burundi	29	165	Bermuda	1
98	Nicaragua	194	133	Guyana	28	166	Cape Verde	1
99	Panama	163	134	Mauritius	25	167	Congo	1
100	Angola	160	135	Lesotho	24	168	Gabon	1
101	Niger	154	136	Malta	24	169	Grenada	1
102	Yemen	150	137	Ghana	23	170	Liberia	1
103	Bolivia	139	138	Haiti	22	171	St. Lucia	1
104	Lebanon	139	139	Bahrain	20	172	St. Vincent	1
105	Mali	139	140	Cote d'Ivoire	20	173	Solomon Islands	1
106	Burkina	125	141	Cambodia	19	174	Western Samoa	1
107	Chad	125	142	Oman	19			
108	Cyprus	125	143	Sierra Leone	17			

Source: FAO

95. PIGS

Pigs, more properly known as swine and sometimes as hogs, are native to the Old World and were introduced into America by the Spanish explorers. They are commonly grouped as meat-type, lard-type and bacon-type: meat-type breeds include the Hereford and Berkshire; lard-type breeds include Poland China, Duroc and Spotted Swine; and bacon type breeds include Tamworth, Yorkshire and American Landrace. Male domestic swines suitable for breeding are know as boars.

TOP 10 Hogs

Rank	Country	(000 head)	Rank	Country	(000 head)
1	China	402,846	4	Germany	26,044
			5	Russia	23,800
			6	Poland	19,466
2	United States	57,904	7	Spain	18,188
			8	Mexico	18,000
3	Brazil	30,450	9	Ukraine	15,298
			10	Vietnam	15,043

Agriculture **131**

Rank	Country	Hogs (000 head)	Rank	Country	Hogs (000 head)	Rank	Country	Hogs (000 head)
	UPPER MIDDLE		64	Togo	934	116	Albania	86
11	Netherlands	13,991	65	Dominican Republic	900	117	Armenia	80
12	France	13,383	66	Uganda	880	118	Burundi	80
13	India	11,780	67	Angola	820	119	Lesotho	78
14	Canada	11,200	68	Norway	745	120	Bhutan	75
15	Denmark	10,864	69	Latvia	737	121	Mali	63
16	Japan	10,621	70	Guatemala	720	122	Vanuatu	59
17	Taiwan	10,066	71	Georgia	650	123	Congo	56
18	Romania	9,262	72	Slovenia	620	124	Solomon Islands	55
19	Indonesia	8,720	73	Nepal	612	125	Sierra Leone	51
20	Philippines	8,227	74	Honduras	603	126	Guyana	50
21	Italy	8,200	75	Ghana	595	127	Mongolia	49
22	United Kingdom	7,910	76	Benin	555	128	Trinidad and Tobago	48
23	Belgium	6,948	77	Burkina	551	129	Lebanon	41
24	Nigeria	6,926	78	Nicaragua	535	130	Brunei	40
25	Korea, South	6,300				131	Tajikistan	40
26	Hungary	5,002		**LOWER MIDDLE**		132	Niger	39
27	Thailand	4,931	79	Central African Republic	480	133	Suriname	37
28	Belarus	4,175	80	New Zealand	430	134	Guinea	33
29	Czech Republic	4,071	81	Estonia	424	135	Swaziland	32
30	Yugoslavia	4,000	82	Cote d'Ivoire	404	136	Barbados	30
31	Austria	3,800	83	Uzbekistan	391	137	Egypt	27
32	Korea, North	3,368	84	Cyprus	370	138	Belize	26
33	Paraguay	3,300	85	Tanzania	335	139	Iceland	22
34	Malaysia	3,098	86	Ethiopia	329	140	Ethiopia	20
35	Australia	2,740	87	El Salvador	325	141	Namibia	18
36	Colombia	2,635	88	Guinea-Bissau	312	142	Seychelles	18
37	Myanmar (Burma)	2,589	89	Panama	295	143	Botswana	17
38	Ecuador	2,540	90	Zambia	295	144	Chad	17
39	Kazakhstan	2,445	91	Zimbabwe	280	145	Mauritius	17
40	Peru	2,405	92	Costa Rica	252	146	Bahamas	15
41	Bolivia	2,331	93	Malawi	245	147	St. Lucia	13
42	Venezuela	2,250	94	Uruguay	230	148	Tuvalu	13
43	Argentina	2,200	95	Bosnia & Herzegovina	223	149	Gambia	11
44	Slovakia	2,179	96	Haiti	200	150	Morocco	10
45	Sweden	2,168	97	Puerto Rico	196	151	Kiribati	9
46	Cambodia	2,154	98	Macedonia	181	152	St. Vincent	9
47	Bulgaria	2,071	99	Jamaica	180	153	Somalia	9
48	Switzerland	1,680	100	Western Samoa	179	154	Turkey	9
49	Laos	1,605	101	Mozambique	174	155	Algeria	6
50	Madagascar	1,558	102	Gabon	165	156	Tunisia	6
51	South Africa	1,511	103	Kyrgyzstan	165			
52	Cuba	1,503	104	Turkmenistan	159		**BOTTOM 10**	
53	Ireland	1,487	105	Singapore	150	157	Dominica	5
54	Portugal	1,487	106	Rwanda	136	158	Equatorial Guinea	5
55	Chile	1,407	107	Liberia	120	159	Antigua and Barbuda	4
56	Cameroon	1,380	108	Azerbaijan	115	160	Grenada	3
57	Croatia	1,347	109	Fiji	115	161	Liechtenstein	3
58	Finland	1,300	110	Cape Verde	111	162	Nauru	3
59	Lithuania	1,200	111	Malta	111	163	St. Kitts and Nevis	2
60	Zaire	1,185	112	Kenya	107	164	Sao Tome e Principe	2
61	Moldova	1,165	113	Israel	100	165	Bermuda	1
62	Greece	1,143	114	Tonga	94	166	Syria	1
63	Papua New Guinea	1,033	115	Sri Lanka	90			

Source: FAO

96. SHEEP

Sheep, first domesticated about 7,000 years ago, are found mostly in temperate climates. The present-day breeds vary because they were bred for different environments, but most of them are derived from the wild mouflon of Sardinia and Corsica and from the urial of Asia. They are raised for their wool, meat (called mutton or lamb according to age) and skins; in some countries their milk is drunk and made into cheese.

Among the major species of wild sheep are the argali, the Barbary sheep or aoudad of North Africa, and the North American bighorn or Rocky Mountain sheep. The more important breeds of domesticated sheep are Columbia, Cotswold, Dorset, Hampshire, Karakul, Leicester, Lincoln, Merino, Oxford, Rambouillet, Shropshire, Southdown and Suffolk.

Rank	Country	Sheep (000 head)	Rank	Country	Sheep (000 head)	Rank	Country	Sheep (000 head)
TOP 10			57	Estonia	3,382	114	Angola	255
1	Australia	132,609	58	Ghana	3,288	115	Liberia	210
2	China	111,649	59	Yugoslavia	2,752	116	Czech Republic	196
3	New Zealand	50,135	60	Namibia	2,620	117	Malawi	196
4	Iran	45,400	61	Colombia	2,540	118	Gabon	170
5	India	44,809	62	Macedonia	2,444	119	Qatar	170
6	Russia	41,078	63	Germany	2,360	120	Belgium	160
7	Turkey	37,541	64	Norway	2,316	121	Central African Republic	152
8	Kazakhstan	33,524	65	Netherlands	2,174	122	Kuwait	150
9	United Kingdom	29,300	66	Chad	2,152	123	Oman	149
10	South Africa	29,134	67	Jordan	2,100	124	Dominican Republic	134
			68	Tajikistan	2,000	125	Latvia	133
UPPER MIDDLE			69	Uganda	1,980	126	Guyana	131
11	Pakistan	28,975	70	Albania	1,900	127	Gambia	121
12	Spain	23,838	71	Ecuador	1,728	128	Mozambique	119
13	Uruguay	23,441	72	Lesotho	1,691	129	Congo	111
14	Sudan	22,870	73	Eritrea	1,510	130	Thailand	98
15	Ethiopia	21,700	74	Moldova	1,373	131	Haiti	85
16	Brazil	20,500				132	Estonia	83
17	Argentina	20,000	**LOWER MIDDLE**			133	Denmark	82
18	Algeria	17,850	75	Georgia	1,300	134	Finland	79
19	Morocco	15,594	76	Hungary	1,280	135	Zambia	69
20	Nigeria	14,455	77	Cote d'Ivoire	1,251	136	Bhutan	59
21	Mongolia	14,392	78	Togo	1,250	137	Lithuania	48
22	Afghanistan	14,200	79	Bangladesh	1,070	138	Barbados	41
23	Somalia	13,000	80	Zaire	1,012	139	Bahamas	40
24	Syria	12,000	81	Benin	940	140	Equatorial Guinea	36
25	Peru	11,600	82	Nepal	914	141	Philippines	30
26	Romania	11,499	83	Poland	870	142	Bahrain	29
27	France	10,452	84	Madagascar	740	143	Swaziland	27
28	Italy	10,370	85	Armenia	720	144	Japan	25
29	Greece	9,604	86	Canada	691	145	Slovenia	21
30	United States	9,600	87	Bosnia & Herzegovina	600	146	Sri Lanka	19
31	Uzbekistan	8,600	88	Venezuela	550	147	Comoros	15
32	Bolivia	7,789	89	Zimbabwe	550	148	Honduras	14
33	Saudi Arabia	7,257	90	Iceland	500	149	St. Kitts and Nevis	14
34	Tunisia	7,100	91	Sweden	483	150	Trinidad and Tobago	14
35	Kyrgyzstan	7,077	92	Djibouti	470	151	Antigua and Barbuda	13
36	Indonesia	6,411	93	Croatia	444	152	Grenada	12
37	Iraq	6,320	94	Guatemala	440	153	St. Vincent	12
38	Ukraine	6,118	95	Guinea	435	154	St. Lucia	10
39	Turkmenistan	6,000	96	Switzerland	425	155	Suriname	9
40	Ireland	5,991	97	Rwanda	400	156	Dominica	8
41	Portugal	5,991	98	Slovakia	397	157	Puerto Rico	8
42	Mexico	5,905	99	Korea, North	396	158	Cape Verde	7
43	Burkina	5,686	100	Paraguay	386	159	Mauritius	7
44	Kenya	5,500	101	Burundi	350	160	Fiji	6
45	Mali	5,173	102	Botswana	344			
46	Mauritania	4,800	103	Malaysia	336	**BOTTOM 10**		
47	Chile	4,649	104	United Arab Emirates	333	161	Malta	6
48	Senegal	4,600	105	Israel	330	162	El Salvador	5
49	Azerbaijan	4,339	106	Austria	324	163	Belize	4
50	Tanzania	3,955	107	Cuba	310	164	Korea, South	4
51	Cameroon	3,770	108	Myanmar (Burma)	304	165	Nicaragua	4
52	Bulgaria	3,763	109	Sierra Leone	302	166	Papua New Guinea	4
53	Yemen	3,715	110	Belarus	289	167	Costa Rica	3
54	Niger	3,700	111	Cyprus	285	168	Liechtenstein	3
55	Libya	3,500	112	Guinea-Bissau	263	169	Jamaica	2
56	Egypt	3,382	113	Lebanon	258	170	Sao Tome e Principe	2

Source: FAO

97. CATTLE

Of all domesticated animals, cattle are the most numerous and the most productive. Throughout the world they are the principal source of meat and milk, and in the developing world they also serve as draft animals. In many places even today wealth consists chiefly of cattle (the word pecuniary is derived from the Latin word for cattle, *pecus*, and the words *capital* and *cattle* are etymologically related). Since the 18th century, new types of breeds have been developed. The principal beef breeds include the Angus and the Hereford, and the principal dairy breeds the Ayrshire, Brown Swiss, Guernsey, Holstein-Friesian and Jersey. The dual purpose breeds include Devon, Red Poll and Shorthorn.

Rank	Country	Livestock (000 head)
TOP 10		
1	India	192,980
2	Brazil	151,600
3	United States	100,988
4	China	90,906
5	Argentina	50,000
6	Russia	48900
7	Mexico	30,702
8	Ethiopia	29,450
9	Colombia	25,700
10	Australia	24,732
UPPER MIDDLE		
11	Bangladesh	24,130
12	Sudan	21,751
13	Ukraine	21,607
14	France	20,112
15	Pakistan	18,146
16	Nigeria	16,717
17	Germany	15,891
18	Venezuela	15,071
19	Tanzania	13,376
20	South Africa	12,584
21	Canada	12,306
22	Turkey	11,910
23	United Kingdom	11,735
24	Indonesia	11,595
25	Kenya	11,000
26	Uruguay	10,316
27	Madagascar	10,288
28	Myanmar (Burma)	9,691
29	Kazakhstan	9,347
30	New Zealand	8,550
31	Paraguay	8,000
32	Italy	7,683
33	Thailand	7,593
34	Poland	7,696
35	Iran	7,100
36	Nepal	6,546
37	Ireland	6,308
38	Bolivia	6,012
39	Belarus	5,851
40	Mali	5,554
41	Uzbekistan	5,291
42	Uganda	5,100
43	Somalia	5,000
44	Spain	5,000
45	Japan	4,989
46	Ecuador	4,963
47	Cameroon	4,867
48	Netherlands	4,629
49	Chad	4,621
50	Cuba	4,500
51	Zimbabwe	4,500
52	Burkina	4,261
53	Peru	4,000
54	Chile	3,692
55	Romania	3,597
56	Vietnam	3,438
57	Zambia	3,300
58	Belgium	3,289
59	Angola	3,280
60	Korea, South	3,200
61	Egypt	3,070
62	Botswana	2,800
63	Central African Republic	2,800
64	Senegal	2,800
65	Mongolia	2,779
66	Cambodia	2,589
67	Dominican Republic	2,450
68	Morocco	2,431
69	Austria	2,430
70	Honduras	2,286
71	Guatemala	2,210
72	Czech Republic	2,113
73	Denmark	2,082
74	Namibia	2,036
75	Niger	1,996
76	Sweden	1,830
77	Philippines	1,825
78	Yugoslavia	1,809
79	Switzerland	1,700
80	Zaire	1,696
LOWER MIDDLE		
81	Ghana	1,680
82	Guinea	1,658
83	Lithuania	1,650
84	Nicaragua	1,650
85	Azerbaijan	1,621
86	Sri Lanka	1,600
87	Costa Rica	1,594
88	Eritrea	1,550
89	Afghanistan	1,500
90	Panama	1,437
91	Algeria	1,370
92	Korea, North	1,330
93	Portugal	1,322
94	El Salvador	1,256
95	Mozambique	1,250
96	Tajikistan	1,250
97	Benin	1,233
98	Cote d'Ivoire	1,232
99	Finland	1,230
100	Laos	1,137
101	Yemen	1,128
102	Turkmenistan	1,104
103	Iraq	1,100
104	Kyrgyzstan	1,061
105	Georgia	1,050
106	Mauritania	1,011
107	Norway	1,003
108	Hungary	1,002
109	Latvia	995
110	Malawi	980
111	Moldova	916
112	Slovakia	916
113	Haiti	800
114	Syria	770
115	Bulgaria	750
116	Malaysia	686
117	Lesotho	663
118	Tunisia	660
119	Albania	630
120	Swaziland	620
121	Rwanda	610
122	Greece	608
123	Croatia	519
124	Slovenia	504
125	Armenia	502
126	Guinea-Bissau	494
127	Estonia	463
128	Bhutan	435
129	Puerto Rico	429
130	Gambia	414
131	Bosnia & Herzegovina	390
132	Burundi	380
133	Israel	362
134	Sierra Leone	362
135	Jamaica	335
136	Fiji	334
137	Macedonia	276
138	Togo	250
139	Saudi Arabia	203
140	Djibouti	190
141	Guyana	190
142	Taiwan	164
143	Oman	144
144	Vanuatu	132
145	Papua New Guinea	105
146	Suriname	98
147	Lebanon	80
148	Iceland	77
149	Congo	68
150	United Arab Emirates	65
151	Cyprus	61
152	Belize	59
153	Trinidad and Tobago	55
154	Comoros	50
155	Libya	50
156	Jordan	42
157	Gabon	36
158	Liberia	36
159	Mauritius	34
160	Western Samoa	26
161	Barbados	25
162	Malta	20
163	Cape Verde	18
164	Antigua and Barbuda	16
165	Bahrain	16
166	Solomon Islands	13
167	Kuwait	12
168	Qatar	12
169	St. Lucia	12
170	Tonga	10
171	Dominica	9
BOTTOM 10		
172	Bahamas	6
173	Liechtenstein	6
174	St. Vincent	6
175	Equatorial Guinea	5
176	St. Kitts and Nevis	5
177	Grenada	4
178	Sao Tome e Principe	4
179	Seychelles	2
180	Bermuda	1
181	Brunei	1

Source: FAO

98. FERTILIZER CONSUMPTION

The contribution that fertilizers make to agricultural production has never been determined precisely, but it is bound to be enormous, particularly in countries where the soil is being constantly impoverished through poor soil management practices and intensive cultivation techniques. Three types of fertilizers are used, sometimes in combination, according to the needs of the soil: nitrogenous fertilizers, phosphate fertilizers (such as superphosphates and ammonium phosphates) and potash fertilizers (such as muriate, nitrate and sulfate of potash). In addition to these inorganics, various organic fertilizers are being added to the soil, but no statistics are available on them. In the following ranking all three types of inorganic fertilizers have been combined and presented in terms of hectares of cultivated land.

Rank	Country	Artificial Fertilizer (kg per hectare)	Rank	Country	Artificial Fertilizer (kg per hectare)	Rank	Country	Artificial Fertilizer (kg per hectare)
TOP 10			48	Spain	101	96	Zambia	15
1	Singapore	5,600	49	United States	99	97	Lesotho	14
2	Iceland	2,529	50	Bangladesh	98	98	Algeria	13
3	Ireland	741	51	Slovakia	98	99	Mauritania	12
4	New Zealand	741	52	Fiji	96	100	Mongolia	12
5	Netherlands	628	53	Barbados	91	101	Nigeria	12
6	Belgium	496	54	Pakistan	91	102	Yemen	12
7	Korea, South	454	55	Belize	88	103	Cote d'Ivoire	11
8	Switzerland	430	56	Oman	83	104	Mali	9
9	Japan	414	57	Vietnam	82	105	Paraguay	9
10	Korea, North	407	58	Iran	80	106	Tanzania	9
			59	Lebanon	79	107	Myanmar (Burma)	8
UPPER MIDDLE			60	India	75	108	Togo	8
11	Taiwan	400				109	Afghanistan	7
12	Saudi Arabia	398	**LOWER MIDDLE**			110	Angola	7
13	Egypt	384	61	Portugal	73	111	Ethiopia	7
14	Germany	384	62	Mexico	70	112	Liberia	7
15	United Kingdom	376	63	Chile	69	113	Burkina	6
16	Bahrain	333	64	Philippines	67	114	Cameroon	6
17	France	319	65	Guatemala	66	115	Argentina	4
18	Czech Republic	314	66	Turkey	64	116	Burundi	4
19	Mauritius	304	67	Jordan	63	117	Greece	4
20	China	261	68	South Africa	59	118	Haiti	4
21	Dominica	259	69	Panama	58	119	Sudan	4
22	Denmark	255	70	Brunei	57	120	Bolivia	3
23	Israel	252	71	Trinidad and Tobago	57	121	Congo	3
24	Norway	242	72	Uruguay	54	122	Gambia	3
25	Hungary	231	73	Zimbabwe	53	123	Ghana	3
26	Poland	219	74	Dominican Republic	50	124	Guinea-Bissau	3
27	Finland	210	75	Kenya	48	125	Somalia	3
28	Costa Rica	203	76	Canada	47	126	Benin	2
29	Austria	201	77	Swaziland	46	127	Central African Republic	2
30	Qatar	200	78	Syria	46	128	Chad	2
31	Cuba	199	79	Brazil	43	129	Latvia	2
32	Bulgaria	195	80	Peru	41	130	Madagascar	2
33	Malaysia	170	81	Papua New Guinea	40	131	Senegal	2
34	Kuwait	167	82	Libya	39			
35	Albania	158	83	Malta	39	**BOTTOM 10**		
36	Italy	151	84	Morocco	36	132	Tonga	2
37	Cyprus	144	85	Thailand	36	133	Bhutan	1
38	Venezuela	138	86	Guyana	33	134	Botswana	1
39	Romania	133	87	Iraq	30	135	Cambodia	1
40	Sweden	127	88	Ecuador	29	136	Guinea	1
41	United Arab Emirates	120	89	Australia	28	137	Mozambique	1
42	Jamaica	116	90	Nicaragua	28	138	Niger	1
43	Yugoslavia	115	91	Suriname	26	139	Rwanda	1
44	Sri Lanka	111	92	Nepal	25	140	Sierra Leone	1
45	Indonesia	110	93	Malawi	23	141	Zaire	1
46	El Salvador	106	94	Tunisia	20			
47	Colombia	101	95	Honduras	18			

Source: *FAO Fertilizer Yearbook*

99. TRACTORS

Agriculture is generally divided into two sectors: modern and traditional. The traditional sector is characterized by intensive labor and the law of diminishing returns. As a result, traditional agriculture is one of the least productive of all economic activities. The modern sector, on the other hand, is characterized by large-scale mechanization, application of fertilizers, soil conservation, irrigation and the use of improved seeds, among other things. Mechanization is best measured by the number of tractors in use per hectare of land actually under cultivation.

TOP 10
Tractors

Rank	Country		(per 1000 hectares)	Rank	Country		(per 1000 hectares)
1	Iceland		1,809.0	5	Bosnia & Herzegovina		214.0
2	Japan		507.0	6	Slovenia		204.0
3	Switzerland		288.0	7	Netherlands		201.0
4	Austria		242.0	8	New Zealand		197.0
				9	Ireland		182.0
				10	Norway		175.0

1 tractor = 100 tractors

Rank	Country	Tractors (per 1000 hectares)	Rank	Country	Tractors (per 1000 hectares)	Rank	Country	Tractors (per 1000 hectares)
UPPER MIDDLE			50	Papua New Guinea	28.5	88	Bulgaria	11.7
11	Italy	158.0	51	St. Kitts and Nevis	27.0	89	Argentina	11.2
12	Belgium	145.3	52	Uruguay	26.2	90	Chile	10.5
13	Luxembourg	143.0	53	United States	25.9	91	Panama	10.1
14	Cyprus	125.0	54	Belize	25.6	92	Bahamas	10.0
15	Liechtenstein	112.0	55	Egypt	24.9	93	Qatar	9.9
16	Germany	111.3	56	Costa Rica	24.6	94	South Africa	9.8
17	Yugoslavia	108.0	57	Czech Republic	24.6	95	Thailand	9.6
18	Finland	89.9	58	Swaziland	24.1	96	Oman	9.4
19	Greece	89.3	59	Brunei	24.0	97	Colombia	9.3
20	Macedonia	83.8	60	Suriname	23.3	98	Russia	9.3
21	United Kingdom	82.2	61	Azerbaijan	22.2	99	Tunisia	9.2
22	Poland	80.8	62	Azerbaijan	20.6	100	Mongolia	8.4
23	France	80.0	63	Belarus	20.2	101	Hungary	8.2
24	Israel	72.6	64	Kuwait	20.0	102	China	8.0
25	Singapore	65.0	65	Lithuania	20.0	103	Guyana	7.6
26	Sao Tome e Principe	62.5	66	Nepal	20	104	Paraguay	7.5
27	Puerto Rico	61.5	67	St. Vincent	20.0	105	Mexico	7.4
28	Denmark	61.4	68	Jamaica	19.9	106	India	7.2
29	Sweden	59.3	69	Libya	19.0	107	Iran	7.1
30	Portugal	55.5	70	Jordan	18.4	108	Australia	6.8
31	Spain	51.7	71	Brazil	17.5	109	Tonga	6.8
32	Korea, North	44.2	72	St. Lucia	17.4	110	Vietnam	6.7
33	Uzbekistan	41.5	73	Kyrgyzstan	16.4	111	United Arab Emirates	6.4
34	Korea, South	40.9	74	Canada	16.3	112	El Salvador	6.1
35	Seychelles	40.0	75	Albania	15.7	113	Iraq	6.1
36	Fiji	39.4	76	Romania	15.7	114	Grenada	6.0
37	Barbados	38.0	77	Venezuela	15.2	115	Zimbabwe	5.9
38	Malta	37.5	78	Botswana	14.3	116	Lesotho	5.8
39	Turkmenistan	37.4	79	Lebanon	13.9	117	Ecuador	5.5
40	Tajikistan	37.0	80	Syria	13.9	118	Kazakhstan	5.2
41	Sri Lanka	35.5	81	Pakistan	13.6	119	Gabon	5.1
42	Trinidad and Tobago	35.3	82	Estonia	13.3	120	Congo	4.9
43	Armenia	33.4	83	Dominica	12.9	121	Peru	4.9
44	Latvia	31.0				122	Namibia	4.8
45	Moldova	31.0	**LOWER MIDDLE**			123	Morocco	4.5
46	Turkey	30.5	84	Ukraine	12.8	124	Yemen	4.0
47	Antigua and Barbuda	30.0	85	Algeria	12.5	125	Vanuatu	3.8
48	Cuba	30.0	86	Bermuda	12.5	126	Mauritius	3.7
49	Georgia	28.6	87	Malaysia	12.0	127	Kenya	3.5

Rank	Country	Tractors (per 1000 hectares)	Rank	Country	Tractors (per 1000 hectares)	Rank	Country	Tractors (per 1000 hectares)
128	Angola	3.4	146	Madagascar	1.1	164	Zaire	0.3
129	Croatia	3.4	147	Myanmar (Burma)	1.1	165	Gambia	0.2
130	Guatemala	3.2	148	Sierra Leone	1.1	166	Senegal	0.2
131	Honduras	2.9	149	Zambia	1.1	167	Togo	0.2
132	Liberia	2.6	150	Uganda	0.9		**BOTTOM 10**	
133	Bolivia	2.5	151	Equatorial Guinea	0.8	168	Afghanistan	0.1
134	Dominican Republic	2.4	152	Malawi	0.8	169	Benin	0.1
135	Nicaragua	2.4	153	Sudan	0.8	170	Burundi	0.1
136	Tanzania	2.2	154	Eritrea	0.7	171	Cameroon	0.1
137	Philippines	2.1	155	Bangladesh	0.6	172	Central African Republic	0.1
138	Somalia	2.1	156	Cambodia	0.6	173	Guinea-Bissau	0.1
139	Indonesia	1.9	157	Saudi Arabia	0.6	174	Rwanda	0.1
140	Mozambique	1.9	158	Guinea	0.5	175	Chad	0.05
141	Mauritania	1.6	159	Cape Verde	0.4	176	Niger	0.05
142	Cote d'Ivoire	1.5	160	Haiti	0.4	177	Burkina	0.04
143	Ghana	1.5	161	Nigeria	0.4			
144	Western Samoa	1.4	162	Ethiopia	0.3			
145	Laos	1.1	163	Mali	0.3			

Source: *United Nations Statistical Yearbook*

100. AVERAGE SIZE OF FARMS

Next to land tenure, the most important factor in agricultural economics is the average size of farms. The size of farms is determined by land colonization practices. In Latin America, for example, the ease with which the conquistadors could establish large estates called latifundios or haciendas led to a system in which large farms were the rule rather than the exception. On the other hand, in countries where Muslim or Hindu inheritance laws prevail, the division of farms among all male heirs has led to fragmentation of holdings into minute parcels. In Asia and Africa, the current trend is to consolidate individual holdings into contiguous blocks of land without actually changing the distribution of land ownership. It is now generally conceded that although smaller farms are worked more intensively, larger farms are more efficient in terms of mechanization and application of fertilizers.

Rank	Country	Average Size of Farms (hectares)	Rank	Country	Average Size of Farms (hectares)	Rank	Country	Average Size of Farms (hectares)
	TOP 10		28	Luxembourg	38.0	58	Turkmenistan	10.0
1	Mongolia	85,000.0	29	Denmark	35.9	59	Switzerland	9.9
2	Russia	7,088.0	30	Sweden	29.5	60	Peru	9.5
3	Romania	3,900.0	31	Germany	28.0	61	Syria	8.9
4	Australia	3,710.0	32	Vietnam	28.0	62	Liechtenstein	8.7
5	Bulgaria	2,467.0	33	Belize	26.7	63	Sao Tome e Principe	8.7
6	South Africa	1,319.0	34	France	26.6	64	Bahamas	8.5
7	Albania	1,182.0	35	Austria	26.4	65	Czech Republic	8.1
8	Cuba	1,047.0	36	Colombia	26.3	66	Italy	7.5
9	Papua New Guinea	483.0	37	Ireland	25.0			
10	Argentina	469.0	38	New Zealand	21.7		**LOWER MIDDLE**	
			39	Belarus	21.0	67	Suriname	7.5
	UPPER MIDDLE		40	Ukraine	20.0	68	Poland	7.0
11	Kazakhstan	412.0	41	Spain	19.0	69	Qatar	7.0
12	Uruguay	280.5	42	Belgium	16.5	70	San Marino	7.0
13	Canada	242.0	43	Latvia	16.5	71	Senegal	7.0
14	United States	190.0	44	Lithuania	16.0	72	Uzbekistan	7.0
15	United Kingdom	107.3	45	Netherlands	15.5	73	Vanuatu	6.9
16	Barbados	95.8	46	Ecuador	15.4	74	Guatemala	6.8
17	Chile	94.1	47	Puerto Rico	14.5	75	Dominican Republic	6.3
18	Paraguay	88.0	48	Libya	14.0	76	Jordan	6.3
19	Venezuela	82.0	49	Panama	13.8	77	Algeria	6.2
20	Bolivia	72.1	50	Tunisia	13.6	78	Western Samoa	6.1
21	Brazil	64.5	51	Honduras	13.5	79	El Salvador	5.4
22	Swaziland	51.0	52	Iraq	13.3	80	Botswana	5.0
23	Mexico	49.0	53	Finland	12.6	81	Cote d'Ivoire	5.0
24	Kyrgyzstan	44.0	54	Israel	11.3	82	Niger	4.9
25	Azerbaijan	39.0	55	Portugal	10.5	83	Burkina	4.8
26	Zimbabwe	38.7	56	Norway	10.2	84	Bahrain	4.4
27	Costa Rica	38.3	57	Saudi Arabia	10.1	85	Lebanon	4.3

Rank	Country	Average Size of Farms (hectares)	Rank	Country	Average Size of Farms (hectares)	Rank	Country	Average Size of Farms (hectares)
86	Trinidad and Tobago	4.3	110	Kenya	2.5	134	Japan	1.4
87	Fiji	4.2	111	Guinea	2.4	135	Ethiopia	1.3
88	Mali	4.0	112	Kuwait	2.4	136	Madagascar	1.3
89	Angola	3.9	113	Myanmar (Burma)	2.3	137	Korea, South	1.2
90	Morocco	3.9	114	United Arab Emirates	2.3	138	Malawi	1.2
91	Uganda	3.9	115	Yemen	2.3	139	Rwanda	1.2
92	Cyprus	3.8	116	Zaire	2.3	140	Taiwan	1.2
93	Thailand	3.7	117	Malaysia	2.2	141	Malta	1.1
94	Cambodia	3.6	118	Antigua and Barbuda	2.1	142	Mauritius	1.1
95	Somalia	3.6	119	Armenia	2.0	143	Nepal	1.1
96	Afghanistan	3.5	120	Lesotho	2.0			
97	Greece	3.5	121	Mauritania	2.0		**BOTTOM 10**	
98	Tonga	3.3	122	St. Lucia	2.0	144	Sri Lanka	1.1
99	Ghana	3.2	123	St. Vincent	1.8	145	Gabon	1.0
100	Bermuda	3.1	124	Sierra Leone	1.8	146	Indonesia	1.0
101	Mozambique	3.1	125	Central African Republic	1.7	147	Solomon Islands	1.0
102	Zambia	3.1	126	Grenada	1.7	148	Bangladesh	0.9
103	Guinea-Bissau	3.0	127	India	1.7	149	Tanzania	0.9
104	Liberia	3.0	128	Tuvalu	1.7	150	Bhutan	0.8
105	Moldova	3.0	129	Cameroon	1.6	151	Singapore	0.8
106	Jamaica	2.9	130	Oman	1.6	152	Egypt	0.7
107	Brunei	2.6	131	Togo	1.5	153	Djibouti	0.4
108	Chad	2.6	132	Congo	1.4			
109	Philippines	2.6	133	Haiti	1.4			

Source: *World Data*

101. FARMLAND

Farmland consists of cropland (land under permanent and temporary crops and fallow), meadows and pastures and wooded lands. Farmland makes up more than half the total land area in about 52 countries. At the bottom of the scale are countries of the Arabian Peninsula where only 1% of the land area is cultivable.

Rank	Country	Farmland as Percent of Total Land Area	Rank	Country	Farmland as Percent of Total Land Area	Rank	Country	Farmland as Percent of Total Land Area
	TOP 10		33	Paraguay	59.9	68	Comoros	44.3
1	Austria	91.0	34	Poland	59.6	69	Slovenia	42.6
2	Uruguay	89.7	35	Senegal	59.1	70	Malta	41.2
3	Burundi	85.8	36	Netherlands	58.1	71	United States	41.1
4	Hungary	85.5	37	Spain	57.6	72	Grenada	40.2
5	Ireland	82.6	38	Croatia	57.0	73	Albania	40.0
6	Mongolia	79.6	39	Haiti	57.0	74	Panama	39.0
7	Sao Tome e Principe	79.2	40	Uzbekistan	57.0	75	Puerto Rico	38.7
8	Taiwan	78.5	41	Bulgaria	55.7	76	Latvia	38.5
9	Cuba	78.3	42	France	55.0	77	Guatemala	38.1
10	United Kingdom	76.9	43	Germany	54.9	78	Sierra Leone	38.1
			44	Jamaica	54.8	79	St. Lucia	38.0
	UPPER MIDDLE		45	Czech Republic	54.3			
11	Zimbabwe	76.6	46	Lithuania	53.9		**LOWER MIDDLE**	
12	San Marino	76.5	47	Mauritius	53.8	80	Nigeria	37.1
13	Italy	75.3	48	Luxembourg	53.3	81	Cyprus	35.6
14	Moldova	73.5	49	India	52.6	82	Colombia	34.7
15	Mexico	72.7	50	Portugal	52.4	83	Venezuela	34.3
16	Bangladesh	70.2	51	Macedonia	51.3	84	Thailand	34.2
17	Ukraine	69.7	52	Rwanda	51.3	85	Syria	32.8
18	El Salvador	69.0	53	Kyrgyzstan	50.9	86	Burkina	32.6
19	Kazakhstan	66.7	54	Barbados	50.2	87	Malaysia	31.2
20	South Africa	66.5	55	Slovakia	49.9	88	St. Vincent	30.8
21	Turkmenistan	66.2	56	Dominican Republic	49.8	89	Sri Lanka	30.6
22	Argentina	64.8	57	Azerbaijan	49.6	90	Swaziland	30.6
23	New Zealand	64.7	58	Bosnia & Herzegovina	49.4	91	Ecuador	30.5
24	Tunisia	64.6	59	Finland	47.7	92	Turkey	30.5
25	Denmark	64.5	60	Nicaragua	47.7	93	Philippines	30.1
26	Romania	64.2	61	Armenia	46.1	94	Tajikistan	30.1
27	Iran	63.8	62	Chad	45.8	95	Honduras	29.8
28	Maldives	63.5	63	Georgia	45.7	96	Benin	29.3
29	Yugoslavia	61.1	64	Belgium	45.6	97	Seychelles	27.8
30	Afghanistan	61.0	65	Belarus	45.1	98	Pakistan	27.7
31	Costa Rica	60.0	66	Brazil	44.5	99	Vietnam	27.4
32	Australia	59.9	67	Tonga	44.5	100	Switzerland	27.1

Rank	Country	Farmland as Percent of Total Land Area	Rank	Country	Farmland as Percent of Total Land Area	Rank	Country	Farmland as Percent of Total Land Area
101	Lebanon	27.0	129	Iraq	13.1	157	Guinea-Bissau	3.4
102	Dominica	26.3	130	Lesotho	12.3	158	Solomon Islands	3.4
103	Guyana	26.2	131	Russia	12.3	159	Cameroon	3.3
104	Greece	26.0	132	Kenya	11.9	160	Norway	3.3
105	Trinidad and Tobago	25.8	133	Chile	11.7	161	Niger	3.0
106	Indonesia	25.3	134	Peru	11.6	162	Brunei	2.8
107	St. Kitts and Nevis	24.7	135	Ghana	10.8	163	Zaire	2.6
108	Liechtenstein	24.2	136	Cape Verde	10.2	164	Andorra	2.0
109	Western Samoa	23.7	137	Belize	10.0	165	Mali	1.8
110	Estonia	22.7	138	Antigua and Barbuda	9.0	166	Bahamas	1.5
111	Israel	21.2	139	Singapore	9.0	167	Zambia	1.3
112	Korea, South	21.2	140	Cote d'Ivoire	8.6	168	Saudi Arabia	1.0
113	Morocco	20.7	141	Tanzania	8.5	169	Suriname	1.0
114	Bolivia	20.6	142	Canada	7.3	170	Central African Republic	0.8
115	Sweden	19.1	143	Laos	7.1	171	Namibia	0.8
116	Nepal	19.0	144	Togo	7.1			
117	Myanmar (Burma)	18.6	145	Guinea	6.5		**BOTTOM 10**	
118	Uganda	18.4	146	Ethiopia	6.4	172	Papua New Guinea	0.8
119	Mozambique	17.8	147	Botswana	5.9	173	Congo	0.7
120	China	17.4	148	Bahrain	5.2	174	Djibouti	0.5
121	Algeria	16.7	149	Egypt	5.2	175	Qatar	0.5
122	Cambodia	16.5	150	Libya	5.1	176	Kuwait	0.4
123	Gambia	16.5	151	Bermuda	4.4	177	Oman	0.4
124	Fiji	15.2	152	Jordan	4.1	178	Gabon	0.3
125	Vanuatu	15.0	153	Liberia	3.8	179	Mauritania	0.2
126	Malawi	14.1	154	Madagascar	3.5	180	United Arab Emirates	0.2
127	Japan	13.7	155	Angola	3.4	181	Yemen	0.1
128	Sudan	13.3	156	Bhutan	3.4			

Source: *World Data*

102. CHICKENS

Chickens provide a cheaper source of proteins than beef and are thus popular in both developed and developing countries. They are valuable for both their meat and their eggs. In developing countries chickens are raised in traditional farms or in small subsistence plots. In developed countries they are raised in large commercialized batteries where they are hatched, fed, raised, killed and processed in mechanized assembly lines.

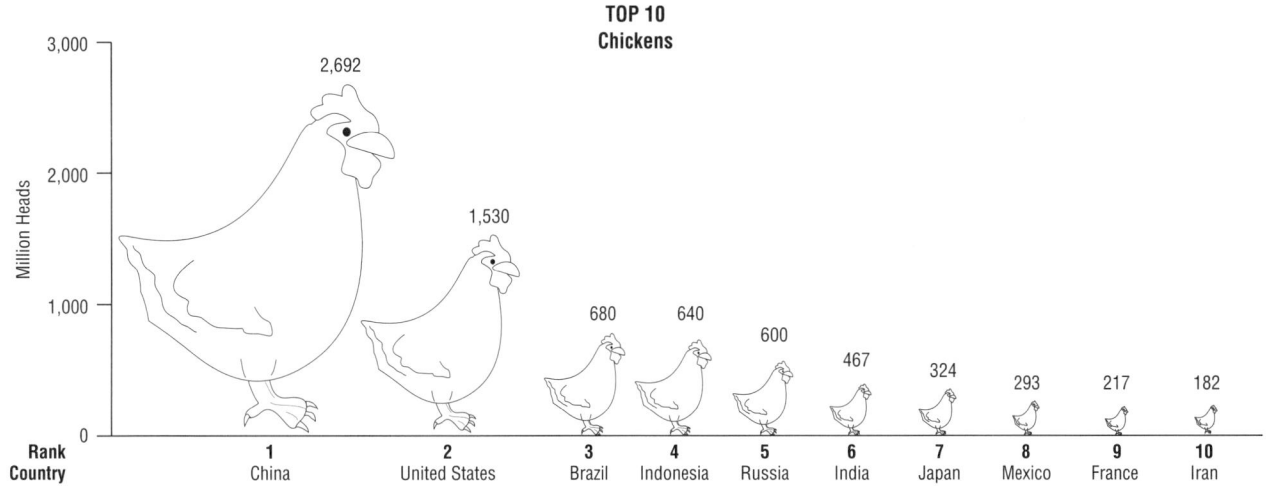

TOP 10
Chickens

Rank	1	2	3	4	5	6	7	8	9	10
Country	China	United States	Brazil	Indonesia	Russia	India	Japan	Mexico	France	Iran
Million Heads	2,692	1,530	680	640	600	467	324	293	217	182

Rank	Country	Chickens (million heads)	Rank	Country	Chickens (million heads)	Rank	Country	Chickens (million heads)
UPPER MIDDLE			63	Iraq	24	114	Bosnia & Herzegovina	7
11	Turkey	178	64	Lebanon	24	115	Lithuania	7
12	Ukraine	159	65	Azerbaijan	23	116	Nicaragua	7
13	Italy	137	66	Israel	23	117	Turkmenistan	7
14	Thailand	127	67	Korea, North	23	118	Angola	6
15	United Kingdom	126	68	Madagascar	23	119	Finland	6
16	Nigeria	122	69	Mali	23	120	Sierra Leone	6
17	Bangladesh	116	70	Mozambique	22	121	Suriname	6
18	Netherlands	110	71	Portugal	22	122	Switzerland	6
19	Malaysia	98	72	Yemen	22	123	Togo	6
20	Pakistan	98	73	Zambia	22	124	Haiti	5
21	Taiwan	98	74	Yugoslavia	21	125	Tajikistan	5
22	Canada	96	75	Cameroon	20	126	Burundi	4
23	Germany	96	76	Niger	20	127	Chad	4
24	Morocco	91				128	El Salvador	4
25	Venezuela	90	**LOWER MIDDLE**			129	Eritrea	4
26	Vietnam	85	77	Uganda	20	130	Latvia	4
27	Saudi Arabia	81	78	Burkina	19	131	Liberia	4
28	Algeria	78	79	Denmark	19	132	Macedonia	4
29	Jordan	77	80	Syria	19	133	Mauritania	4
30	Romania	77	81	Georgia	17	134	Norway	4
31	Colombia	75	82	Guatemala	16	135	Albania	3
32	Korea, South	74	83	Bulgaria	15	136	Armenia	3
33	Peru	68	84	Costa Rica	15	137	Barbados	3
34	Philippines	68	85	Libya	15	138	Botswana	3
35	Australia	65	86	Guinea	14	139	Central African Republic	3
36	Argentina	59	87	Kuwait	14	140	Cyprus	3
37	Ecuador	59	88	Moldova	14	141	Estonia	3
38	Chile	58	89	Austria	13	142	Fiji	3
39	Kazakhstan	55	90	Croatia	13	143	Gabon	3
40	Ethiopia	54	91	Paraguay	13	144	Mauritius	3
41	Spain	51	92	Puerto Rico	13	145	Oman	3
42	Belarus	45	93	Sweden	13	146	Papua New Guinea	3
43	Poland	44	94	Zimbabwe	13	147	Qatar	3
44	South Africa	42	95	Ghana	12	148	Somalia	3
45	Tunisia	39	96	Honduras	12	149	Bahamas	2
46	Egypt	38	97	Kyrgyzstan	12	150	Brunei	2
47	Senegal	38	98	Slovakia	12	151	Congo	2
48	Zaire	37	99	Cambodia	11	152	Namibia	2
49	Bolivia	36	100	Guyana	11			
50	Belgium	35	101	Ireland	11	**BOTTOM 10**		
51	Sudan	35	102	Slovenia	11	153	Singapore	2
52	Dominican Republic	34	103	Trinidad and Tobago	11	154	Bahrain	1
53	Hungary	31	104	New Zealand	10	155	Belize	1
54	Benin	30	105	Uruguay	10	156	Cape Verde	1
55	Uzbekistan	30	106	Laos	9	157	Gambia	1
56	Cote d'Ivoire	27	107	Malawi	9	158	Guinea-Bissau	1
57	Greece	27	108	Panama	9	159	Lesotho	1
58	Kenya	26	109	Sri Lanka	9	160	Malta	1
59	Cuba	25	110	Jamaica	8	161	Rwanda	1
60	Myanmar (Burma)	25	111	Nepal	8	162	Swaziland	1
61	Tanzania	25	112	United Arab Emirates	8			
62	Czech Republic	24	113	Afghanistan	7			

Source: FAO

AGRICULTURAL CROPS

Agriculture is a statistical nightmare. Despite FAO's efforts over the past 50 years to promote and standardize statistical reporting in this field, few farmers take the trouble to keep tabs on their output and few national agricultural departments and agencies bother to check on the accuracy of the data reported to them. Traditional definitions also persist in distorting reported data. Worldwide agricultural production is more often underreported than overreported, which is perhaps the one reason that even in countries with reported food shortages, people seldom starve. Most countries report only commercial sales of foodstuffs and ignore subsistence crops or barter. In some developed countries, domestic production statistics are collected only for holdings above a certain size. Cereals statistics often relate to estimated yields rather than harvests. European and North American countries exclude from cereals totals millet and sorghum used primarily as livestock or poultry feed, but in most developing countries millet and sorghum are used for human consumption and reported as cereals. Statistics for tropical fruits are not compiled by producing countries, while wild fruits and berries are completely ignored even by FAO. Almost all countries exclude the production of kitchen gardens and small plots, even though they may account for up to 40% of the total output.

103. AGRICULTURAL CROPS: VEGETABLES

Rank	Country	Vegetable Production (000 metric tons)	Rank	Country	Vegetable Production (000 metric tons)	Rank	Country	Vegetable Production (000 metric tons)
TOP 10			42	Australia	1,618	84	Uganda	413
1	India	65,137	43	Hungary	1,584	85	Malaysia	396
2	United States	36,443	44	Tunisia	1,550	86	Guatemala	386
3	China	28,811	45	Moldova	1,477	87	Papua New Guinea	383
4	Turkey	19,354	46	Bangladesh	1,459	88	Ecuador	376
5	Japan	13,870	47	Bulgaria	1,293	89	Albania	352
6	Italy	13,629	48	Israel	1,287	90	Madagascar	333
7	Spain	10,680	49	Colombia	1,264	91	Kyrgyzstan	328
8	Korea, South	10,503	50	Nepal	1,252	92	Denmark	316
9	Russia	10,190	51	Georgia	1,130	93	Croatia	300
10	Iran	10,050	52	Kazakhstan	1,065	94	Switzerland	298
			53	Peru	1,037	95	Lithuania	280
UPPER MIDDLE			54	Tanzania	1,001	96	Mali	271
11	Egypt	9,402	55	Belarus	981	97	Zambia	269
12	France	7,223	56	Lebanon	964	98	Malawi	265
13	Brazil	6,181	57	Sudan	922	99	Niger	264
14	Mexico	6,078	58	Jordan	883	100	Benin	257
15	Nigeria	5,670	59	Yugoslavia	883	101	Burkina	254
16	Ukraine	5,506	60	Azerbaijan	813	102	Paraguay	253
17	Poland	5,313	61	Venezuela	739	103	Angola	249
18	Indonesia	5,280	62	Sri Lanka	685	104	Honduras	241
19	Philippines	4,440	63	Turkmenistan	672	105	Dominican Republic	239
20	Pakistan	4,029	64	Kenya	655	106	Sweden	238
21	Vietnam	4,028	65	Libya	614	107	Latvia	232
22	Korea, North	3,988	66	Tajikistan	595	108	Haiti	219
23	Greece	3,870	67	New Zealand	590	109	Ireland	218
24	United Kingdom	3,791	68	Zaire	583	110	Burundi	210
25	Romania	3,755	69	United Arab Emirates	576	111	Finland	201
26	Uzbekistan	3,737	70	Ethiopia	565	112	Sierra Leone	182
27	Germany	3,630	71	Czech Republic	522	113	Costa Rica	175
28	Netherlands	3,561	72	Slovakia	499	114	Togo	170
29	Morocco	3,102	73	Afghanistan	492	115	Oman	169
30	Argentina	2,882	74	Cambodia	488	116	Norway	166
31	Iraq	2,799	75	Cuba	484	117	Laos	154
32	Chile	2,660	76	Ghana	473	118	Jamaica	151
33	Thailand	2,603	77	Yemen	460	119	Zimbabwe	143
34	Myanmar (Burma)	2,217	78	Cote d'Ivoire	454	120	Uruguay	136
35	Saudi Arabia	2,138	79	Macedonia	448	121	El Salvador	128
36	Portugal	2,047	80	Austria	440	122	Cyprus	123
37	Canada	2,017				123	Rwanda	120
38	South Africa	1,980	**LOWER MIDDLE**			124	Senegal	115
39	Algeria	1,958	81	Bolivia	429	125	Mozambique	114
40	Belgium	1,885	82	Armenia	424	126	Estonia	83
41	Syria	1,806	83	Guinea	420	127	Panama	75

Rank	Country	Vegetable Production (000 metric tons)	Rank	Country	Vegetable Production (000 metric tons)	Rank	Country	Vegetable Production (000 metric tons)
128	Chad	74	147	Djibouti	22	166	Dominica	6
129	Somalia	72	148	Guinea-Bissau	20	167	Solomon Islands	6
130	Liberia	71	149	Maldives	19	168	Belize	5
131	Kuwait	69	150	Trinidad and Tobago	18	169	Kiribati	5
132	Slovenia	67	151	Botswana	16	170	Singapore	5
133	Central African Republic	65	152	Bahrain	15	171	Comoros	4
134	Bosnia & Herzegovina	59	153	Mongolia	15			
135	Mauritius	57	154	Fiji	13		**BOTTOM 10**	
136	Nicaragua	57	155	Guyana	12	172	Antigua and Barbuda	3
137	Malta	54	156	Swaziland	12	173	Bermuda	3
138	Cameroon	46	157	Bhutan	10	174	St. Vincent	3
139	Congo	44	158	Barbados	9	175	Sao Tome e Principe	3
140	Qatar	38	159	Cape Verde	9	176	Grenada	2
141	Puerto Rico	37	160	Mauritania	9	177	Iceland	2
142	Suriname	35	161	Brunei	8	178	Seychelles	2
143	Gabon	31	162	Gambia	8	179	St. Kitts and Nevis	1
144	Bahamas	28	163	Namibia	8	180	St. Lucia	1
145	Lesotho	26	164	Tonga	8	181	Western Samoa	1
146	Eritrea	25	165	Vanuatu	8			

Source: FAO

104. AGRICULTURAL CROPS: FRUITS

Rank	Country	Fruit Production (000 metric tons)
TOP 10		
1	China	37,298
2	India	33,235
3	Brazil	32,515
4	United States	25,854
5	Italy	17,972
6	Spain	11,648
7	France	10,649
8	Turkey	9,700
9	Mexico	9,547
10	Uganda	9,239
UPPER MIDDLE		
11	Iran	9,021
12	Nigeria	7,911
13	Indonesia	7,125
14	Philippines	6,799
15	Argentina	6,766
16	Thailand	6,338
17	Ecuador	6,053
18	Colombia	5,935
19	Egypt	4,628
20	Japan	4,564
21	Pakistan	4,428
22	Greece	4,395
23	Germany	4,342
24	Vietnam	4,067
25	Romania	3,930
26	South Africa	3,670
27	Zaire	3,569
28	Chile	3,086
29	Russia	3,026
30	Australia	2,803
31	Rwanda	2,655
32	Costa Rica	2,518
33	Venezuela	2,494
34	Morocco	2,377
35	Tanzania	2,228
36	Poland	2,111
37	Korea, South	2,024
38	Peru	1,945
39	Papua New Guinea	1,833
40	Cote d'Ivoire	1,788
41	Dominican Republic	1,767
42	Hungary	1,748
43	Iraq	1,629
44	Ukraine	1,548
45	Israel	1,516
46	Ghana	1,468
47	Syria	1,426
48	Yugoslavia	1,424
49	Portugal	1,409
50	Lebanon	1,402
51	Korea, North	1,393
52	Bangladesh	1,379
53	Burundi	1,349
54	Honduras	1,331
55	Cuba	1,324
56	Azerbaijan	1,282
57	Moldova	1,281
58	Georgia	1,265
59	Algeria	1,241

Rank	Country	Fruit Production (000 metric tons)
60	Malaysia	1,206
61	Cameroon	1,138
62	Panama	1,076
63	Guinea	1,054
64	Myanmar (Burma)	1,020
65	Uzbekistan	1,005
66	Kenya	974
67	New Zealand	933
68	Saudi Arabia	919
69	Haiti	893
70	Bolivia	878
71	Netherlands	873
72	Tunisia	871
73	Guatemala	852
74	Bulgaria	845
75	Sudan	804
76	Austria	788
77	Belgium	766
78	Sri Lanka	762
79	Madagascar	760
LOWER MIDDLE		
80	Canada	720
81	Paraguay	717
82	Afghanistan	614
83	Nepal	587
84	Switzerland	579
85	Malawi	507
86	Croatia	495
87	United Kingdom	477
88	Czech Republic	476
89	Uruguay	458
90	Angola	417
91	Jamaica	377
92	Yemen	361
93	Macedonia	338
94	El Salvador	322
95	Cyprus	320
96	Belarus	298
97	United Arab Emirates	297
98	Jordan	295
99	Mozambique	292
100	Armenia	275
101	Slovakia	270
102	Cambodia	269
103	Gabon	266
104	Slovenia	260
105	Turkmenistan	249
106	Libya	247
107	Nicaragua	236
108	Ethiopia	227
109	Tajikistan	225
110	Puerto Rico	218
111	Oman	210
112	Central African Republic	208
113	Somalia	207
114	St. Lucia	199
115	Congo	188
116	Kazakhstan	177
117	Belize	167
118	Benin	162
119	Sierra Leone	157

Rank	Country	Fruit Production (000 metric tons)
120	Zimbabwe	157
121	Laos	152
122	Swaziland	149
123	Lithuania	133
124	Kyrgyzstan	132
125	Senegal	132
126	Liberia	130
127	Denmark	118
128	Norway	118
129	Zambia	103
130	Bosnia & Herzegovina	102
131	Chad	100
132	St. Vincent	98
133	Albania	97
134	Sweden	96
135	Finland	90
136	Suriname	82
137	Latvia	78
138	Burkina	74
139	Guyana	73
140	Guinea-Bissau	67
141	Trinidad and Tobago	65
142	Bhutan	64
143	Comoros	60
144	Estonia	49
145	Togo	49
146	Niger	47
147	Western Samoa	43
148	Mauritania	25
149	Bahrain	24
150	Grenada	23
151	Vanuatu	20
152	Dominica	19
153	Ireland	19
154	Lesotho	18
155	Equatorial Guinea	17
156	Cape Verde	16
157	Mali	16
158	Sao Tome e Principe	14
159	Solomon Islands	14
160	Bahamas	13
161	Tonga	13
162	Fiji	12
163	Malta	12
164	Qatar	12
165	Botswana	11
166	Mauritius	11
167	Maldives	10
168	Namibia	10
169	Antigua and Barbuda	9
BOTTOM 10		
170	Brunei	5
171	Kiribati	5
172	Eritrea	4
173	Gambia	4
174	Barbados	3
175	St. Kitts and Nevis	2
176	Seychelles	2
177	Bermuda	1
178	Kuwait	1
179	Tuvalu	1

Source: FAO

105. AGRICULTURAL CROPS: PULSES

Rank	Country	Pulses Production (000 metric tons)	Rank	Country	Pulses Production (000 metric tons)	Rank	Country	Pulses Production (000 metric tons)
TOP 10			50	Japan	113	100	Croatia	24
1	India	14,536	51	Mozambique	99	101	Zambia	23
2	China	6,678	52	South Africa	94	102	Ghana	20
3	France	3,450	53	Chile	91	103	Senegal	18
4	Brazil	3,307	54	Yugoslavia	91	104	Mauritania	17
5	Russia	3,000	55	Dominican Republic	90	105	Bosnia & Herzegovina	16
6	Ukraine	2,636	56	Haiti	89	106	Central African Republic	16
7	Canada	2,028	57	Moldova	86	107	Cambodia	14
8	Turkey	1,752	58	New Zealand	85	108	Finland	14
9	Nigeria	1,750	59	Kazakhstan	80	109	Botswana	13
10	Mexico	1,702	60	Romania	76	110	Eritrea	13
			61	Nicaragua	75	111	Libya	12
UPPER MIDDLE			62	Benin	71	112	Somalia	12
11	United States	1,552	63	Yemen	69	113	Panama	10
12	Australia	1,252	64	Sweden	67	114	Switzerland	10
13	Myanmar (Burma)	960				115	Congo	9
14	Ethiopia	800	**LOWER MIDDLE**			116	Comoros	8
15	United Kingdom	743	65	Mali	65	117	Cote d'Ivoire	8
16	Iran	730	66	Tunisia	65	118	Jordan	8
17	Poland	624	67	Burkina	63	119	Ireland	7
18	Pakistan	621	68	Portugal	62	120	Jamaica	7
19	Uganda	572	69	Guinea	60	121	Namibia	7
20	Bangladesh	517	70	Madagascar	60	122	Saudi Arabia	7
21	Indonesia	504	71	El Salvador	57	123	Israel	6
22	Denmark	454	72	Paraguay	56	124	Latvia	6
23	Thailand	441	73	Venezuela	50	125	Tajikistan	6
24	Niger	433	74	Zimbabwe	49	126	Uruguay	6
25	Egypt	380	75	Algeria	48	127	Slovenia	5
26	Tanzania	302	76	Greece	45	128	Gambia	4
27	Korea, North	293	77	Bulgaria	43	129	Swaziland	4
28	Burundi	287	78	Laos	43	130	Guinea-Bissau	3
29	Argentina	277	79	Togo	43	131	Lesotho	3
30	Malawi	268	80	Honduras	41	132	Liberia	3
31	Morocco	261	81	Sierra Leone	40	133	Mongolia	3
32	Vietnam	217	82	Ecuador	39	134	Armenia	2
33	Spain	211	83	Sri Lanka	39	135	Belize	2
34	Germany	204	84	Iraq	38	136	Bhutan	2
35	Kenya	200	85	Lebanon	38	137	Cyprus	2
36	Zaire	198	86	Philippines	37	138	Mauritius	2
37	Nepal	197	87	Afghanistan	35			
38	Colombia	194	88	Costa Rica	35	**BOTTOM 10**		
39	Italy	184	89	Korea, South	35	139	Papua New Guinea	2
40	Syria	174	90	Angola	34	140	Solomon Islands	2
41	Slovakia	165	91	Chad	34	141	Trinidad and Tobago	2
42	Czech Republic	163	92	Belgium	31	142	Bahamas	1
43	Rwanda	142	93	Lithuania	30	143	Barbados	1
44	Belarus	140	94	Bolivia	29	144	Fiji	1
45	Hungary	119	95	Cameroon	28	145	Grenada	1
46	Sudan	116	96	Netherlands	28	146	Guyana	1
47	Austria	114	97	Cuba	26	147	Malta	1
48	Peru	114	98	Macedonia	26	148	Puerto Rico	1
49	Guatemala	113	99	Albania	25			

Source: FAO

106. AGRICULTURAL CROPS: ROOTS AND TUBERS

Rank	Country	Roots and Tubers Production (000 metric tons)
TOP 10		
1	China	150,098
2	Nigeria	44,415
3	Russia	33,780
4	Brazil	27,274
5	Poland	23,058
6	India	21,490
7	United States	21,432
8	Zaire	20,447
9	Thailand	19,309
10	Indonesia	17,914
UPPER MIDDLE		
11	Ukraine	16,102
12	Germany	9,257
13	Belarus	8,241
14	Netherlands	7,748
15	Tanzania	7,716
16	United Kingdom	7,065
17	Ghana	6,650
18	Uganda	5,923
19	France	5,456
20	Vietnam	5,431
21	Japan	5,244
22	Colombia	5,139
23	Cote d'Ivoire	4,761
24	Turkey	4,352
25	Spain	4,084
26	Romania	3,889
27	Canada	3,518
28	Mozambique	3,426
29	Iran	2,850
30	Phillipines	2,777
31	Peru	2,672
32	Paraguay	2,658
33	Argentina	2,550
34	Benin	2,510
35	Korea, North	2,266
36	Madagascar	2,210
37	Belgium	2,080
38	Ethiopia	2,018
39	Italy	1,984
40	Cameroon	1,967
41	Kazakhstan	1,950
42	Bangladesh	1,865
43	Egypt	1,859
44	Denmark	1,826
45	Kenya	1,752
46	Rwanda	1,616
47	South Africa	1,564
48	Pakistan	1,460
49	Bolivia	1,371
50	Mexico	1,348
51	Paqua New Guinea	1,303
52	Portugal	1,278
53	Czech Republic	1,231
54	Angola	1,203
55	Guinea	1,203
56	Algeria	1,200
57	Lithuania	1,200
58	Australia	1,158
59	Burundi	1,124

Rank	Country	Roots and Tubers Production (000 metric tons)
60	Greece	1,002
61	Sweden	991
62	Latvia	944
63	Chile	907
64	Central African Republic	901
65	Nepal	891
66	Morocco	887
67	Togo	848
68	Hungary	826
69	Switzerland	800
70	Haiti	789
71	Austria	750
72	Cuba	744
73	Finland	726
74	Korea, South	721
75	Congo	703
76	Estonia	700
77	Yugoslavia	700
78	Venezuela	655
LOWER MIDDLE		
79	Zambia	648
80	Ireland	600
81	Croatia	563
82	Uzbekistan	562
83	Malawi	550
84	Malaysia	543
85	Chad	534
86	Ecuador	513
87	Sri Lanka	485
88	Bulgaria	476
89	Norway	471
90	Slovakia	455
91	Liberia	441
92	Moldova	435
93	Iraq	410
94	Armenia	400
95	Syria	377
96	Gabon	374
97	Slovenia	360
98	Lebanon	296
99	Kyrgyzstan	288
100	New Zealand	276
101	Myanmar (Burma)	265
102	Niger	260
103	Namibia	253
104	Dominican Republic	249
105	Israel	241
106	Cambodia	233
107	Jamaica	232
108	Georgia	229
109	Afghanistan	228
110	Uruguay	226
111	Laos	221
112	Tunisia	200
113	Yemen	181
114	Bosnia & Herzegovina	180
115	Saudi Arabia	169
116	Zimbabwe	163
117	Sudan	157
118	Cyprus	154
119	Azerbaijan	150

Rank	Country	Roots and Tubers Production (000 metric tons)
120	Costa Rica	146
121	Mali	145
122	Tajikistan	140
123	Macedonia	134
124	Libya	130
125	Sierra Leone	115
126	Solomon Islands	110
127	Eritrea	109
128	Tonga	102
129	Albania	100
130	Senegal	91
131	Burkina	86
132	Equatorial Guinea	84
133	Nicaragua	79
134	Panama	72
135	Jordan	70
136	Guinea-Bissau	65
137	Fiji	64
138	Comoros	63
139	Guatemala	63
140	Bhutan	56
141	Mongolia	54
142	El Salvador	51
143	Vanuatu	51
144	Western Samoa	41
145	Somalia	39
146	Guyana	32
147	Honduras	30
148	Turkmenistan	30
149	Malta	25
150	Dominica	23
151	Mauritius	20
152	St. Vincent	18
153	Puerto Rico	13
154	Liechtenstein	12
155	St. Lucia	12
156	Trinidad and Tobago	12
157	Sao Tome e Principe	10
158	Botswana	9
159	Cape Verde	8
160	Iceland	8
161	Kiribati	8
162	Lesotho	8
163	Maldives	8
164	Swaziland	8
165	Gambia	6
166	Oman	6
167	Mauritania	5
BOTTOM 10		
168	Belize	4
169	Grenada	4
170	Suriname	4
171	United Arab Emirates	4
172	Barbados	3
173	Bahamas	2
174	Bermuda	1
175	Brunei	1
176	Kuwait	1
177	St. Kitts and Nevis	1

Source: FAO

107. AGRICULTURAL CROPS: GRAINS

Rank	Country	Grain Production (000 metric tons)	Rank	Country	Grain Production (000 metric tons)	Rank	Country	Grain Production (000 metric tons)
TOP 10			55	Mali	2,705	110	Togo	526
1	China	397,212	56	Afghanistan	2,662	111	Sierra Leone	515
2	United States	357,377	57	Sri Lanka	2,620	112	Mongolia	443
3	India	212,482	58	Chile	2,619	113	Slovenia	409
4	Russia	78,709	59	Croatia	2,595	114	Somalia	405
5	France	53,641	60	Madagascar	2,517	115	Haiti	380
6	Indonesia	52,862	61	Burkina	2,509	116	Georgia	353
7	Canada	47,054	62	Lithuania	2,412	117	Guyana	343
8	Brazil	45,930	63	Peru	2,396	118	Panama	327
9	Germany	36,353	64	Uzbekistan	2,306	119	Cuba	277
10	Ukraine	32,862	65	Belgium	2,273	120	Angola	274
			66	Iraq	2,250	121	Libya	263
UPPER MIDDLE			67	Niger	2,221	122	Lesotho	258
11	Bangladesh	28,741	68	Algeria	2,195	123	Tajikistan	254
12	Mexico	27,412	69	Malaysia	2,080	124	Armenia	240
13	Turkey	27,001	70	Venezuela	2,069	125	Suriname	225
14	Argentina	24,668	71	Uganda	2,036	126	Costa Rica	215
15	Vietnam	23,455				127	Burundi	213
16	Thailand	22,576	**LOWER MIDDLE**			128	Guinea-Bissau	201
17	Pakistan	22,256	72	Ecuador	1,937	129	Mauritania	188
18	Poland	21,763	73	Cambodia	1,864	130	Rwanda	158
19	United Kingdom	19,670	74	Zaire	1,798	131	Israel	157
20	Myanmar (Burma)	19,607	75	Laos	1,730	132	Cyprus	148
21	Italy	18,918	76	Ireland	1,700	133	Namibia	120
22	Iran	17,522	77	Turkmenistan	1,573	134	Jordan	119
23	Romania	17,512	78	Portugal	1,546	135	Gambia	109
24	Kazakhstan	16,395	79	Guatemala	1,507	136	Bermuda	106
25	Japan	15,787	80	Ghana	1,450	137	Central African Republic	92
26	Philippines	15,550	81	Uruguay	1,428	138	Eritrea	72
27	Spain	15,341	82	Moldova	1,423	139	Lebanon	67
28	Egypt	14,766	83	Cote d'Ivoire	1,359	140	Swaziland	67
29	Australia	14,462	84	Netherlands	1,355	141	Botswana	50
30	South Africa	14,422	85	Norway	1,268	142	Liberia	50
31	Nigeria	13,517	86	Switzerland	1,218	143	Fiji	32
32	Hungary	11,911	87	Guinea	1,172	144	Congo	27
33	Morocco	9,789	88	Zambia	1,168	145	Belize	26
34	Yugoslavia	8,910	89	Bolivia	1,110	146	Gabon	24
35	Denmark	7,885	90	Malawi	1,110	147	Trinidad and Tobago	21
36	Korea, South	7,588	91	Bhutan	1,047	148	Comoros	19
37	Czech Republic	6,777	92	Kyrgyzstan	1,047	149	Malta	9
38	Ethiopia	6,734	93	Azerbaijan	1,012	150	United Arab Emirates	7
39	Bulgaria	6,424	94	Cameroon	985	151	Cape Verde	6
40	Belarus	5,930	95	Chad	963	152	Jamaica	6
41	Nepal	5,929	96	Senegal	952	153	Qatar	5
42	Syria	5,660	97	El Salvador	943			
43	Greece	4,896	98	Paraguay	941	**BOTTOM 10**		
44	Sudan	4,805	99	Mozambique	819	154	Sao Tome e Principe	4
45	Austria	4,681	100	Yemen	802	155	Oman	3
46	Sweden	4,571	101	Latvia	799	156	Papua New Guinea	3
47	Korea, North	4,525	102	New Zealand	779	157	Barbados	2
48	Saudi Arabia	4,509	103	Albania	692	158	Kuwait	2
49	Slovakia	3,730	104	Estonia	661	159	Mauritius	2
50	Colombia	3,703	105	Tunisia	660	160	Bahamas	1
51	Tanzania	3,534	106	Benin	646	161	Brunei	1
52	Kenya	3,481	107	Honduras	639	162	St. Vincent	1
53	Finland	3400	108	Nicaragua	623	163	Vanuatu	1
54	Zimbabwe	2,764	109	Dominican Republic	610			

Source: FAO

108. VALUE ADDED IN AGRICULTURE

Worldwide, the agricultural sector has become more productive, yet at the same time, its share of the national wealth has shrunk. The sector has also witnessed structural changes as a result of food crops being displaced in many countries by cash crops. The value of these cash crops is determined not by the producing nations as much as by cartels and commodities exchanges. More agricultural land is being converted into industrial and residential use. The value added in agriculture may remain stable because of increased productivity and better prices, but its share of GDP will continue to decline.

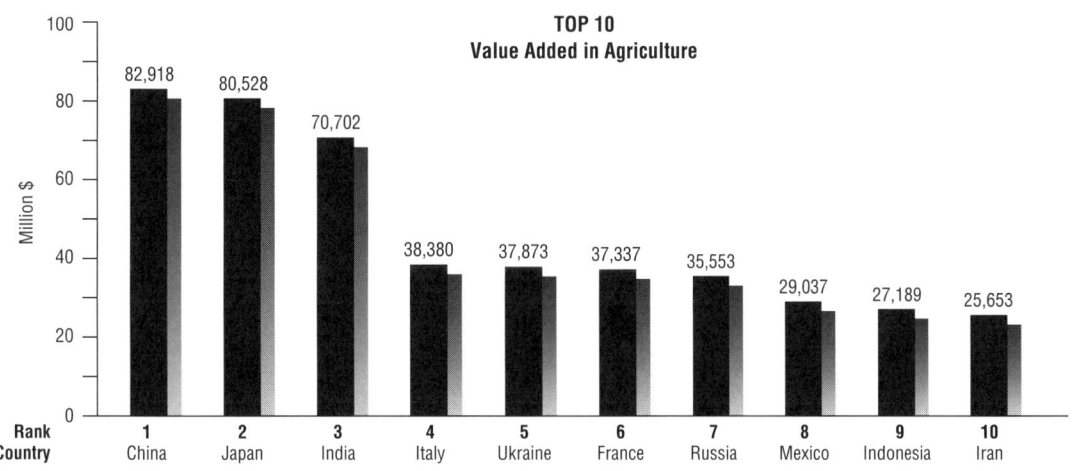

TOP 10
Value Added in Agriculture

Rank	1	2	3	4	5	6	7	8	9	10
Country	China	Japan	India	Italy	Ukraine	France	Russia	Mexico	Indonesia	Iran
Million $	82,918	80,528	70,702	38,380	37,873	37,337	35,553	29,037	27,189	25,653

Rank	Country	Value Added in Agriculture (million $)
UPPER MIDDLE		
11	Turkey	23,609
12	Korea, South	23,403
13	Germany	23,267
14	Spain	20,295
15	United Kingdom	16,383
16	Argentina	15,312
17	Thailand	12,441
18	Greece	12,014
19	Philippines	11,723
20	Netherlands	11,636
21	Pakistan	11,500
22	Nigeria	10,505
23	Australia	9,404
24	Colombia	7,607
25	Bangladesh	7,306
26	Egypt	6,396
27	Poland	5,434
28	Algeria	5,366
29	Romania	5,327
30	Sweden	5,208
31	South Africa	4,815
32	Finland	4,717
33	Uzbekistan	4,693
34	Belarus	4,643
35	Peru	4,518
36	Austria	4,491
37	Denmark	4,360
38	Morocco	3,809
39	Vietnam	3,759
40	Belgium	3,644
41	Ethiopia	3,476
42	Cameroon	3,170
43	Cote d'Ivoire	3,026
44	Venezuela	3,024

Rank	Country	Value Added in Agriculture (million $)
45	Ghana	2,893
46	Guatemala	2,845
47	Yemen	2,511
48	Sri Lanka	2,311
49	Tunisia	2,287
50	Hungary	2,135
LOWER MIDDLE		
51	Czech Republic	1,952
52	Paraguay	1,802
53	Ecuador	1,746
54	Georgia	1,738
55	Uganda	1,599
56	Nepal	1,532
57	Moldova	1,485
58	Dominican Republic	1,473
59	Kenya	1,357
60	Bulgaria	1,346
61	Papua New Guinea	1,321
62	Azerbaijan	1,304
63	Zambia	1,242
64	Uruguay	1,187
65	Tanzania	1,168
66	Costa Rica	1,158
67	Mali	1,128
68	Senegal	1,126
69	Madagascar	1,062
70	Armenia	1,051
71	Lithuania	890
72	Niger	855
73	United Arab Emirates	773
74	Benin	760
75	Guinea	759
76	Zimbabwe	757
77	Slovakia	741

Rank	Country	Value Added in Agriculture (million $)
78	Malawi	709
79	Laos	685
80	Latvia	685
81	Panama	667
82	El Salvador	654
83	Togo	607
84	Central African Republic	584
85	Slovenia	583
86	Honduras	566
87	Rwanda	551
88	Nicaragua	545
89	Chad	494
90	Mozambique	453
91	Gabon	447
92	Burundi	443
93	Estonia	411
94	Puerto Rico	410
95	Oman	374
96	Jordan	353
97	Jamaica	321
98	Albania	277
99	Mauritius	274
100	Congo	273
BOTTOM 10		
101	Mauritania	238
102	Botswana	216
103	Namibia	207
104	Trinidad and Tobago	114
105	Mongolia	112
106	Kuwait	110
107	Guinea-Bissau	108
108	Singapore	103
109	Gambia	83
110	Lesotho	61

Source: *World Development Report*

109. FOOD IMPORTS—CEREALS

Historically, nations that had poor crops in any year had only one choice: starvation for many of its poorer people. However, in the latter part of the 20th century, imports from food-rich nations have offered a dramatic solution to this problem, leading to the virtual disappearance of widespread starvation. There are more nations in the world suffering chronic food deficits than there are nations with overflowing surpluses of food. But worldwide, the FAO has concluded that the world produces more than enough food for all its inhabitants—it is only a matter of distribution.

Rank	Country	Food Imports: Cereal (000 tons)	Rank	Country	Food Imports: Cereal (000 tons)	Rank	Country	Food Imports: Cereal (000 tons)
TOP 10			43	Chile	983	86	Papua New Guinea	227
1	Japan	28,035	44	Dominican Republic	961	87	Tanzania	215
2	Korea, South	11,271	45	Turkmenistan	940	88	Sweden	202
3	Russia	11,238	46	Singapore	798	89	Moldova	200
4	Brazil	7,848	47	Greece	708	90	Honduras	197
5	China	7,332	48	India	694	91	Austria	184
6	Egypt	7,206	49	Albania	647	92	Mongolia	182
7	Italy	6,249	50	Thailand	638	93	Panama	159
8	Mexico	6,223	51	Cote d'Ivoire	590	94	Congo	148
9	Algeria	5,821	52	United Arab Emirates	583	95	Namibia	141
10	Belgium	5,291	53	Denmark	579	96	Hungary	137
						97	Niger	136
UPPER MIDDLE			**LOWER MIDDLE**			98	Sierra Leone	136
11	Saudi Arabia	5,186	54	Senegal	579	99	Benin	134
12	Spain	4,955	55	Kenya	569	100	Botswana	133
13	Iran	4,840	56	Slovenia	549	101	Lesotho	131
14	United States	4,684	57	Zimbabwe	538	102	Nicaragua	125
15	Netherlands	4,431	58	Costa Rica	535	103	Burkina	121
16	Uzbekistan	4,151	59	Czech Republic	519	104	Kyrgyzstan	120
17	Morocco	3,653	60	Malawi	514	105	Macedonia	117
18	United Kingdom	3,534	61	Mozambique	507	106	Rwanda	115
19	Germany	3,533	62	Georgia	500	107	Madagascar	111
20	Malaysia	3,288	63	Guatemala	486	108	Uruguay	110
21	Poland	3,142	64	Azerbaijan	480	109	Finland	108
22	Indonesia	3,105	65	Switzerland	455	110	Kazakhstan	100
23	Pakistan	2,893	66	Tajikistan	450	111	Gambia	87
24	Romania	2,649	67	Jamaica	429	112	Mali	83
25	Venezuela	2,314	68	Ecuador	428	113	Paraguay	82
26	Israel	2,293	69	Ireland	409	114	Gabon	77
27	South Africa	2,225	70	Ghana	396	115	Uganda	76
28	Portugal	2,147	71	Oman	369	116	Guinea-Bissau	70
29	Turkey	2,107	72	Zambia	353			
30	Philippines	2,036	73	Armenia	350	**BOTTOM 10**		
31	Peru	1,920	74	Guinea	335	117	Togo	63
32	Yemen	1,843	75	Norway	302	118	Chad	59
33	Colombia	1,702	76	Bolivia	298	119	Estonia	46
34	Jordan	1,596	77	Vietnam	289	120	Australia	32
35	Nigeria	1,584	78	El Salvador	286	121	Central African Republic	32
36	Ukraine	1,500	79	Mauritania	286	122	Nepal	27
37	Belarus	1,250	80	New Zealand	282	123	Burundi	22
38	France	1,188	81	Cameroon	281	124	Latvia	11
39	Bangladesh	1,175	82	Kuwait	251	125	Argentina	8
40	Sri Lanka	1,149	83	Bulgaria	241	126	Laos	8
41	Canada	1,095	84	Mauritius	240			
42	Tunisia	1,044	85	Trinidad and Tobago	232			

Source: *World Development Report*

FOOD PRODUCTION PER CAPITA GROWTH RATE

The natural process in food production is decline rather than growth. First, there are more mouths to feed, so that there is less food per capita. Second, the nutrients in the soil are being constantly depleted, as a result of which there is less of a harvest. Third, as more agricultural land is being converted to industrial and residential uses, the total acreage under crops is shrinking. Faced with these negative factors, it is surprising that per capita food production is stable in many countries, and slightly increasing in others. The positive factor on the side of the farmers is technology in the form of better fertilizers, better seeds, better irrigation facilities, and better marketing support.

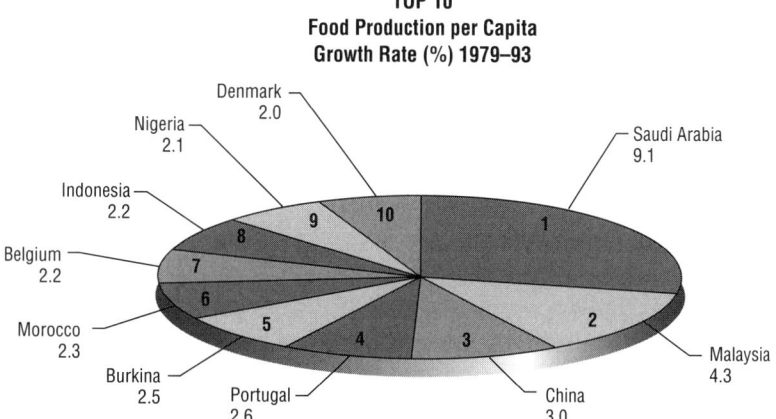

TOP 10
Food Production per Capita
Growth Rate (%) 1979–93

- Denmark 2.0
- Nigeria 2.1
- Indonesia 2.2
- Belgium 2.2
- Morocco 2.3
- Burkina 2.5
- Portugal 2.6
- China 3.0
- Malaysia 4.3
- Saudi Arabia 9.1

Rank	Country	Food Production per Capita Growth Rate (%) 1979–93
UPPER MIDDLE		
11	Benin	1.9
12	Chile	1.9
13	Ireland	1.9
14	India	1.5
15	Tunisia	1.5
16	Egypt	1.3
17	Paraguay	1.3
18	Algeria	1.2
19	Brazil	1.2
20	Nepal	1.2
21	Pakistan	1.2
22	Spain	1.1
23	Colombia	1.0
24	Iran	1.0
25	Jamaica	1.0
26	Guinea-Bissau	0.9
27	Bolivia	0.7
28	Costa Rica	0.7
29	El Salvador	0.7
30	Hungary	0.7
31	Poland	0.7
32	Canada	0.6
33	Ecuador	0.6
34	Georgia	0.5
35	Korea, South	0.5
36	Netherlands	0.4
37	Australia	0.3
38	Chad	0.3
39	Ghana	0.3
40	Turkey	0.3
41	Uganda	0.3
42	Uruguay	0.3
43	Austria	0.2
44	Jordan	0.2

Rank	Country	Food Production per Capita Growth Rate (%) 1979–93
45	Norway	0.2
46	Venezuela	0.2
47	France	0.1
48	Greece	0.0
49	Mauritius	0.0
LOWER MIDDLE		
50	New Zealand	0.0
51	Senegal	0.0
52	Thailand	0.0
53	United Kingdom	0.0
54	Bangladesh	−0.1
55	Cote d'Ivoire	−0.1
56	Laos	−0.2
57	Papua New Guinea	−0.2
58	Argentina	−0.3
59	Burundi	−0.3
60	Finland	−0.3
61	Guinea	−0.3
62	Italy	−0.3
63	Japan	−0.3
64	Puerto Rico	−0.3
65	Switzerland	−0.3
66	United States	−0.3
67	Zambia	−0.3
68	Kenya	−0.4
69	Peru	−0.4
70	Guatemala	−0.5
71	Yemen	−0.5
72	Togo	−0.6
73	Trinidad and Tobago	−0.6
74	Dominican Republic	−0.9
75	Mali	−0.9
76	Mexico	−0.9
77	Central African Republic	−1.0

Rank	Country	Food Production per Capita Growth Rate (%) 1979–93
78	Ethiopia	−1.2
79	Panama	−1.2
80	Sierra Leone	−1.2
81	Honduras	−1.3
82	Myanmar (Burma)	−1.3
83	Philippines	−1.3
84	Tanzania	−1.3
85	Gabon	−1.4
86	Sweden	−1.4
87	Congo	−1.5
88	Madagascar	−1.5
89	Mauritania	−1.6
90	Israel	−1.8
91	Niger	−1.8
92	Sri Lanka	−1.8
93	Bulgaria	−1.9
94	Cameroon	−1.9
95	Namibia	−2.0
96	South Africa	−2.0
97	Botswana	−2.1
98	Mozambique	−2.1
99	Lesotho	−2.2
BOTTOM 10		
100	Vietnam	−2.2
101	Albania	−2.3
102	Romania	−2.4
103	Mongolia	−2.5
104	Rwanda	−2.5
105	Nicaragua	−2.7
106	Zimbabwe	−3.0
107	Gambia	−4.0
108	Malawi	−4.2
109	Singapore	−6.4

Source: FAO

Section

XI

INDUSTRY & MINING

Compared to agriculture, industry, particularly manufacturing, is a glamour sector, and the terms industrialize and modernize are often used as synonyms. Developing nations including the oil-rich ones are anxious to move into the industrial age and experience their own version of the Industrial Revolution. The secret is that industrialization creates a multiplier or ripple effect; each factory leads to the establishment of satellite factories supplying parts; to the building of townships; to the construction of the infrastructure, such as roads; to increased energy consumption; to the refinement of vocational skills and to a number of other similar improvements.

Industrial strength may not always ensure economic independence, as many nations are discovering; in fact, it may have the opposite effect of reinforcing dependence because of the more critical need to find and maintain markets and suppliers of raw materials. Industrial progress is therefore a complex phenomenon, which can be measured only at certain middle levels. Technological capability, supply of raw materials, infrastructure support and downstream facilities form the base, while industrial production forms only the top of the pyramid. There are only a handful of countries where all these conditions are so ideally combined that they can be called industrial nations. The United States, already described as a postindustrial nation, leads the list, with Germany and Japan close runners-up. The United Kingdom, France, Sweden and Italy complete the list; all the other nations are far behind.

111. VALUE ADDED IN MANUFACTURING

Value added in manufacturing expresses the difference between the cost of the finished manufactured products and the sum total of the cost of individual parts and materials that went into their making. It is an important index of industrialization.

Rank	Country	Value Added in Manufacturing (million $)
TOP 10		
1	Japan	1,023,048
2	Germany	565,703
3	France	271,133
4	Italy	250,345
5	United Kingdom	201,859
6	Russia	200,337
7	China	147,302
8	Spain	100,672
9	Brazil	90,062
10	Korea, South	85,454
UPPER MIDDLE		
11	Mexico	67,157
12	Netherlands	58,476
13	Argentina	50,009
14	Ukraine	48,872
15	Austria	46,739
16	Australia	43,679
17	Sweden	43,605
18	India	41,558
19	Thailand	31,185
20	Indonesia	27,854
21	Turkey	27,465
22	South Africa	26,050
23	Denmark	23,478

Rank	Country	Value Added in Manufacturing (million $)
24	Finland	20,785
25	Iran	15,363
26	Norway	14,282
27	Singapore	13,568
28	Puerto Rico	13,392
29	Philippines	12,811
30	Greece	12,398
31	Belarus	12,179
32	Romania	10,623
33	Kazakhstan	10,571
34	Colombia	9,618
35	Venezuela	8,838
36	Pakistan	7,538
37	Hungary	7,381
38	Egypt	5,747
39	Uzbekistan	5,494
LOWER MIDDLE		
40	Morocco	5,118
41	Algeria	4,010
42	Slovenia	3,670
43	Ecuador	2,790
44	United Arab Emirates	2,708
45	Tunisia	2,576
46	Azerbaijan	2,557
47	Uruguay	2,476

Rank	Country	Value Added in Manufacturing (million $)
48	Bangladesh	2,164
49	Vietnam	2,139
50	Nigeria	2,012
51	Latvia	1,738
52	Kuwait	1,731
53	Ireland	1,511
54	Cameroon	1,384
55	Costa Rica	1,380
56	Zimbabwe	1,379
57	Sri Lanka	1,354
58	Estonia	1,265
59	El Salvador	1,238
60	Paraguay	1,103
61	Dominican Republic	1,094
62	Zambia	1,057
63	Yemen	977
64	Georgia	861
65	Senegal	809
66	Kenya	764
67	Gabon	653
68	Jamaica	620
69	Mauritius	602
70	Ghana	598
71	Jordan	598
72	Honduras	510
73	Panama	502

Rank	Country	Value Added in Manufacturing (million $)	Rank	Country	Value Added in Manufacturing (million $)	Rank	Country	Value Added in Manufacturing (million $)
74	Trinidad and Tobago	496	84	Rwanda	180	92	Guinea	135
75	Oman	495	85	Namibia	173	93	Tanzania	121
76	Papua New Guinea	404	86	Benin	170	94	Mauritania	115
77	Nepal	322	87	Botswana	161	95	Lesotho	97
78	Nicaragua	306	88	Togo	161	96	Burundi	93
79	Malawi	244	89	Uganda	155	97	Sierra Leone	34
80	Mali	234				98	Gambia	21
81	Congo	228	**BOTTOM 10**			99	Guinea-Bissau	19
82	Ethiopia	210	90	Niger	151			
83	Chad	198	91	Laos	149			

Source: *World Development Report*

112. INDUSTRY'S SHARE OF GDP

The industrial sector comprises mining, manufacturing, construction, electricity, water and gas. It is one of three principal sectors contributing to GDP, the other two being agriculture and services.

Rank	Country	Industry's Share of GDP (%)	Rank	Country	Industry's Share of GDP (%)	Rank	Country	Industry's Share of GDP (%)
TOP 10			43	South Africa	25	86	New Zealand	17
1	Tajikistan	60	44	Luxembourg	24	87	Paraguay	17
2	Bosnia & Herzegovina	58	45	Philippines	24	88	Seychelles	17
3	Slovakia	53	46	Switzerland	24	89	Sri Lanka	17
4	Azerbaijan	48	47	Belgium	23	90	Tunisia	17
5	Armenia	46	48	Brazil	23	91	Bolivia	16
6	China	45	49	Hungary	23	92	Australia	15
7	Romania	45	50	Mauritius	23	93	Belize	15
8	Yugoslavia	45	51	Peru	23	94	Burkina	15
9	Belarus	44	52	Spain	23	95	Greece	15
10	Croatia	44	53	Argentina	22	96	Guatemala	15
			54	Finland	22	97	Jordan	15
UPPER MIDDLE			55	Israel	22	98	Malawi	15
11	Czech Republic	44	56	Mexico	22	99	Pakistan	15
12	Ukraine	43	57	Nicaragua	22	100	Senegal	15
13	Brunei	42	58	United Kingdom	22	101	Cameroon	14
14	Bulgaria	39	59	Uruguay	22	102	Cyprus	14
15	Cuba	39	60	Indonesia	21	103	Iran	14
16	Ireland	39	61	Venezuela	21	104	Kuwait	14
17	Mongolia	39	62	Colombia	20	105	Albania	13
18	Puerto Rico	39	63	Ecuador	20	106	Laos	13
19	Poland	38	64	France	20	107	Lebanon	13
20	Russia	36	65	Italy	20	108	Lesotho	13
21	Kyrgyzstan	34	66	Jamaica	20	109	Norway	13
22	Moldova	33	67	Netherlands	20	110	Qatar	13
23	Taiwan	33	68	Sweden	20	111	Burundi	12
24	Japan	31	69	Turkmenistan	20	112	Eritrea	12
25	Malaysia	30	70	Vietnam	20	113	Fiji	12
26	Slovenia	30	71	Costa Rica	19	114	Iceland	12
27	Zimbabwe	30	72	Denmark	19	115	Macedonia	12
28	Portugal	29	73	El Salvador	19	116	Madagascar	12
29	Uzbekistan	29	74	Lithuania	19	117	Rwanda	12
30	Estonia	28	75	Turkey	19	118	St. Kitts and Nevis	12
31	Germany	28	76	United States	19	119	Western Samoa	12
32	Kazakhstan	28	77	Canada	18	120	Haiti	11
33	Singapore	28	78	Chile	18	121	Sierra Leone	11
34	Thailand	28	79	Dominican Republic	18	122	Suriname	11
35	Zambia	28	80	Georgia	18	123	Algeria	10
36	Korea, South	27				124	Guyana	10
37	Swaziland	27	**LOWER MIDDLE**			125	Kenya	10
38	Afghanistan	26.0	81	Morocco	18	126	St. Vincent	10
39	Austria	26	82	Bahrain	17	127	Yemen	10
40	Latvia	26	83	Egypt	17	128	Bangladesh	9
41	Malta	26	84	Honduras	17	129	Bhutan	9
42	Mozambique	25	85	India	17	130	Chad	9

Rank	Country	Industry's Share of GDP (%)	Rank	Country	Industry's Share of GDP (%)	Rank	Country	Industry's Share of GDP (%)
131	Congo	9	149	Niger	7	167	Benin	4
132	Ethiopia	9	150	Sao Tome e Principe	7	168	Comoros	4
133	Ghana	9	151	Saudi Arabia	7	169	Guinea	4
134	Mali	9	152	Solomon Islands	7	170	Iraq	4
135	Mauritania	9	153	Togo	7	171	Namibia	4
136	Panama	9	154	Barbados	6	172	Oman	4
137	Papua New Guinea	9	155	Cape Verde	6			
138	Sudan	9	156	Cote d'Ivoire	6	**BOTTOM 10**		
139	Trinidad and Tobago	9	157	Gambia	6	173	Somalia	4
140	Libya	8	158	Grenada	6	174	Tonga	4
141	Nepal	8	159	Maldives	6	175	Uganda	4
142	St. Lucia	8	160	Nigeria	6	176	Angola	3
143	United Arab Emirates	8	161	Syria	6	177	Antigua and Barbuda	3
144	Central African Republic	7	162	Vanuatu	6	178	Bahamas	3
145	Dominica	7	163	Botswana	5	179	Tuvalu	3
146	Gabon	7	164	Djibouti	5	180	Kiribati	2
147	Liberia	7	165	Guinea-Bissau	5	181	Equatorial Guinea	1
148	Myanmar (Burma)	7	166	Tanzania	5	182	Zaire	1

Source: *World Development Report*

113. MINERAL PRODUCTION

Mining statistics tend to be as reliable as industrial statistics because they are reported at various stages to the authorities: first during mining, then during transport, trade and final industrial processing. The sector has also the benefit of numerous associations and publications reporting data relating to their par-

ticular metal or mineral. Metals are ferrous and non-ferrous metallic ores, concentrates and scrap; non-metals include all nonmetallic minerals, (stone, clay, precious gems, etc.). Value added by the mineral industry measures the importance of the sector within the national economy.

TOP 10
Mineral Production Value Added (million $)

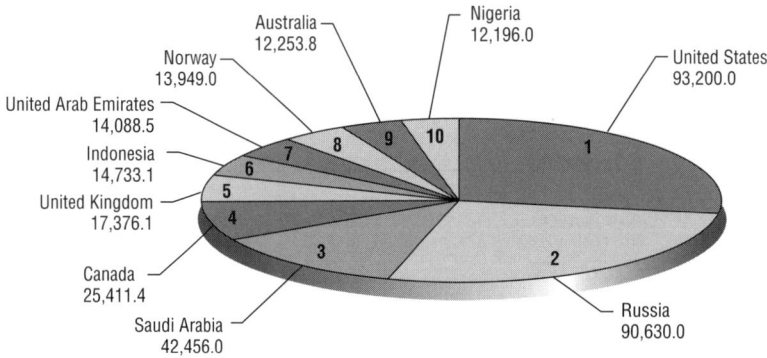

Australia 12,253.8
Nigeria 12,196.0
United States 93,200.0
Norway 13,949.0
United Arab Emirates 14,088.5
Indonesia 14,733.1
United Kingdom 17,376.1
Canada 25,411.4
Saudi Arabia 42,456.0
Russia 90,630.0

Rank	Country	Mineral Production (million $)
UPPER MIDDLE		
11	Germany	11,803.2
12	Iran	11,264.3
13	Japan	10,509.3
14	Libya	9,988.9
15	China	9,885.2
16	Algeria	9,880.5
17	Kuwait	9,640.7
18	Netherlands	9,396.1
19	South Africa	9,012.6
20	Venezuela	8,942.5
21	France	6,233.7
22	Mexico	5,946.9
23	Brazil	5,738.7
24	Malaysia	5,542.9
25	India	4,827.9
26	Oman	4,382.1
27	Argentina	4,108.1
28	Spain	3,786.9
29	Syria	3,657.1
30	Colombia	2,952.4
31	Qatar	2,678.6
32	Angola	2,609.0
33	Italy	2,554.5
34	Czech Republic	2,225.4
35	Yugoslavia	2,205.9
36	Turkey	2,077.0
37	Chile	2,066.4
38	Egypt	1,960.0
39	Poland	1,903.5
40	Thailand	1,541.4
41	Brunei	1,476.0
42	Papua New Guinea	1,471.6
43	Cameroon	1,441.0
44	Korea, South	1,384.7
45	Romania	1,315.6
46	Botswana	1,234.1
47	Denmark	1,232.1
48	Taiwan	1,194.1
49	Peru	1,098.1
50	Vietnam	1,062.9
51	Gabon	1,055.9
52	Hungary	939.5
53	Tunisia	889.9
54	Ecuador	882.6
55	Bahrain	779.8
56	Zaire	708.0
57	Trinidad and Tobago	706.6

Rank	Country	Mineral Production (million $)
58	Greece	666.2
59	Philippines	637.5
60	Morocco	629.0
61	Guinea	592.8
62	Congo	586.2
63	Bulgaria	582.1
64	Bolivia	576.1
65	Sweden	560.5
66	New Zealand	552.8
67	Yemen	551.5
68	Zambia	546.8
69	Ireland	512.1
LOWER MIDDLE		
70	Iraq	480.6
71	Belgium	433.6
72	Austria	385.0
73	Finland	374.6
74	Israel	352.6
75	Namibia	319.0
76	Pakistan	301.5
77	Zimbabwe	290.5
78	Jamaica	279.0
79	Cote d'Ivoire	248.1
80	Myanmar (Burma)	223.0
81	Slovenia	207.7
82	Togo	146.8
83	Jordan	145.2
84	Dominican Republic	141.0
85	Ghana	130.7
86	Portugal	129.2
87	Niger	124.0
88	Liberia	122.3
89	Croatia	119.7
90	Sri Lanka	112.4
91	Mauritania	86.5
92	Suriname	85.0
93	Sierra Leone	84.2
94	Albania	81.4
95	Guyana	81.1
96	Honduras	52.3
97	Central African Republic	49.1
98	Senegal	42.3
99	Mali	40.1
100	Uruguay	31.6
101	Estonia	31.0
102	Puerto Rico	31.0
103	Latvia	30.9

Rank	Country	Mineral Production (million $)
104	Luxembourg	29.2
105	Burkina	28.4
106	Singapore	25.5
107	Paraguay	24.2
108	Nepal	22.3
109	Tanzania	22.0
110	Cyprus	17.2
111	Sudan	17.1
112	Nicaragua	16.5
113	Afghanistan	16.2
114	Benin	13.1
115	Kenya	12.1
116	Uganda	11.8
117	Fiji	11.2
118	Ethiopia	11.0
119	El Salvador	10.8
120	Swaziland	8.9
121	Madagascar	8.1
122	Antigua and Barbuda	6.1
123	Chad	5.0
124	Panama	5.0
125	Burundi	4.7
126	Costa Rica	3.8
127	Malta	3.1
128	Mauritius	3.1
129	Bhutan	2.9
130	St. Lucia	2.6
131	Mozambique	2.4
132	Belize	2.3
133	Rwanda	2.2
134	Belarus	2.0
135	Maldives	1.9
136	Laos	1.8
137	Dominica	1.3
BOTTOM 10		
138	Haiti	1.2
139	Grenada	1.1
140	Lesotho	1.1
141	Somalia	1.0
142	Cape Verde	0.8
143	St. Vincent	0.7
144	St. Kitts and Nevis	0.5
145	Tonga	0.4
146	Malawi	0.1
147	Solomon Islands	−0.5

Source: *World Data*

114. STEEL PRODUCTION

Steel has long been acknowledged as the bellwether of industrial development, and its production is an indicator of the general level of industrial activity. Steel derives its importance from its status as the basic raw material of the hard-technology manufacturing sector, and its price and production levels influence those of a host of other products, appliances and vehicles. The following ranking reveals as closely as any single ranking can the degree of a nation's industrialization.

Rank	Country	Steel Production Monthly (000 million tons)	Rank	Country	Steel Production Monthly (000 million tons)	Rank	Country	Steel Production Monthly (000 million tons)
TOP 10			**LOWER MIDDLE**			45	Trinidad and Tobago	60
1	China	8,343	22	Romania	540	46	Qatar	52
2	Japan	8,246	23	Netherlands	528	47	Colombia	50
3	United States	7,850	24	Czech Republic	495	48	Peru	50
4	Russia	4,200	25	Iran	449	49	New Zealand	48
5	Germany	3,731	26	Sweden	430	50	Moldova	40
6	Korea, South	3,224	27	Argentina	351	51	Uzbekistan	39
7	Brazil	2,062	28	Venezuela	350	52	Ireland	31
8	Italy	1,974	29	Austria	349	53	Slovenia	31
9	Ukraine	1,885	30	Kazakhstan	301			
10	United Kingdom	1,559	31	Slovakia	238	**BOTTOM 10**		
			32	Egypt	230	54	Norway	30
UPPER MIDDLE			33	Saudi Arabia	223	55	Cuba	22
11	India	1,534	34	Finland	221	56	Zimbabwe	20
12	France	1,469	35	Luxembourg	211	57	Denmark	15
13	Spain	1,220	36	Bulgaria	190	58	Tunisia	15
14	Canada	1,190	37	Hungary	159	59	Azerbaijan	9
15	Mexico	1,075	38	Chile	90	60	Croatia	5
16	Turkey	1,060	39	Greece	80	61	Georgia	5
17	Taiwan	1,000	40	Libya	80	62	El Salvador	3
18	Poland	850	41	Belarus	76	63	Macedonia	3
19	Belgium	797	42	Yugoslavia	70			
20	Australia	710	43	Algeria	60			
21	South Africa	654	44	Portugal	60			

Source: *Steel Statistical Yearbook*

115. INDUSTRIAL ROBOTS

Assembly line repetitive work and the consequent monotony are the bane of industrial society. During the 1980s, it was thought that robots could be created to undertake much of this monotonous and repetitive work and that they would do it more efficiently and more quickly. Although the hope has not been borne out, there are more than half a million robots cheerfully doing the work that humans hate, and further they do not receive any overtime or Social Security benefits. They do not need coffee breaks either.

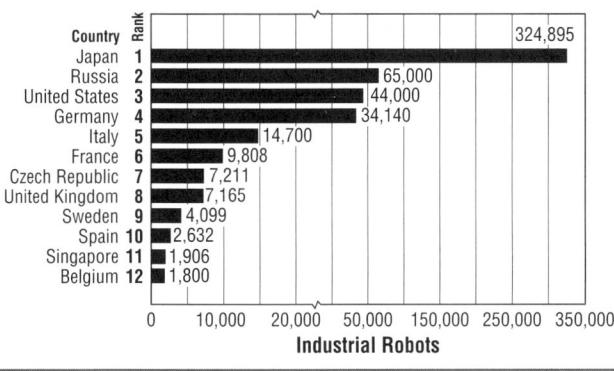

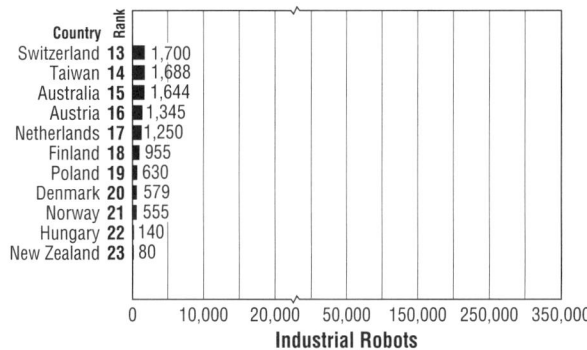

Source: *World Industrial Robot Statistics*

116. PASSENGER CAR PRODUCTION AND ASSEMBLY

Production of passenger cars is almost entirely confined to the developed world and is therefore one of the true indices of industrial development. The data include units shipped in knocked-down form for local assembly in other countries.

Rank	Country	Passenger Car Production and Assembly	Rank	Country	Passenger Car Production and Assembly	Rank	Country	Passenger Car Production and Assembly
TOP 10			**MIDDLE**			**BOTTOM 10**		
1	Japan	9,378,694	11	Mexico	778,413	25	Portugal	60,990
2	United States	5,663,284	12	Brazil	338,322	26	Malaysia	49,153
3	Germany	4,419,797	13	Sweden	293,499	27	Colombia	38,021
4	France	3,329,490	14	Switzerland	271,044	28	Hungary	30,099
5	Spain	1,790,615	15	Turkey	265,245	29	Indonesia	29,650
6	Italy	1,476,627	16	Poland	221,072	30	Yugoslavia	25,271
7	Korea, South	1,306,752	17	Argentina	220,502	31	Austria	23,479
8	United Kingdom	1,291,880	18	Australia	217,218	32	Taiwan	20,985
9	Canada	1,019,633	19	Czech Republic	202,455	33	Chile	18,014
10	Belgium	840,263	20	India	153,867	34	Peru	819
			21	Netherlands	94,019			
			22	Venezuela	92,179			
			23	China	81,055			
			24	Ireland	70,775			

Source: *World Motor Vehicle Data*

Section

XII

ENERGY

Energy may be described as a doomsday indicator—one that is bound to get worse before it gets worse! It therefore needs to be looked at closely, even if with quiet desperation. Energy is bound up with the whole mythology of industrial civilization; it is inconceivable that civilization as we know it can exist without energy, certainly not its marvels, its conveniences, its extravagances, and its 1,001 useless luxuries. What is wrong with energy is that both its production and consumption are lopsided. The production is monopolized by the Arabs; the consumption is monopolized by the Americans, many of whom believe they have a constitutional right to a third of the world's energy supplies. The energy shortage, the first phase of which we are now in, has been triggered by two phenomena that will soon converge: the first is the finite supply of the non-renewable fossil fuels that generate most of the energy presently consumed; the second is the soaring demand caused by a growing population, the greater number and variety of technological goods available and the increased affluence that has brought these goods within the reach of a larger proportion of the population.

The principal objective of this section is to present a global framework of data on energy supply and demand. The first group of rankings is an overview presenting production of energy in terms of total production, annual growth rate of production, annual growth rate of energy consumption and consumption per capita. The share of fuel in imports is examined in another ranking. The next four groups of rankings deal with the principal source of energy: coal, petroleum, natural gas and electricity. For coal and natural gas there are rankings on production and reserves; for petroleum, rankings on production, reserves and refinery capacity.

117. COMMERCIAL ENERGY EFFICIENCY

Because energy is a finite resource when produced from non-renewable source, its efficient use is as important as its conservation. One way of assessing the efficiency of energy use is relative of the GDP. In other words, the efficiency rate is expressed in terms of its production of GDP. The greater the nonproductive uses of the energy measured, the less the efficiency rate.

Rank	Country	Commercial Energy Efficiency (energy consumption in kg of oil equivalent per $100 CDP)
TOP 10		
1	Bulgaria	403
2	Romania	254
3	China	187
4	Poland	155
5	Algeria	154
6	India	132
7	Trinidad and Tobago	130
8	Egypt	105
9	South Africa	97
10	Hungary	95
UPPER MIDDLE		
11	Zimbabwe	94
12	Venezuela	93
13	Jordan	90
14	Zambia	80
15	Mozambique	78
16	Panama	75
17	Pakistan	70
18	Saudi Arabia	69
19	Syria	69
20	Iran	64

Rank	Country	Commercial Energy Efficiency (energy consumption in kg of oil equivalent per $100 CDP)
21	Colombia	61
22	Jamaica	59
23	Ecuador	56
24	Argentina	50
25	Canada	50
26	Turkey	48
27	Nigeria	45
28	Oman	45
29	Indonesia	43
30	Singapore	43
31	Sierra Leone	42
32	Tanzania	42
33	Malaysia	41
34	Mexico	41
35	New Zealand	39
36	Tunisia	39
37	Chile	38
38	Greece	38
39	Bolivia	37
40	Norway	37
41	Sri Lanka	37
42	Honduras	36

Rank	Country	Commercial Energy Efficiency (energy consumption in kg of oil equivalent per $100 CDP)
LOWER MIDDLE		
43	Kenya	36
44	United States	35
45	Dominican Republic	34
46	Brazil	33
47	Costa Rica	32
48	Ghana	31
49	Philippines	31
50	Australia	30
51	Korea, North	30
52	Cyprus	29
53	Gabon	28
54	Bangladesh	27
55	Netherlands	27
56	Thailand	27
57	Uruguay	27
58	Finland	25
59	Ireland	25
60	Papua New Guinea	25
61	Sweden	25
62	Portugal	24
63	United Kingdom	24
64	Morocco	23

Rank	Country	Commercial Energy Efficiency (energy consumption in kg of oil equivalent per $100 CDP)	Rank	Country	Commercial Energy Efficiency (energy consumption in kg of oil equivalent per $100 CDP)	Rank	Country	Commercial Energy Efficiency (energy consumption in kg of oil equivalent per $100 CDP)
65	Mauritania	22	79	Guatemala	16	93	Burundi	13
66	El Salvador	21	80	Paraguay	16	94	Japan	13
67	Peru	20	81	Spain	16		**BOTTOM 10**	
68	Madagascar	19	82	Yemen	16	95	Rwanda	13
69	Mauritius	19	83	Botswana	15	96	Benin	12
70	Congo	18	84	Cameroon	15	97	Haiti	12
71	Ethiopia	18	85	Israel	15	98	Hong Kong	12
72	France	18	86	Belgium	14	99	Switzerland	12
73	Germany	18	87	Guinea	14	100	Togo	11
74	Laos	18	88	Italy	14	101	Chad	8
75	Malawi	18	89	Nepal	14	102	Mali	8
76	Austria	17	90	Nicaragua	14	103	Central African Republic	7
77	Denmark	17	91	Niger	14	104	Burkina	6
78	Uganda	17	92	Senegal	14			

Source: *World Development Report*

118. NUCLEAR REACTORS

The Nuclear Club is one of the exclusive groups in the world. The major powers are the senior members of the club and, despite the ban on proliferation of nuclear weapons, more than 20 small countries have managed to get their foot in the door. Most nuclear reactors are designed for the production of electricity, but their existence and operations continue to pose a serious threat to the safety of the general population.

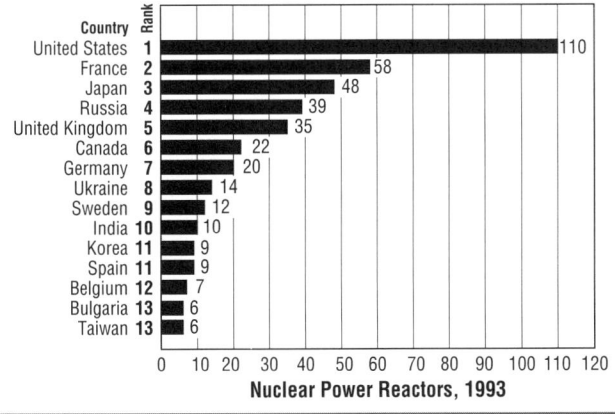

Nuclear Power Reactors, 1993

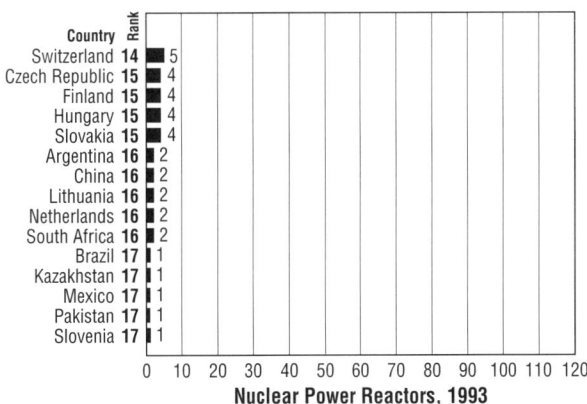

Nuclear Power Reactors, 1993

Source: "It's Business, Not Religion." *Nuclear Engineering International* (June 1994), p. 16.

119. ELECTRICITY PRODUCTION

There are many standard terms used by public utilities to measure electric power generation. One is the installed capacity expressed in kW. Total installed capacity is multiplied by 8760 hours per year to yield total production capacity (kW-hr). Annual production of electricty meausured in millions of kW-hrs ranges generally between 50% and 60% of total production capacity.

Rank	Country	Electricity Produced (million kW-hr)	Rank	Country	Electricity Produced (million kW-hr)	Rank	Country	Electricity Produced (million kW-hr)
TOP 10			61	Tajikistan	17,741	122	Sudan	1,328
1	United States	3,145,892	62	United Arab Emirates	17,578	123	Ethiopia	1,293
2	Russia	956,587	63	Libya	17,000	124	Brunei	1,285
3	Japan	906,705	64	Puerto Rico	16,540	125	Luxembourg	1,067
4	China	839,453	65	Ireland	16,416	126	Mauritius	988
5	Canada	527,316	66	Peru	14,326	127	Bahamas	980
6	Germany	525,721	67	Lithuania	14,122	128	Nepal	936
7	France	471,448	68	Syria	12,638	129	Gabon	922
8	India	356,519	69	Turkmenistan	12,637	130	Tanzania	907
9	United Kingdom	323,029	70	Nigeria	11,800	131	Laos	900
10	Brazil	251,484	71	Slovenia	11,692	132	Malawi	795
			72	Kyrgyzstan	11,091	133	Uganda	788
UPPER MIDDLE			73	Cuba	11,054	134	Senegal	765
11	Ukraine	229,907	74	Bosnia & Herzegovina	11,000	135	Afghanistan	695
12	Italy	222,788	75	Vietnam	10,854	136	Madagascar	599
13	South Africa	175,910	76	Moldova	10,369	137	Barbados	548
14	Australia	163,557	77	Morocco	9,917	138	Guinea	536
15	Korea, South	163,449	78	Georgia	9,700	139	Botswana	522
16	Spain	156,529	79	Bangladesh	9,685	140	Bermuda	518
17	Sweden	144,311				141	Mozambique	490
18	Mexico	134,925	**LOWER MIDDLE**			142	Fiji	485
19	Poland	133,867	80	Croatia	9,359	143	Liberia	480
20	Norway	120,001	81	Estonia	9,118	144	Congo	431
21	Taiwan	101,784	82	Uruguay	7,989	145	Haiti	394
22	Kazakhstan	77,444	83	Zambia	7,785	146	Mali	330
23	Netherlands	76,992	84	Zimbabwe	7,643	147	Somalia	258
24	Turkey	73,808	85	Ecuador	7,447	148	Guyana	240
25	Iran	71,980	86	Oman	7,048	149	Rwanda	234
26	Venezuela	71,388	87	Tunisia	6,416	150	Sierra Leone	233
27	Belgium	69,845	88	Armenia	6,300	151	Burkina	196
28	Thailand	66,305	89	Zaire	6,189	152	Djibouti	182
29	Saudi Arabia	63,331	90	Ghana	6,154	153	Cambodia	180
30	Argentina	63,038	91	Macedonia	5,980	154	Niger	173
31	Finland	61,172	92	Dominican Republic	5,874	155	Mauritania	146
32	Switzerland	61,070	93	Qatar	5,560	156	Burundi	117
33	Indonesia	58,888	94	Jordan	4,761	157	Belize	110
34	Czech Republic	58,882	95	Iceland	4,727	158	Seychelles	110
35	Romania	55,476	96	Costa Rica	4,386	159	St. Lucia	107
36	Pakistan	55,311	97	Bahrain	4,330	160	Central African Republic	97
37	Austria	52,675	98	Sri Lanka	3,979	161	Antigua and Barbuda	95
38	Uzbekistan	49,149	99	Lebanon	3,950	162	Togo	91
39	Egypt	47,470	100	Latvia	3,924	163	Chad	87
40	Colombia	40,298	101	Trinidad and Tobago	3,817	164	Gambia	73
41	Greece	38,396	102	Albania	3,450	165	Grenada	65
42	Korea, North	38,000	103	Kenya	3,396	166	St. Vincent	52
43	Bulgaria	37,997	104	Panama	3,286	167	Western Samoa	50
44	Malaysia	35,579	105	Mongolia	3,200	168	Guinea-Bissau	42
45	Yugoslavia	34,156	106	Guatemala	3,084	169	St. Kitts and Nevis	42
46	Denmark	33,738	107	Myanmar (Burma)	3,030	170	Maldives	40
47	Belarus	33,369	108	El Salvador	2,858	171	Cape Verde	37
48	Hungary	32,784	109	Cameroon	2,726			
49	Paraguay	31,454	110	Cyprus	2,581	**BOTTOM 10**		
50	New Zealand	31,248	111	Honduras	2,464	172	Dominica	31
51	Portugal	31,205	112	Bolivia	2,445	173	Nauru	30
52	Iraq	26,300	113	Jamaica	2,298	174	Solomon Islands	30
53	Israel	26,000	114	Cote d'Ivoire	1,910	175	Vanuatu	29
54	Chile	24,004	115	Angola	1,855	176	Tonga	27
55	Slovakia	23,881	116	Yemen	1,850	177	Equatorial Guinea	19
56	Philippines	21,885	117	Papua New Guinea	1,790	178	Comoros	16
57	Algeria	19,415	118	Nicaragua	1,683	179	Sao Tome e Principe	15
58	Azerbaijan	19,051	119	Bhutan	1,627	180	Kiribati	7
59	Singapore	18,962	120	Malta	1,500	181	Benin	5
60	Kuwait	18,200	121	Suriname	1,392			

Source: *UN Energy Statistics Yearbook*

120. PETROLEUM REFINERY CAPACITY

Petroleum refinery capacity is the theoretical maximum capability of crude oil distillation plants. The actual capacity may vary, depending on the density of the crude oil, and may be less than the theoretical by 2 to 3% on the average.

TOP 10
Petroleum Refinery Capacity

Rank	Country	(000 barrels per day)	Rank	Country	(000 barrels per day)
1	United States	15,319	6	Italy	2,260
2	Russia	6,527	7	Canada	1,908
3	Japan	4,847	8	United Kingdom	1,869
4	China	2,867	9	France	1,768
5	Germany	2,317	10	Saudi Arabia	1,661

1 barrel = 1,000,000 barrels

Rank	Country	Petreleum Refinery Capacity (000 barrels per day)
UPPER MIDDLE		
11	Mexico	1,524
12	Spain	1,283
13	Ukraine	1,259
14	Brazil	1,253
15	Netherlands	1,187
16	Iran	1,184
17	Korea, South	1,170
18	Venezuela	1,167
19	Singapore	1,091
20	India	1,086
21	Belarus	835
22	Indonesia	805
23	Kuwait	759
24	Turkey	713
25	Australia	705
26	Argentina	665
27	Romania	651
28	Belgium	614
29	Taiwan	543
30	Egypt	532
31	Algeria	485
32	Azerbaijan	442
33	Nigeria	433
34	Sweden	428
35	Greece	401
36	South Africa	401
37	Kazakhstan	394
38	Poland	352
39	Iraq	348
40	Libya	348
41	Thailand	347
42	Czech Republic	307
43	Portugal	304
44	Bulgaria	300
45	Croatia	294
46	Malaysia	286
47	Norway	285

Rank	Country	Petreleum Refinery Capacity (000 barrels per day)
48	Cuba	280
49	Philippines	280
50	Lithuania	267
51	Bahrain	250
52	Colombia	249
53	Trinidad and Tobago	245
54	Hungary	242
LOWER MIDDLE		
55	Syria	242
56	Turkmenistan	234
57	Israel	220
58	Austria	210
59	Finland	200
60	Slovakia	193
61	United Arab Emirates	193
62	Denmark	188
63	Peru	184
64	Uzbekistan	175
65	Yugoslavia	168
66	Chile	165
67	Morocco	155
68	Ecuador	148
69	Pakistan	139
70	Switzerland	132
71	Puerto Rico	127
72	Yemen	120
73	Georgia	106
74	Jordan	100
75	Kenya	90
76	New Zealand	89
77	Oman	85
78	Cote d'Ivoire	64
79	Qatar	58
80	Ireland	53
81	Macedonia	51
82	Sri Lanka	50
83	Dominican Republic	48

Rank	Country	Petreleum Refinery Capacity (000 barrels per day)
84	Bolivia	45
85	Cameroon	42
86	Korea, North	42
87	Albania	40
88	Panama	40
89	Lebanon	38
90	Jamaica	36
91	Uruguay	35
92	Tunisia	34
93	Angola	32
94	Myanmar (Burma)	32
95	Bangladesh	31
96	Ghana	25
97	Zambia	24
98	Cyprus	22
99	Sudan	22
100	Congo	21
101	Guatemala	20
102	El Salvador	19
103	Eritrea	18
104	Gabon	17
105	Nicaragua	17
106	Senegal	17
107	Tanzania	17
108	Zaire	17
BOTTOM 10		
109	Madagascar	16
110	Costa Rica	15
111	Liberia	15
112	Honduras	14
113	Slovenia	11
114	Sierra Leone	10
115	Somalia	10
116	Brunei	9
117	Paraguay	8
118	Barbados	3

Source: *UN Energy Statistics Yearbook*

121. CRUDE PETROLEUM PRODUCTION

Petroleum production is the world's largest industry in terms of the value of output, estimated at between $700 and $800 billion annually (based on current OPEC prices). Of this amount close to one-fifth is estimated to go into OPEC coffers and the rest is accounted for by tankerage, refineries, distribution markups, and oil company profits. It is significant that of the top *Fortune* 40 companies in the world, 17 are in the petroleum sector and each of these companies has an annual revenue that exceeds the GNP of over half the nations of the world.

The production figures are given in metric tons following U.N. usage, although barrels and gallons are the more popular units. Because of differences in the specific gravity of crude petroleum, tons can be converted into barrels only approximately. Middle East crude petroleum has an average conversion rate of about 7.5 barrels to a metric ton.

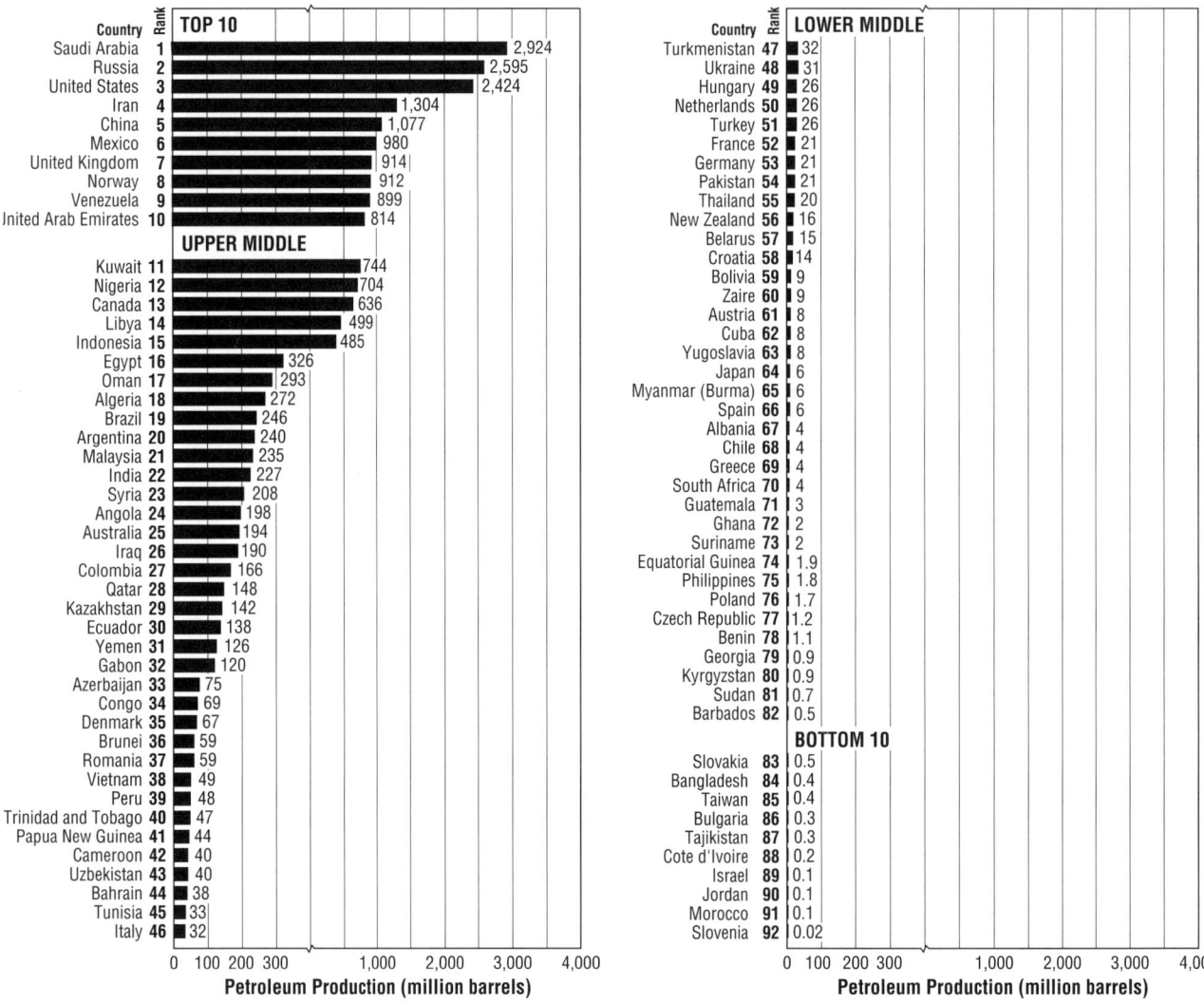

Source: *UN Energy Statistics Yearbook*

122. PETROLEUM RESERVES

Industrial civilization is heavily dependent on petroleum for motive power, lubrication, fuel, dyes, drugs and many synthetics. Estimates of the total petroleum reserves have been revised upward almost every year since its exploitation began on a commercial basis in the 1860s. Yet the demand is so great that oil companies have been unable to recover and refine sufficient quantities to meet all needs. Petroleum has also acquired in recent years a political and strategic dimension, conferring on the few nations with disproportionately vast reserves a degree of leverage and clout that they could never possess otherwise. Oil-exporting nations have also learned to manipulate their oil wealth as a bargaining chip in international negotiations, thus converting oil into a sword of Damocles hanging over the industrialized West. On the other hand, the widespread use of petroleum has also caused serious environmental problems and in many cases perhaps irreversible damage to air, land and water resources.

Rank	Country	Petroleum Reserves (million barrels)	Rank	Country	Petroleum Reserves (million barrels)	Rank	Country	Petroleum Reserves (million barrels)
TOP 10			28	Syria	2,500	56	France	152
1	Saudi Arabia	261,203	29	Argentina	2,217	57	Croatia	150
2	Russia	156,700	30	Ecuador	2,014	58	Bolivia	139
3	Iraq	100,000	31	Australia	1,615	59	New Zealand	137
4	United Arab Emirates	98,100				60	Hungary	132
5	Kuwait	96,500	**LOWER MIDDLE**			61	Netherlands	113
6	Iran	89,250	32	Romania	1,606	62	Austria	101
7	Venezuela	64,477	33	Brunei	1,350	63	Cuba	100
8	Mexico	50,776	34	Gabon	1,340	64	Suriname	82
9	China	24,000	35	Congo	830	65	Yugoslavia	78
10	United States	22,957	36	Peru	800	66	Cote d'Ivoire	50
			37	Turkmenistan	740	67	Myanmar (Burma)	50
UPPER MIDDLE			38	Denmark	736	68	Japan	49
11	Libya	22,800	39	Italy	621	69	Greece	41
12	Nigeria	17,900	40	Vietnam	500	70	South Africa	40
13	Norway	9,416	41	Guatemala	488	71	Poland	35
14	Algeria	9,200	42	Trinidad and Tobago	488	72	Benin	27
15	Indonesia	5,779	43	Turkey	488	73	Spain	20
16	India	5,776	44	Tunisia	416			
17	Angola	5,412	45	Cameroon	400	**BOTTOM 10**		
18	Canada	5,038	46	Germany	368	74	Bulgaria	15
19	Oman	4,828	47	Chile	300	75	Czech Republic	15
20	United Kingdom	4,517	48	Sudan	300	76	Equatorial Guinea	12
21	Malaysia	4,300	49	Philippines	239	77	Slovakia	7
22	Yemen	4,000	50	Papua New Guinea	229	78	Bangladesh	4
23	Brazil	3,797	51	Thailand	218	79	Taiwan	4
24	Qatar	3,700	52	Bahrain	210	80	Barbados	3
25	Colombia	3,393	53	Pakistan	203	81	Israel	3
26	Azerbaijan	3,300	54	Zaire	187	82	Ghana	0.5
27	Egypt	3,260	55	Albania	165	83	Jordan	0.3

Source: *UN Energy Statistics Yearbook*

123. NATURAL GAS PRODUCTION

The production of natural gas has become critical in industrial countries, where it is being used extensively as an illuminant and a fuel. The main constraint is that the construction of pipelines—until recently the only means of transporting natural gas—involves enormous engineering problems and expense. Because of the short life span of proved resources, the construction of new pipelines is not commercially viable. Since its boiling point is very low, natural gas is not easy to liquefy or maintain in its liquid state. Although cryogenic technology has now advanced to the point where such liquefaction is technologically possible, the weight of the containers (made of stainless steel) necessary to contain liquefied natural gas (LNG) limits its usefulness.

Rank	Country	Natural Gas Production (million cubic meters)
TOP 10		
1	Russia	643,000
2	United States	558,978
3	Canada	166,011
4	Turkmenistan	84,300
5	Netherlands	83,000
6	United Kingdom	76,294
7	Indonesia	55,252
8	Algeria	50,376
9	Uruguay	40,226
10	Mexico	37,514
UPPER MIDDLE		
11	Saudi Arabia	35,510
12	Australia	28,025
13	Iran	28,025
14	Norway	26,570
15	Malaysia	24,887
16	United Arab Emirates	23,948
17	Venezuela	23,591
18	Italy	20,337
19	Ukraine	19,502
20	Romania	18,746
21	Germany	18,304
22	Argentina	17,435
23	India	17,024
24	China	16,605
25	Pakistan	16,316
26	Qatar	12,224
27	Thailand	9,330
28	Brunei	9,042
29	Egypt	8,427
30	Libya	6,402
31	Bangladesh	6,315
32	Trinidad and Tobago	6,054
LOWER MIDDLE		
33	Hungary	5,992
34	Azerbaijan	5,921
35	Bahrain	5,193
36	New Zealand	4,933
37	Colombia	4,797
38	Poland	4,686
39	Kuwait	4,664
40	Nigeria	4,582
41	Denmark	4,565
42	Syria	4,151
43	Oman	3,752
44	Kazakhstan	3,349
45	Bolivia	3,231
46	Brazil	2,965
47	Iraq	2,917
48	Ireland	2,500
49	Japan	2,180
50	Croatia	1,897
51	Austria	1,328
52	Peru	1,303
53	Chile	1,138
54	Myanmar (Burma)	1,102
55	Taiwan	827
56	Yugoslavia	765
57	Czech Republic	699
58	Vietnam	697
59	Spain	600
60	Angola	561
61	Slovakia	313
62	Afghanistan	300
63	Tunisia	235
64	Jordan	229
65	Belarus	210
66	Turkey	195
67	Armenia	170
68	Greece	139
69	Albania	136
70	Ecuador	102
71	Gabon	102
72	Papua New Guinea	93
73	Kyrgyzstan	68
74	Tajikistan	49
75	Georgia	45
BOTTOM 10		
76	Cuba	31
77	Morocco	25
78	Slovenia	24
79	Israel	20
80	Barbados	16
81	Belgium	14
82	Bulgaria	11
83	Guatemala	8
84	Congo	2
85	Rwanda	0.2

Source: *UN Energy Statistics Yearbook*

124. NATURAL GAS RESERVES

Because of its flammability and its high caloric value, natural gas is used widely. Although generally believed to be a by-product of petroleum, it is found sometimes at a distance from petroleum fields, leading some geologists to conclude that it has a separate origin. Until recently it was flared off in many countries, but the construction of natural gas pipelines has enabled the maximum utilization of this important source of energy.

Rank	Country	Natural Gas Reserves (billion cubic meters)
TOP 10		
1	Russia	48,677
2	Iran	21,000
3	Qatar	7,079
4	United Arab Emirates	5,794
5	Saudi Arabia	5,264
6	United States	4,599
7	Venezuela	3,693
8	Algeria	3,625
9	Nigeria	3,396
10	Iraq	3,101
UPPER MIDDLE		
11	Canada	2,244
12	Norway	2,008
13	Mexico	1,973
14	Malaysia	1,926
15	Netherlands	1,875
16	Indonesia	1,823
17	China	1,671
18	Kuwait	1,498
19	Libya	1,297
20	Pakistan	779
21	Bangladesh	714
22	India	707
23	Oman	630
24	United Kingdom	630
25	Australia	555
26	Egypt	546
27	Argentina	517
28	Papua New Guinea	425
29	Yemen	425
30	Brunei	396
31	Italy	374
32	Romania	348
33	Turkmenistan	326
34	Germany	303
35	Myanmar (Burma)	278
36	Trinidad and Tobago	240
LOWER MIDDLE		
37	Colombia	223
38	Peru	199
39	Syria	198
40	Thailand	174
41	Azerbaijan	170
42	Poland	155
43	Bahrain	150
44	Brazil	137
45	Bolivia	126
46	Denmark	121
47	Tanzania	116
48	Cameroon	110
49	Chile	110
50	Ecuador	108
51	Vietnam	105
52	Afghanistan	99
53	Hungary	98
54	Philippines	98
55	New Zealand	85

Rank	Country	Natural Gas Reserves (billion cubic meters)	Rank	Country	Natural Gas Reserves (billion cubic meters)	Rank	Country	Natural Gas Reserves (billion cubic meters)
56	Sudan	85	69	South Africa	27	82	Bulgaria	7
57	Mozambique	77	70	Guinea	24		**BOTTOM 10**	
58	Congo	76	71	Ethiopia	23	83	Jordan	6
59	Taiwan	68	72	Ghana	23	84	Somalia	6
60	Namibia	57	73	Austria	22	85	Cuba	3
61	Rwanda	57	74	Spain	19	86	Albania	2
62	Angola	51	75	Ireland	15	87	Madagascar	2
63	Yugoslavia	45	76	Cote d'Ivoire	14	88	Morocco	1.5
64	Equatorial Guinea	37	77	Gabon	14	89	Zaire	1.4
65	France	36	78	Czech Republic	13	90	Israel	0.4
66	Croatia	35	79	Turkey	11	91	Guatemala	0.3
67	Tunisia	30	80	Greece	8	92	Barbados	0.1
68	Japan	27	81	Slovakia	8			

Source: *UN Energy Statistics Yearbook*

125. COAL PRODUCTION

Coal is the least efficient and the most ecologically harmful of all fossil fuels. Its production, especially through strip mining, often disfigures the landscape and leaves permanent scars. Its burning adds to air pollution. Nevertheless, it is the most plentiful of all fossil fuels and as such may be the most significant source of energy after other sources have been depleted. Because it is providentially located in consuming countries, coal offers these countries a viable alternative to overdependence on petroleum-exporting nations.

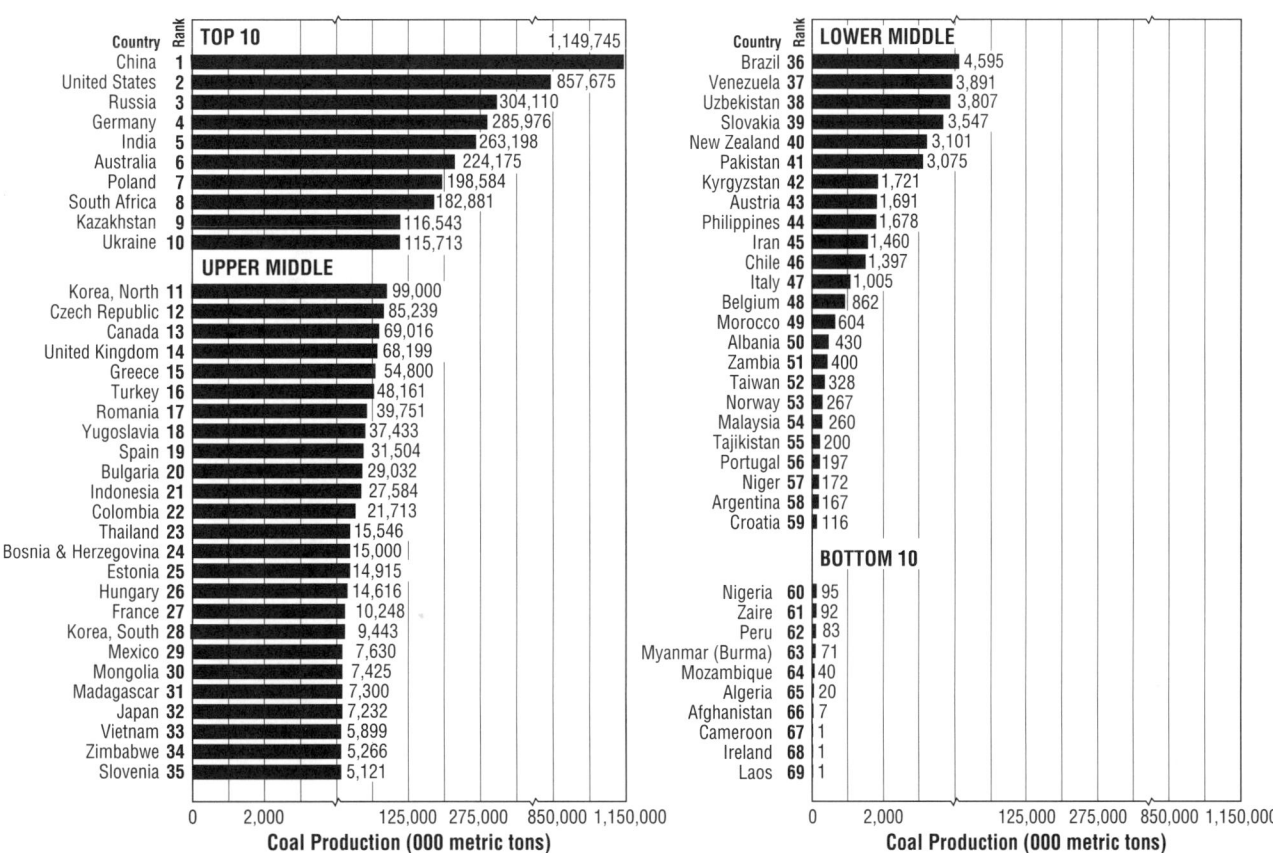

Country	Rank	Coal Production (000 metric tons)
TOP 10		
China	1	1,149,745
United States	2	857,675
Russia	3	304,110
Germany	4	285,976
India	5	263,198
Australia	6	224,175
Poland	7	198,584
South Africa	8	182,881
Kazakhstan	9	116,543
Ukraine	10	115,713
UPPER MIDDLE		
Korea, North	11	99,000
Czech Republic	12	85,239
Canada	13	69,016
United Kingdom	14	68,199
Greece	15	54,800
Turkey	16	48,161
Romania	17	39,751
Yugoslavia	18	37,433
Spain	19	31,504
Bulgaria	20	29,032
Indonesia	21	27,584
Colombia	22	21,713
Thailand	23	15,546
Bosnia & Herzegovina	24	15,000
Estonia	25	14,915
Hungary	26	14,616
France	27	10,248
Korea, South	28	9,443
Mexico	29	7,630
Mongolia	30	7,425
Madagascar	31	7,300
Japan	32	7,232
Vietnam	33	5,899
Zimbabwe	34	5,266
Slovenia	35	5,121
LOWER MIDDLE		
Brazil	36	4,595
Venezuela	37	3,891
Uzbekistan	38	3,807
Slovakia	39	3,547
New Zealand	40	3,101
Pakistan	41	3,075
Kyrgyzstan	42	1,721
Austria	43	1,691
Philippines	44	1,678
Iran	45	1,460
Chile	46	1,397
Italy	47	1,005
Belgium	48	862
Morocco	49	604
Albania	50	430
Zambia	51	400
Taiwan	52	328
Norway	53	267
Malaysia	54	260
Tajikistan	55	200
Portugal	56	197
Niger	57	172
Argentina	58	167
Croatia	59	116
BOTTOM 10		
Nigeria	60	95
Zaire	61	92
Peru	62	83
Myanmar (Burma)	63	71
Mozambique	64	40
Algeria	65	20
Afghanistan	66	7
Cameroon	67	1
Ireland	68	1
Laos	69	1

Coal Production (000 metric tons)

Source: *UN Energy Statistics Yearbook*

126. ELECTRICITY CONSUMPTION

It often takes a blackout to demonstrate how basic electricity is; few things can stop a whole town dead in its tracks as completely as a suspension of electric power. This ranking examines the phenomenon of a plugged-in civilization with an insatiable appetite for power.

Rank	Country	Electric Consumption per Capita (kW–hr)	Rank	Country	Electric Consumption per Capita (kW–hr)	Rank	Country	Electric Consumption per Capita (kW–hr)
TOP 10			61	Macedonia	2,940	122	Ghana	357
1	Norway	26,079	62	Tajikistan	2,873	123	Bolivia	348
2	Canada	17,347	63	Croatia	2,615	124	Philippines	338
3	Sweden	16,531	64	Azerbaijan	2,580	125	Djibouti	327
4	Finland	13,594	65	Romania	2,491	126	Guyana	309
5	Luxembourg	12,957	66	Latvia	2,461	127	Guatemala	308
6	United States	12,308	67	Kyrgyzstan	2,263	128	Indonesia	307
7	Iceland	11,973	68	Uzbekistan	2,242	129	Western Samoa	299
8	Qatar	10,510	69	Moldova	2,179	130	Tonga	276
9	Kuwait	10,254	70	Barbados	2,108	131	Sri Lanka	222
10	United Arab Emirates	9,680	71	Argentina	1,903	132	Congo	221
			72	Malaysia	1,847	133	Cameroon	218
UPPER MIDDLE			73	Georgia	1,838	134	Angola	181
11	Australia	9,284	74	Armenia	1,803	135	Vanuatu	180
12	New Zealand	8,966	75	Uruguay	1,802	136	Liberia	169
13	Bermuda	8,222	76	Brazil	1,783	137	Maldives	168
14	Bahrain	8,093	77	Chile	1,737	138	Vietnam	152
15	Switzerland	7,602	78	Korea, North	1,649	139	Zaire	145
16	Japan	7,281	79	Seychelles	1,528	140	Cote d'Ivoire	143
17	Belgium	7,175				141	Yemen	140
18	France	7,126	**LOWER MIDDLE**			142	Kenya	139
19	Singapore	6,770	80	Mexico	1,486	143	Sao Tome e Principe	118
20	Denmark	6,761	81	Antigua and Barbuda	1,462	144	Bhutan	116
21	Austria	6,606	82	Lebanon	1,426	145	Nigeria	111
22	Germany	6,513	83	Mongolia	1,406	146	Togo	104
23	Russia	6,342	84	Iraq	1,352	147	Cape Verde	100
24	United Kingdom	5,843	85	Costa Rica	1,340	148	Senegal	97
25	Netherlands	5,711	86	Panama	1,330	149	Kiribati	92
26	Czech Republic	5,515	87	Turkey	1,232	150	Guinea	85
27	Slovenia	5,304	88	Colombia	1,195	151	Solomon Islands	85
28	Kazakhstan	5,259	89	Thailand	1,162	152	Bangladesh	84
29	Estonia	4,897	90	Iran	1,122	153	Malawi	76
30	Israel	4,888	91	Cuba	1,016	154	Gambia	70
31	Slovakia	4,874	92	St. Kitts and Nevis	1,000	155	Mauritania	68
32	Brunei	4,690	93	Jordan	965	156	Myanmar (Burma)	68
33	Ireland	4,658	94	Jamaica	953	157	Laos	64
34	Italy	4,588	95	Syria	923	158	Haiti	57
35	Puerto Rico	4,572	96	Mauritius	906	159	Mozambique	54
36	Ukraine	4,430	97	Zimbabwe	890	160	Sierra Leone	54
37	Taiwan	4,397	98	Albania	850	161	Equatorial Guinea	50
38	Bulgaria	4,296	99	Egypt	797	162	Sudan	50
39	Malta	4,155	100	Dominican Republic	779	163	Benin	48
40	Spain	4,037	101	St. Lucia	770	164	Afghanistan	47
41	Belarus	3,865	102	Tunisia	747	165	Nepal	45
42	South Africa	3,830	103	Gabon	739	166	Madagascar	43
43	Greece	3,778	104	China	719	167	Niger	43
44	Korea, South	3,704	105	Paraguay	709	168	Guinea-Bissau	41
45	Saudi Arabia	3,699	106	Grenada	707	169	Uganda	34
46	Bahamas	3,657	107	Zambia	706	170	Mali	33
47	Cyprus	3,555	108	Algeria	680			
48	Oman	3,538	109	Ecuador	678	**BOTTOM 10**		
49	Hungary	3,453	110	Peru	626	171	Rwanda	32
50	Poland	3,432	111	Fiji	613	172	Tanzania	32
51	Venezuela	3,399	112	Belize	539	173	Central African Republic	31
52	Libya	3,368	113	El Salvador	532	174	Somalia	29
53	Suriname	3,362	114	St. Vincent	473	175	Comoros	26
54	Yugoslavia	3,253	115	Honduras	465	176	Ethiopia	25
55	Turkmenistan	3,223	116	Dominica	437	177	Burundi	23
56	Portugal	3,190	117	Papua New Guinea	436	178	Burkina	20
57	Lithuania	3,069	118	Morocco	421	179	Cambodia	19
58	Nauru	3,000	119	Pakistan	416	180	Chad	14
59	Bosnia & Herzegovina	2,988	120	Nicaragua	409			
60	Trinidad and Tobago	2,987	121	India	397			

Source: *UN Energy Statistics Yearbook*

127. ENERGY CONSUMPTION PER CAPITA

Energy is consumed in many forms and obtained from a variety of sources, such as coal and lignite, gasoline, kerosene, fuel oils, natural gas, and hydro-electric power and also derivatives, such as briquettes, refinery gases, coke, manufactured gas, thermal electric power, liquefied petroleum gases and benzols.

Rank	Country	Energy Use per Capita (kg)	Rank	Country	Energy Use per Capita (kg)	Rank	Country	Energy Use per Capita (kg)
TOP 10			59	Korea, North	1,701	118	Nicaragua	241
1	United Arab Emirates	16,878	60	Seychelles	1,681	119	Papua New Guinea	238
2	Qatar	16,196	61	Malaysia	1,545	120	Pakistan	226
3	Bahrain	11,925	62	Slovenia	1,531	121	El Salvador	222
4	Luxembourg	9,879	63	Mexico	1,439	122	Paraguay	214
5	United States	7,918	64	Barbados	1,381	123	St. Vincent	200
6	Canada	7,821	65	Argentina	1,351	124	Sao Tome e Principe	189
7	Brunei	7,687	66	Moldova	1,345	125	Tonga	184
8	Bahamas	6,900	67	Iran	1,235	126	Honduras	180
9	Finland	5,635	68	Croatia	1,109	127	Congo	165
10	Singapore	5,563	69	Iraq	1,103	128	Solomon Islands	164
			70	Jamaica	1,096	129	Guatemala	159
UPPER MIDDLE			71	Mongolia	1,089	130	Zambia	146
11	Sweden	5,385	72	Turkey	983	131	Afghanistan	145
12	Australia	5,316	73	Djibouti	975	132	Nigeria	141
13	Norway	5,096	74	Kyrgyzstan	965	133	Maldives	139
14	Iceland	5,025	75	Algeria	955	134	Senegal	115
15	Belgium	4,989	76	Gabon	953	135	Sri Lanka	110
16	Trinidad and Tobago	4,696	77	Jordan	922	136	Cote d'Ivoire	109
17	Saudi Arabia	4,552				137	Kiribati	105
18	Netherlands	4,533	**LOWER MIDDLE**			138	Mauritania	105
19	Kazakhstan	4,435	78	Chile	911	139	Kenya	99
20	Russia	4,411	79	Armenia	897	140	Angola	96
21	New Zealand	4,299	80	Georgia	891	141	Ghana	96
22	Kuwait	4,217	81	Cuba	839	142	Cameroon	87
23	Germany	4,170	82	Syria	798	143	Equatorial Guinea	82
24	France	4,031	83	Lebanon	727	144	Vietnam	77
25	Ukraine	3,960	84	Uruguay	715	145	Sierra Leone	72
26	Denmark	3,861	85	Thailand	673	146	Sudan	68
27	United Kingdom	3,718	86	Brazil	666	147	Guinea	66
28	Japan	3,642	87	Colombia	661	148	Bangladesh	59
29	Switzerland	3,491	88	Tajikistan	634	149	Gambia	57
30	Belarus	3,427	89	China	632	150	Cambodia	52
31	Austria	3,277	90	Panama	599	151	Zaire	48
32	Ireland	3,016	91	Egypt	576	152	Haiti	47
33	Korea, South	2,863	92	Tunisia	576	153	Togo	47
34	Bermuda	2,798	93	Ecuador	561	154	Mozambique	43
35	Italy	2,697	94	Costa Rica	558	155	Laos	39
36	Israel	2,607	95	Fiji	525	156	Myanmar (Burma)	39
37	Lithuania	2,596	96	St. Kitts and Nevis	476	157	Liberia	38
38	Cyprus	2,517	97	Zimbabwe	471	158	Niger	38
39	Azerbaijan	2,470	98	Albania	455	159	Guinea-Bissau	37
40	Oman	2,408	99	Belize	426	160	Malawi	35
41	South Africa	2,399	100	Western Samoa	425	161	Tanzania	35
42	Poland	2,390	101	Mauritius	391	162	Madagascar	34
43	Hungary	2,385	102	Botswana	388	163	Bhutan	33
44	Spain	2,373	103	St. Lucia	373	164	Comoros	30
45	Venezuela	2,369	104	Guyana	349			
46	Yugoslavia	2,353	105	Dominican Republic	340	**BOTTOM 10**		
47	Turkmenistan	2,268	106	Peru	332	165	Central African Republic	29
48	Greece	2,160	107	Indonesia	330	166	Rwanda	27
49	Malta	2,107	108	Philippines	328	167	Burundi	24
50	Uzbekistan	2,033	109	Bolivia	310	168	Uganda	23
51	Puerto Rico	2,018	110	Cape Verde	305	169	Nepal	22
52	Antigua and Barbuda	2,000	111	Morocco	299	170	Benin	20
53	Bulgaria	1,954	112	Dominica	296	171	Mali	20
54	Libya	1,883	113	Yemen	285	172	Burkina	16
55	Suriname	1,877	114	Grenada	283	173	Chad	16
56	Romania	1,785	115	Swaziland	283	174	Somalia	7
57	Portugal	1,781	116	Vanuatu	280			
58	Latvia	1,717	117	India	243			

Source: *UN Energy Statistics Yearbook*

Energy **169**

128. RATIO OF FUEL IMPORTS TO EXPORTS

The plight of oil-consuming countries and nonoil-producing developing countries is nowhere more dramatically highlighted than in the growing share of fuel in their import bills. The crippling costs of importing fuel for domestic needs has also served to widen the gap between the rich and the poor nations and to create a new class of rich nations. The severe economic imbalances and dislocations, which this division of the world into oil producers and oil consumers has caused, became fully apparent only during the 1980s and 1990s.

Rank	Country	Energy Imports as Percentage of Merchandise Exports
TOP 10		
1	Saudi Arabia	69
2	Nicaragua	61
3	Panama	51
4	Lithuania	43
5	Kyrgyzstan	41
6	El Salvador	39
7	Jordan	37
8	India	36
9	Romania	34
10	Tajikistan	31
UPPER MIDDLE		
11	Paraguay	30
12	Uzbekistan	30
13	Bangladesh	26
14	Guatemala	26
15	Turkey	26
16	Greece	24
17	Morocco	24
18	Pakistan	24
19	Poland	20
20	Hungary	19
21	Philippines	19
22	Korea, South	18
23	Honduras	16
24	Zimbabwe	15
25	Japan	14
LOWER MIDDLE		
26	Trinidad and Tobago	14
27	Portugal	13
28	Singapore	13
29	Spain	13
30	Sri Lanka	13
31	Tunisia	13
32	United States	13
33	Costa Rica	12
34	Uruguay	12
35	Belarus	11
36	Brazil	11
37	Chile	11
38	Israel	11
39	Mauritius	11
40	Finland	10
41	France	9
42	Italy	9
43	Thailand	9
44	Bolivia	8
45	Netherlands	8
46	Peru	8
47	Sweden	8
48	Germany	7
49	Australia	6
50	Austria	6
51	China	6
52	Egypt	6
53	Indonesia	6
54	New Zealand	6
55	United Kingdom	6
56	Colombia	5
57	Denmark	5
58	Canada	4
59	Ireland	4
60	Malaysia	4
61	Mexico	4
BOTTOM 10		
62	Switzerland	4
63	Argentina	3
64	Azerbaijan	3
65	Norway	2
66	Algeria	1
67	Ecuador	1
68	Kuwait	1
69	Oman	1
70	Venezuela	1
71	South Africa	0

Source: *World Development Report*

129. ENERGY CONSUMPTION GROWTH RATE

One of the fallouts of the energy crisis is the adoption in most countries of an energy policy designed to increase production and reduce consumption at the same time. After 20 years it is interesting to examine whether the latter thrust has borne fruit. How many countries have successfully managed the transition from profusion to parsimony in their use of energy?

Rank	Country	Average Annual Energy Consumption Growth Rate 1980–93 (%)
TOP 10		
1	Thailand	10.5
2	United Arab Emirates	10.5
3	Malaysia	9.8
4	Oman	9.7
5	Korea, South	9.5
6	Nepal	8.1
7	Bangladesh	7.9
8	Yemen	7.8
9	Singapore	7.7
10	Indonesia	7.5
UPPER MIDDLE		
11	Burundi	7.0
12	Pakistan	6.8
13	India	6.7
14	Iran	6.7
15	Ethiopia	6.0
16	Paraguay	5.9
17	Egypt	5.8
18	Zimbabwe	5.5
19	Saudi Arabia	5.3
20	China	5.1
21	Turkey	5.1
22	Algeria	5.0
23	Jordan	5.0
24	Portugal	4.8
25	Chile	4.7
26	New Zealand	4.6
27	Israel	4.4
28	Colombia	4.0
29	Tunisia	4.0
30	Morocco	3.8
31	Brazil	3.7
32	Costa Rica	3.6
33	Philippines	3.5
34	Greece	3.4
35	Trinidad and Tobago	3.4
36	Uganda	3.3
37	Mexico	3.1
38	Mauritius	3.0
39	South Africa	3.0
40	Central African Republic	2.9
41	Kenya	2.9
42	Spain	2.9
43	Ecuador	2.8
44	Botswana	2.7
45	Ghana	2.7
46	Japan	2.7
LOWER MIDDLE		
47	Laos	2.6
48	Vietnam	2.6
49	Nicaragua	2.4

Rank	Country	Average Annual Energy Consumption Growth Rate 1980–93 (%)
50	Papua New Guinea	2.4
51	Australia	2.3
52	El Salvador	2.3
53	Venezuela	2.3
54	Mongolia	2.2
55	Niger	2.2
56	Guinea-Bissau	2.1
57	Ireland	2.1
58	France	2.0
59	Jamaica	1.9
60	Mali	1.9
61	Nigeria	1.9
62	Sri Lanka	1.9
63	Gabon	1.8
64	Guatemala	1.8
65	Switzerland	1.8
66	Finland	1.7
67	Honduras	1.7
68	Madagascar	1.7
69	Belgium	1.6
70	Cameroon	1.6
71	Canada	1.5
72	Congo	1.5
73	Italy	1.5
74	Malawi	1.5
75	Norway	1.5
76	Austria	1.4
77	Guinea	1.4
78	United States	1.4
79	Dominican Republic	1.3
80	Netherlands	1.3
81	Sweden	1.3
82	Argentina	1.1
83	Burkina	1.1
84	United Kingdom	1.0
85	Uruguay	1.0
86	Bolivia	0.9
87	Togo	0.9
88	Gambia	0.8
89	Denmark	0.7
90	Puerto Rico	0.7
91	Tanzania	0.6
92	Chad	0.5
93	Mauritania	0.4
94	Senegal	0.4
95	Sierra Leone	0.4
96	Cote d'Ivoire	0.3
97	Panama	0.3
98	Germany	0.0
99	Rwanda	−0.1
100	Hungary	−0.6

BOTTOM 10

Rank	Country	Average Annual Energy Consumption Growth Rate 1980–93 (%)
101	Peru	−0.6
102	Myanmar (Burma)	−0.8
103	Poland	−2.0
104	Zambia	−2.5
105	Romania	−2.7
106	Bulgaria	−3.0
107	Mozambique	−3.0
108	Albania	−3.1
109	Benin	−3.3
110	Kuwait	−4.2

Source: *World Development Report*

130. ENERGY PRODUCTION GROWTH RATE

No natural resource is being exploited so thoroughly as energy, especially fossil fuels. All commercial forms of primary energy are included under this rubric: coal and lignite, crude petroleum, natural gas and natural gas liquids, and hydro and nuclear electricity. This ranking covers a long period, emphasizing long-range patterns at the expense of recent developments.

Rank	Country	Energy Production Growth Rate 1980–93 (%)
TOP 10		
1	Paraguay	45.5
2	Thailand	26.0
3	Denmark	24.1
4	Papua New Guinea	20.1
5	Kenya	15.6
6	Nepal	14.1
7	Bangladesh	12.2
8	Colombia	11.9
9	Malaysia	11.6
10	Benin	11.2
UPPER MIDDLE		
11	Panama	10.4
12	Vietnam	9.7
13	Norway	9.0
14	Niger	8.5
15	Oman	8.3
16	Brazil	7.5
17	Korea, South	7.5
18	New Zealand	7.5
19	Pakistan	7.3
20	Mauritius	7.1
21	Zimbabwe	7.1
22	Burundi	6.9
23	Congo	6.9
24	Iran	6.8
25	France	6.7
26	Sri Lanka	6.7
27	India	6.6
28	Ethiopia	6.5
29	Uruguay	6.5
30	Greece	6.2
31	United Arab Emirates	5.9
32	Costa Rica	5.8
33	Gabon	5.7
34	Madagascar	5.7
35	Australia	5.6
36	Philippines	5.6
37	Cameroon	5.3
38	Mali	5.2
39	Spain	5.1
40	Tanzania	5.1
41	China	4.9
42	Algeria	4.6
43	Japan	4.6
44	Mongolia	4.6
45	Sweden	4.5
46	Egypt	4.1
47	Ecuador	3.9
48	Guatemala	3.8
49	Guinea	3.8
LOWER MIDDLE		
50	Canada	3.7
51	Dominican Republic	3.7
52	Indonesia	3.7
53	Malawi	3.6
54	El Salvador	3.5
55	Turkey	3.5
56	Rwanda	3.4
57	Honduras	3.3
58	South Africa	3.1
59	Belgium	3.0
60	Finland	2.7
61	Ireland	2.7
62	Nicaragua	2.7
63	Switzerland	2.6
64	Argentina	2.5
65	Central African Republic	2.5
66	Italy	2.4
67	Nigeria	2.4
68	Portugal	2.4
69	Ghana	2.1
70	Uganda	2.1
71	Puerto Rico	1.9
72	Mexico	1.8
73	Venezuela	1.8
74	Chile	1.5
75	Austria	1.4
76	Bolivia	0.8
77	Saudi Arabia	0.7
78	United States	0.7
79	Bulgaria	0.4
80	United Kingdom	0.1
81	Netherlands	−0.1
82	Botswana	−0.2
83	Hungary	−0.3
84	Trinidad and Tobago	−0.3
85	Tunisia	−0.8
86	Laos	−1.2
87	Germany	−1.3
88	Myanmar (Burma)	−1.5
89	Poland	−2.2
BOTTOM 10		
90	Kuwait	−2.3
91	Morocco	−2.7
92	Zambia	−3.0
93	Peru	−3.9
94	Romania	−4.6
95	Albania	−5.4
96	Jamaica	−5.6
97	Cote d'Ivoire	−6.1
98	Israel	−10.4
99	Mozambique	−15.6

Source: *UN Energy Statistics Yearbook*

131. GDP OUTPUT PER KG OF ENERGY

Energy is measured in many ways, but none more illuminating than that which measures GDP output per kg of energy. It essentially measures how much energy adds to the national wealth. Since energy is the key element adding value in the primary and secondary sectors (agriculture, manufacturing, transportation, etc.) and transforming raw materials into consumer and industrial goods, the measurement of the GDP per kg of energy used is an indicator of efficiency in the major sectors of the economy.

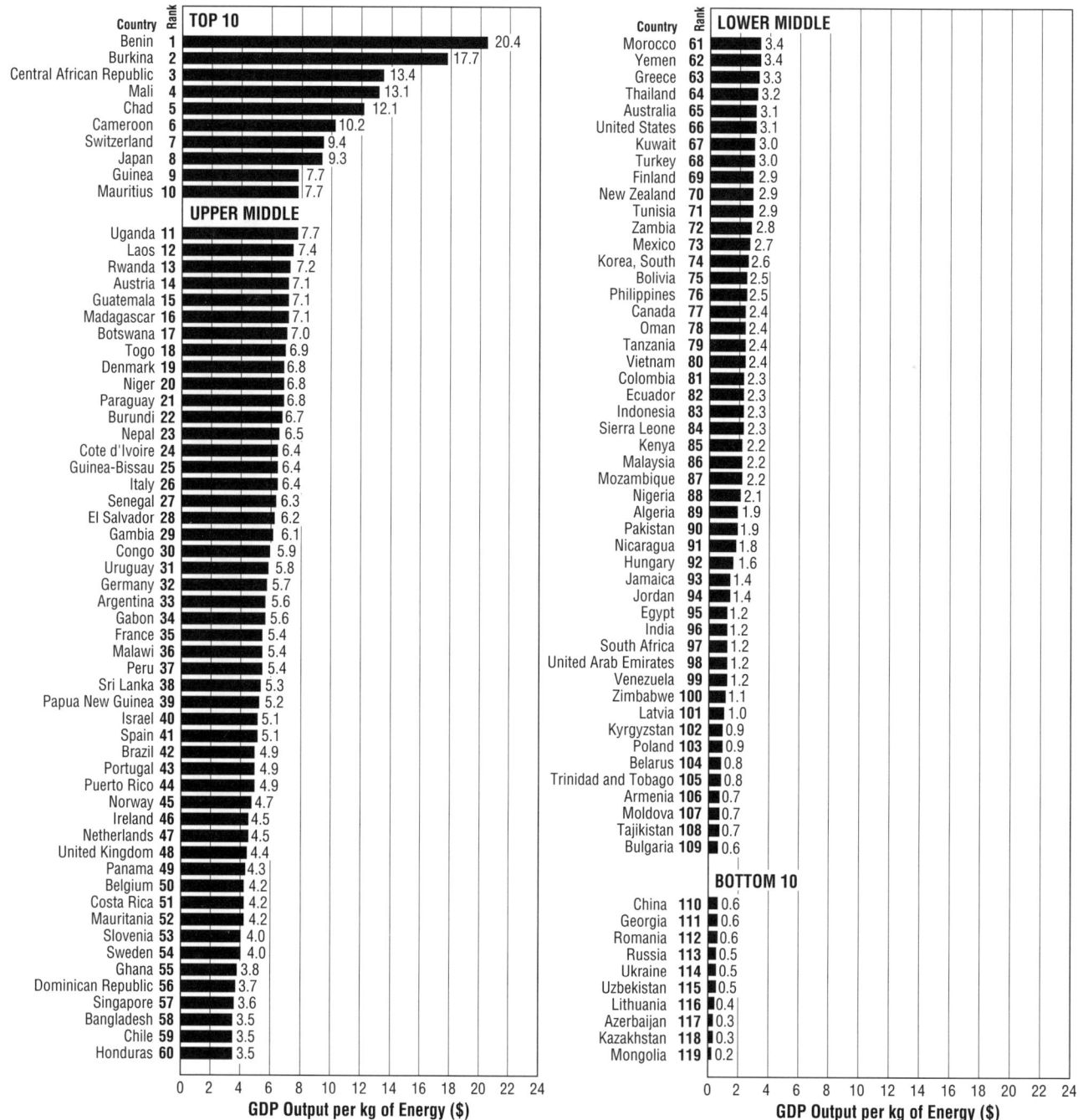

TOP 10

Country	Rank	GDP Output per kg of Energy ($)
Benin	1	20.4
Burkina	2	17.7
Central African Republic	3	13.4
Mali	4	13.1
Chad	5	12.1
Cameroon	6	10.2
Switzerland	7	9.4
Japan	8	9.3
Guinea	9	7.7
Mauritius	10	7.7

UPPER MIDDLE

Country	Rank	GDP Output per kg of Energy ($)
Uganda	11	7.7
Laos	12	7.4
Rwanda	13	7.2
Austria	14	7.1
Guatemala	15	7.1
Madagascar	16	7.1
Botswana	17	7.0
Togo	18	6.9
Denmark	19	6.8
Niger	20	6.8
Paraguay	21	6.8
Burundi	22	6.7
Nepal	23	6.5
Cote d'Ivoire	24	6.4
Guinea-Bissau	25	6.4
Italy	26	6.4
Senegal	27	6.3
El Salvador	28	6.2
Gambia	29	6.1
Congo	30	5.9
Uruguay	31	5.8
Germany	32	5.7
Argentina	33	5.6
Gabon	34	5.6
France	35	5.4
Malawi	36	5.4
Peru	37	5.4
Sri Lanka	38	5.3
Papua New Guinea	39	5.2
Israel	40	5.1
Spain	41	5.1
Brazil	42	4.9
Portugal	43	4.9
Puerto Rico	44	4.9
Norway	45	4.7
Ireland	46	4.5
Netherlands	47	4.5
United Kingdom	48	4.4
Panama	49	4.3
Belgium	50	4.2
Costa Rica	51	4.2
Mauritania	52	4.2
Slovenia	53	4.0
Sweden	54	4.0
Ghana	55	3.8
Dominican Republic	56	3.7
Singapore	57	3.6
Bangladesh	58	3.5
Chile	59	3.5
Honduras	60	3.5

LOWER MIDDLE

Country	Rank	GDP Output per kg of Energy ($)
Morocco	61	3.4
Yemen	62	3.4
Greece	63	3.3
Thailand	64	3.2
Australia	65	3.1
United States	66	3.1
Kuwait	67	3.0
Turkey	68	3.0
Finland	69	2.9
New Zealand	70	2.9
Tunisia	71	2.9
Zambia	72	2.8
Mexico	73	2.7
Korea, South	74	2.6
Bolivia	75	2.5
Philippines	76	2.5
Canada	77	2.4
Oman	78	2.4
Tanzania	79	2.4
Vietnam	80	2.4
Colombia	81	2.3
Ecuador	82	2.3
Indonesia	83	2.3
Sierra Leone	84	2.3
Kenya	85	2.2
Malaysia	86	2.2
Mozambique	87	2.2
Nigeria	88	2.1
Algeria	89	1.9
Pakistan	90	1.9
Nicaragua	91	1.8
Hungary	92	1.6
Jamaica	93	1.4
Jordan	94	1.4
Egypt	95	1.2
India	96	1.2
South Africa	97	1.2
United Arab Emirates	98	1.2
Venezuela	99	1.2
Zimbabwe	100	1.1
Latvia	101	1.0
Kyrgyzstan	102	0.9
Poland	103	0.9
Belarus	104	0.8
Trinidad and Tobago	105	0.8
Armenia	106	0.7
Moldova	107	0.7
Tajikistan	108	0.7
Bulgaria	109	0.6

BOTTOM 10

Country	Rank	GDP Output per kg of Energy ($)
China	110	0.6
Georgia	111	0.6
Romania	112	0.6
Russia	113	0.5
Ukraine	114	0.5
Uzbekistan	115	0.5
Lithuania	116	0.4
Azerbaijan	117	0.3
Kazakhstan	118	0.3
Mongolia	119	0.2

Source: *UN Energy Statistics Yearbook*

132. NUCLEAR POWER PRODUCTION

The total world production of nuclear energy is less than one-twentieth of the world production of electric energy. However, nuclear energy has grown by over 1,000% since 1980. This growth has been achieved despite the continuing opposition of environmentalists and formidable technological problems.

Rank	Country	World Nuclear Power Production (Exa (10^{18}) Joules)	Rank	Country	World Nuclear Power Production (Exa (10^{18}) Joules)	Rank	Country	World Nuclear Power Production (Exa (10^{18}) Joules)
TOP 10			**MIDDLE**			19	Bulgaria	0.13
1	United States	7.01	11	Spain	0.57	20	South Africa	0.10
2	France	3.53	12	Belgium	0.45	21	Argentina	0.08
3	Japan	2.24	13	Taiwan	0.33	22	India	0.08
4	Germany	1.62	14	Czech Republic	0.30	23	Mexico	0.04
5	Russia	1.39	15	Switzerland	0.25	24	Netherlands	0.04
6	United Kingdom	0.97	16	Finland	0.20	25	Yugoslavia	0.04
7	Canada	0.93				26	Brazil	0.02
8	Ukraine	0.81	**BOTTOM 10**					
9	Sweden	0.65	17	Lithuania	0.18			
10	Korea, South	0.57	18	Hungary	0.14			

Source: *Nuclear Power Plants Worldwide*

Section
XIII

LABOR

The employed segment of the population is usually called the work force, labor force or economically active population, although these terms are not strictly interchangeable. The term labor is not used in these rankings in the conventional Marxian sense of workers as opposed to capitalists, but rather in the sense of persons engaged in any form of gainful activity, as distinguished from children and senior citizens who may not be so engaged. On any given working day, about 2 billion persons may be working (including housewives, whose work, of course, is never done) to make the world go round. This equals about 16 billion person-hours a day—a staggering thought in itself. In the following rankings we are trying to describe this 16-billion-person-hour figure.

What are the emerging trends and prospects in the labor field? First, the median age of the labor force has been rising along with a downswing in the growth of the economically active population; second, there has been increased participation by women in the labor force leading to a proportionate reduction in the dependency rate; third, there has been a universal reduction in working hours and improvement in working conditions; and lastly, there has been an increase in measured unemployment, but much of this increase is accounted for by those seeking work for the first time, by disadvantaged minorities and by women.

133. LABOR FORCE

The labor force refers to the total population between 15 and 64 years of age. It should be distinguished from the economically active population because the latter term includes housewives, students and other economically unproductive groups.

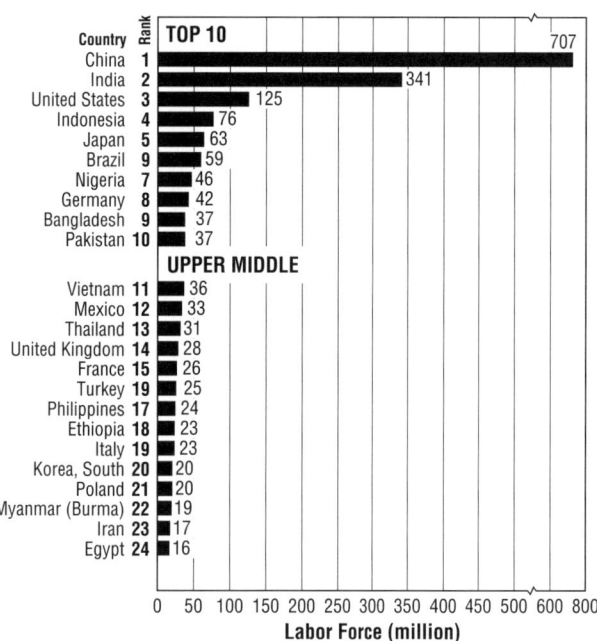

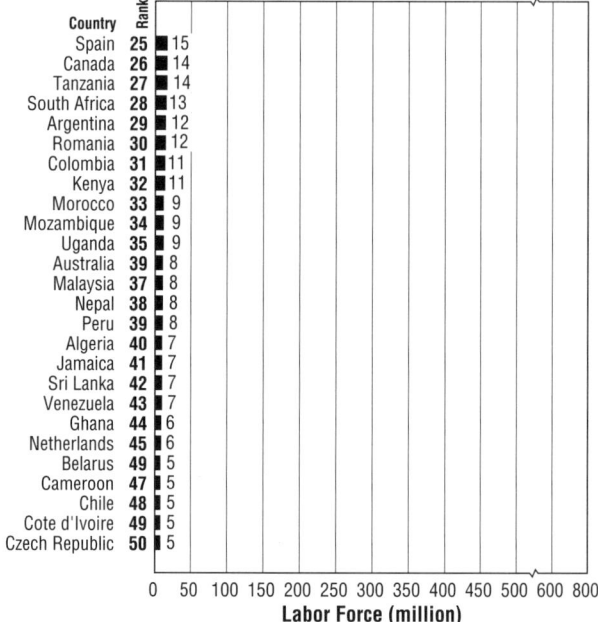

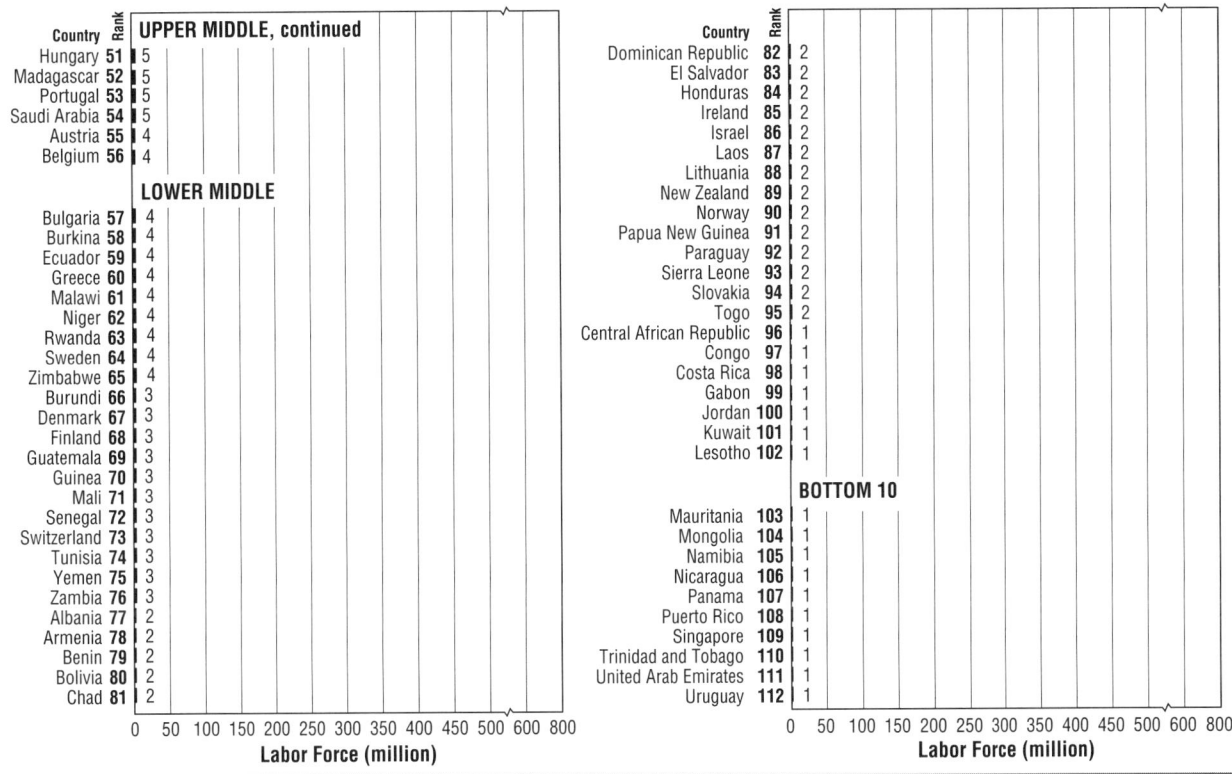

UPPER MIDDLE, continued

Country	Rank	Labor Force (million)
Hungary	51	5
Madagascar	52	5
Portugal	53	5
Saudi Arabia	54	5
Austria	55	4
Belgium	56	4

LOWER MIDDLE

Country	Rank	Labor Force (million)
Bulgaria	57	4
Burkina	58	4
Ecuador	59	4
Greece	60	4
Malawi	61	4
Niger	62	4
Rwanda	63	4
Sweden	64	4
Zimbabwe	65	4
Burundi	66	3
Denmark	67	3
Finland	68	3
Guatemala	69	3
Guinea	70	3
Mali	71	3
Senegal	72	3
Switzerland	73	3
Tunisia	74	3
Yemen	75	3
Zambia	76	3
Albania	77	2
Armenia	78	2
Benin	79	2
Bolivia	80	2
Chad	81	2

Country	Rank	Labor Force (million)
Dominican Republic	82	2
El Salvador	83	2
Honduras	84	2
Ireland	85	2
Israel	86	2
Laos	87	2
Lithuania	88	2
New Zealand	89	2
Norway	90	2
Papua New Guinea	91	2
Paraguay	92	2
Sierra Leone	93	2
Slovakia	94	2
Togo	95	2
Central African Republic	96	1
Congo	97	1
Costa Rica	98	1
Gabon	99	1
Jordan	100	1
Kuwait	101	1
Lesotho	102	1

BOTTOM 10

Country	Rank	Labor Force (million)
Mauritania	103	1
Mongolia	104	1
Namibia	105	1
Nicaragua	106	1
Panama	107	1
Puerto Rico	108	1
Singapore	109	1
Trinidad and Tobago	110	1
United Arab Emirates	111	1
Uruguay	112	1

Labor Force (million)

Source: *Yearbook of Labour Statistics*

134. ORGANIZED LABOR AS PERCENTAGE OF LABOR FORCE

The strength of the organized labor movement varies from country to country and from sector to sector within a country. The political power of organized labor is greatest in democratic countries, such as the United States and the United Kingdom, where it operates either as a pressure group or overt political party and where it influences legislation through intensive lobbying; labor is weakest, ironically, in Communist countries, where it has been incorporated into the ruling political apparatus and has virtually no independent existence of its own. However, the political power of organized labor can be measured only very imprecisely; on the other hand, the strength of unionization within the labor force can be measured rather accurately and expressed as a percentage of dues-paying members in relation to the wage-earning work force.

Rank	Country	Percent of Labor Force Unionized	Rank	Country	Percent of Labor Force Unionized	Rank	Country	Percent of Labor Force Unionized
TOP 10			9	Luxembourg	50	16	Portugal	30
1	Sweden	85	10	Austria	46	17	Japan	27
2	Iceland	78	11	Australia	42	18	Switzerland	26
3	Denmark	73	12	United Kingdom	42	19	Greece	25
4	Finland	71	13	Italy	40	20	Netherlands	25
5	Norway	55				21	United States	17
6	Belgium	53	**BOTTOM 10**			22	Spain	16
7	Ireland	52	14	Canada	35	23	France	12
8	New Zealand	51	15	Germany	34			

Source: *Yearbook of Labour Statistics*

Labor **177**

135. CIVIL SERVANTS AS PERCENTAGE OF THE WORK FORCE

Bureaucrats form a significant part of the work force world wide. As in other sectors, there are variations in the percentage of the labor market accounted for by civil servants. In socialist or command economies, the percentage is naturally higher, while in democratic countries where there is a natural antipathy to increasing government roles in society, the percentage is lower. Growing budgetary constraints also have fostered privatization of essential services and a reduction in the number of civil servants.

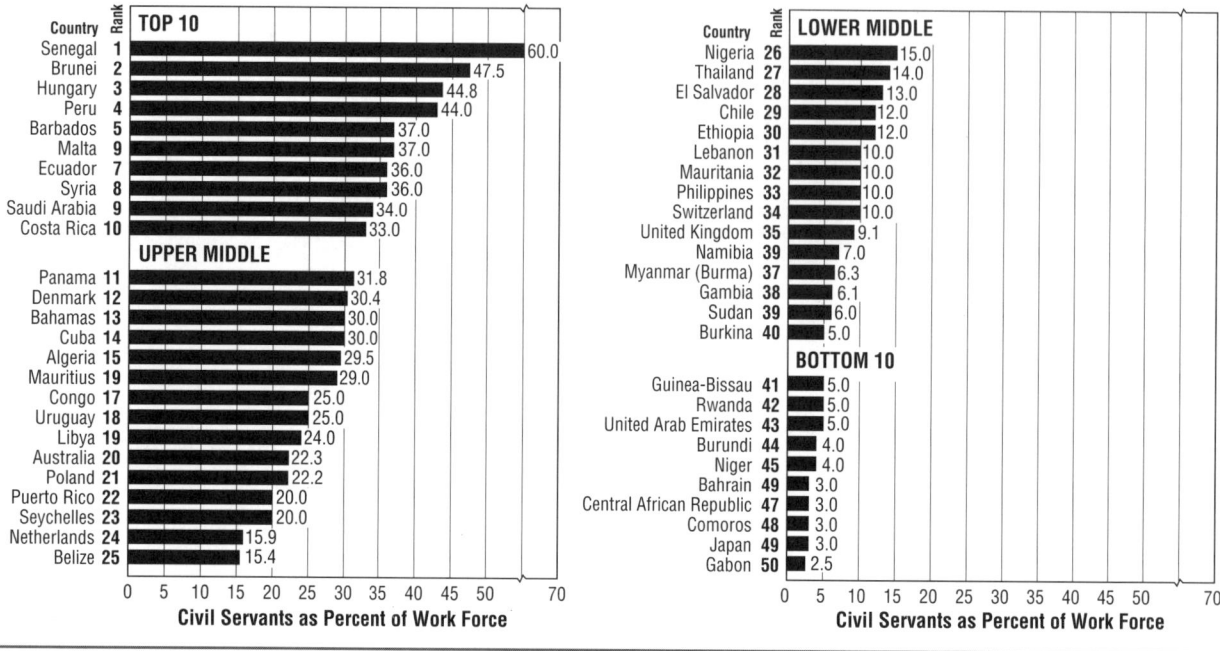

Country	Rank	TOP 10	
Senegal	1		60.0
Brunei	2		47.5
Hungary	3		44.8
Peru	4		44.0
Barbados	5		37.0
Malta	9		37.0
Ecuador	7		36.0
Syria	8		36.0
Saudi Arabia	9		34.0
Costa Rica	10		33.0
UPPER MIDDLE			
Panama	11		31.8
Denmark	12		30.4
Bahamas	13		30.0
Cuba	14		30.0
Algeria	15		29.5
Mauritius	19		29.0
Congo	17		25.0
Uruguay	18		25.0
Libya	19		24.0
Australia	20		22.3
Poland	21		22.2
Puerto Rico	22		20.0
Seychelles	23		20.0
Netherlands	24		15.9
Belize	25		15.4

Country	Rank	LOWER MIDDLE	
Nigeria	26		15.0
Thailand	27		14.0
El Salvador	28		13.0
Chile	29		12.0
Ethiopia	30		12.0
Lebanon	31		10.0
Mauritania	32		10.0
Philippines	33		10.0
Switzerland	34		10.0
United Kingdom	35		9.1
Namibia	39		7.0
Myanmar (Burma)	37		6.3
Gambia	38		6.1
Sudan	39		6.0
Burkina	40		5.0
BOTTOM 10			
Guinea-Bissau	41		5.0
Rwanda	42		5.0
United Arab Emirates	43		5.0
Burundi	44		4.0
Niger	45		4.0
Bahrain	49		3.0
Central African Republic	47		3.0
Comoros	48		3.0
Japan	49		3.0
Gabon	50		2.5

Civil Servants as Percent of Work Force

Source: *Yearbook of Labour Statistics*

---

136. YOUTH UNEMPLOYMENT RATE MALE/FEMALE

In almost every country, the unemployment rates for youth (ages 18 to 21) are greater than those of any other age segments. The causes may vary from country to country, but employers tend to prefer workers with work experience, even if they have to pay slightly higher wages. Generally, young workers of both sexes who look for work between the ages of 18 to 21 are unskilled workers who have dropped out of school. Within this age group females tend to be worse off than males, and minority workers are triple disadvantaged.

Rank	Country	Percentage of Unemployment Male 1991–1992 (age 15–24)	Rank	Country	Percentage of Unemployment Male 1991–1992 (age 15–24)	Rank	Country	Percentage of Unemployment Male 1991–1992 (age 15–24)
TOP 10			7	Canada	20	12	Sweden	12
1	Spain	27	8	New Zealand	20	13	Denmark	11
2	Italy	26	9	Austria	19	14	Netherlands	11
3	Finland	25	10	France	15	15	Norway	11
4	Ireland	23				16	Portugal	8
5	Australia	21	**BOTTOM 10**			17	Japan	5
6	Israel	21	11	United States	14	18	Germany	4

Source: *Yearbook of Labour Statistics*

Rank	Country	Percentage of Unemployment Female 1991–1992 (age 15–24)
TOP 10		
1	Spain	40
2	Italy	36
3	Israel	25
4	France	23
5	Finland	21
6	Ireland	19
7	Australia	18
8	Austria	17
9	New Zealand	17
10	Canada	15
BOTTOM 10		
11	Norway	13
12	United States	13
13	Denmark	12
14	Portugal	12
15	Netherlands	9
16	Sweden	9
17	Germany	4
18	Japan	4

Source: *Yearbook of Labour Statistics*

137. PERCENTAGE OF LABOR IN SERVICES

The percentage of labor in the services sector of the economy has been gaining in all industrialized countries and may constitute a significant post-industrial trend. This shift is bound to be more dramatic in the future, as industry and agriculture become less labor-intensive and the service needs of society grow more sophisticated.

Rank	Country	Percentage of Labor Force in Services
TOP 10		
1	Libya	57.1
2	Jordan	55.6
3	Kuwait	52.6
4	Iraq	52.3
5	Qatar	51.1
6	Brunei	46.6
7	Canada	42.7
8	Puerto Rico	42.4
9	Malta	40.0
10	Georgia	38.8
UPPER MIDDLE		
11	Suriname	38.6
12	Sweden	37.1
13	Saudi Arabia	36.6
14	Uruguay	35.4
15	United States	35.3
16	United Arab Emirates	35.0
17	Cote d'Ivoire	34.2
18	Brazil	33.7
19	Israel	33.5
20	Bermuda	33.4
21	Belgium	32.9
22	Netherlands	32.7
23	Denmark	32.5
24	Lesotho	31.1
25	Norway	30.4
26	Barbados	30.2
27	France	30.1
28	Bahamas	29.6
29	Lebanon	28.8
30	Trinidad and Tobago	28.5
31	Peru	27.6
32	Iceland	27.3
33	Syria	27.3
34	Finland	26.8
35	Cameroon	26.5
36	Mongolia	26.5
37	Panama	26.4
38	Chile	26.3
39	Germany	26.3
40	Australia	26.0
41	New Zealand	26.0
42	Venezuela	25.8
43	Solomon Islands	25.6
44	United Kingdom	25.5
45	Ecuador	24.9
46	Italy	24.9
47	Mauritania	24.8
48	Botswana	24.2
49	Liechtenstein	24.2
50	Portugal	24.1
51	Antigua and Barbuda	23.9
52	Argentina	23.9
53	Iran	23.7
54	Colombia	23.6
55	Austria	23.4
56	Costa Rica	23.4
57	Korea, North	22.9
58	South Africa	22.7
59	Algeria	22.1
60	Tonga	22.0
61	Tuvalu	22.0
62	Ukraine	22.0
63	Uzbekistan	21.8
64	Jamaica	21.7
65	Japan	21.7
66	Poland	21.6
67	Ireland	21.5
68	Mexico	21.4
69	Estonia	21.3
70	Lithuania	21.3
71	Maldives	21.0
72	Singapore	21.0
73	Bulgaria	20.9
74	Hungary	20.9
75	Western Samoa	20.7
76	Kyrgyzstan	20.5
77	Sierra Leone	20.4
78	Armenia	20.3
79	Mauritius	20.3
80	Kazakhstan	20.2
81	Angola	20.1
82	Egypt	20.1
LOWER MIDDLE		
83	Swaziland	20.1
84	Seychelles	20.0
85	Spain	20.0
86	Zambia	20.0
87	Malaysia	19.9
88	Tajikistan	19.8
89	Cyprus	19.7
90	Togo	19.6
91	Belarus	19.5
92	Russia	19.5
93	Honduras	19.3
94	Afghanistan	19.0
95	Bahrain	19.0
96	Zaire	19.0
97	Cambodia	18.9
98	Dominican Republic	18.9
99	Greece	18.9
100	Gabon	18.8
101	St. Lucia	18.8
102	Somalia	18.8
103	Tunisia	18.8
104	Chad	18.7
105	Luxembourg	18.7
106	Slovenia	18.7
107	Switzerland	18.7
108	Dominica	18.6
109	St. Vincent	18.5
110	Moldova	18.1
111	Sri Lanka	18.0
112	Czech Republic	17.7
113	Guinea-Bissau	17.5
114	Turkmenistan	17.5
115	Latvia	17.4
116	Laos	17.2
117	Oman	17.1
118	St. Kitts and Nevis	17.0
119	Paraguay	16.8
120	Andorra	16.7
121	Nigeria	15.9
122	El Salvador	15.7
123	Philippines	15.6
124	Kenya	15.5
125	Slovakia	15.4
126	Grenada	15.3
127	Fiji	15.2
128	Bosnia & Herzegovina	15.1
129	Congo	15.1
130	Tanzania	15.0
131	Monaco	14.9
132	Senegal	14.7
133	Cape Verde	14.4
134	Guatemala	14.4
135	Taiwan	14.2
136	Comoros	14.1
137	Korea, South	14.1
138	Uganda	13.9
139	Bolivia	13.8
140	Djibouti	13.8
141	Turkey	12.9
142	Yemen	12.9
143	Nicaragua	12.7
144	Pakistan	12.4
145	Zimbabwe	12.2
146	Madagascar	12.0
147	Guyana	11.9
148	Indonesia	11.9
149	Romania	11.9
150	Vanuatu	11.8
151	Thailand	11.6
152	Sao Tome e Principe	11.3
153	Yugoslavia	10.9
154	Albania	10.8

Rank	Country	Percentage of Labor Force in Services	Rank	Country	Percentage of Labor Force in Services	Rank	Country	Percentage of Labor Force in Services
155	Papua New Guinea	10.5	167	Kiribati	7.0	177	Malawi	4.3
156	Belize	10.3	168	Bangladesh	6.8	178	Mozambique	4.3
157	Croatia	10.0	169	Ghana	6.7	179	Burundi	3.1
158	India	9.3	170	Central African Republic	5.9	180	China	3.0
159	Liberia	9.0	171	Haiti	5.8	181	Gambia	2.9
160	Sudan	8.7	172	Rwanda	5.7	182	Myanmar (Burma)	2.9
161	San Marino	8.3	173	Niger	5.3	183	Burkina	2.4
162	Equatorial Guinea	8.2	174	Ethiopia	5.1	184	Mali	2.4
163	Benin	7.9	175	Nepal	4.6	185	Namibia	1.2
164	Morocco	7.9	**BOTTOM 10**					
165	Guinea	7.5	176	Vietnam	4.5			
166	Macedonia	7.4						

Source: *Yearbook of Labour Statistics*

138. PERCENTAGE OF LABOR IN MANUFACTURING

The structure of the economically active population has been shifting in favor of industry in most countries of the world, although in no country does industrial labor constitute more than 51% of the total labor force. This trend is more marked in developed countries because of the ability of the industrial sector to absorb and train workers. Unlike agricultural workers, industrial workers require specialized skills, are more intensively unionized and are covered by an array of regulations and laws governing wages, work periods, occupational health and fringe benefits. The industrial work force constitutes the core of the organized labor movement in many countries and therefore wields a disproportionately large influence in national affairs.

Rank	Country	Percentage of Labor in Manufacturing	Rank	Country	Percentage of Labor in Manufacturing	Rank	Country	Percentage of Labor in Manufacturing
TOP 10			37	Malaysia	21.2	76	Brazil	15.9
1	Bosnia & Herzegovina	50.5	38	Israel	21.1	77	Mexico	15.9
2	Romania	38.4	39	Italy	20.4	78	Venezuela	15.9
3	Czech Republic	37.3	40	United Kingdom	20.4	79	Zaire	15.9
4	Slovenia	35.4	41	South Africa	20.3	80	Luxembourg	15.8
5	Korea, North	33.0	42	Greece	20.2	81	Tonga	15.8
6	Liechtenstein	32.1	43	Kazakhstan	20.2	82	Honduras	15.3
7	San Marino	31.9	44	Moldova	20.2			
8	Libya	31.8	45	Finland	20.0	**LOWER MIDDLE**		
9	Estonia	31.5	46	Spain	20.0	83	Trinidad and Tobago	15.2
10	Mauritius	31.5	47	Costa Rica	19.5	84	Turkey	15.1
			48	Georgia	19.4	85	Egypt	15.0
UPPER MIDDLE			49	Lebanon	18.9	86	Bahrain	14.6
11	Ukraine	30.8	50	Belgium	18.6	87	Colombia	14.5
12	Yugoslavia	30.1	51	Maldives	18.6	88	Thailand	14.5
13	Belarus	29.5	52	Ireland	18.4	89	Gabon	14.1
14	Russia	29.4	53	Chile	18.3	90	Bangladesh	14.0
15	Malta	28.8	54	France	18.2	91	Guatemala	14.0
16	Lesotho	28.2	55	United States	18.1	92	Uzbekistan	13.9
17	Croatia	28.0	56	Sierra Leone	18.0	93	Sri Lanka	13.7
18	Germany	28.0	57	Macedonia	17.9	94	United Arab Emirates	13.6
19	Taiwan	28.0	58	Puerto Rico	17.9	95	Syria	13.5
20	Bulgaria	27.9	59	Sweden	17.9	96	Cameroon	13.2
21	Austria	27.5	60	Mongolia	17.8	97	Peru	13.2
22	Slovakia	27.5	61	Iceland	17.7	98	Tajikistan	13.1
23	Singapore	26.7	62	Tunisia	17.7	99	Dominican Republic	12.7
24	Hungary	26.0	63	Cyprus	17.5	100	Afghanistan	12.5
25	Latvia	25.4	64	Netherlands	17.4	101	Pakistan	12.4
26	Lithuania	25.3	65	Denmark	17.3	102	Paraguay	12.4
27	Poland	25.0	66	Morocco	16.9	103	Iran	12.3
28	Portugal	24.9	67	Canada	16.8	104	Nicaragua	12.3
29	Korea, South	23.8	68	Guyana	16.8	105	Belize	12.0
30	Japan	23.7	69	Norway	16.5	106	Ecuador	12.0
31	Armenia	23.3	70	China	16.4	107	Swaziland	12.0
32	Switzerland	23.2	71	El Salvador	16.4	108	Madagascar	11.9
33	St. Kitts and Nevis	22.3	72	Seychelles	16.4	109	Dominica	11.8
34	Uruguay	22.2	73	Kyrgyzstan	16.3	110	Algeria	11.6
35	Monaco	21.8	74	New Zealand	16.3	111	Zambia	11.4
36	Argentina	21.3	75	Australia	15.9	112	Ghana	11.3

Rank	Country	Percentage of Labor in Manufacturing
113	Togo	11.2
114	Bolivia	11.1
115	Indonesia	11.1
116	Saudi Arabia	11.1
117	Vietnam	11.1
118	Andorra	11.0
119	Djibouti	11.0
120	Mauritania	11.0
121	Cote d'Ivoire	10.9
122	Botswana	10.7
123	Iraq	10.6
124	Panama	10.6
125	Angola	10.5
126	Somalia	10.5
127	Suriname	10.5
128	Brunei	10.4
129	Philippines	10.0
130	Jamaica	9.8
131	Turkmenistan	9.8
132	India	9.7
133	Kuwait	9.4
134	Fiji	9.0
135	Solomon Islands	9.0
136	Barbados	8.9
137	Congo	8.8
138	St. Lucia	8.7
139	Grenada	8.6
140	Jordan	8.6
141	St. Vincent	8.4
142	Namibia	8.2
143	Kenya	8.0
144	Benin	7.8
145	Qatar	7.5
146	Chad	7.4
147	Myanmar (Burma)	7.4
148	Antigua and Barbuda	7.3
149	Laos	7.1
150	Senegal	7.0
151	Haiti	6.8
152	Cambodia	6.7
153	Comoros	6.5
154	Albania	6.3
155	Sao Tome e Principe	6.2
156	Mozambique	6.1
157	Cape Verde	5.7
158	Uganda	5.7
159	Mali	5.6
160	Zimbabwe	5.5
161	Western Samoa	5.4
162	Oman	5.1
163	Bermuda	5.0
164	Sudan	5.0
165	Bahamas	4.9
166	Tanzania	4.7
167	Guinea-Bissau	4.5
168	Nigeria	4.5
169	Liberia	4.4
170	Yemen	4.3
171	Rwanda	3.5
172	Malawi	3.3
173	Niger	3.1
174	Gambia	2.9
175	Papua New Guinea	2.9
BOTTOM 10		
176	Kiribati	2.8
177	Central African Republic	2.6
178	Tuvalu	2.0
179	Equatorial Guinea	1.8
180	Ethiopia	1.7
181	Guinea	1.5
182	Vanuatu	1.5
183	Burundi	1.3
184	Burkina	1.2
185	Nepal	0.5

Source: *Yearbook of Labour Statistics*

139. PERCENTAGE OF LABOR IN AGRICULTURE

Traditionally, agricultural labor is the least skilled and the least productive segment of the labor force. In most countries agricultural laborers are excluded from the purview of labor laws, have no guaranteed minimum wage and receive no social security. Because of their diffusion, they are rarely organized and play only a marginal role in social or labor union movements. Agricultural labor is also characterized by a greater proportion of women, most of whom serve as unpaid family workers. They are often required to work for longer hours each day than workers in industrial or service establishments. Work may be seasonal, resulting in serious underemployment or long periods of inactivity.

Rank	Country	Percentage of Labor Force in Agriculture
TOP 10		
1	Burundi	92.6
2	Burkina	91.8
3	Nepal	91.1
4	Rwanda	90.8
5	Ethiopia	88.3
6	Malawi	85.8
7	Mozambique	83.8
8	Mali	81.5
9	Uganda	80.4
10	Tanzania	80.3
UPPER MIDDLE		
11	Comoros	79.4
12	Senegal	78.3
13	Guinea	78.1
14	Guinea-Bissau	78.0
15	Papua New Guinea	77.0
16	Kenya	76.6
17	Niger	76.2
18	Madagascar	76.1
19	Laos	75.7
20	Djibouti	75.2
21	Cambodia	74.4
22	Vanuatu	74.4
23	Central African Republic	74.2
24	Chad	73.9
25	Gambia	73.7
26	Yemen	71.1
27	China	71.0
28	Kiribati	71.0
29	Somalia	70.8
30	Angola	69.4
31	Togo	69.2
32	Zambia	68.6
33	Liberia	68.3
34	Gabon	67.1
35	Myanmar (Burma)	67.1
36	Vietnam	67.1
37	Swaziland	66.0
38	Zaire	65.1
39	Zimbabwe	64.7
40	Mauritania	64.3
41	Bangladesh	64.2
42	Western Samoa	63.6
43	Sudan	63.5
44	Oman	62.0
45	Sierra Leone	61.7
46	India	60.9
47	Cameroon	60.3
48	Afghanistan	60.1
49	Ghana	59.3
50	Tuvalu	58.0
51	Equatorial Guinea	57.9
52	Haiti	57.3
53	Benin	55.0
54	Cote d'Ivoire	54.9
55	Sao Tome e Principe	53.9
56	Indonesia	52.9
57	Congo	52.2
58	Thailand	49.1
59	Guatemala	48.9
60	Tajikistan	44.7
61	Pakistan	44.5
62	Turkmenistan	44.2
63	Fiji	44.1
64	Korea, North	44.1
65	Uzbekistan	43.5
66	Nigeria	43.1
67	Paraguay	42.9
68	Philippines	41.7
69	Turkey	40.2
70	El Salvador	40.0
71	Albania	39.9
72	Morocco	39.2
73	Bolivia	38.9
74	Moldova	38.5
75	Namibia	38.5

Rank	Country	Percentage of Labor Force in Agriculture
76	Kyrgyzstan	38.2
77	Honduras	37.0
78	Tonga	36.5
79	Sri Lanka	33.2
80	Peru	32.5
81	Belize	31.4
82	Ecuador	30.8
LOWER MIDDLE		
83	Armenia	30.2
84	Nicaragua	28.8
85	Colombia	28.5
86	Mongolia	27.6
87	Georgia	27.1
88	Egypt	26.3
89	Mexico	26.3
90	Syria	26.3
91	St. Kitts and Nevis	26.1
92	Malaysia	26.0
93	Lesotho	25.9
94	St. Lucia	25.5
95	Dominica	25.2
96	Iran	25.0
97	Maldives	25.0
98	Cape Verde	24.8
99	Kazakhstan	24.3
100	Solomon Islands	23.7
101	Romania	23.1
102	Poland	23.0
103	Macedonia	22.9
104	Panama	22.9
105	Costa Rica	22.5
106	Botswana	22.1
107	Lithuania	22.1
108	Brazil	22.0
109	Dominican Republic	22.0
110	Tunisia	21.6
111	Ukraine	20.8

Rank	Country	Percentage of Labor Force in Agriculture
112	Guyana	20.4
113	Greece	20.1
114	St. Vincent	20.1
115	Jamaica	20.0
116	Belarus	19.9
117	Lebanon	19.1
118	Mauritius	17.5
119	Latvia	17.0
120	Croatia	16.7
121	Chile	15.8
122	Korea, South	14.4
123	Grenada	14.3
124	Russia	14.2
125	Algeria	13.6
126	Slovenia	12.8
127	Cyprus	12.2
128	Argentina	12.0
129	Bulgaria	12.0
130	Estonia	11.7
131	Czech Republic	11.6
132	Iraq	11.6
133	Ireland	11.6
134	Portugal	11.2
135	Libya	11.0
136	Taiwan	10.7
137	South Africa	10.5
138	Trinidad and Tobago	10.0
139	Venezuela	9.9
140	New Zealand	9.5
141	Spain	9.2
142	Slovakia	9.0
143	Hungary	8.6
144	Iceland	8.4
145	Finland	7.7
146	Seychelles	7.7
147	Italy	7.5
148	Austria	6.9
149	United Arab Emirates	6.3

Rank	Country	Percentage of Labor Force in Agriculture
150	Japan	5.8
151	Norway	5.4
152	Switzerland	5.4
153	Australia	5.1
154	Jordan	5.1
155	Denmark	4.8
156	Bahamas	4.7
157	Uruguay	4.5
158	France	4.4
159	Barbados	4.2
160	Antigua and Barbuda	3.9
161	Bosnia & Herzegovina	3.8
162	Yugoslavia	3.7
163	Netherlands	3.6
164	Saudi Arabia	3.6
165	Suriname	3.5
166	Canada	3.4
167	Israel	3.4
168	Germany	3.2
169	Luxembourg	3.2
170	Sweden	3.1
171	Puerto Rico	2.9
172	United States	2.7
173	Malta	2.5
174	Bahrain	2.3
175	Belgium	2.2
BOTTOM 10		
176	Liechtenstein	2.2
177	San Marino	2.0
178	Brunei	1.9
179	Qatar	1.6
180	United Kingdom	1.6
181	Kuwait	1.3
182	Andorra	1.2
183	Bermuda	1.2
184	Monaco	0.3
185	Singapore	0.2

Source: *Yearbook of Labour Statistics*

140. SELF-EMPLOYED AND EMPLOYERS

In most developed countries employees make up the largest category by employment status. However, developing countries generally have a larger proportion of persons listed as employers or self-employed, because these countries have poor, largely agrarian economies where there are no large-scale industrial or commercial establishments. In some developed countries, where downsizing has become a feature of the economy, there is a greater transfer of the workforce from the employee to the self-employed sector, but this trend has not become statistically significant.

Rank	Country	Percentage of Self Employed and Employers in Labor Force
TOP 10		
1	Nepal	86.2
2	Bahamas	76.5
3	Central African Republic	75.3
4	Papua New Guinea	72.7
5	Kiribati	71.9
6	Togo	70.3
7	Ghana	67.7
8	Nigeria	64.6
9	Congo	64.3
10	Burundi	62.8
UPPER MIDDLE		
11	Cameroon	60.2

Rank	Country	Percentage of Self Employed and Employers in Labor Force
12	Haiti	59.1
13	Liberia	59.1
14	Ethiopia	58.5
15	Benin	58.4
16	Niger	51.4
17	Comoros	47.6
18	Ecuador	45.7
19	Indonesia	43.2
20	Paraguay	43.1
21	Bolivia	41.2
22	Pakistan	41.2
23	Peru	39.8
24	Maldives	39.7
25	Philippines	38.6

Rank	Country	Percentage of Self Employed and Employers in Labor Force
26	Iran	36.9
27	Dominican Republic	36.5
28	Honduras	36.5
29	Guinea	36.2
30	Mali	35.4
31	Tonga	33.7
32	Fiji	33.6
33	Guatemala	32.7
34	Jamaica	32.7
35	Greece	32.5
36	Syria	31.0
37	Thailand	30.3
38	Venezuela	30.2
39	Mexico	30.1

Rank	Country	Percentage of Self Employed and Employers in Labor Force
40	Solomon Islands	29.6
41	Bangladesh	29.3
42	Dominica	29.2
43	El Salvador	29.2
44	Equatorial Guinea	29.0
45	Panama	28.4
46	Argentina	28.0
47	Korea, South	27.6
48	Turkey	27.6
49	Morocco	27.1
50	Sri Lanka	27.0
51	Brazil	26.3
LOWER MIDDLE		
52	Belize	26.2
53	Chile	25.9
54	Iraq	25.4
55	Cape Verde	24.7
56	Malaysia	23.6
57	Portugal	23.1
58	Uruguay	22.9
59	Zambia	22.9
60	Jordan	22.8
61	San Marino	22.2
62	Taiwan	22.2
63	Poland	21.9
64	Italy	21.6
65	Western Samoa	21.1
66	St. Lucia	21.0
67	Tunisia	20.9

Rank	Country	Percentage of Self Employed and Employers in Labor Force
68	Costa Rica	20.1
69	Egypt	19.6
70	Cyprus	18.7
71	Trinidad and Tobago	18.3
72	Ireland	18.2
73	New Zealand	18.2
74	St. Vincent	18.2
75	Namibia	17.8
76	Monaco	17.4
77	Spain	17.1
78	Algeria	16.8
79	Lesotho	16.8
80	Sao Tome e Principe	15.8
81	Israel	14.6
82	Australia	14.3
83	Guyana	14.3
84	Malta	14.1
85	Puerto Rico	14.0
86	Romania	13.9
87	Belgium	12.7
88	Croatia	12.7
89	Finland	12.6
90	Japan	12.3
91	Singapore	12.3
92	Mauritius	12.2
93	Antigua and Barbuda	12.1
94	United Kingdom	11.2
95	France	10.6
96	Austria	9.8
97	St. Kitts and Nevis	9.7

Rank	Country	Percentage of Self Employed and Employers in Labor Force
98	Switzerland	9.7
99	Sweden	9.5
100	Netherlands	9.4
101	Luxembourg	9.2
102	Canada	9.6
103	Barbados	8.8
104	India	8.8
105	Denmark	8.4
106	Norway	8.3
107	United States	8.2
108	Bermuda	7.7
109	Germany	7.6
110	South Africa	7.0
111	United Arab Emirates	6.8
112	Botswana	6.5
113	Liechtenstein	6.2
BOTTOM 10		
114	Slovakia	5.7
115	Bahrain	5.1
116	Malawi	4.9
117	Kuwait	3.9
118	Brunei	3.5
119	Czech Republic	2.2
120	Slovenia	2.2
121	Qatar	1.8
122	Gambia	0.5
123	Tuvalu	0.3

Source: *Yearbook of Labour Statistics*

141. ACTIVITY RATE

ILO defines economically active population as "persons of all ages who are either employed or looking for work." It does not include students, housekeepers, retired persons and persons wholly dependent on others. In some cases, the definition also excludes smugglers, prostitutes, drug dealers, bootleggers, blackmarketeers, members of the armed forces, prisoners, inmates of mental institutions, and persons engaged in informal, subsistence or part-time economic activities. The ratio of the working population to the total population is the activity rate. Activity rates are high in countries with certain demographic characteristics, such as a higher proportion of people between 15 and 65 or countries with a good employment market. Also women tend to have a lower activity rate because of gender differentials.

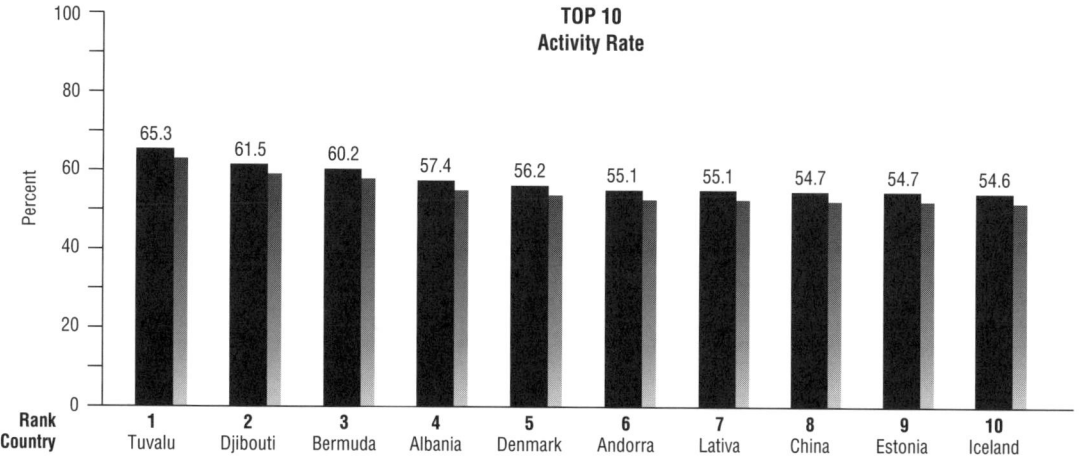

TOP 10 Activity Rate

Rank	1	2	3	4	5	6	7	8	9	10
Country	Tuvalu	Djibouti	Bermuda	Albania	Denmark	Andorra	Lativa	China	Estonia	Iceland
Percent	65.3	61.5	60.2	57.4	56.2	55.1	55.1	54.7	54.7	54.6

Rank	Country	Economically Active Population Activity Rate (%)
	UPPER MIDDLE	
11	Thailand	54.3
12	Qatar	53.7
13	San Marino	53.4
14	Japan	53.1
15	Czech Republic	52.6
16	Burundi	52.5
17	Canada	51.7
18	Bahamas	51.1
19	Burkina	50.9
20	Switzerland	50.8
21	Barbados	50.2
22	Rwanda	50.2
23	Germany	49.9
24	United States	49.9
25	Singapore	49.6
26	Finland	49.5
27	Norway	49.4
28	Sweden	49.4
29	United Kingdom	49.4
30	Liechtenstein	49.3
31	Australia	49.0
32	Russia	49.0
33	Laos	48.9
34	New Zealand	48.7
35	Hungary	48.6
36	Mozambique	48.6
37	Lithuania	48.5
38	Central African Republic	48.2
39	Suriname	48.2
40	Slovenia	48.1
41	Portugal	47.9
42	United Arab Emirates	47.6
43	Vietnam	47.4
44	Gambia	47.3
45	Slovakia	47.2
46	Moldova	47.1
47	Vanuatu	47.0
48	Bangladesh	46.9
49	Belarus	46.9
50	Mongolia	46.9
51	Austria	46.7
52	Georgia	46.4
53	Bulgaria	46.3
54	Cyprus	46.3
55	Ukraine	46.2
56	Tanzania	46.0
57	Guinea-Bissau	45.9
58	Romania	45.9
59	Azerbaijan	45.4
60	Ghana	45.4
61	Korea, South	45.4
62	Nepal	45.4
63	Croatia	45.3
64	Macedonia	45.2
65	Antigua and Barbuda	45.1
66	Kiribati	45.1
67	Poland	45.1
68	Uruguay	45.0
69	France	44.8
70	Mali	44.7

Rank	Country	Economically Active Population Activity Rate (%)
71	Bahrain	44.6
72	Korea, North	44.6
73	Mauritius	44.5
74	Comoros	44.4
75	Gabon	43.9
76	Brazil	43.8
77	Jamaica	43.7
78	Kazakhstan	43.7
79	Armenia	43.6
80	Uganda	43.6
81	Luxembourg	43.5
82	Malawi	43.3
83	Cambodia	43.1
84	Benin	43.0
85	Brunei	43.0
86	Taiwan	43.0
87	Indonesia	42.9
88	Madagascar	42.8
	LOWER MIDDLE	
89	Senegal	42.6
90	Italy	42.5
91	Belgium	42.2
92	Netherlands	42.1
93	Zimbabwe	42.1
94	Monaco	42.0
95	Ethiopia	41.3
96	Kyrgyzstan	41.2
97	Haiti	41.1
98	Sri Lanka	41.0
99	Somalia	40.9
100	Turkmenistan	40.9
101	Greece	40.6
102	Argentina	40.5
103	Trinidad and Tobago	40.5
104	Angola	40.3
105	Myanmar (Burma)	40.2
106	Cameroon	40.0
107	Togo	40.0
108	Grenada	39.9
109	Swaziland	39.8
110	Philippines	39.7
111	St. Kitts and Nevis	39.5
112	Bolivia	39.4
113	Spain	39.4
114	Equatorial Guinea	39.2
115	Uzbekistan	39.2
116	Guinea	39.1
117	St. Vincent	39.1
118	Cote d'Ivoire	39.0
119	Kenya	39.0
120	Kuwait	38.9
121	Mexico	38.9
122	Seychelles	38.9
123	Chile	38.6
124	Oman	38.2
125	Costa Rica	38.1
126	Ireland	37.8
127	Malaysia	37.6
128	Dominica	37.5
129	India	37.5

Rank	Country	Economically Active Population Activity Rate (%)
130	South Africa	37.5
131	Panama	37.4
132	Malta	37.2
133	St. Lucia	37.2
134	Israel	36.9
135	Tajikistan	36.9
136	Saudi Arabia	36.3
137	Venezuela	36.3
138	Peru	36.2
139	Zaire	36.1
140	Sierra Leone	35.9
141	Guyana	35.7
142	El Salvador	35.4
143	Cape Verde	35.3
144	Chad	35.3
145	Turkey	35.3
146	Namibia	35.2
147	Sudan	35.1
148	Ecuador	34.8
149	Honduras	34.8
150	Nicaragua	34.7
151	Colombia	34.3
152	Paraguay	34.3
153	Dominican Republic	33.9
154	Fiji	33.7
155	Tonga	33.6
156	Guatemala	33.5
157	Liberia	33.5
158	Puerto Rico	33.5
159	Zambia	33.4
160	Botswana	33.3
161	Belize	33.1
162	Niger	31.9
163	Sao Tome e Principe	31.7
164	Lesotho	31.6
165	Nigeria	31.1
166	Mauritania	30.8
167	Nauru	30.5
168	Afghanistan	30.3
169	Tunisia	29.8
170	Yugoslavia	29.8
171	Congo	29.5
172	Morocco	29.3
173	Egypt	29.2
174	Western Samoa	29.0
175	Iran	28.0
176	Pakistan	28.0
177	Syria	27.8
	BOTTOM 10	
178	Lebanon	26.5
179	Maldives	26.5
180	Yemen	26.4
181	Libya	24.8
182	Iraq	24.7
183	Papua New Guinea	24.6
184	Algeria	23.6
185	Jordan	22.8
186	Bosnia & Herzegovina	22.7
187	Solomon Islands	13.7

Source: *Yearbook of Labour Statistics*

142. WOMEN IN THE LABOR FORCE

Historically, women have been part of the labor force only since the Industrial Revolution, and the struggle to ensure their fair share of jobs and equal rights in the labor market continues even today in most countries. Not only are women openly and often legally discriminated against, but they receive unequal wages and unequal treatment under existing labor laws. Female labor, therefore, has always been cheaper. It has also been confined to certain sectors, dressmaking for example, where women may have certain aptitudes.

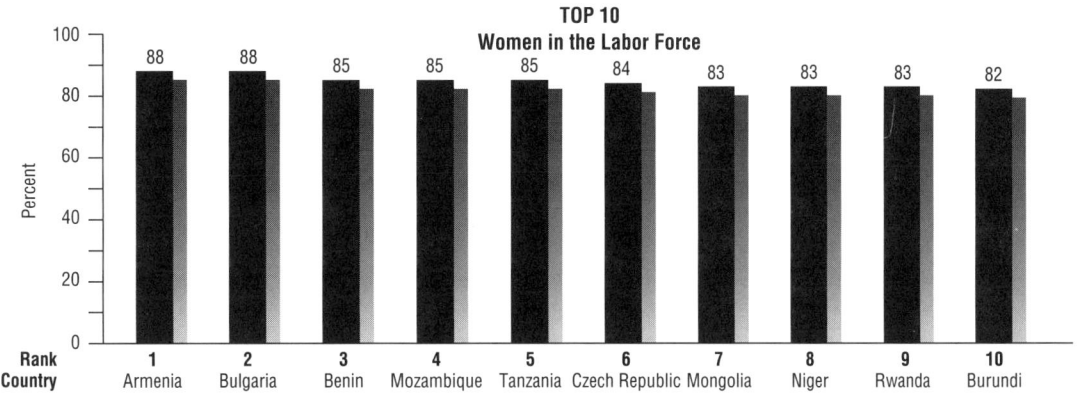

TOP 10
Women in the Labor Force

Rank	1	2	3	4	5	6	7	8	9	10
	88	88	85	85	85	84	83	83	83	82
Country	Armenia	Bulgaria	Benin	Mozambique	Tanzania	Czech Republic	Mongolia	Niger	Rwanda	Burundi

Rank	Country	Female Economic Participation as Percentage of Male	Rank	Country	Female Economic Participation as Percentage of Male	Rank	Country	Female Economic Participation as Percentage of Male
UPPER MIDDLE			51	Djibouti	64	90	Korea, South	52
11	Finland	82	52	France	64	91	Togo	52
12	Jamaica	82	53	Haiti	64	92	Zaire	52
13	Vietnam	82	54	Japan	64	93	Nigeria	51
14	Burkina	81	55	Canada	63	94	Portugal	51
15	China	81	56	Comoros	63	95	Cuba	50
16	Moldova	81	57	Equatorial Guinea	63	96	Botswana	49
17	Slovakia	81	58	Ghana	63	97	Israel	49
18	Grenada	80	59	Gambia	62	98	Zimbabwe	49
19	Korea, North	79	60	Kenya	62	99	Bahamas	48
20	Barbados	78	61	Malawi	62	100	Nepal	48
21	Uzbekistan	78	62	Australia	61	101	Belgium	47
22	Denmark	77	63	Congo	61	102	Bhutan	47
23	Laos	77	64	Guinea	61	103	Cameroon	46
24	Poland	77	65	Guinea-Bissau	61	104	Sierra Leone	45
25	Romania	77	66	Austria	60	105	Indonesia	44
26	Sweden	77	67	Madagascar	60	106	Italy	44
27	Thailand	77	68	Senegal	60	107	Luxembourg	44
28	Belarus	75	69	Solomon Islands	60	108	Philippines	44
29	Central African Republic	74	70	Swaziland	60	109	Uruguay	44
30	Estonia	74	71	United Kingdom	60	110	Netherlands	42
31	Iceland	74	72	Vanuatu	60	111	Trinidad and Tobago	42
32	Kyrgyzstan	74	73	Cambodia	59	112	Ireland	41
33	Turkmenistan	74	74	Somalia	59	113	Liberia	41
34	Bangladesh	73	75	Western Samoa	59	114	Suriname	41
35	Latvia	73	76	Angola	58	115	Zambia	41
36	Tajikstan	73	77	Singapore	58	116	Panama	40
37	Seychelles	72	78	Dominica	57	117	Chile	39
38	Georgia	71				118	Venezuela	39
39	Lithuania	71	**LOWER MIDDLE**			119	Argentina	38
40	Azerbaijan	70	79	Brazil	56	120	Brazil	38
41	Hungary	70	80	Cyprus	56	121	Mexico	37
42	Russia	70	81	Ethiopia	56	122	Nicaragua	37
43	Albania	69	82	Myanmar (Burma)	56	123	Belize	36
44	Lesotho	69	83	Gabon	55	124	Cape Verde	36
45	Ukraine	69	84	Malaysia	55	125	Sri Lanka	36
46	Norway	68	85	Cote d'Ivoire	54	126	El Salvador	35
47	Kazakhstan	67	86	South Africa	54	127	Greece	35
48	Papua New Guinea	65	87	Turkey	54	128	Mauritius	35
49	Uganda	65	88	New Zealand	53	129	Guyana	34
50	United States	65	89	Switzerland	53	130	India	34

Rank	Country	Female Economic Participation as Percentage of Male	Rank	Country	Female Economic Participation as Percentage of Male	Rank	Country	Female Economic Participation as Percentage of Male
131	Lebanon	34	145	Fiji	27	**BOTTOM 10**		
132	Kuwait	33	146	Honduras	27	158	Mali	17
133	Tunisia	33	147	Morocco	26	159	Pakistan	16
134	Peru	32	148	Paraguay	26	160	Jordan	13
135	Bolivia	31	149	Chad	25	161	Yemen	13
136	Spain	31	150	Ecuador	24	162	Egypt	12
137	Maldives	30	151	Iran	24	163	Libya	12
138	Namibia	30	152	United Arab Emirates	23	164	Afghanistan	11
139	Sudan	30	153	Guatemala	21	165	Algeria	11
140	Costa Rica	29	154	Syria	21	166	Oman	11
141	Iraq	29	155	Bahrain	20	167	Saudi Arabia	11
142	Malta	29	156	Qatar	20			
143	Mauritania	29	157	Dominican Republic	19			
144	Colombia	28						

Source: *Yearbook of Labour Statistics*

143. WORKERS' REMITTANCES FROM ABROAD

Historically, workers had little mobility and were forced to take on whatever work was available locally. With the spread of railways and automobiles, it became possible for workers to move from one city or state to another within the same country. It is only after World War II that the concept of labor imports and exports became an international reality. The tendency of workers to gravitate toward work became an international and borderless phenomenon. It surfaced first in Western Europe, whose booming economies were hit by the effects of the loss of manpower in World War II. Workers from Southern Europe and Turkey began to move north and were at first welcomed as *Gastarbeiter* or guest workers. Although the welcome soon wore thin, hordes of workers continued to flow into France, Netherlands, Germany, Switzerland and other countries. These workers kept their families in their native countries and sent them remittances periodically until such time when they were economically capable of maintaining a household. Thus workers' remittances entered the economics lexicon as a term signifying the transfer of wealth from labor importers to labor exporters. Today workers' remittances are a major source of income for many developing countries, such as Turkey, (from Germany and Austria) Philippines and Egypt (from oil-rich Arab countries), Botswana (from South Africa) and Mexico (from the United States).

Rank	Country	Net Workers' Remittance from Abroad (million $)	Rank	Country	Net Workers' Remittance from Abroad (million $)	Rank	Country	Net Workers' Remittance from Abroad (million $)
TOP 10						42	Guinea-Bissau	−2
1	Egypt	4,960				43	Kenya	−3
2	Portugal	3,844	**LOWER MIDDLE**			44	Guinea	−20
3	India	3,050	21	Albania	278	45	Niger	−34
4	Turkey	2,919	22	New Zealand	256	46	Chad	−35
5	Greece	2,360	23	Ethiopia	248	47	Congo	−78
6	Morocco	1,945	24	Peru	220	48	Gabon	−141
7	Pakistan	1,562	25	Guatemala	199	49	Norway	−234
8	Spain	1,495	26	China	93	50	Netherlands	−353
9	Jordan	1,040	27	Sweden	90			
10	Algeria	993	28	Benin	87	**BOTTOM 10**		
			29	Mali	87	51	Belgium	−365
UPPER MIDDLE			30	Burkina	71	52	Cote d'Ivoire	−394
11	Bangladesh	942	31	Papua New Guinea	69	53	Venezuela	−746
12	El Salvador	789	32	Mozambique	60	54	Kuwait	−1229
13	Sri Lanka	632	33	Austria	44	55	Oman	−1329
14	Tunisia	590	34	Senegal	40	56	France	−1530
15	Colombia	455	35	Nicaragua	25	57	Switzerland	−2007
16	Italy	432	36	Mauritania	23	58	Germany	−4375
17	Dominican Republic	362	37	Nigeria	22	59	United States	−7660
18	Yemen	347	38	Ghana	8	60	Saudi Arabia	−15717
19	Indonesia	346	39	Trinidad and Tobago	6			
20	Philippines	279	40	Rwanda	4			
			41	Togo	2			

Source: *World Development Report*

Section
XIV

TRANSPORTATION & COMMUNICATIONS

Scene 1: The Concorde leaves Heathrow Airport, London, at 9 A.M. and arrives at Kennedy Airport, New York, at 7 A.M. local time the same day.

Scene II: A man from Koro Toro in Ennedi Province in Chad walks hundreds of miles of pathless wild to D'jamena, then sails down the Lagone River to the Cameroon border town of Yagoua, from where he travels by cart, if he is lucky, to the railhead at Betare Oya and then takes the train to the port of Douala. The distance: over 2,500 km (1,550 mi); the time taken: over three weeks.

Between these two extremes the world of transportation presents a picture of contrasts. It is not often realized that a good transportation system is not merely a convenience or facility; it is a prerequisite for industrial development and military power. A nation is only as efficient as its transportation system. Even in developed countries, transportation is the weakest sector in the economy. The trains that breakdown, the black star airports (those with poor air traffic controls) and the potholed roads are symptoms of arterial weakening; it can impair mobility and slow more than the traffic. The plight of the railroads in the United States is as good an illustration as any of the deterioration of a once-proud system through nothing more than simple neglect.

The situation is less encouraging in many developing countries, where the transportation policies are directed toward the creation of showcase projects rather than an integrated national grid. There are countries with only a few kilometers of paved roads spending a good part of their GNP on national airlines; in others four-lane concrete highways end at the city limits.

We have followed conventional practice in bunching transportation and communications, although the latter is a field that is bound to outstrip the former in importance in coming decades, with the emergence of satellite communications and other technological breakthroughs.

144. AIRFIELDS

One of the principal indicators of development is accessibility by air. The inherent advantages of air travel are demonstrated most dramatically not in urban areas, but in remote jungles and deserts inaccessible by road, rail or river. During the post-World War II period, thousands of airfields and airstrips have been built even in countries without a civil air fleet. Many of them are not properly maintained.

Rank	Country	Airports	Rank	Country	Airports	Rank	Country	Airports
TOP 10			62	Spain	105	124	Estonia	29
1	United States	14,177	63	Syria	104	125	Mauritania	29
2	Brazil	3,613	64	Korea, South	103	126	Tunisia	29
3	Russia	2,550	65	Norway	103	127	Lesotho	28
4	Mexico	1,841	66	Tanzania	103	128	Netherlands	28
5	Argentina	1,700	67	Botswana	100	129	Niger	28
6	Canada	1,420	68	Vietnam	100	130	Bosnia & Herzegovina	27
7	Colombia	1,233	69	Lithuania	96	131	Moldova	26
8	Bolivia	1,225	70	Egypt	92	132	Fiji	25
9	South Africa	899	71	Hungary	92	133	Senegal	25
10	Paraguay	862	72	Iceland	90	134	Swaziland	23
			73	Uruguay	88	135	Kiribati	21
UPPER MIDDLE			74	Myanmar (Burma)	83	136	Jordan	19
11	Ukraine	594	75	Mongolia	81	137	Macedonia	17
12	Papua New Guinea	504	76	Greece	78	138	Bangladesh	16
13	Germany	499	77	Nigeria	76	139	Cambodia	15
14	United Kingdom	496	78	Croatia	75	140	Guinea	15
15	Zimbabwe	485	79	Czech Republic	75	141	Seychelles	14
16	Australia	481	80	Morocco	73	142	Sri Lanka	14
17	Guatemala	474	81	Chad	69	143	Cyprus	13
18	France	471	82	Somalia	69	144	Djibouti	13
19	Indonesia	435				145	Haiti	13
20	Chile	396	**LOWER MIDDLE**			146	Slovenia	13
21	Bulgaria	380	83	Gabon	68	147	Albania	12
22	Kazakhstan	365	84	Sudan	68	148	Armenia	12
23	Venezuela	360	85	Bahamas	66	149	Sierra Leone	11
24	India	336	86	Central African Republic	66	150	Ghana	10
25	China	330	87	Switzerland	66	151	Singapore	10
26	Angola	302	88	Azerbaijan	65	152	Togo	9
27	Zaire	281	89	Portugal	64	153	Rwanda	8
28	Philippines	270	90	Cameroon	59	154	Benin	7
29	Uzbekistan	265	91	Liberia	59	155	Kuwait	7
30	Sweden	253	92	Tajikistan	58	156	Turkmenistan	7
31	Kenya	247	93	Austria	55	157	Cape Verde	6
32	Peru	228	94	Korea, North	55	158	St. Vincent	6
33	Nicaragua	226	95	Laos	54	159	Tonga	6
34	Iran	219	96	Guyana	53	160	Trinidad and Tobago	6
35	Saudi Arabia	213	97	Israel	53	161	Burundi	5
36	Mozambique	194	98	Kyrgyzstan	52	162	Eritrea	5
37	Cuba	186	99	Latvia	50	163	Mauritius	5
38	Ecuador	174	100	Burkina	48	164	Comoros	4
39	Honduras	165	101	Yugoslavia	48	165	Qatar	4
40	Poland	163	102	Malawi	47	166	Antigua and Barbuda	3
41	Costa Rica	162	103	Suriname	46	167	Bahrain	3
42	Japan	162	104	Yemen	45	168	Equatorial Guinea	3
43	Finland	160	105	Congo	44	169	Grenada	3
44	Romania	158	106	Belgium	42	170	Western Samoa	3
45	Madagascar	146	107	Belize	42	171	Bhutan	2
46	Algeria	141	108	Cote d'Ivoire	42	172	Brunei	2
47	Lebanon	138	109	Afghanistan	41	173	Dominica	2
48	Libya	138	110	Ireland	40	174	Luxembourg	2
49	Italy	137	111	Taiwan	40	175	Maldives	2
50	Namibia	137	112	Georgia	37			
51	Belarus	124	113	Nepal	37	**BOTTOM 10**		
52	Ethiopia	121	114	United Arab Emirates	37	176	Sao Tome e Principe	2
53	New Zealand	120	115	Dominican Republic	36	177	St. Kitts and Nevis	2
54	Zambia	116	116	Jamaica	36	178	St. Lucia	2
55	Iraq	114	117	Mali	34	179	Barbados	1
56	Panama	112	118	Slovakia	34	180	Bermuda	1
57	Malaysia	111	119	Guinea-Bissau	33	181	Gambia	1
58	Pakistan	111	120	Uganda	31	182	Malta	1
59	Turkey	110	121	Vanuatu	31	183	Monaco	1
60	Thailand	106	122	Puerto Rico	30	184	Nauru	1
61	El Salvador	105	123	Solomon Islands	30	185	Tuvalu	1

Source: *World Factbook*

145. CYCLING

Cycling is one of the most universal modes of transport and it is the principal mode of urban personal transport in the two most populous countries of the world: China and India. It has also the advantage of being the most environment-friendly and nonpolluting means of transport. Cycling is recommended by doctors as a good exercise for the heart and the foot.

Even in Western countries, cycling has made a comeback for its recreational value.

Worldwatch Institute predicts that by the middle of the 21st century, cycling will become more popular even as automobiles become more fuel inefficient and destructive of the environment.

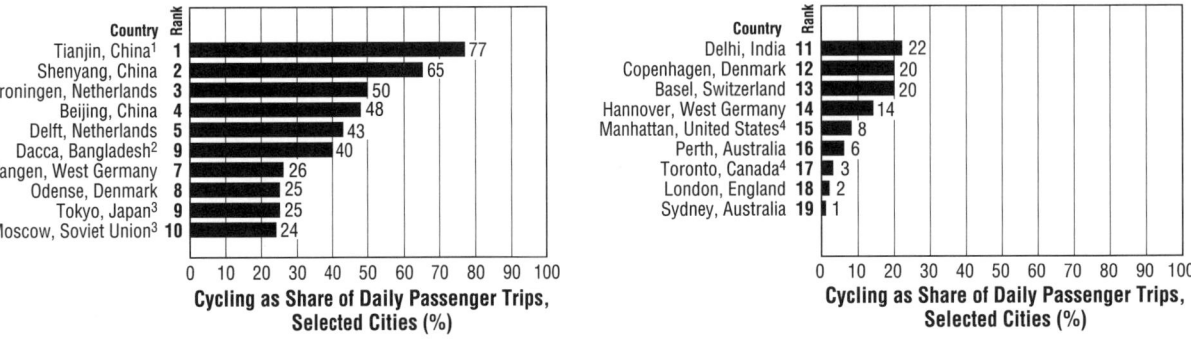

Cycling as Share of Daily Passenger Trips, Selected Cities (%)

[1]Share of nonwalking trips. [2]Trips by cycle rickshaw only. [3]Share cycling or walking to work. [4]Vehicle trips (versus passenger trips). Source: Worldwatch Institute, based on various sources.

146. INLAND WATERWAYS

One of a nation's most important natural resources is its waterways, but, as in other things, nations are not equally endowed. They differ not only in the length of the waterways but also in their quality. Some, like the Amazon in Brazil, are so deep that giant steamers can sail up the river for thousands of miles, while others may be so shallow that even canoes and similar craft navigate with difficulty. Some are navigable year round, while others dry up in the summer and are subject to floods in the rainy season. The usefulness of many of the largest rivers, such as the Nile and the Zaire, is diminished by intervening rapids. Therefore in interpreting the following ranking, it must be remembered that length is only one of the many attributes of a usable inland waterway system.

Rank	Country	Canals and Inland Waterways (mi)	Rank	Country	Canals and Inland Waterways (mi)	Rank	Country	Canals and Inland Waterways (mi)
TOP 10			**UPPER MIDDLE**			21	Venezuela	4,400
1	China	86,100	11	Myanmar (Burma)	7,954	22	Finland	4,148
2	Russia	63,380	12	Argentina	6,800	23	Netherlands	3,939
3	Brazil	31,069	13	Papua New Guinea	6,798	24	Guyana	3,700
4	United States	25,482	14	Bolivia	6,214	25	Sudan	3,300
5	Indonesia	13,409	15	Nigeria	5,328	26	Laos	2,850
6	Vietnam	11,000	16	Peru	5,300	27	Poland	2,484
7	India	10,054	17	Australia	5,200	28	Mozambique	2,330
8	Zaire	9,300	18	Bangladesh	5,000	29	Cambodia	2,300
9	France	9,278	19	Germany	4,686	30	Thailand	2,300
10	Colombia	8,900	20	Malaysia	4,534	31	Egypt	2,175

Rank	Country	Canals and Inland Waterways (mi)
32	Philippines	2,000
33	Paraguay	1,900
34	Canada	1,860
35	Mexico	1,800
36	Yugoslavia	1,616
37	Italy	1,500
38	United Kingdom	1,424
39	Korea, North	1,400
40	Zambia	1,398
LOWER MIDDLE		
41	Nicaragua	1,379
42	Cameroon	1,299
43	Sweden	1,275
44	Belgium	1,269
45	Chad	1,240
46	Mali	1,128
47	Japan	1,100
48	Romania	1,071
49	Ukraine	1,039
50	Hungary	1,008
51	Korea, South	1,000
52	New Zealand	1,000
53	Uruguay	1,000
54	Gabon	994
55	Norway	980
56	Ecuador	932
57	Malawi	891
58	Angola	805
59	Guinea	805
60	Afghanistan	750
61	Turkey	750
62	Suriname	746
63	Congo	696
64	Spain	649
65	Iraq	631
66	Cote d'Ivoire	609
67	Ghana	603
68	Iran	562
69	Senegal	557
70	Syria	541
71	Belize	513
72	Portugal	510
73	Central African Republic	500
74	Sierra Leone	500
75	Panama	497
76	Croatia	488
77	Costa Rica	454
78	Chile	450
79	Lithuania	373
80	Estonia	311
81	Czech Republic	295
82	Bulgaria	292
83	Honduras	289
84	Austria	277
85	Sri Lanka	267
86	Gambia	260
87	Denmark	259
88	Mongolia	247
89	Latvia	186
90	Niger	186
91	Guatemala	182
BOTTOM 10		
92	Cuba	149
93	Brunei	130
94	Fiji	126
95	Haiti	60
96	Greece	50
97	Switzerland	40
98	Togo	31
99	Albania	27
100	Luxembourg	23
101	Kiribati	3

Source: *World Data*

147. CIVIL AVIATION: PASSENGERS

The data in this table rank countries according to the number of passengers carried annually by domestic and international scheduled services operated by airlines registered in the respective countries.

Rank	Country	Air Transport Passengers (mi million)
TOP 10		
1	United States	480,463
2	Japan	69,346
3	Germany	60,997
4	United Kingdom	58,825
5	Russia	44,900
6	China	33,100
7	France	33,012
8	Singapore	27,929
9	Australia	25,649
10	Canada	25,633
UPPER MIDDLE		
11	Korea, South	24,395
12	Netherlands	23,713
13	Taiwan	22,848
14	Brazil	20,264
15	Italy	18,429
16	Spain	16,614
17	Thailand	15,688
18	Indonesia	12,273
19	Mexico	11,879
20	Saudi Arabia	11,540
21	Switzerland	11,505
22	India	10,878
23	Malaysia	10,853
24	Philippines	8,679
25	Kazakhstan	7,800
26	New Zealand	7,799
27	South Africa	6,588
28	Uzbekistan	6,500
29	Pakistan	6,152
30	Norway	6,023
31	Israel	5,930
32	Turkey	5,675
33	Finland	5,142
34	Sweden	5,097
35	Greece	4,908
36	Argentina	4,816
37	Portugal	4,745
38	Belgium	4,658
39	Austria	4,552
40	Venezuela	4,168
41	Belarus	3,487
42	United Arab Emirates	3,470
43	Egypt	3,437
44	Georgia	3,291
45	Tajikistan	3,214
46	Colombia	3,200
47	Iran	3,121
48	Azerbaijan	3,025
49	Kuwait	2,805
50	Chile	2,750
51	Morocco	2,731
52	Denmark	2,714
53	Ireland	2,660
54	Sri Lanka	2,289
55	Poland	2,270
56	Bulgaria	2,239
57	Trinidad and Tobago	2,030
58	Turkmenistan	2,021
59	Algeria	2,010
60	Ukraine	1,988
61	Cuba	1,908
62	Cyprus	1,903
63	Latvia	1,863
64	Mauritius	1,841
65	Kyrgyzstan	1,602
66	Bangladesh	1,588
67	Czech Republic	1,588
68	Bahrain	1,515
69	Iceland	1,474
70	Moldova	1,461
71	Jordan	1,455
72	Brunei	1,261
LOWER MIDDLE		
73	Tunisia	1,227
74	Oman	1,194
75	Romania	1,171
76	Kenya	1,079
77	Qatar	1,042
78	Hungary	1,027
79	Costa Rica	999
80	Ethiopia	998
81	Lebanon	987
82	Iraq	976
83	Jamaica	934.8
84	Peru	803
85	El Salvador	801
86	Paraguay	791
87	Ecuador	780
88	Malta	777
89	Angola	771
90	Bolivia	729
91	Yemen	698
92	Fiji	671
93	Nigeria	619
94	Syria	521
95	Zimbabwe	514
96	Papua New Guinea	458.8
97	Nepal	439

Rank	Country	Air Transport Passengers (mi million)
98	Seychelles	388.9
99	Sudan	382.1
100	Suriname	336
101	Namibia	332
102	Zambia	313
103	Ghana	296.7
104	Slovenia	295
105	Uruguay	293
106	Gabon	276.7
107	Madagascar	268.2
108	Libya	264.2
109	Mozambique	253
110	Guatemala	239
111	Honduras	221
112	Bahamas	215
113	Panama	209
114	Guyana	200
115	Croatia	196
116	Cameroon	187
117	Zaire	183
118	Macedonia	181.7
119	Mongolia	179.9
120	Cote d'Ivoire	178
121	Dominican Republic	174

Rank	Country	Air Transport Passengers (mi million)
122	Mauritania	171
123	Malawi	165.2
124	Congo	157
125	Nauru	148
126	Burkina	146
127	Estonia	141.8
128	Armenia	138.1
129	Senegal	138
130	Myanmar (Burma)	137.7
131	Lithuania	135.1
132	Benin	135
133	Togo	135
134	Mali	134.9
135	Central African Republic	134
136	Chad	131
137	Afghanistan	127
138	Niger	126
139	Antigua and Barbuda	121
140	Cape Verde	106
141	Tanzania	94
142	Barbados	93
143	Yugoslavia	93
144	Somalia	81
145	Luxembourg	79.5

Rank	Country	Air Transport Passengers (mi million)
146	Sierra Leone	68.3
147	Vietnam	54
148	Solomon Islands	40.5
149	Botswana	36.3
150	Nicaragua	35.8
151	Laos	27
152	Swaziland	25.6
153	Guinea	17.9
154	Uganda	15
155	Slovakia	9.5
BOTTOM 10		
156	Guinea-Bissau	6
157	Tonga	5.8
158	Kiribati	5.3
159	Sao Tome e Principe	5.0
160	Lesotho	4.8
161	Liberia	4.3
162	Equatorial Guinea	4
163	Bhutan	2.7
164	Comoros	1.9
165	Maldives	1.9

Source: *Air Transport Statistics*

CARGO HANDLED BY PORTS

Much of international trade is seaborne, and a nation's share of this traffic is represented by the cargo handled by its ports. The figures include the total weight of cargo unloaded and loaded from seagoing vessels of all flags at the ports of a country, but exclude ballast, bunkers, ships' stores and transshipment goods.

148. CARGO HANDLED BY PORTS: LOADED

Rank	Country	Maritime International Cargo Loaded (000 metric tons)
TOP 10		
1	United States	340,344
2	Australia	332,124
3	Indonesia	226,980
4	Saudi Arabia	214,070
5	Brazil	168,026
6	Canada	153,795
7	Taiwan	140,705
8	Mexico	129,696
9	Norway	125,184
10	Singapore	114,788
UPPER MIDDLE		
11	Iran	113,207
12	Japan	111,180
13	China	105,852
14	Panama	105,744
15	Venezuela	101,435
16	Iraq	97,830
17	South Africa	95,904
18	Netherlands	88,476
19	United Arab Emirates	88,153
20	Nigeria	80,607
21	Korea, South	74,736

Rank	Country	Maritime International Cargo Loaded (000 metric tons)
22	United Kingdom	68,076
23	Libya	67,000
24	Malaysia	66,025
25	Germany	64,980
26	France	61,200
27	Algeria	57,607
28	Belgium	57,168
29	India	53,220
30	Italy	51,420
31	Kuwait	51,400
32	Sweden	48,048
33	Spain	40,836
34	Argentina	36,792
35	Finland	35,604
36	Ukraine	34,200
37	Poland	33,984
38	Oman	33,843
39	Russia	25,476
40	Angola	23,288
41	Turkey	22,956
42	Latvia	22,548
43	Colombia	22,332
44	Chile	21,768
45	Thailand	21,192

Rank	Country	Maritime International Cargo Loaded (000 metric tons)
46	Morocco	19,476
47	Greece	18,465
48	Qatar	18,145
49	Syria	17,868
50	New Zealand	17,748
51	Denmark	17,508
52	Liberia	14,900
53	Egypt	14,808
54	Brunei	13,554
55	Bahrain	13,285
56	Romania	13,164
57	Philippines	12,864
58	Gabon	12,828
59	Guinea	12,210
60	Ecuador	11,783
61	Lithuania	11,736
62	Peru	10,197
LOWER MIDDLE		
63	Mauritania	10,037
64	Trinidad and Tobago	9,622
65	Congo	8,987
66	Jordan	8,868
67	Jamaica	8,802

Rank	Country	Maritime International Cargo Loaded (000 metric tons)
68	Yugoslavia	8,520
69	Israel	8,448
70	Cuba	8,092
71	Estonia	7,068
72	Ireland	6,367
73	Tunisia	6,060
74	Pakistan	5,976
75	Bahamas	5,920
76	Suriname	5,776
77	Bulgaria	5,290
78	Sri Lanka	5,220
79	Croatia	4,140
80	Portugal	4,068
81	Cote d'Ivoire	3,853
82	Mozambique	2800
83	Senegal	2591
84	Dominican Republic	2550
85	Papua New Guinea	2463
86	Zaire	2395
87	Togo	2362
88	Cyprus	2184
89	Yemen	1936
90	Guatemala	1818
91	Ghana	1810
92	Sierra Leone	1802
93	Bangladesh	1,740
94	Guyana	1,730

Rank	Country	Maritime International Cargo Loaded (000 metric tons)
95	Nauru	1,650
96	Costa Rica	1,605
97	Kenya	1,596
98	Myanmar (Burma)	1,343
99	Honduras	1,316
100	Austria	1,267
101	Cameroon	1,260
102	Tanzania	1,249
103	Sudan	1,195
104	Albania	1,055
105	Mauritius	956
106	Iceland	927
107	Uruguay	770
108	Korea, North	635
109	Ethiopia	582
110	Fiji	568
111	Madagascar	540
112	Namibia	483
113	Djibouti	414
114	Somalia	324
115	Nicaragua	320
116	Vietnam	303
117	Solomon Islands	278
118	Benin	246
119	El Salvador	221
120	Barbados	206
121	Belize	178

Rank	Country	Maritime International Cargo Loaded (000 metric tons)
122	Haiti	170
123	Gambia	169
124	Lebanon	152
125	St. Lucia	150
126	Bermuda	130
127	Dominica	103
128	Equatorial Guinea	100
129	Malta	90
130	Cape Verde	87
131	St. Vincent	80
132	Vanuatu	80
133	Central African Republic	53
134	Guinea-Bissau	40
135	Burundi	35
136	Antigua and Barbuda	28
BOTTOM 10		
137	Maldives	27
138	Grenada	25
139	St. Kitts and Nevis	24
140	Kiribati	15
141	Sao Tome e Principe	15
142	Tonga	15
143	Comoros	12
144	Western Samoa	12
145	Cambodia	11
146	Seychelles	11

Source: *UN Statistical Yearbook*

149. CARGO HANDLED BY PORTS: OFF-LOADED

Rank	Country	Maritime International Cargo Off-Loaded (000 metric tons)
TOP 10		
1	Japan	751,404
2	United States	598,116
3	Netherlands	277,008
4	Korea, South	273,672
5	Taiwan	243,019
6	Italy	222,060
7	France	182,400
8	Singapore	164,400
9	Spain	133,956
10	Germany	124,824
UPPER MIDDLE		
11	United Kingdom	117,804
12	China	101,688
13	Belgium	88,908
14	India	75,000
15	Panama	70,572
16	Canada	69,080
17	Turkey	61,728
18	Sweden	56,976
19	Mexico	52,716
20	Brazil	52,570
21	Saudi Arabia	46,437
22	Australia	40,284
23	Thailand	40,152
24	Finland	38,640
25	Indonesia	36,252
26	Malaysia	35,760
27	Denmark	34,368
28	Philippines	34,128
29	Greece	32,429
30	Pakistan	24,684
31	Egypt	22,860
32	Norway	22,116
33	Morocco	21,120

Rank	Country	Maritime International Cargo Off-Loaded (000 metric tons)
34	Israel	20,964
35	Bulgaria	20,080
36	Romania	18,144
37	Venezuela	17,932
38	Ireland	17,637
39	Iran	16,719
40	Portugal	16,044
41	Cuba	15,440
42	Algeria	14,284
43	South Africa	13,560
44	Poland	13,524
45	Chile	13,464
46	Libya	12,200
47	Colombia	11,268
48	Trinidad and Tobago	10,961
49	Nigeria	10,812
50	New Zealand	10,776
51	Tunisia	10,200
52	Yugoslavia	10,176
53	United Arab Emirates	9,595
54	Bangladesh	9,000
55	Sri Lanka	8,796
56	Iraq	8,638
57	Yemen	7,829
58	Argentina	6,864
59	Croatia	6,252
60	Jordan	6,168
61	Cote d'Ivoire	5,936
62	Bahamas	5,705
63	Syria	5,676
LOWER MIDDLE		
64	Korea, North	5,520
65	Jamaica	5,285
66	Peru	5,077
67	Cyprus	4,968

Rank	Country	Maritime International Cargo Off-Loaded (000 metric tons)
68	Kenya	4,884
69	Kuwait	4,522
70	Austria	4,419
71	Estonia	4,308
72	Dominican Republic	4,182
73	Latvia	3,984
74	Bahrain	3,512
75	Sudan	3,467
76	Mozambique	3,400
77	Ethiopia	3,120
78	Guatemala	3,025
79	Ghana	2,842
80	Lithuania	2,784
81	Tanzania	2,721
82	Qatar	2,588
83	Oman	2,492
84	Senegal	2,477
85	Malta	2,458
86	Cameroon	2,328
87	Mauritius	2,232
88	Ecuador	1,958
89	Russia	1,896
90	Costa Rica	1,892
91	Papua New Guinea	1,784
92	Lebanon	1,750
93	Iceland	1,633
94	Nicaragua	1,629
95	Liberia	1,520
96	Vietnam	1,510
97	Benin	1,489
98	Zaire	1,453
99	Uruguay	1,450
100	Brunei	1,325
101	Suriname	1,286
102	Myanmar (Burma)	1,284
103	Angola	1,261

Rank	Country	Maritime International Cargo Off-Loaded (000 metric tons)
104	Togo	1,050
105	El Salvador	1,023
106	Somalia	1,007
107	Honduras	1,002
108	Madagascar	984
109	Djibouti	958
110	Mauritania	874
111	Congo	736
112	Guinea	712
113	Haiti	704
114	Guyana	673
115	Albania	664
116	Fiji	625
117	Cape Verde	580
118	Barbados	538

Rank	Country	Maritime International Cargo Off-Loaded (000 metric tons)
119	Sierra Leone	533
120	Bermuda	470
121	Solomon Islands	349
122	Seychelles	348
123	Guinea-Bissau	315
124	Namibia	260
125	Belize	241
126	St. Lucia	234
127	Gabon	212
128	Gambia	212
129	Western Samoa	192
130	Grenada	190
131	Burundi	189
132	Dominica	181
133	St. Vincent	140

Rank	Country	Maritime International Cargo Off-Loaded (000 metric tons)
134	Central African Republic	126
135	Antigua and Barbuda	113
136	Comoros	107
BOTTOM 10		
137	Tonga	104
138	Cambodia	95
139	Maldives	78
140	Equatorial Guinea	60
141	Nauru	59
142	Vanuatu	55
143	St. Kitts and Nevis	36
144	Kiribati	26
145	Sao Tome e Principe	26

Source: *UN Statistical Yearbook*

150. MERCHANT MARINE

The data in this table rank merchant fleets registered in each country in terms of gross registered tons (GRT)—100 cubic feet or 2.83 cubic meters. Vessels without mechanical means of propulsion are excluded, but sailing vessels with auxiliary power are included. Because of the existence of flags of convenience, the data must be interpreted with caution, at least as far as countries such as Liberia and Panama are concerned. The figures, however, are extremely precise because of the care with which Lloyd's of London compiles its shipping register.

Rank	Country	Merchant Marine Deadweight Tonnage (000)
TOP 10		
1	Liberia	97,374.0
2	Panama	79,255.6
3	Greece	45,276.6
4	Japan	37,815.8
5	Cyprus	36,198.1
6	Bahamas	33,081.7
7	United States	25,646.4
8	China	20,658
9	Belarus	18,373
10	Malta	17,073.2
UPPER MIDDLE		
11	Russia	16,592.3
12	Singapore	14,929.2
13	Philippines	13,807.1
14	Korea, South	11,724.9
15	Italy	10,940.1
16	India	10,365.9
17	Brazil	9,348.3
18	Taiwan	9,241.3
19	Iran	8,345.3
20	Denmark	7,569.1
21	Turkey	7,114.3
22	St. Vincent	7,044.2
23	Germany	6,832.3
24	Bermuda	5,206.5
25	Yugoslavia	5,173.1
26	Spain	5,077.3
27	France	4,981.0
28	Romania	4,845.5
29	United Kingdom	4,687.3
30	Poland	4,314.3
31	Netherlands	4,191
32	Australia	3,857.3
33	Sweden	3,327.7
34	Vanuatu	3,259.6

Rank	Country	Merchant Marine Deadweight Tonnage (000)
35	Kuwait	3,188.5
36	Indonesia	3,130.2
37	Malaysia	2,916.3
38	Canada	2,896.8
39	Luxembourg	2,603.6
40	Norway	2,143.3
41	Bulgaria	1,938.2
42	Egypt	1,685.2
43	Iraq	1,578.8
44	Mexico	1,495.3
45	United Arab Emirates	1,491.7
46	Honduras	1,437.3
47	Latvia	1,436.9
48	Saudi Arabia	1,381.7
49	Venezuela	1,355.4
50	Myanmar (Burma)	1,354
51	Libya	1,223.6
52	Thailand	1,194.5
53	Argentina	1,173.1
54	Portugal	1,129.3
55	Algeria	1,093.4
56	Antigua and Barbuda	997.4
57	Finland	989.3
58	Korea, North	951.2
59	Peru	924.6
60	Vietnam	872.8
61	Chile	854.9
62	Nigeria	733.3
63	Israel	723.4
64	Estonia	680.4
65	Qatar	635.6
66	Peru	615.6
67	Switzerland	602.8
LOWER MIDDLE		
68	Slovenia	596.9
69	Morocco	586.2

Rank	Country	Merchant Marine Deadweight Tonnage (000)
70	Bangladesh	566.8
71	Pakistan	513.8
72	Ecuador	504.1
73	Sri Lanka	472.6
74	Czech Republic	446.2
75	Tunisia	443.3
76	Lebanon	438.2
77	Colombia	403
78	Lithuania	373.9
79	Brunei	349.7
80	South Africa	282.5
81	New Zealand	279.8
82	Belgium	218.5
83	Syria	210.4
84	Ireland	208.6
85	Austria	208.5
86	Bahrain	192.5
87	Uruguay	172.5
88	Mauritius	152.2
89	Croatia	140.9
90	Hungary	134.5
91	Ghana	131.0
92	Angola	123.5
93	Iceland	114.9
94	Jordan	113.6
95	Cote d'Ivoire	98.6
96	Ethiopia	84.3
97	Barbados	84
98	Madagascar	82.1
99	Albania	81.0
100	Maldives	79.0
101	Sudan	62.2
102	Fiji	60.4
103	Tanzania	48.5
104	Belize	45.7
105	Papua New Guinea	40.9
106	Cameroon	39.8

Rank	Country	Merchant Marine Deadweight Tonnage (000)
107	Paraguay	38.5
108	Mozambique	31.6
109	Cape Verde	30.9
110	Zaire	30.7
111	Gabon	30.2
112	Senegal	27.5
113	Mauritania	23.9
114	Togo	20.6
115	Somalia	18.5
116	Sierra Leone	18.4
117	Trinidad and Tobago	17.5
118	Tuvalu	16.0
119	Bolivia	15.8
120	Suriname	15.7
121	Tonga	13.7
122	Yemen	13.7
123	Guyana	13.5

Rank	Country	Merchant Marine Deadweight Tonnage (000)
124	Oman	11.7
125	Kenya	11.6
126	Congo	10.8
127	Dominican Republic	10.4
128	Jamaica	10.2
129	Costa Rica	8.4
130	Equatorial Guinea	6.7
131	Western Samoa	6.5
132	Namibia	5.9
133	Nauru	5.8
134	Solomon Islands	5.0
135	Djibouti	4.1
136	Cambodia	3.8
137	Comoros	3.6
138	Seychelles	3.3
139	Dominica	3.2
140	Kiribati	2.7

Rank	Country	Merchant Marine Deadweight Tonnage (000)
141	Sao Tome e Principe	2.3
142	St. Lucia	2.1
143	Gambia	2.0
144	Guinea-Bissau	1.8
BOTTOM 10		
145	Guinea	1.7
146	Laos	1.5
147	Nicaragua	1.3
148	St. Kitts and Nevis	0.6
149	Grenada	0.5
150	Burundi	0.4
151	Guatemala	0.4
152	Haiti	0.4
153	Malawi	0.3
154	Benin	0.2

Source: *Lloyd's World Fleet Statistics*

151. RAIL; FREIGHT TRAFFIC

In all but a few countries, freight traffic is not only the principal source of railway revenues but also the only cause for its continued existence. Recent developments in streamlining the capability of rail systems to carry more freight faster have given them a slight competitive edge over trucking and inland waterways. Particularly, raw materials such as pig iron and coal depend largely on railways for movement from the pits to the factories.

Rank	Country	Rail Cargo Short Ton (mi million)
TOP 10		
1	United States	1,183,000
2	China	853,576
3	Ukraine	232,000
4	India	171,213
5	Canada	166,057
6	Brazil	85,439
7	South Africa	62,605
8	Australia	61,000
9	Uzbekistan	48,400
10	Germany	46,254
UPPER MIDDLE		
11	Poland	44,082
12	Belarus	38,659
13	France	31,414
14	Mexico	23,973
15	Czech Republic	17,520
16	Japan	17,420
17	Russia	17,244
18	Italy	15,091
19	Sweden	12,725
20	Slovakia	11,436
21	United Kingdom	10,623
22	Moldova	10,279
23	Korea, South	9,633
24	Azerbaijan	9,439
25	Austria	8,080
26	Tajikistan	7,617
27	Lithuania	7,555
28	Hungary	6,860
29	Latvia	6,732
30	Finland	6,345
31	Korea, North	6,200
32	Argentina	5,790
33	Turkey	5,654
34	Bulgaria	5,325

Rank	Country	Rail Cargo Short Ton (mi million)
35	Spain	5,303
36	Iran	5,277
37	Belgium	5,184
38	Switzerland	5,022
39	Pakistan	4,011
40	Mauritania	3,860
41	Morocco	3,025
42	Estonia	2,844
43	Indonesia	2,803
44	Thailand	2,095
45	Swaziland	1,993
46	Netherlands	1,836
47	Liberia	1,746
48	Mongolia	1,734
49	Chile	1,732
50	New Zealand	1,700
51	Egypt	1,597
52	Norway	1,575
LOWER MIDDLE		
53	Algeria	1,569
54	Slovenia	1,549
55	Tunisia	1,380
56	Taiwan	1,334
57	Nigeria	1,281
58	Portugal	1,279
59	Zaire	1,258
60	Denmark	1,231
61	Croatia	1,212
62	Angola	1,178
63	Syria	1,167
64	Kyrgyzstan	1,088
65	Tanzania	1021
66	Yugoslavia	950
67	Malaysia	945
68	Cuba	937
69	Kenya	899

Rank	Country	Rail Cargo Short Ton (mi million)
70	Botswana	867
71	Namibia	840
72	Romania	819
73	Zambia	735.6
74	Israel	734
75	Sudan	666
76	Vietnam	661
77	Peru	605.8
78	Jordan	542
79	Saudi Arabia	523
80	Bolivia	521.9
81	Bangladesh	492
82	Cote d'Ivoire	466
83	Myanmar (Burma)	444
84	Luxembourg	443
85	Mozambique	421.9
86	Senegal	418
87	Cameroon	405
88	Albania	400
89	Macedonia	395
90	Ireland	393.6
91	Greece	358
92	Burkina	322
93	Armenia	308
94	Congo	273
95	Kazakhstan	256.3
96	Mali	187.2
97	Colombia	166.4
98	Uruguay	139.2
99	Gabon	126
100	Benin	111.3
101	Sri Lanka	106.9
102	Ghana	93.9
103	Guatemala	92.5
104	Madagascar	90
105	Ethiopia	86
106	Djibouti	81.7

Rank	Country	Rail Cargo Short Ton (mi million)	Rank	Country	Rail Cargo Short Ton (mi million)	Rank	Country	Rail Cargo Short Ton (mi million)
107	Iraq	79	114	El Salvador	24.2	119	Paraguay	4.3
108	Uganda	60				120	Zimbabwe	3.7
109	Nicaragua	46.6		**BOTTOM 10**		121	Ecuador	3.6
110	Costa Rica	45.8	115	Honduras	20.7	122	Philippines	3.5
111	Lebanon	29	116	Togo	12	123	Jamaica	1.7
112	Malawi	29	117	Cambodia	6.9	124	Panama	0.5
113	Venezuela	24.8	118	Nauru	4.7			

Source: *International Railway Statistics*

152. RAILWAY TRACKAGE

The following listing ranks countries by rail trackage in relation to the national territory. It should be borne in mind that length is only one element in determining adequacy of trackage; nevertheless, it is the most widely used and the most important. Other elements include the gauge; proportion of double tracks, electrified tracks, etc.; the type of beds; and regular maintenance and upgrading.

No less than 15 track widths are in use in the world, from 7 ft in Australia, 5.5 ft in Spain, and 5 ft in Russia to 3.3 ft in use in all of Africa except Egypt. The most famous railroads have been the transcontinental ones, such as the Trans-Siberian, the legendary Orient Express, the Trans-Australian from Sydney to Freemantle, the Trans-Andean from Buenos Aires to Valparaiso, the Beijing-Canton, the TanZam from Lusaka to Dar es Salaam, and the four major transcontinental routes in the United States. During the last 30 years total trackage has declined in most developed nations.

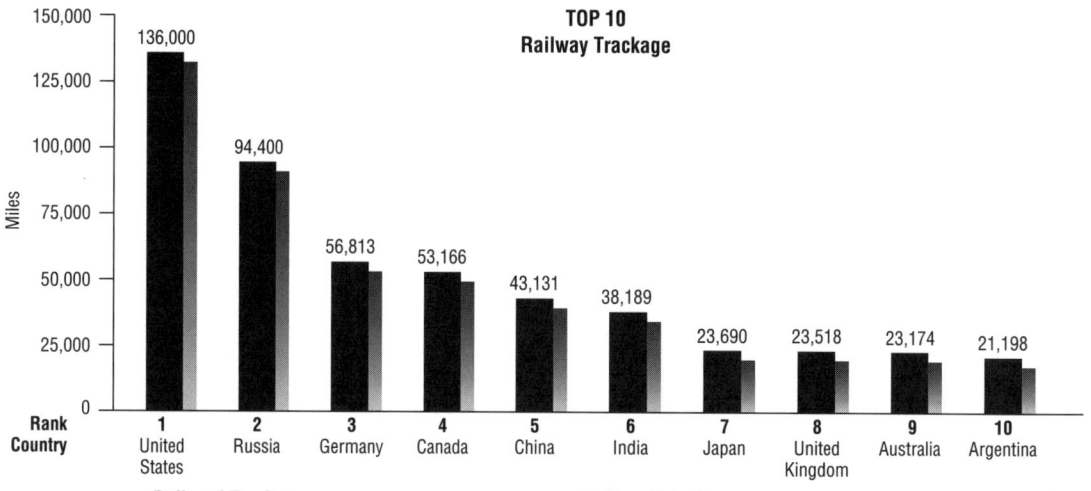

TOP 10 Railway Trackage

Rank	Country	Railroad Trackage Length (mi)	Rank	Country	Railroad Trackage Length (mi)	Rank	Country	Railroad Trackage Length (mi)
	UPPER MIDDLE		25	Pakistan	5,453	40	Sudan	2,960
11	France	21,173	26	Korea, North	5,302	41	Myanmar (Burma)	2,945
12	Brazil	18,877	27	Egypt	5,274	42	Norway	2,502
13	Poland	15,488	28	Uzbekistan	4,200	43	New Zealand	2,469
14	Ukraine	14,509	29	Indonesia	4,090	44	Yugoslavia	2,461
15	Kazakhstan	13,200	30	Chile	4,076	45	Taiwan	2,410
16	Mexico	12,784	31	Korea, South	4,049	46	Thailand	2,405
17	South Africa	12,399	32	Bulgaria	4,044	47	Bolivia	2,295
18	Italy	12,176	33	Finland	3,657	48	Slovakia	2,275
19	Hungary	8,200	34	Belarus	3,410	49	Nigeria	2,210
20	Spain	7,830	35	Zaire	3,162	50	Belgium	2,119
21	Romania	7,051	36	Switzerland	3,125	51	Portugal	2,066
22	Sweden	7,012	37	Cuba	3,033	52	Colombia	2,007
23	Turkey	6,470	38	Iran	3,014	53	Mozambique	1,946
24	Czech Republic	5,866	39	Algeria	2,965	54	Kenya	1,885

Rank	Country	Railroad Trackage Length (mi)
55	Uruguay	1,867
56	Lithuania	1,862
57	Denmark	1,763
58	Ireland	1,749
59	Angola	1,739
60	Zimbabwe	1,714
61	Netherlands	1,713
62	Azerbaijan	1,706
63	Croatia	1,676
64	Vietnam	1,619
LOWER MIDDLE		
65	Tanzania	1,600
66	Greece	1,552
67	Latvia	1,499
68	Iraq	1,493
69	Namibia	1,481
70	Mongolia	1,445
71	Syria	1,405
72	Tunisia	1,404
73	Malaysia	1,381
74	Austria	1,322
75	Peru	1,318
76	Turkmenistan	1,317
77	Morocco	1,099
78	Georgia	976
79	Sri Lanka	928
80	Saudi Arabia	864
81	Zambia	791
82	Uganda	770

Rank	Country	Railroad Trackage Length (mi)
83	Slovenia	746
84	Moldova	715
85	Guatemala	708
86	Cameroon	686
87	Philippines	658
88	Bosnia & Herzegovina	646
89	Madagascar	640
90	Estonia	636
91	Honduras	614
92	Ecuador	594
93	Ghana	592
94	Costa Rica	590
95	Macedonia	573
96	Senegal	562
97	Tajikistan	554
98	Botswana	551
99	Armenia	511
100	Malawi	495
101	Congo	494
102	Jordan	490
103	Kyrgyzstan	490
104	Ethiopia	486
105	Albania	447
106	Mauritania	416
107	Gabon	414
108	Guinea	411
109	Cote d'Ivoire	410
110	Mali	399
111	Cambodia	380
112	El Salvador	374

Rank	Country	Railroad Trackage Length (mi)
113	Fiji	370
114	Benin	359
115	Israel	356
116	Togo	326
117	Burkina	308
118	Liberia	304
119	Paraguay	274
120	Venezuela	226
121	Panama	220
122	Swaziland	199
123	Suriname	187
124	Nicaragua	186
125	Luxembourg	171
126	Lebanon	138
127	Jamaica	129
128	Guyana	116
129	Djibouti	66
BOTTOM 10		
130	Dominican Republic	65
131	Sierra Leone	52
132	Singapore	42
133	Nepal	33
134	Afghanistan	16
135	Brunei	12
136	Liechtenstein	12
137	Nauru	3
138	Lesotho	1.6
139	Monaco	1

Source: *International Railway Statistics*

153. RAIL PASSENGER TRAFFIC

Railway passenger traffic has been steadily declining over the years until it has ceased to be economically viable in many countries, requiring state intervention and subsidies on a large sale. Where state support has not been forthcoming, the systems have been rationalized—involving the closing of unprofitable lines and reduction in other facilities.

Rank	Country	Rail Passengers Miles (million)
TOP 10		
1	Japan	250,242
2	China	225,590
3	India	195,926
4	Russia	141,100
5	Ukraine	47,200
6	France	36,276
7	Germany	35,567
8	Italy	30,050
9	Egypt	29,821
10	United Kingdom	19,693
UPPER MIDDLE		
11	Poland	19,179
12	Korea, South	18,775
13	United States	14,000
14	Kazakhstan	12,100
15	Romania	12,057
16	Belarus	11,195
17	Pakistan	10,208
18	Spain	9,605
19	Netherlands	9,472
20	Thailand	9,145
21	Brazil	8,723
22	Indonesia	7,690
23	Switzerland	7,464

Rank	Country	Rail Passengers Miles (million)
24	Australia	7,152
25	Argentina	6,618
26	Tajikistan	6,094
27	Austria	5,988
28	Taiwan	5,906
29	Hungary	5,706
30	Moldova	5,515
31	Czech Republic	5,311
32	Belgium	4,159
33	Turkey	3,967
34	Sweden	3,712
35	Portugal	3,538
36	Slovakia	3,444
37	Bangladesh	3,323
38	Uzbekistan	3,300
39	Bulgaria	3,144
40	Azerbaijan	3,025
41	Myanmar (Burma)	2,908
42	Iran	2,848
43	Denmark	2,793
44	Mexico	2,408
45	Tanzania	2,324
46	Korea, North	2,100
47	Sri Lanka	1,894
48	Algeria	1,720
49	Cuba	1,680

Rank	Country	Rail Passengers Miles (million)
50	Yugoslavia	1,569
51	Finland	1,514
LOWER MIDDLE		
52	Latvia	1,484
53	Norway	1,437
54	Namibia	1,248
55	Morocco	1,186
56	Malaysia	1,148
57	Vietnam	1,140
58	Greece	1,072
59	Canada	852
60	Syria	775
61	Cote d'Ivoire	752
62	Swaziland	752
63	Tunisia	670
64	Ireland	665.5
65	Croatia	610
66	Chile	582
67	Iraq	572
68	South Africa	556
69	Lithuania	547
70	Albania	484.2
71	Estonia	449
72	Burkina	422
73	Mongolia	361.9

Rank	Country	Rail Passengers Miles (million)	Rank	Country	Rail Passengers Miles (million)	Rank	Country	Rail Passengers Miles (million)
74	Zaire	360	92	Botswana	160	110	Mozambique	16.2
75	Zimbabwe	355.1	93	Madagascar	152	111	Nicaragua	15.8
76	Slovenia	352	94	Israel	134	112	Jamaica	12.1
77	Congo	340	95	Senegal	108	113	Georgia	10.6
78	Sudan	330	96	Peru	102.7			
79	Mali	304.2	97	Saudi Arabia	94		**BOTTOM 10**	
80	Kenya	288	98	Uruguay	87.4	114	Colombia	9.6
81	New Zealand	285	99	Togo	82	115	Guatemala	6.3
82	Nigeria	281	100	Kyrgyzstan	81.5	116	Lebanon	5.3
83	Armenia	270	101	Philippines	75.2	117	Honduras	4.8
84	Cameroon	247	102	Ghana	73.1	118	Mauritania	4.4
85	Bolivia	216.8	103	Macedonia	64	119	El Salvador	3.8
86	Uganda	205	104	Benin	39.4	120	Jordan	3.7
87	Angola	203	105	Cambodia	33.6	121	Costa Rica	3.6
88	Djibouti	182	106	Ecuador	29.9	122	Paraguay	2.9
89	Luxembourg	176	107	Venezuela	29	123	Panama	0.3
90	Ethiopia	172	108	Malawi	28.3			
91	Zambia	166.7	109	Gabon	21			

Source: *International Railway Statistics*

154. COMMERCIAL VEHICLES

Commercial vehicles include vans, trucks, buses, tractor and semitrailer combinations. The data are based on registration figures as reported by national motor vehicle departments. This ranking has more relevance than the passenger car ranking as an indication of the relative economic strength of road transportation systems in the countries listed.

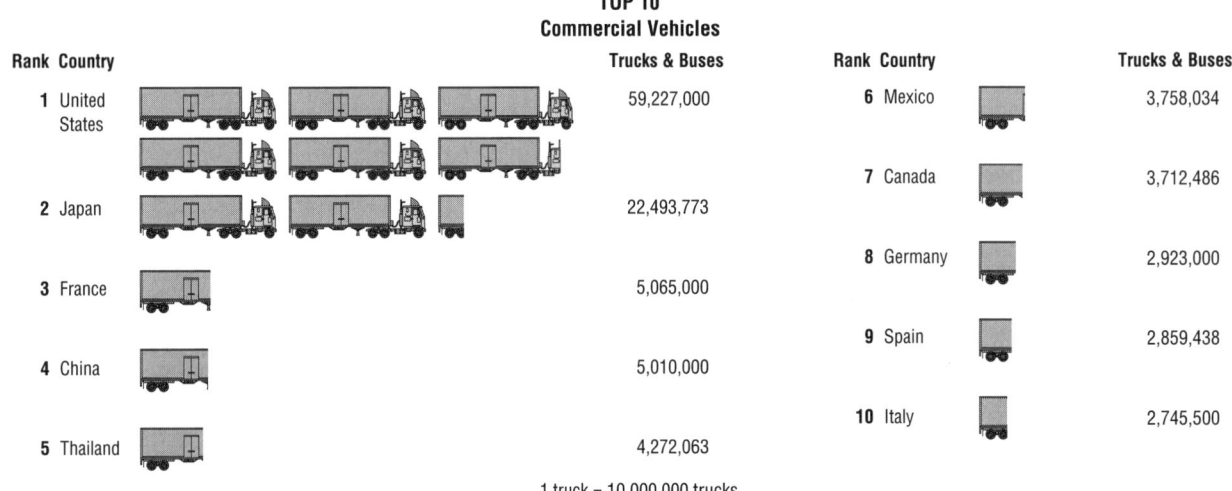

TOP 10
Commercial Vehicles

Rank	Country		Trucks & Buses
1	United States		59,227,000
2	Japan		22,493,773
3	France		5,065,000
4	China		5,010,000
5	Thailand		4,272,063
6	Mexico		3,758,034
7	Canada		3,712,486
8	Germany		2,923,000
9	Spain		2,859,438
10	Italy		2,745,500

1 truck = 10,000,000 trucks

Rank	Country	Trucks and Buses	Rank	Country	Trucks and Buses	Rank	Country	Trucks and Buses
	UPPER MIDDLE		68	Yugoslavia	132,100	124	Togo	16,100
11	United Kingdom	2,733,000	69	Bulgaria	130,000	125	Suriname	15,742
12	Saudi Arabia	2,286,541	70	Honduras	128,264	126	Iceland	15,644
13	Australia	2,225,659	71	Costa Rica	114,911	127	Burundi	14,914
14	Korea, South	2,002,755	72	Oman	108,600	128	Bahamas	14,000
15	India	1,980,000	73	Azerbaijan	104,006	129	Brunei	13,658
16	South Africa	1,899,721	74	Bangladesh	96,853	130	Guinea	13,500
17	Argentina	1,664,000	75	Guatemala	95,000	131	Burkina	13,300
18	Indonesia	1,554,582	76	Lithuania	93,920	132	Laos	12,987
19	Brazil	1,371,127	77	Jordan	91,600	133	Benin	12,200
20	Poland	1,321,000	78	Cote d'Ivoire	90,300	134	Somalia	12,000
21	Philippines	1,024,051	79	Cyprus	90,209	135	Sierra Leone	11,902
22	Turkey	942,000	80	Zaire	86,000	136	Belarus	10,279
23	Greece	848,903	81	Latvia	85,000	137	Mauritius	9,846
24	Taiwan	815,500	82	Estonia	82,800	138	Cambodia	9,247
25	Portugal	759,100	83	Panama	82,800	139	St. Lucia	9,200
26	Austria	745,987				140	Guyana	9,000
27	Netherlands	679,000		**LOWER MIDDLE**		141	Niger	8,768
28	Nigeria	606,000	84	Cameroon	79,000	142	Barbados	8,479
29	Iran	584,100	85	Dominican Republic	78,900	143	Mali	8,400
30	Algeria	480,000	86	United Arab Emirates	72,824	144	Swaziland	7,734
31	Venezuela	474,466	87	Zambia	68,000	145	Chad	7,200
32	Malaysia	472,414	88	Namibia	59,000	146	Central African Republic	6,300
33	Egypt	466,650	89	Qatar	59,000	147	Belize	6,294
34	Chile	437,520	90	Tanzania	57,200	148	Dominica	5,500
35	Colombia	430,611	91	Sudan	57,000	149	Mauritania	5,500
36	Russia	407,000	92	Bosnia & Herzegovina	50,578	150	Comoros	5,000
37	Norway	404,108	93	Lebanon	49,560	151	Andorra	4,362
38	Belgium	389,812	94	Senegal	48,000	152	Equatorial Guinea	4,100
39	Iraq	368,000	95	Ghana	44,200	153	Tonga	3,900
40	Czech Republic	354,690	96	Slovenia	43,824	154	San Marino	3,843
41	New Zealand	352,997	97	Nicaragua	43,600	155	Antigua and Barbuda	3,800
42	Romania	342,492	98	Croatia	43,513	156	Monaco	3,700
43	Libya	322,000	99	Angola	42,200	157	Paraguay	3,375
44	Morocco	316,941	100	Botswana	42,136	158	Nepal	3,363
45	Sweden	315,994	101	Myanmar (Burma)	36,000	159	Bermuda	3,300
46	Ecuador	292,830	102	Mozambique	35,000	160	Gambia	3,100
47	Hungary	288,914	103	Madagascar	33,300	161	Liberia	3,100
48	Switzerland	286,501	104	Albania	32,900	162	Djibouti	3,000
49	Peru	275,094	105	Fiji	30,899	163	St. Vincent	2,878
50	Yemen	269,819	106	Papua New Guinea	30,800	164	Guinea-Bissau	2,600
51	Finland	261,364	107	Jamaica	30,548	165	Solomon Islands	2,574
52	Denmark	260,833	108	Zimbabwe	30,182	166	Vanuatu	2,200
53	Pakistan	252,023	109	Mongolia	29,794	167	Cape Verde	2,099
54	Puerto Rico	227,100	110	Malta	27,978			
55	Israel	222,108	111	Bahrain	26,771		**BOTTOM 10**	
56	Cuba	208,400	112	Macedonia	25,574	168	Rwanda	2,048
57	Syria	186,366	113	Uganda	25,246	169	Seychelles	2,000
58	Bolivia	185,922	114	Luxembourg	25,050	170	Liechtenstein	1,817
59	Tunisia	180,500	115	Afghanistan	25,000	171	Bhutan	1,367
60	Sri Lanka	165,228	116	Trinidad and Tobago	23,828	172	Grenada	981
61	Slovakia	160,328	117	Haiti	21,000	173	Maldives	869
62	El Salvador	150,385	118	Ethiopia	20,939	174	Western Samoa	863
63	Uruguay	148,644	119	Moldova	20,409	175	St. Kitts and Nevis	700
64	Ireland	146,204	120	Congo	20,100	176	Sao Tome e Principe	300
65	Kuwait	144,300	121	Malawi	18,900	177	Kiribati	130
66	Singapore	134,042	122	Lesotho	17,785			
67	Kenya	133,968	123	Gabon	17,500			

Source: *World Data*

155. PASSENGER CARS

Passenger cars are defined as vehicles seating not more than nine persons (counting the driver) and include taxis, jeeps and station wagons. The data are based on registration figures as reported by national motor vehicle departments.

TOP 10
Passenger Cars

Rank	Country	Automobiles
1	United States	146,314,000
2	Japan	40,772,407
3	Germany	39,086,000
4	Italy	29,600,000
5	France	24,385,000
6	United Kingdom	20,479,000
7	Canada	13,477,896
8	Spain	13,440,694
9	Brazil	12,974,991
10	Russia	10,499,000

1 car = 10,000,000 automobiles

Rank	Country	Automobiles
	UPPER MIDDLE	
11	Australia	8,280,211
12	Mexico	8,014,143
13	Poland	6,771,000
14	Netherlands	5,755,000
15	Argentina	4,856,000
16	Korea, South	4,271,253
17	Belgium	4,109,601
18	Taiwan	3,798,800
19	Sweden	3,566,040
20	South Africa	3,488,570
21	Austria	3,367,626
22	India	3,330,000
23	Switzerland	3,137,619
24	Ukraine	2,920,000
25	Turkey	2,862,000
26	China	2,859,800
27	Greece	2,807,447
28	Saudi Arabia	2,762,132
29	Czech Republic	2,693,905
30	Portugal	2,210,000
31	Malaysia	2,147,974
32	Hungary	2,058,334
33	Finland	1,872,933
34	Romania	1,793,054
35	Indonesia	1,676,781
36	Denmark	1,674,939
37	Norway	1,653,678
38	New Zealand	1,600,499
39	Iran	1,557,000
40	Venezuela	1,507,309
41	Puerto Rico	1,420,000
42	Yugoslavia	1,406,000
43	Bulgaria	1,358,976
44	Egypt	1,119,727
45	Thailand	1,091,085
46	Philippines	1,078,895
47	Slovakia	994,933
48	Israel	988,176
49	Ireland	891,027
50	Morocco	864,652

Rank	Country	Automobiles
51	Colombia	854,160
52	Chile	826,794
53	Uzbekistan	790,800
54	Belarus	773,582
55	Nigeria	773,000
56	Kazakhstan	734,800
57	Pakistan	732,100
58	Algeria	725,000
59	Iraq	672,000
60	Croatia	646,210
61	Slovenia	632,563
62	Lithuania	597,735
63	Kuwait	530,000
64	Lebanon	473,372
65	Libya	448,000
66	Bosnia & Herzegovina	438,080
67	Georgia	427,400
68	Peru	418,648
69	Latvia	351,000
70	Singapore	340,647
71	Bolivia	340,365
72	Tunisia	320,000
73	Estonia	317,400
74	Uruguay	310,833
75	Zimbabwe	310,412
76	United Arab Emirates	297,128
77	Macedonia	279,861
78	Azerbaijan	251,192
79	Korea, North	248,000
80	Cuba	241,300
81	Armenia	230,100
82	Moldova	221,883
83	Costa Rica	220,142
84	Luxembourg	217,754
85	Yemen	214,561
86	Tajikistan	209,100
87	Cyprus	203,610
	LOWER MIDDLE	
88	Sri Lanka	197,300
89	Ecuador	191,746

Rank	Country	Automobiles
90	Oman	180,700
91	Kyrgyzstan	173,800
92	Turkmenistan	170,600
93	Jordan	162,000
94	Panama	161,500
95	Kenya	157,166
96	Cote d'Ivoire	155,300
97	Syria	125,807
98	Qatar	123,200
99	Trinidad and Tobago	122,201
100	Brunei	122,104
101	Angola	122,000
102	Malta	120,320
103	Dominican Republic	117,800
104	Paraguay	117,067
105	Iceland	116,195
106	Sudan	116,000
107	Bahrain	114,045
108	Senegal	102,000
109	Guatemala	98,700
110	Zambia	96,000
111	El Salvador	95,670
112	Zaire	94,000
113	Cameroon	90,000
114	Ghana	90,000
115	Bangladesh	75,409
116	Jamaica	73,015
117	Bahamas	69,000
118	Honduras	62,777
119	Namibia	54,000
120	Madagascar	47,000
121	Tanzania	44,000
122	Fiji	43,979
123	Barbados	43,077
124	Suriname	42,509
125	Ethiopia	37,799
126	Andorra	36,660
127	Myanmar (Burma)	36,000
128	Mozambique	35,000
129	Mauritius	33,613
130	Sierra Leone	32,415

Rank	Country	Automobiles	Rank	Country	Automobiles	Rank	Country	Automobiles
131	Haiti	32,000	151	Albania	16,000	171	Seychelles	5,000
132	Niger	31,427	152	Malawi	15,000	172	Nepal	4,949
133	Nicaragua	31,300	153	Burundi	14,483	173	Grenada	4,784
134	Afghanistan	31,000	154	Antigua and Barbuda	14,300	174	Dominica	4,700
135	Cambodia	28,919	155	Central African Republic	14,000	175	St. Vincent	4,591
136	Congo	26,000	156	Djibouti	13,500	176	St. Kitts and Nevis	4,000
137	Swaziland	25,946	157	Papua New Guinea	11,500			
138	Togo	25,000	158	Burkina	11,000		**BOTTOM 10**	
139	Gabon	24,000	159	Somalia	10,700	177	Vanuatu	4,000
140	Guinea	24,000	160	St. Lucia	10,000	178	Guinea-Bissau	3,700
141	Guyana	24,000	161	Belize	9,989	179	Tonga	3,400
142	San Marino	22,945	162	Chad	9,500	180	Sao Tome e Principe	2,600
143	Benin	22,000	163	Liberia	8,000	181	Bhutan	2,590
144	Mali	21,000	164	Mauritania	8,000	182	Solomon Islands	2,052
145	Botswana	20,785	165	Rwanda	7,868	183	Comoros	2,000
146	Laos	20,233	166	Gambia	7,300	184	Western Samoa	962
147	Bermuda	20,148	167	Cape Verde	6,479	185	Maldives	823
148	Uganda	17,804	168	Equatorial Guinea	6,200	186	Kiribati	307
149	Liechtenstein	17,767	169	Lesotho	5,944			
150	Monaco	17,000	170	Mongolia	5,660			

Source: *World Motor Vehicle Data*

156. LENGTH OF ROADS

In terms of length and intensity of use, roads dwarf both railroads and inland waterways. Ranging from the great national highways of the world, which are engineering marvels, to small dusty paths, they form arterial networks for almost every conceivable kind of vehicular traffic. To be meaningful, the length of roads has to be read in relation to the size of the national territory.

Rank	Country	Roads (length—mi)	Rank	Country	Roads (length—mi)	Rank	Country	Roads (length—mi)
	TOP 10		28	Iran	94,130	58	Latvia	37,421
1	United States	3,904,721	29	Zaire	91,200	59	Morocco	36,955
2	India	1,342,000	30	Belgium	85,672	60	Thailand	35,358
3	Brazil	1,031,693	31	Sweden	84,419	61	Czech Republic	34,742
4	Japan	702,702	32	Netherlands	73,908	62	Lithuania	34,550
5	China	673,239	33	Greece	72,170	63	Uruguay	32,311
6	Russia	585,000	34	Nigeria	69,680	64	Yemen	32,130
7	Canada	527,794	35	Austria	68,400	65	Belarus	31,390
8	France	504,055	36	Colombia	66,721	66	Mongolia	30,600
9	Australia	503,474	37	Vietnam	65,200	67	Cameroon	30,074
10	Germany	395,367	38	Algeria	59,388	68	Yugoslavia	29,771
			39	New Zealand	58,605	69	Egypt	29,445
	UPPER MIDDLE		40	Venezuela	58,081	70	Cuba	28,928
11	Turkey	240,286	41	Malaysia	57,505	71	Iraq	28,305
12	United Kingdom	240,241	42	Ireland	57,369	72	Ecuador	28,200
13	Poland	225,629	43	Zimbabwe	56,593	73	Bolivia	26,370
14	Spain	206,271	44	Norway	56,031	74	Namibia	26,024
15	Indonesia	196,016	45	Uzbekistan	55,431	75	Chad	24,855
16	Italy	188,597	46	Tanzania	55,000	76	Tanzania	23,214
17	Ukraine	170,069	47	Chile	49,270	77	Bulgaria	22,942
18	Mexico	157,036	48	Finland	47,763	78	Ghana	22,800
19	Argentina	133,954	49	Angola	45,128	79	Syria	22,528
20	Pakistan	121,119	50	Switzerland	44,201	80	Costa Rica	22,084
21	Bangladesh	120,100	51	Denmark	44,186	81	Madagascar	21,586
22	South Africa	117,010	52	Portugal	43,605	82	Korea, North	18,600
23	Kazakhstan	102,500	53	Peru	43,460	83	Paraguay	18,217
24	Philippines	98,860	54	Cote d'Ivoire	42,250	84	Tunisia	18,133
25	Hungary	98,618	55	Kenya	39,400			
26	Romania	95,099	56	Azerbaijan	38,972		**LOWER MIDDLE**	
27	Saudi Arabia	94,157	57	Korea, South	38,087	85	Uganda	17,808

Rank	Country	Roads (length—mi)	Rank	Country	Roads (length—mi)	Rank	Country	Roads (length—mi)
86	Ethiopia	17,381	122	El Salvador	7,791	158	Belize	1,684
87	Mozambique	16,955	123	Malawi	7,590	159	Equatorial Guinea	1,667
88	Croatia	16,732	124	Gambia	7,483	160	Bhutan	1,502
89	Oman	16,372	125	Guatemala	7,363	161	Brunei	1,502
90	Sri Lanka	16,158	126	Sierra Leone	7,254	162	Bahamas	1,491
91	Myanmar (Burma)	15,118	127	Dominican Republic	7,100	163	Western Samoa	1,296
92	Central African Republic	14,750	128	Iceland	7,008	164	Mauritius	1,138
93	Puerto Rico	14,089	129	Cyprus	6,746	165	Malta	988
94	Somalia	13,500	130	Moldova	6,400	166	Barbados	977
95	Bosnia & Herzegovina	13,153	131	Panama	6,304	167	Solomon Islands	840
96	Sudan	12,400	132	Nepal	5,884	168	Antigua and Barbuda	721
97	Papua New Guinea	12,263	133	Suriname	5,687	169	Vanuatu	702
98	Niger	12,244	134	Macedonia	5,223	170	Cape Verde	680
99	Libya	12,000	135	Trinidad and Tobago	4,970	171	Qatar	671
100	Botswana	11,933	136	Armenia	4,800	172	Grenada	650
101	Afghanistan	11,930	137	Togo	4,688	173	Eritrea	621
102	Kyrgyzstan	11,900	138	Mauritania	4,683	174	St. Vincent	586
103	Taiwan	11,830	139	Gabon	4,671	175	St. Lucia	500
104	Mali	11,185	140	Albania	4,629	176	Comoros	466
105	Slovakia	11,110	141	Lebanon	4,579	177	Dominica	466
106	Jamaica	10,212	142	Guyana	4,474	178	Kiribati	398
107	Guinea	9,974	143	Jordan	3,958	179	Tonga	240
108	Senegal	9,625	144	Liberia	3,787			
109	Nicaragua	9,499	145	Benin	3,770		**BOTTOM 10**	
110	Slovenia	9,198	146	Lesotho	3,308	180	Liechtenstein	201
111	Estonia	9,178	147	Luxembourg	3,190	181	Seychelles	201
112	Burundi	8,993	148	Fiji	2,996	182	Andorra	187
113	Honduras	8,825	149	United Arab Emirates	2,830	183	St. Kitts and Nevis	186
114	Laos	8,780	150	Kuwait	2,655	184	Sao Tome e Principe	149
115	Israel	8,620	151	Guinea-Bissau	2,579	185	San Marino	147
116	Tajikistan	8,324	152	Haiti	2,485	186	Bermuda	120
117	Turkmenistan	8,300	153	Georgia	2,100	187	Monaco	31
118	Cambodia	8,296	154	Singapore	1,857	188	Nauru	17
119	Rwanda	8,283	155	Swaziland	1,839	189	Tuvalu	5
120	Burkina	8,161	156	Djibouti	1,789			
121	Congo	7,919	157	Bahrain	1,719			

Source: *World Road Statistics*

157. PIPELINES

There are three types of pipelines: those carrying crude petroleum, those carrying refined products and those carrying natural gas. The construction and maintenance of pipelines has become strategic and key industries, although pipelines remain the least studied form of transportation.

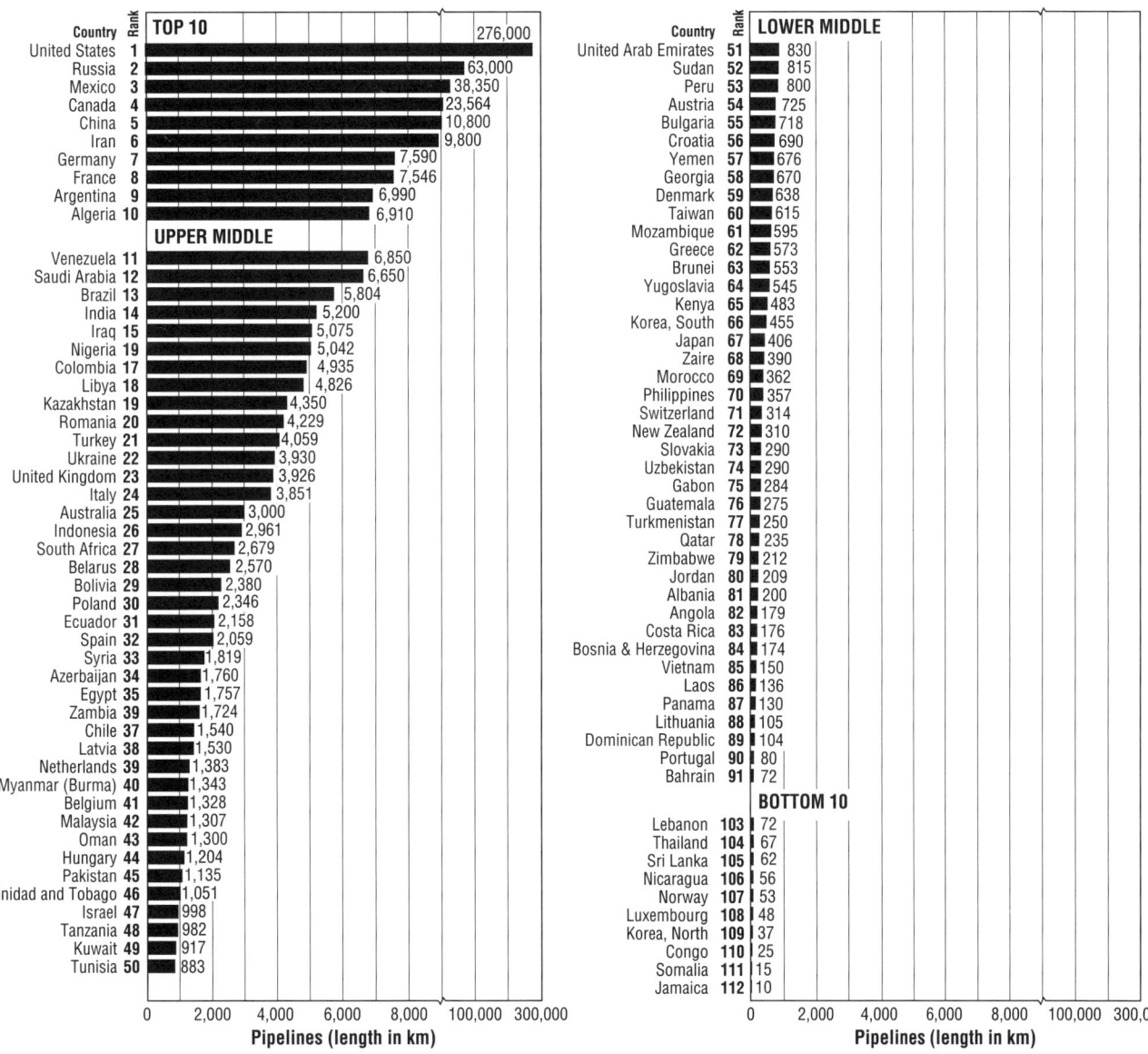

Country	Rank	TOP 10
United States	1	276,000
Russia	2	63,000
Mexico	3	38,350
Canada	4	23,564
China	5	10,800
Iran	6	9,800
Germany	7	7,590
France	8	7,546
Argentina	9	6,990
Algeria	10	6,910
		UPPER MIDDLE
Venezuela	11	6,850
Saudi Arabia	12	6,650
Brazil	13	5,804
India	14	5,200
Iraq	15	5,075
Nigeria	19	5,042
Colombia	17	4,935
Libya	18	4,826
Kazakhstan	19	4,350
Romania	20	4,229
Turkey	21	4,059
Ukraine	22	3,930
United Kingdom	23	3,926
Italy	24	3,851
Australia	25	3,000
Indonesia	26	2,961
South Africa	27	2,679
Belarus	28	2,570
Bolivia	29	2,380
Poland	30	2,346
Ecuador	31	2,158
Spain	32	2,059
Syria	33	1,819
Azerbaijan	34	1,760
Egypt	35	1,757
Zambia	39	1,724
Chile	37	1,540
Latvia	38	1,530
Netherlands	39	1,383
Myanmar (Burma)	40	1,343
Belgium	41	1,328
Malaysia	42	1,307
Oman	43	1,300
Hungary	44	1,204
Pakistan	45	1,135
inidad and Tobago	46	1,051
Israel	47	998
Tanzania	48	982
Kuwait	49	917
Tunisia	50	883

Country	Rank	LOWER MIDDLE
United Arab Emirates	51	830
Sudan	52	815
Peru	53	800
Austria	54	725
Bulgaria	55	718
Croatia	56	690
Yemen	57	676
Georgia	58	670
Denmark	59	638
Taiwan	60	615
Mozambique	61	595
Greece	62	573
Brunei	63	553
Yugoslavia	64	545
Kenya	65	483
Korea, South	66	455
Japan	67	406
Zaire	68	390
Morocco	69	362
Philippines	70	357
Switzerland	71	314
New Zealand	72	310
Slovakia	73	290
Uzbekistan	74	290
Gabon	75	284
Guatemala	76	275
Turkmenistan	77	250
Qatar	78	235
Zimbabwe	79	212
Jordan	80	209
Albania	81	200
Angola	82	179
Costa Rica	83	176
Bosnia & Herzegovina	84	174
Vietnam	85	150
Laos	86	136
Panama	87	130
Lithuania	88	105
Dominican Republic	89	104
Portugal	90	80
Bahrain	91	72
		BOTTOM 10
Lebanon	103	72
Thailand	104	67
Sri Lanka	105	62
Nicaragua	106	56
Norway	107	53
Luxembourg	108	48
Korea, North	109	37
Congo	110	25
Somalia	111	15
Jamaica	112	10

Pipelines (length in km)

Source: *World Data*

158. TOURIST RECEIPTS

Data on tourist receipts are derived from two sources: the International Monetary Fund (IMF) and the World Tourism Organization (WTO) in Madrid. The IMF includes tourist receipts in its balance of payments reports on the basis of information supplied by member countries. It covers receipts for goods and services provided to foreigners and also transportation expenses. In other countries the WTO estimates travel receipts by applying an average per diem expenditure to the number of days spent by foreigners. Per diem expenditures are based on inquiries made of travel agents, banks, hotels and shops. Many countries keep systematic records of the number of nights spent by foreign tourists in their hotels.

Rank	Country	Tourist Receipts from Foreign Nationals (million $)	Rank	Country	Tourist Receipts from Foreign Nationals (million $)	Rank	Country	Tourist Receipts from Foreign Nationals (million $)
TOP 10			52	Syria	700	104	Grenada	45
1	United States	56,501	53	Malta	653	105	Papua New Guinea	45
2	France	23,410	54	Costa Rica	577	106	Yemen	45
3	Italy	20,521	55	Jordan	563	107	Zambia	44
4	Spain	19,425	56	Bermuda	505	108	Madagascar	41
5	Austria	13,566	57	Barbados	502	109	Iran	39
6	United Kingdom	13,451	58	Uruguay	447	110	Benin	38
7	Germany	10,509	59	Venezuela	432	111	Guyana	36
8	Switzerland	7,001	60	Kenya	413	112	Brunei	32
9	Mexico	6,167	61	Slovakia	390	113	Honduras	32
10	Canada	5,897	62	Antigua and Barbuda	372	114	Nigeria	31
			63	Bulgaria	307	115	Nicaragua	30
UPPER MIDDLE			64	Mauritius	301	116	Swaziland	30
11	Singapore	5,793	65	Luxembourg	290	117	Vanuatu	30
12	Thailand	5,014	66	Peru	268	118	Dominica	29
13	Netherlands	4,690	67	Guatemala	265	119	Gambia	26
14	China	4,683				120	Chad	23
15	Australia	4,655	**LOWER MIDDLE**			121	Yugoslavia	23
16	Poland	4,500	68	Fiji	236	122	Western Samoa	21
17	Portugal	4,176	69	Ecuador	230	123	Angola	20
18	Belgium	4,017	70	Panama	222	124	Ethiopia	20
19	Indonesia	3,988	71	St. Lucia	221	125	Myanmar (Burma)	19
20	Turkey	3,959	72	Sri Lanka	208	126	Sierra Leone	18
21	Argentina	3,614	73	Ghana	206	127	Togo	18
22	Japan	3,557	74	Paraguay	204	128	Lesotho	17
23	Korea, South	3,510	75	Romania	197	129	Niger	16
24	Greece	3,293	76	Bahrain	177	130	Bangladesh	15
25	Denmark	3,052	77	Senegal	173	131	Mauritania	15
26	Taiwan	2,934	78	Nepal	157	132	Djibouti	13
27	Sweden	2,650	79	Tanzania	147	133	Malawi	13
28	Philippines	2,122	80	Maldives	146	134	Macedonia	11
29	Israel	2,110	81	Iceland	132	135	Mali	11
30	Saudi Arabia	1,884	82	El Salvador	121	136	Suriname	11
31	Malaysia	1,876	83	Seychelles	116	137	Tonga	10
32	Norway	1,849	84	Bolivia	115	138	Central African Republic	9
33	Ireland	1,639	85	Pakistan	111	139	Albania	8
34	Puerto Rico	1,629	86	Zimbabwe	103	140	Burkina	8
35	India	1,487	87	Namibia	91	141	Comoros	8
36	Brazil	1,449	88	Oman	85	142	Zaire	7
37	Cyprus	1,396	89	Vietnam	85	143	Guinea	6
38	Egypt	1,332	90	Kuwait	83	144	Solomon Islands	6
39	Bahamas	1,304	91	Trinidad and Tobago	80			
40	Morocco	1,243	92	Botswana	79	**BOTTOM 10**		
41	Finland	1,239	93	Belize	73	145	Gabon	5
42	Dominican Republic	1,234	94	St. Kitts and Nevis	69	146	Libya	5
43	South Africa	1,190	95	Cote d'Ivoire	64	147	Bhutan	.3
44	Hungary	1,181	96	Algeria	55	148	Burundi	3
45	New Zealand	1,165	97	Iraq	55	149	Sudan	3
46	Tunisia	1,114	98	St. Vincent	55	150	Congo	2
47	Jamaica	942	99	Estonia	51	151	Rwanda	2
48	Chile	824	100	Uganda	50	152	Afghanistan	1
49	Slovenia	734	101	Cambodia	48	153	Kiribati	1
50	Cuba	720	102	Cameroon	47	154	Sao Tome e Principe	1
51	Colombia	705	103	Haiti	46	155	Tuvalu	

Source: *Yearbook of Tourism Statistics*

159. TOURIST EXPENDITURES BY NATIONALS ABROAD

Tourism encourages spending, international tourism even more so. In many countries tourists sustain the retail shops and service establishments and provide windfalls to governments and local authorities. In countries with nonconvertible currencies, such spending is hedged by tight regulations. But big spenders like Germans, Japanese and Americans tend to be a boon to developing countries. In fact, tourist spending is as important as aid as a mechanism for the transfer of wealth across national borders.

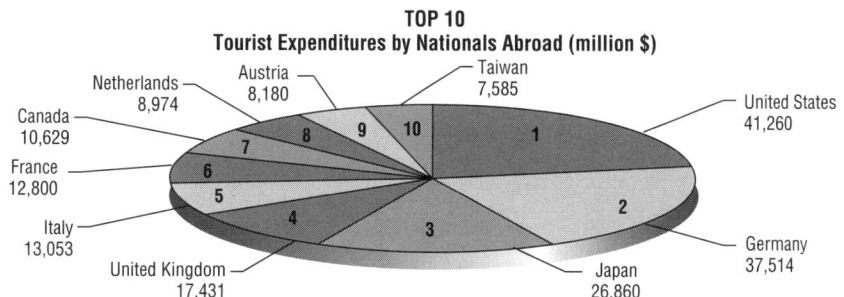

TOP 10
Tourist Expenditures by Nationals Abroad (million $)

- Taiwan 7,585
- Austria 8,180
- Netherlands 8,974
- Canada 10,629
- France 12,800
- Italy 13,053
- United Kingdom 17,431
- Japan 26,860
- Germany 37,514
- United States 41,260

Rank	Country	Tourist Expenditures by Nationals Abroad (million $)	Rank	Country	Tourist Expenditures by Nationals Abroad (million $)	Rank	Country	Tourist Expenditures by Nationals Abroad (million $
UPPER MIDDLE			56	Malta	211	100	Honduras	39
11	Belgium	6,363	57	Tunisia	203	101	Madagascar	37
12	Switzerland	5,803	58	Cote d'Ivoire	199	102	Burkina	35
13	Mexico	5,562	59	Bahamas	195	103	Nicaragua	34
14	Spain	4,706	60	Romania	195	104	Haiti	33
15	Sweden	4,464	61	Ecuador	190	105	Sudan	33
16	Korea, South	4,105	62	Poland	181	106	Mauritania	31
17	Australia	4,100	63	Algeria	163	107	Togo	30
18	Norway	3,565	64	Libya	154	108	Maldives	29
19	Denmark	3,214				109	Niger	29
20	Singapore	3,022	**LOWER MIDDLE**			110	Estonia	26
21	Argentina	2,445	65	Bangladesh	153	111	Guinea	26
22	Israel	2,313	66	Bolivia	151	112	Antigua and Barbuda	23
23	Thailand	2,092	67	Bahrain	141	113	Belize	21
24	Malaysia	1,960	68	Bermuda	139	114	St. Lucia	21
25	Kuwait	1,888	69	Paraguay	138	115	Burundi	20
26	Portugal	1,846	70	Cyprus	133	116	Ghana	17
27	Brazil	1,842	71	Gabon	132	117	Rwanda	17
28	Finland	1,617	72	Philippines	130	118	Swaziland	17
29	South Africa	1,598	73	Uruguay	129	119	Seychelles	16
30	Indonesia	1,539	74	Mauritius	128	120	Zaire	16
31	Venezuela	1,428	75	Sri Lanka	121	121	Benin	13
32	Ireland	1,256	76	Panama	120	122	Gambia	13
33	Iran	1,109	77	Dominican Republic	118	123	Malawi	13
34	Egypt	1,048	78	Guatemala	116	124	Chad	12
35	Greece	1,003	79	Trinidad and Tobago	115	125	Solomon Islands	11
36	New Zealand	1,003	80	Senegal	106	126	Suriname	11
37	Turkey	934	81	Tanzania	102	127	Ethiopia	10
38	China	812	82	Zimbabwe	97	128	Lesotho	7
39	Puerto Rico	774	83	Nepal	93	129	Comoros	6
40	Colombia	641	84	Congo	81	130	Albania	5
41	Pakistan	633	85	Namibia	81	131	Dominica	5
42	Chile	568	86	Yemen	81	132	St. Kitts and Nevis	5
43	India	393	87	Angola	75	133	Cambodia	4
44	Jordan	345	88	Jamaica	64			
45	Peru	304	89	El Salvador	61	**BOTTOM 10**		
46	Slovenia	304	90	Mali	61	134	Grenada	4
47	Syria	300	91	Zambia	56	135	St. Vincent	4
48	Costa Rica	267	92	Kenya	48	136	Sierra Leone	4
49	Iceland	264	93	Oman	47	137	Tonga	3
50	Slovakia	262	94	Papua New Guinea	42	138	Kiribati	2
51	Bulgaria	257	95	Barbados	41	139	Sao Tome e Principe	2
52	Morocco	245	96	Central African Republic	41	140	Western Samoa	2
53	Hungary	241	97	Botswana	40	141	Afghanistan	1
54	Nigeria	234	98	Uganda	40	142	Myanmar (Burma)	1
55	Cameroon	225	99	Fiji	39	143	Vanuatu	1

Source: *Yearbook of Tourism Statistics*

160. PERSONS PER MOTOR VEHICLE

A car in every garage has been the goal of the 20th century society in developed countries, just as a chicken in every pot was the goal in late 19th century. But outside North America, Western Europe, and parts of Asia and Latin America, the automobile is still a luxury affordable only by the very rich. But in countries ranking low in passenger car ownership, buses are correspondingly more numerous.

Rank	Country	Persons per Motor Vehicle	Rank	Country	Persons per Motor Vehicle	Rank	Country	Persons per Motor Vehicle
TOP 10			60	Yugoslavia	6.8	120	Cape Verde	43
1	San Marino	0.9	61	Oman	6.9	121	Syria	43
2	United States	1.3	62	Dominica	7.0	122	Sri Lanka	49
3	Andorra	1.5	63	Korea, South	7.0	123	Guatemala	52
4	Liechtenstein	1.5	64	Malaysia	7.1	124	Congo	53
5	Monaco	1.5	65	Suriname	7.1	125	Senegal	53
6	Australia	1.7	66	St. Lucia	7.3	126	Cote d'Ivoire	54
7	Canada	1.7	67	Mexico	7.4	127	Zambia	54
8	Luxembourg	1.7	68	South Africa	7.4	128	Nicaragua	57
9	Italy	1.8	69	Trinidad and Tobago	8.6	129	Mongolia	58
10	New Zealand	1.8	70	Bosnia & Herzegovina	8.9	130	Indonesia	59
			71	Costa Rica	9.6	131	Angola	65
UPPER MIDDLE			72	Fiji	10	132	Nigeria	66
11	Austria	1.9	73	Panama	10	133	Comoros	68
12	Germany	1.9	74	St. Kitts and Nevis	10	134	Cameroon	74
13	Brunei	2.0	75	Seychelles	10	135	Solomon Islands	75
14	France	2.0	76	Brazil	11	136	Lesotho	82
15	Iceland	2.0	77	Chile	11	137	Albania	88
16	Japan	2.0	78	Romania	11	138	Kenya	88
17	Switzerland	2.0	79	Venezuela	11	139	Western Samoa	89
18	Norway	2.1				140	Togo	95
19	Qatar	2.1	**LOWER MIDDLE**			141	Papua New Guinea	97
20	Belgium	2.2	80	Belize	12	142	Sierra Leone	97
21	Kuwait	2.2	81	Belarus	13	143	Gambia	99
22	Puerto Rico	2.2	82	Bolivia	13	144	Ghana	117
23	Sweden	2.2	83	Namibia	14	145	Haiti	120
24	Finland	2.4	84	Russia	14	146	Laos	135
25	Malta	2.4	85	Tonga	14	147	Pakistan	135
26	Netherlands	2.4	86	Jordan	15	148	Maldives	141
27	Spain	2.4	87	St. Vincent	15	149	Sudan	143
28	United Kingdom	2.5	88	Grenada	16	150	Kiribati	147
29	Bermuda	2.6	89	Thailand	16	151	Central African Republic	148
30	Cyprus	2.7	90	Turkey	16	152	Benin	149
31	Denmark	2.7	91	Tunisia	17	153	China	150
32	Greece	2.8	92	Iraq	18	154	Mauritania	160
33	Slovenia	2.9	93	Moldova	18	155	Guinea-Bissau	163
34	Bahamas	3.2	94	Azerbaijan	21	156	Guinea	168
35	Portugal	3.3	95	Algeria	22	157	India	170
36	Saudi Arabia	3.3	96	Botswana	22	158	Madagascar	172
37	Czech Republic	3.4	97	El Salvador	22	159	Burundi	188
38	Ireland	3.4	98	Morocco	22	160	Niger	192
39	Antigua and Barbuda	3.5	99	Cuba	23	161	Liberia	214
40	Bahrain	3.8	100	Ecuador	23	162	Mozambique	224
41	Estonia	3.8	101	Guyana	23	163	Zaire	229
42	Israel	4.3	102	Jamaica	24	164	Cambodia	240
43	Hungary	4.4	103	Mauritius	25	165	Tanzania	262
44	Slovakia	4.6	104	Swaziland	25	166	Somalia	287
45	Taiwan	4.6	105	Yemen	25	167	Mali	294
46	Poland	4.8	106	Colombia	26	168	Afghanistan	295
47	Lebanon	5.0	107	Honduras	26			
48	Barbados	5.1	108	Vanuatu	26	**BOTTOM 10**		
49	Argentina	5.2	109	Gabon	27	169	Malawi	315
50	Lithuania	5.4	110	Iran	27	170	Bhutan	348
51	United Arab Emirates	5.6	111	Zimbabwe	30	171	Chad	361
52	Bulgaria	5.8	112	Philippines	32	172	Burkina	402
53	Latvia	5.9	113	Djibouti	33	173	Uganda	402
54	Singapore	6.2	114	Peru	33	174	Myanmar (Burma)	619
55	Libya	6.3	115	Egypt	36	175	Bangladesh	655
56	Nauru	6.3	116	Paraguay	36	176	Rwanda	697
57	Croatia	6.5	117	Equatorial Guinea	37	177	Ethiopia	856
58	Macedonia	6.7	118	Dominican Republic	38	178	Nepal	2259
59	Uruguay	6.8	119	Sao Tome e Principe	39			

Source: *World Data*

161. CARGO BY ROAD

Freight transport by road offers many benefits over rail, especially in countries whre gasoline prices are competitive. Freight can be delivered to precise destinations without the additional costs of secondary transport. Road freight is also the transport of choice in the case of non-bulk materials and in areas where rail transport is not available.

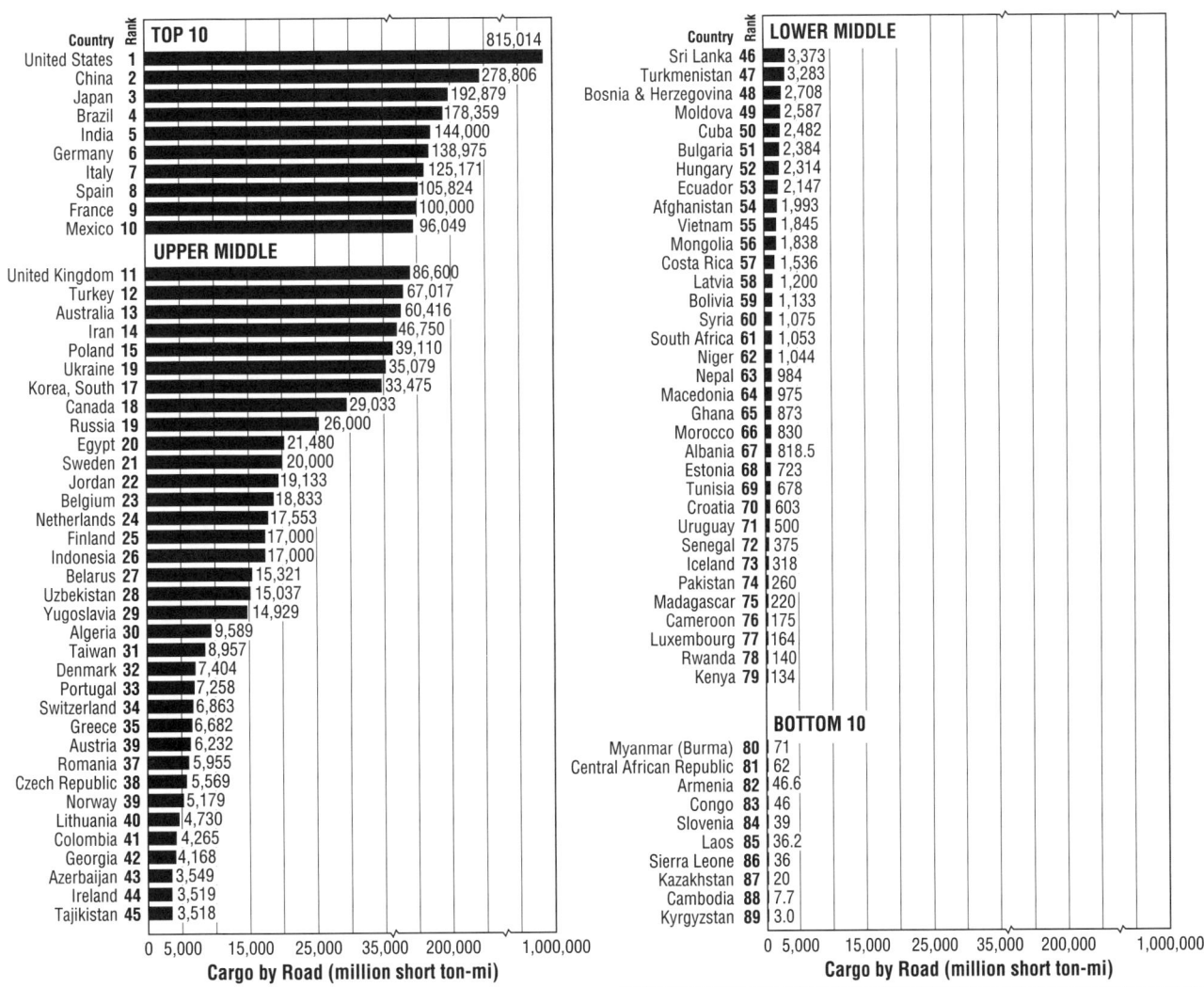

TOP 10

Rank	Country	Cargo by Road (million short ton-mi)
1	United States	815,014
2	China	278,806
3	Japan	192,879
4	Brazil	178,359
5	India	144,000
6	Germany	138,975
7	Italy	125,171
8	Spain	105,824
9	France	100,000
10	Mexico	96,049

UPPER MIDDLE

Rank	Country	Cargo by Road (million short ton-mi)
11	United Kingdom	86,600
12	Turkey	67,017
13	Australia	60,416
14	Iran	46,750
15	Poland	39,110
19	Ukraine	35,079
17	Korea, South	33,475
18	Canada	29,033
19	Russia	26,000
20	Egypt	21,480
21	Sweden	20,000
22	Jordan	19,133
23	Belgium	18,833
24	Netherlands	17,553
25	Finland	17,000
26	Indonesia	17,000
27	Belarus	15,321
28	Uzbekistan	15,037
29	Yugoslavia	14,929
30	Algeria	9,589
31	Taiwan	8,957
32	Denmark	7,404
33	Portugal	7,258
34	Switzerland	6,863
35	Greece	6,682
39	Austria	6,232
37	Romania	5,955
38	Czech Republic	5,569
39	Norway	5,179
40	Lithuania	4,730
41	Colombia	4,265
42	Georgia	4,168
43	Azerbaijan	3,549
44	Ireland	3,519
45	Tajikistan	3,518

LOWER MIDDLE

Rank	Country	Cargo by Road (million short ton-mi)
46	Sri Lanka	3,373
47	Turkmenistan	3,283
48	Bosnia & Herzegovina	2,708
49	Moldova	2,587
50	Cuba	2,482
51	Bulgaria	2,384
52	Hungary	2,314
53	Ecuador	2,147
54	Afghanistan	1,993
55	Vietnam	1,845
56	Mongolia	1,838
57	Costa Rica	1,536
58	Latvia	1,200
59	Bolivia	1,133
60	Syria	1,075
61	South Africa	1,053
62	Niger	1,044
63	Nepal	984
64	Macedonia	975
65	Ghana	873
66	Morocco	830
67	Albania	818.5
68	Estonia	723
69	Tunisia	678
70	Croatia	603
71	Uruguay	500
72	Senegal	375
73	Iceland	318
74	Pakistan	260
75	Madagascar	220
76	Cameroon	175
77	Luxembourg	164
78	Rwanda	140
79	Kenya	134

BOTTOM 10

Rank	Country	Cargo by Road (million short ton-mi)
80	Myanmar (Burma)	71
81	Central African Republic	62
82	Armenia	46.6
83	Congo	46
84	Slovenia	39
85	Laos	36.2
86	Sierra Leone	36
87	Kazakhstan	20
88	Cambodia	7.7
89	Kyrgyzstan	3.0

Source: *World Data*

162. AIR FREIGHT

Air freight is gaining in popularity as a viable alternative to rail and road freight, despite the fact that it is still the most expensive mode and is possible only in cases where such a delivery is warranted by the value of the commodities. Perishable commodities like fruits and flowers may be best transported by air. Air freight companies have worked with aircraft manufacturers to design new planes that can transport more goods over short hauls. The gap between land and air freight transport is therefore narrowing.

Rank	Country	Air Transport—Cargo (Short-ton km million)	Rank	Country	Air Transport—Cargo (Short-ton km million)	Rank	Country	Air Transport—Cargo (Short-ton km million)
TOP 10			54	Jordan	81.9	108	Tunisia	11.8
1	United States	13,320	55	Sri Lanka	79.6	109	Romania	11.4
2	Germany	9,725	56	Yemen	78	110	Zambia	11.4
3	France	6,230	57	Ethiopia	75.5	111	Burkina	11.0
4	Japan	3,697	58	Bahrain	73.4	112	Central African Republic	11.0
5	Korea, South	3,306	59	Ireland	69.3	113	Chad	11.0
6	Slovenia	2,556	60	Egypt	68.8	114	Cote d'Ivoire	11.0
7	Singapore	2,254	61	Ukraine	68	115	Niger	11.0
8	United Kingdom	2,000	62	Mauritius	67.4	116	Malawi	10.1
9	Netherlands	1,895	63	Brunei	64.7	117	Trinidad and Tobago	10.1
10	Taiwan	1,892	64	Papua New Guinea	56.4	118	Nigeria	7.9
			65	Iran	54.0	119	Syria	7.9
UPPER MIDDLE			66	Kazakhstan	48.0	120	Nepal	7.5
11	Australia	1,766	67	Oman	47.8	121	Mozambique	7.1
12	Brazil	1,452	68	Seychelles	47.7	122	Cameroon	6.8
13	China	1,336	69	Czech Republic	46.7	123	Myanmar (Burma)	5.6
14	Mexico	1,249	70	Madagascar	45.2	124	Afghanistan	5.5
15	New Zealand	1,100	71	Ecuador	44	125	Malta	5.0
16	Russia	1,027	72	Namibia	40	126	El Salvador	4.8
17	Switzerland	964.4	73	Kenya	39.2	127	Mongolia	4.0
18	Italy	914.3	74	Fiji	38.2	128	Panama	3.6
19	Thailand	872.2				129	Laos	3.0
20	South Africa	863	**LOWER MIDDLE**			130	Somalia	3.0
21	Canada	856	75	Zaire	38	131	Honduras	2.0
22	Israel	654.4	76	Poland	37.7	132	Dominican Republic	1.9
23	Colombia	619	77	Iraq	37.4	133	Guyana	1.9
24	Uzbekistan	608	78	Morocco	36.5	134	Croatia	1.8
25	Norway	591.7	79	Qatar	35.1	135	Nicaragua	1.8
26	Malaysia	524.6	80	Bulgaria	32.2	136	Uruguay	1.8
27	Saudi Arabia	492	81	Costa Rica	29.7	137	Guinea	1.7
28	Indonesia	458.4	82	Angola	28.8	138	Sierra Leone	1.4
29	Chile	422	83	Iceland	28.8	139	Tanzania	1.3
30	Spain	410	84	Mauritania	28	140	Nauru	1.1
31	India	379.7	85	Zimbabwe	27	141	Slovakia	0.9
32	Luxembourg	338	86	Sudan	26.8	142	Solomon Islands	0.9
33	Belgium	289.1	87	Lebanon	26.3	143	Barbados	0.8
34	Pakistan	285.8	88	Senegal	25.0	144	Lithuania	0.8
35	Philippines	260.3	89	Cyprus	24.5	145	Equatorial Guinea	0.7
36	Turkmenistan	222	90	Cuba	23.8	146	Guinea-Bissau	0.7
37	Kuwait	195.1	91	Benin	23.4	147	Liberia	0.7
38	United Arab Emirates	190	92	Mali	23.4	148	Sao Tome e Principe	0.7
39	Kyrgyzstan	158.8	93	Togo	23.4	149	Vietnam	0.7
40	Turkey	143.7	94	Belarus	23			
41	Sweden	123.1	95	Tajikistan	22.1	**BOTTOM 10**		
42	Portugal	123	96	Suriname	18.2	150	Kiribati	0.5
43	Argentina	120.8	97	Gabon	17.9	151	Botswana	0.3
44	Finland	115.4	98	Armenia	17.6	152	Estonia	0.3
45	Bolivia	108.5	99	Paraguay	16.5	153	Bahamas	0.2
46	Jamaica	107.2	100	Ghana	16.3	154	Lesotho	0.2
47	Venezuela	102	101	Latvia	15.1	155	Libya	0.2
48	Peru	101	102	Guatemala	14	156	Antigua and Barbuda	0.1
49	Bangladesh	100	103	Algeria	13.8	157	Swaziland	0.1
50	Austria	94.6	104	Cape Verde	13.2	158	Uganda	0.1
51	Yugoslavia	92	105	Moldova	13.0	159	Tonga	0.01
52	Denmark	91.2	106	Hungary	12.1			
53	Greece	87.0	107	Congo	12			

Source: *Air Transport Statistics*

163. TOURIST ARRIVALS

Tourists are defined as persons traveling for pleasure, domestic reasons, health, meetings, business and study, and stopping for a period of 24 hours or more in a country other than that in which they usually reside. These figures do not include immigrants, transport crews or troops passing through a country.

The data are generally based on frontier checks. In the absence of such checks, hotel registration figures are used. These two sources are not strictly comparable because some tourists stay in private houses and others move from one hotel to another.

Rank	Country	Tourist Arrivals (000)	Rank	Country	Tourist Arrivals (000)	Rank	Country	Tourist Arrivals (000)
TOP 10			52	Finland	866	104	Haiti	120
1	France	53,157	53	Botswana	844	105	Bangladesh	115
2	United States	39,772	54	Jamaica	841	106	Togo	115
3	Spain	34,300	55	Saudi Arabia	827	107	Zambia	113
4	Italy	26,679	56	Luxembourg	820	108	Burundi	109
5	Hungary	20,510	57	Colombia	813	109	Gabon	108
6	Austria	19,011	58	Kenya	801	110	Nicaragua	106
7	United Kingdom	18,021	59	Iraq	747	111	Gambia	101
8	Germany	17,045	60	Sweden	731	112	Cameroon	100
9	Mexico	15,695	61	Brunei	625	113	Qatar	100
10	Canada	15,258	62	United Arab Emirates	616	114	Libya	96
			63	San Marino	582	115	Seychelles	86
UPPER MIDDLE			64	Syria	562	116	Sierra Leone	86
11	Switzerland	13,200	65	Venezuela	525	117	Grenada	82
12	China	10,484	66	Guatemala	508	118	Liechtenstein	78
13	Greece	8,873				119	St. Kitts and Nevis	76
14	Czech Republic	8,100	**LOWER MIDDLE**			120	Ethiopia	73
15	Portugal	8,020	67	Zimbabwe	474	121	Guyana	67
16	Yugoslavia	7,880	68	Costa Rica	435	122	St. Vincent	54
17	Malaysia	7,446	69	Bermuda	434	123	Madagascar	53
18	Romania	6,533	70	Barbados	432	124	Yemen	52
19	Netherlands	5,795	71	Pakistan	424	125	Zaire	51
20	Thailand	5,299	72	Ecuador	362	126	Benin	50
21	Singapore	4,842	73	Peru	317	127	Kuwait	50
22	Turkey	4,799	74	Cuba	300	128	Djibouti	47
23	Bulgaria	4,500	75	Sri Lanka	298	129	Angola	46
24	Morocco	4,024	76	Mauritius	292	130	Burkina	46
25	Ireland	3,666	77	Paraguay	280	131	Congo	46
26	Poland	3,400	78	Fiji	279	132	Dominica	45
27	Tunisia	3,222	79	Swaziland	270	133	Mali	44
28	Belgium	3,163	80	Senegal	259	134	Uganda	44
29	Korea, South	2,959	81	Nepal	255	135	Rwanda	43
30	Argentina	2,728	82	Monaco	245	136	Papua New Guinea	41
31	Jordan	2,633	83	Belize	222	137	Somalia	40
32	Puerto Rico	2,554	84	Bolivia	217	138	Vanuatu	35
33	Egypt	2,411	85	Panama	214	139	Chad	29
34	Australia	2,215	86	Honduras	202	140	Suriname	29
35	Indonesia	2,178	87	Antigua and Barbuda	197	141	Laos	25
36	Norway	1,955	88	Cote d'Ivoire	196	142	Sudan	23
37	Japan	1,879	89	Bahrain	195	143	Myanmar (Burma)	21
38	India	1,707	90	Maldives	195			
39	Bahamas	1,562	91	El Salvador	194	**BOTTOM 10**		
40	Cyprus	1,561	92	Trinidad and Tobago	194	144	Niger	21
41	Dominican Republic	1,533	93	Nigeria	190	145	Tonga	21
42	Denmark	1,275	94	Vietnam	180	146	Solomon Islands	9
43	Uruguay	1,267	95	Lesotho	171	147	Afghanistan	8
44	Algeria	1,137	96	Iran	154	148	Comoros	8
45	Brazil	1,079	97	Oman	149	149	Central African Republic	6
46	Israel	1,063	98	Mongolia	147	150	Kiribati	3
47	New Zealand	976	99	St. Lucia	147	151	Bhutan	2
48	Chile	950	100	Ghana	146	152	Sao Tome e Principe	1
49	South Africa	930	101	Iceland	142	153	Tuvalu	1
50	Philippines	893	102	Tanzania	138			
51	Malta	872	103	Malawi	130			

Source: *Yearbook of Tourism Statistics*

164. TELEPHONES PER CAPITA

Telephones per capita has been cited (K. Finsterbusch and T. Caplow in A *Matrix of Modernization*) as the most reliable index of economic development.

Rank	Country	Persons per Telephone	Rank	Country	Persons per Telephone	Rank	Country	Persons per Telephone
TOP 10			64	Trinidad and Tobago	6.7	128	Honduras	48
1	Bermuda	1.5	65	Ukraine	6.7	129	Sao Tome e Principe	52
2	Sweden	1.5	66	Macedonia	6.8	130	Swaziland	56
3	Liechtenstein	1.6	67	Hungary	6.9	131	Nicaragua	60
4	San Marino	1.6	68	Belize	7.1	132	Gambia	63
5	Switzerland	1.6	69	Bosnia & Herzegovina	7.3	133	Solomon Islands	65
6	Canada	1.7	70	Malaysia	7.9	134	China	68
7	Denmark	1.7	71	Argentina	8.1	135	Albania	70
8	United States	1.7	72	Moldova	8.3	136	Pakistan	76
9	Finland	1.8	73	Nauru	8.3	137	Philippines	76
10	Iceland	1.8	74	Oman	8.6	138	Tuvalu	77
			75	Suriname	8.6	139	Djibouti	78
UPPER MIDDLE			76	Poland	8.7	140	Yemen	83
11	Norway	1.8	77	Romania	8.7	141	Zimbabwe	83
12	France	1.9	78	Colombia	8.9	142	Papua New Guinea	100
13	Luxembourg	1.9	79	Chile	9.1	143	India	110
14	Cyprus	2.0	80	Jamaica	9.5	144	Indonesia	110
15	Netherlands	2.0	81	Georgia	9.6	145	Zambia	110
16	United Kingdom	2.0	82	Panama	9.8	146	Sri Lanka	111
17	Australia	2.1	83	Mauritius	10	147	Guinea-Bissau	120
18	Japan	2.1	84	Venezuela	10	148	Kenya	120
19	Monaco	2.1	85	Azerbaijan	11	149	Comoros	130
20	Austria	2.2				150	Congo	130
21	Germany	2.2	**LOWER MIDDLE**			151	Senegal	130
22	Greece	2.2	86	Costa Rica	11	152	Cote d'Ivoire	140
23	New Zealand	2.2	87	Fiji	11	153	Haiti	150
24	Belgium	2.3	88	Kazakhstan	11	154	Eritrea	170
25	Malta	2.3	89	Lebanon	11	155	Lesotho	179
26	Singapore	2.3	90	Mexico	11	156	Angola	190
27	Andorra	2.4	91	Saudi Arabia	11	157	Cameroon	220
28	Italy	2.4	92	South Africa	11	158	Togo	230
29	Taiwan	2.6	93	Kyrgyzstan	12	159	Benin	260
30	United Arab Emirates	2.6	94	Brazil	13	160	Mozambique	270
31	Israel	2.7	95	Dominican Republic	13	161	Vietnam	270
32	Korea, South	2.7	96	Jordan	14	162	Malawi	290
33	Spain	2.7	97	Turkmenistan	15	163	Mauritania	290
34	Puerto Rico	3.0	98	Uzbekistan	15	164	Nepal	290
35	Ireland	3.1	99	Tonga	16	165	Nigeria	300
36	Barbados	3.2	100	Iran	17	166	Sierra Leone	310
37	Portugal	3.2	101	Ecuador	19	167	Tanzania	313
38	Bahamas	3.3	102	Guyana	20	168	Equatorial Guinea	330
39	St. Kitts and Nevis	3.4	103	Tunisia	20	169	Ghana	333
40	Antigua and Barbuda	3.5	104	Korea, North	21	170	Madagascar	370
41	Latvia	3.7	105	Libya	21	171	Burundi	390
42	Bulgaria	3.8	106	Namibia	22	172	Bhutan	400
43	Slovenia	3.9	107	Tajikistan	22	173	Ethiopia	400
44	Kuwait	4.1	108	Egypt	24	174	Bangladesh	440
45	Bahrain	4.3	109	Maldives	24	175	Sudan	440
46	Estonia	4.3	110	Syria	24	176	Burkina	460
47	Lithuania	4.4	111	Algeria	25	177	Central African Republic	480
48	Croatia	4.5	112	Western Samoa	25	178	Laos	530
49	Grenada	4.5	113	Cape Verde	26	179	Liberia	530
50	Qatar	4.7	114	El Salvador	26	180	Guinea	560
51	Brunei	5.1	115	Thailand	27			
52	Czech Republic	5.3	116	Iraq	29	**BOTTOM 10**		
53	Dominica	5.3	117	Cuba	31	181	Myanmar (Burma)	560
54	Turkey	5.4	118	Botswana	32	182	Somalia	560
55	Yugoslavia	5.6	119	Morocco	32	183	Rwanda	630
56	Belarus	5.7	120	Bolivia	33	184	Mali	670
57	Uruguay	5.9	121	Paraguay	33	185	Afghanistan	770
58	Slovakia	6.0	122	Peru	34	186	Niger	830
59	Seychelles	6.2	123	Mongolia	36	187	Uganda	830
60	Russia	6.3	124	Vanuatu	39	188	Zaire	1110
61	Armenia	6.4	125	Gabon	41	189	Chad	1430
62	St. Lucia	6.5	126	Guatemala	43	190	Cambodia	1670
63	St. Vincent	6.7	127	Kiribati	43			

Source: *World's Telephones*

165. DOMESTIC MAIL PER CAPITA

The mail is perhaps the most universal form of communication and also the cheapest and the most convenient. Because the post office is a state monopoly in all countries of the world, it has acquired some of the characteristics of a public service, which despite many shortcomings is generally acknowledged as the smoothest and the most efficient public service everywhere in the world. It is also one operation where the methods and techniques do not vary greatly among countries. Mail gets stamped, collected, transported and delivered in more or less the same way in the United States as it is in Western Samoa or Botswana.

TOP 10
Domestic Mail per Capita

Rank	Country	Pieces of Mail	Rank	Country	Pieces of Mail
1	Sweden	962	6	Norway	500
2	Russia	700	7	France	436
3	United States	662	8	Austria	420
4	Switzerland	614	9	Netherlands	410
5	Liechtenstein	580	10	Greece	400

1 envelope = 100 pieces of mail

Rank	Country	Postal Service Pieces of Mail per Capita	Rank	Country	Postal Service Pieces of Mail per Capita	Rank	Country	Postal Service Pieces of Mail per Capita
UPPER MIDDLE			45	Korea, South	67	80	Djibouti	21
11	Luxembourg	400	46	Taiwan	66			
12	Bermuda	380	47	Turkmenistan	65	**LOWER MIDDLE**		
13	Canada	372	48	Namibia	64	81	Saudi Arabia	21
14	Denmark	356	49	Seychelles	64	82	Mali	20
15	Belgium	344	50	Tajikistan	59	83	Nauru	20
16	Jamaica	320	51	Brunei	57	84	Oman	20
17	United Kingdom	290	52	Haiti	57	85	Sri Lanka	20
18	Iceland	250	53	Grenada	55	86	Gabon	19
19	New Zealand	250	54	Malaysia	53	87	Trinidad and Tobago	19
20	Australia	240	55	Barbados	49	88	Belize	18
21	Germany	240	56	Qatar	48	89	Guatemala	17
22	Bahamas	220	57	St. Kitts and Nevis	48	90	Tunisia	17
23	Singapore	200	58	Lesotho	44	91	Algeria	16
24	Japan	190	59	Croatia	43	92	India	16
25	Finland	153	60	Liberia	40	93	Nepal	16
26	Hungary	150	61	Tonga	40	94	Slovakia	16
27	United Arab Emirates	145	62	Mauritius	37	95	Thailand	16
28	Ireland	130	63	St. Lucia	34	96	Comoros	15.0
29	Malta	130	64	Fiji	31	97	Estonia	15
30	Italy	120	65	Jordan	31	98	Malawi	15
31	Czech Republic	114	66	Poland	31	99	Philippines	15
32	Slovenia	110	67	Bosnia & Herzegovina	30	100	Armenia	14
33	Spain	110	68	Zimbabwe	30	101	Kenya	13
34	Kazakhstan	95	69	Ukraine	29	102	Solomon Islands	12
35	Portugal	92	70	Bulgaria	28	103	Lithuania	11
36	Andorra	90	71	Moldova	28	104	Romania	11
37	Bahrain	90	72	Dominica	27	105	Mexico	10
38	Israel	87	73	Turkey	27	106	Papua New Guinea	10
39	Sao Tome e Principe	86	74	Botswana	26	107	Tuvalu	10
40	Kyrgyzstan	80	75	Brazil	26	108	Argentina	9.8
41	Azerbaijan	75	76	Georgia	25	109	Kiribati	9.7
42	Cyprus	74	77	Swaziland	25	110	Ghana	9.5
43	Uzbekistan	73	78	Belarus	23	111	Morocco	9.0
44	Kuwait	69	79	Chile	22	112	Macedonia	8.3

Rank	Country	Postal Service Pieces of Mail per Capita	Rank	Country	Postal Service Pieces of Mail per Capita	Rank	Country	Postal Service Pieces of Mail per Capita
113	Costa Rica	8.2	133	Tanzania	2.9	153	Zaire	1.3
114	Maldives	8.2	134	Cuba	2.6	154	Benin	1.2
115	Western Samoa	6.8	135	Afghanistan	2.5	155	Bhutan	1.2
116	Colombia	6.7	136	Iraq	2.5	156	Burundi	1.1
117	Libya	6.7	137	Albania	2.4	157	Guinea	1
118	Latvia	6.5	138	Madagascar	2.2	158	Uganda	1
119	Pakistan	5.9	139	Egypt	2.0	159	Togo	0.9
120	Nigeria	5.7	140	Senegal	2.0	160	Yemen	0.9
121	Panama	5.7	141	Cameroon	1.9		**BOTTOM 10**	
122	China	5.6	142	Bangladesh	1.8	161	Laos	0.8
123	Guyana	5.6	143	Burkina	1.7	162	Chad	0.7
124	Zambia	5.5	144	Myanmar (Burma)	1.7	163	Mozambique	0.6
125	Cape Verde	5.1	145	Peru	1.7	164	Niger	0.6
126	Iran	5.0	146	Ecuador	1.6	165	Ethiopia	0.5
127	St. Vincent	4.9	147	Paraguay	1.6	166	Sierra Leone	0.5
128	Uruguay	4.9	148	Syria	1.4	167	Guinea-Bissau	0.4
129	Venezuela	4.8	149	Bolivia	1.3	168	Mongolia	0.4
130	El Salvador	3.3	150	Congo	1.3	169	Angola	0.2
131	Cote d'Ivoire	3.0	151	Dominican Republic	1.3	170	Sudan	0.2
132	Indonesia	3.0	152	Rwanda	1.3			

Source: *Postal Statistics*

166. VOLUME OF MAIL

Ironically, the volume of mail has been increasing at a pace that has surprised observers, despite competition from telephones and fax machines. The reason is the growth in junk mail, direct mail, greeting cards, newspapers and magazines. Worldwide the volume of mail is estimated at over 1 trillion pieces. The share of personal communications is dwindling, while the reverse is true of business communications.

Rank	Country	Volume of Mail (1000 pieces)	Rank	Country	Volume of Mail (1000 pieces)	Rank	Country	Volume of Mail (1000 pieces)
	TOP 10		34	Mexico	889,827	70	Tunisia	144,522
1	United States	170,544,202	35	New Zealand	838,656	71	Georgia	138,000
2	France	25,176,530	36	Finland	779,000	72	Jordan	136,740
3	Japan	24,283,947	37	Pakistan	722,293	73	Bosnia & Herzegovina	128,886
4	Germany	19,200,413	38	Nigeria	681,977	74	Moldova	122,879
5	United Kingdom	16,651,000	39	Singapore	577,419			
6	India	13,314,660	40	Indonesia	545,972		**LOWER MIDDLE**	
7	Canada	10,714,615	41	Azerbaijan	538,885	75	Egypt	114,874
8	Russia	10,390,706	42	Ireland	473,450	76	Malawi	113,975
9	Sweden	8,418,751	43	Israel	456,000	77	Sao Tome e Principe	101,525
10	Italy	6,929,647	44	Greece	455,549	78	Kuwait	98,888
			45	Algeria	417,362	79	Liberia	98,455
	UPPER MIDDLE		46	Haiti	398,873	80	Venezuela	94,854
11	China	6,753,807	47	Kenya	377,356	81	Namibia	89,743
12	Netherlands	6,105,000	48	Saudi Arabia	365,522	82	Slovakia	85,620
13	Spain	4,318,678	49	Kyrgyzstan	355,300	83	Tanzania	82,171
14	Switzerland	4,234,907	50	Sri Lanka	350,748	84	Jamaica	81,086
15	Australia	4,131,260	51	Nepal	327,905	85	Lesotho	77,615
16	Brazil	3,908,203	52	Argentina	326,111	86	Myanmar (Burma)	70,499
17	Belgium	3,441,741	53	Zimbabwe	321,825	87	Iceland	64,877
18	Austria	3,313,573	54	Tajikistan	320,049	88	Bahamas	59,365
19	Korea, South	2,966,731	55	Iran	313,151	89	Armenia	49,000
20	Norway	2,164,233	56	Chile	279,526	90	Zambia	48,868
21	Denmark	1,846,000	57	Bulgaria	254,813	91	Iraq	48,807
22	Taiwan	1,754,119	58	Romania	250,509	92	Bahrain	48,730
23	Turkey	1,651,700	59	United Arab Emirates	249,058	93	Malta	47,240
24	Kazakhstan	1,602,917	60	Turkmenistan	244,027	94	Zaire	45,394
25	Uzbekistan	1,537,874	61	Belarus	240,412	95	Lithuania	40,865
26	Ukraine	1,506,173	62	Morocco	235,783	96	Mauritius	40,448
27	Hungary	1,487,375	63	Colombia	220,456	97	Cote d'Ivoire	39,791
28	Poland	1,188,495	64	Slovenia	218,625	98	Papua New Guinea	38,686
29	Czech Republic	1,188,226	65	Croatia	206,702	99	Peru	37,751
30	Malaysia	1,011,206	66	Bangladesh	197,363	100	Botswana	37,387
31	Philippines	986,027	67	Guatemala	173,047	101	Afghanistan	36,981
32	Portugal	907,170	68	Luxembourg	151,000	102	Oman	34,292
33	Thailand	904,878	69	Ghana	145,576	103	Libya	31,578

Rank	Country	Volume of Mail (1000 pieces)	Rank	Country	Volume of Mail (1000 pieces)	Rank	Country	Volume of Mail (1000 pieces)
104	Madagascar	29,048	127	Burkina	13,689	150	Laos	3,809
105	Cuba	27,868	128	Barbados	12,788	151	Togo	3,511
106	Ethiopia	27,078	129	Yemen	9,999	152	Andorra	3,483
107	Qatar	27,051	130	Rwanda	9,972	153	Congo	3,240
108	Costa Rica	26,093	131	Djibouti	9,904	154	Belize	3,096
109	Fiji	23,562	132	Dominican Republic	9,800	155	Angola	2,063
110	Trinidad and Tobago	23,288	133	Comoros	9,007	156	Dominica	2,051
111	Estonia	22,939	134	Bolivia	8,879	157	Mali	2,040
112	Bermuda	22,700	135	Mozambique	8,573	158	Sierra Leone	2,018
113	Cameroon	22,590	136	Albania	7,936	159	Cape Verde	1,997
114	Swaziland	20,085	137	Paraguay	7,333	160	Maldives	1,962
115	Gabon	19,190	138	Guinea	6,688			
116	El Salvador	18,572	139	Burundi	6,300	**BOTTOM 10**		
117	Syria	17,974	140	Benin	6,088	161	St. Kitts and Nevis	1,906
118	Ecuador	17,310	141	Sudan	5,309	162	Bhutan	1,817
119	Uganda	17,239	142	Cyprus	5,300	163	Western Samoa	1,089
120	Liechtenstein	17,192	143	St. Lucia	5,095	164	Mongolia	1,016
121	Latvia	16,912	144	Niger	4,647	165	Kiribati	707
122	Macedonia	16,644	145	Guyana	4,582	166	St. Vincent	526
123	Brunei	15,839	146	Seychelles	4,502	167	Guinea-Bissau	410
124	Uruguay	15,370	147	Solomon Islands	4,289	168	Yugoslavia	210
125	Senegal	15,150	148	Chad	4,270	169	Nauru	168
126	Panama	14,456	149	Tonga	4,014	170	Tuvalu	88

Source: *Postal Statistics*

167. POST OFFICE

Post offices were the hub of communications until the end of World War II. In almost all countries, postal services are a state monopoly. Historically, post masters were important local officials and they provided services for which there was no competition. However, the telecommunications revolution has displaced the post office and sidelined it. Its parcel shipments face severe competition and its letter delivery system appears antiquated in relation to the speed of fax and other electronic means of communication. Nevertheless, the postal system will survive, just as the rail system has survived in the transportation field. It will certainly be forced to become more efficient through technology. It remains the truly universal means of communication, a claim that even telephones cannot make.

Rank	Country	Post Offices	Rank	Country	Post Offices	Rank	Country	Post Offices
TOP 10			24	Romania	4,884	50	Belgium	1,756
1	India	152,382	25	Kazakhstan	4,591	51	Saudi Arabia	1,754
2	China	52,969	26	Thailand	4,265	52	Slovakia	1,744
3	United States	51,193	27	Australia	4,233	53	Yugoslavia	1,569
4	Russia	48,061	28	Sri Lanka	4,043	54	Cuba	1,546
5	Turkey	42,541	29	Belarus	4,002	55	Peru	1,373
6	Indonesia	26,291	30	Colombia	3,806	56	Morocco	1,329
7	Japan	24,359	31	Uzbekistan	3,800	57	Moldova	1,320
8	United Kingdom	19,782	32	Switzerland	3,733	58	Denmark	1,293
9	Canada	19,102	33	Nigeria	3,619	59	Greece	1,262
10	France	16,877	34	Netherlands	3,567	60	New Zealand	1,242
			35	Czech Republic	3,504	61	Myanmar (Burma)	1,152
UPPER MIDDLE			36	Korea, South	3,309	62	Kenya	1,102
11	Ukraine	16,500	37	Ireland	3,250	63	Croatia	1,082
12	Italy	14,447	38	Hungary	3,208	64	Latvia	1,048
13	Taiwan	13,233	39	Bulgaria	3,119	65	Lithuania	1,037
14	Pakistan	13,196	40	Algeria	2,877	66	Kyrgyzstan	1,020
15	Brazil	12,766	41	Austria	2,670	67	Ghana	1,011
16	Iran	8,053	42	Norway	2,541	68	Singapore	998
17	Bangladesh	7,985	43	Nepal	2,461	69	Madagascar	921
18	Mexico	7,275	44	Philippines	2,147	70	Tunisia	906
19	Portugal	7,272	45	Finland	2,073	71	Armenia	898
20	Poland	7,119	46	Germany	2,043	72	Tanzania	885
21	Egypt	7,106	47	Malaysia	1,970	73	Tajikistan	785
22	Spain	5,894	48	Sweden	1,836	74	Cyprus	774
23	Argentina	5,489	49	Azerbaijan	1,821	75	Jamaica	728

Rank	Country	Post Offices	Rank	Country	Post Offices	Rank	Country	Post Offices
	LOWER MIDDLE		108	Dominican Republic	206	142	Burundi	68
76	Israel	692	109	Zimbabwe	202	143	Burkina	66
77	Bosnia & Herzegovina	656	110	Equatorial Guinea	201	144	Niger	64
78	Mozambique	627	111	Grenada	191	145	Cape Verde	63
79	Syria	626	112	Benin	180	146	Dominica	63
80	Sudan	619	113	Botswana	167	147	St. Lucia	62
81	Albania	615	114	Uruguay	167	148	Mauritania	60
82	Chile	602	115	United Arab Emirates	161	149	Central African Republic	52
83	Estonia	590	116	Lesotho	140	150	Gabon	52
84	Turkmenistan	580	117	Fiji	139	151	Malta	50
85	Ethiopia	561	118	Senegal	139	152	Liberia	44
86	Venezuela	556	119	Bahamas	136	153	Rwanda	43
87	Guatemala	540	120	Bolivia	133	154	Togo	43
88	Slovenia	504	121	Haiti	132	155	Maldives	40
89	Zambia	421	122	Laos	127	156	Western Samoa	40
90	Mongolia	420	123	Mali	127	157	Chad	36
91	Cote d'Ivoire	386	124	Iceland	120	158	Comoros	36
92	Libya	373	125	Solomon Islands	117	159	Qatar	28
93	Afghanistan	358	126	Congo	114	160	Guinea-Bissau	24
94	Iraq	343	127	Belize	112	161	Kiribati	24
95	Ecuador	332	128	Papua New Guinea	108	162	Barbados	17
96	Paraguay	321	129	Tonga	108	163	Bermuda	14
97	Uganda	319	130	Luxembourg	106			
98	El Salvador	307	131	Mauritius	105		**BOTTOM 10**	
99	Zaire	304	132	St. Vincent	103	164	Bahrain	13
100	Costa Rica	276	133	Guyana	91	165	Liechtenstein	12
101	Macedonia	263	134	Kuwait	89	166	Sao Tome e Principe	11
102	Malawi	263	135	Namibia	87	167	San Marino	10
103	Cameroon	259	136	Bhutan	83	168	Djibouti	9
104	Trinidad and Tobago	232	137	Angola	76	169	Tuvalu	9
105	Panama	231	138	Oman	76	170	St. Kitts and Nevis	8
106	Yemen	217	139	Guinea	75	171	Brunei	6
107	Jordan	216	140	Sierra Leone	71	172	Seychelles	5
			141	Swaziland	69	173	Nauru	3

Source: *Postal Statistics*

168. TELEPHONES

Worldwide there are over 300 million telephone access lines, of which the United States accounts for more than half. Advances in communications technology have helped the industry, about 78% of which is privately owned, to provide better service more efficiently and at less cost. Whereas the cost of postage has increased tenfold in most countries, the cost of phone calls has come down tenfold in the past 75 years. Countries with efficient phone service are also more productive industrially. The spread of answering machines, cellular phones, and fax machines are also positive factors in making telephones a central feature of modern life.

Rank	Country	Telephones (000)	Rank	Country	Telephones (000)	Rank	Country	Telephones (000)
	TOP 10		14	Australia	8,540	30	Denmark	3,060
1	United States	148,084	15	India	8,037	31	Finland	2,761
2	Japan	58,459	16	Taiwan	7,951	32	Romania	2,624
3	Germany	36,900	17	Netherlands	7,630	33	Malaysia	2,411
4	France	30,900	18	Mexico	7,621	34	Egypt	2,375
5	United Kingdom	28,681	19	Sweden	5,903	35	Norway	2,335
6	Italy	24,176	20	Greece	4,744	36	Bulgaria	2,300
7	Russia	23,397	21	Poland	4,419	37	Ukraine	2,225
8	China	17,332	22	Belgium	4,396	38	Thailand	2,185
9	Korea, South	16,633	23	Switzerland	4,266	39	Venezuela	2,083
10	Canada	16,471	24	Argentina	4,115	40	Czech Republic	1,961
			25	Colombia	3,828	41	Israel	1,958
	UPPER MIDDLE		26	South Africa	3,660	42	Yugoslavia	1,923
11	Spain	14,254	27	Iran	3,598	43	Belarus	1,814
12	Brazil	11,744	28	Austria	3,579	44	Indonesia	1,713
13	Turkey	10,936	29	Portugal	3,260	45	Pakistan	1,605

Rank	Country	Telephones (000)	Rank	Country	Telephones (000)	Rank	Country	Telephones (000)
46	New Zealand	1,593	94	Bolivia	234	144	St. Lucia	24
47	Saudi Arabia	1,575	95	Guatemala	231	145	Burkina	22
48	Kazakhstan	1,559	96	Kenya	215	146	Uganda	21
49	Chile	1,520	97	Luxembourg	215	147	Benin	20
50	Hungary	1,498	98	Trinidad and Tobago	193	148	Eritrea	20
51	Uzbekistan	1,452	99	El Salvador	174	149	Grenada	20
52	Singapore	1,246	100	Yemen	162	150	Antigua and Barbuda	19
53	Puerto Rico	1,207	101	Malta	158	151	Congo	19
54	Ireland	1,170	102	Sri Lanka	158	152	Liechtenstein	19
55	Korea, North	1,089	103	Oman	148	153	St. Vincent	17
56	Algeria	1,068	104	Iceland	144	154	Togo	17
57	Croatia	1,027	105	Paraguay	142	155	Burundi	16
58	Slovakia	893	106	Ethiopia	133	156	Gambia	16
59	Philippines	860	107	Zimbabwe	128	157	Swaziland	16
60	Lithuania	858	108	Bahrain	124	158	Cape Verde	15
61	Azerbaijan	847	109	Honduras	117	159	Sierra Leone	15
62	Latvia	694	110	Qatar	111	160	Somalia	15
63	Iraq	675	111	Mauritius	107	161	Dominica	14
64	Peru	670	112	Cote d'Ivoire	94	162	Mali	14
65	United Arab Emirates	624	113	Tanzania	85	163	Monaco	14
66	Bosnia & Herzegovina	600	114	Barbados	83	164	San Marino	14
67	Ecuador	598	115	Bahamas	80	165	Guinea	12
68	Armenia	584	116	Myanmar (Burma)	80	166	Rwanda	12
69	Georgia	571	117	Zambia	78	167	St. Kitts and Nevis	12
70	Dominican Republic	552	118	Nepal	72	168	Niger	11
71	Syria	550	119	Namibia	70	169	Seychelles	11
72	Uruguay	530	120	Nicaragua	67	170	Lesotho	10.5
73	Moldova	524	121	Mongolia	66	171	Maldives	10
74	Slovenia	516	122	Senegal	64	172	Guinea-Bissau	8.6
75	Tunisia	421	123	Sudan	64	173	Laos	8.6
76	Kyrgyzstan	367	124	Mozambique	62	174	Mauritania	7.6
77	Costa Rica	364	125	Cameroon	57	175	Djibouti	7.3
78	Estonia	358	126	Brunei	55	176	Central African Republic	6.7
79	Kuwait	358	127	Fiji	54	177	Western Samoa	6.5
80	Lebanon	350	128	Angola	53	178	Cambodia	5.9
81	Cuba	344	129	Albania	49	179	Tonga	5.9
82	Nigeria	342	130	Ghana	49	180	Solomon Islands	5.3
83	Macedonia	324	131	Suriname	47			
84	Cyprus	311	132	Haiti	45	**BOTTOM 10**		
			133	Botswana	44	181	Chad	4.6
LOWER MIDDLE			134	Bermuda	42	182	Liberia	4.5
85	Jordan	288	135	Guyana	41	183	Vanuatu	4.1
86	Morocco	281	136	Papua New Guinea	40	184	Comoros	4.0
87	Bangladesh	268	137	Zaire	36	185	Bhutan	3.8
88	Turkmenistan	265	138	Madagascar	35	186	Sao Tome e Principe	2.4
89	Panama	262	139	Malawi	33	187	Kiribati	1.8
90	Tajikistan	260	140	Gabon	30	188	Equatorial Guinea	1.3
91	Vietnam	260	141	Afghanistan	29	189	Nauru	1.2
92	Jamaica	255	142	Andorra	29	190	Tuvalu	0.12
93	Libya	240	143	Belize	29			

Source: *World's Telephones*

FAX MACHINES AND CELLULAR PHONES

Among the marvels of modern communications technology are the fax machines and cellular phones which have made instantaneous communication possible any time or from any place, without cumbersome mechanical procedures. They also are remarkable for the speed with which they spread throughout the world in a matter of years. For developing countries they offer a boon, enabling them to skip several generations of technology and move right into the age of high tech communications.

169. FAX MACHINES

Rank	Country	Fax Machines	Rank	Country	Fax Machines	Rank	Country	Fax Machines
TOP 10			42	Yugoslavia	8,200	84	Togo	600
1	United States	6,000,000	43	Sri Lanka	8,100	85	Bahamas	500
2	Japan	5,533,000	44	Slovenia	7,600	86	Ethiopia	500
3	Germany	1,172,700	45	Indonesia	7,100	87	Kuwait	500
4	United Kingdom	1,005,000	46	Uruguay	7,000	88	Philippines	500
5	France	630,000	47	Jordan	6,000	89	Rwanda	500
6	Australia	600,000	48	Pakistan	5,300	90	Zambia	500
7	Canada	500,000	49	Luxembourg	5,000	91	Antigua and Barbuda	400
8	Netherlands	372,800	50	Vietnam	5,000	92	Belize	400
9	Sweden	300,000	51	Guatemala	4,000	93	Cuba	400
10	Italy	230,000				94	Gambia	400
			LOWER MIDDLE			95	Lesotho	400
UPPER MIDDLE			52	Iceland	4,000	96	Cape Verde	300
11	Spain	195,000	53	Qatar	4,000	97	Grenada	300
12	Denmark	170,000	54	Bahrain	3,800	98	Guinea-Bissau	300
13	Brazil	160,000	55	Ghana	3,800	99	Mauritania	300
14	Belgium	150,000	56	El Salvador	3,500	100	Niger	300
15	Switzerland	135,000	57	Cyprus	3,000	101	St. Lucia	300
16	Austria	130,000	58	Lebanon	3,000	102	Seychelles	300
17	Norway	120,000	59	Lithuania	3,000	103	Solomon Islands	300
18	Finland	105,000	60	Fiji	2,200	104	Sudan	300
19	China	89,300	61	Malta	2,200	105	Suriname	300
20	Ireland	75,000	62	Peru	2,100	106	Gabon	200
21	Turkey	62,900	63	Tanzania	2,000	107	Guyana	200
22	Israel	60,000	64	Zimbabwe	2,000	108	Kenya	200
23	Colombia	53,000	65	Mauritius	1,800	109	Laos	200
24	Puerto Rico	49,560	66	Paraguay	1,700	110	Maldives	200
25	Singapore	48,300	67	Jamaica	1,600	111	Moldova	200
26	Malaysia	46,000	68	Oman	1,600	112	Sierra Leone	200
27	New Zealand	40,000	69	Uganda	1,600	113	Chad	100
28	Czech Republic	29,400	70	Barbados	1,500			
29	Portugal	26,800	71	Belarus	1,500	**BOTTOM 10**		
30	Poland	25,100	72	Estonia	1,500	114	Comoros	100
31	Ecuador	25,000	73	Trinidad and Tobago	1,500	115	Congo	100
32	Hungary	24,700	74	Ukraine	1,500	116	Djibouti	100
33	United Arab Emirates	23,900	75	Macedonia	1,400	117	Kiribati	100
34	Iran	22,000	76	Andorra	1,300	118	Mali	100
35	Slovakia	16,200	77	Brunei	1,200	119	Nepal	100
36	Egypt	15,600	78	Mozambique	1,200	120	Sao Tome e Principe	100
37	Greece	13,300	79	Swaziland	800	121	Tonga	100
38	Chile	12,500	80	Yemen	800	122	Western Samoa	100
39	Romania	10,200	81	Malawi	700	123	Bolivia	10
40	Tunisia	10,000	82	Albania	600			
41	Croatia	9,100	83	Latvia	600			

Source: *World Telecommunication Indicators*

170. CELLULAR PHONES

Rank	Country	Cellular Phones	Rank	Country	Cellular Phones	Rank	Country	Cellular Phones
TOP 10			31	United Arab Emirates	48,900	62	Slovenia	3,500
1	United States	11,033,000	32	Argentina	45,000	63	Morocco	3,200
2	Japan	1,712,500	33	Ireland	44,000	64	Costa Rica	3,000
3	United Kingdom	1,496,000	34	Portugal	37,300	65	Mauritius	2,900
4	Canada	1,022,800	35	Israel	36,100	66	Poland	2,800
5	Germany	951,900				67	Bahamas	2,600
6	Italy	783,000	**LOWER MIDDLE**			68	Guatemala	2,100
7	Sweden	656,000	36	Indonesia	35,500	69	Bermuda	1,900
8	France	441,700	37	Brazil	30,700	70	Tunisia	1,900
9	Australia	440,000	38	Peru	27,100	71	Uruguay	1,700
10	Taiwan	384,800	39	Hungary	23,300	72	Bolivia	1,600
			40	Venezuela	20,900	73	Yemen	1,600
UPPER MIDDLE			41	Saudi Arabia	15,800	74	Jordan	1,500
11	Finland	354,200	42	Iceland	15,300	75	Paraguay	1,500
12	Norway	280,000	43	Pakistan	13,500	76	Slovakia	1,500
13	Korea, South	271,900	44	South Africa	12,500	77	Trinidad and Tobago	1,300
14	Mexico	267,200	45	Nigeria	10,000	78	Kiribati	1,100
15	Thailand	248,700	46	Cyprus	9,700	79	Luxembourg	1,100
16	Switzerland	220,600	47	Colombia	8,500	80	Latvia	1,000
17	Denmark	206,500	48	Jamaica	7,900	81	Andorra	800
18	Spain	180,300	49	Dominican Republic	7,000	82	Bangladesh	800
19	China	176,900	50	Egypt	6,900			
20	Austria	172,500	51	Croatia	6,300	**BOTTOM 10**		
21	Netherlands	166,000	52	Russia	6,000	83	Guyana	800
22	Singapore	120,000	53	Algeria	4,800	84	Bahrain	700
23	New Zealand	100,200	54	Czech Republic	4,700	85	Ghana	400
24	Malaysia	83,100	55	Oman	4,700	86	Laos	300
25	Chile	64,400	56	Estonia	4,300	87	Lithuania	300
26	Belgium	61,500	57	Qatar	4,200	88	Cuba	200
27	Turkey	61,400	58	Brunei	4,100	89	Gambia	200
28	Philippines	52,000	59	Sri Lanka	4,000	90	Grenada	200
29	Puerto Rico	51,100	60	Lebanon	3,800	91	Moldova	100
30	Kuwait	51,000	61	Malta	3,500	92	St. Vincent	100

Source: *World Telecommunication Indicators*

171. INTERNATIONAL TELEPHONE TRAFFIC

Nowhere is the term borderless world a powerful reality than in communications. The telephone is one of the great tools of globalization, and in many countries more calls are international than domestic. It is not merely businesses that are becoming transnational, but also individual families who make international calls to reach out and touch their kith and kin living in different countries.

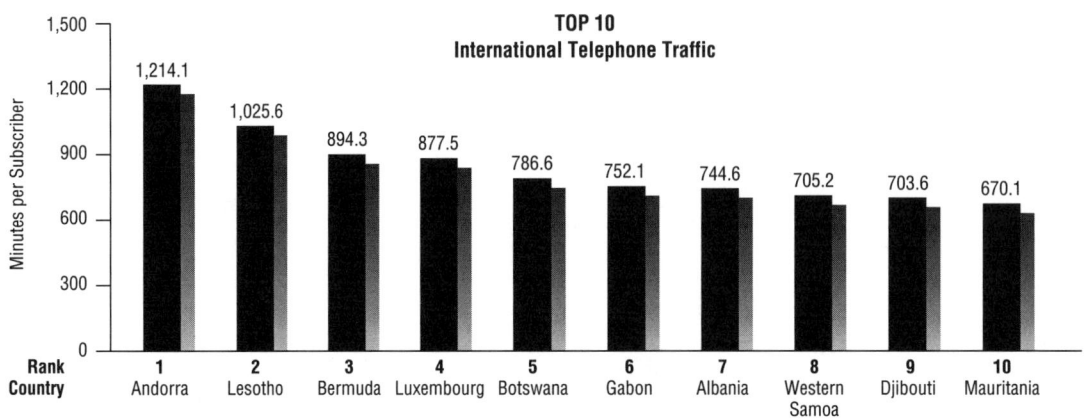

TOP 10 International Telephone Traffic

Rank	Country	Minutes per Subscriber
1	Andorra	1,214.1
2	Lesotho	1,025.6
3	Bermuda	894.3
4	Luxembourg	877.5
5	Botswana	786.6
6	Gabon	752.1
7	Albania	744.6
8	Western Samoa	705.2
9	Djibouti	703.6
10	Mauritania	670.1

Rank	Country	International Telephone Traffic (minutes per subscriber)
	UPPER MIDDLE	
11	Bahrain	658.3
12	Swaziland	620.0
13	Papua New Guinea	566.7
14	United Arab Emirates	553.2
15	Antigua and Barbuda	515.8
16	Liberia	508.9
17	Togo	502.4
18	Qatar	496.0
19	Brunei	453.9
20	Haiti	422.1
21	Bahamas	421.9
22	Chad	398.6
23	Mali	390.2
24	Dominica	365.0
25	Switzerland	364.3
26	Congo	354.6
27	Guyana	350.8
28	Nicaragua	350.0
29	Singapore	342.1
30	Cameroon	336.5
31	Solomon Islands	330.5
32	Zimbabwe	311.6
33	Oman	303.0
34	Honduras	300.8
35	Comoros	298.2
36	Cyprus	293.2
37	St. Lucia	290.7
38	Barbados	287.4
39	Central African Republic	285.1
40	Senegal	275.1
41	Maldives	270.4
42	Saudi Arabia	270.4
43	Ireland	266.5
44	Niger	248.6
45	Cote d'Ivoire	248.1
46	Rwanda	239.8
47	Fiji	234.7
48	Trinidad and Tobago	227.8
49	Malawi	225.2
50	Guinea-Bissau	218.7
51	Mauritius	218.4
52	Belgium	213.7

Rank	Country	International Telephone Traffic (minutes per subscriber)
53	Austria	205.8
54	El Salvador	202.9
55	Belize	202.6
56	Cape Verde	200.8
57	Gambia	191.4
58	Philippines	191.3
59	Suriname	190.5
60	Kiribati	187.2
61	Angola	186.1
62	Benin	183.9
63	St. Kitts and Nevis	181.8
64	Tunisia	181.4
65	Jordan	165.3
66	Mozambique	163.2
67	Seychelles	163.1
68	Grenada	162.1
69	Sao Tome e Principe	162.0
70	Iceland	157.8
71	Morocco	156.9
72	Sudan	155.4
73	Norway	153.6
74	Yemen	153.4
75	Netherlands	153.3
76	Nepal	151.0
	LOWER MIDDLE	
77	St. Vincent	150.8
78	Zambia	149.8
79	Ghana	149.0
80	Panama	148.5
81	Burundi	146.3
82	Dominican Republic	145.2
83	Guatemala	143.3
84	Hungary	142.9
85	Denmark	141.4
86	Estonia	134.2
87	Costa Rica	132.4
88	Sri Lanka	131.2
89	Laos	130.1
90	Malta	128.8
91	Burkina	123.3
92	Uganda	123.0
93	Algeria	122.6

Rank	Country	International Telephone Traffic (minutes per subscriber)
94	Germany	115.4
95	Sweden	115.2
96	Croatia	109.7
97	United Kingdom	109.2
98	Kenya	107.8
99	Paraguay	107.2
100	Sierra Leone	99.9
101	New Zealand	99.3
102	Libya	96.1
103	Slovenia	93.5
104	Syria	92.6
105	Madagascar	89.9
106	Macedonia	88.9
107	Mexico	88.7
108	Indonesia	86.0
109	Finland	85.7
110	Czech Republic	85.2
111	Israel	83.0
112	Australia	79.8
113	Yugoslavia	78.4
114	Bolivia	78.0
115	France	77.6
116	Vietnam	75.4
117	Thailand	74.0
118	Ethiopia	71.4
119	United States	70.2
120	Namibia	67.7
121	Greece	66.5
122	South Africa	62.9
123	Uruguay	62.2
124	Italy	62.1
125	Venezuela	60.9
126	Spain	58.3
127	Bangladesh	58.1
128	China	55.4
129	Poland	54.0
130	Ecuador	53.6
131	Peru	52.3
132	Portugal	51.8
133	Chile	50.9
134	Malaysia	50.5
135	Tanzania	50.4
136	Taiwan	49.5

Rank	Country	International Telephone Traffic (minutes per subscriber)	Rank	Country	International Telephone Traffic (minutes per subscriber)	Rank	Country	International Telephone Traffic (minutes per subscriber)
137	Canada	44.5	147	Turkey	24.2	155	Moldova	10.7
138	Iran	43.8	148	Japan	22.4	156	Russia	5.5
139	Colombia	38.9	149	Romania	19.4	157	Lithuania	4.5
140	India	38.1	150	Korea, South	19.3	158	Kyrgyzstan	3.2
141	Bulgaria	37.9	151	Afghanistan	16.5	159	Latvia	2.8
142	Cuba	36.0	152	Brazil	15.9	160	Turkmenistan	1.3
143	Pakistan	35.5				161	Georgia	1.2
144	Argentina	34.5		**BOTTOM 10**		162	Tajikistan	0.8
145	Lebanon	34.3	153	Myanmar (Burma)	13.3			
146	Egypt	32.7	154	Mongolia	12.5			

Source: *World's Telephones*

Section
XV

ENVIRONMENT

The first three editions of this book (1979, 1984, 1992) had no section on the Environment. It is significant that such a section is being included in this edition and it is an acknowledgment of the growing importance of environment as a key determinant of not only the present but also the future of the planet.

There is a new awareness of the connectedness of things. Our smallest actions have consequences that we may not fully comprehend and may affect the quality of life of other human beings and the welfare of other nations and future generations. Thus, disposal of urban wastes, destruction of trees and plants, the use of certain chemicals, the consumption of ivory ornaments or coats made from the skins of endangered animals are not merely individual or parochial decisions: they affect the web of life and may have irreparable ecological consequences. If the present pattern of human activities in certain areas continues, it will lead to a major decline in the condition of nature and the quality of human life. Among the vast array of environmental problems that we face are global warming as a result of indiscriminate consumption of fuels, unchecked population growth, biological impoverishment from the destruction of tropical forests, the degradation of marine environments and wetlands, and the growing loss of biological diversity. Eventually, concern for the environment boils down to the right lifestyle choices: how much waste, how much energy, how much water and what type of food. Some matters are beyond the realm of individual choices, although the adoption of more austere and low-consumption lifestyles is the first step. Governments and industries have a role in promoting better and more efficient standards for environmental safety. Sometimes, the proper concern extends from our impact on the environment to the environment's impact on us—pesticide residues in food, lead and other contaminants in drinking water, polluted air in cities. These environmental hazards may force human beings to take more drastic action later if they are ignored now.

172. DEFORESTATION

Deforestation is a cause as well as a symptom of environmental degradation. Air pollution, soil erosion and desertification can cause irreversible loss of forest stands, even in areas where forests have been growing for centuries. Deforestation is also caused by clearcutting by lumber companies who do not replant. In many Third World countries, indiscriminate exploitation of forest wealth has led to permanent loss of both trees and the biospecies for which the forest was a home.

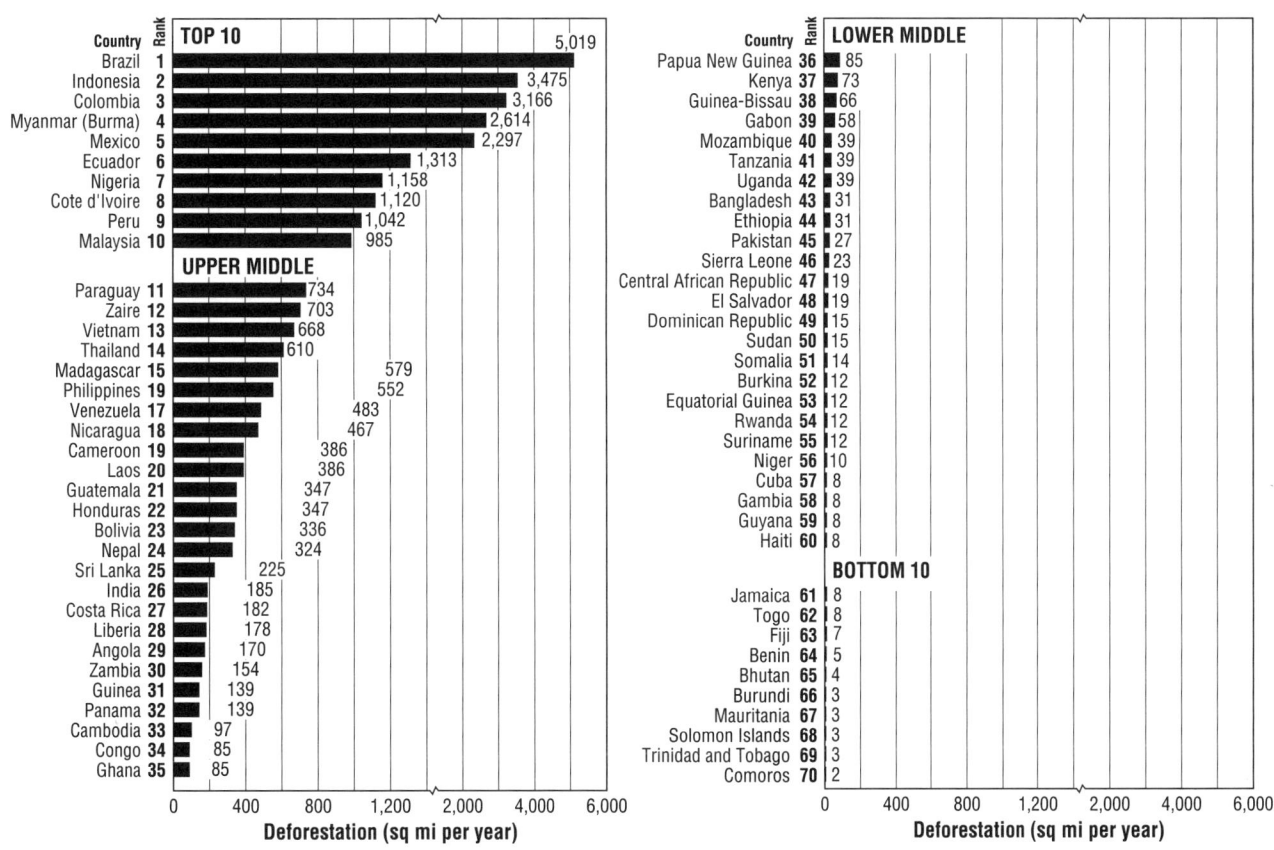

Country	Rank	TOP 10
Brazil	1	5,019
Indonesia	2	3,475
Colombia	3	3,166
Myanmar (Burma)	4	2,614
Mexico	5	2,297
Ecuador	6	1,313
Nigeria	7	1,158
Cote d'Ivoire	8	1,120
Peru	9	1,042
Malaysia	10	985

UPPER MIDDLE

Country	Rank	
Paraguay	11	734
Zaire	12	703
Vietnam	13	668
Thailand	14	610
Madagascar	15	579
Philippines	19	552
Venezuela	17	483
Nicaragua	18	467
Cameroon	19	386
Laos	20	386
Guatemala	21	347
Honduras	22	347
Bolivia	23	336
Nepal	24	324
Sri Lanka	25	225
India	26	185
Costa Rica	27	182
Liberia	28	178
Angola	29	170
Zambia	30	154
Guinea	31	139
Panama	32	139
Cambodia	33	97
Congo	34	85
Ghana	35	85

Deforestation (sq mi per year)

Country	Rank	LOWER MIDDLE
Papua New Guinea	36	85
Kenya	37	73
Guinea-Bissau	38	66
Gabon	39	58
Mozambique	40	39
Tanzania	41	39
Uganda	42	39
Bangladesh	43	31
Ethiopia	44	31
Pakistan	45	27
Sierra Leone	46	23
Central African Republic	47	19
El Salvador	48	19
Dominican Republic	49	15
Sudan	50	15
Somalia	51	14
Burkina	52	12
Equatorial Guinea	53	12
Rwanda	54	12
Suriname	55	12
Niger	56	10
Cuba	57	8
Gambia	58	8
Guyana	59	8
Haiti	60	8

BOTTOM 10

Country	Rank	
Jamaica	61	8
Togo	62	8
Fiji	63	7
Benin	64	5
Bhutan	65	4
Burundi	66	3
Mauritania	67	3
Solomon Islands	68	3
Trinidad and Tobago	69	3
Comoros	70	2

Deforestation (sq mi per year)

Source: *World Resources*

173. PROTECTED AREAS

Protected areas are those established under national or international auspices for the protection of biospecies, endangered animals, natural vegetation and plants, and rare geographic or geologic phenomena, including conservancies, national parks and sanctuaries for wildlife. To promote the establishment of such areas in the developing world, international organizations and Western donor countries have an incentive program under which certain types of debt are forgiven in return. Most states prohibit commercial exploitation of protected areas and the willful destruction of their animal and plant life.

Rank	Country	Protected Areas (sq mi)	Rank	Country	Protected Areas (sq mi)	Rank	Country	Protected Areas (sq mi)
TOP 10			41	Cameroon	6,572	82	Turkey	950
1	United States	305,172	42	Niger	6,387	83	Israel	911
2	Pakistan	297,279	43	Austria	6,154	84	Myanmar (Burma)	668
3	Australia	140,854	44	Mauritania	5,726	85	Libya	598
4	Canada	130,831	45	Congo	5,224	86	Romania	588
5	Brazil	77,591	46	Uganda	5,143	87	Netherlands	583
6	Indonesia	54,313	47	Panama	5,063	88	Afghanistan	550
7	India	50,851	48	Italy	4,890	89	Liberia	505
8	Chile	46,266	49	Ghana	4,537	90	Bulgaria	499
9	Tanzania	45,996	50	Paraguay	4,326	91	Switzerland	467
10	Argentina	42,374				92	Chad	440
			LOWER MIDDLE			93	Sierra Leone	389
UPPER MIDDLE			51	Malaysia	4,252	94	Guatemala	383
11	Ecuador	41,001	52	Malawi	4,119	95	Bangladesh	374
12	Botswana	38,707	53	Madagascar	3,982	96	Jordan	359
13	Zaire	34,081	54	Cuba	3,946	97	Belgium	324
14	Venezuela	33,277	55	Nigeria	3,707	98	Luxembourg	251
15	Sudan	31,334	56	Nepal	3,701	99	Korea, North	224
16	China	30,516	57	Angola	3,435	100	Albania	210
17	Ethiopia	26,535	58	Mali	3,383	101	Oman	208
18	Zambia	24,552	59	Bhutan	3,382	102	Tunisia	173
19	South Africa	22,401	60	Vietnam	3,314	103	Nicaragua	167
20	Colombia	21,676	61	Benin	3,257	104	Swaziland	153
21	Mexico	21,556	62	Saudi Arabia	3,118	105	Uruguay	117
22	Peru	21,170	63	Finland	3,114	106	United Kingdom	99
23	Bolivia	18,676	64	Iceland	3,047	107	Ireland	93
24	Norway	18,385	65	Portugal	2,893	108	El Salvador	86
25	Thailand	18,057	66	Sri Lanka	2,856	109	Trinidad and Tobago	62
26	France	17,378	67	Burkina	2,853	110	Guinea	50
27	Central African Republic	15,073	68	Suriname	2,837			
28	Iran	14,001	69	Egypt	2,546	**BOTTOM 10**		
29	Kenya	11,950	70	Costa Rica	2,354	111	Guyana	45
30	New Zealand	10,919	71	Honduras	2,241	112	Djibouti	39
31	Germany	10,915	72	Korea, South	2,154	113	Haiti	30
32	Zimbabwe	10,657	73	Dominican Republic	2,125	114	Cyprus	29
33	Spain	9,889	74	Philippines	2,011	115	Papua New Guinea	28
34	Japan	9,269	75	Hungary	1,974	116	Lesotho	26
35	Poland	8,467	76	Algeria	1,918	117	Fiji	21
36	Senegal	8,406	77	Togo	1,788	118	Lebanon	14
37	Czech Republic	7,668	78	Mongolia	1,227	119	Mauritius	14
38	Cote d'Ivoire	7,560	79	Morocco	1,152	120	Singapore	10
39	Gabon	6,768	80	Denmark	1,089			
40	Sweden	6,590	81	Rwanda	1,012			

Source: *World Resources*

174. GREENHOUSE EMISSIONS PER CAPITA

Greenhouse gas emission is the principal culprit in the global warming phenomenon which contributes to a warming of the surface and lower atmosphere. The principal greenhouse gases are carbon dioxide, methane, nitrous oxide, chlorofluorocarbons and ozone and other trace gases. Of these, carbon dioxide alone contributes 54% to global warming.

Rank	Country	Greenhouse Gas Emissions per Capita (tons)
TOP 10		
1	Laos	49.6
2	Bahrain	23.5
3	Cote d'Ivoire	23.1
4	United States	21.0
5	Australia	18.9
6	Canada	18.8
7	Trinidad and Tobago	17.2
8	Singapore	16.8
9	Kuwait	16.7
10	Germany	14.7
UPPER MIDDLE		
11	Ecuador	14.1
12	Myanmar (Burma)	13.9
13	Nicaragua	13.8
14	Denmark	13.5
15	Paraguay	13.0
16	Liberia	13.0
17	Czech Republic	12.9
18	United Kingdom	12.7
19	New Zealand	12.7
20	Malaysia	12.7
21	Ireland	12.1
22	Belgium	12.0
23	Gabon	11.9
24	Brazil	11.9
25	Bulgaria	11.8
26	Finland	11.7
27	Saudi Arabia	11.5
28	Netherlands	11.5
29	Poland	11.3
30	Colombia	11.3
31	Norway	10.7
32	Greece	9.8
33	Switzerland	9.5
34	Italy	9.5
35	Madagascar	9.4
36	Iceland	9.4
37	Israel	9.2
38	France	9.2
39	Austria	9.2
40	Japan	9.1
41	Spain	8.5
42	Romania	8.5
43	Venezuela	8.3

Rank	Country	Greenhouse Gas Emissions per Capita (tons)
44	South Africa	8.3
45	Panama	8.3
46	Costa Rica	8.1
47	Sweden	7.4
48	Honduras	7.4
49	Portugal	7.1
50	Hungary	6.9
51	Peru	6.7
52	Libya	6.6
53	Thailand	6.5
54	Oman	6.3
55	Congo	6.3
LOWER MIDDLE		
56	Mexico	5.9
57	Zaire	5.8
58	Yugoslavia	5.7
59	Malawi	5.7
60	Suriname	5.4
61	Bolivia	5.4
62	Mongolia	5.1
63	Guinea	5.1
64	Cyprus	5.1
65	Indonesia	4.9
66	Argentina	4.9
67	Cameroon	4.6
68	Korea, South	4.5
69	Barbados	4.3
70	Guatemala	4.2
71	Sudan	4.0
72	Central African Republic	3.9
73	Botswana	3.9
74	Zimbabwe	3.5
75	Iran	3.5
76	Cuba	3.5
77	Angola	3.5
78	Philippines	3.4
79	Zambia	3.3
80	Nigeria	3.2
81	Iraq	3.2
82	Algeria	2.9
83	Vietnam	2.8
84	Chad	2.8
85	Lebanon	2.6
86	Turkey	2.4
87	Somalia	2.4

Rank	Country	Greenhouse Gas Emissions per Capita (tons)
88	Jamaica	2.4
89	Ghana	2.4
90	Papua New Guinea	2.3
91	Nepal	2.3
92	Chile	2.3
93	Syria	2.2
94	Mauritania	2.2
95	China	2.2
96	Senegal	2.1
97	Tunisia	2.0
98	Guyana	2.0
99	Jordan	1.9
100	Cambodia	1.9
101	Benin	1.9
102	Egypt	1.8
103	Sri Lanka	1.7
104	Burkina	1.7
105	India	1.6
106	Dominican Republic	1.5
107	Sierra Leone	1.3
108	Mali	1.3
109	Fiji	1.3
110	Niger	1.2
111	El Salvador	1.2
112	Guinea-Bissau	1.1
113	Swaziland	0.9
114	Kenya	0.9
115	Ethiopia	0.9
116	Bangladesh	0.9
117	Yemen	0.8
118	Pakistan	0.8
119	Morocco	0.8
120	Uganda	0.7
BOTTOM 10		
121	Mauritius	0.7
122	Afghanistan	0.6
123	Solomon Islands	0.5
124	Gambia	0.5
125	Bhutan	0.5
126	Rwanda	0.4
127	Haiti	0.3
128	Burundi	0.3
129	Mozambique	0.2
130	Cape Verde	0.2

Source: *World Resources*

175. FOREST LAND

Throughout history, the percentage of land under forests has been declining, and this process has been hastened in the 20th century by the requirements of industrial civilization for forest and agricultural products. Nevertheless, as conservationists have been reminding us, the ecological value of forests makes it dangerous to reduce further the present area under them. The debate on the building of the Trans-Amazonian Highway through the forests of Brazil illustrates the worldwide concern over the deforestation of the earth in the name of economic development.

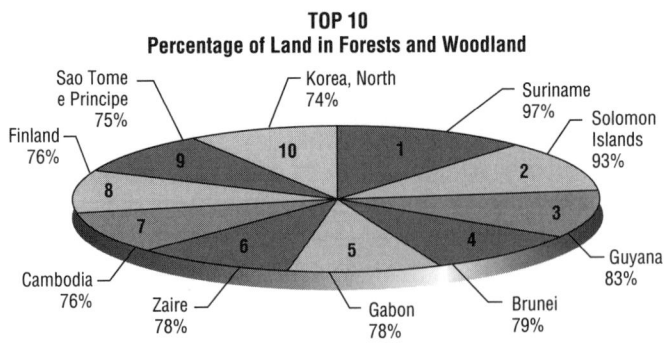

TOP 10
Percentage of Land in Forests and Woodland

Rank	Country	Land in Forests and Woodland (%)
UPPER MIDDLE		
11	Papua New Guinea	71
12	Bhutan	70
13	Brazil	67
14	Indonesia	67
15	Japan	67
16	Korea, South	67
17	Fiji	65
18	Central African Republic	64
19	Sweden	64
20	Malaysia	63
21	Congo	62
22	Zimbabwe	62
23	Laos	58
24	Peru	55
25	Taiwan	55
26	Cameroon	54
27	Panama	54
28	Bolivia	52
29	Ecuador	51
30	Equatorial Guinea	51
31	Malawi	50
32	Colombia	49
33	Myanmar (Burma)	49
34	Tanzania	47
35	Western Samoa	47
36	Slovenia	45
37	Belize	44
38	Trinidad and Tobago	44
39	Angola	43
40	Guinea	42
41	Dominica	41
42	St. Vincent	41
43	Guatemala	40
44	Philippines	40
45	Portugal	40
46	Vietnam	40
47	Austria	39
48	Latvia	39
49	Liberia	39
50	Venezuela	39
51	Albania	38
52	Guinea-Bissau	38
53	New Zealand	38
54	Ghana	37
55	Sri Lanka	37
56	Bosnia & Herzegovina	36
57	Benin	35
58	Bulgaria	35
59	Canada	35
60	Nicaragua	35
61	Paraguay	35

Rank	Country	Land in Forests and Woodland (%)
62	Costa Rica	34
63	Honduras	34
64	Nepal	33
65	Bahamas	32
66	Estonia	31
67	Mauritius	31
68	Senegal	31
69	Spain	31
70	Germany	30
71	Macedonia	30
72	Thailand	30
73	Uganda	30
74	Sierra Leone	29
75	United States	29
LOWER MIDDLE		
76	Jamaica	28
77	Poland	28
78	Romania	28
79	Togo	28
80	France	27
81	Norway	27
82	Zambia	27
83	Burkina	26
84	Cote d'Ivoire	26
85	Madagascar	26
86	Switzerland	26
87	Turkey	26
88	Yugoslavia	25
89	Ethiopia	24
90	Mexico	24
91	India	23
92	Andorra	22
93	Argentina	22
94	Italy	22
95	Namibia	22
96	Chile	21
97	Luxembourg	21
98	Bermuda	20
99	Gambia	20
100	Greece	20
101	Mozambique	20
102	Puerto Rico	20
103	Sudan	20
104	Liechtenstein	19
105	Cyprus	18
106	Hungary	18
107	Seychelles	18
108	Cuba	17
109	St. Kitts and Nevis	17
110	Lithuania	16.3
111	Antigua and Barbuda	16

Rank	Country	Land in Forests and Woodland (%)
112	Bangladesh	16
113	Comoros	16
114	Croatia	15
115	Nigeria	15
116	Australia	14
117	China	14
118	Somalia	14
119	Dominican Republic	13
120	St. Lucia	13
121	Denmark	12
122	Morocco	12
123	Tonga	12
124	Chad	11
125	Iran	11
126	Saudi Arabia	11
127	Mongolia	10
128	Rwanda	10
129	Grenada	9
130	Netherlands	9
131	United Kingdom	9
132	Lebanon	8
133	Mali	7
134	Yemen	7
135	El Salvador	6
136	Israel	6
137	Swaziland	6
138	Eritrea	5
139	Ireland	5
140	Mauritania	5
141	Singapore	5
142	Haiti	4
143	Kazakhstan	4
144	Kenya	4
145	Pakistan	4
146	Tunisia	4
147	Uruguay	4
148	Afghanistan	3
149	Iraq	3
150	Kiribati	3
BOTTOM 10		
151	Maldives	3
152	South Africa	3
153	Syria	3
154	Algeria	2
155	Botswana	2
156	Burundi	2
157	Niger	2
158	Iceland	1
159	Vanuatu	1
160	Jordan	0.5

Source: *Human Development Report*

176. POPULATION SERVED BY WASTEWATER TREATMENT PLANTS

It has been said that one cannot breathe the air in the developed world and one cannot drink the water in the developing world. Lacking capital to build filtration plants, most urban residents in developing countries are forced to drink polluted water containing disease-causing organisms. As a result, the governments in these countries are forced to spend on healthcare what they "save" by not building filtration plants.

Rank	Country	Population Served by Wastewater Treatment Plants 1990 (%)	Rank	Country	Population Served by Wastewater Treatment Plants 1990 (%)	Rank	Country	Population Served by Wastewater Treatment Plants 1990 (%)
TOP 10			10	United States	74	18	Japan	42
1	Denmark	98	11	Austria	72	19	Slovakia	42
2	Sweden	95	12	Canada	70	20	Poland	34
3	Netherlands	93	13	France	68	21	Hungary	31
4	Luxembourg	90	14	Italy	61	22	Belgium	23
5	Switzerland	90	15	Norway	57	23	Portugal	21
6	New Zealand	88	16	Spain	53	24	Ireland	11
7	United Kingdom	87				25	Greece	10
8	Germany	86	**BOTTOM 10**			26	Iceland	6
9	Finland	76	17	Czech Republic	51			

Source: Worldwatch Institute

177. WASTE RECYCLING OF PAPER AND PAPERBOARD

Despite forecasts of a paperless society, the use of paper has been mushrooming in developed countries. Environmental activists have used paper and paperboard recycling as one of the main items in their agenda to save trees and forests. They have achieved remarkable success. It is expected that within the next 10 years about 50% of all paper and paperboard will be recycled.

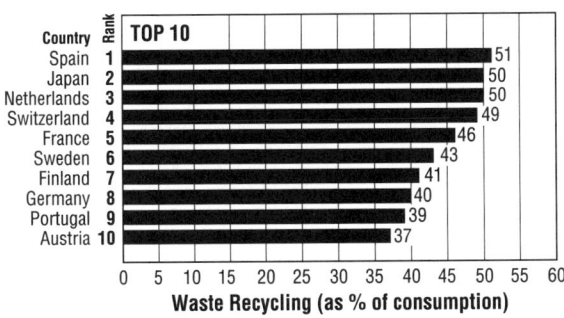

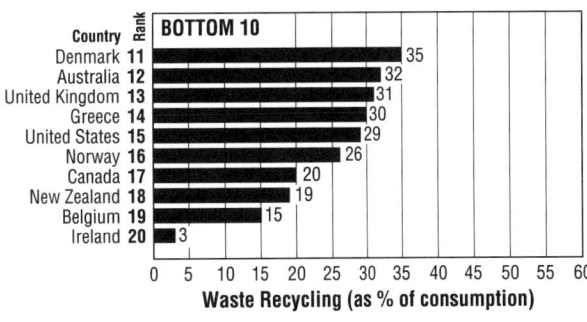

Source: Worldwatch Institute

178. HAZARDOUS WASTE PRODUCTION

Hazardous waste production occurs almost entirely in developed countries, where they are a byproduct of the chemical and weapons industries. The disposal of such hazardous wastes is a problem for which no clear and permanent solution has been found. In some cases they are buried undergroud or under the ocean floor, but these sites have a potential for leaks at a later time. The United States is believed to produce about 25% of all hazardous wastes in the world.

Rank	Country	Hazardous Waste Production 1990 (1,000 metric tons)
TOP 10		
1	United States	18,000
2	Czech Republic	8,317
3	Canada	6,080
4	Germany	6,000
5	Hungary	4,000
6	France	3,958
7	Italy	3,246
8	Slovakia	2,704

Rank	Country	Hazardous Waste Production 1990 (1,000 metric tons)
9	United Kingdom	2,540
10	Spain	1,708
11	Portugal	1,043
12	Netherlands	1,040
BOTTOM 10		
13	Austria	616
14	Switzerland	520
15	Sweden	500

Rank	Country	Hazardous Waste Production 1990 (1,000 metric tons)
16	Greece	450
17	Finland	314
18	Norway	200
19	New Zealand	110
20	Denmark	106
21	Poland	64
22	Iceland	5

Source: *Human Development Report*

179. POPULATION SERVED BY MUNICIPAL WASTE SERVICES

Municipal functions vary from country to country as do the income and powers of municipalities. In the majority of developing countries, waste services do not exist and households devise their own means of dealing with waste. Generally, in such countries, waste is dumped on public property and in rivers, where they accumulate and pose serious health hazards.

Rank	Country	Population Served by Municipal Waste Services 1990 (%)
TOP 10		
1	Belgium	100
2	Canada	100
3	Greece	100
4	Japan	100
5	Luxembourg	100
6	Sweden	100
7	United Kingdom	100
8	United States	100

Rank	Country	Population Served by Municipal Waste Services 1990 (%)
9	Austria	99
10	France	99
11	Netherlands	99
12	Switzerland	98
13	Germany	96
BOTTOM 10		
14	New Zealand	91
15	Spain	90

Rank	Country	Population Served by Municipal Waste Services 1990 (%)
16	Portugal	88
17	Norway	85
18	Ireland	77
19	Finland	75
20	Czech Republic	70
21	Hungary	63
22	Poland	55
23	Slovakia	55

Source: *Human Development Report*

180. NUCLEAR WASTES FROM SPENT FUEL

Certain nuclear wastes present hazards to human life for several millennia to come. Therefore their disposal is one of the principal worries of the nuclear powers, of whom the United States and Russia are the largest. In the United States, the Superfund has been estab-lished to meet the enormous costs involved in both the transport of nuclear wastes from nuclear plants to the disposal sites and their burial in containers designed to withstand radiation and prevent leakage. There is no comparable program in Russia.

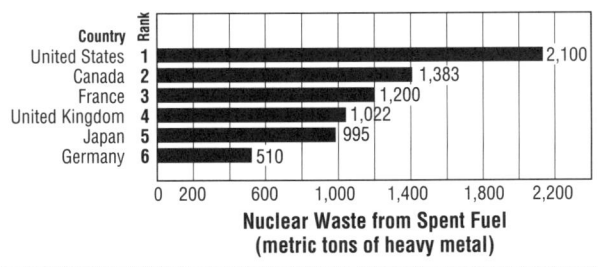

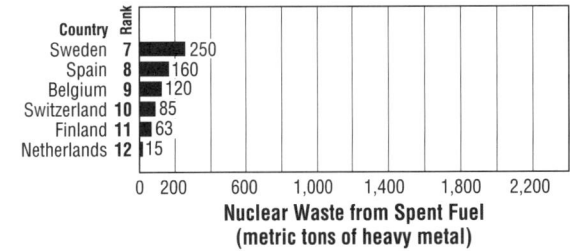

Source: Worldwatch Institute

181. ANNUAL FRESHWATER WITHDRAWALS

Freshwater withdrawals represent human, agricul-tural and industrial consumption of water. In most cases, agricultural industrial consumption levels are high in countries where, ironically, water is in short supply. Thus, desert or near desert regions like Iraq and Sudan have high water withdrawal rates.

Rank	Country	Annual Fresh Water Withdrawals per Capita 1980–89 (m³)
TOP 10		
1	Guyana	7,564
2	Iraq	4,575
3	Pakistan	2,053
4	United States	1,952
5	Afghanistan	1,706
6	Canada	1,684
7	Madagascar	1,642
8	Chile	1,623
9	Bulgaria	1,600
10	Iran	1,362
UPPER MIDDLE		
11	Australia	1,280
12	Germany	1,274
13	Egypt	1,213
14	Spain	1,184
15	Suriname	1,155
16	Romania	1,144
17	Sudan	1,092
18	Portugal	1,075
19	Argentina	1,042
20	Netherlands	993
21	Italy	984
22	Belgium	917
23	Mexico	875

Rank	Country	Annual Fresh Water Withdrawals per Capita 1980–89 (m³)
24	Cuba	870
25	Cyprus	812
26	France	783
27	Costa Rica	780
28	Malaysia	768
29	Panama	744
30	Bahrain	735
31	Japan	733
32	Greece	720
33	Philippines	693
34	Libya	692
35	Korea, South	687
36	India	612
37	Finland	605
38	Thailand	600
39	New Zealand	585
40	Ecuador	567
41	Oman	561
42	Honduras	510
43	Sri Lanka	503
44	Hungary	502
45	Morocco	499
46	Mauritania	494
47	Norway	490
48	Poland	472
49	China	462

Rank	Country	Annual Fresh Water Withdrawals per Capita 1980–89 (m³)
50	Dominican Republic	443
51	Israel	441
52	Syria	434
53	Turkey	434
54	United Arab Emirates	414
55	Mauritius	410
56	South Africa	410
57	Swaziland	408
58	Venezuela	387
59	Czech Republic	379
60	Nicaragua	370
61	Iceland	366
62	Sweden	356
63	Saudi Arabia	321
64	Tunisia	317
65	Peru	301
LOWER MIDDLE		
66	Korea, North	299
67	Austria	279
68	Mongolia	273
69	Lebanon	271
70	Laos	260
71	United Kingdom	253
72	Brazil	248
73	El Salvador	245

Rank	Country	Annual Fresh Water Withdrawals per Capita 1980–89 (m^3)
74	Uruguay	241
75	Ireland	235
76	Qatar	234
77	Denmark	228
78	Bangladesh	211
79	Senegal	202
80	Bolivia	184
81	Jordan	173
82	Colombia	172
83	Switzerland	170
84	Mali	162
85	Algeria	160
86	Jamaica	159
87	Luxembourg	159
88	Nepal	151
89	Trinidad and Tobago	148
90	Cape Verde	147
91	Guinea	140
92	Guatemala	139
93	Zimbabwe	138
94	Somalia	119
95	Barbados	117
96	Paraguay	110
97	Saint Vincent	108
98	Belize	104
99	Myanmar (Burma)	101
100	Botswana	100

Rank	Country	Annual Fresh Water Withdrawals per Capita 1980–89 (m^3)
101	Sierra Leone	96
102	Indonesia	95
103	Albania	94
104	Saint Lucia	89
105	Zambia	86
106	Namibia	84
107	Singapore	84
108	Vietnam	81
109	Cambodia	68
110	Cote d'Ivoire	66
111	Malta	66
111	Gabon	57
113	Liberia	56
114	Mozambique	53
115	Angola	52
116	Kenya	50
117	Ethiopia	49
118	Fiji	41
119	Niger	41
120	Cameroon	37
121	Nigeria	37
122	Tanzania	36
123	Ghana	35
124	Chad	34
125	Lesotho	31
126	Djibouti	29
127	Gambia	29

Rank	Country	Annual Fresh Water Withdrawals per Capita 1980–89 (m^3)
128	Papua New Guinea	28
129	Togo	28
130	Benin	26
131	Central African Republic	25
132	Rwanda	23
133	Zaire	22
134	Burundi	20
135	Malawi	20
136	Uganda	20
137	Congo	19
138	Burkina	18
139	Solomon Islands	18
140	Grenada	16
BOTTOM 10		
141	Equatorial Guinea	15
142	Seychelles	15
143	Bhutan	14
144	Comoros	14
145	Dominica	14
146	Brunei	13
147	Guinea-Bissau	11
148	Kuwait	11
149	Sao Tome e Principe	10
150	Haiti	7

Source: *World Resources*

182. INTERNAL RENEWABLE WATER RESOURCES

Internal renewable water resources consist of rivers, lakes, aquifers, wells and other features all dependent on rain for their supply. Since rainfall is variable, these resources tend to vary as well between regions and between seasons.

Rank	Country	Internal Renewable Water Resources per Capita 1992 (1,000 m^3 per year)
TOP 10		
1	Iceland	653.9
2	Suriname	456.6
3	Guyana	298.3
4	Papua New Guinea	197.5
5	Gabon	132.6
6	Solomon Islands	130.7
7	New Zealand	114.9
8	Canada	106.0
9	Norway	94.5
10	Liberia	84.3
UPPER MIDDLE		
11	Equatorial Guinea	81.3
12	Belize	80.8
13	Congo	76.4
14	Laos	60.4
15	Bhutan	58.9
16	Panama	57.3
17	Central African Republic	44.4
18	Nicaragua	44.3
19	Venezuela	42.4
20	Bolivia	39.9
21	Fiji	38.6
22	Guinea	37.0
23	Sierra Leone	36.6
24	Chile	34.4
25	Brazil	33.7

Rank	Country	Internal Renewable Water Resources per Capita 1992 (1,000 m^3 per year)
26	Colombia	32.0
27	Guinea-Bissau	30.8
28	Costa Rica	29.8
29	Ecuador	28.4
30	Russia	27.1
31	Zaire	25.6
32	Myanmar (Burma)	24.8
33	Malaysia	24.3
34	Finland	22.0
35	Argentina	21.0
36	Paraguay	20.8
37	Sweden	20.3
38	Australia	19.5
39	Uruguay	18.9
40	Cameroon	17.0
41	Angola	16.0
42	Ireland	14.3
43	Indonesia	13.2
44	Guatemala	11.9
45	Honduras	11.6
46	Bangladesh	11.4
47	Zambia	11.1
48	Kyrgyzstan	10.8
49	Mongolia	10.7
50	Cambodia	10.0
51	Georgia	9.8
52	United States	9.7
53	Swaziland	8.8

Rank	Country	Internal Renewable Water Resources per Capita 1992 (1,000 m^3 per year)
54	Tajikistan	8.5
55	Nepal	8.3
56	Austria	7.2
57	Estonia	6.9
58	Chad	6.6
59	Mali	6.3
60	Switzerland	6.2
61	Namibia	5.9
62	Cote d'Ivoire	5.7
63	Latvia	5.7
64	Vietnam	5.4
65	Benin	5.3
LOWER MIDDLE		
66	Philippines	5.0
67	Greece	4.4
68	Japan	4.4
69	Kazakhstan	4.1
70	Mexico	4.1
71	Trinidad and Tobago	4.0
72	Mozambique	3.9
73	El Salvador	3.5
74	Portugal	3.5
75	Uganda	3.5
76	Jamaica	3.4
77	Lithuania	3.4
78	Belarus	3.3
79	Gambia	3.3

Rank	Country	Internal Renewable Water Resources per Capita 1992 (1,000 m³ per year)	Rank	Country	Internal Renewable Water Resources per Capita 1992 (1,000 m³ per year)	Rank	Country	Internal Renewable Water Resources per Capita 1992 (1,000 m³ per year)
80	Ghana	3.3	105	United Kingdom	2.1	130	Rwanda	0.8
81	Cuba	3.2	106	Bulgaria	2.0	131	Algeria	0.7
82	Turkey	3.2	107	Mauritius	2.0	132	Netherlands	0.7
83	Italy	3.1	108	Thailand	2.0	133	Burundi	0.6
84	Madagascar	3.1	109	Iran	1.9	134	Djibouti	0.6
85	Togo	3.1	110	Armenia	1.8	135	Hungary	0.6
86	Albania	3.0	111	Iraq	1.8	136	Kenya	0.6
87	France	3.0	111	Peru	1.8	137	Syria	0.6
88	Korea, South	3.0	113	Lebanon	1.7	138	Tunisia	0.5
89	Senegal	3.0	114	Niger	1.7	139	Uzbekistan	0.4
90	Burkina	2.9	115	Haiti	1.6	140	Israel	0.3
91	Spain	2.8	116	Romania	1.6		**BOTTOM 10**	
92	Dominican Republic	2.7	117	Korea, North	1.5	141	Moldova	0.3
93	Luxembourg	2.7	118	Poland	1.3	142	Turkmenistan	0.3
94	Tanzania	2.7	119	Somalia	1.3	143	Jordan	0.2
95	Afghanistan	2.6	120	South Africa	1.3	144	Mauritania	0.2
96	Sri Lanka	2.5	121	Germany	1.2	145	Singapore	0.2
97	China	2.4	122	Oman	1.2	146	United Arab Emirates	0.2
98	Pakistan	2.4	123	Azerbaijan	1.1	147	Yemen	0.2
99	Nigeria	2.3	124	Morocco	1.1	148	Egypt	0.1
100	Lesotho	2.2	125	Sudan	1.1	149	Libya	0.1
101	Zimbabwe	2.2	126	Ukraine	1.0	150	Saudi Arabia	0.1
102	Denmark	2.1	127	Malawi	0.9			
103	Ethiopia	2.1	128	Belgium	0.8			
104	India	2.1	129	Botswana	0.8			

Source: *World Resources*

183. SULFUR AND NITROGEN EMISSIONS

Sulfur and nitrogen emissions affect environmental quality, pollute air, and make humans and animals more susceptible to illnesses. The rankings show that this is a serious problem only in developed countries and is related to the levels of industrialization.

Rank	Country	Sulfur and Nitrogen Emissions 1990 (1,000 metric tons of SO_2 and NO_2)	Rank	Country	Sulfur and Nitrogen Emissions 1990 (1,000 metric tons of SO_2 and NO_2)	Rank	Country	Sulfur and Nitrogen Emissions 1990 (1,000 metric tons of SO_2 and NO_2)
	TOP 10		10	Japan	2,177	18	Denmark	464
1	United States	40,440	11	Hungary	1,248	19	Portugal	353
2	Germany	8,931	12	Belarus	855	20	Ireland	315
3	United Kingdom	6,559	13	Netherlands	760	21	Austria	312
4	Canada	5,249	14	Belgium	720	22	Norway	284
5	Poland	4,496	15	Greece	650	23	Switzerland	247
6	Italy	4,402				24	Iceland	36
7	Ukraine	3,879		**BOTTOM 10**		25	Luxembourg	25
8	France	2,687	16	Finland	540			
9	Spain	2,190	17	Sweden	524			

Source: Worldwatch Institute

184. CARBON MONOXIDE EMISSIONS

Carbon monoxide is one of the principal air pollutants in urban areas. In the ranking this pollutant gas is weighted according to its heat-trapping quality and is expressed in metric tons of carbon per capita.

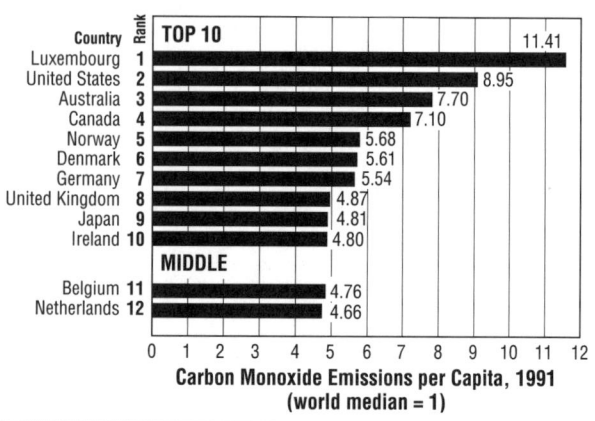

Carbon Monoxide Emissions per Capita, 1991
(world median = 1)

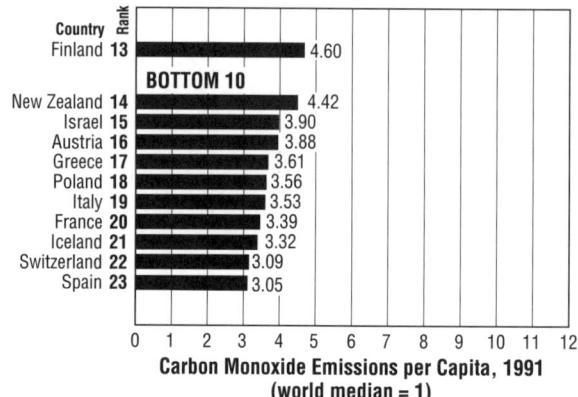

Carbon Monoxide Emissions per Capita, 1991
(world median = 1)

Source: *World Resources*

185. SPACE OBJECTS IN ORBIT

The pollution and clutter on earth has its counterpart in space, which is increasingly littered with space satellites and their debris. Some of the debris eventually fall to the earth and pose hazards to buildings and humans.

Rank	Country	Space Objects	Rank	Country	Space Objects	Rank	Country	Space Objects
TOP 10			**MIDDLE**			19	Mexico	2
1	Russia	3,291	11	Germany	12	20	Saudi Arabia	2
2	United States	3,219	12	India	9	21	Sweden	2
3	European Space Agency	161	13	North Atlantic Treaty Organization	9	22	Argentina	1
4	Japan	94	14	Indonesia	5	23	Czech Republic	1
5	China	90	15	Australia	4	24	Spain	1
6	International Telecommunications					25	Israel	
7	Satellite Organization	42	**BOTTOM 10**					
8	France	32	16	Brazil	3			
9	United Kingdom	19	17	Italy	2			
10	Canada	16	18	Luxembourg	2			

Source: National Aeronautics and Space Administration. Project Operations Branch, Code 513. Goddard Space Flight Center (Greenbelt, MD). *Satellite Situation Report* 31, no. 4 (31 December 1991), p. iii.

186. CARBON EMISSIONS

Carbon emissions from fossil fuel burning are among the main culprits of global warming and the depletion of the ozone layer. The ranking follows roughly auto ownership levels, but the relationship between the two is also affected by technological innovations. Catalytic converters have helped to reduce carbon emission, even as automobile driving has expanded in many of the industrialized countries.

Rank	Country	Total Emissions (000 tons)	Emissions Per Person (tons)	Emissions Per Dollar GNP[1] (tons per 000 $)	Emissions Growth 1990–94 (%)
1	United States	1,371	5.26	210	4.4
2	China	835	0.71	330	13.0
3	Russia	455	3.08	590	−24.1
4	Japan	299	2.39	110	0.1
5	Germany	234	2.89	140	−9.9
6	India	222	0.24	160	23.5
7	United Kingdom	153	2.62	150	−0.3
8	Ukraine	125	2.43	600	−43.5
9	Canada	116	3.97	200	5.3
10	Italy	104	1.81	110	0.8
11	France	90	1.56	80	−3.2
12	Poland	89	2.31	460	−4.5
13	South Korea	88	1.98	200	43.7
14	Mexico	88	0.96	140	7.1
15	South Africa	85	2.07	680	9.1
16	Kazakstan	81	4.71	1,250	n.a.
17	Australia	75	4.19	230	4.2
18	North Korea	67	2.90	960	n.a.
19	Iran	62	1.09	270	n.a.
20	Brazil	60	0.39	70	15.8

Sources: G. Marland, R.J. Andres, and T.A. Boden, "Global, Regional, and National CO_2 Emission Estimates From Fossil Fuel Burning, Cement Production, and Gas Flaring: 1950–1992" (electronic database) (Oak Ridge, Tenn.: Carbon Dioxide Information Analysis Center, Oak Ridge National Laboratory, 1995); Worldwatch estimates based on *ibid.*, and on British Petroleum, *BP Statistical Review of World Energy* (London: Group Media & Publications, 1995); Population Reference Bureau, 1994 World Population Data Sheet (Washington, D.C.: 1994); World Bank, *The World Bank Atlas 1995* (Washington, D.C.: 1995).

187. DOMESTIC WATER SHORTAGE

Disputes between nations about water are among the oldest causes for war. Because of the quirks of geography, many nations are dependent for their water on rivers originating outside their borders. Thus Egypt is dependent on the Nile, Hungary and Bulgaria on the Danube and Bangladesh on the Ganges and the Brahmaputra, all of which may be blocked at the source or near the source by modern dams. In a world where water is scarce, disputes about transnational water sources may become more frequent.

Rank	Country	Share of Total Flow Originating Outside of Border (%)	Rank	Country	Share of Total Flow Originating Outside of Border (%)	Rank	Country	Share of Total Flow Originating Outside of Border (%)
1	Turkmenistan	98	8	Netherlands	89	15	Bangladesh	42
2	Egypt	97	9	Gambia	86	16	Thailand	39
3	Hungary	95	10	Cambodia	82	17	Jordan	36
4	Mauritania	95	11	Syria	79	18	Senegal	34
5	Botswana	94	12	Sudan	77	19	Israel[1]	
6	Bulgaria	91	13	Niger	68			
7	Uzbekistan	91	14	Iraq	66			

[1]Includes only flows originating outside current borders; a significant additional share of Israel's fresh water originates from occupied, disputed territories.
Sources: Turkmenistan and Uzbekistan figures from David R. Smith, *"Climate Change, Water Supply, and Conflict in the Aral Sea Basin,"* presented at the PriAral Workshop 1994, San Diego State University, March 1994; others from Peter H. Gleick, *Water in Crisis: A Guide to the World's Fresh Water Resources* (New York: Oxford University Press, 1993).

188. ENDANGERED SPECIES

All life is fragile. The fragility affects not only individuals but also groups and species. Because of the incredible biodiversity of life, it is difficult to realize that hundreds, and possibly thousands, of species are dying out every year. Generally the weakest species are the first to die out, and it is possible that humans, being the strongest of them all, may survive just a little longer. But the habitat is getting crowded, more polluted and the ecological web is being cut at many points. Nothing brings out this tragic phenomenon as clearly as the list of endangered species prepared by the World Conservation Union. More alarming is the fact that this list has grown steadily ever since it was first created.

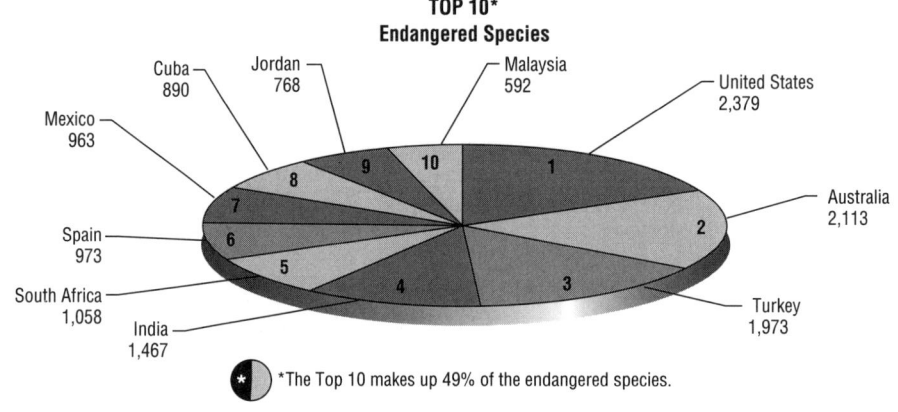

TOP 10*
Endangered Species

Cuba 890 — Jordan 768 — Malaysia 592 — United States 2,379
Mexico 963
Australia 2,113
Spain 973
South Africa 1,058
India 1,467
Turkey 1,973

*The Top 10 makes up 49% of the endangered species.

Rank	Country	Endangered Species	Rank	Country	Endangered Species	Rank	Country	Endangered Species
UPPER MIDDLE			49	Puerto Rico	96	86	Bhutan	41
11	Panama	578	50	Albania	93	87	Austria	40
12	Greece	552	51	Guyana	92	88	Uganda	40
13	China	481	52	Seychelles	90	89	Hungary	39
14	Peru	471	53	Bangladesh	89	90	Chad	38
15	Costa Rica	445	54	Bolivia	88	91	Mali	37
16	Colombia	431	55	Romania	88	92	Namibia	37
17	Vietnam	409	56	Suriname	86	93	Fiji	36
18	Brazil	392	57	Nicaragua	85	94	Poland	36
19	Ecuador	349	58	Ethiopia	84	95	Switzerland	36
20	Iran	340	59	Nepal	84	96	El Salvador	35
21	Chile	311	60	Libya	80	97	Sudan	35
22	Guatemala	306	61	Malawi	79	98	Sierra Leone	34
23	Mauritius	288	62	Japan	78	99	Bahamas	33
24	Madagascar	282	63	Somalia	77	100	Zambia	33
25	Indonesia	267	64	Myanmar (Burma)	75	101	Afghanistan	32
26	Portugal	265	65	Paraguay	67	102	Uruguay	32
27	New Zealand	263	66	Dominica	65	103	Liberia	31
28	Italy	241	67	Honduras	64	104	Swaziland	31
29	Argentina	240	68	Zaire	63	105	Syria	31
30	Sri Lanka	238	69	Brunei	62	106	Korea, North	30
31	Morocco	217	70	Cyprus	62	107	Equatorial Guinea	29
32	Tanzania	217	71	Guinea	61	108	Singapore	29
33	Philippines	216	72	Korea, South	61	109	Israel	28
34	Yugoslavia	213	73	Dominican Republic	60	110	Iraq	27
35	Kenya	181	74	Pakistan	60	111	Finland	26
36	France	173	75	Ghana	57	112	Jamaica	26
37	Algeria	172	76	Solomon Islands	53	113	Lebanon	25
38	Venezuela	162	77	Belize	51	114	Sweden	25
39	Yemen	149				115	Belgium	24
40	Thailand	137	**LOWER MIDDLE**			116	Denmark	24
41	Cameroon	121	78	Cambodia	51	117	Norway	24
42	Papua New Guinea	119	79	Senegal	50	118	Canada	23
43	Egypt	118	80	Czech Republic	49	119	Mauritania	23
44	Zimbabwe	112	81	Laos	49	120	Saudi Arabia	23
45	Bulgaria	107	82	United Kingdom	49	121	Haiti	22
46	Mozambique	106	83	Angola	47	122	Mongolia	22
47	Gabon	103	84	Tunisia	47	123	Netherlands	22
48	Cote d'Ivoire	99	85	Nigeria	46	124	Congo	21

Rank	Country	Endangered Species	Rank	Country	Endangered Species	Rank	Country	Endangered Species
125	Botswana	20	140	Djibouti	12	155	Barbados	3
126	Rwanda	20	141	Togo	12			
127	Germany	19	142	Comoros	11		**BOTTOM 10**	
128	Niger	18	143	United Arab Emirates	11	156	Liechtenstein	3
129	Benin	17	144	Burundi	10	157	Qatar	3
130	Malta	17	145	Luxembourg	10	158	St. Vincent	3
131	Central African Republic	16	146	Guinea-Bissau	9	159	Tonga	3
132	Gambia	16	147	Sao Tome e Principe	9	160	Kiribati	2
133	Lesotho	16	148	Trinidad and Tobago	9	161	Maldives	2
134	Oman	16	149	St. Lucia	8	162	Nauru	2
135	Ireland	14	150	Grenada	6	163	Andorra	1
136	Bermuda	13	151	Bahrain	5	164	St. Kitts and Nevis	1
137	Burkina	13	152	Cape Verde	5	165	Tuvalu	1
138	Kuwait	13	153	Iceland	5			
139	Vanuatu	13	154	Antigua and Barbuda	3			

Source: *World Resources*

Section
XVI

CONSUMPTION

Consumption is important in a consumer-oriented economy because consumption generates demand, and demand in turn governs supply. Unfortunately, few consumption statistics are published, although they are collected regularly by market research organizations for their own confidential use. The U.N. data that are available relate to what is called apparent consumption, which is based on a simple formula: production minus exports plus imports. It is logical to assume that the resulting figure represents actual consumption in a broad sense; however, in the case of perishables, it does not tell how much was wasted or, in the case of consumer durables, show much was held in stock. But this should not cause undue concern so long as the usual precautions are adopted.

189. GOLD

Currencies are no longer backed by gold, but gold remains in various other forms the most important precious metal for investors. It also is the most common metal used in ornaments. The latter use explains the high ranking of India in the table. Even in ancient times, India was known as the "Gold Sink" because Indian women use more gold ornaments then their peers in other countries.

Rank	Country	Gold Product Use (tons)	Rank	Country	Gold Product Use (tons)	Rank	Country	Gold Product Use (tons)
TOP 10			22	Singapore	37.3	45	Bangladesh	6.0
1	Italy	473.3				46	Libya	4.2
2	India	306.6	**LOWER MIDDLE**			47	Sri Lanka	4.0
3	United States	219.4	23	Pakistan[3]	35.0	48	Yugoslavia	4.0
4	Japan	190.3	24	Spain	32.1	49	Cyprus[5]	3.6
5	China	181.4	25	Austria	29.3	50	Bolivia	2.9
6	Taiwan	164.1	26	Mexico	26.7	51	Sweden	2.9
7	Saudi Arabia[1]	157.1	27	Canada	26.1	52	Czechoslovakia	2.7
8	Turkey	118.5	28	Syria	25.1	53	Colombia	2.6
9	Hong Kong	99.1	29	Morocco	25.0	54	Philippines	2.5
10	Malaysia	99.0	30	Australia	19.7	55	Belgium	2.4
			31	Israel	17.9	56	Argentina	2.2
UPPER MIDDLE			32	Kuwait	15.5			
11	Thailand	81.0	33	Vietnam	15.0	**BOTTOM 10**		
12	Germany	76.8	34	Jordan	14.2	57	Poland	2.2
13	South Korea	72.1	35	Portugal	11.4	58	Chile	2.0
14	Commonwealth of		36	Brazil	10.6	59	Ecuador	1.9
	Independent States	66.2	37	Lebanon	9.9	60	Venezuela	1.7
15	Indonesia	56.0	38	Greece	9.4	61	Denmark	1.0
16	Iran	51.8	39	Dominican Republic	8.4	62	Hungary	1.0
17	Egypt	50.9	40	Peru	8.2	63	Iraq	1.0
18	Gulf States[2]	48.0	41	Burma[4]	8.0	64	Nepal	1.0
19	Switzerland	44.5	42	Netherlands	8.0	65	Norway	0.9
20	France	43.3	43	South Africa	7.9	66	Tunisia	0.9
21	Great Britain	39.1	44	Algeria	6.5			

Source: "Asia's Gold Coast." *Asiaweek* (2 June 1993), P. 15. Primary sources: Gold Fields Mineral Services Ltd; *Asiaweek* Research. Notes: 1. Include Yemen. 2. Includes United Arab Emirates, Bahrain, Oman, and Qatar. 3. Includes Afghanistan 4. Includes Laos and Cambodia. 5. Includes Malta.

190. ALCOHOLIC LIQUORS

The consumption of alcoholic liquors is one of the oldest social traditions in the world. Interestingly, it is as prevalent in primitive as in civilized societies. As a stimulant of undoubted potency, it shares many characteristics with mood-altering drugs of later origin, such as the ability to produce temporary elation (hence the custom of a "happy hour" in bars), habit-uation and creation of dependence, withdrawal symptoms, and impairment of many motor and cognitive functions. Medically, the consumption of alcoholic beverages cannot be considered separately from alcoholism, the thin line between them being too blurred for definition.

Rank	Country	Alcohol Consumption per Capita 1991 (liters)	Rank	Country	Alcohol Consumption per Capita 1991 (liters)	Rank	Country	Alcohol Consumption per Capita 1991 (liters)
TOP 10			**MIDDLE**			**BOTTOM 10**		
1	Luxembourg	12.3	11	Greece	8.6	19	United Kingdom	7.4
2	France	11.9	12	Italy	8.4	20	Canada	7.1
3	Portugal	11.6	13	Netherlands	8.2	21	Poland	7.1
4	Germany	10.9	14	Bulgaria	7.8	22	United States	7.0
5	Switzerland	10.7	15	New Zealand	7.8	23	Romania	6.4
6	Hungary	10.5	16	Australia	7.7	24	Japan	6.3
7	Spain	10.4	17	Finland	7.4	25	Sweden	5.5
8	Austria	10.3	18	Ireland	7.4	26	Norway	4.1
9	Denmark	9.9				27	Iceland	3.9
10	Belgium	9.4				28	Israel	0.9

Source: World Drink Trends

191. MEAT

The consumption of meat is critical in any nutritional system because it is an incomparable source of protein. There is therefore a strong correlation between this ranking and the ranking by per capita protein consumption. (See Health rankings) Meat itself is a broad term that includes beef, mutton and lamb and pork but generally excludes poultry.

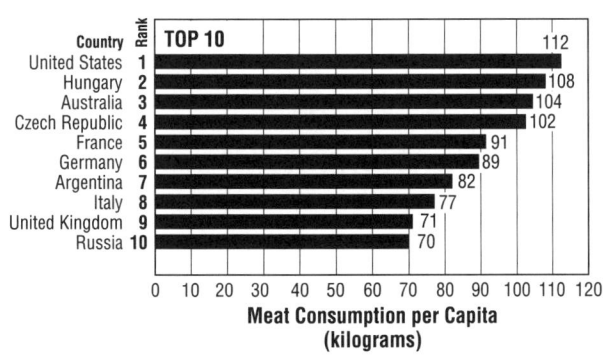

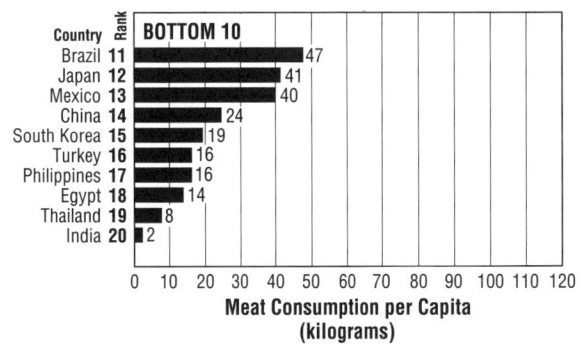

[1]Includes beef, pork, mutton, lamb, and poultry; based on carcass weights.
Sources: U.S. Department of Agriculture (USDA).

192. CHOCOLATE

Chocolate consumption is an index of affluence. Associated with commercialized holiday gift giving, it is also used in ice creams and cakes. Cocoa-producing economies, such as Ghana, are the principal beneficiaries of chocolate consumption.

Rank	Country	Chocolate Consumption (in pounds)
TOP 10		
1	Switzerland	21.7
2	Norway	17.3
3	Austria	17.1
4	Netherlands	16.9
5	United Kingdom	16.2
6	Belgium	15.8
7	Germany	12.9

Rank	Country	Chocolate Consumption (in pounds)
8	Ireland	12.5
9	Denmark	12.1
10	Sweden	11.8
BOTTOM		
11	Australia	11.2
12	France	10.3
13	United States	10.1

Rank	Country	Chocolate Consumption (in pounds)
14	Finland	7.1
15	Italy	4.1
16	Japan	3.7
17	Spain	3.3

Source: "Chocolate Consumption Is Sweet Success." *Restaurants & Institutions,* 1 December 1993, p. 46. Primary source: Chocolate Manufacturers Association.

193. BUTTER

Butter, along with other milk products, is one of the staples of diet in all countries of the world. Its sales have been slumping in recent years because of the association of butter with fat, making it taboo for dieters. India, United States and Germany have remained in the front rank of butter consumers for many decades.

Rank	Country	Quantity of Domestic Use (in metric tons)
TOP 10		
1	India	1,060,000
2	Germany	544,000
3	United States	495,000
4	France	470,000
5	Poland-Danzig	213,000
6	United Kingdom-Northern Ireland	163,000
7	Czech Republic	139,000
8	Japan	105,000
9	Italy	100,000
10	Netherlands	90,000

Rank	Country	Quantity of Domestic Use (in metric tons)
MIDDLE		
11	Canada	86,000
12	Belgium-Luxembourg	73,000
13	Brazil	71,000
14	New Zealand	55,000
15	Australia	52,000
16	Romania	51,000
17	Argentina	48,000
18	Sweden	43,000
19	Switzerland	42,000
20	Austria	39,000
21	Mexico	38,000
22	Finalnd	37,000
23	Egypt	34,000

Rank	Country	Quantity of Domestic Use (in metric tons)
BOTTOM 10		
24	Denmark	33,000
25	Spain	28,000
26	Hungary	21,000
27	Ireland	18,000
28	Norway	17,000
29	South Africa	15,000
30	Yugoslavia	14,000
31	Greece	12,000
32	Portugal	9,000
33	Venezuela	3,000

Source: *UN Statistical Yearbook*

194. CIGARETTES

Worldwide production of cigarettes reached an all-time high of 5.5 trillion in 1995 reversing some years of decline in the early 1990s. Production per capita, however, declined to 966 pieces, 63 below the peak in 1988. With 1.7 trillion pieces, China is now the world's largest producer. China is also the largest market, with more than 300 million smokers. In the course of a year, tobacco kills about 3 million people—2 million in industrialized countries and 1 million in developed countries. By 2000, the death toll is expected to reach 10 million annually.

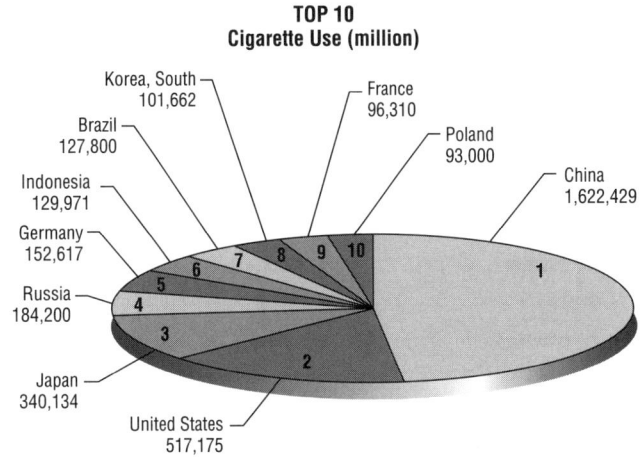

TOP 10
Cigarette Use (million)

Korea, South 101,662
France 96,310
Brazil 127,800
Poland 93,000
Indonesia 129,971
China 1,622,429
Germany 152,617
Russia 184,200
Japan 340,134
United States 517,175

Rank	Country	Cigarette Use (million)	Rank	Country	Cigarette Use (million)	Rank	Country	Cigarette Use (million)
UPPER MIDDLE			54	Uzbekistan	10,700	96	Nicaragua	2,400
11	United Kingdom	92,538	55	Tunisia	9,746	97	Zimbabwe	2,244
12	Italy	88,220	56	Denmark	8,317	98	Uganda	2,200
13	India	84,930	57	Israel	7,900	99	Ghana	2,133
14	Sweden	83,160	58	Moldova	7,500	100	Estonia	2,097
15	Ukraine	78,708	59	Finland	6,703	101	Honduras	2,083
16	Turkey	77,316	60	Azerbaijan	6,689	102	Costa Rica	2,010
17	Philippines	67,145	61	United Arab Emirates	6,500	103	Guatemala	1,858
18	Mexico	51,396	62	Georgia	6,250	104	El Salvador	1,620
19	Yugoslavia	45,000				105	Zambia	1,500
20	South Africa	40,740	**LOWER MIDDLE**			106	Mauritius	1,417
21	Thailand	40,662	63	Ireland	6,200	107	Afghanistan	1,400
22	Argentina	39,400	64	New Zealand	6,190	108	Nepal	1,400
23	Egypt	37,710	65	Libya	5,700	109	Malta	1,311
24	Canada	35,762	66	Syria	5,682	110	Trinidad and Tobago	1,270
25	Taiwan	35,719	67	Kenya	5,610	111	Jamaica	1,235
26	Australia	34,402	68	Turkmenistan	5,551	112	Bolivia	1,200
27	Bulgaria	31,853	69	Lebanon	5,300	113	Laos	1,200
28	Greece	30,050	70	Zaire	5,200	114	Cyprus	1,170
29	Czech Republic	29,150	71	Kyrgyzstan	5,100	115	Sudan	1,150
30	Pakistan	28,861	72	Sri Lanka	5,050	116	Mozambique	1,100
31	Romania	27,500	73	Cameroon	4,905	117	Congo	1,027
32	Hungary	27,330	74	Lithuania	4,881	118	Sierra Leone	1,013
33	Netherlands	26,082	75	Dominican Republic	4,730	119	Kuwait	1,000
34	Vietnam	24,600	76	Armenia	4,627	120	Malawi	950
35	Iran	24,000	77	Cote d'Ivoire	4,570	121	Togo	950
36	Colombia	21,742	78	Ecuador	4,500	122	Haiti	900
37	Algeria	20,000	79	Yemen	4,500	123	Panama	840
38	Cuba	19,500	80	Peru	4,210	124	Brunei	800
39	Saudi Arabia	18,880	81	Cambodia	4,200	125	Niger	700
40	Nigeria	18,500	82	Myanmar (Burma)	4,000			
41	Malaysia	17,945	83	Uruguay	3,938	**BOTTOM 10**		
42	Belgium	16,988	84	Senegal	3,820	126	Fiji	652
43	Switzerland	15,972	85	Latvia	3,737	127	Guyana	600
44	Portugal	15,823	86	Jordan	3,700	128	Benin	400
45	Korea, North	15,300	87	Tanzania	3,625	129	Suriname	390
46	Kazakhstan	15,289	88	Singapore	3,520	130	Liberia	222
47	Bangladesh	14,031	89	Tajikistan	3,450	131	Barbados	220
48	Venezuela	13,600	90	Paraguay	2,940	132	Belize	175
49	Belarus	13,540	91	Albania	2,700	133	Guinea	100
50	Morocco	13,508	92	Angola	2,700	134	Papua New Guinea	54
51	Austria	13,392	93	Norway	2,683	135	Chad	50
52	Iraq	13,000	94	Ethiopia	2,500			
53	Chile	10,745	95	Madagascar	2,451			

Source: Worldwatch Institute

Rank	Country	Percent of Male Smokers	Rank	Country	Percent of Male Smokers	Rank	Country	Percent of Male Smokers
TOP 10			6	Japan	61	**BOTTOM**		
1	Cambodia	90	7	Thailand	47	11	Singapore	30
2	South Korea	70	8	Malaysia	41	12	Hong Kong	29
3	Indonesia	65	9	India	40	13	New Zealand	28
4	Philippines	64	10	Australia	30	14	United States	28
5	China	61				15	Vietnam	24

Source: "The Cigarette's Open Frontier." *New York Times,* 15 May 1994, p. E16. Primary source: World Health Organization. Provisional Estimates for 1994.

Rank	Country	Percent of Women Smokers	Rank	Country	Percent of Women Smokers	Rank	Country	Percent of Women Smokers
TOP 10			6	China	7	**BOTTOM**		
1	Australia	27	7	South Korea	7	11	Cambodia	3
2	New Zealand	27	8	Indonesia	5	12	Hong Kong	3
3	United States	24	9	Malaysia	5	13	India	3
4	Philippines	19	10	Thailand	4	14	Singapore	2
5	Japan	14				15	Vietnam	1

Source: "The Cigarette's Open Frontier." *New York Times,* 15 May 1994, p. E16. Primary source: World Health Organization. Provisional Estimates for 1994.

195. NEWSPRINT

The consumption of newsprint, which is used in the printing of newspapers, journals and travel literature, is one of the yardsticks by which print media penetration in a country may be measured.

Rank	Country	Newsprint Consumption (per 1000 inhabitants—kg)	Rank	Country	Newsprint Consumption (per 1000 inhabitants—kg)	Rank	Country	Newsprint Consumption (per 1000 inhabitants—kg)
TOP 10			31	South Africa	5,913	62	Nicaragua	1,683
1	Canada	56,809	32	Mexico	5,141	63	Dominican Republic	1,667
2	United States	52,026	33	Czech Republic	5,106	64	Egypt	1,648
3	Switzerland	45,448	34	Venezuela	4,992	65	Paraguay	1,614
4	Finland	44,189	35	Malaysia	4,480	66	Bahamas	1,606
5	Denmark	42,568	36	Cyprus	4,473	67	Brunei	1,563
6	New Zealand	41,409	37	Russia	4338	68	Honduras	1,466
7	Australia	39,074	38	Bulgaria	4,137	69	Lebanon	1,447
8	Sweden	38,517	39	Peru	4,023	70	Guatemala	1,342
9	Norway	38,152	40	Trinidad and Tobago	3,965	71	Yugoslavia	1,257
10	United Kingdom	35,972	41	Chile	3,812	72	Tunisia	1,252
			42	Cuba	3,670	73	Bolivia	1,138
UPPER MIDDLE			43	Malta	3,419	74	Belize	1,099
11	Netherlands	34,855	44	Romania	3375	75	Poland	1,022
12	Austria	31,503	45	Costa Rica	2,893	76	China	891
13	Singapore	29,274	46	Fiji	2,530	77	Indonesia	740
14	Japan	28,977	47	Brazil	2,508	78	Panama	717
15	Belgium	28,554				79	Guyana	629
16	Germany	27,704	**LOWER MIDDLE**			80	India	610
17	Iceland	19,124	48	Thailand	2,490	81	Sri Lanka	588
18	Ireland	16,802	49	Turkey	2,485	82	Kenya	578
19	Israel	15,269	50	Jordan	2,290	83	Nigeria	503
20	France	13,554	51	Colombia	2,248	84	Morocco	483
21	Jamaica	11,893	52	El Salvador	2,226	85	Libya	457
22	Italy	10,683	53	Suriname	2,174	86	Pakistan	445
23	Kuwait	10,204	54	Ecuador	2,130	87	Tanzania	437
24	Korea, South	10,070	55	Saudi Arabia	2,064	88	Bangladesh	435
25	Barbados	9,412	56	Zimbabwe	2,052	89	Oman	416
26	Greece	8,718	57	Mauritius	1,959	90	Syria	380
27	Argentina	8,222	58	Iraq	1,860	91	Zambia	369
28	Spain	7,386	59	Uruguay	1,785	92	Myanmar (Burma)	284
29	Hungary	6,348	60	Mongolia	1,783	93	Guinea-Bissau	212
30	Portugal	6,327	61	Philippines	1,696	94	Cote d'Ivoire	191

Rank	Country	Newsprint Consumption (per 1000 inhabitants—kg)	Rank	Country	Newsprint Consumption (per 1000 inhabitants—kg)	Rank	Country	Newsprint Consumption (per 1000 inhabitants—kg)
95	Iran	188	103	Nepal	70	109	Sierra Leone	49
96	Algeria	181	104	Niger	67	110	Ethiopia	48
97	Vietnam	168	105	Haiti	63	111	Liberia	40
98	Korea, North	150	106	Malawi	59	112	Zaire	29
99	Senegal	140				113	Benin	22
100	Ghana	124		**BOTTOM 10**		114	Madagascar	21
101	Yemen	124	107	Mozambique	52	115	Somalia	14
102	Sudan	94	108	Angola	51	116	Uganda	11

Source: *UNESCO Statistical Yearbook*

196. SUGAR

The data in this table rank countries by their consumption of sugar, including both sugar consumed directly and that used in the manufacture of soft drinks, candies and other products.

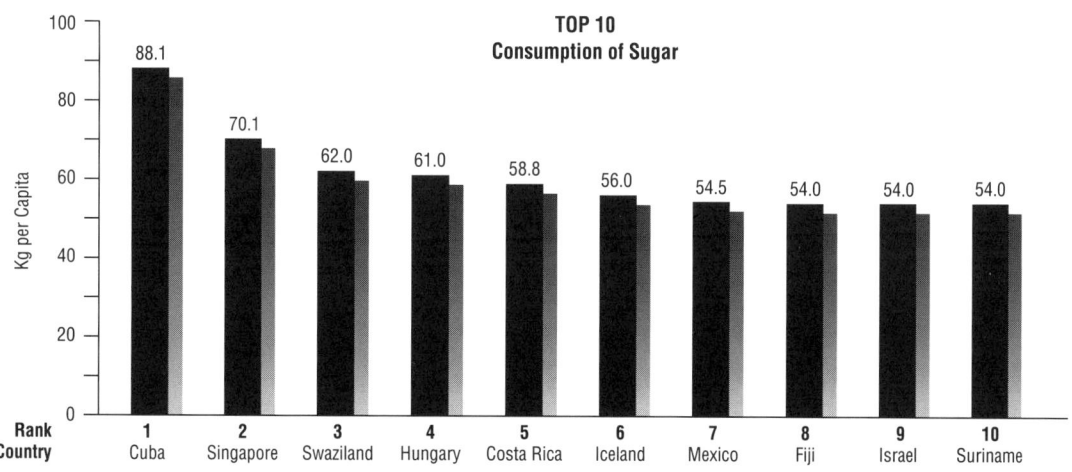

TOP 10 Consumption of Sugar

Kg per Capita

Rank	1	2	3	4	5	6	7	8	9	10
Country	Cuba	Singapore	Swaziland	Hungary	Costa Rica	Iceland	Mexico	Fiji	Israel	Suriname
	88.1	70.1	62.0	61.0	58.8	56.0	54.5	54.0	54.0	54.0

Rank	Country	Sugar Consumption per Capita (kg)	Rank	Country	Sugar Consumption per Capita (kg)	Rank	Country	Sugar Consumption per Capita (kg)
	UPPER MIDDLE		31	Norway	40.3	52	Honduras	34.2
11	Gambia	52.7	32	Jordan	40.1	53	South Africa	34.0
12	Malta	51.0	33	Yugoslavia	39.9	54	Bermuda	33.3
13	New Zealand	50.7	34	Canada	39.7	55	Argentina	33.1
14	Australia	50.6	35	Guatemala	39.1	56	El Salvador	32.9
15	Panama	49.6	36	Brunei	38.8	57	Egypt	32.4
16	Czech Republic	49.0	37	Nicaragua	38.8	58	Morocco	31.8
17	Barbados	48.2	38	Botswana	38.3	59	Algeria	31.7
18	Trinidad and Tobago	48.2	39	Mauritius	38.1	60	United States	31.4
19	Jamaica	48.0	40	St. Kitts and Nevis	38.1			
20	Yemen	47.0	41	Finland	38.0		**LOWER MIDDLE**	
21	Germany	46.3	42	Malaysia	37.9	61	Syria	30.9
22	Russia	46.2	43	Bulgaria	37.7	62	Zimbabwe	30.7
23	Switzerland	45.6	44	Lebanon	37.4	63	Romania	30.2
24	Belize	45.4	45	Chile	37.2	64	Turkey	30.2
25	Sweden	44.3	46	Venezuela	37.1	65	Cape Verde	28.9
26	Bahamas	44.0	47	Poland	37.0	66	Dominican Republic	28.5
27	Brazil	44.0	48	Colombia	35.7	67	Iraq	28.5
28	Libya	41.8	49	Cyprus	35.7	68	Kuwait	28.0
29	Maldives	41.0	50	Guyana	34.8	69	Peru	27.8
30	Austria	40.9	51	Ecuador	34.4	70	Mauritania	27.2

Rank	Country	Sugar Consumption per Capita (kg)	Rank	Country	Sugar Consumption per Capita (kg)	Rank	Country	Sugar Consumption per Capita (kg)
71	Saudi Arabia	26.9	93	India	13.3	115	Nigeria	3.6
72	Djibouti	25.3	94	Cote d'Ivoire	12.8	116	Benin	3.2
73	Bolivia	25.0	95	Malawi	12.6	117	Ethiopia	3.2
74	Tunisia	25.0	96	Togo	10.1	118	Burundi	3.1
75	Philippines	24.5	97	Congo	10.0	119	Guinea-Bissau	3.1
76	Uruguay	24.3	98	Angola	9.5	120	Zaire	2.7
77	Japan	23.0	99	Guinea	9.3	121	Mozambique	2.5
78	Mongolia	22.4	100	Mali	9.2			
79	Albania	21.6	101	Chad	8.8		**BOTTOM 10**	
80	Iran	21.5	102	Vietnam	7.9	122	Niger	2.5
81	Pakistan	20.4	103	Madagascar	7.3	123	Afghanistan	2.4
82	Thailand	19.6	104	Papua New Guinea	7.3	124	Bangladesh	2.3
83	Kenya	19.1	105	Cameroon	6.3	125	Nepal	2.1
84	Paraguay	18.5	106	China	6.2	126	Tuvalu	1.9
85	Sudan	17.8	107	Ghana	6.2	127	Laos	1.5
86	Gabon	17.1	108	Comoros	5.7	128	Rwanda	1.4
87	Korea, South	17.0	109	Somalia	5.3	129	Central African Republic	1.0
88	Zambia	15.5	110	Korea, North	5.2	130	Cambodia	0.6
89	Haiti	14.9	111	Sierra Leone	4.3	131	Myanmar (Burma)	0.6
90	Indonesia	14.8	112	Liberia	4.2			
91	Senegal	14.6	113	Burkina	3.9			
92	Sri Lanka	14.1	114	Tanzania	3.7			

Source: International Sugar Organization

197. COFFEE

The bulk of the world's coffee production is consumed in 24 countries ranked below, and the remainder in over 150 countries where the per capita consumption is insignificant. Because coffee is used principally in affluent countries, its demand and popularity have not been seriously affected by the steep rise in the prices in recent years.

Rank	Country	Coffee Consumption per Capita (kg)	Rank	Country	Coffee Consumption per Capita (kg)	Rank	Country	Coffee Consumption per Capita (kg)
	TOP 10		8	Germany	7.86	14	Belgium	3.76
1	Finland	11.58	9	France	5.89	15	Portugal	2.96
2	Sweden	11.18	10	United States	4.52	16	Japan	2.92
3	Denmark	10.61				17	United Kingdom	2.44
4	Norway	10.35		**BOTTOM 10**		18	Greece	2.29
5	Austria	9.99	11	Italy	4.39	19	Ireland	1.94
6	Netherlands	9.90	12	Spain	4.08	20	Fiji	0.08
7	Switzerland	8.41	13	Cyprus	4.03			

Source: *UN Statistical Yearbook*

198. PER CAPITA CONSUMPTION

Per capita consumption is perhaps one of the most useful in the vast arsenal of economic indexes. It measures total private and public expenditures in a nation. Because it does not distinguish between various types of expenditures (such as food, durables, etc.), it presents a more reliable guide to a country's total spending. Needs and spending patterns vary in individual areas; some spend more on clothing, some more on leisure; some more on food. The question this index answers is a broader one: Is the nation on a spending spree, or is it exercising some kind of spending restraint?

Rank	Country	Per Capita Consumption ($)
TOP 10		
1	Japan	19,700
2	Switzerland	19,570
3	United States	16,500
4	Iceland	15,550
5	Luxembourg	13,880
6	Germany	13,680
7	France	13,400
8	Norway	13,400
9	Belgium	13,060
10	Bermuda	12,690
UPPER MIDDLE		
11	Netherlands	12,570
12	Austria	12,520
13	Denmark	12,230
14	Italy	10,790
15	Sweden	10,190
16	Australia	10,130
17	Canada	10,040
18	United Kingdom	9,040
19	New Zealand	8,740
20	United Arab Emirates	8,560
21	Finland	8,450
22	Israel	8,230
23	Singapore	7,900
24	Spain	7,730
25	Cyprus	6,500
26	Argentina	6,310
27	Ireland	6,010
28	Puerto Rico	5,640
29	Portugal	5,570
30	Croatia	5,050
31	Taiwan	4,670
32	Barbados	4,540
33	Greece	4,490
34	Kuwait	4,140
35	Malta	4,100
36	Korea, South	4,060
37	Bahamas	3,950
38	Qatar	3,600
39	Uruguay	3,150
40	Seychelles	3,110
41	Trinidad and Tobago	2,960
42	Slovenia	2,890
43	Mexico	2,860
44	Saudi Arabia	2,860
45	Bahrain	2,800
46	Gabon	2,600
47	St. Kitts and Nevis	2,580
48	Yugoslavia	2,480
49	Hungary	2,360
50	Libya	2,330
51	Suriname	2,260
52	Brazil	2,250
53	Antigua and Barbuda	2,170
54	Venezuela	2,090
55	Chile	2,060
56	Oman	1,990
57	Bosnia & Herzegovina	1,890
58	Mauritius	1,810
59	Dominica	1,800

Rank	Country	Per Capita Consumption ($)
60	Macedonia	1,800
61	Czech Republic	1,710
62	Iraq	1,710
63	Turkey	1,690
64	Ukraine	1,680
65	Malaysia	1,660
66	Syria	1,630
67	Grenada	1,610
68	South Africa	1,580
69	Cuba	1,510
70	Costa Rica	1,490
71	Poland	1,470
72	Estonia	1,450
73	Belarus	1,400
74	Peru	1,400
75	Belize	1,350
76	Namibia	1,300
77	Botswana	1,290
78	Panama	1,290
LOWER MIDDLE		
79	Fiji	1,280
80	St. Vincent	1,240
81	Jamaica	1,200
82	Slovakia	1,200
83	Thailand	1,200
84	Russia	1,150
85	Colombia	1,050
86	Paraguay	1,050
87	Djibouti	1,030
88	Jordan	1,000
89	Guatemala	960
90	Ecuador	930
91	Iran	920
92	Algeria	900
93	Kazakhstan	900
94	Tunisia	890
95	Cape Verde	880
96	Latvia	870
97	Dominican Republic	840
98	Congo	835
99	Lithuania	820
100	Solomon Islands	820
101	Moldova	790
102	Lebanon	780
103	Bulgaria	760
104	Sudan	760
105	Myanmar (Burma)	750
106	Romania	740
107	Western Samoa	710
108	Albania	680
109	Morocco	670
110	Vanuatu	660
111	Papua New Guinea	650
112	Swaziland	650
113	Philippines	640
114	Yemen	630
115	Bolivia	620
116	Cameroon	620
117	Senegal	580
118	Turkmenistan	570
119	Georgia	530

Rank	Country	Per Capita Consumption ($)
120	Egypt	510
121	Armenia	500
122	Indonesia	460
123	Guinea	440
124	Tajikstan	440
125	Comoros	430
126	Angola	420
127	El Salvador	420
128	Kyrgyzstan	410
129	Nicaragua	410
130	Uzbekistan	410
131	Honduras	400
132	Sao Tome e Principe	400
133	Cote d'Ivoire	390
134	Sri Lanka	390
135	Azerbaijan	380
136	Equatorial Guinea	380
137	Haiti	370
138	Kiribati	370
139	Benin	360
140	Central African Republic	360
141	Ghana	340
142	Mauritania	340
143	Liberia	330
144	Lesotho	320
145	Zambia	310
146	Zimbabwe	290
147	Pakistan	280
148	Maldives	270
149	Togo	270
150	Guyana	240
151	Bhutan	220
152	Burkina	220
153	Gambia	220
154	Guinea-Bissau	220
155	Mali	220
156	Madagascar	200
157	Nigeria	190
158	Uganda	190
159	Zaire	190
160	Chad	180
161	China	180
162	Mongolia	180
163	Bangladesh	170
164	India	170
165	Niger	160
166	Rwanda	150
167	Vietnam	150
BOTTOM 10		
168	Laos	140
169	Sierra Leone	140
170	Nepal	135
171	Burundi	130
172	Malawi	130
173	Kenya	120
174	Ethiopia	95
175	Mozambique	87
176	Tanzania	61
177	Somalia	17

Source: *World Development Report*

199. PAPER

The world is rapidly approaching a "paperless society," just as it is on the verge of a "cashless society." Nonprint media are encroaching on the print media and reducing the monopoly that the latter had for centuries on the transmission of knowledge and information. In offices, paperwork is being taken over by automated functions performed by computers and word processors. Nevertheless, we are still living in an age when paper is a basic need for all literate men and women.

Rank	Country	Consumption of Paper (per 1000 inhabitants kg)	Rank	Country	Consumption of Paper (per 1000 inhabitants kg)	Rank	Country	Consumption of Paper (per 1000 inhabitants kg)
TOP 10			43	Brazil	6,612	86	Philippines	940
1	Sweden	115,331	44	Mauritius	6,077	87	Maldives	909
2	Switzerland	107,645	45	Poland	5,769	88	Pakistan	873
3	Finland	95,896	46	Brunei	5,682	89	Zimbabwe	737
4	Belgium	92,339	47	Thailand	5,188	90	Honduras	707
5	United States	84,579	48	Saudi Arabia	5,022	91	Cameroon	700
6	Canada	83,392	49	Argentina	4,952	92	Nigeria	678
7	Netherlands	80,012	50	Jordan	4,781	93	Cote d'Ivoire	675
8	Japan	76,892	51	Cuba	4,687	94	Vietnam	615
9	Germany	72,749	52	Tunisia	4,427	95	Zambia	596
10	Austria	60,046	53	Colombia	4,425	96	Angola	429
						97	Rwanda	413
UPPER MIDDLE			**LOWER MIDDLE**			98	Guyana	375
11	Singapore	59,620	54	Dominican Republic	4,245	99	Bangladesh	365
12	Denmark	57,362	55	Oman	3,924	100	Madagascar	364
13	France	54,930	56	China	3,853	101	Togo	329
14	United Kingdom	52,335	57	Bulgaria	3,655	102	Nicaragua	315
15	Australia	45,074	58	Turkey	3,576	103	Haiti	303
16	Italy	43,098	59	Iran	3,486	104	Ghana	291
17	Norway	41,575	60	Egypt	3,448	105	Tanzania	266
18	Spain	35,152	61	Jamaica	3,316	106	Romania	258
19	New Zealand	33,100	62	Barbados	3,101	107	Mongolia	242
20	Ireland	27,146	63	Panama	2,960	108	Bolivia	237
21	Portugal	24,126	64	El Salvador	2,840	109	Ethiopia	162
22	Cyprus	22,426	65	Suriname	2,749	110	Laos	156
23	Korea, South	21,198	66	Algeria	2,457	111	Malawi	155
24	Israel	20,324	67	Indonesia	2,405	112	Myanmar (Burma)	154
25	Malta	17,978	68	Sri Lanka	2,334	113	Benin	151
26	Iceland	16,342	69	Morocco	2,285	114	Sierra Leone	141
27	Greece	15,641	70	Peru	2,200	115	Congo	131
28	Trinidad and Tobago	12,870	71	Paraguay	2,024	116	Burundi	124
29	South Africa	11,385	72	Ecuador	1,852	117	Central African Republic	108
30	Malaysia	10,856	73	Iraq	1,713			
31	Bahrain	10,685	74	Belize	1,546	**BOTTOM 10**		
32	Fiji	9,290	75	Albania	1,369	118	Sudan	85
33	Qatar	9,023	76	India	1,350	119	Chad	70
34	Kuwait	8,922	77	Syria	1,302	120	Uganda	70
35	Hungary	8,640	78	Libya	1,271	121	Mozambique	69
36	Lebanon	8,564	79	Gabon	1,253	122	Korea, North	68
37	Chile	8,553	80	Guatemala	1,183	123	Zaire	52
38	Yugoslavia	8,183	81	Senegal	1,180	124	Niger	38
39	Venezuela	6,860	82	Kenya	1,166	125	Mali	32
40	Mexico	6,800	83	Bahamas	1,154	126	Somalia	17
41	Czech Republic	6,728	84	Liberia	991	127	Afghanistan	14
42	Uruguay	6,716	85	Costa Rica	964			

Source: *Pulp and Paper Industry; UNESCO Statistical Yearbook*

200. GASOLINE

Gasoline is the weakest link in the energy chain, and it is the resource that is being depleted at the fastest pace and the one that will be exhausted first. Consumption of gasoline has become critical in the world economy for a number of reasons. The first is that consumption rates are lopsidedly in favor of developed countries. The United States, for example, consumes 1,346 times more gasoline per capita than Nepal. Much of this consumption is undoubtedly squandered; it is acknowledged that even simple conservation measures can help to reduce per capita consumption in the United States by one-quarter to one-third. The second reason is that because the gasoline deficit has gown so rapidly in developed countries (and is bound to grow more in the future), they are being subjected to a variety of threats and measures that can only be described as energy blackmail by the oil-producing countries. It is this political dimension of the oil shortage that is even more alarming than the economic one. This ranking tells us which nations will be hurt most when the Arabs and the Iranians decide to turn off the spigot.

TOP 10
Gasoline Consumption

Rank	Country	(000 barrels per day)
1	United States	17,033
2	Japan	5,454
3	Russia	4,301
4	Germany	2,843
5	China	2,632
6	Italy	1,936
7	France	1,929
8	Mexico	1,845
9	United Kingdom	1,803
10	Canada	1,644

1 barrel = 1,000,000 barrels

Rank	Country	Gasoline Consumption (000 barrels per day)	Rank	Country	Gasoline Consumption (000 barrels per day)	Rank	Country	Gasoline Consumption (000 barrels per day)
UPPER MIDDLE			42	Austria	229	72	Moldova	69
11	Korea, South	1,508	43	Poland	227	73	Vietnam	64
12	Brazil	1,410	44	Finland	221	74	Jordan	63
13	India	1,252	45	Colombia	218	75	Dominican Republic	62
14	Iran	1,118				76	Sudan	60
15	Spain	1,108	**LOWER MIDDLE**			77	Georgia	55
16	Saudi Arabia	1,102	46	Algeria	208	78	Lebanon	53
17	Indonesia	770	47	Czech Republic	206	79	Jamaica	50
18	Australia	712	48	Ukraine	199	80	Latvia	46
19	Taiwan	579	49	Denmark	193	81	Cote d'Ivoire	39
20	Belgium	511	50	Uzbekistan	189	82	Luxembourg	39
21	Egypt	494	51	Norway	183	83	Turkmenistan	38
22	Turkey	492	52	Israel	180	84	Armenia	37
23	Thailand	478	53	Syria	178	85	Kyrgyzstan	35
24	Belarus	471	54	Libya	171	86	Estonia	34
25	Venezuela	430	55	Cuba	160	87	Kenya	34
26	Argentina	420	56	Azerbaijan	158	88	Sri Lanka	34
27	South Africa	406	57	Yugoslavia	153	89	Panama	33
28	Singapore	400	58	Puerto Rico	150	90	Cyprus	32
29	Iraq	360	59	Chile	147	91	Uruguay	30
30	Kazakhstan	356	60	Hungary	140			
31	Sweden	342	61	Morocco	117	**BOTTOM 10**		
32	United Arab Emirates	332	62	Peru	113	92	Myanmar (Burma)	29
33	Greece	331	63	New Zealand	110	93	Bahrain	27
34	Nigeria	300	64	Ecuador	105	94	Bolivia	26
35	Malaysia	291	65	Ireland	104	95	Guatemala	26
36	Switzerland	287	66	Kuwait	100	96	Angola	25
37	Portugal	277	67	Lithuania	85	97	Tajikstan	24
38	Romania	277	68	Yemen	78	98	Zaire	22
39	Netherlands	266	69	Korea, North	76	99	Trinidad and Tobago	21
40	Pakistan	246	70	Bulgaria	72	100	Bahamas	15
41	Philippines	235	71	Tunisia	72	101	Albania	12

Source: *Energy Statistics Yearbook*

201. FISH

This ranking compares the national consumption of fish in any form. The most popular types of fish are cod, herring, haddock, mackerel, shrimp, tuna and salmon.

Rank	Country	Annual Fish Consumption (lbs)	Rank	Country	Annual Fish Consumption (lbs)	Rank	Country	Annual Fish Consumption (lbs)
TOP 10			22	Singapore	64.6	44	Malta	44.8
1	Maldives	293.4	23	Brunei	63.9	45	Italy	44.3
2	Iceland	203.0				46	United Kingdom	43.9
3	Japan	158.7	**LOWER MIDDLE**			47	Cuba	43.7
4	Portugal	132.7	24	New Zealand	63.7	48	Bahrain	43.2
5	Solomon Islands	131.8	25	Tonga	61.7	49	Equatorial Guinea	42.1
6	Seychelles	127.2	26	Russia	61.1	50	Greece	42.1
7	Korea, South	104.9	27	Malaysia	60.0	51	Mauritius	42.1
8	Antigua and Barbuda	99.9	28	Peru	60.0	52	Australia	41.4
9	Fiji	98.3	29	Sweden	59.3	53	Belgium	41.4
10	Korea, North	97.4	30	Ghana	58.2	54	Jamaica	40.1
			31	United Arab Emirates	58.0	55	Gambia	39.2
UPPER MIDDLE			32	Grenada	56.2			
11	Guyana	91.0	33	Canada	53.6	**BOTTOM 10**		
12	Norway	90.6	34	Chile	52.9	56	Ireland	35.1
13	Taiwan	86.2	35	Oman	52.2	57	Cote d'Ivoire	34.2
14	Spain	83.8	36	Angola	51.4	58	Myanmar (Burma)	33.7
15	Congo	78.7	37	Papua New Guinea	50.3	59	Panama	33.7
16	Philippines	76.3	38	Western Samoa	47.8	60	Cyprus	32.2
17	Sao Tome e Principe	71.0	39	United States	47.0	61	France	31.1
18	Gabon	68.8	40	Denmark	46.7	62	Venezuela	31.1
19	Finland	67.5	41	Thailand	45.6	63	Poland	27.3
20	Barbados	67	42	Israel	45.4	64	Mexico	24.3
21	Vanuatu	67.0	43	Bahamas	45.0	65	Kuwait	20.1

Source: *Fishery Statistics Yearbook*

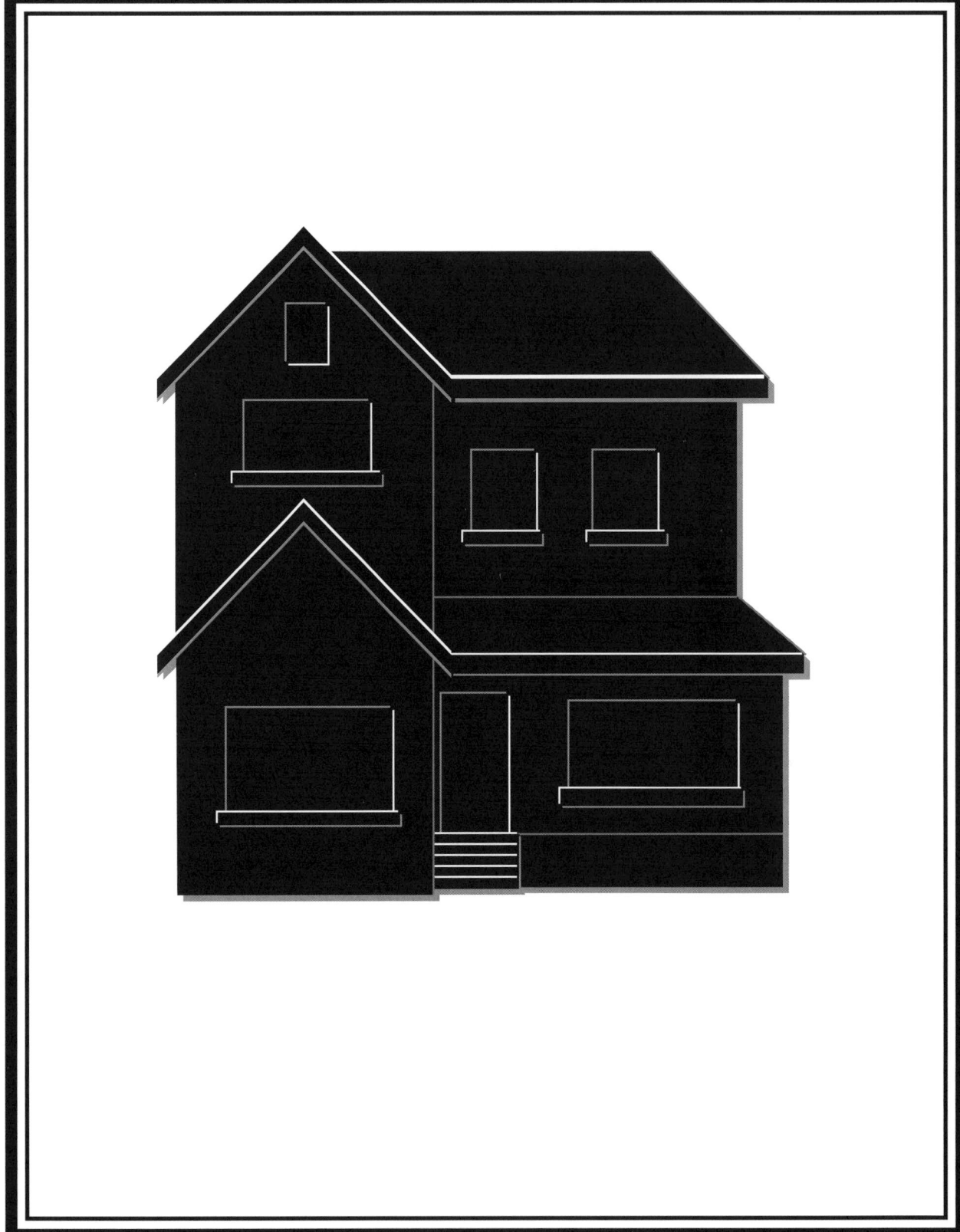

Section
XVII

HOUSING

Housing censuses have been carried out under U.N. auspices in 152 countries and have yielded a wealth of data on the quality of housing in each country, particularly with referene to minimum standards of what may be described as habitability. These include the provision of the 5Cs (to coin a term), that is, the five basic conveniences or facilities: piped water, electric light, kitchen, toilet and bath. The censuses also dealt with new homes built per 1,000 inhabitants, tenure, i.e., whether the homes are rented or owned, the number of persons per room and the number of rooms per house. Unfortunately, no effort was made to determine what might have been considered an important and interesting fact: the condition of the roof and the nature of the construction materials used.

The general trend in these rankings is toward more and better housing. In almost all countries, the 5Cs have become the norm rather than the exception and the number of countries reporting 100% of homes with these facilities has doubled since 1960. Subsidized housing is now almost universal for industrial workers. Mortgages, financed partly by state funds, have made home construction and ownership practicable even for the less well-to-do.

202. SIZE OF DWELLINGS

The size of a dwelling in terms of the number of rooms has an important bearing not only on levels of density but also on construction costs. Although no statistics are available on the size of the rooms themselves, it is assumed that they conform to normal building codes and regulations in force in each country or city. The data are also assumed to include rooms used for business and professional purposes, although only a few countries specifically state that this is the case. However, extremely crowded housing conditions are reported in all Third World Cities.

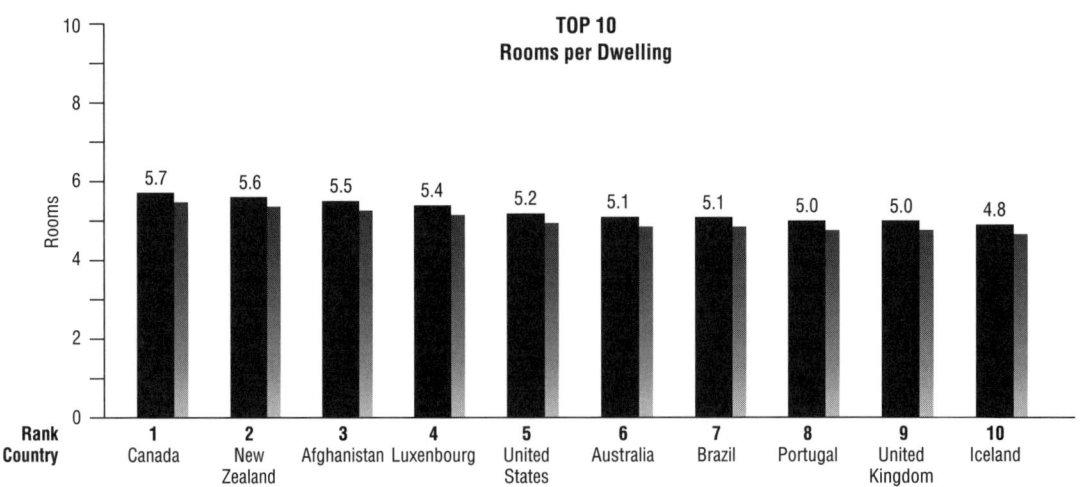

TOP 10
Rooms per Dwelling

Rank	1	2	3	4	5	6	7	8	9	10
Rooms	5.7	5.6	5.5	5.4	5.2	5.1	5.1	5.0	5.0	4.8
Country	Canada	New Zealand	Afghanistan	Luxembourg	United States	Australia	Brazil	Portugal	United Kingdom	Iceland

Rank	Country	Rooms per Dwelling	Rank	Country	Rooms per Dwelling	Rank	Country	Rooms per Dwelling
UPPER MIDDLE			52	Uruguay	3.4	92	Estonia	2.5
11	Puerto Rico	4.8	53	Colombia	3.3	93	Sri Lanka	2.5
12	Cyprus	4.6	54	Dominica	3.3	94	Tanzania	2.5
13	Liechtenstein	4.5	55	Egypt	3.3	95	Burundi	2.4
14	San Marino	4.5	56	Fiji	3.3	96	Honduras	2.4
15	Chile	4.4	57	Greece	3.3	97	Iraq	2.4
16	Maldives	4.4	58	Libya	3.3	98	Jamaica	2.4
17	Spain	4.4	59	Trinidad and Tobago	3.3	99	Japan	4.9
18	Austria	4.3	60	Bermuda	3.2	100	Philippines	2.4
19	Barbados	4.3				101	Turkey	2.4
20	Belgium	4.3	**LOWER MIDDLE**			102	Guatemala	2.4
21	Germany	4.3	61	Malta	3.2	103	Korea, South	2.3
22	Bahrain	4.2	62	Poland	3.2	104	Liberia	2.3
23	Brunei	4.2	63	Gabon	3.0	105	Malaysia	2.3
24	Venezuela	4.2	64	Indonesia	3.3	106	Senegal	2.3
25	Cameroon	4.1	65	Israel	3.0	107	Solomon Islands	2.3
26	Cuba	4.1	66	St. Kitts and Nevis	3.0	108	China	2.2
27	Netherlands	4.1	67	Slovenia	3.0	109	Haiti	2.3
28	Norway	4.1	68	Syria	3.0	110	India	2.2
29	Qatar	4.1	69	Algeria	2.9	111	Nicaragua	2.2
30	Seychelles	4.1	70	Grenada	2.9	112	Paraguay	2.2
31	Taiwan	4.1	71	Guyana	2.9	113	Sudan	2.2
32	Bahamas	4.0	72	Slovakia	2.9	114	Suriname	2.1
33	Costa Rica	4.0	73	Yugoslavia	2.9	115	Bangladesh	2.0
34	Italy	4.0	74	Croatia	2.8	116	Gambia	2.0
35	Kuwait	4.0	75	Dominican Republic	2.8	117	Yemen	2.0
36	Argentina	3.9	76	Ecuador	2.8	118	Djibouti	1.9
37	France	3.9	77	Hungary	2.6	119	Ethiopia	1.9
38	Western Samoa	3.9	78	Iran	2.8	120	Malawi	1.9
39	Denmark	3.8	79	Monaco	2.8	121	Pakistan	1.9
40	Congo	3.7	80	Panama	2.8			
41	Ireland	3.7	81	St. Vincent	2.8	**BOTTOM 10**		
42	Nepal	3.7	82	United Arab Emirates	2.8	122	Tunisia	1.9
43	Switzerland	3.7	83	Zimbabwe	2.8	123	Zambia	1.9
44	Antigua and Barbuda	3.6	84	Czech Republic	2.7	124	Albania	1.8
45	Mauritius	3.6	85	Morocco	2.7	125	Cape Verde	1.8
46	Nauru	3.6	86	Mali	2.6	126	Singapore	1.8
47	Finland	3.5	87	Peru	2.6	127	Togo	1.8
48	Mexico	3.4	88	Romania	2.6	128	Thailand	1.6
49	St. Lucia	3.4	89	Botswana	2.5	129	El Salvador	1.5
50	South Africa	3.4	90	Bulgaria	2.5	130	Guinea-Bissau	1.4
51	Sweden	3.4	91	Comoros	2.5	131	Nigeria	1.4

Source: *UN Construction Statistics Yearbook*

203. DWELLINGS WITH TOILETS

A primary indicator of public health and sanitation is the extent to which dwellings, especially in urban areas, are equipped with or connected to satisfactory means of disposing human waste. The ideal means is the flush toilet, although in rural and sparsely populated areas other, less satisfactory, means may be commonly and safely used, even if they do not always come up to the standards considered acceptable by public health authorities. In the following ranking both flush and other types of toilets are combined unless otherwise indicated.

Rank	Country	Homes with Inside Toilets (%)	Rank	Country	Homes with Inside Toilets (%)	Rank	Country	Homes with Inside Toilets (%)
TOP 10			**UPPER MIDDLE**			21	Taiwan	94.2
1	Netherlands	100.0	11	Sweden	98.0	22	Italy	94.0
2	Canada	99.4	12	New Zealand	97.1	23	Iceland	93.6
3	United Kingdom	99.8	13	Spain	97.1	24	France	93.5
4	Luxembourg	99.4	14	Bermuda	96.7	25	Switzerland	93.3
5	Denmark	99.2	15	Monaco	96.2	26	Greece	93.0
6	United States	98.9	16	Argentina	95.1	27	Finland	92.7
7	Israel	98.8	17	Seychelles	95.0	28	Australia	92.2
8	Malta	98.8	18	Puerto Rico	94.7	29	Belgium	91.9
9	Germany	98.3	19	Norway	94.6	30	Ireland	90.0
10	San Marino	98.3	20	Brunei	94.2	31	Solomon Islands	89.2

Rank	Country	Homes with Inside Toilets (%)
32	Austria	88.7
33	Czech Republic	88.5
34	Slovenia	86.8
35	Liechtenstein	86.7
36	United Arab Emirates	84.5
37	Venezuela	84.4
38	Lebanon	82.9
39	Djibouti	82.0
40	Croatia	80.3
41	Slovakia	80.1
42	Bahrain	78.2
43	Portugal	78.1
44	Colombia	77.9
45	Hungary	75.9
46	Japan	74.7
47	Cyprus	74.5
48	Panama	74.3
49	Uruguay	73.3
LOWER MIDDLE		
50	Western Samoa	71.0
51	Turkey	70.6
52	Sudan	70.2
53	Algeria	68.9
54	Poland	68.9
55	Barbados	66.2
56	Singapore	63.6
57	Mauritius	63.3
58	Macedonia	56.3
59	Fiji	56.0
60	Jordan	55.4
61	Ethiopia	55.2
62	Kiribati	53.3
63	Yugoslavia	53.3
64	Bosnia & Herzegovina	53.2
65	Korea, South	51.3
66	Morocco	50.2
67	Ecuador	49.6
68	Haiti	45.8
69	Cuba	45.2
70	Mexico	45.0
71	Iran	43.6
72	Tunisia	43.3
73	Bolivia	42.8
74	Tonga	42.3
75	Trinidad and Tobago	41.1
76	Thailand	40.9
77	Libya	40.6
78	Suriname	40.4
79	Papua New Guinea	40.0
80	El Salvador	39.7
81	Tuvalu	37.3
82	Dominica	36.8
83	Peru	35.7
84	St. Lucia	35.7
85	Jamaica	35.2
86	Philippines	35.0
87	Belize	34.7
88	St. Kitts and Nevis	33.5
89	Malawi	33.4
90	Bulgaria	33.2
91	Guyana	29.0
92	Vanuatu	27.5
93	Indonesia	26.6
94	Paraguay	26.4
95	Botswana	25.4
96	China	25.2
97	Cape Verde	25.1
98	Pakistan	25.1
99	Cote d'Ivoire	23.9
100	India	23.7
101	Grenada	23.0
102	Swaziland	21.4
103	Albania	21.3
104	Nicaragua	19.3
105	Congo	16.6
106	Zambia	15.1
107	Guatemala	14.3
108	Dominican Republic	14.1
BOTTOM 10		
109	Honduras	13.0
110	Bangladesh	12.5
111	Sao Tome e Principe	9.2
112	Cambodia	7.0
113	Nigeria	7.0
114	Nepal	6.1
115	Afghanistan	5.5
116	Sri Lanka	4.7
117	Cameroon	2.2
118	Mali	1.3

Source: *UN Construction Statistics Yearbook*

204. DWELLINGS WITH ELECTRIC LIGHTS

The data in this table rank countries by percentage of occupied buildings with access to electricity. Access to electricity refers to electric lights only in all countries; however, in developed countries it also refers to the whole range of electric appliances, such as refrigerators, air conditioners, washing machines, and even electric toothbrushes and hairdryers.

Rank	Country	Homes with Electricity (%)
TOP 10		
1	Belgium	100
2	Canada	100
3	Czech Republic	100
4	Denmark	100
5	Monaco	100
6	San Marino	100
7	Estonia	99.9
8	Bulgaria	99.8
9	Germany	99.7
10	Taiwan	99.7
UPPER MIDDLE		
11	Kuwait	99.5
12	Slovenia	99.5
13	Portugal	99.4
14	Spain	99.2
15	Italy	99.0
16	Hungary	98.8
17	Croatia	98.6
18	Australia	98.4
19	Singapore	98.3
20	Cyprus	98.1
21	Malta	98.0
22	Netherlands	98.0
23	Puerto Rico	97.4
24	Costa Rica	97.3
25	Bahrain	97.1
26	United States	96.9
27	Liechtenstein	96.6
28	Israel	96.5
29	Macedonia	96.4
30	Mauritius	96.2
31	Poland	96.2
32	Sweden	96.2
33	Finland	95.9
34	Senegal	95.9
35	Yugoslavia	95.7
36	Ireland	94.7
37	Iceland	94.6
38	Bosnia & Herzegovina	94.2
39	Lebanon	93.4
40	Qatar	93.2
41	Barbados	92.6
42	Chile	90.2
43	Venezuela	89.8
44	Thailand	89.7
45	Greece	89.0
46	Brazil	87.8
47	Mexico	87.5
48	Egypt	87.0
49	Argentina	86.8
50	Uruguay	84.7
51	Iran	84.1
52	Trinidad and Tobago	83.3
53	Cuba	82.9
LOWER MIDDLE		
54	Suriname	82.0
55	Nigeria	81.3
56	Solomon Islands	79.6
57	Colombia	78.5
58	Bahamas	77.9
59	Ecuador	77.7
60	Jordan	77.3
61	Seychelles	75.8
62	St. Lucia	72.9
63	Algeria	72.7
64	Libya	72.1
65	El Salvador	69.3
66	Guyana	69.0
67	Belize	67.2

Rank	Country	Homes with Electricity (%)	Rank	Country	Homes with Electricity (%)	Rank	Country	Homes with Electricity (%)
68	Afghanistan	66.5	89	India	42.4	110	Bangladesh	14.3
69	Panama	65.7	90	Syria	41.7	111	Vanuatu	14.2
70	Malaysia	64.4	91	Nicaragua	40.9	112	Guinea	12.5
71	Brunei	64.2	92	Cote d'Ivoire	39.6	113	Swaziland	11.6
72	Tunisia	63.4	93	Western Samoa	37.7	114	Togo	10.3
73	Djibouti	58.0	94	Morocco	37.2	115	Sudan	9.9
74	St. Kitts and Nevis	57.5	95	Guatemala	37.0	116	Zimbabwe	9.3
75	Turkey	56.8	96	Dominican Republic	36.7	117	Congo	8.8
76	Papua New Guinea	56.0	97	Pakistan	30.6		**BOTTOM 10**	
77	Bolivia	55.5	98	Nepal	30.2	118	Tuvalu	7.4
78	Philippines	55.1	99	Zambia	27.5	119	Tanzania	6.3
79	Peru	54.9	100	Honduras	25.0	120	Cameroon	5.9
80	Maldives	53.4	101	Cape Verde	24.9	121	Comoros	5.7
81	Gabon	50.5	102	United Arab Emirates	24.2	122	Botswana	5.4
82	Korea, South	49.9	103	Kiribati	23.7	123	Yemen	4.6
83	Nauru	49.2	104	Malawi	22.8	124	Mozambique	4.2
84	Jamaica	48.6	105	Sao Tome e Principe	22.0	125	Guinea-Bissau	3.9
85	Romania	48.6	106	Haiti	21.9	126	Mali	3.6
86	Fiji	48.5	107	Tonga	20.9	127	Burundi	0.6
87	Mongolia	47.5	108	Iraq	17.1			
88	Indonesia	44.0	109	Sri Lanka	14.9			

Source: *UN Construction Statistics Yearbook*

205. DWELLINGS WITH PIPED WATER

The data is this table rank countries by the percentage of occupied dwellings with safe water piped inside or within 100 meters.

Rank	Country	Homes with Piped Water (%)	Rank	Country	Homes with Piped Water (%)	Rank	Country	Homes with Piped Water (%)
	TOP 10		36	Estonia	92.7	72	Macedonia	72.0
1	Cyprus	100.0	37	New Zealand	92.7	73	Colombia	70.5
2	Denmark	100.0	38	Solomon Islands	92.7	74	Libya	70.1
3	Germany	100.0	39	Slovakia	91.8	75	Turkey	68.0
4	Monaco	100.0	40	Antigua and Barbuda	91.5	76	Ethiopia	67.9
5	Netherlands	100.0	41	Singapore	90.6	77	Yugoslavia	67.8
6	Switzerland	100.0	42	Brunei	90.3	78	Bosnia & Herzegovina	66.2
7	Canada	99.8	43	Hungary	90.1	79	Tuvalu	65.4
8	San Marino	99.8	44	China	89.4	80	Malaysia	65.0
9	France	99.7	45	Uruguay	89.3	81	St. Lucia	64.7
10	Belgium	99.6	46	Chile	88.2	82	Dominican Republic	64.4
	UPPER MIDDLE		47	Algeria	87.4	83	Trinidad and Tobago	64.3
11	Luxembourg	99.4	48	Dominica	87.4	84	Suriname	62.9
12	Iceland	99.1	49	Senegal	87.7	85	Ecuador	62.7
13	Portugal	99.1	50	Costa Rica	86.9	86	Tonga	61.3
14	Sweden	99.0	51	Grenada	86.5	87	Bolivia	57.5
15	Italy	98.7	52	Croatia	86.2	88	Bangladesh	56.8
16	Spain	98.7	53	Venezuela	86.2	89	Honduras	55.0
17	United States	98.5	54	Poland	84.3	90	Belize	54.9
18	Malta	98.0	55	Bahamas	83.0	91	Kuwait	53.9
19	Norway	97.5	56	Greece	81.3	92	Guatemala	52.0
20	Bermuda	97.4	57	Panama	80.7	93	Kazakhstan	50.0
21	Slovenia	97.4	58	Western Samoa	80.7	94	Papua New Guinea	50.0
22	Australia	97.1	59	Mexico	79.4	95	Nepal	47.7
23	Czech Republic	96.9		**LOWER MIDDLE**		96	Peru	46.7
24	Israel	96.5	60	Taiwan	79.4	97	El Salvador	46.4
25	Liechtenstein	96.5	61	Argentina	77.4	98	St. Kitts and Nevis	46.3
26	Lithuania	95.7	62	Jordan	77.2	99	Djibouti	45.0
27	Puerto Rico	95.6	63	Botswana	77.0	100	Swaziland	42.5
28	Finland	95.1	64	Seychelles	77.0	101	Syria	40.2
29	Austria	95.0	65	Jamaica	76.9	102	Vanuatu	39.2
30	St. Vincent	95.0	66	Bulgaria	74.6	103	Philippines	38.8
31	Ireland	94.8	67	Iran	74.6	104	Guyana	38.1
32	Mauritius	94.7	68	Korea, South	74.1	105	Tanzania	37.2
33	Barbados	94.0	69	Fiji	73.7	106	Ghana	34.0
34	Japan	94.0	70	Brazil	73.4	107	Kiribati	33.1
35	Bahrain	92.8	71	Egypt	73.1	108	Albania	33.0
						109	India	32.3

Rank	Country	Homes with Piped Water (%)		Rank	Country	Homes with Piped Water (%)		Rank	Country	Homes with Piped Water (%)
110	United Arab Emirates	30.9		122	Gambia	21.9		132	Burundi	11.0
111	Congo	30.5		123	Iraq	20.8		133	Cambodia	11.0
112	Morocco	30.5		124	Pakistan	20.3		134	Haiti	5.8
113	Thailand	29.7		125	Sri Lanka	18.2		135	Yemen	5.7
114	Sudan	29.4		126	Cape Verde	16.2		136	Togo	4.1
115	Nicaragua	27.9		127	Comoros	12.9		137	Mali	3.8
116	Tunisia	26.4		128	Indonesia	12.9		138	Guinea-Bissau	3.7
117	Afghanistan	25.3		129	Mozambique	12.7		139	Mongolia	0.3
118	Cuba	24.1								
119	Malawi	23.6		**BOTTOM 10**						
120	Cote d'Ivoire	23.0		130	Zambia	12.4				
121	Cameroon	22.0		131	Guinea	11.9				

Source: *UN Construction Statistics Yearbook*

206. HOME OWNERSHIP

The extent to which households own or rent accommodation is of special significance for housing programs. It provides an indication of the adequacy and quality of housing and also provides a basis for estimating housing needs. The ranking is restricted to households occupying conventional dwellings, but in a few countries mobile units or semi-permanent units are considered acceptable as places of habitation. Data are tabulated in terms of conventional dwellings by tenure of households; the percentage of renters is not shown separately because it may be safely assumed that those who do not own buildings either rent them or use them under some comparable arrangements.

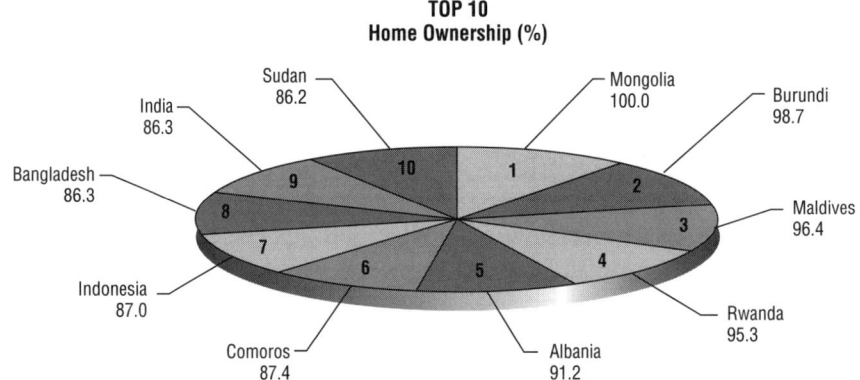

TOP 10
Home Ownership (%)

Sudan 86.2
India 86.3
Bangladesh 86.3
Indonesia 87.0
Comoros 87.4
Albania 91.2
Mongolia 100.0
Burundi 98.7
Maldives 96.4
Rwanda 95.3

Rank	Country	Home Ownership (%)		Rank	Country	Home Ownership (%)		Rank	Country	Home Ownership (%)
	UPPER MIDDLE			25	Norway	80.3		40	Hungary	75.9
11	Thailand	86.0		26	Western Samoa	80.1		41	Mauritius	75.9
12	Mali	84.2		27	Korea, South	79.0		42	Fiji	75.5
13	Yemen	83.9		28	Tunisia	78.9		43	Panama	75.5
14	Brunei	83.8		29	Zambia	78.8		44	Tanzania	75.4
15	Lithuania	83.5		30	Romania	78.6		45	Nepal	75.3
16	Cameroon	83.4		31	Taiwan	78.5		46	Grenada	74.5
17	Iraq	83.0		32	Pakistan	78.4		47	Israel	74.3
18	Philippines	83.0		33	Argentina	78.0		48	Cambodia	74.0
19	Peru	82.0		34	Mexico	77.9		49	San Marino	73.5
20	Tonga	82.0		35	Bulgaria	77.3		50	Haiti	73.2
21	Syria	81.6		36	Turkey	77.2		51	Greece	73.1
22	Tuvalu	81.6		37	Iran	77.0		52	St. Vincent	72.1
23	Guinea	81.3		38	Benin	76.8		53	New Zealand	72.4
24	Paraguay	80.4		39	Barbados	76.1		54	St. Lucia	72.4

Rank	Country	Home Ownership (%)	Rank	Country	Home Ownership (%)	Rank	Country	Home Ownership (%)
55	Venezuela	75.8	82	Trinidad and Tobago	64.6	111	Liechtenstein	53.6
56	Puerto Rico	72.1	83	Belgium	64.5	112	Bahamas	51.4
57	Dominican Republic	72.0	84	Nicaragua	64.4	113	Austria	50.0
58	Dominica	71.9	85	United States	64.2	114	Ethiopia	48.8
59	Honduras	71.8	86	Croatia	64.0	115	Bahrain	48.2
60	Finland	71.5	87	Egypt	64.0	116	Ghana	47.7
61	Iceland	70.3	88	Gambia	63.9	117	Zaire	47.4
62	Oman	70.2	89	Seychelles	63.7	118	Jamaica	46.7
63	El Salvador	69.6	90	Malaysia	63.4	119	Czech Republic	44.7
			91	Algeria	63.0	120	Bermuda	43.4
LOWER MIDDLE			92	Jordan	62.6	121	Netherlands	43.2
64	Sri Lanka	69.4	93	Libya	62.5	122	Morocco	41.2
65	Chile	68.3	94	Canada	62.1	123	Vanuatu	40.9
66	Kiribati	68.2	95	Congo	61.4	124	Papua New Guinea	40.0
67	Ecuador	68.1	96	Cyprus	60.0	125	Malawi	39.6
68	Ireland	67.9	97	Japan	59.8	126	Germany	39.0
69	Colombia	67.6	98	Botswana	59.2	127	Kuwait	38.2
70	Spain	67.5	99	Italy	58.9			
71	Australia	67.1	100	Uruguay	57.6	**BOTTOM 10**		
72	Yugoslavia	67.1	101	Guyana	57.2	128	Nigeria	37.0
73	Brazil	67.0	102	Portugal	56.7	129	United Arab Emirates	36.2
74	United Kingdom	66.4	103	Sweden	55.9	130	Poland	35.2
75	Luxembourg	66.1	104	Afghanistan	55.2	131	Switzerland	31.3
76	Belize	65.9	105	Singapore	55.0	132	Solomon Islands	27.4
77	Costa Rica	65.8	106	St. Kitts and Nevis	54.7	133	Monaco	23.3
78	Bolivia	65.5	107	South Africa	54.5	134	Qatar	21.9
79	Zimbabwe	65.1	108	France	54.4	135	China	18.5
80	Guatemala	64.7	109	Malta	53.9	136	Estonia	18.3
81	Antigua and Barbuda	64.6	110	Denmark	53.8	137	Nauru	11.0

Source: *UN Construction Statistics Yearbook*

Section
XVIII

HEALTH
& FOOD

Health is one area where measurable and undeniable progress has been achieved in every country since the end of World War II. The incidence of major epidemic diseases and once-dreaded killers, such as plague, smallpox and malaria, is down in almost all countries. There are more hospitals and more trained professionals to staff them, more medical research and more transfer of medical technology, and more people covered by medical insurance today than at any time in history. Much of this improvement has been the direct result of better nutrition, sanitation and water supply, and better monitoring procedures.

It is against this background that the following rankings should be considered. But there are a number of negative factors that the rankings may conceal or reveal rather imperfectly. One is the scandalous and prohibitive cost of medical care, especially in developing countries, restricting its availability to the well-to-do. Medical insurance, originally designed to enlarge the reach of health care and delivery services, has been, paradoxically, a contributory factor in these spiraling costs. Medical care in almost all countries remains very much of an urban phenomenon, with little or no penetration of rural areas. Even the per capita rankings of medical personnel in this section do not reveal the heavy concentration of health services in towns and cities.

207. PUBLIC HEALTH EXPENDITURES AS PERCENTAGE OF GDP

Until recently defense was the major item in every national budget, but with the end of the Cold War, social expenditures have taken a larger slice of the budget pie. Social expenditures comprise expenditures on education, health, housing and social welfare, and other areas affecting national well being and future. Health expenditures vary from country to country, based on the existence or absence of a national health service as well as personnel and technology costs. The optimum health expenditures as percentage of GDP is suggested by WHO at 4%.

Rank	Country	Health Expenditures as Percentage of GDP	Rank	Country	Health Expenditures as Percentage of GDP	Rank	Country	Health Expenditures as Percentage of GDP
TOP 10			22	Italy	7.54	46	Seychelles	6.03
1	United States	12.71	23	Gambia	7.53	47	India	6.00
2	Guyana	10.37	24	Switzerland	7.52	48	St. Kitts and Nevis	5.99
3	France	9.40	25	Belgium	7.50	49	Tajikistan	5.98
4	Sao Tome e Principe	9.22	26	New Zealand	7.37	50	Grenada	5.96
5	Canada	9.05	27	Norway	7.35	51	Hungary	5.95
6	Sweden	8.79	28	Swaziland	7.22	52	Czech Republic	5.94
7	Germany	8.73	29	St. Lucia	7.18	53	Uzbekistan	5.90
8	Nicaragua	8.61	30	Panama	7.13	54	Belize	5.88
9	Burkina	8.46	31	Haiti	6.99	55	El Salvador	5.86
10	Austria	8.38	32	Portugal	6.99	56	Mozambique	5.86
			33	Algeria	6.95	57	St. Vincent	5.69
UPPER MIDDLE			34	Mongolia	6.63	58	Vanuatu	5.68
11	Iceland	8.34	35	Korea, South	6.61	59	South Africa	5.56
12	Lesotho	8.32	36	Spain	6.59	60	Comoros	5.40
13	Liberia	8.24	37	Luxembourg	6.56	61	Greece	5.39
14	Zimbabwe	8.23	38	Costa Rica	6.51	62	Malta	5.38
15	Guinea-Bissau	8.15	39	Tonga	6.46	63	Bulgaria	5.36
16	Dominica	8.06	40	Japan	6.45	64	Mali	5.19
17	Netherlands	8.03	41	Cape Verde	6.32	65	Yugoslavia	5.11
18	Finland	7.82	42	Denmark	6.30	66	Poland	5.07
19	Ireland	7.72	43	Chad	6.22	67	Bhutan	5.05
20	Australia	7.67	44	Botswana	6.19	68	Barbados	5.04
21	Equatorial Guinea	7.60	45	United Kingdom	6.11	69	Jamaica	5.04

Rank	Country	Health Expenditures as Percentage of GDP	Rank	Country	Health Expenditures as Percentage of GDP	Rank	Country	Health Expenditures as Percentage of GDP
70	Turkmenistan	4.99	101	Ecuador	4.14	134	Burundi	3.28
71	Malawi	4.98	102	Gabon	4.10	135	Peru	3.21
LOWER MIDDLE			103	Togo	4.10	136	Bangladesh	3.19
72	Niger	4.98	104	Bolivia	4.01	137	Belarus	3.19
73	Thailand	4.98	105	Albania	4.0	138	Yemen	3.19
74	Kyrgyzstan	4.97	106	Congo	3.99	139	Mexico	3.17
75	Tunisia	4.91	107	Colombia	3.98	140	Zambia	3.16
76	Kuwait	4.86	108	Cyprus	3.96	141	Russia	3.02
77	Saudi Arabia	4.76	109	Turkey	3.94	142	Paraguay	2.97
78	Chile	4.73	110	Namibia	3.92	143	Malaysia	2.96
79	Qatar	4.73	111	Moldova	3.91	144	Western Samoa	2.94
80	Tanzania	4.73	112	Guinea	3.90	145	Suriname	2.88
81	Bahrain	4.62	113	Latvia	3.87	146	Nigeria	2.72
82	Uruguay	4.62	114	Romania	3.87	147	United Arab Emirates	2.66
83	Antigua and Barbuda	4.55	115	Ethiopia	3.80	148	Cameroon	2.62
84	Honduras	4.54	116	Mauritania	3.80	149	Egypt	2.61
85	Nepal	4.54	117	Jordan	3.77	150	Madagascar	2.56
86	Trinidad and Tobago	4.54	118	Fiji	3.76	151	Tuvalu	2.56
87	Georgia	4.45	119	Sri Lanka	3.74	152	Morocco	2.55
88	Kazakhstan	4.44	120	Dominican Republic	3.72	153	Iran	2.54
89	Papua New Guinea	4.44	121	Guatemala	3.70	**BOTTOM 10**		
90	Mauritius	4.40	122	Senegal	3.66	154	Laos	2.53
91	Kenya	4.33	123	Estonia	3.62	155	Sierra Leone	2.43
92	Benin	4.32	124	Venezuela	3.60	156	Zaire	2.38
93	Taiwan	4.30	125	Lithuania	3.58	157	Solomon Islands	2.18
94	Azerbaijan	4.27	126	China	3.51	158	Philippines	2.15
95	Oman	4.22	127	Ghana	3.50	159	Vietnam	2.11
96	Argentina	4.21	128	Pakistan	3.48	160	Syria	2.07
97	Brazil	4.20	129	Rwanda	3.44	161	Indonesia	2.01
98	Israel	4.20	130	Uganda	3.40	162	Singapore	1.87
99	Central African Republic	4.19	131	Cote d'Ivoire	3.35	163	Somalia	1.51
100	Armenia	4.17	132	Sudan	3.33			
			133	Ukraine	3.30			

Source: *Human Development Report*

208. HEALTH EXPENDITURES PER CAPITA

Public health expenditures represent current and capital expenditures by governments for medical care and other health services. They include national health insurance, public health, health expenditures under workmen's compensation, and in some countries public expenditures for family planning. Health expenditures are understated for some countries because of incomplete reporting at intermediate and local levels of government.

Rank	Country	Health Expenditures per Capita ($)	Rank	Country	Health Expenditures per Capita ($)	Rank	Country	Health Expenditures per Capita ($)
TOP 10			15	United Kingdom	1,039	32	Barbados	323
1	United States	2,765	16	New Zealand	925	33	Taiwan	323
2	Switzerland	2,520	17	Iceland	884	34	Seychelles	289
3	Sweden	2,343	18	Ireland	876	35	Yugoslavia	264
4	Finland	2,046	19	Spain	831	36	Saudi Arabia	260
5	Canada	1,945	20	Luxembourg	662	37	Iran	244
6	France	1,869	21	Qatar	630	38	Antigua and Barbuda	241
7	Norway	1,835	22	Kuwait	541	39	Estonia	228
8	Austria	1,711	23	Israel	480	40	Latvia	220
9	Denmark	1,588	24	Tuvalu	472	41	Singapore	215
10	Japan	1,538	25	United Arab Emirates	472	42	St. Kitts and Nevis	212
UPPER MIDDLE			26	Italy	449	43	Oman	209
11	Germany	1,511	27	Portugal	383	44	Dominica	192
12	Netherlands	1,501	28	Korea, South	365	45	Hungary	185
13	Belgium	1,449	29	Greece	359	46	Trinidad and Tobago	180
14	Australia	1,294	30	Malta	349	47	Czech Republic	169
			31	Bahrain	324	48	St. Lucia	169

Rank	Country	Health Expenditures per Capita ($)
49	Gabon	164
50	Lithuania	159
51	Russia	159
52	Belarus	157
53	Kazakhstan	154
54	Armenia	152
55	Georgia	152
56	Algeria	149
57	Brazil	146
58	Moldova	143
59	Panama	142
60	Botswana	139
61	Argentina	137
62	Grenada	133
63	Costa Rica	132
64	Ukraine	131
65	Turkmenistan	125
66	Uruguay	123
67	Bulgaria	121
68	Kyrgyzstan	118
69	Solomon Islands	117
70	Uzbekistan	116
71	St. Vincent	102
LOWER MIDDLE		
72	Chile	100
73	Mauritius	100
74	Tajikistan	100
75	Azerbaijan	99
76	Suriname	93
77	Mexico	89
78	Venezuela	88
79	Poland	84
80	South Africa	77
81	Tunisia	76
82	Turkey	76
83	Thailand	72
84	Malaysia	71
85	Fiji	70
86	Cyprus	69

Rank	Country	Health Expenditures per Capita ($)
87	Vanuatu	67
88	Cape Verde	64
89	Swaziland	64
90	Jamaica	63
91	Tonga	63
92	Peru	61
93	El Salvador	58
94	Mongolia	58
95	Romania	58
96	Jordan	55
97	Honduras	52
98	Colombia	51
99	Congo	50
100	Namibia	45
101	Ecuador	44
102	Guyana	42
103	Syria	41
104	Zimbabwe	39
105	Dominican Republic	38
106	Sao Tome e Principe	38
107	Papua New Guinea	37
108	Paraguay	35
109	Nicaragua	34
110	Sudan	34
111	Burundi	30
112	Senegal	29
113	Comoros	28
114	Cote d'Ivoire	28
115	Egypt	28
116	Equatorial Guinea	28
117	Cameroon	27
118	Guatemala	27
119	Haiti	27
120	Albania	26
121	Lesotho	26
122	Morocco	26
123	Bolivia	25
124	Belize	23
125	Gambia	22
126	India	21

Rank	Country	Health Expenditures per Capita ($)
127	Western Samoa	20
128	Yemen	20
129	Benin	19
130	Central African Republic	18
131	Mauritania	18
132	Sri Lanka	18
133	Togo	18
134	Guinea	17
135	Zambia	17
136	Guinea-Bissau	16
137	Kenya	16
138	Niger	16
139	Philippines	16
140	Ghana	15
141	Mali	15
142	Chad	12
143	Indonesia	12
144	Pakistan	12
145	China	11
146	Malawi	11
147	Bhutan	10
148	Nigeria	10
149	Rwanda	10
150	Somalia	8
151	Uganda	8
152	Burkina	7
153	Madagascar	7
BOTTOM 10		
154	Nepal	7
155	Bangladesh	6
156	Laos	5
157	Mozambique	5
158	Zaire	5
159	Ethiopia	4
160	Liberia	4
161	Sierra Leone	4
162	Tanzania	4
163	Vietnam	3

Source: *Human Development Report*

209. UNDERWEIGHT CHILDREN

The birth weight of children as well as their weight during the early years of life have a bearing on their general health. Malnutrition begins in the womb and many pregnant women in developing countries receive less nutrition than they need. The effects of the lack of nutrition in mothers is felt by the child, reducing his or her ability to fight illness and maintain adequate levels of mental and physical health.

Rank	Country	Underweight Children Under Age Five, 1990 (%)
TOP 10		
1	Bangladesh	66
2	India	63
3	Nepal	51
4	Mozambique	47
5	Niger	44
6	Pakistan	42
7	Sri Lanka	42
8	Vietnam	42
9	Afghanistan	40
10	Ethiopia	40
UPPER MIDDLE		
11	Iran	39
12	Somalia	39
13	Cambodia	38

Rank	Country	Underweight Children Under Age Five, 1990 (%)
14	Indonesia	38
15	Madagascar	38
16	Papua New Guinea	36
17	Angola	35
18	Nigeria	35
19	Laos	34
20	Philippines	34
21	Sudan	34
22	Myanmar (Burma)	33
23	Zaire	33
24	Central African Republic	32
25	Rwanda	32
26	Chad	31
27	Burundi	29
28	Congo	28
29	Botswana	27

Rank	Country	Underweight Children Under Age Five, 1990 (%)
30	Burkina	27
31	Ghana	27
32	Yemen	27
33	Sierra Leone	26
34	Uganda	26
35	Zambia	26
36	Guatemala	25
LOWER MIDDLE		
37	Benin	24
38	Guinea	24
39	Haiti	24
40	Malawi	24
41	Tanzania	24
42	Mali	22
43	China	21

Rank	Country	Underweight Children Under Age Five, 1990 (%)
44	Honduras	20
45	Liberia	20
46	Senegal	20
47	El Salvador	19
48	Nicaragua	19
49	Guyana	18
50	Lesotho	18
51	Malaysia	18
52	Togo	18
53	Cameroon	17
54	Gambia	17
55	Kenya	17
56	Mauritius	17
57	Mauritania	16
58	Gabon	15
59	Mexico	14
60	Zimbabwe	14
61	Ecuador	13

Rank	Country	Underweight Children Under Age Five, 1990 (%)
62	Jordan	13
63	Peru	13
64	Saudi Arabia	13
65	Syria	13
66	Thailand	13
67	Algeria	12
68	Cote d'Ivoire	12
69	Dominican Republic	12
70	Iraq	12
71	Morocco	12
72	Bolivia	11
73	Panama	11
74	Turkey	11
75	Colombia	10
76	Egypt	10
77	Lebanon	9
78	Swaziland	9
79	Trinidad and Tobago	9

Rank	Country	Underweight Children Under Age Five, 1990 (%)
80	Tunisia	9
81	Costa Rica	8
82	Cuba	8
83	Cyprus	8
BOTTOM 10		
84	Brazil	7
85	Jamaica	7
86	United Arab Emirates	7
87	Uruguay	7
88	Venezuela	6
89	Kuwait	5
90	Libya	4
91	Paraguay	4
92	Chile	2
93	Argentina	1

Source: *UNICEF: State of the World's Children*

LOW BIRTH WEIGHT CHILDREN

Rank	Country	Low Birth Weight Infants, 1990 (%)
TOP 10		
1	Bangladesh	50
2	India	33
3	Pakistan	25
4	Sri Lanka	25
5	Papua New Guinea	23
6	Burkina	21
7	Guinea	21
8	Afghanistan	20
9	Guinea-Bissau	20
10	Malawi	20
UPPER MIDDLE		
11	Mozambique	20
12	Togo	20
13	Angola	19
14	Yemen	19
15	Laos	18
16	Ghana	17
17	Mali	17
18	Rwanda	17
19	Sierra Leone	17
20	Vietnam	17
21	Congo	16
22	Dominican Republic	16
23	Ethiopia	16
24	Kenya	16
25	Myanmar (Burma)	16
26	Nigeria	16
27	Somalia	16
28	Central African Republic	15

Rank	Country	Low Birth Weight Infants, 1990 (%)
29	Haiti	15
30	Iraq	15
31	Nicaragua	15
32	Niger	15
33	Philippines	15
34	Sudan	15
35	Zaire	15
36	Cote d'Ivoire	14
37	Guatemala	14
38	Indonesia	14
39	Tanzania	14
LOWER MIDDLE		
40	Zimbabwe	14
41	Cameroon	13
42	Thailand	13
43	Zambia	13
44	Bolivia	12
45	Mexico	12
46	Namibia	12
47	Brazil	11
48	Ecuador	11
49	El Salvador	11
50	Jamaica	11
51	Lesotho	11
52	Mauritania	11
53	Peru	11
54	Senegal	11
55	Syria	11
56	Colombia	10
57	Egypt	10

Rank	Country	Low Birth Weight Infants, 1990 (%)
58	Lebanon	10
59	Madagascar	10
60	Malaysia	10
61	Mongolia	10
62	Oman	10
63	Panama	10
64	Trinidad and Tobago	10
65	Algeria	9
66	China	9
67	Honduras	9
68	Iran	9
69	Korea, North	9
70	Mauritius	9
71	Morocco	9
72	Venezuela	9
73	Argentina	8
74	Botswana	8
75	Cuba	8
76	Hong Kong	8
BOTTOM 10		
77	Paraguay	8
78	Tunisia	8
79	Turkey	8
80	Uruguay	8
81	Chile	7
82	Jordan	7
83	Kuwait	7
84	Singapore	7
85	Costa Rica	6
86	United Arab Emirates	6

Source: *UNICEF: State of the World's Children*

210. BREAST CANCER RATE

Breast cancer is a disease typically affecting women in developed societies. It is one of the leading causes of death in mature women.

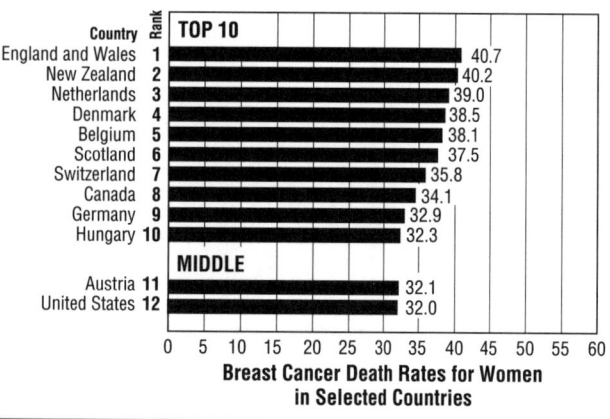

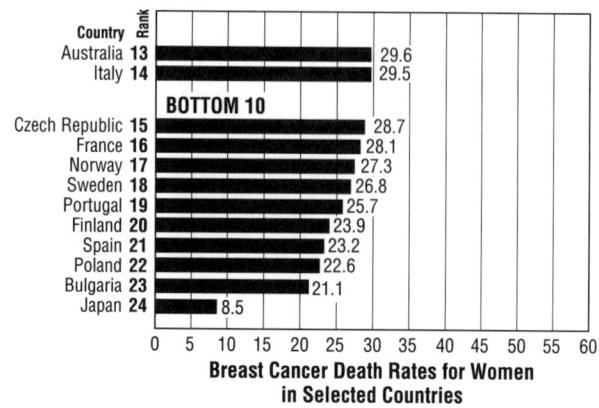

Breast Cancer Death Rates for Women in Selected Countries

Source: *World Health Statistics*

211. SUICIDES

Suicide is one of the leading causes of death in many countries, and it is the only one which is not classifiable as a medical malady and one for which there is no cure. Because psychiatrists and sociologists are divided on the nature and causes of suicide, no inferences may be drawn from the prevalence of suicide in certain countries. However, certain age groups (especially adolescents) and social classes are more prone to suicide than others.

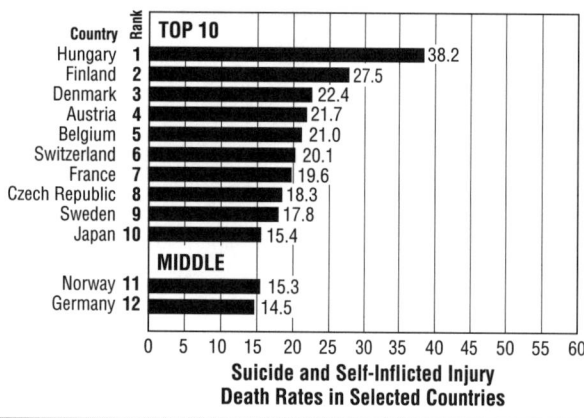

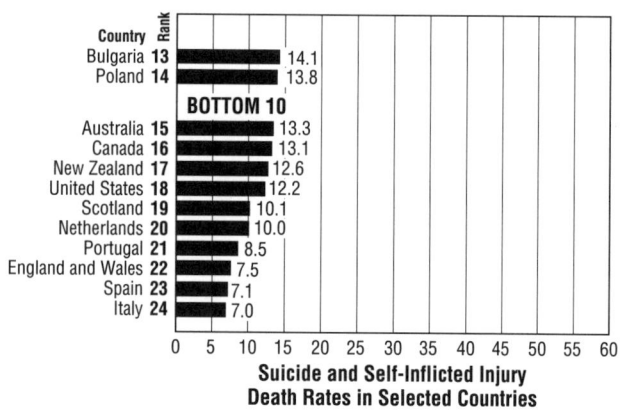

Suicide and Self-Inflicted Injury Death Rates in Selected Countries

Source: *World Health Statistics*

212. DEATH RATE FROM CANCER

The most widely available and uniformly compiled statistics relating to cancer are mortality rates. Such data cover about 36% of the world population; in the case of developed countries the data are virtually complete, but in the case of developing countries the coverage is below 5%. Statistics reveal a decreasing incidence of cancer in the principal female site, the breast, and an increasing incidence in the principal male site, the lung.

Rank	Country	Causes of Death per 100,000	Rank	Country	Causes of Death per 100,000	Rank	Country	Causes of Death per 100,000
TOP 10			40	Malta	173.8	80	Colombia	62.9
1	Hungary	312.8	41	Iceland	171.0	81	Paraguay	61.0
2	Denmark	298.5	42	Romania	163.4	82	Suriname	57.0
3	United Kingdom	280.8	43	Thailand	162.0	83	Nicaragua	56.0
4	Czech Republic	270.5	44	Yugoslavia	155.8	84	Tonga	54.9
5	Belgium	270.1	45	Argentina	143.0	85	Vietnam	54.0
6	Germany	263.7	46	Kazakhstan	135.2	86	Albania	53.5
7	Italy	260.6	47	Liechtenstein	133.9	87	Belize	52.4
8	Luxembourg	254.5	48	Moldova	131.6	88	Uzbekistan	51.5
9	France	245.7	49	Israel	130.5	89	Venezuela	51.1
10	Austria	244.3				90	Mexico	50.6
			LOWER MIDDLE			91	Ecuador	50.0
UPPER MIDDLE			50	Cuba	128.7	92	Tajikistan	48.3
11	Netherlands	236.8	51	Seychelles	128.6	93	South Africa	48.0
12	Switzerland	236.1	52	Singapore	128.0	94	Antigua and Barbuda	44.5
13	Sweden	235.0	53	Bosnia & Herzegovina	122.6	95	Cape Verde	43.8
14	Slovenia	228.9	54	Puerto Rico	122.2	96	El Salvador	43.0
15	Norway	228.4	55	Dominica	116.6	97	Nauru	38.0
16	Croatia	226.1	56	China	115.9	98	Guyana	37.1
17	Uruguay	222.8	57	Chile	111.5	99	Fiji	35.5
18	San Marino	221.1	58	Korea, South	105.6	100	Philippines	35.2
19	Estonia	218.1	59	Armenia	102.8	101	Bahrain	32.3
20	Latvia	211.3	60	Taiwan	101.5	102	Guatemala	29.8
21	Ireland	211.2	61	St. Vincent	99.7	103	Vanuatu	29.2
22	United States	206.0	62	Georgia	98.6	104	Zimbabwe	28.4
23	Russia	203.4	63	St. Kitts and Nevis	95.5	105	Dominican Republic	27.4
24	Greece	202.3	64	Grenada	90.5	106	Kuwait	27.4
25	Spain	202.1	65	Panama	85.7	107	Brunei	27.0
26	Ukraine	201.8	66	Jamaica	84.1	108	Malawi	27.0
27	Lithuania	200.8	67	Trinidad and Tobago	83.4			
28	Slovakia	200.0	68	Bahamas	80.4	**BOTTOM 10**		
29	New Zealand	199.9	69	Turkey	79.0	109	Sri Lanka	26.7
30	Finland	198.9	70	Brazil	75.0	110	Egypt	22.0
31	Poland	196.8	71	Costa Rica	74.6	111	Qatar	21.4
32	Canada	196.7	72	Peru	73.0	112	Malaysia	21.0
33	Portugal	195.5	73	Azerbaijan	72.1	113	Sao Tome e Principe	19.6
34	Japan	189.1	74	Tuvalu	70.0	114	Morocco	14.0
35	Belarus	184.5	75	Korea, North	69.0	115	Honduras	12.4
36	Bulgaria	183.9	76	Kyrgyzstan	67.9	116	Syria	12.0
37	Bermuda	181.5	77	Turkmenistan	65.1	117	Western Samoa	11.2
38	Australia	179.9	78	St. Lucia	64.4	118	Macedonia	6.2
39	Barbados	178.5	79	Mauritius	64.0			

Source: *World Health Statistics Annual*

CAUSES OF DEATH

Death rates or mortality rates are among the most widely available and uniformly compiled. These rates are primarily used by demographers, actuaries and statisticians for a variety of purposes. But for medical purposes, the causes of death are even more important. Causes of death data reveal the incidence of certain types of disease in a country, their spread, and their peculiarities and gender differences, as well as the way they affect certain social classes and age groups. Certain death-causing diseases are peculiar to developed countries and others to developing countries. Certain diseases, like tuberculosis, have been contained through medical advances, while others, like AIDS, have emerged as scourges.

213. CAUSES OF DEATH—ACCIDENTS

Rank	Country	Accidents Rate per 100,000	Rank	Country	Accidents Rate per 100,000	Rank	Country	Accidents Rate per 100,000
TOP 10			39	Ecuador	66.7	78	Kuwait	41.3
1	Russia	249.3	40	Chile	66.1	79	Bahamas	40.8
2	Estonia	232.2	41	Bulgaria	65.3	80	Australia	40.3
3	Latvia	212.3	42	Belgium	65.1	81	Barbados	40.3
4	Lithuania	167.2	43	Taiwan	63.7	82	Brunei	39.8
5	El Salvador	137.0	44	Austria	63.4	83	Costa Rica	39.7
6	Sri Lanka	135.7	45	St. Vincent	62.8	84	Egypt	39.1
7	Kazakhstan	133.0	46	Turkmenistan	62.4	85	Bermuda	38.6
8	Belarus	132.6	47	Uruguay	61.7	86	Ireland	38.5
9	Colombia	132.3	48	Venezuela	61.4	87	Israel	38.4
10	Ukraine	128.8				88	Iceland	38.3
			LOWER MIDDLE			89	Korea, North	38.2
UPPER MIDDLE			49	Portugal	61.2	90	Qatar	36.0
11	Hungary	119.5	50	Georgia	58.2	91	Liechtenstein	35.9
12	Nauru	116.0	51	Norway	57.0	92	Netherlands	35.7
13	Moldova	105.3	52	Yugoslavia	57.0	93	Macedonia	35.3
14	Thailand	104.0	53	Guyana	56.5	94	St. Lucia	34.7
15	South Africa	99.3	54	China	55.6	95	United Kingdom	34.2
16	Kyrgyzstan	95.7	55	United States	54.9	96	Puerto Rico	34.1
17	Slovenia	95.1	56	Italy	53.2	97	Dominican Republic	33.7
18	Belize	92.6	57	Sweden	52.9	98	Singapore	32.5
19	Croatia	91.8	58	Uzbekistan	52.9	99	Fiji	32.2
20	Brazil	91.0	59	Germany	52.6	100	Albania	31.7
21	Finland	85.2	60	New Zealand	52.6	101	Cape Verde	30.1
22	Czech Republic	82.3	61	Guatemala	52.0	102	St. Kitts and Nevis	29.5
23	France	81.1	62	Argentina	51.6	103	Malaysia	28.5
24	Cuba	79.9	63	Trinidad and Tobago	51.4	104	Turkey	28.0
25	Panama	78.7	64	Paraguay	49.0	105	Syria	27.0
26	Malawi	78.0	65	Grenada	47.9	106	Malta	21.9
27	Slovakia	76.0	66	Spain	47.6			
28	Romania	74.3	67	Japan	47.3	**BOTTOM 10**		
29	Denmark	74.1	68	Canada	47.2	107	Morocco	19.2
30	Armenia	73.8	69	Bosnia & Herzegovina	47.1	108	Bahrain	19.0
31	Korea, South	73.0	70	San Marino	45.7	109	Dominica	18.0
32	Poland	73.0	71	Zimbabwe	44.9	110	Sao Tome e Principe	14.3
33	Philippines	71.8	72	Mauritius	44.7	111	Maldives	9.9
34	Mexico	69.5	73	Tajikistan	43.5	112	Vanuatu	9.1
35	Suriname	69.0	74	Seychelles	43.3	113	Jamaica	8.4
36	Switzerland	68.7	75	Honduras	42.2	114	Antigua and Barbuda	5.1
37	Luxembourg	67.6	76	Azerbaijan	42.1	115	Tonga	4.1
38	Peru	67.0	77	Greece	41.5	116	Western Samoa	2.5

Source: *World Health Statistics Annual*

214. CAUSES OF DEATH—RESPIRATORY DISEASES

Rank	Country	Respiratory Diseases Rate per 100,000	Rank	Country	Respiratory Diseases Rate per 100,000	Rank	Country	Respiratory Diseases Rate per 100,000
TOP 10			40	Luxembourg	69.3	80	Barbados	39.9
1	Malawi	265.0	41	Hungary	68.8	81	Guyana	39.8
2	Turkmenistan	160.6	42	Mauritius	68.6	82	Zimbabwe	39.5
3	Guatemala	145.7	43	Switzerland	68.2	83	Costa Rica	38.5
4	Egypt	140.7	44	Maldives	66.2	84	South Africa	38.2
5	China	131.9	45	France	65.8	85	El Salvador	38.0
6	Kyrgyzstan	131.5	46	Germany	65.2	86	Colombia	37.9
7	Tajikistan	125.4	47	Chile	64.9	87	Liechtenstein	35.9
8	United Kingdom	120.4	48	Netherlands	64.8	88	Poland	35.8
9	Tuvalu	120.0	49	Moldova	64.2	89	Dominican Republic	35.4
10	Uzbekistan	119.2				90	Macedonia	34.5
			LOWER MIDDLE			91	Suriname	34.0
UPPER MIDDLE			50	Brazil	64.0	92	St. Vincent	33.2
11	Ireland	116.7	51	Bulgaria	63.3	93	Fiji	31.7
12	Norway	106.7	52	Canada	62.8	94	Tonga	31.5
13	Peru	100.0	53	Slovenia	60.3	95	Sri Lanka	31.1
14	Denmark	98.9	54	Italy	59.6	96	Trinidad and Tobago	31.1
15	Seychelles	98.8	55	Malta	58.4	97	Vanuatu	30.4
16	Romania	94.0	56	Cuba	58.0	98	Jamaica	30.2
17	Japan	93.6	57	Belize	57.1	99	Croatia	29.5
18	Iceland	89.5	58	Australia	56.8	100	Bosnia & Herzegovina	29.0
19	Azerbaijan	88.9	59	Thailand	55.0	101	Turkey	29.0
20	Belgium	88.1	60	Grenada	54.1	102	Venezuela	29.0
21	Singapore	86.9	61	Greece	53.9	103	Bahrain	27.7
22	Sao Tome e Principe	86.5	62	Paraguay	53.0	104	Panama	26.9
23	Finland	85.6	63	Bahamas	52.2	105	Honduras	26.3
24	Kazakhstan	85.5	64	Georgia	51.4	106	Bermuda	25.2
25	Sweden	82.9	65	Argentina	49.0	107	Taiwan	24.3
26	St. Kitts and Nevis	81.8	66	St. Lucia	48.5	108	Korea, South	24.0
27	New Zealand	81.7	67	Austria	48.2			
28	Spain	80.7	68	Lithuania	48.2	**BOTTOM 10**		
29	Puerto Rico	80.5	69	Armenia	48.0	109	Brunei	23.4
30	Russia	80.3	70	Yugoslavia	47.5	110	Philippines	20.5
31	Portugal	78.9	71	Korea, North	46.7	111	Syria	19.0
32	Slovakia	77.0	72	Czech Republic	46.6	112	Nauru	16.0
33	Uruguay	76.3	73	Mexico	45.9	113	Kuwait	13.7
34	Albania	75.0	74	Antigua and Barbuda	44.5	114	San Marino	13.6
35	Ukraine	74.0	75	Estonia	44.3	115	Western Samoa	9.9
36	Nicaragua	73.0	76	Israel	44.1	116	Morocco	9.5
37	Cape Verde	72.3	77	Dominica	43.0	117	Malaysia	7.5
38	United States	70.1	78	Latvia	41.7	118	Qatar	7.5
39	Belarus	69.7	79	Ecuador	40.6			

Source: *World Health Statistics Annual*

215. CAUSES OF DEATH—CIRCULATORY DISEASES

Rank	Country	Circulatory Diseases Rate per 100,000
TOP 10		
1	Ukraine	915.5
2	Russia	832.6
3	Estonia	816.0
4	Bulgaria	810.4
5	Hungary	751.7
6	Romania	707.7
7	Lithuania	670.2
8	Czech Republic	638.9
9	Belarus	624.7
10	Croatia	571.8
UPPER MIDDLE		
11	Georgia	553.2
12	Sweden	549.7
13	Austria	544.5
14	Germany	543.1
15	Poland	529.7
16	Yugoslavia	528.3
17	Slovakia	521.0
18	Denmark	513.9
19	Latvia	503.8
20	United Kingdom	501.0
21	Finland	485.2
22	Norway	482.9
23	Portugal	469.1
24	Greece	460.2
25	Slovenia	454.7
26	Moldova	452.2
27	St. Kitts and Nevis	443.2
28	Italy	425.3
29	Kazakhstan	425.1
30	Luxembourg	416.5
31	Belgium	398.9
32	Ireland	393.3
33	Switzerland	390.8
34	Macedonia	385.8
35	Armenia	383.9
36	Uruguay	378.4
37	Barbados	366.8
38	United States	364.7
39	Turkey	358.0

Rank	Country	Circulatory Diseases Rate per 100,000
40	Malta	354.5
41	Spain	353.2
42	New Zealand	351.1
43	Bermuda	344.4
44	Bosnia & Herzegovina	344.1
45	Netherlands	339.6
46	Argentina	337.3
47	Kyrgyzstan	330.8
48	Liechtenstein	326.4
49	San Marino	325.6
LOWER MIDDLE		
50	Egypt	314.4
51	Australia	307.8
52	France	298.2
53	Mauritius	297.1
54	Cuba	294.7
55	Iceland	294.6
56	Azerbaijan	292.4
57	Grenada	290.3
58	Seychelles	288.4
59	Uzbekistan	283.4
60	Turkmenistan	275.3
61	Canada	274.4
62	Dominica	273.5
63	Israel	268.4
64	Trinidad and Tobago	260.0
65	Japan	253.4
66	Thailand	250.0
67	Puerto Rico	242.3
68	Antigua and Barbuda	237.5
69	Korea, North	224.9
70	St. Vincent	222.5
71	Brazil	206.0
72	St. Lucia	205.6
73	Guyana	202.5
74	Paraguay	201.0
75	China	199.4
76	Jamaica	189.5
77	Albania	187.9
78	Tajikistan	185.8
79	Singapore	185.3

Country		Circulatory Diseases Rate per 100,000
80	Suriname	179.0
81	Maldives	170.1
82	Panama	167.0
83	Belize	164.0
84	Tonga	158.5
85	Chile	157.4
86	Fiji	153.4
87	Tuvalu	150.0
88	Korea, South	149.0
89	Colombia	144.7
90	Sao Tome e Principe	143.5
91	Nicaragua	142.0
92	Taiwan	140.1
93	Cape Verde	135.8
94	Bahamas	126.3
95	Vietnam	123.8
96	El Salvador	120.0
97	Peru	115.0
98	Venezuela	115.0
99	Costa Rica	111.3
100	Sri Lanka	104.4
101	Mexico	101.2
102	Dominican Republic	100.3
103	Ecuador	93.1
104	South Africa	91.2
105	Nauru	89.0
106	Bahrain	86.6
107	Syria	86.0
108	Philippines	82.2
109	Kuwait	82.1
BOTTOM 10		
110	Brunei	80.0
111	Qatar	59.9
112	Guatemala	57.2
113	Malaysia	54.1
114	Malawi	50.0
115	Honduras	48.4
116	Zimbabwe	40.8
117	Vanuatu	39.0
118	Morocco	35.5
119	Western Samoa	24.2

Source: *World Health Statistics Annual*

216. FOOD SUPPLY—PROTEINS

The FAO and WHO recommendation for per capita daily consumption of protein is 65 grams, subject to variations because of age, climate, occupation and other factors. This requirements is exceeded in most industrialized countries.

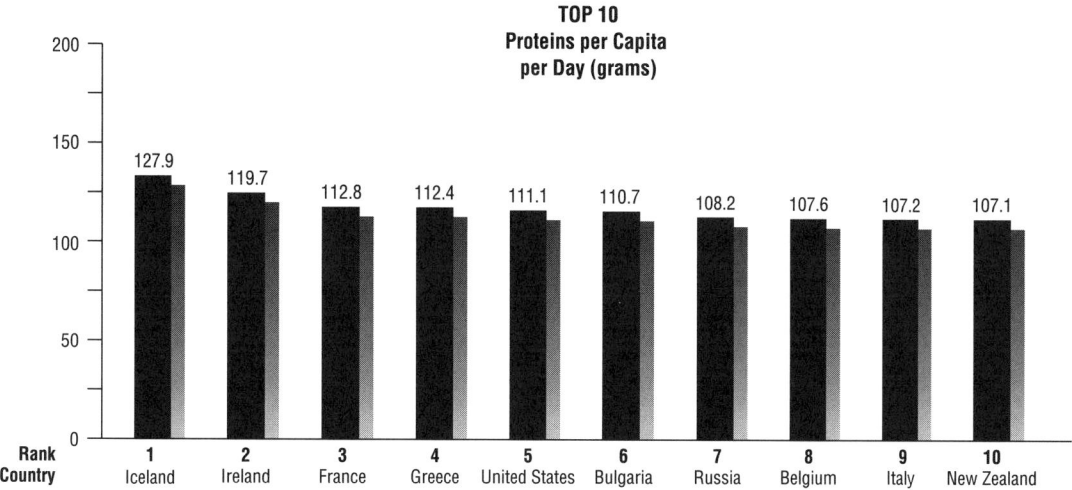

TOP 10
Proteins per Capita
per Day (grams)

Rank	1	2	3	4	5	6	7	8	9	10
Country	Iceland	Ireland	France	Greece	United States	Bulgaria	Russia	Belgium	Italy	New Zealand
	127.9	119.7	112.8	112.4	111.1	110.7	108.2	107.6	107.2	107.1

Rank	Country	Proteins per Capita per Day (grams)	Rank	Country	Proteins per Capita per Day (grams)	Rank	Country	Proteins per Capita per Day (grams)
UPPER MIDDLE			60	Albania	73.7	108	Gambia	56.2
11	United Arab Emirates	105.8	61	Mauritius	72.1	109	Benin	56.0
12	Bermuda	105.6	62	Mauritania	71.7	110	India	55.7
13	Czech Republic	105.4	63	Cuba	71.6	111	Kenya	55.7
14	Israel	103.1	64	Iraq	71.0	112	Cameroon	55.3
15	Germany	102.9	65	St. Kitts and Nevis	69.7	113	El Salvador	55.2
16	Canada	101.4	66	St. Lucia	69.7	114	Guatemala	55.0
17	Spain	101.4	67	Chile	69.6	115	Honduras	55.0
18	Australia	100.7	68	Botswana	69.0	116	Tanzania	54.2
19	Hungary	100.6	69	Jordan	68.4	117	Zambia	53.9
20	Poland	100.2	70	Paraguay	67.9	118	Zimbabwe	53.7
21	Norway	99.9	71	Belize	67.8	119	Malaysia	53.6
22	Barbados	98.9	72	Cape Verde	66.7	120	Burundi	53.4
23	Denmark	98.6				121	Nicaragua	53.3
24	Yugoslavia	98.4	**LOWER MIDDLE**			122	Solomon Islands	53.3
25	Argentina	98.3	73	Kiribati	66.2	123	Uganda	53.0
26	Portugal	97.9	74	China	66.0	124	Ethiopia	52.9
27	Finland	97.6	75	Burkina	65.8	125	Madagascar	52.3
28	Austria	97.3	76	Senegal	65.3	126	Papua New Guinea	51.7
29	Japan	95.6	77	Guyana	65.2	127	Bolivia	51.3
30	Switzerland	94.5	78	Yemen	65.0	128	Vietnam	51.2
31	Sweden	93.7	79	Pakistan	64.6	129	Guinea	51.1
32	United Kingdom	93.7	80	Trinidad and Tobago	64.6	130	Togo	51.1
33	Romania	92.9	81	Fiji	64.4	131	Cambodia	50.8
34	Malta	90.0	82	Niger	64.4	132	Peru	50.8
35	Netherlands	89.6	83	Costa Rica	64.0	133	Cote d'Ivoire	50.4
36	Saudi Arabia	88.6	84	Vanuatu	63.5	134	Dominican Republic	50.4
37	Maldives	88.0	85	Swaziland	62.3	135	Ecuador	50.0
38	Singapore	87.1	86	Namibia	62.2	136	Chad	49.6
39	Turkey	85.5	87	Mali	62.0	137	Rwanda	48.9
40	Mongolia	85.1	88	Brazil	61.7	138	Afghanistan	47.6
41	Egypt	84.5	89	Jamaica	61.6	139	Sri Lanka	47.6
42	Tunisia	83.3	90	Grenada	61.5	140	Thailand	47.5
43	Uruguay	82.5	91	Myanmar (Burma)	61.5	141	Congo	47.0
44	Lebanon	82.2	92	Gabon	61.3	142	Central African Republic	46.9
45	Korea, North	82.0	93	Laos	60.8	143	Haiti	46.7
46	Kuwait	81.9	94	Suriname	60.0	144	Sao Tome e Principe	45.6
47	Morocco	81.9	95	Djibouti	59.9			
48	Mexico	81.5	96	Somalia	59.6	**BOTTOM 10**		
49	Syria	81.5	97	Panama	59.3	145	Angola	44.3
50	Iran	81.1	98	Lesotho	59.1	146	Ghana	43.8
51	Libya	80.3	99	Seychelles	58.7	147	Bangladesh	43.6
52	Antigua and Barbuda	79.5	100	Malawi	58.4	148	Guinea-Bissau	43.4
53	Bahamas	79.0	101	Venezuela	57.9	149	Nigeria	42.9
54	Korea, South	79.0	102	Nepal	57.5	150	Sierra Leone	39.9
55	South Africa	79.0	103	Indonesia	57.3	151	Comoros	38.3
56	Tonga	77.5	104	St. Vincent	57.2	152	Liberia	37.1
57	Algeria	75.7	105	Colombia	56.5	153	Zaire	33.7
58	Dominica	75.3	106	Philippines	56.5	154	Mozambique	30.3
59	Brunei	75.2	107	Sudan	56.5			

Source: *UN Statistical Yearbook*

217. FOOD SUPPLY—CALORIES

The FAO and WHO recommendation of per capita daily consumption of calories is 2,600, but there are considerable variations in requirements because of age, climate, occupation and other factors.

Rank	Country	Caloric Consumption per Capita	Rank	Country	Caloric Consumption per Capita	Rank	Country	Caloric Consumption per Capita
TOP 10			55	Saudi Arabia	2,932	110	Gambia	2,290
1	Ireland	3,951	56	Japan	2,921	111	Pakistan	2,283
2	Belgium	3,925	57	Dominica	2,911	112	Thailand	2,280
3	Luxembourg	3,925	58	Mauritius	2,897	113	Solomon Islands	2,277
4	Greece	3,775	59	Taiwan	2,872	114	Panama	2,269
5	Bulgaria	3,695	60	Brunei	2,859	115	Togo	2,269
6	United States	3,642	61	Korea, North	2,843	116	Liberia	2,264
7	Denmark	3,639	62	Korea, South	2,826	117	Botswana	2,260
8	Hungary	3,608	63	Cape Verde	2,780	118	Mali	2,259
9	France	3,593	64	Bahamas	2,776	119	Zimbabwe	2,256
10	Monaco	3,593	65	Trinidad and Tobago	2,769	120	Guatemala	2,254
			66	Fiji	2,768	121	Sri Lanka	2,246
UPPER MIDDLE			67	Vanuatu	2,736	122	Guinea	2,243
11	Czech Republic	3,574	68	Brazil	2,730	123	Niger	2,240
12	Andorra	3,567	69	Costa Rica	2,711	124	Guinea-Bissau	2,235
13	Yugoslavia	3,545	70	Jordan	2,710	125	Nicaragua	2,234
14	Germany	3,522	71	Paraguay	2,684	126	Yemen	2,231
15	Switzerland	3,508				127	India	2,229
16	Italy	3,498	**LOWER MIDDLE**			128	Burkina	2,218
17	San Marino	3,498	72	Malaysia	2,671	129	Vietnam	2,216
18	Austria	3,486	73	Uruguay	2,668	130	Honduras	2,211
19	Iceland	3,473	74	China	2,642	131	Cameroon	2,208
20	Spain	3,472	75	Swaziland	2,634	132	Nepal	2,206
21	New Zealand	3,460	76	Indonesia	2,605	133	Nigeria	2,199
22	Poland	3,426	77	Papua New Guinea	2,589	134	Tanzania	2,195
23	Russia	3,380	78	Albania	2,585	135	Uganda	2,179
24	Portugal	3,342	79	Belize	2,575	136	Madagascar	2,156
25	Egypt	3,310	80	Cote d'Ivoire	2,565	137	Sao Tome e Principe	2,153
26	Australia	3,302	81	Jamaica	2,558	138	Ghana	2,141
27	Libya	3,293	82	Kiribati	2,516	139	Zaire	2,129
28	United Arab Emirates	3,286	83	Guyana	2,495	140	Cambodia	2,122
29	United Kingdom	3,270	84	Latvia	2,490	141	Lesotho	2,121
30	Canada	3,242	85	Chile	2,484	142	Lithuania	2,110
31	Norway	3,221	86	Western Samoa	2,469	143	Kenya	2,064
32	Israel	3,220	87	Laos	2,465	144	Malawi	2,048
33	Barbados	3,217	88	St. Vincent	2,460	145	Sudan	2,042
34	Turkey	3,197	89	Colombia	2,453	146	Bangladesh	2,038
35	Malta	3,169	90	Myanmar (Burma)	2,453	147	Peru	2,035
36	Lebanon	3,142	91	Mauritania	2,447	148	Zambia	2,016
37	South Africa	3,134	92	Gabon	2,442	149	Bolivia	2,012
38	Cuba	3,129	93	Venezuela	2,440	150	Haiti	2,005
39	Tunisia	3,123	94	Suriname	2,436	151	Namibia	1,968
40	Singapore	3,121	95	St. Kitts and Nevis	2,435	152	Burundi	1,947
41	Syria	3,121	96	St. Lucia	2,424			
42	Iraq	3,092	97	Grenada	2,400	**BOTTOM 10**		
43	Romania	3,081	98	Maldives	2,400	153	Rwanda	1,915
44	Netherlands	3,078	99	Ecuador	2,399	154	Sierra Leone	1,899
45	Argentina	3,068	100	Benin	2,383	155	Angola	1,880
46	Finland	3,066	101	Djibouti	2,363	156	Somalia	1,873
47	Mexico	3,061	102	Mongolia	2,361	157	Central African Republic	1,847
48	Kuwait	3,057	103	Seychelles	2,356	158	Mozambique	1,804
49	Morocco	3,031	104	Philippines	2,343	159	Afghanistan	1,764
50	Iran	3,022	105	El Salvador	2,331	160	Comoros	1,760
51	Sweden	2,976	106	Senegal	2,323	161	Chad	1,733
52	Tonga	2,967	107	Dominican Republic	2,310	162	Ethiopia	1,699
53	Bermuda	2,960	108	Antigua and Barbuda	2,307			
54	Algeria	2,945	109	Congo	2,295			

Source: *UN Statistical Yearbook*

218. DEATHS FROM MOTOR VEHICLE ACCIDENTS

Motor vehicle accidents have become a leading cause of fatalities in many countries of the world. Such accidents are not only due to the number of motor vehicles on the road but are also affected by the condition of the roads, national driving habits, lack of driver education, pedestrian habits and the type of cars (smaller cars result in fewer accidents but in a larger proportion of fatalities). Other factors include the effectiveness of the traffic police and the availability of medical and ambulance services.

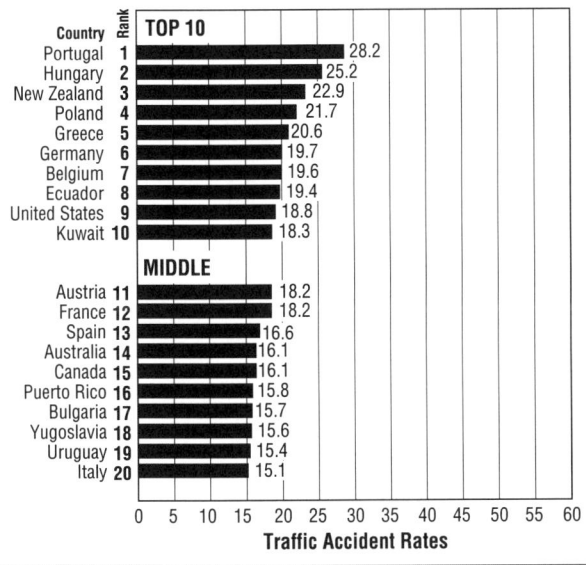

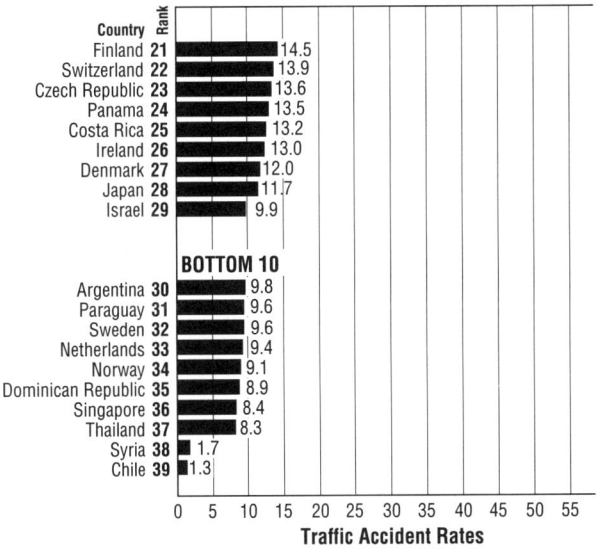

Source: *World Health Statistics Annual*

219. MATERNAL MORTALITY RATE

Maternal deaths are defined as deaths caused by complications of childbirth and pregnancy. They include maternal deaths caused by the death of the fetus and induced abortion. The data are compiled from civil registers and are thus subject to the same limitations as other vital statistics.

Rank	Country	Maternal Mortality Rate per 100,000 Live Births	Rank	Country	Maternal Mortality Rate per 100,000 Live Births	Rank	Country	Maternal Mortality Rate per 100,000 Live Births
TOP 10			14	Italy	4.8	30	Israel	8.5
1	Iceland	0.0	15	Slovenia	5.1	31	Japan	9.2
2	Luxembourg	0.0	16	Germany	5.5	32	Hungary	9.9
3	Malta	0.0	17	Spain	5.5	33	Cyprus	10
4	Sweden	0.0	18	Norway	5.8	34	Solomon Islands	10
5	Kuwait	1.9	19	Portugal	6.1	35	Czech Republic	11.6
6	Greece	2.5	20	Macedonia	6.2	36	Poland	11.8
7	Canada	2.9	21	Belgium	6.6	37	Armenia	12.8
8	Finland	3.1	22	United Kingdom	6.7	38	France	12.9
9	Australia	3.4	23	Netherlands	7.1	39	Korea, South	13.7
10	Croatia	3.6	24	Denmark	7.4	40	Uruguay	15.9
			25	Ireland	7.6	41	Puerto Rico	20.1
UPPER MIDDLE			26	Taiwan	7.8	42	Lithuania	20.5
11	Singapore	4.1	27	Bahrain	7.9	43	Belarus	21.1
12	Austria	4.2	28	United States	8.2	44	Bulgaria	21.3
13	Switzerland	4.6	29	New Zealand	8.4	45	Barbados	26.7

Rank	Country	Maternal Mortality Rate per 100,000 Live Births	Rank	Country	Maternal Mortality Rate per 100,000 Live Births	Rank	Country	Maternal Mortality Rate per 100,000 Live Births
46	Azerbaijan	28.6	86	Sao Tome e Principe	76.7	128	Indonesia	450
47	Uzbekistan	30.1	87	South Africa	84	129	Sierra Leone	450
48	Suriname	31.1	88	Guatemala	92.3	130	India	460
49	Ukraine	31.3	89	China	95	131	Myanmar (Burma)	460
50	Estonia	33	90	Mauritius	99.2	132	Cambodia	500
51	Moldova	34.1	91	Philippines	100	133	Comoros	500
52	Costa Rica	34.5	92	Iran	120	134	Pakistan	500
53	El Salvador	37.4	93	Iraq	120	135	Sudan	550
54	Chile	40.5	94	Jamaica	120	136	Uganda	550
55	Korea, North	41	95	Vietnam	120	137	Ethiopia	560
56	Saudi Arabia	41	96	United Arab Emirates	130	138	Madagascar	570
57	Fiji	41.1	97	Algeria	140	139	Bangladesh	600
58	Cuba	41.8	98	Syria	140	140	Bolivia	600
59	Albania	43.1	99	Turkey	150	141	Central African Republic	600
60	Sri Lanka	46.5	100	Zambia	150	142	Haiti	600
61	Jordan	48	101	Ecuador	152.2	143	Liberia	600
62	Trinidad and Tobago	49.2	102	Benin	160	144	Senegal	600
63	Kazakhstan	49.6	103	Kenya	170	145	Cote d'Ivoire	680
64	Thailand	50	104	Gabon	190	146	Guinea-Bissau	700
65	Russia	50.8	105	Guyana	200	147	Niger	700
66	Mexico	51.3	106	Lebanon	200	148	Djibouti	740
67	Argentina	52.0	107	Mongolia	200	149	Burundi	800
68	Tajikistan	53.2	108	Rwanda	210	150	Equatorial Guinea	800
69	Georgia	54.9	109	Honduras	220	151	Guinea	800
70	Turkmenistan	55.2	110	Oman	220	152	Mauritania	800
71	Bosnia & Herzegovina	56.0	111	Kiribati	225	153	Nigeria	800
72	Malaysia	59	112	Botswana	250	154	Yemen	800
73	Romania	60.3	113	Paraguay	280.3	155	Zaire	800
			114	Latvia	299	156	Burkina	810
LOWER MIDDLE			115	Laos	300			
74	Nicaragua	61.2	116	Morocco	300	**BOTTOM 10**		
75	Panama	62.6	117	Mozambique	300	157	Nepal	830
76	Kyrgyzstan	62.9	118	Peru	300	158	Angola	900
77	Afghanistan	64.0	119	Maldives	313.4	159	Congo	900
78	Venezuela	64.1	120	Zimbabwe	330	160	Papua New Guinea	900
79	Brazil	64.7	121	Tanzania	340	161	Chad	960
80	Egypt	65.2	122	Lesotho	350	162	Gambia	1000
81	Grenada	65.4	123	Namibia	370	163	Ghana	1000
82	Colombia	69.2	124	Malawi	400	164	Somalia	1100
83	Bahamas	69.3	125	Swaziland	400	165	Bhutan	1310
84	Libya	70	126	Togo	420	166	Mali	2000
85	Tunisia	70	127	Cameroon	430			

Source: *World Development Report*

220. HOSPITAL ADMISSIONS

Western medicine has been historically oriented toward the provision of medical infrastructures as well as inpatient hospital care. Much of its admired technology is available—alas—only within the walls of a hospital, where the physicians' skills are augmented by an increasingly sophisticated array of medical hardware. It is often the machine and not the physician that does the work and deserves the credit, if not the check. Hospital admissions, which this ranking examines, does not so much show which nations have more sick people than others, but rather which people have more access to and rely more on inpatient medical care. Some of these hospital admissions may not have been strictly necessary or may have been avoidable if other therapeutic procedures were followed, but for many modern medical shamans as well as their patients, hospital admission is the first step toward cure and recovery.

Rank	Country	Hospital Admissions Rate per 10,000
TOP 10		
1	Iceland	2,781
2	Austria	2,619
3	France	2,318
4	Finland	2,276
5	Hungary	2,234
6	Russia	2,150
7	Latvia	2,106
8	Lithuania	1,966
9	Belgium	1,963
10	Luxembourg	1,956
UPPER MIDDLE		
11	Czech Republic	1,938
12	Israel	1,935
13	Sweden	1,881
14	Germany	1,843
15	Kyrgyzstan	1,775
16	Estonia	1,773
17	Slovakia	1,679
18	Seychelles	1,605
19	Slovenia	1,579
20	Norway	1,569
21	Italy	1,554
22	Tajikistan	1,492
23	Sri Lanka	1,464
24	Ireland	1,448
25	Mauritius	1,440
26	United Kingdom	1,434
27	Cuba	1,376
28	New Zealand	1,374
29	Tuvalu	1,368
30	Greece	1,367
31	Bermuda	1,319
32	Poland	1,288

Rank	Country	Hospital Admissions Rate per 10,000
33	Brazil	1,277
34	Bahrain	1,274
35	Denmark	1,253
36	Zambia	1,249
37	Oman	1,226
38	United States	1,191
LOWER MIDDLE		
39	Singapore	1,174
40	Croatia	1,172
41	Portugal	1,146
42	Trinidad and Tobago	1,114
43	Puerto Rico	1,101
44	St. Kitts and Nevis	1,068
45	Yugoslavia	1,060
46	Netherlands	1,057
47	Chile	1,041
48	Dominica	1,026
49	Spain	997
50	Costa Rica	958
51	Kuwait	950
52	Macedonia	913
53	Grenada	910
54	Western Samoa	894
55	St. Lucia	890
56	Fiji	886
57	Bangladesh	853
58	Bahamas	822
59	Barbados	810
60	St. Vincent	776
61	Panama	773
62	Suriname	766
63	Cyprus	747
64	Malaysia	717
65	Iraq	645

Rank	Country	Hospital Admissions Rate per 10,000
66	Tonga	622
67	Korea, South	620
68	Colombia	614
69	Venezuela	601
70	Nicaragua	596
71	Turkey	568
72	Vanuatu	567
73	Jamaica	550
74	Zimbabwe	546
75	Philippines	538
76	Bosnia & Herzegovina	529
77	Argentina	520
78	Ecuador	518
79	Honduras	503
80	Syria	474
81	Dominican Republic	470
82	Malawi	436
83	China	418
84	Jordan	408
85	Mexico	403
86	Uruguay	401
87	Guatemala	284
BOTTOM 10		
88	Maldives	256
89	Papua New Guinea	253
90	Bolivia	252
91	Angola	238
92	Morocco	238
93	Lesotho	221
94	Burundi	109
95	Rwanda	85
96	Antigua and Barbuda	63
97	Nepal	54

Source: *World Health Statistics Annual*

221. HOSPITAL BEDS

Hospital establishments include general and specialized hospitals, as well as other medical establishments with beds, such as medical centers, bedded dispensaries, leprosaria, rehabilitation and physiotherapy centers, establishments for alcoholics and convalescent homes. Care should be taken in interpreting the data in this ranking because in almost all countries of the world hospitals are unduly concentrated in urban areas so that the rural population does not receive the medical advantages their urban counterparts enjoy. Also, it must be kept in mind that the very definition of what constitutes a hospital can vary widely.

TOP 10
Hospital Beds

1 bed = 100,000 beds

Rank	Country	10,000 Beds
1	Monaco	168
2	Japan	136
3	Korea, North	135
4	Kazakhstan	134
5	Ukraine	130
6	Belarus	122
7	Moldova	122
8	Latvia	121
9	Nigeria	121
10	France	120

Rank	Country	Hospital Beds per 10,000
UPPER MIDDLE		
11	Russia	119
12	Lithuania	117
13	Luxembourg	115
14	Turkmenistan	115
15	Iceland	111
16	Bulgaria	106
17	Azerbaijan	105
18	Georgia	105
19	Mongolia	105
20	Kyrgyzstan	99
21	Czech Republic	98
22	Hungary	98
23	Romania	95
24	Austria	92
25	Slovakia	91
26	Finland	90
27	Tajikistan	88
28	Uzbekistan	85
29	Estonia	84
30	Armenia	83
31	Germany	80
32	Switzerland	78
33	New Zealand	77
34	Belgium	76
35	Barbados	75
36	Italy	68
37	St. Kitts and Nevis	67
38	San Marino	66
39	Antigua and Barbuda	65
40	Israel	63
41	Poland	63
42	Croatia	61
43	Cuba	61
44	Malta	58
45	Slovenia	58
46	Albania	57
47	Netherlands	57
48	Seychelles	56
49	Yugoslavia	55
50	United Kingdom	54
51	Norway	53
52	Solomon Islands	53
53	Macedonia	52
54	Sweden	52
55	Gabon	51
56	Australia	50
57	Canada	50
58	Greece	50
59	Lebanon	50
60	Taiwan	48
61	Suriname	47
62	Bosnia & Herzegovina	46
63	United States	46
64	Namibia	45
65	Uruguay	45
66	Argentina	44
67	St. Vincent	44
68	Bermuda	42
69	Portugal	42

Rank	Country	Hospital Beds per 10,000
70	Spain	42
71	Libya	41
72	Bahamas	40
73	Kiribati	40
74	Papua New Guinea	40
75	South Africa	39
76	Grenada	38
77	Brazil	37
78	St. Lucia	37
79	Brunei	36
80	Singapore	36
81	Tuvalu	36
82	Denmark	35
83	Liechtenstein	35
84	Ireland	34
85	Western Samoa	34
86	Congo	33
87	Trinidad and Tobago	33
LOWER MIDDLE		
88	Chile	32
89	Tonga	31
90	Belize	29
91	Equatorial Guinea	29
92	Korea, South	29
93	Panama	29
94	Zambia	29
95	Mauritius	28
96	Sri Lanka	28
97	Cameroon	27
98	Djibouti	27
99	Vietnam	27
100	Kuwait	26
101	Puerto Rico	26
102	Venezuela	26
103	Botswana	25
104	Comoros	25
105	Dominica	25
106	Laos	25
107	China	24
108	Turkey	24
109	Bahrain	23
110	Guyana	23
111	Oman	23
112	Algeria	22
113	Fiji	22
114	Jamaica	22
115	Malaysia	22
116	Vanuatu	22
117	Costa Rica	21
118	Saudi Arabia	21
119	United Arab Emirates	21
120	Zaire	21
121	Andorra	20
122	Dominican Republic	20
123	Egypt	20
124	Qatar	20
125	Tunisia	20
126	Burundi	19
127	Cyprus	18

Rank	Country	Hospital Beds per 10,000
128	Iraq	18
129	El Salvador	17
130	Peru	17
131	Thailand	17
132	Cambodia	16
133	Ecuador	16
134	Guatemala	16
135	Malawi	16
136	Togo	16
137	Bolivia	15
138	Cape Verde	15
139	Central African Republic	15
140	Iran	15
141	Lesotho	15
142	Zimbabwe	15
143	Colombia	14
144	Kenya	14
145	Ghana	13
146	Guinea-Bissau	13
147	Angola	12
148	Bhutan	12
149	Honduras	12
150	Nicaragua	12
151	Paraguay	12
152	Syria	12
153	Uganda	12
154	Jordan	11
155	Morocco	11
156	Philippines	11
157	Tanzania	11
158	Mexico	10
159	Senegal	10
160	Sierra Leone	10
161	Eritrea	9
162	Madagascar	9
163	Mozambique	9
164	Rwanda	9
165	Cote d'Ivoire	8
166	Haiti	8
167	India	8
168	Maldives	8
169	Sudan	8
170	Yemen	8
171	Chad	7
172	Gambia	7
173	Mauritania	7
174	Somalia	7
175	Guinea	6
BOTTOM 10		
176	Indonesia	6
177	Myanmar (Burma)	6
178	Pakistan	6
179	Burkina	5
180	Niger	5
181	Mali	4
181	Afghanistan	3
182	Bangladesh	3
183	Ethiopia	3
184	Nepal	3

Source: *World Health Statistics Annual*

222. PHARMACISTS

Pharmacists constitute an important link in the chain of health care and delivery services, but their role is often ignored or obscured by the greater visibility of other medical personnel. In only a few countries do pharmacists undergo rigorous training, but in almost all countries they are licensed and also subject to penalties for dispensing illegal drugs or improper prescriptions.

Rank	Country	Pharmacists	Rank	Country	Pharmacists	Rank	Country	Pharmacists
TOP 10			48	Switzerland	1,547	96	Bahrain	121
1	China	413,000	49	Denmark	1,498	97	Panama	115
2	United States	182,000	50	Lebanon	1,390	98	Burkina	113
3	Japan	162,021	51	Costa Rica	1,152	99	Namibia	91
4	Brazil	57,047	52	Kyrgyzstan	1,122	100	Benin	86
5	Italy	53,948	53	Mongolia	1,113	101	Gabon	71
6	France	51,613	54	Malaysia	1,084	102	Ghana	67
7	Germany	42,887	55	Slovenia	1,019	103	Jamaica	65
8	Korea, South	40,779	56	Uruguay	948	104	Togo	65
9	Spain	39,608	57	Estonia	930	105	Monaco	64
10	United Kingdom	37,832	58	Kuwait	903	106	Lesotho	60
			59	Honduras	792	107	Zaire	59
UPPER MIDDLE			60	Bosnia & Herzegovina	781	108	Mali	57
11	Egypt	34,700				109	Burundi	55
12	Canada	22,121	**LOWER MIDDLE**			110	Bahamas	52
13	Poland	19,208	61	Singapore	773	111	Botswana	40
14	Taiwan	18,762	62	Albania	772	112	Guyana	29
15	Turkey	15,792	63	Philippines	730	113	Niger	29
16	Belgium	13,657	64	Tajikistan	709	114	Bermuda	28
17	Australia	10,637	65	Cuba	650	115	Grenada	28
18	South Africa	9,388	66	Kenya	605	116	St. Vincent	27
19	Greece	7,948	67	Malta	600	117	Rwanda	25
20	Bangladesh	7,485	68	Finland	579	118	Zambia	24
21	Russia	7,300	69	Trinidad and Tobago	529	119	Central African Republic	22
22	Vietnam	6,500	70	Sri Lanka	520	120	Madagascar	19
23	Romania	6,432	71	Afghanistan	510	121	Belize	16
24	Portugal	5,950	72	Slovakia	499	122	Djibouti	14
25	Peru	5,940	73	Nepal	427	123	St. Kitts and Nevis	14
26	Venezuela	5,615	74	Cyprus	423	124	Antigua and Barbuda	13
27	Sweden	5,603	75	Zimbabwe	411	125	Swaziland	13
28	Nigeria	5,318	76	Ethiopia	364	126	Dominica	12
29	Hungary	4,806	77	Macedonia	358	127	Guinea-Bissau	12
30	Thailand	4,609	78	Oman	350	128	Brunei	10
31	Israel	4,127	79	Luxembourg	336	129	Chad	10
32	Syria	4,041	80	Mozambique	332	130	Cape Verde	9
33	Pakistan	3,772	81	Latvia	292	131	Comoros	6
34	Indonesia	3,520	82	Cambodia	262			
35	New Zealand	3,483	83	Guinea	261	**BOTTOM 10**		
36	Algeria	2,575	84	Yemen	231	132	Mauritania	6
37	Netherlands	2,464	85	Chile	230	133	Vanuatu	6
38	Bulgaria	2,376	86	Cameroon	206	134	Western Samoa	6
39	Jordan	2,220	87	Mauritius	206	135	Bhutan	5
40	Morocco	2,214	88	Senegal	200	136	Malawi	5
41	Yugoslavia	2,209	89	Somalia	180	137	Seychelles	5
42	Puerto Rico	2,111	90	Congo	175	138	Kiribati	3
43	Austria	2,043	91	Qatar	175	139	Liechtenstein	2
44	Saudi Arabia	1,811	92	Barbados	138	140	Tonga	2
45	Croatia	1,696	93	Cote d'Ivoire	135	141	Sao Tome e Principe	1
46	Tunisia	1,596	94	Iceland	132			
47	Iraq	1,552	95	Dominican Republic	129			

Source: *World Data*

223. NURSES

Nursing personnel include graduate, practical and assistant nurses. Because definitions of nursing personnel vary widely from country, to country the data may not be strictly comparable.

Rank	Country	Nurses	Rank	Country	Nurses	Rank	Country	Nurses
TOP 10			54	Costa Rica	7,021	108	Barbados	889
1	China	1,056,000	55	Laos	6,753	109	Lesotho	874
2	Japan	795,810	56	Jordan	6,466	110	Tunisia	836
3	Germany	708,000	57	Romania	6,414	111	Mauritania	819
4	India	340,208	58	Honduras	6,288	112	Singapore	767
5	France	313,374	59	Cameroon	6,053	113	Gabon	759
6	Canada	262,288	60	Dominican Republic	6,035	114	Guyana	708
7	Kazakhstan	229,600	61	Chile	5,653	115	Bahamas	682
8	Australia	188,600	62	Macedonia	5,638	116	Guinea-Bissau	674
9	United States	187,000	63	El Salvador	5,094	117	Burundi	670
10	Italy	170,409	64	Norway	5,088	118	Panama	570
			65	Sweden	4,900	119	Bermuda	534
UPPER MIDDLE			66	Syria	4,495	120	Eritrea	488
11	Mexico	141,404	67	Yugoslavia	4,478	121	Gambia	430
12	Finland	123,456	68	Switzerland	4,400	122	United Arab Emirates	388
13	Indonesia	118,555	69	Ecuador	4,215	123	Grenada	347
14	Belarus	115,700	70	Malta	4,100	124	Sri Lanka	333
15	Korea, South	107,883				125	Nicaragua	332
16	Cuba	73,943	**LOWER MIDDLE**			126	Belize	303
17	Azerbaijan	72,200	71	South Africa	4,024	127	Monaco	293
18	Georgia	64,100	72	Uruguay	3,712	128	Malawi	284
19	Denmark	63,841	73	Cote d'Ivoire	3,691	129	Guinea	243
20	Hungary	54,472	74	Ethiopia	3,496	130	Chad	239
21	Bulgaria	52,038	75	Madagascar	3,124	131	Bhutan	233
22	Iran	48,639	76	Mozambique	2,847	132	Dominica	218
23	Moldova	48,600	77	Thailand	2,669	133	Cape Verde	205
24	Russia	47,100	78	Burkina	2,627	134	Zimbabwe	194
25	Colombia	46,376	79	Mauritius	2,575	135	Antigua and Barbuda	179
26	Kyrgyzstan	41,939	80	Haiti	2,489	136	Yemen	163
27	Poland	37,296	81	Botswana	2,488	137	Comoros	155
28	Malaysia	36,076	82	Slovakia	2,444	138	Equatorial Guinea	154
29	Austria	35,533	83	Pakistan	2,401	139	Maldives	153
30	Greece	34,314	84	Cyprus	2,356	140	Kiribati	147
31	Armenia	34,000	85	Saudi Arabia	1,967	141	Oman	142
32	Lithuania	28,179	86	New Zealand	1,916	142	Trinidad and Tobago	136
33	Kenya	27,143	87	Bolivia	1,869	143	Qatar	114
34	Ireland	23,127	88	Iceland	1,793	144	Senegal	58
35	Argentina	18,000	89	Jamaica	1,687	145	Namibia	51
36	Guatemala	14,401	90	Fiji	1,631	146	Zaire	41
37	Libya	13,849	91	Congo	1,624	147	Zambia	26
38	Morocco	13,358	92	Philippines	1,614	148	Togo	22
39	Iraq	13,206	93	Bahrain	1,607	149	Seychelles	11
40	Latvia	12,559	94	Mali	1,509	150	Tonga	11
41	Spain	12,247	95	Portugal	1,509	151	St. Kitts and Nevis	8
42	Ghana	11,808	96	Afghanistan	1,451			
43	Bangladesh	10,607	97	Benin	1,384	**BOTTOM 10**		
44	Turkey	10,514	98	Central African Republic	1,353	152	Rwanda	7
45	Angola	9,334	99	Lebanon	1,248	153	Swaziland	7
46	Mongolia	9,183	100	Brunei	1,228	154	Western Samoa	7
47	Peru	7,945	101	Paraguay	1,160	155	St. Lucia	6
48	Venezuela	7,945	102	Slovenia	1,148	156	St. Vincent	6
49	Netherlands	7,800	103	Nigeria	1,088	157	Niger	5
50	Kuwait	7,406	104	Myanmar (Burma)	1,062	158	Sao Tome e Principe	5
51	Estonia	7,302	105	Tajikistan	926	159	Vanuatu	3
52	Cambodia	7,271	106	Liberia	908	160	Somalia	2
53	Taiwan	7,095	107	Puerto Rico	902	161	Tuvalu	2

Source: *World Data*

224. DENTISTS

The quality of dental care is best measured by the number of practicing dentists. Other factors influencing dental care delivery are the availability of dental instruments and prosthetic devices as well as fluoridation of water. Dental service appears to be the most neglected of all medical services in many parts of the world.

Rank	Country	Dentists
TOP 10		
1	United States	187,000
2	Brazil	118,609
3	Japan	77,416
4	Germany	58,194
5	Russia	47,100
6	France	38,451
7	Argentina	21,900
8	Poland	17,296
9	Egypt	15,150
10	Canada	14,621
UPPER MIDDLE		
11	Colombia	13,815
12	Spain	12,247
13	Korea, South	12,180
14	India	11,300
15	Italy	10,814
16	Greece	10,731
17	Turkey	10,514
18	Cuba	8,057
19	Peru	7,945
20	Venezuela	7,945
21	Netherlands	7,900
22	Algeria	7,563
23	Taiwan	7,095
24	Belgium	7,070
25	Israel	6,956
26	Australia	6,700
27	Romania	6,414
28	Czech Republic	6,015
29	Bulgaria	5,727
30	Chile	5,200
31	Denmark	5,088
32	Norway	5,088
33	Sweden	4,900
34	Iran	4,770
35	Hungary	4,754
36	Mexico	4,730
37	Finland	4,602
38	Syria	4,495
39	Yugoslavia	4,478
40	Switzerland	4,400
41	South Africa	4,024
42	Indonesia	3,821
43	Uruguay	3,712
44	Austria	3,517
45	Thailand	2,669
46	Slovakia	2,444
47	Pakistan	2,401
48	Saudi Arabia	1,967
49	Lithuania	1,952
50	Croatia	1940
51	New Zealand	1,916
52	Dominican Republic	1,898

Rank	Country	Dentists
53	Ecuador	1,826
54	Bolivia	1,643
55	Philippines	1,614
56	Iraq	1,577
57	Portugal	1,509
58	Jordan	1,477
59	Bosnia & Herzegovina	1,368
60	Malaysia	1,288
61	Ireland	1,205
62	Costa Rica	1,200
63	El Salvador	1,182
64	Paraguay	1,160
65	Slovenia	1,148
66	Morocco	1,132
67	Albania	1,099
LOWER MIDDLE		
68	Nigeria	1,088
69	Macedonia	1,078
70	Guatemala	1,065
71	Myanmar (Burma)	1,062
72	Lebanon	1,015
73	Latvia	968
74	Tajikistan	926
75	Puerto Rico	902
76	Tunisia	836
77	Estonia	820
78	Singapore	767
79	Bangladesh	702
80	Libya	686
81	Kenya	664
82	Honduras	622
83	Panama	570
84	Cyprus	498
85	Kuwait	399
86	United Arab Emirates	388
87	Sri Lanka	333
88	Nicaragua	332
89	Mongolia	299
90	Jamaica	270
91	Afghanistan	267
92	Kyrgyzstan	226
93	Cote d'Ivoire	219
94	Iceland	219
95	Luxembourg	203
96	Zimbabwe	194
97	Yemen	163
98	Mauritius	148
99	Oman	142
100	Trinidad and Tobago	136
101	Malta	115
102	Qatar	114
103	Madagascar	89
104	Haiti	81
105	Bahamas	58

Rank	Country	Dentists
106	Senegal	58
107	Cameroon	55
108	Namibia	51
109	Zaire	41
110	Fiji	40
111	Ghana	39
112	Bahrain	38
113	Barbados	38
114	Cambodia	36
115	Congo	35
116	Gabon	32
117	Monaco	31
118	Brunei	27
119	Zambia	26
120	Bermuda	23
121	Guinea	22
122	Togo	22
123	Botswana	21
124	Mauritania	20
125	Burkina	19
126	Mozambique	17
127	Benin	16
128	Guyana	15
129	Antigua and Barbuda	13
130	Guinea-Bissau	13
131	Mali	13
132	Belize	12
133	Liechtenstein	12
134	Seychelles	11
135	Tonga	11
136	Angola	10
137	Djibouti	10
138	Bhutan	9
139	Burundi	9
140	Tuvalu	9
141	Central African Republic	8
142	St. Kitts and Nevis	8
143	Grenada	7
144	Rwanda	7
145	Swaziland	7
146	Comoros	6
BOTTOM 10		
147	St. Lucia	6
148	St. Vincent	6
149	Chad	5
150	Liberia	5
151	Niger	5
152	Sao Tome e Principe	5
153	Dominica	4
154	Somalia	2
155	Kiribati	1
156	Maldives	1

Source: *World Health Statistics Annual*

225. PHYSICIANS

The number of physicians is a usually reliable index of the quality of national medical and health care. Because all countries require physicians to be licensed, the number of licensed and practicing physicians is in most cases reported accurately. The index is, however, weak in two respects. It does not reflect the continuing and deplorable drain of physicians from developing countries (where they are so badly needed) to developed countries such as the United States. It also does not reflect the concentration of physicians in urban centers and the resulting disparity between urban and rural health care.

Medical statistics, especially those relating to physicians, are subject to numerous qualifications.

Although virtually every country requires physicians to be licensed, the terms of such license and the quality of education that precedes the license are likely to vary substantially from one country to another. These variations result not merely because of available education resources but also as a consequence of public policy. Maintenance of high standards may drastically limit the total number of physicians entering the medical marketplace every year, and therefore many developing countries, such as Albania, have relaxed the standards of medical education. In other countries paraprofessionals are included in the data.

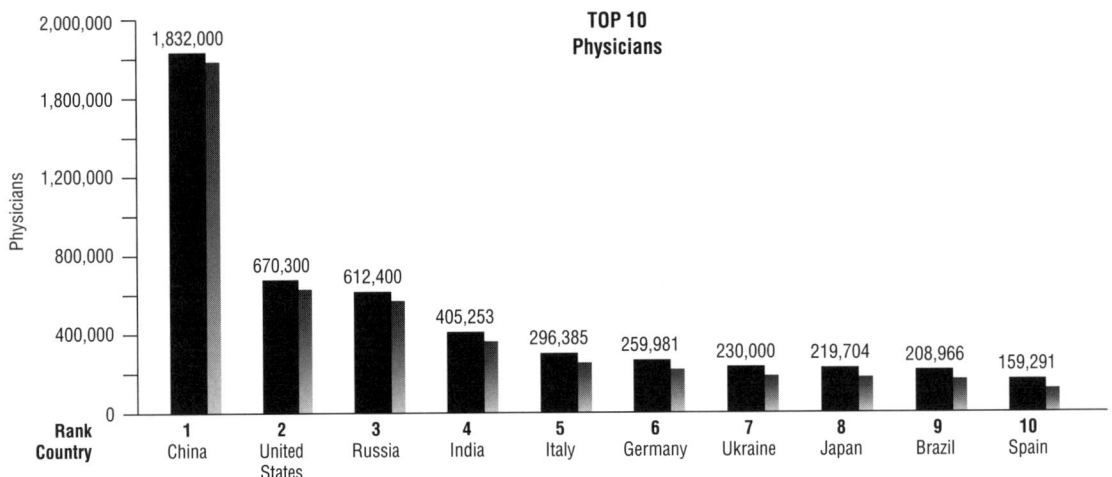

TOP 10
Physicians

Rank	1	2	3	4	5	6	7	8	9	10
Country	China	United States	Russia	India	Italy	Germany	Ukraine	Japan	Brazil	Spain
Physicians	1,832,000	670,300	612,400	405,253	296,385	259,981	230,000	219,704	208,966	159,291

Rank	Country	Phisicians	Rank	Country	Phisicians	Rank	Country	Phisicians
	UPPER MIDDLE		34	Colombia	36,551	58	Kyrgyzstan	14,674
11	France	155,896	35	Venezuela	32,616	59	Lithuania	14,670
12	Mexico	149,432	36	Czech Republic	31,897	60	Denmark	14,497
13	Egypt	101,500	37	Georgia	30,000	61	Norway	14,497
14	Argentina	88,800	38	Azerbaijan	29,000	62	Armenia	14,000
15	Poland	87,706	39	Vietnam	28,500	63	Turkmenistan	14,000
16	United Kingdom	87,000	40	Bulgaria	28,457	64	Thailand	13,398
17	Uzbekistan	79,000	41	Taiwan	27,288	65	Finland	13,344
18	Philippines	78,445	42	Austria	26,121	66	Tajikistan	13,084
19	Kazakhstan	66,000	43	South Africa	25,967	67	Ecuador	12,853
20	Pakistan	63,033	44	Saudi Arabia	25,543	68	Myanmar (Burma)	12,245
21	Canada	60,559	45	Algeria	25,304	69	Syria	11,808
22	Korea, North	57,690	46	Indonesia	25,135	70	New Zealand	11,413
23	Korea, South	51,518	47	Yugoslavia	24,698	71	Uruguay	11,201
24	Turkey	50,639	48	Portugal	24,499	72	Dominican Republic	11,130
25	Cuba	46,860	49	Israel	24,344	73	Iraq	9,366
26	Belarus	45,000	50	Peru	23,771	74	Croatia	9,280
27	Romania	42,808	51	Switzerland	23,000	75	Latvia	7,714
28	Greece	40,116	52	Sweden	22,200	76	Morocco	7,695
29	Netherlands	39,069	53	Bangladesh	21,749	77	Guatemala	7,601
30	Australia	38,800	54	Moldova	18,000	78	Malaysia	7,012
31	Belgium	37,792	55	Nigeria	17,954	79	Bosnia & Herzegovina	6,929
32	Iran	37,000	56	Slovakia	15,767	80	Lebanon	6,638
33	Hungary	36,643	57	Chile	15,015	81	Jordan	6,395

Rank	Country	Phisicians
82	Puerto Rico	6,269
83	Ireland	6,036
84	Mongolia	5,911
85	Libya	4,749
86	Estonia	4,680
87	Tunisia	4,670
88	Macedonia	4,528
89	El Salvador	4,525
LOWER MIDDLE		
90	Albania	4,467
91	Singapore	4,301
92	Slovenia	4,086
93	Costa Rica	4,027
94	Honduras	3,803
95	Kenya	3,794
96	Bolivia	3,392
97	Sri Lanka	3,345
98	Panama	3,168
99	United Arab Emirates	3,090
100	Yemen	3,065
101	Paraguay	2,924
102	Kuwait	2,717
103	Nicaragua	2,554
104	Zaire	2,469
105	Sudan	2,400
106	Afghanistan	2,233
107	Oman	2,095
108	Cote d'Ivoire	2,020
109	Jamaica	1,589
110	Zimbabwe	1,551
111	Nepal	1,497
112	Ethiopia	1,466
113	Cyprus	1,441
114	Madagascar	1,392
115	Laos	1,173
116	Tanzania	1,065
117	Trinidad and Tobago	1,051

Rank	Country	Phisicians
118	Cameroon	945
119	Mauritius	941
120	Malta	900
121	Luxembourg	848
122	Uganda	774
123	Guinea	773
124	Qatar	758
125	Iceland	726
126	Zambia	713
127	Angola	662
128	Ghana	628
129	Congo	613
130	Cambodia	600
131	Haiti	564
132	Bahrain	542
133	Senegal	520
134	Somalia	450
135	Gabon	448
136	Mali	435
137	Sierra Leone	404
138	Mozambique	368
139	Bahamas	357
140	Burkina	341
141	Suriname	329
142	Fiji	326
143	Namibia	324
144	Benin	323
145	Togo	319
146	Burundi	317
147	Barbados	312
148	Papua New Guinea	301
149	Guinea-Bissau	274
150	Rwanda	272
151	Botswana	240
152	Chad	217
153	Brunei	197
154	Malawi	186
155	Central African Republic	170

Rank	Country	Phisicians
156	Niger	142
157	Bhutan	141
158	Guyana	138
159	Lesotho	136
160	Mauritania	135
161	Cape Verde	112
162	Monaco	112
163	Andorra	110
164	Belize	110
165	Equatorial Guinea	99
166	Djibouti	97
167	Bermuda	91
168	Liberia	89
169	Swaziland	83
170	Seychelles	72
171	Eritrea	68
172	St. Lucia	64
173	Gambia	61
174	Sao Tome e Principe	61
175	San Marino	60
176	Antigua and Barbuda	59
177	Comoros	57
178	Solomon Islands	52
179	Western Samoa	50
BOTTOM 10		
180	Grenada	47
181	Tonga	46
182	Maldives	45
183	St. Vincent	40
184	St. Kitts and Nevis	39
185	Dominica	38
186	Liechtenstein	32
187	Vanuatu	12
188	Kiribati	10
189	Tuvalu	8

Source: *World Health Statistics Annual*

226. POPULATION PER PHYSICIAN

One of the ironies of the global health situation is that it is precisely those nations in dire need of health care that have less of it, while those countries with relatively healthy populations have more health professionals. Further, the brain drain of medical professionals from developing countries to the developed world has made this imbalance even more severe. Ideally, one physician will be able to care for no more than 700 persons, including children and older citizens. But in most developing countries, there is only one physician for several thousand. Lack of physicians also drives the population of many of these countries into the hands of shamans, witch doctors and alternative sources of relief or cure.

Rank	Country	Population per Physician
TOP 10		
1	Georgia	183
2	Italy	193
3	Israel	214
4	Ukraine	226
5	Cuba	231
6	Belarus	233
7	Moldova	241
8	Russia	241
9	Spain	246
10	Hungary	248

Rank	Country	Population per Physician
UPPER MIDDLE		
11	Lithuania	255
12	Azerbaijan	256
13	Kazakhstan	256
14	Greece	259
15	Armenia	263
16	Belgium	267
17	Monaco	270
18	Turkmenistan	286
19	Uruguay	286
20	Uzbekistan	286

Rank	Country	Population per Physician
21	Bulgaria	298
22	Norway	298
23	Switzerland	299
24	Kyrgyzstan	305
25	Austria	307
26	New Zealand	309
27	Germany	312
28	Estonia	319
29	Czech Republic	324
30	Latvia	330
31	Slovakia	336

Rank	Country	Population per Physician	Rank	Country	Population per Physician	Rank	Country	Population per Physician
32	Iceland	353	86	Oman	910	142	Bhutan	5,226
33	Denmark	358	87	Colombia	914	143	Djibouti	5,258
34	Korea, North	370	88	Chile	920	144	Maldives	5,297
35	Argentina	373	89	Peru	944	145	Guyana	5,314
36	San Marino	375	90	Bahrain	953	146	Cote d'Ivoire	5,931
37	Mongolia	376	91	Liechtenstein	957	147	Solomon Islands	6,154
38	Finland	380	92	Algeria	1,014	148	Zimbabwe	6,909
39	United States	385	93	Seychelles	1,026	149	Kenya	7,022
40	France	387	94	St. Kitts and Nevis	1,057	150	Indonesia	7,402
41	Netherlands	391	95	Syria	1,061	151	Afghanistan	7,414
42	Sweden	393	96	Antigua and Barbuda	1,085	152	Guinea	7,445
43	Portugal	403	97	Turkey	1,108	153	Kiribati	7,687
44	Lebanon	407	98	Tuvalu	1,152	154	Comoros	8,135
45	Malta	409	99	Mauritius	1,187	155	Madagascar	8,628
46	Yugoslavia	420	100	Trinidad and Tobago	1,191	156	Swaziland	9,265
47	Cyprus	433	101	El Salvador	1,219	157	Sudan	10,000
48	Tajikistan	439	102	Suriname	1,247	158	Sierra Leone	10,832
49	Poland	440	103	Guatemala	1,282	159	Haiti	11,113
50	Australia	445	104	Honduras	1,358	160	Togo	11,270
51	Macedonia	458	105	Brunei	1,359	161	Zambia	11,414
52	Canada	464	106	Paraguay	1,522	162	Cameroon	11,848
53	Luxembourg	473	107	South Africa	1,527	163	Nepal	12,623
54	Croatia	486	108	Jamaica	1,541	164	Papua New Guinea	12,874
55	Slovenia	489	109	Iran	1,600	165	Somalia	13,315
56	Saudi Arabia	523	110	Nicaragua	1,668	166	Benin	13,879
57	Romania	531	111	Tunisia	1,799	167	Vanuatu	14,025
58	Andorra	548	112	Belize	1,809	168	Mauritania	14,259
59	Egypt	552	113	Fiji	1,829	169	Cambodia	14,300
60	Puerto Rico	558	114	Sao Tome e Principe	1,881	170	Lesotho	14,306
61	Japan	566	115	Dominica	1,889	171	Gambia	14,536
62	Jordan	574	116	Iraq	1,922	172	Senegal	14,817
63	Mexico	578	117	Grenada	1,949	173	Angola	15,136
64	Ireland	588	118	Bolivia	2,083	174	Zaire	15,584
65	Kuwait	596	119	Pakistan	2,107	175	Central African Republic	16,447
66	United Arab Emirates	618	120	Tonga	2,139	176	Burundi	16,657
67	Bosnia & Herzegovina	624	121	India	2,140	177	Mali	18,046
68	Venezuela	626	122	St. Lucia	2,235	178	Tanzania	19,775
69	China	633	123	Malaysia	2,475	179	Uganda	20,720
70	Bermuda	662	124	Vietnam	2,490			
71	United Kingdom	667	125	Gabon	2,504	**BOTTOM 10**		
72	Dominican Republic	671	126	St. Vincent	2,708	180	Ghana	22,452
73	Qatar	671	127	Cape Verde	2,931	181	Liberia	24,600
74	Singapore	681	128	Western Samoa	3,183	182	Rwanda	24,697
75	Libya	690	129	Guinea-Bissau	3,245	183	Burkina	27,158
76	Bahamas	714	130	Morocco	3,361	184	Chad	27,765
77	Brazil	715	131	Equatorial Guinea	3,532	185	Ethiopia	30,195
78	Albania	729	132	Laos	3,555	186	Mozambique	36,428
79	Taiwan	772	133	Myanmar (Burma)	3,721	187	Malawi	49,118
80	Costa Rica	792	134	Yemen	3,900	188	Eritrea	49,200
81	Panama	800	135	Congo	4,028	189	Niger	54,472
82	Ecuador	836	136	Thailand	4,245			
83	Barbados	842	137	Namibia	4,594			
84	Philippines	849	138	Nigeria	4,692			
			139	Botswana	4,964			
LOWER MIDDLE			140	Bangladesh	5,184			
85	Korea, South	855	141	Sri Lanka	5,203			

Source: *World Health Statistics Annual*

227. HOSPITALS

Hospitals remain the primary health delivery mechanism in the world. In most countries, (the United States is a major exception) hospitals are run by the state or by national organizations funded by the state, and their role and purpose are defined in humanitarian terms. The American model, however, is different.

Hospitals have become a profit-driven big business in the United States, and consequently the percentage of people without access to affordable healthcare is almost as large as in any developing country. Hospitals in the West also have become large, impersonal and technology-based.

Rank	Country	Hospitals	Rank	Country	Hospitals	Rank	Country	Hospitals
TOP 10			52	Turkmenistan	368	104	Puerto Rico	72
1	China	60,784	53	Belgium	363	105	Ireland	63
2	Brazil	35,701	54	Norway	350	106	Macedonia	61
3	India	15,067	55	Bolivia	336	107	Panama	60
4	Vietnam	12,500	56	Moldova	335	108	Angola	58
5	Russia	12,265	57	Portugal	335	109	Nicaragua	56
6	Nigeria	11,588	58	New Zealand	330	110	Dominica	53
7	Pakistan	10,905	59	Austria	324	111	Jordan	53
8	Japan	9,963	60	Finland	317	112	Namibia	47
9	United States	6,580	61	Bulgaria	287	113	Guinea	38
10	Egypt	6,418	62	Algeria	284	114	Western Samoa	36
			63	Burundi	264	115	United Arab Emirates	35
UPPER MIDDLE			64	Malaysia	264	116	Luxembourg	34
11	Ukraine	3,900	65	Cuba	244	117	Costa Rica	33
12	France	3,834	66	Israel	244	118	Trinidad and Tobago	31
13	United Kingdom	2,423	67	Mozambique	238	119	Botswana	30
14	Germany	2,381				120	Jamaica	30
15	Italy	1,926	**LOWER MIDDLE**			121	Bhutan	27
16	Kazakhstan	1,805	68	Czech Republic	237	122	Gabon	27
17	Philippines	1,723	69	Netherlands	236	123	Iceland	26
18	Mexico	1,539	70	Saudi Arabia	229	124	Fiji	25
19	Uzbekistan	1,388	71	Rwanda	220	125	Slovenia	24
20	Zimbabwe	1,378	72	Sierra Leone	219	126	Swaziland	24
21	Thailand	1,097	73	Chile	217	127	Mauritius	23
22	Canada	1,079	74	Syria	213	128	Kuwait	22
23	Laos	1,074	75	Morocco	203	129	Lesotho	22
24	Australia	1,071	76	Lithuania	198	130	Singapore	22
25	Indonesia	971	77	Cambodia	188	131	Guinea-Bissau	16
26	Zambia	965	78	Armenia	183	132	Mauritania	16
27	Colombia	947	79	Oman	180	133	Gambia	13
28	Albania	895	80	Iraq	177	134	Bahrain	12
29	Bangladesh	891	81	Latvia	170	135	Barbados	10
30	Kenya	877	82	Denmark	163	136	Brunei	10
31	Belarus	868	83	Hungary	148	137	St. Vincent	9
32	Turkey	857	84	Tunisia	138	138	Djibouti	8
33	South Africa	834	85	Central African Republic	133	139	Solomon Islands	8
34	Spain	813	86	Ghana	121	140	Tuvalu	8
35	Taiwan	810	87	Estonia	115	141	Belize	7
36	Poland	752	88	Nepal	114	142	Malta	7
37	Azerbaijan	749	89	Uruguay	112	143	Seychelles	7
38	Myanmar (Burma)	717	90	Slovakia	111	144	Bahamas	5
39	Cameroon	629	91	Cyprus	110	145	Maldives	5
40	Venezuela	610	92	Dominican Republic	103			
41	Iran	609	93	Croatia	98	**BOTTOM 10**		
42	Mongolia	475	94	Liberia	92	146	St. Kitts and Nevis	4
43	Tajikistan	449	95	Vanuatu	90	147	St. Lucia	4
44	Ecuador	429	96	Uganda	89	148	Tonga	4
45	Peru	427	97	Haiti	87	149	Grenada	3
46	Georgia	422	98	Ethiopia	86	150	Qatar	3
47	Sri Lanka	422	99	Honduras	86	151	Antigua and Barbuda	2
48	Zaire	400	100	Burkina	78	152	Bermuda	2
49	Kyrgyzstan	396	101	El Salvador	78	153	Andorra	1
50	Malawi	395	102	Cape Verde	75	154	Liechtenstein	1
51	Greece	372	103	Yemen	75	155	Monaco	1

Source: *World Health Statistics Annual*

228. HOSPITAL BED OCCUPANCY RATE

Hospital stay has become financially ruinous for many people not covered by medical insurance and for a few who are covered. This is one of the reasons for the decline in hospital bed occupancy rate in recent years. Another reason is improving health among all classes and age-groups. A third factor is that technology has made many surgical procedures faster and post-operation hospital stays shorter. In fact, ambulatory medical care is becoming so common that hospitals, like corporations, have been forced to downsize.

Rank	Country	Hospital Bed Occupancy Rate	Rank	Country	Hospital Bed Occupancy Rate	Rank	Country	Hospital Bed Occupancy Rate
TOP 10			30	Spain	76.7	60	Chile	64.9
1	Dominica	94.6	31	Bermuda	76.4	61	Kuwait	64.9
2	New Zealand	93.3	32	Cyprus	75.7	62	Mexico	64.7
3	Botswana	93.1	33	Kyrgyzstan	75.6	63	United States	64.6
4	Finland	91.5				64	Jamaica	63.8
5	Israel	91.2	**LOWER MIDDLE**			65	Puerto Rico	63.1
6	Malawi	90.6	34	Seychelles	75.2	66	Philippines	62.1
7	Barbados	88.3	35	Korea, South	75.1	67	Panama	58.4
8	Iceland	87.8	36	Mauritania	74.6	68	Syria	57.9
9	Belgium	84.4	37	Portugal	74.5	69	Guatemala	57.7
10	Macedonia	84.2	38	Hungary	73.9	70	Ecuador	57.5
			39	Czech Republic	73.8	71	Colombia	57.2
UPPER MIDDLE			40	Luxembourg	73.4	72	Tonga	56.2
11	Estonia	83.9	41	Slovakia	73.2	73	Dominican Republic	55.3
12	Germany	83.9	42	Singapore	73.1	74	El Salvador	54.9
13	Bahamas	83.7	43	Fiji	72.6	75	Morocco	52.9
14	Russia	83.2	44	Poland	72.5	76	Argentina	51.9
15	Norway	83.1	45	Qatar	71.7	77	Tuvalu	51.5
16	France	83.0	46	Yugoslavia	71.6			
17	Oman	83.0	47	Maldives	71.4	**BOTTOM 10**		
18	Slovenia	82.7	48	China	71.1	78	Antigua and Barbuda	49.9
19	Bosnia & Herzegovina	82.4	49	Trinidad and Tobago	70.7	79	St. Kitts and Nevis	49.3
20	United Kingdom	80.6	50	Tajikistan	70.2	80	Bolivia	45.9
21	Denmark	80.4	51	Greece	69.8	81	Grenada	45.6
22	Bahrain	80.0	52	Italy	69.8	82	Angola	44.5
23	Croatia	78.9	53	Zimbabwe	69.8	83	Rwanda	42.8
24	Latvia	78.7	54	Venezuela	69.7	84	Iraq	42.4
25	Netherlands	78.5	55	Uruguay	69.1	85	Vanuatu	41.9
26	Costa Rica	78.2	56	Suriname	68.8	86	Algeria	38.4
27	Sweden	78.0	57	Jordan	68.7	87	Western Samoa	32.9
28	Ireland	77.7	58	Zambia	68.5			
29	Austria	77.3	59	St. Vincent	67.9			

Source: *World Health Statistics Annual*

229. POPULATION WITH ACCESS TO SAFE WATER

Water, like air, is easily subject to contamination. Particularly so in communities where there are no filtration or water purification systems and water and sewage are not separated. In many countries of the Third World, people bathe in the river or lake from which they draw their drinking water, and they also use the same source for doing laundry and cooking. In the absence of a septic system, sewage flows into the same rivers and lakes, and then is used for household purposes. In many Western countries, the problem is less severe although of a different order. Chemicals and toxic substances leach into the underground reservoirs and contaminate the wellsprings. Ensuring safe water is essential for maintaining public health, and the task is becoming more difficult in the absence of proper environmental controls.

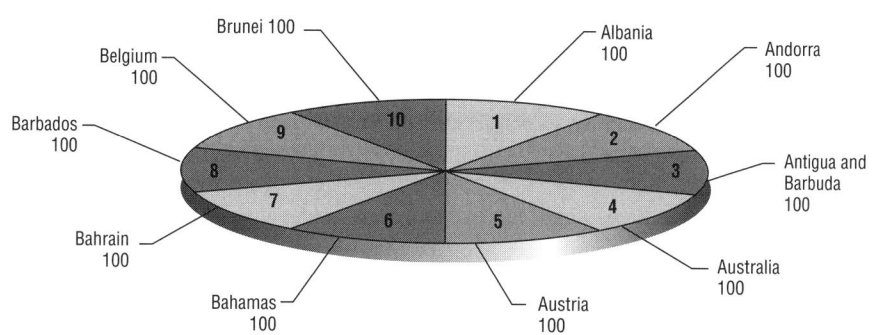

TOP 10
Population with Access to Safe Water

- Brunei 100
- Belgium 100
- Barbados 100
- Bahrain 100
- Bahamas 100
- Albania 100
- Andorra 100
- Antigua and Barbuda 100
- Australia 100
- Austria 100

Rank	Country	Population with Access to Safe Water (%)
UPPER MIDDLE		
11	Bulgaria	100
12	Canada	100
13	Cyprus	100
14	Czech Republic	100
15	Denmark	100
16	Finland	100
17	France	100
18	Germany	100
19	Greece	100
20	Hungary	100
21	Iceland	100
22	Ireland	100
23	Israel	100
24	Italy	100
25	Jamaica	100
26	Korea, North	100
27	Kuwait	100
28	Lithuania	100
29	Malta	100
30	Monaco	100
31	Netherlands	100
32	New Zealand	100
33	Norway	100
34	Poland	100
35	Portugal	100
36	Qatar	100
37	Romania	100
38	St. Kitts and Nevis	100
39	Seychelles	100
40	Singapore	100
41	Slovakia	100
42	Spain	100
43	Sweden	100
44	Switzerland	100
45	United Kingdom	100
46	United States	100
47	Vanuatu	100
48	Jordan	99
49	Tunisia	99
50	Cuba	98
51	Japan	97
52	Libya	97
53	Mauritius	97
54	Trinidad and Tobago	97
55	Maldives	95
56	Saudi Arabia	95
57	United Arab Emirates	95
58	Costa Rica	93
59	Korea, South	93
60	Latvia	92
61	Egypt	90

Rank	Country	Population with Access to Safe Water (%)
62	Botswana	89
63	Iran	89
64	Venezuela	89
65	Brazil	87
66	Chile	86
67	Colombia	86
68	Grenada	85
69	Bangladesh	84
70	Mexico	84
71	Oman	84
72	Panama	84
73	Zimbabwe	84
74	Western Samoa	83
75	Philippines	82
LOWER MIDDLE		
76	Solomon Islands	82
77	Fiji	80
78	Mongolia	80
79	India	79
80	Malaysia	78
81	Turkey	78
82	Dominica	77
83	Gambia	77
84	Iraq	77
85	Thailand	77
86	Cote d'Ivoire	76
87	Belize	75
88	St. Vincent	75
89	Tonga	75
90	Uruguay	75
91	Syria	74
92	Peru	72
93	Argentina	71
94	Cape Verde	71
95	China	69
96	Algeria	68
97	Gabon	68
98	Honduras	68
99	Pakistan	68
100	Suriname	68
101	St. Lucia	67
102	Mauritania	66
103	Rwanda	66
104	Comoros	63
105	Guatemala	62
106	Guyana	61
107	Sri Lanka	60
108	Togo	60
109	Dominican Republic	59
110	Niger	59
111	Burundi	57

Rank	Country	Population with Access to Safe Water (%)
112	Chad	57
113	Burkina	56
114	Malawi	56
115	Ecuador	55
116	Guinea	55
117	Bolivia	54
118	Morocco	54
119	Nicaragua	54
120	Zambia	53
121	Ghana	52
122	Namibia	52
123	Sao Tome e Principe	52
124	Benin	51
125	Indonesia	51
126	Cameroon	50
127	Liberia	50
128	Tanzania	50
129	Kenya	49
130	Senegal	48
131	Sudan	48
132	El Salvador	47
133	Lebanon	47
134	Djibouti	45
135	Kiribati	44
136	Nepal	42
137	Angola	41
138	Guinea-Bissau	41
139	Mali	41
140	Haiti	39
141	Zaire	39
142	Congo	38
143	Sierra Leone	37
144	Somalia	37
145	Cambodia	36
146	Kyrgyzstan	36
147	Nigeria	36
148	Yemen	36
149	Paraguay	35
150	Bhutan	34
BOTTOM 10		
151	Papua New Guinea	33
152	Myanmar (Burma)	32
153	Uganda	31
154	Swaziland	30
155	Estonia	25
156	Central African Republic	24
157	Vietnam	24
158	Afghanistan	23
159	Madagascar	23
160	Mozambique	22

Source: *World Resources*

230. FOOD SUPPLY AS PERCENTAGE OF FAO REQUIREMENTS

Daily food intake is based on many factors, including age, climate, type of work, and average body weight. The FAO has broadly determined the minimum daily nutritional requirements for each major geographic region as follows: Africa (2,320 calories), former Soviet Union (2,300 calories), Far East (2,240 calories), Latin America (2,360 calories), Middle East (2,440 calories) and Developed Countries of Europe and North America (2,600 calories). The following table shows the actual food intake of the countries as a percentage of FAO recommendations. Generally, food consumption is based on availability and price, and, to a lesser extent, on food preferences and traditions.

Rank	Country	Food Supply (as % of FAO requirement)
TOP 10		
1	Ireland	153
2	Cyprus	152
3	Spain	151
4	Portugal	148
5	France	144
6	Greece	143
7	Italy	141
8	Malta	141
9	United States	141
10	Korea, South	140
UPPER MIDDLE		
11	Libya	140
12	United Arab Emirates	140
13	Belgium	139
14	Luxembourg	139
15	New Zealand	139
16	Tunisia	139
17	Denmark	136
18	Turkey	136
19	Fiji	135
20	Mexico	135
21	Lebanon	134
22	Barbados	133
23	Egypt	133
24	Hungary	133
25	Austria	132
26	United Kingdom	132
27	Malaysia	130
28	Costa Rica	129
29	Tonga	129
30	Syria	128
31	Indonesia	127
32	Germany	126
33	Poland	126
34	Switzerland	126
35	Japan	124
36	Western Samoa	124
37	Argentina	123
38	Brunei	123
39	Cuba	123
40	Jordan	123
41	Morocco	123
42	Algeria	121
43	Korea, North	121
44	Norway	121
45	Australia	120
46	Myanmar (Burma)	120
47	Netherlands	120
48	Vanuatu	120
49	Cape Verde	119
50	Iran	119
51	Israel	119

Rank	Country	Food Supply (as % of FAO requirement)
52	Mauritius	119
53	Belize	118
54	Brazil	118
55	Maldives	117
56	Swaziland	117
57	Canada	116
58	China	116
59	El Salvador	116
60	Jamaica	116
61	Kiribati	116
62	Mauritania	116
63	Paraguay	116
64	Colombia	115
65	Dominica	115
66	Iceland	115
LOWER MIDDLE		
67	Papua New Guinea	115
68	Romania	115
69	Bulgaria	113
70	Ecuador	113
71	Saudi Arabia	113
72	Suriname	113
73	Finland	111
74	Guinea-Bissau	111
75	Benin	110
76	South Africa	110
77	Sweden	110
78	Thailand	110
79	Albania	108
80	Bahamas	108
81	Cote d'Ivoire	108
82	India	108
83	Gabon	107
84	St. Lucia	107
85	Trinidad and Tobago	107
86	Bermuda	106
87	Chile	106
88	Venezuela	106
89	Antigua and Barbuda	105
90	Guyana	105
91	Kuwait	104
92	Vietnam	104
93	Congo	103
94	Guatemala	103
95	Guinea	103
96	Uruguay	103
97	Honduras	102
98	Laos	102
99	Nicaragua	102
100	Sri Lanka	102
101	Burkina	101
102	Djibouti	101
103	Dominican Republic	101

Rank	Country	Food Supply (as % of FAO requirement)
104	Pakistan	100
105	Philippines	100
106	St. Kitts and Nevis	100
107	Gambia	99
108	Grenada	99
109	Botswana	98
110	Seychelles	98
111	Lesotho	97
112	Mali	97
113	Panama	97
114	St. Vincent	97
115	Togo	97
116	Ghana	96
117	Niger	96
118	Senegal	95
119	Solomon Islands	95
120	Madagascar	94
121	Namibia	94
122	Sudan	94
123	Uganda	93
124	Zaire	93
125	Cambodia	91
126	Sao Tome e Principe	91
127	Yemen	91
128	Nigeria	90
129	Kenya	89
130	Nepal	89
131	Bolivia	88
132	Iraq	88
133	Bangladesh	87
134	Tanzania	87
135	Cameroon	85
136	Chad	84
137	Zambia	84
138	Burundi	83
139	Zimbabwe	83
140	Comoros	81
141	Peru	80
142	Malawi	79
143	Angola	78
BOTTOM 10		
144	Mongolia	78
145	Rwanda	78
146	Central African Republic	75
147	Haiti	75
148	Sierra Leone	74
149	Mozambique	72
150	Liberia	71
151	Ethiopia	69
152	Somalia	65
153	Afghanistan	62

Source: *UN Statistical Yearbook*

231. AIDS

AIDS has been described as the Black Plague of the 20th century, and, in the absence of a cure, may continue to be the scourge of the 21st century. Almost all countries have been affected by AIDS to some degree, and the toll has been heavy in many countries, especially in Africa, the home of the disease. The disease has not only challenged the ability of medical researchers, but has also changed forever sexual and social mores. The number of reported cases in the following table is only the tip of the iceberg. More cases are unreported because of social stigma, and the global total may be considerably higher than indicated in the list.

Rank	Country	Total Reported AIDS Cases
TOP 10		
1	United States	215,263
2	Uganda	30,190
3	Tanzania	27,396
4	Brazil	24,536
5	France	17,836
6	Zaire	14,762
7	Malawi	12,079
8	Italy	11,609
9	Spain	11,555
10	Cote d'Ivoire	10,792
UPPER MIDDLE		
11	Zimbabwe	10,551
12	Kenya	9,139
13	Mexico	9,073
14	Germany	7,533
15	Rwanda	6,578
16	Canada	6,076
17	Zambia	5,803
18	United Kingdom	5,451
19	Congo	3,482
20	Burundi	3,305
21	Australia	3,171
22	Ghana	3,140
23	Haiti	3,086
24	Switzerland	2,228
25	Colombia	2,189
26	Netherlands	2,020
27	Central African Republic	1,864
28	Romania	1,704
29	Ethiopia	1,631
30	Dominican Republic	1,622
31	Honduras	1,595
32	Venezuela	1,573
33	Argentina	1,298
34	Togo	1,278
35	Belgium	1,046
36	South Africa	1,019
37	Burkina	978
38	Trinidad and Tobago	971
39	Denmark	947
40	Bahamas	834
41	Portugal	816
42	Austria	707
43	Sweden	645
44	Greece	559
45	Senegal	552
46	Peru	541
47	Chile	500
48	Sudan	500
49	Niger	497

Rank	Country	Total Reported AIDS Cases
50	Japan	453
51	Cameroon	429
52	Angola	421
53	Guinea	338
54	Mali	338
55	Jamaica	334
56	Panama	330
57	Namibia	311
58	New Zealand	310
59	Costa Rica	300
60	Yugoslavia	254
61	Norway	252
62	Barbados	250
63	Botswana	250
LOWER MIDDLE		
64	El Salvador	250
65	Uruguay	245
66	Ireland	241
67	Guatemala	236
68	Guyana	230
69	Chad	224
70	Gabon	215
71	Bermuda	191
72	Benin	185
73	Nigeria	184
74	Gambia	180
75	Ecuador	179
76	Thailand	179
77	Israel	169
78	Djibouti	165
79	Guinea-Bissau	137
80	Tunisia	105
81	Cuba	103
82	India	102
83	Finland	100
84	Suriname	99
85	Morocco	98
86	Algeria	92
87	Poland	87
88	Hungary	82
89	Swaziland	71
90	Philippines	67
91	Turkey	62
92	Malaysia	47
93	Luxembourg	45
94	Iran	44
95	Lesotho	44
96	Papua New Guinea	42
97	Bolivia	41
98	St. Lucia	40
99	Saudi Arabia	40

Rank	Country	Total Reported AIDS Cases
100	Sierra Leone	40
101	Egypt	39
102	St. Vincent	39
103	Paraguay	36
104	Singapore	35
105	St. Kitts and Nevis	33
106	Cape Verde	32
107	Grenada	31
108	Qatar	31
109	Lebanon	29
110	Czech Republic	26
111	Mauritania	26
112	Liberia	24
113	Nicaragua	24
114	Oman	24
115	Cyprus	23
116	Iceland	22
117	Malta	22
118	Indonesia	21
119	Pakistan	18
120	Jordan	17
121	Syria	17
122	Bulgaria	13
123	Somalia	13
124	Belize	12
125	Dominica	12
126	Mauritius	10
127	Myanmar (Burma)	10
128	Sri Lanka	10
129	China	8
130	Korea, South	8
131	Equatorial Guinea	7
132	Iraq	7
133	Libya	7
134	Monaco	7
135	Antigua and Barbuda	6
136	Kuwait	6
137	Sao Tome e Principe	6
BOTTOM 10		
138	United Arab Emirates	6
139	Nepal	5
140	Fiji	4
141	Comoros	3
142	Brunei	2
143	Madagascar	2
144	Tonga	2
145	Bangladesh	1
146	Laos	1
147	San Marino	1

Source: *World Health Statistics Annual*

Section

XIX

EDUCATION

Consider the size of the world's educational system: a total enrollment of 992.286 million (fully 14% of the world's population), a teaching staff of 47.659 million and a gross public expenditure of $1.119 trillion.

What these figures do not tell is the quality of education achieved at such enormous cost and effort. There are a number of intangibles in any educational system: the training of the teaching staff, the quality of the textbooks, the pedagogical techniques, the examination system, to mention a few. These intangibles are, of course, very difficult to define and cannot be evaluated by fixed or objective criteria.

The rankings begin appropriately with male and female literacy rates, and then proceed level by level. At the first level, the rankings deal with the primary school enrollment ratio, and the teacher-pupil ratio. At the secondary level, they deal with the school enrollment ratio and at the third level, with the graduate population and university enrollment per 10,000. Other rankings cover educational expenditures as a percentage of GNP and per capita.

The subsection on science and technology is designed to measure the size of the pool of scientific manpower.

232. MALE LITERACY RATE

Literacy has conflicting definitions in different countries. UNESCO defines literacy as the ability to read and write a simple sentence. In some countries, such as Japan, Sudan, Uganda and Zambia, illiteracy is defined as never having attended school. In Tunisia literacy is defined as the ability to read but not necessarily to write. In developed countries literacy is defined in functional terms as the ability to fill out a simple application form. Literacy figures are also qualified by the age groups to which they refer. Data for most countries relate to populations aged 15 and over; but in the case of others, such as Italy, the figures are based on the population over age six. Other kinds of error and bias include the exclusion of segments of the population, such as nomads in the Middle East and Africa and Indians in South America. Furthermore, because of the great prestige attached to literacy, governments in developing countries have shown a tendency to inflate, distort or even fabricate literacy ratios. Caution must therefore be exercised in evaluating literacy figures at their face value.

Rank	Country	Male Literacy (over age 15–%)	Rank	Country	Male Literacy (over age 15–%)	Rank	Country	Male Literacy (over age 15–%)
TOP 10			14	Netherlands	100	30	Hungary	99.2
1	Albania	100	15	New Zealand	100	31	Poland	99.2
2	Andorra	100	16	Norway	100	32	Kazakhstan	99.1
3	Austria	100	17	Slovakia	100	33	Korea, South	99.1
4	Belgium	100	18	Sweden	100	34	Azerbaijan	98.9
5	Czech Republic	100	19	Switzerland	100	35	Croatia	98.9
6	Denmark	100	20	United Kingdom	100	36	France	98.9
7	Finland	100	21	Western Samoa	100	37	Tajikstan	98.8
8	Germany	100	22	Estonia	99.9	38	Turkmenistan	98.8
9	Iceland	100	23	Latvia	99.8	39	Kyrgyzstan	98.6
10	Ireland	100	24	Georgia	99.5	40	Romania	98.6
			25	Russia	99.5	41	Uzbekistan	98.5
UPPER MIDDLE			26	Ukraine	99.5	42	Jamaica	98.2
11	Japan	100	27	Armenia	99.4	43	San Marino	98.2
12	Liechtenstein	100	28	Belarus	99.4	44	Cyprus	98
13	Luxembourg	100	29	Slovenia	99.3	45	Italy	97.8

Rank	Country	Male Literacy (over age 15–%)	Rank	Country	Male Literacy (over age 15–%)	Rank	Country	Male Literacy (over age 15)–%)
46	Greece	97.6	86	Colombia	87.5	128	Egypt	62.9
47	Guyana	97.5	87	China	87.0	129	Lesotho	62.4
48	Israel	97.1	88	Portugal	86.7	130	Solomon Islands	62.4
49	Spain	97.0	89	Malaysia	86.5	131	Uganda	62.2
50	Taiwan	96.9	90	Myanmar (Burma)	85.8	132	India	61.8
51	Bermuda	96.7	91	Indonesia	85.6	133	Cape Verde	61.4
52	Moldova	96.6	92	Mauritius	85.2	134	Morocco	61.3
53	Bosnia & Herzegovina	96.5	93	Cambodia	85.0	135	Somalia	60.9
54	Malta	96.2	94	Dominican Republic	84.8	136	Haiti	59.1
55	Peru	95.9	95	Bolivia	84.7	137	Oman	58.0
56	Singapore	95.7	96	Botswana	83.7	138	Algeria	57.4
57	United States	95.7	97	Zaire	83.6	139	Vanuatu	57.3
58	Canada	95.6	98	Kuwait	83.3	140	Togo	56.0
59	Argentina	95.5	99	Seychelles	82.9	141	Angola	55.6
60	Tuvalu	95.5	100	Brazil	82.1	142	Comoros	54.2
61	Yugoslavia	95.4	101	Zimbabwe	81.5	143	Nigeria	53.8
62	Suriname	95.1	102	Zambia	80.8	144	Yemen	53.3
63	Uruguay	94.5	103	Kenya	79.8	145	Central African Republic	51.8
64	Macedonia	94.2	104	Syria	78.3	146	Nepal	51.7
65	Chile	93.5	105	Equatorial Guinea	77.8	147	Guinea-Bissau	50.2
66	Venezuela	93.5	106	South Africa	77.8	148	Liberia	49.8
67	Thailand	93.2	107	Qatar	76.8	149	Rwanda	49.8
68	Vietnam	93.0	108	Bahrain	76.5	150	Mauritania	47.1
69	Tonga	92.9	109	El Salvador	76.2	151	Bangladesh	45.2
70	Costa Rica	92.6	110	Honduras	75.5	152	Mozambique	45.1
71	Paraguay	92.1	111	Libya	75.4	153	Afghanistan	44.1
72	Laos	92.0	112	United Arab Emirates	74.5	154	Sudan	42.7
73	Brunei	90.9	113	Namibia	74.2	155	Chad	42.2
			114	Tunisia	74.2	156	Gambia	39.0
LOWER MIDDLE			115	Burundi	73.7			
74	Maldives	90.6	116	Gabon	73.5	**BOTTOM 10**		
75	Ecuador	90.5	117	Saudi Arabia	73.1	157	Senegal	38.8
76	Sri Lanka	90.1	118	Sao Tome e Principe	70.2	158	Pakistan	36.0
77	Fiji	90.0	119	Congo	70.0	159	Guinea	34.9
78	Philippines	89.9	120	Ghana	70.0	160	Ethiopia	32.7
79	Turkey	89.9	121	Iraq	69.8	161	Benin	31.7
80	Puerto Rico	89.7	122	Guatemala	69.7	162	Bhutan	31.0
81	Mexico	89.5	123	Swaziland	69.0	163	Sierra Leone	30.7
82	Jordan	89.3	124	Cote d'Ivoire	66.9	164	Burkina	27.9
83	Panama	88.1	125	Cameroon	66.3	165	Mali	26.7
84	Lebanon	87.8	126	Papua New Guinea	64.9	166	Niger	16.7
85	Madagascar	87.7	127	Iran	64.5			

Source: *UNESCO Statistical Yearbook*

233. FEMALE LITERACY RATE

Literacy rate was presented for males and females together in the first edition of this book. It is one of the most widely used rates in the world for determining social and cultural development. But a closer look reveals wide disparities between the rates for males and females, especially in developing countries. The disparity is often as high as 30 to 40 percentage points, and the gap is not seen as closing, despite efforts to promote female education in countries where there are few incentives for women to seek such advancement. A comparative study of this ranking with that of male literacy will reveal those countries where women suffer one of the greatest handicaps of all—that of educational inferiority.

Rank	Country	Female Literay (over age 15–%)
TOP 10		
1	Albania	100
2	Andorra	100
3	Austria	100
4	Belgium	100
5	Czech Republic	100
6	Denmark	100
7	Finland	100
8	Germany	100
9	Iceland	100
10	Ireland	100
UPPER MIDDLE		
11	Japan	100
12	Liechtenstein	100
13	Luxembourg	100
14	Netherlands	100
15	New Zealand	100
16	Norway	100
17	Slovakia	100
18	Sweden	100
19	Switzerland	100
20	United Kingdom	100
21	Western Samoa	100
22	Estonia	99.6
23	Latvia	99.2
24	Slovenia	99.1
25	France	98.7
26	Hungary	98.6
27	Jamaica	98.6
28	Georgia	98.5
29	Poland	98.3
30	Armenia	98.1
31	San Marino	97.7
32	Ukraine	97.4
33	Bermuda	97.0
34	Croatia	97.0
35	Russia	96.8
36	Belarus	96.6
37	Tajikstan	96.6
38	Turkmenistan	96.6
39	Italy	96.4
40	Kazakhstan	96.1
41	Uzbekistan	96.0
42	Azerbaijan	95.9
43	Malta	95.9
44	Canada	95.7
45	Kyrgyzstan	95.5
46	Tuvalu	95.5
47	Guyana	95.4
48	Uruguay	95.4
49	United States	95.3
50	Argentina	95.1
51	Suriname	94.7
52	Moldova	94.4
53	Korea, South	93.5
54	Chile	93.2
55	Costa Rica	93.1

Rank	Country	Female Literay (over age 15–%)
56	Tonga	92.8
57	Israel	92.7
58	Spain	92.5
59	Romania	92.2
60	Venezuela	91.1
61	Maldives	90.1
62	Cyprus	90.0
63	Taiwan	89.2
64	Greece	89.1
65	Puerto Rico	88.5
66	Panama	88.2
67	Paraguay	88.1
68	Philippines	87.5
69	Portugal	86.9
70	Ecuador	86.2
71	Colombia	85.9
72	Seychelles	85.7
73	Singapore	85.6
LOWER MIDDLE		
74	Mexico	85.1
75	Lesotho	84.5
76	Thailand	84.5
77	Fiji	84.0
78	Macedonia	83.8
79	Sri Lanka	83.8
80	Yugoslavia	83.2
81	Vietnam	82.8
82	Peru	82.6
83	Dominican Republic	81.8
84	Brazil	81.2
85	Brunei	78.7
86	Bosnia & Herzegovina	76.7
87	Laos	75.8
88	South Africa	75.1
89	Burundi	74.9
90	Kuwait	74.9
91	Mauritius	74.7
92	Lebanon	73.1
93	Madagascar	72.9
94	Qatar	72.5
95	Myanmar (Burma)	71.6
96	Namibia	70.8
97	Bolivia	70.7
98	Honduras	70.6
99	Malaysia	70.4
100	Jordan	70.3
101	El Salvador	70.0
102	Indonesia	70.0
103	Turkey	68.5
104	United Arab Emirates	68.4
105	China	68.0
106	Zimbabwe	66.8
107	Zambia	65.3
108	Botswana	65.1
109	Cambodia	65.0
110	Swaziland	65.0
111	Zaire	60.7

Rank	Country	Female Literay (over age 15–%)
112	Bahrain	58.6
113	Kenya	58.5
114	Tunisia	56.3
115	Guatemala	51.7
116	Ghana	50.9
117	Rwanda	50.9
118	Syria	50.8
119	Libya	50.4
120	Iraq	49.3
121	Equatorial Guinea	48.6
122	Gabon	48.5
123	Saudi Arabia	48.1
124	Somalia	47.9
125	Vanuatu	47.8
126	Haiti	47.4
127	Algeria	45.5
128	Solomon Islands	44.9
129	Congo	43.9
130	Iran	43.3
131	Cameroon	42.6
132	Cote d'Ivoire	40.2
133	Sao Tome e Principe	39.1
134	Comoros	39.0
135	Cape Verde	38.6
136	Morocco	38.0
137	Papua New Guinea	37.8
138	Uganda	34.9
139	Egypt	33.8
140	India	33.7
141	Nigeria	31.5
142	Togo	31.0
143	Liberia	28.8
144	Angola	28.5
145	Yemen	26.3
146	Central African Republic	24.9
147	Guinea-Bissau	24.0
148	Oman	24.0
149	Bangladesh	23.7
150	Nepal	23.3
151	Mauritania	21.4
152	Mozambique	21.3
153	Senegal	19.4
154	Chad	17.9
155	Ethiopia	16.4
156	Gambia	16.0
BOTTOM 10		
157	Benin	15.6
158	Pakistan	15.2
159	Afghanistan	13.9
160	Guinea	13.4
161	Sudan	11.7
162	Mali	11.4
163	Sierra Leone	11.3
164	Bhutan	9.0
165	Burkina	8.9
166	Niger	5.4

Source: *UNESCO Statistical Yearbook*

234. TERTIARY INSTITUTIONS

Tertiary institutions comprise undergraduate and graduate colleges and universities, and post graduate research institutions, both public and private. Degrees are generally granted only by graduate and postgraduate institutions, but undergraduate institutions may sometimes grant certificates.

Rank	Country	Tertiary Instituions Colleges and Universities
TOP 10		
1	India	7,513
2	United States	3,559
3	Mexico	1,832
4	Argentina	1,540
5	Japan	1,114
6	France	1,062
7	China	1,053
8	Bangladesh	997
9	Brazil	918
10	Indonesia	900
UPPER MIDDLE		
11	Philippines	809
12	Pakistan	797
13	Spain	789
14	Korea, South	605
15	Peru	553
16	Russia	535
17	Turkey	424
18	Germany	314
19	Korea, North	281
20	Canada	272
21	Portugal	250
22	Colombia	235
23	Netherlands	206
24	Chile	201
25	Norway	199
26	Ukraine	156
27	Yugoslavia	141
28	Taiwan	125
29	Poland	124
30	Vietnam	104
31	Venezuela	99
32	Australia	95
33	Austria	94
34	Denmark	94
35	Hungary	91
36	Bulgaria	87
37	Greece	82
38	Saudi Arabia	82
39	Kazakhstan	61
40	Romania	56
41	Jordan	55
42	Croatia	54
43	Malaysia	54
44	Uzbekistan	52
45	Italy	50
46	Ireland	48
47	United Kingdom	48
48	Puerto Rico	45
49	Bosnia & Herzegovina	44
50	Iran	44
51	Syria	44
52	Thailand	43
53	Myanmar (Burma)	40
54	Cuba	35
55	Morocco	35

Rank	Country	Tertiary Instituions Colleges and Universities
56	Belarus	33
57	Cyprus	29
58	Slovenia	28
59	Macedonia	27
60	Sudan	24
61	Czech Republic	23
62	Belgium	21
63	Ecuador	21
64	Finland	20
65	Iraq	20
66	Georgia	19
67	Azerbaijan	18
68	Lebanon	18
69	Senegal	18
70	Lithuania	17
71	South Africa	17
72	Algeria	15
73	Jamaica	15
74	Armenia	14
75	Estonia	14
76	Kenya	14
77	Latvia	14
78	Slovakia	14
LOWER MIDDLE		
79	Benin	13
80	Tajikstan	13
81	Congo	12
82	Egypt	12
83	Kyrgyzstan	12
84	Ethiopia	11
85	Moldova	11
86	Bolivia	10
87	Guinea	10
88	Libya	10
89	Nicaragua	10
90	Burkina	9
91	Cambodia	9
92	Gambia	9
93	Laos	9
94	Mongolia	9
95	Panama	9
96	Turkmenistan	9
97	Uganda	9
98	Albania	8
99	Burundi	8
100	Sri Lanka	8
101	Dominican Republic	7
102	Israel	7
103	Mali	7
104	New Zealand	7
105	Singapore	7
106	El Salvador	6
107	Western Samoa	6
108	Afghanistan	5
109	Cameroon	5
110	Costa Rica	5
111	Equatorial Guinea	5

Rank	Country	Tertiary Instituions Colleges and Universities
112	Fiji	5
113	Guatemala	5
114	Honduras	5
115	Iceland	5
116	Madagascar	5
117	Oman	5
118	Brunei	4
119	Chad	4
120	Malawi	4
121	Mauritania	4
122	Tanzania	4
123	Barbados	3
124	Ghana	3
125	Liberia	3
126	Nepal	3
127	Niger	3
128	Rwanda	3
129	Zimbabwe	3
130	Bahrain	2
131	Bhutan	2
132	Dominica	2
133	Haiti	2
134	Mauritius	2
135	Mozambique	2
136	Papua New Guinea	2
137	Paraguay	2
138	Sierra Leone	2
139	Uruguay	2
140	Zambia	2
141	Angola	1
142	Bahamas	1
143	Bermuda	1
144	Botswana	1
145	Central African Republic	1
146	Cote d'Ivoire	1
147	Djibouti	1
148	Eritrea	1
149	Gabon	1
150	Grenada	1
151	Guyana	1
152	Kuwait	1
153	Lesotho	1
154	Liechtenstein	1
155	Malta	1
156	Nauru	1
157	Qatar	1
BOTTOM 10		
158	St. Kitts and Nevis	1
159	Somalia	1
160	Suriname	1
161	Swaziland	1
162	Togo	1
163	Tonga	1
164	Trinidad and Tobago	1
165	United Arab Emirates	1
166	Vanuatu	1
167	Yemen	1

Source: *World Data*

235. SECONDARY SCHOOLS

Definitions of secondary schools vary. In some countries where there are middle schools, the secondary school consists of fewer grades. But in all cases, secondary school study is the concluding stage of compulsory education and ends with a school-leaving examination. Those who successfully complete secondary school education receive a certificate which forms the basis for admissions to colleges and universities.

Rank	Country	Secondary Schools	Rank	Country	Secondary Schools	Rank	Country	Secondary Schools
TOP 10			56	Morocco	1,080	112	Papua New Guinea	135
1	India	235,793	57	Austria	1,007	113	Oman	128
2	China	84,021	58	Yemen	942	114	Jamaica	126
3	Indonesia	28,834	59	Taiwan	906	115	Mauritius	122
4	Mexico	25,131	60	Hungary	876	116	Burundi	113
5	Spain	22,633	61	Afghanistan	819	117	Cyprus	113
6	United States	20,406	62	Israel	816	118	Niger	105
7	Pakistan	19,117	63	Paraguay	812	119	Trinidad and Tobago	101
8	Iran	18,445	64	Norway	778	120	Malawi	94
9	Japan	16,801	65	Uganda	774	121	Guyana	93
10	France	11,325	66	Laos	750	122	Macedonia	90
			67	Bolivia	724	123	Suriname	89
UPPER MIDDLE			68	Mongolia	634	124	Eritrea	86
11	Brazil	10,160	69	Tunisia	625	125	Somalia	82
12	Australia	9,865	70	Jordan	622	126	Chad	66
13	Italy	9,857	71	Sweden	600	127	Mauritania	56
14	Bangladesh	9,731	72	Honduras	590	128	Gabon	51
15	Sri Lanka	9,041				129	Albania	47
16	Turkey	8,064	**LOWER MIDDLE**			130	Central African Republic	46
17	Argentina	7,224	73	Yugoslavia	539	131	Malta	46
18	Peru	6,617	74	El Salvador	488	132	Tonga	40
19	Egypt	6,558	75	Zambia	480	133	Western Samoa	38
20	Vietnam	6,296	76	Ireland	474	134	Bahamas	37
21	Colombia	6,134	77	Finland	465	135	Qatar	36
22	Nepal	6,124	78	Cambodia	440	136	Bahrain	35
23	Nigeria	5,594	79	Liberia	419	137	Barbados	33
24	Sudan	5,578	80	Nicaragua	407	138	Comoros	32
25	Philippines	5,550	81	Kuwait	390	139	Belize	31
26	Ghana	5,513	82	Cameroon	388	140	Bhutan	31
27	Angola	5,276	83	Panama	363	141	Djibouti	26
28	United Kingdom	4,730	84	Togo	358	142	Brunei	23
29	Korea, South	4,358	85	Uruguay	351	143	Solomon Islands	23
30	Zaire	4,276	86	New Zealand	339	144	St. Vincent	21
31	Saudi Arabia	4,153	87	Senegal	321	145	Vanuatu	21
32	Algeria	3,424	88	Puerto Rico	315	146	Grenada	19
33	Greece	2,988	89	Mali	307	147	Cape Verde	16
34	Myanmar (Burma)	2,920	90	Tanzania	288	148	Gambia	14
35	Iraq	2,746	91	Czech Republic	285	149	St. Lucia	14
36	Kenya	2,639	92	Bosnia & Herzegovina	238	150	Dominica	13
37	Cuba	2,175	93	Congo	238	151	Andorra	12
38	Syria	2,077	94	Slovenia	226	152	Antigua and Barbuda	12
39	Belgium	2,055	95	Guinea	225	153	Bermuda	12
40	Ecuador	2,027	96	Croatia	220	154	Guinea-Bissau	12
41	Thailand	1,859	97	Sierra Leone	217	155	Sao Tome e Principe	11
42	Poland	1,762	98	Mozambique	207			
43	Chile	1,694	99	South Africa	197	**BOTTOM 10**		
44	Venezuela	1,621	100	Rwanda	192	156	Equatorial Guinea	9
45	Libya	1,555	101	Singapore	180	157	Kiribati	9
46	Zimbabwe	1,518	102	Costa Rica	179	158	Maldives	9
47	Kyrgyzstan	1,472	103	Lesotho	179	159	Liechtenstein	8
48	Lebanon	1,405	104	Burkina	173	160	St. Kitts and Nevis	7
49	Portugal	1,368	105	Botswana	169	161	Seychelles	4
50	Malaysia	1,336	106	Slovakia	165	162	Monaco	3
51	Guatemala	1,274	107	Denmark	154	163	San Marino	3
52	Ethiopia	1,209	108	Swaziland	153	164	Nauru	2
53	Romania	1,209	109	Benin	151	165	Tuvalu	1
54	Madagascar	1,142	110	Cote d'Ivoire	147			
55	Netherlands	1,117	111	Fiji	140			

Source: *UNESCO Statistical Yearbook*

236. ACADEMIC ATTAINMENT

Literacy has become virtually universal at least in developed countries. But a college degree remains the privilege of a few. Even in developed countries, with the exception of Canada and the United States, only a small minority can claim to have a complete third-level education. This also reflects the fact that in every country, colleges have seats for only a small percentage of the students who complete their secondary school education.

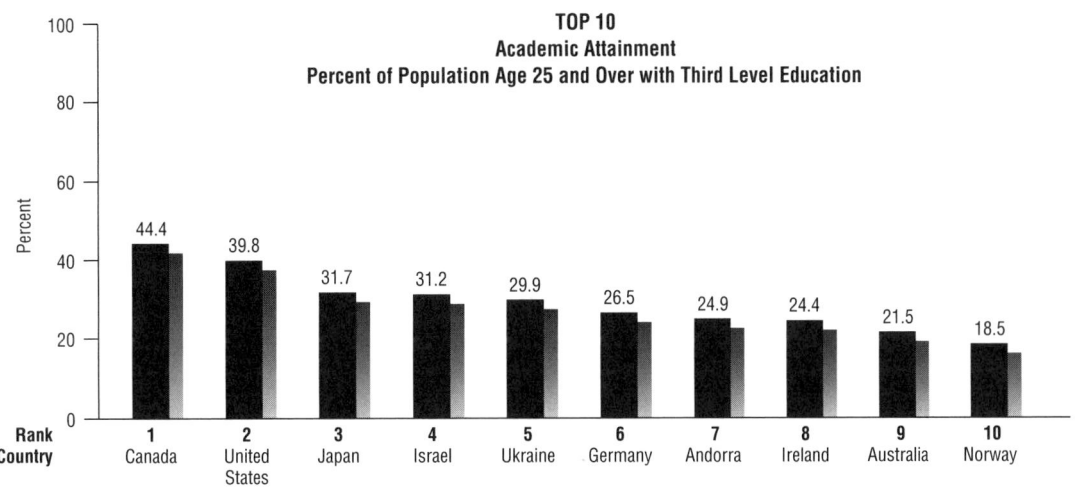

TOP 10
Academic Attainment
Percent of Population Age 25 and Over with Third Level Education

Rank	1	2	3	4	5	6	7	8	9	10
Value	44.4	39.8	31.7	31.2	29.9	26.5	24.9	24.4	21.5	18.5
Country	Canada	United States	Japan	Israel	Ukraine	Germany	Andorra	Ireland	Australia	Norway

Rank	Country	Population Age 25 & Over with Third Level Education (%)	Rank	Country	Population Age 25 & Over with Third Level Education (%)	Rank	Country	Population Age 25 & Over with Third Level Education (%)
UPPER MIDDLE			51	Yugoslavia	5.7	90	Pakistan	1.9
11	Puerto Rico	18.4	52	Macedonia	5.1	91	Guyana	1.8
12	Sweden	15.4	53	Brazil	5.0	92	Dominica	1.7
13	Philippines	15.2	54	Peru	4.8	93	Grenada	1.5
14	Uruguay	14.8	55	Swaziland	4.3	94	Liberia	1.5
15	Costa Rica	14.2	56	Cuba	4.2	95	St. Vincent	1.4
16	Korea, South	14.2	57	Egypt	4.1	96	Bangladesh	1.3
17	Qatar	13.3	58	Italy	4.1	97	Kenya	1.3
18	Panama	13.2	59	Malta	3.9	98	St. Lucia	1.3
19	Ecuador	12.7				99	Togo	1.3
20	Finland	11.2	**LOWER MIDDLE**			100	Indonesia	1.2
21	Liechtenstein	11.2	60	Syria	3.9	101	China	1.1
22	Kuwait	11.1	61	Turkey	3.9	102	Equatorial Guinea	1.1
23	United Kingdom	11.0	62	Bahrain	3.8	103	Sri Lanka	1.1
24	Bolivia	9.8	63	Burkina	3.8	104	Tonga	1.0
25	Brunei	9.4	64	Iceland	3.7	105	Senegal	0.8
26	Croatia	9.4	65	Ghana	3.5	106	Haiti	0.7
27	Slovakia	9.4	66	Paraguay	3.4	107	Kiribati	0.6
28	Mexico	8.3	67	Singapore	3.4	108	Lesotho	0.6
29	Mongolia	8.1	68	Tunisia	3.4	109	Morocco	0.6
30	Iran	7.8	69	Barbados	3.3	110	Botswana	0.5
31	Bermuda	7.4	70	Fiji	3.3	111	Cape Verde	0.5
32	Greece	7.4	71	Honduras	3.3	112	Tuvalu	0.5
33	Romania	7.3	72	Afghanistan	3.2	113	Maldives	0.4
34	Czech Republic	7.2	73	Lebanon	3.1	114	Portugal	0.4
35	Chile	7.1	74	Seychelles	3.1	115	Uganda	0.4
36	Hungary	7.0	75	Congo	3.0			
37	Spain	7.0	76	Guatemala	3.0	**BOTTOM 10**		
38	Venezuela	7.0	77	Thailand	2.9	116	Zambia	0.4
39	Argentina	6.9	78	Trinidad and Tobago	2.7	117	Algeria	0.3
40	New Zealand	6.9	79	Solomon Islands	2.6	118	Benin	0.3
41	Colombia	6.8	80	India	2.5	119	Rwanda	0.3
42	Monaco	6.8	81	Dominican Republic	2.3	120	Sao Tome e Principe	0.3
43	Nauru	6.8	82	El Salvador	2.3	121	Comoros	0.2
44	Vietnam	6.8	83	South Africa	2.3	122	Malawi	0.2
45	Belize	6.6	84	St. Kitts and Nevis	2.1	123	Mozambique	0.2
46	Poland	6.5	85	Jamaica	2.0	124	Niger	0.2
47	Austria	6.1	86	Namibia	2.0	125	Myanmar (Burma)	0.1
48	Taiwan	6.0	87	Western Samoa	2.0			
49	United Arab Emirates	6.0	88	Malaysia	1.9			
50	Slovenia	5.9	89	Mauritius	1.9			

Source: *UNESCO Statistical Yearbook*

237. STUDENTS AT THE TERTIARY LEVEL PER 100,000

The ranking reveals the low percentage of students in colleges and universities relative to the general population. The figures include those who remain in college for any length of time without completing their courses or obtaining a degree. In the case of advanced countries, they also include foreign students in national universities and colleges. In the case of countries such as the United States, the large foreign student population may help to boost the overall national figures.

Rank	Country	Students in Third Level (per 100,000 population)	Rank	Country	Students in Third Level (per 100,000 population)	Rank	Country	Students in Third Level (per 100,000 population)
TOP 10			52	Syria	1,695	104	Sri Lanka	505
1	Canada	7,197	53	Barbados	1,657	105	Botswana	487
2	United States	5,653	54	Uzbekistan	1,650	106	Oman	463
3	New Zealand	4,232	55	Qatar	1,608	107	Myanmar (Burma)	459
4	Korea, South	4,208	56	Estonia	1,593	108	Bangladesh	382
5	Puerto Rico	4,091	57	Turkey	1,569	109	Swaziland	382
6	Norway	3,883	58	Colombia	1,554	110	Gabon	368
7	Finland	3,757	59	Libya	1,548	111	Madagascar	333
8	Peru	3,465	60	Latvia	1,536	112	Nigeria	320
9	France	3,414	61	Poland	1,521	113	Mauritania	281
10	Spain	3,335	62	El Salvador	1,512	114	Namibia	280
			63	Mexico	1,478	115	Yemen	276
UPPER MIDDLE			64	Azerbaijan	1,470	116	Cameroon	268
11	Argentina	3,293	65	Bahrain	1,456	117	Pakistan	266
12	Netherlands	3,280	66	Yugoslavia	1,374	118	Senegal	266
13	Australia	3,178	67	Kyrgyzstan	1,330	119	Togo	260
14	Lebanon	3,071				120	Brunei	259
15	Germany	3,051	**LOWER MIDDLE**			121	Sudan	258
16	Denmark	2,917	68	Tajikstan	1,280	122	Benin	235
17	Ireland	2,895	69	Mongolia	1,254	123	Liberia	220
18	Austria	2,847	70	Moldova	1,250	124	Mauritius	208
19	Venezuela	2,847	71	Iraq	1,240	125	Luxembourg	207
20	Italy	2,795	72	South Africa	1,231	126	Cote d'Ivoire	204
21	Israel	2,790	73	Algeria	1,163	127	Somalia	195
22	Belgium	2,772	74	Kuwait	1,135	128	China	191
23	Philippines	2,596	75	Turkmenistan	1,130	129	Zambia	189
24	Costa Rica	2,584	76	Hungary	1,117	130	Kenya	187
25	Jordan	2,497	77	Fiji	1,080	131	Zaire	176
26	Switzerland	2,417	78	Brazil	1,075	132	Vietnam	153
27	Sweden	2,407	79	Saudi Arabia	1,064	133	Afghanistan	147
28	United Kingdom	2,406	80	Iran	1,061	134	Central African Republic	146
29	Iceland	2,397	81	Tunisia	1,045	135	Papua New Guinea	146
30	Panama	2,377	82	Indonesia	1,032	136	Ghana	126
31	Japan	2,338	83	Cyprus	1,029	137	Guinea	122
32	Cuba	2,285	84	Suriname	1,023	138	Laos	116
33	Taiwan	2,225	85	Romania	1,010	139	Uganda	115
34	Uruguay	2,180	86	Singapore	963	140	Lesotho	114
35	Chile	2,144	87	Morocco	958	141	Sierra Leone	114
36	Bulgaria	2,078	88	Malta	882	142	Haiti	107
37	Thailand	2,060	89	Honduras	854	143	Burundi	73
38	Armenia	2,030	90	Nicaragua	814	144	Mali	73
39	Bolivia	2,028	91	Paraguay	769	145	Angola	71
40	Ecuador	1,958	92	Guatemala	741			
41	Bahamas	1,945	93	Grenada	709	**BOTTOM 10**		
42	Portugal	1,935	94	Albania	689	146	Chad	70
43	Dominican Republic	1,929	95	Malaysia	679	147	Ethiopia	66
44	Greece	1,928	96	Jamaica	662	148	Malawi	63
45	Georgia	1,900	97	United Arab Emirates	637	149	Burkina	60
46	Russia	1,900	98	Trinidad and Tobago	591	150	Niger	60
47	Lithuania	1,758	99	Guyana	588	151	Eritrea	55
48	Kazakhstan	1,710	100	India	556	152	Rwanda	50
49	Belarus	1,700	101	Nepal	549	153	Tanzania	21
50	Ukraine	1,700	102	Zimbabwe	528	154	Bhutan	18
51	Egypt	1,697	103	Congo	524	155	Mozambique	11

Source: *UNESCO Statistical Yearbook*

238. FEMALE ENROLLMENT RATIO

Among the key areas of gender disparity are female enrollment ratios in primary, secondary and tertiary levels. This is also one of the areas where dramatic strides have been made in the past three decades. Better educational access has enabled women to aspire to better career opportunities and to compete with men in fields entirely closed to them before. The effects of such progress are most dramatic in certain Third World societies where women were formerly confined to the home and denied the right to education.

Rank	Country	Female Enrollment Ratio First, Second & Third Level Combined
TOP 10		
1	Canada	110
2	Finland	101
3	United States	98
4	Norway	89
5	Spain	89
6	France	88
7	Netherlands	87
8	Bahrain	86
9	Denmark	86
10	New Zealand	86
UPPER MIDDLE		
11	Ireland	85
12	Belgium	84
13	Namibia	84
14	Portugal	84
15	United Arab Emirates	84
16	Argentina	82
17	Austria	82
18	Iceland	82
19	Uruguay	82
20	Australia	80
21	Germany	79
22	Sweden	79
23	Greece	78
24	Israel	78
25	Philippines	78
26	Qatar	78
27	South Africa	78
28	Bahamas	77
29	Fiji	77
30	United Kingdom	77
31	Japan	76
32	Poland	76
33	Belarus	75
34	Cyprus	75
35	Korea, South	75
36	Dominican Republic	74
37	Peru	74
38	Barbados	73
39	Botswana	73
40	St. Lucia	73
41	Suriname	73
42	Estonia	72
43	Slovakia	72
44	Ukraine	72
45	Venezuela	72
46	Chile	71
47	Lebanon	71
48	Switzerland	71
49	Brazil	70
50	Ecuador	70

Rank	Country	Female Enrollment Ratio First, Second & Third Level Combined
51	Italy	70
52	Malta	70
53	Panama	70
54	Russia	70
55	Colombia	69
56	Czech Republic	69
57	Latvia	69
58	Albania	68
59	Azerbaijan	68
60	Brunei	68
61	Cuba	68
62	Guyana	68
63	Kazakhstan	68
64	Lithuania	68
65	St. Vincent	68
66	Swaziland	68
LOWER MIDDLE		
67	Trinidad and Tobago	68
68	Bulgaria	67
69	Hungary	67
70	Sri Lanka	67
71	Costa Rica	66
72	Libya	66
73	Maldives	66
74	Singapore	66
75	Tajikstan	66
76	Zimbabwe	66
77	Jamaica	65
78	Mexico	64
79	Lesotho	63
80	Mongolia	63
81	Syria	62
82	Bolivia	61
83	Egypt	61
84	Honduras	61
85	Iran	61
86	Malaysia	61
87	Nicaragua	61
88	Romania	61
89	Algeria	60
90	Tunisia	60
91	Mauritius	59
92	Cape Verde	58
93	Paraguay	58
94	Indonesia	57
95	Luxembourg	57
96	Kenya	56
97	Oman	56
98	El Salvador	54
99	Turkey	54
100	Thailand	53
101	China	52

Rank	Country	Female Enrollment Ratio First, Second & Third Level Combined
102	Saudi Arabia	49
103	Iraq	48
104	Kuwait	48
105	Myanmar (Burma)	47
106	Nigeria	47
107	Vietnam	47
108	India	46
109	Zambia	46
110	Cameroon	44
111	Togo	44
112	Malawi	43
113	Nepal	41
114	Laos	40
115	Ghana	39
116	Guatemala	39
117	Solomon Islands	39
118	Rwanda	38
119	Morocco	35
120	Comoros	34
121	Madagascar	34
122	Bangladesh	33
123	Tanzania	33
124	Uganda	32
125	Zaire	32
126	Angola	31
127	Cote d'Ivoire	31
128	Papua New Guinea	30
129	Haiti	28
130	Burundi	27
131	Central African Republic	27
132	Mauritania	27
133	St. Kitts and Nevis	27
134	Sudan	27
135	Gambia	26
136	Senegal	25
137	Yemen	23
138	Benin	22
139	Sierra Leone	22
140	Mozambique	21
141	Guinea-Bissau	20
142	Chad	17
BOTTOM 10		
143	Djibouti	16
144	Pakistan	16
145	Burkina	14
146	Guinea	13
147	Ethiopia	12
148	Liberia	12
149	Mali	11
150	Afghanistan	10
151	Niger	10
152	Somalia	5

Source: *UNESCO Statistical Yearbook*

239. ENROLLMENT RATIO—TERTIARY

Enrollment ratio at the tertiary level is influenced by a number of factors: the cost of attending college, and the availability of seats, the difficulty of living away from home, and public perception of the benefits of a college education in weak labor markets. In almost all countries, free education ends with the last year in secondary school, and for those without scholarships, the cost of attending college can be prohibitive. Another consideration is the sacrifice of potential income for four or more years. College education is less state-subsidized and requires substantial inputs of time and money from the students.

Rank	Country	Enrollment Ratio Tertiary Level
TOP 10		
1	Canada	98.8
2	United States	76.2
3	Finland	50.7
4	Puerto Rico	48.1
5	Norway	45.3
6	New Zealand	44.8
7	Argentina	43.4
8	France	43.2
9	Korea, South	39.9
10	Australia	38.6
UPPER MIDDLE		
11	Belize	38.2
12	Netherlands	37.6
13	Germany	36.1
14	Denmark	35.6
15	Peru	35.6
16	Spain	35.5
17	Austria	34.5
18	Israel	34.4
19	Ireland	33.8
20	Sweden	33.8
21	Uruguay	32.0
22	Italy	31.7
23	Japan	31.3
24	Bulgaria	30.4
25	Venezuela	29.5
26	Iceland	29.2
27	Switzerland	29.1
28	Lebanon	27.8
29	Philippines	27.8
30	United Kingdom	27.8
31	Costa Rica	27.6
32	Qatar	25.9
33	Greece	25.0
34	Panama	23.8
35	Chile	23.3
36	Portugal	22.7
37	Bolivia	22.6
38	Jordan	21.5
39	Poland	21.5
40	Cuba	20.9
41	Ecuador	20.1
42	Bahamas	19.6
43	Egypt	19.2
44	Syria	18.8
45	Dominican Republic	18.6

Rank	Country	Enrollment Ratio Tertiary Level
46	Yugoslavia	18.2
47	Libya	18.0
48	Bahrain	17.5
49	Barbados	17.3
50	Thailand	16.3
51	El Salvador	16.1
52	Hungary	15.3
53	Mexico	15.2
54	Cyprus	15.0
55	Turkey	14.8
56	Iraq	13.8
57	Kuwait	13.8
58	Colombia	13.7
LOWER MIDDLE		
59	Mongolia	13.6
60	Saudi Arabia	13.3
61	Malta	13.1
62	Fiji	12.8
63	Iran	12.2
64	Algeria	11.8
65	Brazil	11.6
66	United Arab Emirates	10.6
67	Morocco	10.2
68	Nicaragua	10.1
69	Tunisia	9.4
70	Suriname	9.2
71	Honduras	9.1
72	Indonesia	8.7
73	Romania	8.7
74	Grenada	8.6
75	Paraguay	8.2
76	Singapore	7.9
77	Albania	7.2
78	Malaysia	7.2
79	India	6.7
80	Nepal	6.6
81	Oman	6.2
82	Zimbabwe	6.1
83	Congo	6.0
84	Jamaica	6.0
85	Trinidad and Tobago	5.5
86	Myanmar (Burma)	5.4
87	Sri Lanka	5.2
88	Guyana	5.1
89	Swaziland	4.7
90	Brunei	4.5
91	Bangladesh	3.8

Rank	Country	Enrollment Ratio Tertiary Level
92	Nigeria	3.7
93	Cameroon	3.4
94	Madagascar	3.4
95	Botswana	3.3
96	Gabon	3.3
97	Mauritania	3.3
98	Namibia	3.3
99	Senegal	2.9
100	Sudan	2.9
101	Yemen	2.9
102	Benin	2.8
103	Pakistan	2.8
104	Lesotho	2.7
105	Togo	2.6
106	Cote d'Ivoire	2.5
107	Liberia	2.5
108	Luxembourg	2.4
109	Somalia	2.3
110	Vietnam	2.3
111	Kenya	2.2
112	Mauritius	2.1
113	Zaire	2.1
114	Zambia	2.1
115	Central African Republic	1.8
116	Afghanistan	1.7
117	Papua New Guinea	1.7
118	China	1.6
119	Ghana	1.5
120	Guinea	1.4
121	Laos	1.3
122	Sierra Leone	1.3
123	Haiti	1.2
124	Uganda	1.1
125	Angola	0.9
126	Burundi	0.8
BOTTOM 10		
127	Chad	0.8
128	Ethiopia	0.8
129	Mali	0.8
130	Burkina	0.7
131	Malawi	0.7
132	Niger	0.7
133	Rwanda	0.6
134	Bhutan	0.3
135	Tanzania	0.2
136	Mozambique	0.1

Source: *UNESCO Statistical Yearbook*

240. NET ENROLLMENT RATIO-SECONDARY

Educational enrollment ratios follow a pyramid pattern. Even with 100% enrollment at the primary level, there is a moderate-to-sharp dropoff at the secondary level, and then a precipitous drop at the tertiary level. These enrollment ratios have strong implications for the labor market. In countries where fewer cohorts enter the second and third levels, the labor force tends to be less skilled. The secondary level ratio excludes the technical and vocational education sector. In many countries, students with less academic aptitude veer off into the technical and vocational stream.

Rank	Country	Net Enrollment Ratio Secondary Level	Rank	Country	Net Enrollment Ratio Secondary Level	Rank	Country	Net Enrollment Ratio Secondary Level
TOP 10			30	Romania	72	60	Bolivia	27
1	Japan	97	31	Qatar	69	61	Nicaragua	25
2	Canada	93	32	Cuba	67	62	Nepal	23
3	Finland	93	33	Denmark	66	63	Gambia	19
4	Austria	90	34	United Arab Emirates	64	64	Honduras	19
5	Cyprus	90				65	Venezuela	19
6	Spain	90	**LOWER MIDDLE**			66	Bangladesh	17
7	Sweden	90	35	Brunei	62	67	Lesotho	17
8	Norway	89	36	Jamaica	61	68	Liberia	17
9	Korea, South	88	37	Bulgaria	60	69	Zaire	17
10	Bahamas	87	38	Luxembourg	60	70	Brazil	16
			39	Philippines	58	71	Zambia	16
UPPER MIDDLE			40	Algeria	53	72	Cambodia	15
11	Belgium	87	41	Chile	53	73	El Salvador	15
12	France	87	42	Oman	50	74	Laos	15
13	Greece	87	43	Panama	50	75	Benin	13
14	Bahrain	86	44	Iran	47	76	Guatemala	13
15	Germany	85	45	Mexico	46	77	Senegal	13
16	New Zealand	85	46	Suriname	45	78	Cameroon	11
17	Ireland	81	47	Botswana	44	79	Djibouti	11
18	Netherlands	81	48	Taiwan	44			
19	Barbados	80	49	Tunisia	44	**BOTTOM 10**		
20	Malta	80	50	Turkey	44	80	Angola	10
21	Switzerland	80	51	Peru	42	81	Rwanda	8
22	United Kingdom	80	52	Costa Rica	39	82	Burkina	7
23	United States	80	53	Colombia	38	83	Guinea	7
24	Australia	79	54	Indonesia	38	84	Niger	6
25	Poland	78	55	Iraq	37	85	Burundi	5
26	Hungary	77	56	Jordan	36	86	Mali	5
27	Yugoslavia	76	57	Saudi Arabia	36	87	Guinea-Bissau	3
28	Estonia	73	58	Monaco	29	88	Somalia	3
29	Trinidad and Tobago	73	59	Paraguay	28	89	Malawi	2

Source: *UNESCO Statistical Yearbook*

241. PRIMARY SCHOOL ENROLLMENT RATIO

In all countries of the world the first level of education (also called primary or elementary education) is the most important and, in nations where compulsory education laws are in force, the most universal. Although primary school age is generally considered six to 11 years, each educational system follows its own definition. Differences among countries in the age and duration of schooling are reflected in the ratios. Enrollment ratios may be either gross or net;

for the purpose of this ranking, the former has been adopted. Gross enrollment ratio is derived by dividing total enrollment by the national population within the specified age group. In the case of countries with differing educational systems (particularly federal countries, such as the United States and Germany), the age group of the most representative system has been used.

Rank	Country	Net Enrollment Ratio Primary Level	Rank	Country	Net Enrollment Ratio Primary Level	Rank	Country	Net Enrollment Ratio Primary Level
TOP 10			40	Denmark	95	80	Togo	76
1	Bahamas	100	41	Netherlands	95	81	Dominican Republic	73
2	Canada	100	42	Peru	95	82	Papua New Guinea	72
3	France	100	43	Mongolia	94	83	Rwanda	72
4	Jamaica	100	44	Brunei	93	84	El Salvador	70
5	Japan	100	45	Greece	93	85	Lesotho	70
6	Korea, South	100	46	Honduras	93	86	Bangladesh	69
7	Mexico	100	47	Panama	92	87	Madagascar	64
8	New Zealand	100	48	Angola	91	88	Saudi Arabia	64
9	Portugal	100				89	Nepal	61
10	Singapore	100	**LOWER MIDDLE**			90	Laos	59
			49	Austria	91	91	Morocco	59
UPPER MIDDLE			50	Costa Rica	91	92	Guatemala	58
11	Spain	100	51	Kenya	91	93	Zaire	58
12	Sri Lanka	100	52	Swaziland	91	94	Central African Republic	56
13	Suriname	100	53	Uruguay	91	95	Comoros	56
14	Sweden	100	54	Venezuela	91	96	Gambia	56
15	Tunisia	100	55	Algeria	90	97	Uganda	55
16	Turkey	100	56	Barbados	90	98	Cote d'Ivoire	52
17	Tuvalu	100	57	Ireland	90	99	Burundi	51
18	United Arab Emirates	100	58	Trinidad and Tobago	90	100	Tanzania	50
19	Zimbabwe	100	59	Germany	89	101	Malawi	48
20	Fiji	99	60	Mauritius	89	102	Senegal	48
21	Jordan	99	61	Qatar	88	103	Benin	45
22	Malta	99	62	Brazil	86	104	Guinea-Bissau	45
23	Oman	99	63	Hungary	86	105	Kuwait	45
24	Australia	98	64	Bahrain	85	106	Mozambique	42
25	Cyprus	98	65	Luxembourg	85	107	Chad	38
26	Iran	98	66	Pakistan	85			
27	Paraguay	98	67	Chile	83	**BOTTOM 10**		
28	United States	98	68	Colombia	83	108	Liberia	35
29	Cuba	97	69	Latvia	82	109	Djibouti	34
30	Indonesia	97	70	Bolivia	81	110	Burkina	29
31	Syria	97	71	Estonia	81	111	Ethiopia	28
32	United Kingdom	97	72	Namibia	81	112	Guinea	26
33	Botswana	96	73	Zambia	81	113	Haiti	26
34	China	96	74	Bulgaria	80	114	Niger	25
35	Philippines	96	75	Nicaragua	80	115	Afghanistan	19
36	Poland	96	76	Yugoslavia	79	116	Mali	19
37	Switzerland	96	77	Iraq	78	117	Somalia	8
38	Belize	95	78	Romania	78			
39	Cape Verde	95	79	Cameroon	76			

Source: *UNESCO Statistical Yearbook*

242. NUMBER OF PRIMARY SCHOOLS

One of the most important educational indicators is the number of primary, or first-level, schools. Because the duration of each level of schooling varies from country to country, the number of grades in these schools fluctuates. Furthermore, in many developing countries, primary schools, especially in rural areas, tend to be one-room and one-teacher institutions providing only the most rudimentary education. This ranking is therefore a quantitative and not a qualitative measurement. It includes all institutions and structures officially accredited as first-level schools but excludes schools for adults and handicapped persons.

Rank	Country	Primary Schools	Rank	Country	Primary Schools	Rank	Country	Primary Schools
TOP 10			62	Cameroon	6,709	124	Mauritania	1,309
1	China	885,479	63	Angola	6,308	125	Lesotho	1,198
2	India	572,541	64	Korea, North	6,122	126	Puerto Rico	1,145
3	Brazil	206,526	65	Korea, South	6,057	127	Namibia	1,134
4	Indonesia	147,064	66	Belarus	5,187	128	Somalia	1,125
5	Pakistan	124,171	67	Dominican Republic	4,854	129	Macedonia	1,067
6	Mexico	86,636	68	Sweden	4,826	130	Latvia	943
7	Russia	70,200	69	Finland	4,819	131	Central African Republic	930
8	United States	61,340	70	Paraguay	4,649	132	Gabon	892
9	Iran	59,280	71	Belgium	4,584	133	Slovenia	845
10	Turkey	50,701	72	Zimbabwe	4,567	134	Jamaica	788
			73	Cambodia	4,539	135	Estonia	715
UPPER MIDDLE			74	Yugoslavia	4,433	136	Equatorial Guinea	703
11	Bangladesh	48,146	75	Nicaragua	4,402	137	Fiji	681
12	France	44,131	76	Azerbaijan	4,332	138	Botswana	654
13	Germany	43,941	77	El Salvador	4,160	139	Guinea-Bissau	632
14	Colombia	41,044	78	Czech Republic	4,142	140	Afghanistan	553
15	Myanmar (Burma)	36,499	79	Morocco	4,052	141	Swaziland	523
16	Nigeria	35,446	80	Tunisia	4,044	142	Solomon Islands	520
17	Philippines	34,081	81	Hungary	3,959	143	Trinidad and Tobago	471
18	Thailand	34,039				144	Eritrea	447
19	Peru	28,265	**LOWER MIDDLE**			145	Oman	436
20	Japan	24,730	82	Georgia	3,788	146	Guyana	423
21	United Kingdom	23,958	83	Austria	3,702	147	Cyprus	390
22	Italy	22,710	84	Zambia	3,489	148	Cape Verde	367
23	Ukraine	22,000	85	Ireland	3,425	149	United Arab Emirates	354
24	Argentina	21,207	86	Mozambique	3,384	150	Suriname	301
25	South Africa	20,648	87	Bulgaria	3,360	151	Mauritius	283
26	Spain	19,821	88	Norway	3,352	152	Vanuatu	272
27	Poland	19,212	89	Costa Rica	3,317	153	Comoros	257
28	Nepal	18,694	90	Tajikstan	3,179	154	Maldives	243
29	Egypt	16,481	91	Benin	2,952	155	Kuwait	239
30	Canada	16,231	92	Niger	2,807	156	Belize	237
31	Ecuador	16,146	93	Libya	2,744	157	Gambia	233
32	Kenya	15,804	94	Panama	2,712	158	Singapore	194
33	Venezuela	15,800	95	Malawi	2,624	159	Malta	168
34	Algeria	13,970	96	Papua New Guinea	2,606	160	Western Samoa	164
35	Madagascar	13,791	97	Burkina	2,587	161	Brunei	161
36	Romania	13,730	98	Chad	2,544	162	Bhutan	156
37	Vietnam	13,092	99	Niger	2,525	163	Qatar	155
38	Portugal	11,771	100	Togo	2,494	164	Tonga	115
39	Ghana	11,056	101	Guinea	2,476	165	Bahrain	114
40	Zaire	10,817	102	Slovakia	2,472	166	Barbados	104
41	Tanzania	10,437	103	Senegal	2,458	167	Bahamas	100
42	Syria	9,934	104	Jordan	2,421	168	Kiribati	95
43	Bolivia	9,758	105	Uruguay	2,419	169	St. Lucia	84
44	Sri Lanka	9,590	106	New Zealand	2,412	170	Djibouti	69
45	Guatemala	9,362	107	Lithuania	2,219	171	Dominica	65
46	Cuba	9,346	108	Bosnia & Herzegovina	2,205	172	Sao Tome e Principe	64
47	Netherlands	9,333	109	Lebanon	2,130	173	St. Vincent	60
48	Iraq	8,875	110	Denmark	2,127			
49	Kazakhstan	8,841	111	Croatia	2,074	**BOTTOM 10**		
50	Saudi Arabia	8,631	112	Kyrgyzstan	1,862	174	Grenada	57
51	Chile	8,626	113	Sierra Leone	1,792	175	Antigua and Barbuda	43
52	Sudan	8,501	114	Turkmenistan	1,791	176	St. Kitts and Nevis	31
53	Ethiopia	8,434	115	Israel	1,735	177	Seychelles	25
54	Honduras	8,074	116	Albania	1,726	178	Bermuda	24
55	Uganda	7,905	117	Rwanda	1,724	179	Liechtenstein	14
56	Greece	7,634	118	Moldova	1,654	180	San Marino	14
57	Yemen	7,313	119	Liberia	1,651	181	Tuvalu	9
58	Haiti	7,306	120	Congo	1,604	182	Monaco	6
59	Laos	7,140	121	Mali	1,514	183	Nauru	3
60	Malaysia	6,891	122	Armenia	1,374			
61	Cote d'Ivoire	6,844	123	Burundi	1,342			

Source: *UNESCO Statistical Yearbook*

243. EDUCATIONAL EXPENDITURES AS PERCENTAGE OF GNP

A government's ultimate commitment to education is best gauged by its treating it as an investment rather than as one of the many social services performed by the state. Many governments, wishing to minimize the claim of education on the national budget, lump it along with health and welfare and do not hesitate to jettison educational programs during every financial squall. But education is a productive sector, just as critical as agriculture, industry and mining, and one which demands substantial investments.

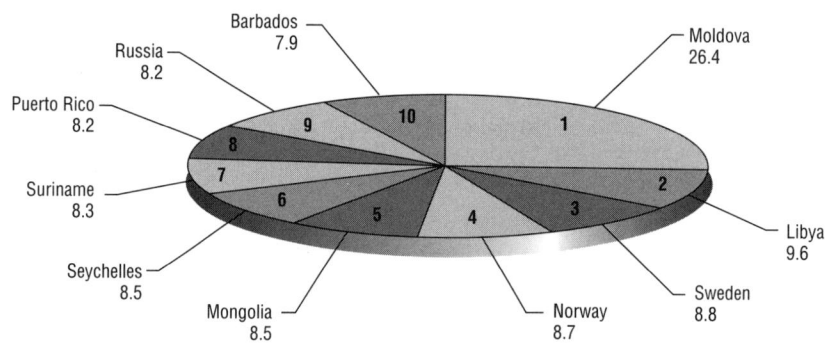

TOP 10
Educational Expenditures as Percentage of GNP

Moldova 26.4
Libya 9.6
Sweden 8.8
Norway 8.7
Mongolia 8.5
Seychelles 8.5
Suriname 8.3
Puerto Rico 8.2
Russia 8.2
Barbados 7.9

Rank	Country	Public Expenditures on Education as Percentage of GNP
UPPER MIDDLE		
11	Botswana	7.5
12	Canada	7.4
13	Denmark	7.4
14	Finland	7.4
15	Zimbabwe	7.4
16	Angola	7.3
17	Cote d'Ivoire	7.2
18	Hungary	7.2
19	New Zealand	7.2
20	Kenya	7.0
21	Slovakia	7.0
22	Maldives	6.9
23	Saudi Arabia	6.8
24	Cuba	6.7
25	St. Vincent	6.7
26	Fiji	6.6
27	Comoros	6.5
28	Kiribati	6.5
29	Bulgaria	6.4
30	Lesotho	6.4
31	Swaziland	6.4
32	Mozambique	6.2
33	Netherlands	6.2
34	Tunisia	6.2
35	Ireland	6.1
36	Yugoslavia	6.1
37	Kuwait	6.0
38	Austria	5.8
39	Belize	5.8
40	Dominica	5.8
41	Iceland	5.8
42	Israel	5.8
43	Morocco	5.8
44	Tanzania	5.8
45	Algeria	5.7
46	France	5.7

Rank	Country	Public Expenditures on Education as Percentage of GNP
47	Liberia	5.7
48	Slovenia	5.7
49	Togo	5.7
50	Congo	5.6
51	Poland	5.6
52	Australia	5.5
53	Malaysia	5.5
54	Panama	5.5
55	St. Lucia	5.5
56	Italy	5.4
57	United States	5.3
58	Belgium	5.2
59	Switzerland	5.2
60	United Kingdom	5.2
61	Venezuela	5.2
62	Benin	5.1
63	Iraq	5.1
64	Bahrain	5.0
65	Czech Republic	5.0
66	Egypt	5.0
67	Ethiopia	4.9
68	Mauritania	4.9
69	Brazil	4.8
70	Portugal	4.8
71	Sudan	4.8
72	Guyana	4.7
73	Japan	4.7
74	Papua New Guinea	4.7
75	Brunei	4.6
76	Grenada	4.6
77	Iran	4.6
78	Spain	4.6
LOWER MIDDLE		
79	Yemen	4.6
80	Costa Rica	4.5
81	Mexico	4.5

Rank	Country	Public Expenditures on Education as Percentage of GNP
82	Vanuatu	4.5
83	Bahamas	4.4
84	Luxembourg	4.3
85	Sao Tome e Principe	4.3
86	Solomon Islands	4.2
87	Syria	4.2
88	Tonga	4.2
89	Western Samoa	4.2
90	Cape Verde	4.1
91	Jamaica	4.1
92	Korea, South	4.1
93	Nicaragua	4.1
94	Trinidad and Tobago	4.1
95	Cyprus	4.0
96	Germany	4.0
97	Honduras	4.0
98	Jordan	4.0
99	Malta	4.0
100	Turkey	4.0
101	India	3.9
102	Oman	3.8
103	Rwanda	3.8
104	South Africa	3.8
105	Burundi	3.7
106	Korea, North	3.7
107	Mauritius	3.7
108	Senegal	3.7
109	Romania	3.6
110	Taiwan	3.6
111	Thailand	3.6
112	Djibouti	3.5
113	Bhutan	3.4
114	Malawi	3.4
115	Singapore	3.4
116	Burkina	3.3
117	Sri Lanka	3.3
118	Bermuda	3.2

Rank	Country	Public Expenditures on Education as Percentage of GNP	Rank	Country	Public Expenditures on Education as Percentage of GNP	Rank	Country	Public Expenditures on Education as Percentage of GNP
119	Mali	3.2	136	Bolivia	2.7	153	El Salvador	1.7
120	Argentina	3.1	137	Ecuador	2.7	154	Equatorial Guinea	1.7
121	Cameroon	3.1	138	Gambia	2.7	155	Nigeria	1.7
122	Colombia	3.1	139	Pakistan	2.7		**BOTTOM 10**	
123	Ghana	3.1	140	Myanmar (Burma)	2.4	156	Uganda	1.7
124	Greece	3.1	141	Bangladesh	2.3	157	Namibia	1.6
125	Niger	3.1	142	Chad	2.3	158	Dominican Republic	1.5
126	Qatar	3.0	143	Zambia	2.3	159	Madagascar	1.5
127	Vietnam	3.0	144	Guinea	2.2	160	Peru	1.5
128	Chile	2.9	145	Indonesia	2.2	161	Sierra Leone	1.4
129	Gabon	2.9	146	Afghanistan	2.0	162	Guatemala	1.2
130	Philippines	2.9	147	Lebanon	2.0	163	Laos	1.2
131	Central African Republic	2.8	148	Nepal	2.0	164	Zaire	1.0
132	Guinea-Bissau	2.8	149	Paraguay	1.9	165	Somalia	0.4
133	St. Kitts and Nevis	2.8	150	United Arab Emirates	1.9			
134	Uruguay	2.8	151	Haiti	1.8			
135	Antigua and Barbuda	2.7	152	China	1.7			

Source: *UNESCO Statistical Yearbook*

244. STUDY ABROAD

Study abroad—the equivalent of the old German *Wanderjahr*—is a significant educational phenomenon in every country. It is more so in underdeveloped countries, where there is a compelling reason for students to seek advanced training in Western countries. Even though scholarships are declining in number and value and college tuition costs are rising, the number of foreign students admitted to North American and European universities has risen every year since the end of World War II. A substantial number of these students fail to return home after completion of studies, thus intensifying the brain drain.

Rank	Country	Teritary Students Abroad (as % of those at home)	Rank	Country	Teritary Students Abroad (as % of those at home)		Country	Teritary Students AbroadRank (as % of those at home)
TOP 10			19	Burkina	30	40	Kenya	17
1	Trinidad and Tobago	62	20	Congo	28			
2	Fiji	54	21	Niger	28		**LOWER MIDDLE**	
3	Chad	50	22	Sudan	27	41	Iran	16
4	Sierra Leone	49	23	Gabon	26	42	Kuwait	16
5	Bahrain	45	24	Togo	26	43	Ghana	15
6	Central African Republic	45	25	Benin	25	44	Zaire	15
7	Jordan	41	26	Singapore	25	45	Laos	14
8	Cameroon	40	27	Tunisia	25	46	Malawi	14
9	Mali	39	28	United Arab Emirates	25	47	Morocco	14
10	Malaysia	38	29	Botswana	24	48	Zambia	14
			30	Senegal	23	49	Barbados	13
UPPER MIDDLE			31	Jamaica	22	50	Madagascar	12
11	Rwanda	38	32	Lebanon	21	51	Swaziland	12
12	Mauritania	34	33	Bhutan	20	52	Lesotho	11
13	Yemen	33	34	Cote d'Ivoire	20	53	Mozambique	11
14	Hong Kong	32	35	Guinea	20	54	Afghanistan	10
15	Guyana	31	36	Qatar	20	55	Nicaragua	10
16	Haiti	31	37	Burundi	19	56	Somalia	10
17	Tanzania	31	38	Liberia	18	57	Uganda	10
18	Angola	30	39	Ethiopia	17	58	Pakistan	9

Rank	Country	Teritary Students Abroad (as % of those at home)	Rank	Country	Teritary Students Abroad (as % of those at home)	Rank	Country	Teritary Students Abroad (as % of those at home)
59	Syria	9	74	Costa Rica	2	89	Mexico	1
60	Zimbabwe	8	75	Egypt	2		**BOTTOM 10**	
61	Algeria	7	76	El Salvador	2	90	Mongolia	1
62	Libya	7	77	Guatemala	2	91	Paraguay	1
63	Nigeria	7	78	Indonesia	2	92	Peru	1
64	Papua New Guinea	6	79	Korea, North	2	93	South Africa	1
65	Saudi Arabia	6	80	Nepal	2	94	Thailand	1
66	Sri Lanka	6	81	Bangladesh	1	95	Uruguay	1
67	Honduras	4	82	Brazil	1	96	Venezuela	1
68	Vietnam	4	83	Chile	1	97	Philippines	0
69	China	3	84	Colombia	1	98	Argentina	(.)
70	Iraq	3	85	Cuba	1	99	Myanmar (Burma)	(.)
71	Panama	3	86	Dominican Republic	1			
72	Turkey	3	87	Ecuador	1			
73	Bolivia	2	88	India	1			

Source: *UNESCO Statistical Yearbook*

245. TERTIARY SCIENCE ENROLLMENT

The percentage of tertiary enrollment is an index of the technological manpower being trained to manage the industrial future of a country. Without trained technical skills, the industrial as well a the knowledge sectors may not be able to grow or modernize. Scientific professionals are needed to transmit important discoveries made in other countries and to conduct research in vital industries. Students in industrializing countries show a greater preference for technical and scientific courses and they also tend to seek further training abroad in their specialties.

Rank	Country	Tertiary Natural and Applied Science Enrollment (as % of total tertiary)	Rank	Country	Tertiary Natural and Applied Science Enrollment (as % of total tertiary)	Rank	Country	Tertiary Natural and Applied Science Enrollment (as % of total tertiary)
	TOP 10		32	Germany	42	64	Cuba	33
1	Romania	72	33	Korea, North	42	65	Iceland	33
2	Algeria	63	34	Madagascar	42	66	Jordan	33
3	Iran	63	35	Sri Lanka	42	67	Poland	33
4	Tanzania	62	36	Belarus	41	68	Turkey	33
5	Guinea	61	37	Ghana	41	69	Ecuador	32
6	Dominica	60	38	Angola	40	70	Israel	32
7	Mozambique	60	39	Burundi	40	71	Kenya	32
8	Guinea-Bissau	58	40	Ethiopia	40	72	Malta	32
9	China	57	41	Greece	40	73	Oman	32
10	Nicaragua	56	42	Saint Lucia	40	74	Paraguay	32
			43	Syria	40	75	Austria	31
	UPPER MIDDLE		44	Belgium	39	76	Brazil	31
11	Mali	55	45	Colombia	39	77	Cyprus	31
12	Argentina	54	46	Liberia	39	78	France	31
13	Bahrain	53	47	Panama	39	79	Italy	31
14	Bolivia	52	48	United Kingdom	39	80	Niger	31
15	Finland	52	49	Senegal	38	81	Barbados	30
16	Guyana	50				82	Cameroon	30
17	Saint Kitts and Nevis	50		**LOWER MIDDLE**		83	Malaysia	30
18	Peru	49	50	Morocco	37	84	Comoros	29
19	Ukraine	49	51	Philippines	37	85	Mauritius	29
20	Trinidad and Tobago	48	52	Central African Republic	36	86	Spain	29
21	Afghanistan	46	53	Iraq	36	87	Zambia	29
22	Chile	46	54	Swaziland	36	88	Burkina	28
23	Honduras	46	55	Jamaica	35	89	Egypt	28
24	Mexico	46	56	Tunisia	35	90	Portugal	28
25	Bulgaria	45	57	Denmark	34	91	Bangladesh	27
26	Russia	44	58	El Salvador	34	92	Norway	27
27	Saint Vincent	44	59	Gabon	34	93	Zimbabwe	27
28	Kuwait	43	60	Ireland	34	94	Japan	26
29	Nigeria	43	61	Switzerland	34	95	Rwanda	26
30	Sweden	43	62	Albania	33	96	Saudi Arabia	26
31	Fiji	42	63	Australia	33	97	Malawi	25

Rank	Country	Tertiary Natural and Applied Science Enrollment (as % of total tertiary)
98	Togo	25
99	Costa Rica	24
100	New Zealand	23
101	Botswana	22
102	Hungary	22
103	Thailand	22
104	Uganda	22
105	Sudan	21

Rank	Country	Tertiary Natural and Applied Science Enrollment (as % of total tertiary)
106	Benin	19
107	Congo	18
108	Netherlands	18
109	Namibia	17
BOTTOM 10		
110	Nepal	17
111	Sierra Leone	17

Rank	Country	Tertiary Natural and Applied Science Enrollment (as % of total tertiary)
112	Brunei	16
113	United Arab Emirates	15
114	Canada	14
115	Suriname	14
116	United States	14
117	Yemen	13
118	Mauritania	12
119	Qatar	10

Source: *World Data*

246. STUDENT-TEACHER RATIO IN SECONDARY SCHOOLS

In most countries, greater importance is attached to primary education because it is the basis for universal literacy. Secondary schools, which form the basis for vocational and higher education, receive short shrift, especially under difficult budgetary conditions. As a result there are fewer teachers per pupil in secondary schools. There is also a dearth in developing countries of training schools for secondary teachers.

TOP 10
Student-Teacher Ratio Secondary Level

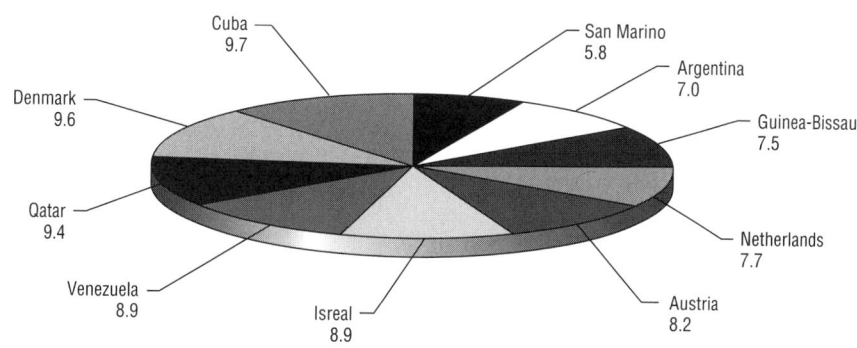

Cuba 9.7
San Marino 5.8
Argentina 7.0
Guinea-Bissau 7.5
Netherlands 7.7
Austria 8.2
Isreal 8.9
Venezuela 8.9
Qatar 9.4
Denmark 9.6

Rank	Country	Student-Teacher Ratio Secondary Level
UPPER MIDDLE		
11	South Africa	9.9
12	Sweden	10.6
13	Bermuda	10.7
14	Kuwait	10.9
15	Belize	11.4
16	India	11.6
17	Norway	11.6
18	United States	11.6
19	France	11.7
20	Slovenia	11.7
21	Libya	12.1
22	Cambodia	12.2
23	Maldives	12.3
24	Australia	12.4
25	United Arab Emirates	12.4
26	Antigua and Barbuda	12.5
27	Cyprus	12.5
28	Portugal	12.6
29	Hungary	12.7

Rank	Country	Student-Teacher Ratio Secondary Level
30	Brunei	13.1
31	Laos	13.1
32	Seychelles	13.3
33	Uruguay	13.4
34	Slovakia	13.6
35	Czech Republic	13.7
36	Ecuador	13.7
37	Paraguay	13.8
38	Saudi Arabia	14.0
39	Yugoslavia	14.1
40	Brazil	14.3
41	Romania	14.8
42	Honduras	14.9
43	Tuvalu	15.0
44	Barbados	15.1
45	China	15.2
46	United Kingdom	15.2
47	Greece	15.3
48	Guatemala	15.3
49	Croatia	15.4

Rank	Country	Student-Teacher Ratio Secondary Level
50	New Zealand	15.4
51	Rwanda	15.5
52	Guinea	15.6
53	St. Kitts and Nevis	15.6
54	Liechtenstein	15.7
55	Kiribati	15.8
56	Suriname	15.8
57	Morocco	16.0
58	Malta	16.2
59	Kenya	16.3
60	Macedonia	16.7
61	Mexico	16.9
62	Algeria	17.0
63	Finland	17.0
64	Oman	17.1
65	Pakistan	17.3
66	Ghana	17.5
67	St. Lucia	17.5
68	St. Vincent	17.5
69	Bolivia	17.6

Rank	Country	Student-Teacher Ratio Secondary Level	Rank	Country	Student-Teacher Ratio Secondary Level	Rank	Country	Student-Teacher Ratio Secondary Level
70	Tonga	17.7	100	Egypt	20.0	132	Togo	27.7
71	Thailand	17.9	101	Solomon Islands	20.2	133	Zambia	27.9
72	Iraq	18.0	102	Somalia	20.3	134	Comoros	28.0
73	Uganda	18.0	103	Mauritius	20.5	135	El Salvador	28.2
74	Japan	18.1	104	Peru	20.6	136	Zimbabwe	28.3
75	Malaysia	18.1	105	Mongolia	21.4	137	Djibouti	28.6
LOWER MIDDLE			106	Poland	21.6	138	Equatorial Guinea	28.9
76	Botswana	18.2	107	Madagascar	21.7	139	Albania	29.3
77	Spain	18.3	108	Zaire	21.7	140	Namibia	29.3
78	Syria	18.4	109	Burundi	21.8	141	Niger	29.3
79	Nauru	18.5	110	Costa Rica	21.8	142	Cape Verde	29.9
80	Sierra Leone	18.5	111	Gabon	21.8	143	Angola	30.2
81	Haiti	19.0	112	Dominica	22.0	144	Cote d'Ivoire	31.3
82	Bahamas	19.1	113	Nigeria	22.1	145	Nepal	31.4
83	Bosnia & Herzegovina	19.1	114	Korea, North	22.2	146	Cameroon	32.2
84	Jamaica	19.2	115	Sudan	22.3	147	Yemen	32.6
85	Lesotho	19.3	116	Vietnam	22.9	148	Philippines	32.9
86	Tanzania	19.3	117	Korea, South	23.1	149	Bangladesh	33.2
87	Italy	19.4	118	Western Samoa	23.2	150	Ethiopia	33.5
88	Mauritania	19.4	119	Sao Tome e Principe	23.4	151	Eritrea	34.1
89	Panama	19.4	120	Swaziland	23.6			
90	Trinidad and Tobago	19.4	121	Bhutan	24.1	**BOTTOM 10**		
91	Vanuatu	19.4	122	Myanmar (Burma)	24.2	152	Congo	34.7
92	Fiji	19.6	123	Iceland	24.3	153	Senegal	34.8
93	Singapore	19.6	124	Tunisia	24.5	154	Chad	35.2
94	Grenada	19.7	125	Iran	24.7	155	Benin	35.2
95	Sri Lanka	19.7	126	Papua New Guinea	25.0	156	Mozambique	40.0
96	Mali	19.8	127	Burkina	25.1	157	Dominican Republic	42.9
97	Colombia	19.9	128	Turkey	25.6	158	Nicaragua	43.0
98	Taiwan	19.9	129	Gambia	26.1	159	Liberia	45.8
99	Bahrain	20.0	130	Indonesia	26.6	160	Afganistan	47.4
			131	Malawi	26.8	161	Central African Republic	55.6

Source: *UNESCO Statistical Yearbook*

247. STUDENT-TEACHER RATIO—TERTIARY

Colleges and universities constituting the tertiary level of education generally have better student-teacher ratios than the two preceding levels. Although college and university teachers are not specifically trained to teach as are primary and secondary school teachers, they tend to be more proficient in their specialties. The classes tend to be smaller in graduate and postgraduate levels than at the undergraduate ones.

Rank	Country	Student-Teacher Ratio Tertiary Level	Rank	Country	Student-Teacher Ratio Tertiary Level	Rank	Country	Student-Teacher Ratio Tertiary Level
TOP 10			21	Poland	7.8	44	Grenada	9.9
1	Liechtenstein	1.3	22	Sierra Leone	7.9	45	Sweden	9.9
2	Tanzania	4.4	23	Slovakia	7.9	46	Nicaragua	10.0
3	Brunei	4.7	24	Costa Rica	8.0	47	South Africa	10.0
4	Rwanda	5.2	25	Gabon	8.0	48	Indonesia	10.5
5	China	5.6	26	Djibouti	8.2	49	Croatia	10.6
6	Mozambique	5.6	27	Estonia	8.2	50	Germany	10.7
7	Mauritius	5.7	28	Gambia	8.4	51	Niger	11.1
8	Vietnam	6.1	29	Barbados	8.6	52	Benin	11.4
9	Guyana	6.5	30	Uganda	8.8	53	Malawi	11.4
10	Hungary	6.8	31	Bermuda	8.9	54	Equatorial Guinea	11.6
			32	Czech Republic	8.9	55	Qatar	11.7
UPPER MIDDLE			33	Bhutan	9.1	56	Swaziland	11.7
11	Laos	6.8	34	Botswana	9.1	57	Brazil	11.8
12	Portugal	6.9	35	Colombia	9.2	58	Namibia	11.8
13	Lesotho	7.0	36	Mongolia	9.4	59	Malaysia	11.9
14	Papua New Guinea	7.1	37	Uruguay	9.4	60	Saudi Arabia	11.9
15	Bahamas	7.3	38	Bulgaria	9.6			
16	Lithuania	7.3	39	Mali	9.6	**LOWER MIDDLE**		
17	Afghanistan	7.5	40	Trinidad and Tobago	9.6	61	Tonga	11.9
18	Burundi	7.8	41	Cuba	9.8	62	United Arab Emirates	11.9
19	Comoros	7.8	42	Malta	9.8	63	St. Kitts and Nevis	12.0
20	Guinea	7.8	43	Mexico	9.8	64	Haiti	12.1

Rank	Country	Student-Teacher Ratio Tertiary Level	Rank	Country	Student-Teacher Ratio Tertiary Level	Rank	Country	Student-Teacher Ratio Tertiary Level
65	Romania	12.2	92	Guatemala	16.0	119	Taiwan	20.8
66	Yugoslavia	12.2	93	Ireland	16.0	120	Turkey	21.6
67	Cyprus	12.3	94	Congo	16.1	121	Nepal	21.8
68	United Kingdom	12.3	95	Ecuador	16.1	122	Jordan	22.4
69	Bahrain	12.6	96	Australia	16.2	123	Philippines	22.6
70	Macedonia	12.6	97	Sri Lanka	16.2	124	New Zealand	23.9
71	Venezuela	12.6	98	Dominican Republic	16.3	125	Pakistan	24.8
72	Zimbabwe	12.8	99	Tunisia	16.4	126	Iran	25.2
73	Ghana	13.2	100	Dominica	16.5	127	Togo	26.6
74	Ethiopia	13.3	101	United States	16.6	128	Italy	27.1
75	Bosnia & Herzegovina	13.4	102	Algeria	16.9	129	Sudan	28.0
76	Argentina	13.7	103	Burkina	16.9	130	Fiji	28.5
77	Iceland	14.0	104	Peru	16.9	131	Morocco	29.2
78	Eritrea	14.1	105	Nigeria	17.1		**BOTTOM 10**	
79	Slovenia	14.2	106	Panama	17.3	132	France	29.6
80	Canada	14.4	107	Puerto Rico	17.3	133	Cameroon	30.5
81	Korea, North	14.4	108	Singapore	17.7	134	Bangladesh	32.9
82	Austria	14.6	109	Jamaica	17.9	135	Mauritania	33.2
83	Honduras	14.7	110	Thailand	18.2	136	Korea, South	34.0
84	Finland	14.8	111	Norway	18.4	137	Madagascar	38.2
85	Greece	14.8	112	Iraq	18.8	138	Myanmar (Burma)	38.9
86	Angola	14.9	113	Japan	18.8	139	Yemen	49.9
87	Albania	15.0	114	Central African Republic	18.9	140	Chad	50.3
88	Zaire	15.1	115	Senegal	19.3	141	Cambodia	82.5
89	Kuwait	15.2	116	El Salvador	19.4			
90	Western Samoa	15.2	117	Zambia	19.5			
91	Lebanon	15.8	118	Spain	19.8			

Source: *UNESCO Statistical Yearbook*

248. READING SCORES—BOYS AND GIRLS

Although literacy has become almost universal in Western countries, reading abilities, including comprehension of written materials and the ability to communicate effectively, vary widely. With the increasing displacement of print by television and electronic media, reading abilities have suffered in many advanced countries. Reading abilities are affected by extraneous factors as well, including physical and mental aptitudes, verbal skills and availability of books and libraries.

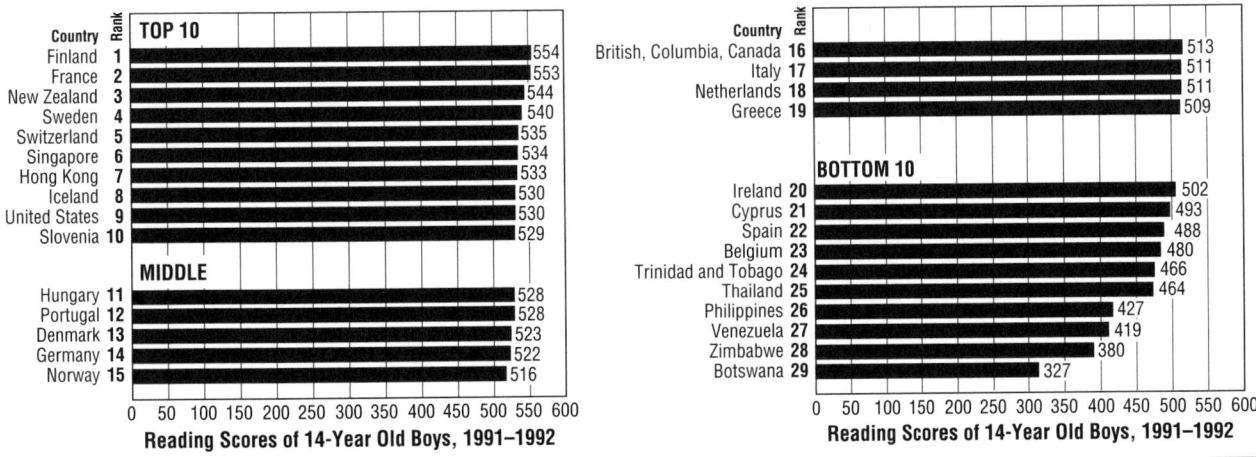

Source: U.S. Department of Education, Office of Educational Research and Improvement. National Center for Education Statistics.

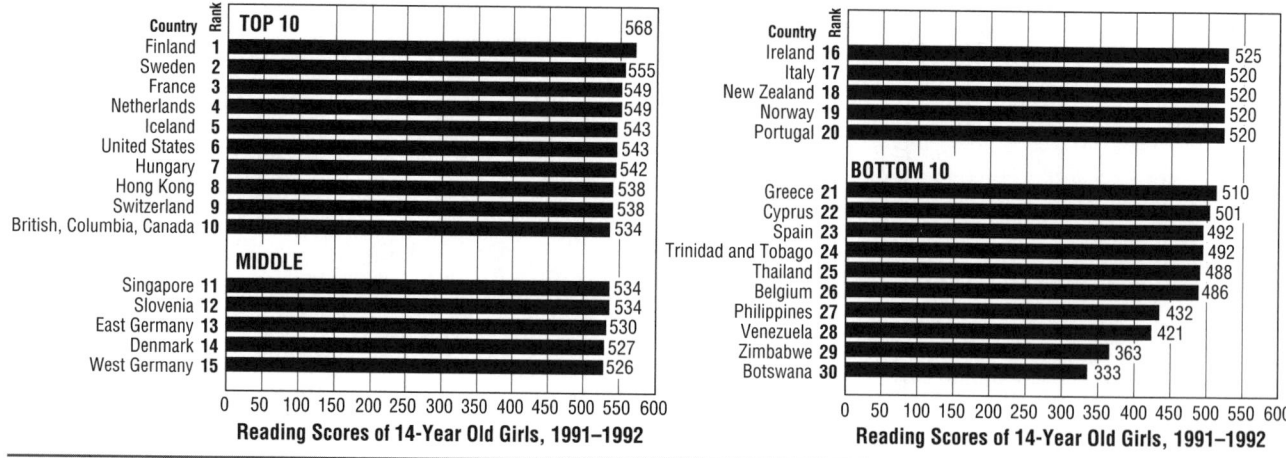

Country	Rank		Country	Rank	
TOP 10			**TOP 10**		
Finland	1	568	Ireland	16	525
Sweden	2	555	Italy	17	520
France	3	549	New Zealand	18	520
Netherlands	4	549	Norway	19	520
Iceland	5	543	Portugal	20	520
United States	6	543			
Hungary	7	542	**BOTTOM 10**		
Hong Kong	8	538	Greece	21	510
Switzerland	9	538	Cyprus	22	501
British, Columbia, Canada	10	534	Spain	23	492
MIDDLE			Trinidad and Tobago	24	492
			Thailand	25	488
Singapore	11	534	Belgium	26	486
Slovenia	12	534	Philippines	27	432
East Germany	13	530	Venezuela	28	421
Denmark	14	527	Zimbabwe	29	363
West Germany	15	526	Botswana	30	333

Reading Scores of 14-Year Old Girls, 1991–1992

Source: U.S. Department of Education, Office of Educational Research and Improvement. National Center for Education Statistics.

249. HIGHER EDUCATION OF WOMEN

One of the most significant indicators of gender disparities is the gap between men and women in access to higher education. This gap has been closing for many years and in some countries and some fields, women are now better represented than men. But overall, the late start of women in joining the educational streams is reflected in the lower percentage of women who complete college and university education. In most developing countries the percentage is much lower.

Rank	Country	Higher Education of Women (%)	Rank	Country	Higher Education of Women (%)	Rank	Country	Higher Education of Women (%)
TOP 10			8	Finland	8.3	14	Ireland	6.5
1	United States	21.3	9	Australia	8.0	15	Austria	5.4
2	Canada	14.8	10	New Zealand	7.9	16	Italy	5.2
3	Sweden	12.1				17	Japan	5.2
4	Denmark	11.4	**BOTTOM 10**			18	Switzerland	4.5
5	Norway	10.0	11	Germany	7.8	19	Netherlands	3.8
6	Spain	9.1	12	United Kingdom	6.8	20	Portugal	3.3
7	France	8.7	13	Belgium	6.6			

Source: U.S. Department of Education, Office of Educational Research and Improvement. National Center for Education Statistics. *The Condition of Education*

250. COMPUTERS

Computers are the icons of the post-industrial age. Their prevalence is a sure indicator of the direction and pace of technological change. There are no surprises in this ranking, which includes only advanced nations. Computer research and manufacturing, similarly, is concentrated in the United States, Japan, and a handful of Western nations. Because of the growing popularity of the Internet, the spread of computers to technology-poor countries will be swift and may be accomplished in less time than it took television and telecommunications to saturate the world.

Rank	Country	Computers (per thousand population) Computers	MIPS[1]
TOP 10			
1	United States	265	516
2	Australia	175	278
3	Canada	162	264
4	Norway	153	256
5	United Kingdom	134	217
6	Switzerland	133	220
7	Ireland	126	208
8	Singapore	116	178
9	France	111	180
10	Germany	104	141
	Japan	84	139
BOTTOM			
11			
12	Italy	57	98
13	Greece	47	71
14	South Korea	33	49
15	Hungary	24	34
16	Mexico	13	19
17	South Africa	9	13
18	Brazil	6	10
19	Former Soviet Union	4	6
20	Indonesia	2	2
21	India	1	1
22	China	1	1
	World Average	27	47

[1]Million instructions per second.
Source: *6th Annual Computer Industry Almanac*

251. SCHOOL YEAR LENGTH

Although no correlation has been established between the length of the school year and the quality of the educational system, longer school years are believed to enhance the intensity of the educational experience in children. Working against longer school years are extraneous factors, such as harsh winters, the density of population, and the nature of school facilities. It is noteworthy that Asian countries generally favor longer school years. Educational experiments in the United States extending the school term have not been successful.

Rank	Country	School Year Length (days)
TOP 10		
1	China	251
2	Japan	243
3	Korea	220
4	Israel	215
5	Russia	210
6	Germany	210
7	Switzerland	207
8	Netherlands	200
9	Scotland	200
10	Thailand	200
BOTTOM		
11	England	192
12	Hungary	192
13	Jordan	191
14	Finland	190
15	New Zealand	190
16	Ontario, Canada	186
17	Sweden	180
18	United States	180

Source: Hornbeck, Mark. "Ringing School Bell Longer." *Detroit News,* 5 December 1993, p. 1C. Primary source: Education Commission of the States.

252. TRADEMARKS AND SERVICEMARKS

The number of trademarks and servicemarks may be used as a rough index of the number of consumer products and services in the market at any given time. In free market economies, where open competition is permitted and encouraged, the growth in the number of such brand names and marks is an indication that the spirit of enterprise is alive and well. It also attests to the choice and variety available to consumers.

Rank	Country	Trademarks and Servicemarks in Force	Rank	Country	Trademarks and Servicemarks in Force	Rank	Country	Trademarks and Servicemarks in Force
TOP 10			23	Austria	79,891	46	Malta	16,776
1	Japan	1,140,933				47	Czech Republic	15,867
2	United States	791,139	**LOWER MIDDLE**			48	Malawi	15,841
3	France	459,797	24	Algeria	72,274	49	Cyprus	15,732
4	Germany	335,509	25	Norway	71,180	50	Hungary	15,216
5	United Kingdom	307,612	26	Finland	60,592	51	Uganda	14,621
6	Brazil	307,247	27	Ireland	58,217	52	Cuba	14,397
7	Switzerland	285,114	28	Uruguay	56,669	53	Tunisia	12,676
8	China	279,397	29	Guyana	55,298	54	Iceland	11,613
9	Canada	251,480	30	Panama	51,578	55	Guatemala	11,034
10	Belgium	188,100	31	Peru	49,463	56	New Zealand	10,322
			32	Paraguay	48,224			
UPPER MIDDLE			33	Vietnam	41,631	**BOTTOM 10**		
11	Indonesia	182,358	34	Philippines	31,756	57	Liechtenstein	7,596
12	Korea, South	163,775	35	Ghana	28,181	58	Mongolia	6,375
13	Romania	158,640	36	Israel	26,802	59	Mauritius	5,945
14	Chile	147,724	37	Bulgaria	25,968	60	Monaco	4,622
15	Australia	139,554	38	Morocco	22,741	61	Yugoslavia	4,298
16	Mexico	135,554	39	Zimbabwe	22,282	62	Burundi	2,552
17	Ecuador	129,878	40	Jamaica	21,585	63	Rwanda	2,501
18	Denmark	105,942	41	Brunei	21,032	64	Seychelles	2,389
19	Thailand	104,392	42	Poland	19,883	65	Ethiopia	1,535
20	Turkey	99,247	43	Zambia	19,707	66	Tuvalu	573
21	Sweden	95,344	44	Sri Lanka	19,214			
22	India	80,789	45	Bangladesh	17,725			

Source: *Industrial Property Statistics*

253. PATENTS IN FORCE

Patents represent the keen edge of technological progress, and their total registrations should give us a clue to the state of research and development in a country, both by individuals working perhaps out of their garages, and those under the auspices of public and quasi-public organizations and private corpora-

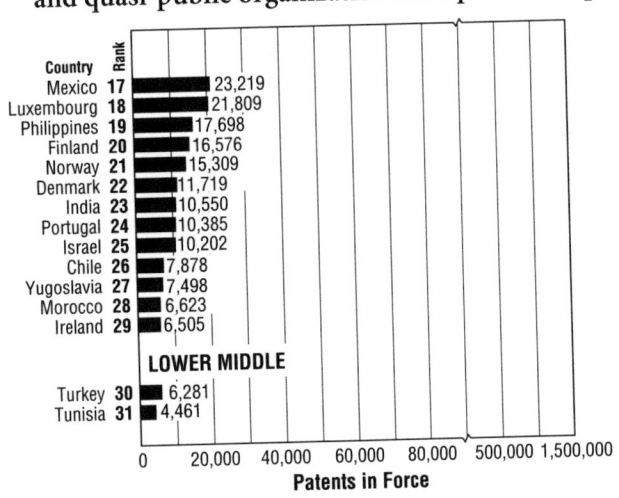

Country	Rank	Patents in Force
TOP 10		
United States	1	1,154,204
Japan	2	589,750
Germany	3	350,890
Canada	4	339,184
France	5	250,051
Czech Republic	6	124,611
Switzerland	7	99,287
Belgium	8	85,935
Sweden	9	84,929
Netherlands	10	76,127
UPPER MIDDLE		
Australia	11	64,070
Korea, North	12	31,972
Bulgaria	13	26,614
Romania	14	26,254
Austria	15	25,738
Korea, South	16	24,803

Country	Rank	Patents in Force
Mexico	17	23,219
Luxembourg	18	21,809
Philippines	19	17,698
Finland	20	16,576
Norway	21	15,309
Denmark	22	11,719
India	23	10,550
Portugal	24	10,385
Israel	25	10,202
Chile	26	7,878
Yugoslavia	27	7,498
Morocco	28	6,623
Ireland	29	6,505
LOWER MIDDLE		
Turkey	30	6,281
Tunisia	31	4,461

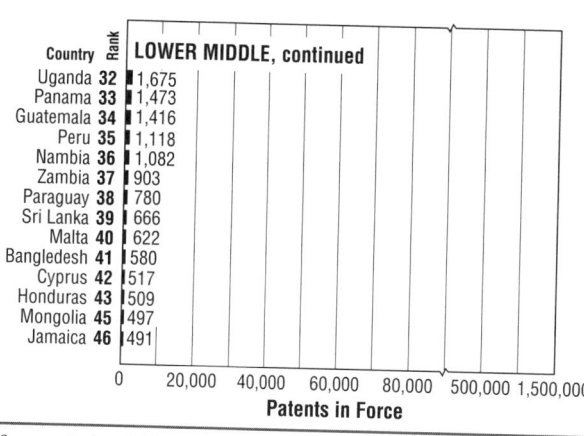

Country	Rank	LOWER MIDDLE, continued
Uganda	32	1,675
Panama	33	1,473
Guatemala	34	1,416
Peru	35	1,118
Nambia	36	1,082
Zambia	37	903
Paraguay	38	780
Sri Lanka	39	666
Malta	40	622
Bangledesh	41	580
Cyprus	42	517
Honduras	43	509
Mongolia	45	497
Jamaica	46	491

Patents in Force

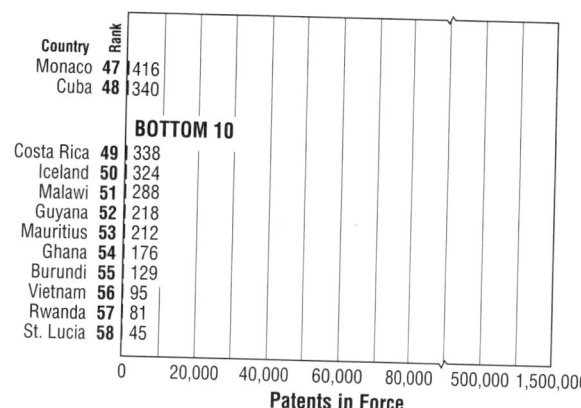

Country	Rank	
Monaco	47	416
Cuba	48	340
BOTTOM 10		
Costa Rica	49	338
Iceland	50	324
Malawi	51	288
Guyana	52	218
Mauritius	53	212
Ghana	54	176
Burundi	55	129
Vietnam	56	95
Rwanda	57	81
St. Lucia	58	45

Patents in Force

Source: *Industrial Property Statistics*

254. SCIENTISTS AND ENGINEERS

Scientific and engineering manpower is a major indicator of a country's technological orientation and capability. This indicator is presented both in terms of scientists and engineers per one million inhabitants and total stock. Statistics on technical personnel are subject to a number of limitations, one of which is the problem of definition. However, in the countries ranked below, technicians and related categories have been excluded.

Rank	Country	Number of Scientists and Engineers	Rank	Country	Number of Scientists and Engineers	Rank	Country	Number of Scientists and Engineers
TOP 10			28	Switzerland	14,910	56	Congo	862
1	United States	949,200	29	Norway	12,100	57	Guatemala	858
2	Japan	638,817	30	Cuba	12,052	58	Paraguay	807
3	Ukraine	348,600	31	Finland	11,317	59	Benin	794
4	Germany	293,063				60	Nicaragua	725
5	India	119,027	**LOWER MIDDLE**			61	Greece	534
6	France	115,163	32	Turkey	11,276	62	Jordan	418
7	Italy	74,833	33	Argentina	11,088	63	Nepal	334
8	Canada	61,130	34	Denmark	10,662	64	Trinidad and Tobago	275
9	Romania	59,670	35	Pakistan	6,641	65	Madagascar	269
10	Korea, South	56,545	36	Ireland	6,351	66	Qatar	229
			37	Thailand	5,539	67	Gabon	199
UPPER MIDDLE			38	Malaysia	5,537	68	Central African Republic	196
11	Czech Republic	55,475	39	Portugal	5,004	69	Mauritius	193
12	Brazil	52,863	40	Peru	4,858	70	Lebanon	180
13	Burkina	50,585	41	Philippines	4,830	71	Burundi	170
14	Belarus	44,100	42	Chile	4,630	72	El Salvador	142
15	Australia	38,568	43	Venezuela	4,568	73	Guyana	89
16	Netherlands	37,520	44	Singapore	3,361			
17	Yugoslavia	34,770	45	Iran	3,194	**BOTTOM 10**		
18	Poland	32,500	46	Sri Lanka	2,790	74	Rwanda	71
19	Indonesia	32,038	47	Uruguay	2,093	75	St. Lucia	53
20	Sweden	22,725	48	Senegal	1,948	76	Cyprus	51
21	Egypt	20,893	49	Austria	1,609	77	Fiji	36
22	Spain	20,890	50	Kuwait	1,511	78	Malta	34
23	Hungary	20,431	51	Nigeria	1,338	79	Brunei	20
24	Israel	20,100	52	Costa Rica	1,328	80	Jamaica	18
25	Vietnam	20,000	53	Guinea	1,282	81	Seychelles	18
26	Mexico	16,679	54	Libya	1,100	82	Tonga	11
27	Belgium	16,646	55	Colombia	1,083	83	Kiribati	2

Source: *UNESCO Statistical Yearbook*

Section

XX

CRIME &
LAW ENFORCEMENT

This section presents seven rankings on crime based on the resources of INTERPOL, which is currently the only organization engaged in the collection of international crime statistics. Because of the limited number of governments cooperating with INTERPOL in its data collection efforts, the rankings are not conclusive and have only limited use for analyses or interpretation. Criminal statistics also suffer from another grave deficiency built into the reporting system. It is well known that only a certain percentage of crimes are reported, and of these only a certain percentage are recorded on the police blotter. Only in a few countries is a copy of this record transmitted regularly to the national headquarters, and in even fewer countries are these criminal statistics published.

There is no way of verifying whether a greater crime rate is simply the result of better law enforcement or a better reporting system. A country could have a low crime rate as the result of inefficient law enforcement or a poor reporting system. It is not clear whether INTERPOL has grappled with this problem. In any case many countries are reluctant to publish criminal statistics or admit law enforcement problems because of fear that it might hurt their image or cause an adverse public reaction.

INTERPOL statistics present two very useful indicators: reported criminal offenses per 10,000 and the criminal ratio, which is essentially a measure of the criminal component of the population. Next it deals with four major crimes: homicides, rapes, burglaries, and drug-related offenses, of which the first three are what are known as index crimes in the FBI lexicon.

255. POPULATION PER POLICE OFFICER

The strengths of police departments in cities and municipalities vary according to the nature of criminal activities they encounter. Since crime is essentially local, the number of police officers nationwide may not be an accurate index of the effectiveness of law enforcement or even of crime trends. But it is a rough indicator of the commitment of the national and local governments to fight crime by deploying the optimum number of police officers.

Rank	Country	Population per Police Officer	Rank	Country	Population per Police Officer	Rank	Country	Population per Police Officer
TOP 10			16	Bahrain	180	34	Tuvalu	290
1	Angola	14	17	Cyprus	180	35	Dominica	300
2	Kuwait	80	18	Panama	180	36	St. Kitts and Nevis	300
3	Nicaragua	90	19	Equatorial Guinea	190	37	Ireland	310
4	Brunei	100	20	Guyana	190	38	Paraguay	310
5	Cape Verde	110	21	Israel	210	39	Venezuela	320
6	Nauru	110	22	Andorra	220	40	Kiribati	330
7	Antigua and Barbuda	120	23	Grenada	230	41	Sweden	330
8	Mongolia	120	24	Malta	230	42	Tonga	330
9	Seychelles	120	25	Singapore	230	43	Tunisia	340
10	Bahamas	125	26	Mauritius	240	44	United States	345
			27	St. Vincent	250	45	Bermuda	370
UPPER MIDDLE			28	Ecuador	260	46	Poland	370
11	Iraq	140	29	Barbados	280	47	Greece	380
12	United Arab Emirates	140	30	Laos	280	48	Puerto Rico	380
13	Yugoslavia	140	31	Saudi Arabia	280	49	Haiti	400
14	Mali	160	32	Trinidad and Tobago	280	50	Sao Tome e Principe	400
15	Uruguay	170	33	Belize	290	51	Colombia	420

Rank	Country	Population per Police Officer	Rank	Country	Population per Police Officer	Rank	Country	Population per Police Officer
52	Korea, South	420	84	Czech Republic	640	118	Honduras	1040
53	United Kingdom	420	85	Finland	640	119	Uganda	1090
54	Jamaica	430	86	Switzerland	640	120	Ethiopia	1100
55	Oman	430	87	Cuba	650	121	Lesotho	1130
56	St. Lucia	430	88	Myanmar (Burma)	650	122	Guinea	1140
57	Fiji	440	89	Liechtenstein	660	123	Nigeria	1140
58	Australia	450	90	Portugal	660	124	Philippines	1160
59	Vanuatu	450	91	Guatemala	670	125	Cameroon	1170
60	Korea, North	460	92	Italy	680	126	Argentina	1270
61	Austria	470	93	Hungary	710	127	Gabon	1290
62	Chile	470	94	Mauritania	710	128	Tanzania	1330
63	Costa Rica	480	95	Pakistan	720	129	Indonesia	1340
64	Japan	480	96	Papua New Guinea	720	130	China	1360
			97	Taiwan	720	131	Kenya	1500
LOWER MIDDLE			98	Luxembourg	730	132	Liberia	1570
65	Netherlands	510	99	Peru	730	133	Turkey	1570
66	Lebanon	530	100	Senegal	730	134	Malawi	1670
67	Thailand	530	101	Sudan	740	135	Yemen	1940
68	Afghanistan	540	102	Botswana	750	136	Syria	1970
69	Somalia	540	103	Zimbabwe	750	137	Togo	1970
70	Zambia	540	104	Malaysia	760	138	Cambodia	1980
71	Albania	550	105	India	820			
72	Dominican Republic	580	106	Algeria	840	**BOTTOM 10**		
73	Egypt	580	107	Morocco	840	139	Niger	2350
74	Spain	580	108	Norway	860	140	Bangladesh	2560
75	Denmark	600	109	Sri Lanka	860	141	Central African Republic	2740
76	Sierra Leone	600	110	Congo	870	142	Madagascar	2900
77	Swaziland	610	111	South Africa	870	143	Benin	3250
78	Ghana	620	112	Zaire	910	144	Gambia	3310
79	Solomon Islands	620	113	Iceland	940	145	Cote d'Ivoire	4640
80	France	630	114	Comoros	960	146	Rwanda	4650
81	Jordan	630	115	Chad	990	147	Canada	8640
82	New Zealand	630	116	El Salvador	1000	148	Maldives	35,710
83	Belgium	640	117	Nepal	1000			

Source: *World Data*

256. CRIME RATE

This ranking presents the general crime rate per 100,000 inhabitants. The figures are only for reported crimes, and they probably constitute the tip of the iceberg in many countries. There may be many reasons why crimes are not reported by victims or why they are not recorded on the police blotter. Nevertheless, these crime rates are fairly valid within limits because the ratio of reported to unreported crimes remains stable in most countries.

Rank	Country	Crime Rate Offenses per 100,000 Population	Rank	Country	Crime Rate Offenses per 100,000 Population	Rank	Country	Crime Rate Offenses per 100,000 Population
TOP 10			19	Austria	6,007	40	Malta	2,802
1	Dominica	22,432	20	United States	5,852	41	Mauritius	2,770
2	Suriname	17,819	21	Norway	5,656	42	Grenada	2,679
3	St. Kitts and Nevis	15,468	22	Andorra	5,430	43	Estonia	2,672
4	Sweden	14,188	23	Trinidad and Tobago	5,335	44	Korea, South	2,637
5	New Zealand	13,247	24	Switzerland	5,275	45	Spain	2,635
6	Canada	11,442	25	Israel	5,234	46	Antigua and Barbuda	2,568
7	Denmark	10,270	26	Monaco	4,614	47	Ireland	2,476
8	Finland	9,631	27	Seychelles	4,583	48	Maldives	2,353
9	United Kingdom	8,986	28	Barbados	4,519	49	Poland	2,311
10	Netherlands	7,613	29	St. Lucia	4,386	50	Tonga	2,100
			30	Italy	4,358	51	Zambia	2,088
UPPER MIDDLE			31	Swaziland	4,310	52	Algeria	2,080
11	Bermuda	7,413	32	St. Vincent	3,977	53	Slovakia	1,982
12	Germany	7,108	33	Bahrain	3,723	54	Guyana	1,980
13	Uruguay	6,806	34	Puerto Rico	3,601	55	Belize	1,968
14	Australia	6,773	35	Belgium	3,338	56	Slovenia	1,930
15	Bahamas	6,752	36	Egypt	3,314	57	Jamaica	1,927
16	Botswana	6,693	37	Greece	3,306	58	Fiji	1,915
17	Luxembourg	6,628	38	Hungary	3,287	59	Czech Republic	1,911
18	France	6,169	39	Zimbabwe	3,033	60	Lesotho	1,896

Rank	Country	Crime Rate Offenses per 100,000 Population	Rank	Country	Crime Rate Offenses per 100,000 Population	Rank	Country	Crime Rate Offenses per 100,000 Population
61	Russia	1,857	91	Panama	703	123	Philippines	230
62	Latvia	1,571	92	Haiti	701	124	Pakistan	221
63	Iceland	1,530	93	Macedonia	686	125	China	201
64	Lithuania	1,507	94	Malaysia	686	126	India	187
65	Singapore	1,507	95	Taiwan	673	127	Yemen	170
			96	Cyprus	671	128	Oman	162
LOWER MIDDLE			97	Belarus	650	129	Senegal	149
66	United Arab Emirates	1,496	98	Argentina	637	130	Somalia	144
67	Thailand	1,449	99	Bosnia & Herzegovina	558	131	Central African Republic	135
68	Japan	1,397	100	Sao Tome e Principe	558	132	Turkey	134.3
69	Chile	1,347	101	Guatemala	510	133	Indonesia	134
70	Tanzania	1,250	102	Sudan	509	134	Saudi Arabia	120
71	Tunisia	1,240	103	Djibouti	487	135	Tajikstan	117
72	Benin	1,234	104	Peru	474	136	Brazil	116
73	Malawi	1,226	105	Paraguay	461	137	Mexico	108
74	Venezuela	1,194	106	Uzbekistan	420	138	Ethiopia	94
75	Yugoslavia	1,135	107	Lebanon	366	139	Iraq	91
76	Croatia	1,087	108	Kenya	364	140	Burundi	87
77	Libya	1,007	109	Armenia	363	141	Iran	76.6
78	Kyrgyzstan	987	110	Brunei	358			
79	Dominican Republic	946	111	Qatar	358	**BOTTOM 10**		
80	Ukraine	923	112	Ecuador	333	142	Syria	73
81	Costa Rica	868	113	Rwanda	327	143	Bulgaria	70
82	Ghana	864	114	Gabon	323	144	Burkina	41
83	Colombia	840	115	Nigeria	312	145	Mali	33
84	Kazakhstan	815	116	Sri Lanka	309	146	Guinea	32.4
85	Portugal	805	117	Azerbaijan	305	147	Congo	32
86	Nicaragua	772	118	Kiribati	285	148	Niger	32
87	Morocco	769	119	Romania	276	149	Nepal	29.1
88	Jordan	762.5	120	Cote d'Ivoire	262	150	Bangladesh	16.8
89	Papua New Guinea	750.6	121	Myanmar (Burma)	262	151	Togo	11
90	Kuwait	709	122	Angola	237			

Source: *International Crime Statistics*

257. PRISONERS

The size of the prison population is a reliable law enforcement index. The United States has been leading this ranking ever since data have been kept in the major countries. Many of the prisoners tend to be recidivists who have a history of criminal activities. The number of first-time offenders is related to the size of the youth population of the country.

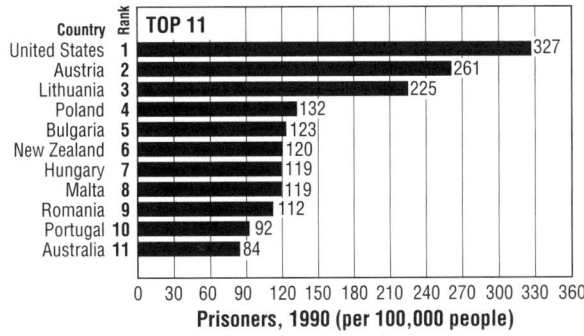

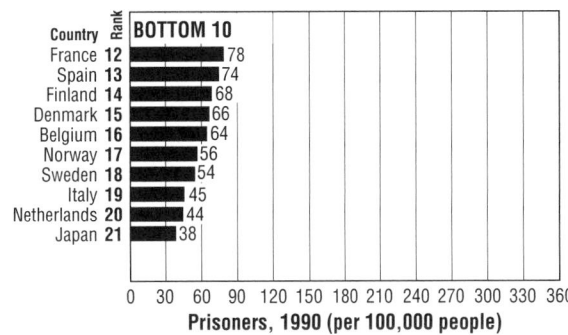

Source: National Criminal Justice Reference Service

258. DRUG OFFENSES

Most nations have laws on their statute books that make it a criminal offense to sell, obtain and use drugs, such as heroin, LSD, marijuana and similar psychoactive substances. The severity and effectiveness of these laws vary from country to country. In technologically advanced countries, the social implications of drug abuse are more severe. Much of this social concern is not merely related to the pharmacological effects of drug addition, but also to the role of drugs as symbols of a deviant subculture that is generally antagonistic to the prevailing moral climate. Drug addiction also has a criminological significance because it feeds and generates other crimes such as shoplifting, prostitution and burglary by addicts who are unable to hold regular jobs and need to obtain several hundreds of dollars a day to support their habits.

Rank	Country	Drug Offenses (per 100,000 inhabitants)	Rank	Country	Drug Offenses (per 100,000 inhabitants)	Rank	Country	Drug Offenses (per 100,000 inhabitants)
TOP 10			28	Spain	52.8	56	Costa Rica	7.33
1	Andorra	1,182	29	Finland	50.9	57	Papua New Guinea	7.3
2	Bahamas	460.1	30	Malta	50.8	58	Cote d'Ivoire	6.8
3	Sweden	326.1				59	Burundi	5.91
4	St. Vincent	320.5	**LOWER MIDDLE**			60	Paraguay	5.6
5	Switzerland	279.6	31	Bahrain	50.5	61	Central African Republic	5.2
6	Denmark	271.1	32	Malaysia	44.6	62	Ghana	5.2
7	Canada	258.9	33	Netherlands	39.6	63	Korea, South	5.1
8	Trinidad and Tobago	236.6	34	Belgium	39.3	64	Maldives	3.7
9	Jamaica	221.8	35	Kenya	27.6	65	Jordan	3.6
10	Barbados	215.9	36	Guatemala	27.4	66	Syria	3.6
			37	Qatar	22.9	67	Peru	3.2
UPPER MIDDLE			38	Saudi Arabia	22.7	68	Guinea	2.8
11	Norway	213.8	39	Gabon	22.1	69	Turkey	1.7
12	Grenada	211.0	40	United Kingdom	19.7	70	Poland	1.6
13	Luxembourg	201.8	41	Greece	19.6	71	Djibouti	1.4
14	Monaco	196.8	42	Japan	17.9			
15	St. Lucia	188.2	43	Fiji	17.1	**BOTTOM 10**		
16	Germany	165.3	44	Senegal	15.8	72	Congo	1.30
17	Israel	161.8	45	Myanmar (Burma)	15.6	73	Ireland	1.3
18	France	99.8	46	Thailand	15.6	74	Czech Republic	1.0
19	Mauritius	89.5	47	Portugal	14.7	75	Nepal	1.0
20	Botswana	85.5	48	Egypt	14.2	76	Argentina	0.9
21	Seychelles	81.6	49	Libya	13.4	77	Hungary	0.4
22	Brunei	80.3	50	Russia	12.3	78	China	0.3
23	Sri Lanka	71.2	51	Chile	12.2	79	Bangladesh	0.2
24	Austria	69.5	52	Malawi	9.6	80	Indonesia	0.2
25	Zimbabwe	62.9	53	Rwanda	9.2	81	Romania	0.01
26	Swaziland	61.1	54	Cyprus	8.9			
27	Italy	53.4	55	Tanzania	7.7			

Source: *International Crime Statistics*

259. THEFT

Larceny generally includes both grand larceny, which is a felony, and petty larceny, which is a misdemeanor. The ranking is limited to grand, or major, larceny comprising robbery and burglary. Historically, grand larceny and petty larceny have led all other crimes since the days of Hammurabi. In almost all countries these offenses outnumber those of every other kind combined.

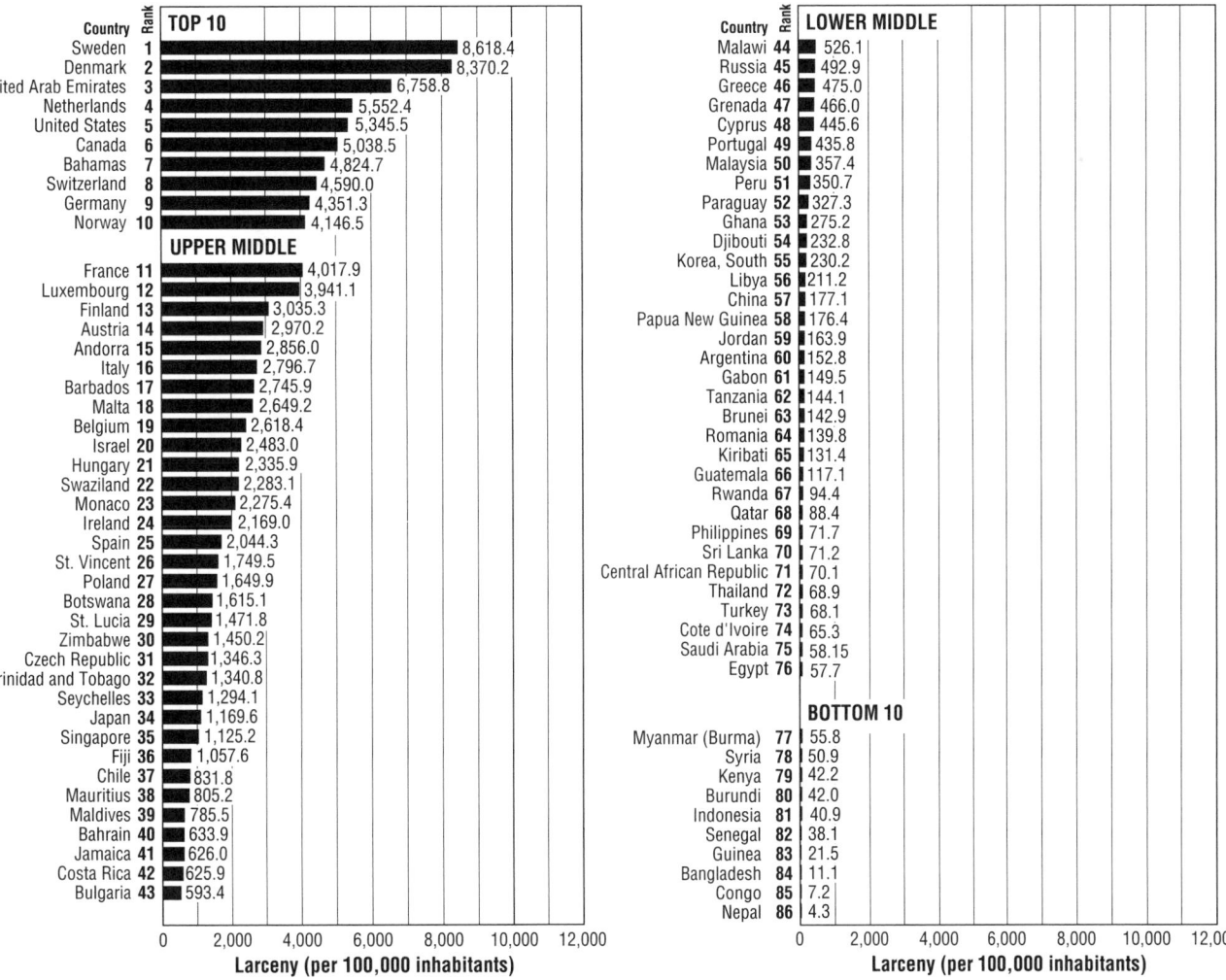

Country	Rank	TOP 10	
Sweden	1		8,618.4
Denmark	2		8,370.2
United Arab Emirates	3		6,758.8
Netherlands	4		5,552.4
United States	5		5,345.5
Canada	6		5,038.5
Bahamas	7		4,824.7
Switzerland	8		4,590.0
Germany	9		4,351.3
Norway	10		4,146.5
		UPPER MIDDLE	
France	11		4,017.9
Luxembourg	12		3,941.1
Finland	13		3,035.3
Austria	14		2,970.2
Andorra	15		2,856.0
Italy	16		2,796.7
Barbados	17		2,745.9
Malta	18		2,649.2
Belgium	19		2,618.4
Israel	20		2,483.0
Hungary	21		2,335.9
Swaziland	22		2,283.1
Monaco	23		2,275.4
Ireland	24		2,169.0
Spain	25		2,044.3
St. Vincent	26		1,749.5
Poland	27		1,649.9
Botswana	28		1,615.1
St. Lucia	29		1,471.8
Zimbabwe	30		1,450.2
Czech Republic	31		1,346.3
Trinidad and Tobago	32		1,340.8
Seychelles	33		1,294.1
Japan	34		1,169.6
Singapore	35		1,125.2
Fiji	36		1,057.6
Chile	37		831.8
Mauritius	38		805.2
Maldives	39		785.5
Bahrain	40		633.9
Jamaica	41		626.0
Costa Rica	42		625.9
Bulgaria	43		593.4

Larceny (per 100,000 inhabitants)

Country	Rank	LOWER MIDDLE	
Malawi	44		526.1
Russia	45		492.9
Greece	46		475.0
Grenada	47		466.0
Cyprus	48		445.6
Portugal	49		435.8
Malaysia	50		357.4
Peru	51		350.7
Paraguay	52		327.3
Ghana	53		275.2
Djibouti	54		232.8
Korea, South	55		230.2
Libya	56		211.2
China	57		177.1
Papua New Guinea	58		176.4
Jordan	59		163.9
Argentina	60		152.8
Gabon	61		149.5
Tanzania	62		144.1
Brunei	63		142.9
Romania	64		139.8
Kiribati	65		131.4
Guatemala	66		117.1
Rwanda	67		94.4
Qatar	68		88.4
Philippines	69		71.7
Sri Lanka	70		71.2
Central African Republic	71		70.1
Thailand	72		68.9
Turkey	73		68.1
Cote d'Ivoire	74		65.3
Saudi Arabia	75		58.15
Egypt	76		57.7
		BOTTOM 10	
Myanmar (Burma)	77		55.8
Syria	78		50.9
Kenya	79		42.2
Burundi	80		42.0
Indonesia	81		40.9
Senegal	82		38.1
Guinea	83		21.5
Bangladesh	84		11.1
Congo	85		7.2
Nepal	86		4.3

Larceny (per 100,000 inhabitants)

Source: *International Crime Statistics*

260. SEX OFFENSES

A variety of offenses are generally grouped together under the rubric "sex offenses," but the most prominent of these is rape. Rape has been described as the most underreported offense in the world. In its psy-chological consequences it is also perhaps the most traumatic. Even today in many countries rape is equated with murder and is punishable by death.

Rank	Country	Sex Offenses (Including Rape) (per 100,000 inhabitants)
TOP 10		
1	Guatemala	253.71
2	Maldives	118.19
3	Bahamas	118.18
4	Canada	116.06
5	St. Vincent	85.05
6	Qatar	76.55
7	Swaziland	73.67
8	Botswana	73.50
9	Netherlands	63.92
10	Sweden	61.07
UPPER MIDDLE		
11	St. Lucia	60.74
12	Germany	60.00
13	Barbados	58.37
14	United Kingdom	57.44
15	Grenada	53.00
16	Denmark	49.09
17	Seychelles	47.49
18	Israel	45.90
19	Switzerland	45.67
20	Norway	42.82
21	Andorra	42.00
22	United States	41.20
23	Papua New Guinea	40.45
24	Monaco	40.04
25	France	39.29
26	Jamaica	38.69
27	Belgium	38.60
28	Fiji	38.10
29	Austria	38.00
30	Jordan	35.80
31	Zimbabwe	35.76
32	Luxembourg	32.25
LOWER MIDDLE		
33	Chile	32.06
34	Singapore	28.60
35	Trinidad and Tobago	23.41
36	Czech Republic	22.70
37	Finland	20.00
38	Kiribati	19.36
39	Argentina	18.34
40	Libya	17.02
41	Saudi Arabia	16.94
42	Costa Rica	16.42
43	Greece	13.83
44	Spain	13.75
45	Hungary	12.90
46	Peru	12.18
47	Ireland	11.21
48	Central African Republic	11.00
49	Rwanda	10.94
50	Russia	10.04
51	Korea, South	9.80
52	Thailand	9.60
53	Poland	8.60
54	Mauritius	8.45
55	Bulgaria	8.33
56	Malta	7.90
57	Syria	7.10
58	Kenya	5.83
59	Burundi	5.75
60	Malawi	5.73
61	Malaysia	5.55
62	Djibouti	5.40
63	Romania	5.30
64	China	4.30
65	Paraguay	3.84
66	Ghana	3.77
67	Brunei	3.61
68	Japan	3.50
69	Philippines	2.99
70	Sri Lanka	2.30
71	Gabon	2.20
72	Cote d'Ivoire	2.15
73	Indonesia	2.10
74	Myanmar (Burma)	1.83
75	Portugal	1.67
76	Cyprus	1.40
BOTTOM 10		
77	Italy	1.20
78	Senegal	1.13
79	Guinea	1.03
80	Congo	1.00
81	Tanzania	0.98
82	Bahrain	0.82
83	Bangladesh	0.65
84	Turkey	0.48
85	Egypt	0.45
86	Nepal	0.45

Source: *International Crime Statistics*

261. MURDER

Murder in the first degree is a calculated act of slaying and generally receives the severest penalty under law, including capital punishment. Most nations distinguish between criminal homicide and manslaughter, the difference being deliberate cold-blooded intent.

Rank	Country	Murders (per 100,000 inhabitants)	Rank	Country	Murders (per 100,000 inhabitants)	Rank	Country	Murders (per 100,000 inhabitants)
TOP 10			29	Canada	5.66	58	Gabon	2.2
1	Swaziland	87.76	30	Costa Rica	5.2	59	Israel	2.2
2	Bahamas	52.61	31	Myanmar (Burma)	4.85	60	Luxembourg	2.15
3	Monaco	36	32	Djibouti	4.8	61	Greece	2.04
4	Philippines	30.12				62	Czech Republic	2.03
5	Guatemala	27.4	**LOWER MIDDLE**			63	Brunei	2.01
6	Jamaica	20.85	33	Denmark	4.56	64	Bangladesh	2.0
7	Botswana	19.5	34	France	4.46	65	Ghana	1.96
8	Zimbabwe	17.88	35	Fiji	4.3	66	China	1.9
9	Netherlands	14.81	36	Kenya	4.16	67	Jordan	1.9
10	Kiribati	12.44	37	Burkina	4.0	68	Maldives	1.88
			38	Germany	3.9	69	Malaysia	1.85
UPPER MIDDLE			39	Seychelles	3.42	70	Turkey	1.66
11	Peru	12.01	40	Romania	3.4	71	Central African Republic	1.6
12	Barbados	11.67	41	Burundi	3.32	72	Egypt	1.59
13	Sri Lanka	11.6	42	Cyprus	3.2	73	Syria	1.55
14	Malta	10.44	43	Switzerland	3.17	74	Korea, South	1.5
15	St. Vincent	10.28	44	Hungary	3.1			
16	Grenada	10.0	45	Qatar	2.96	**BOTTOM 10**		
17	Paraguay	10.0	46	Libya	2.9	75	Singapore	1.5
18	Thailand	9.5	47	Poland	2.8	76	Congo	1.4
19	United States	9.4	48	Cote d'Ivoire	2.78	77	Senegal	1.01
20	Russia	8.67	49	Portugal	2.78	78	Japan	1.0
21	Trinidad and Tobago	8.42	50	Malawi	2.63	79	Guinea	0.98
22	Papua New Guinea	7.87	51	Norway	2.61	80	Indonesia	0.85
23	Sweden	7.02	52	Mauritius	2.47	81	Ireland	0.82
24	St. Lucia	6.75	53	Spain	2.43	82	Saudi Arabia	0.62
25	Italy	6.4	54	Austria	2.3	83	Finland	0.6
26	Tanzania	6.40	55	United Kingdom	2.26	84	Argentina	0.14
27	Rwanda	6.11	56	Nepal	2.21			
28	Chile	5.81	57	Belgium	2.2			

Source: *International Crime Statistics*

Section

XXI

MEDIA

The Japanese call it *johoka,* the information explosion, a word that best describes the deluge of information and ideas transmitted through the print and electronic media throughout the world. Peter Drucker has defined information as a form of energy, and its production is as important as that of other forms of energy. The media function not only as transmission belts conveying information to their ultimate consumers but also, as Lewis A. Coser defines them, as gatekeepers of ideas or sluice gates that determine what will be and will not be published or broadcast. It is this power that makes the media such a terror to errant governments. Marshall McLuhan notwithstanding, the printed word remains the key means of access to the complex world of information and ideas, but the economic status of the print media has been steadily declining over a number of years. Some newspapers may claim larger circulations, but in almost all countries of the world, the daily press stands more or less where it did 20 years ago. Because of the astronomical speed with which news is transmitted, the newspaper has become an obsolescent means of reporting current news. Even the best newspapers— the prestigious *Times* of London, for example—find themselves constantly in financial difficulties and losing advertising revenue to electronic media.

Particularly critical is the short supply of newsprint. It is produced in only 36 countries and only six—Canada, Finland, Sweden, Norway, Russia and New Zealand—produce enough for export. The United States consumes more than three times its own annual production, while Africa produces no newsprint at all.

In terms of circulation the contrasts among regions is striking. In Africa, nine countries and territories have no newspapers and in only 15 of the others does the daily circulation exceed 10 per 1,000 and in none does it exceed 100 per 1,000. Circulation rates are highest in Europe, reaching up to 400 per 1,000. While overall circulation figures have increased in North America, circulation per 1,000 has dropped to around 300 in the United States and 220 in Canada. In Latin America the median circulation is around 100 per 1,000, and the number of newspapers has declined in Brazil, Argentina and Colombia. Asia presents great contrasts. Only Japan approaches Western standards.

In most of the others, including India, the ratio is less than 20 per 1,000. The relative figure is 300 for Oceania and 336 for Russia.

Over 90 countries have national news agencies. Fifty of the news agencies are directly controlled or operated by the state, while the other 40 are either autonomous public corporations or are cooperative organizations controlled by the press and electronic media. The scale, scope and effectiveness of these agencies vary; some are only government information offices under other names. Worldwide, the collection and dissemination of news is dominated by three multinational agencies: Agence France-Presse (AFP), Associated Press (AP) and Reuters. Most of the other news agencies depend on these three for foreign news. Each of the Big Three has between 100 and 200 offices in as many cities or countries.

Broadcasting, unlike the press, is subject to strict state control and legislation in almost all countries of the world. Originally, such control was necessary for technical reasons, particularly the allocation of frequencies; but later, as the impact of broadcasting became more clearly understood, it became a matter of political convenience. The majority of the states operate or directly control radio and television services, which are financed either by state funds or through license fees. In other countries the services are operated by autonomous corporations, which enjoy some freedom in day-to-day operations. In still others the pattern is mixed with private commercial companies, universities, religious organizations and private foundations operating services side by side or in competition with state or autonomous services. In only a few countries, such as the United States, are the services operated almost entirely by private commercial companies and financed solely by advertising revenues.

The number of radio receivers is less than 100 per 1,000 people in 40 African countries, in 17 Asian countries, and in all but 15 of the Latin American countries. Television has spread to many more countries, but there are still no television services in 20 African countries and in 10 Asian countries. In no African country does the number of television receivers exceed 30 per 1,000 people. The number of television receivers is less than 100 per 1,000 people in 19 Asian countries and in 10 Latin American countries. In countries where television has been introduced, it has had an adverse effect on both radio and print media.

Film stands out from other types of media because, although its production is almost entirely in private hands, it is subject to strict surveillance and monitoring by censorship boards that are invariably official bodies. Around 3,600 feature-length entertainment films are produced annually in some 50 countries. More than half of this total are produced by 17 Asian countries, including two giants, India and Japan; Russia and Eastern Europe account for about a third and the rest is divided among the other countries of the world.

The number of cinemas, cinema seats, and annual movie attendance figures are increasing in Asia in contrast to the rest of the world, where they are slipping or have remained stable for a number of years. It is noteworthy that Russia is among the more advanced countries to buck the trend and report better attendance in movie theaters.

Film imports and exports are affected by linguistic, ethnic and cultural affinities as well as political and commercial ties. Dubbing and subtitling, although expensive, are now obligatory in almost all countries for foreign-language films.

On the assumption that the average household consists of four or five persons, the rate of over 200 to 250 per 1,000 inhabitants for both print and electronic media would indicate that the whole population of a country is being reached by that medium. On this basis, the saturation point has been reached for daily newspapers in 30 countries (including 19 in Europe), for radio in 48 (including 26 in Europe) and for television in 22 (including 15 in Europe). In 21 countries (including 14 in Europe, Australia, Canada, Cuba, Japan, New Zealand, the United States and Russia), this point has been reached for all three of the media. In developed countries, the coming decades will witness remarkable breakthroughs in electronic media; these will include the electronic transmission of facsimiles, communication satellites, video-cassettes and cable TV.

The section presents rankings on radio, TV, cinema, periodicals, daily newspapers, and book publishing.

262. INTERNATIONAL PROPAGANDA

Every broadcasting system has an international component consisting of broadcasts in a number of languages to listeners outside national borders. For systems like the BBC, Voice of America and the Voice of Russia, external services are important as a means of influencing world public opinion. The absence of commercials makes international government broadcasting one of the most selective sources of current news, provided the listener is able to sift the news from the slant.

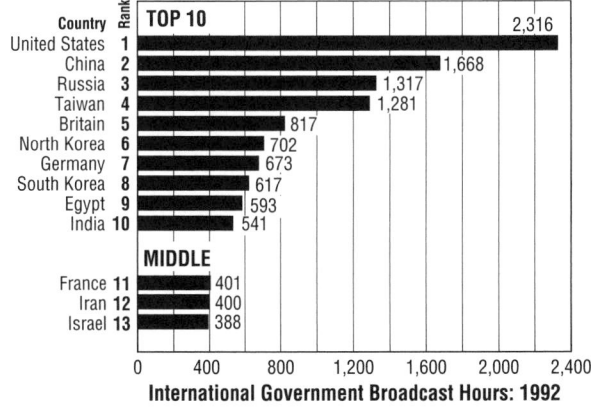

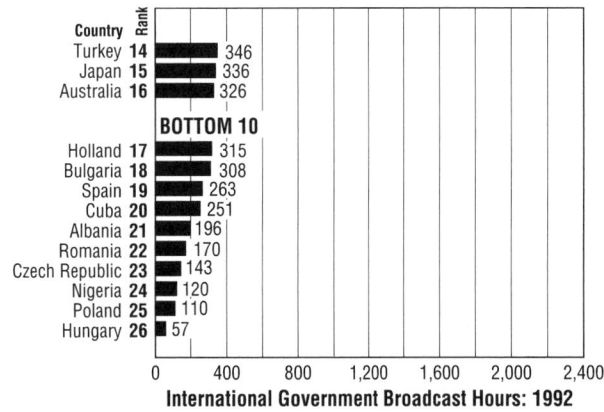

Source: "And Nation Shall Speak Gruff Unto Nation." *The Economist*, 2 May 1992, p. 22. Primary source: British Broadcasting Corporation.

263. BOOK PRODUCTION

National book production statistics are governed by the definitions and classifications set forth in the International Standardization of Statistics Relating to Book Production and Periodicals adopted in 1964 by the General Conference of UNESCO. According to this recommendation, a book is defined as a printed nonperiodical publication of at least 49 pages, exclusive of the cover pages, published in the country and made available to the public. Book production statistics cover publications included in the national bibliographies of their respective countries and cover also government publications, school textbooks, offprints, publications that form part of a series and illustrated works. However, it excludes publications issued for advertising purposes, publications of a transitory character, such as timetables, price lists and telephone directories, and publications in which the text is not the most important part, such as musical scores.

In the 40-year period from 1955 to 1995, Asia, Europe and Russia have reduced their share of the world book market, while North America has more than tripled its share and Africa, Latin America and Oceania have made significant gains.

Rank	Country	Number of Books Published Titles
TOP 10		
1	United Kingdom	80,787
2	China	73,923
3	Germany	67,277
4	United States	49,276
5	France	45,379
6	Japan	42,245
7	Spain	37,325
8	Italy	26,620
9	Korea, South	25,017
10	Russia	22,028
UPPER MIDDLE		
11	Taiwan	16,156
12	Switzerland	14,663
13	Brazil	13,973
14	Belgium	13,913
15	Canada	12,750
16	Netherlands	11,844
17	India	11,170
18	Sweden	9,902
19	Poland	9,172
20	Finland	8,228
21	Denmark	8,132
22	Hungary	7,629
23	Thailand	7,565
24	Australia	6,800
25	Czech Republic	6,743
26	Portugal	6,430
27	Indonesia	6,128
28	Turkey	5,854
29	Argentina	5,628
30	Iran	5,018
31	Norway	4,079
32	Greece	4,066
33	Bulgaria	4,045
34	Austria	3,786
35	Malaysia	3,682
36	Romania	3,662
37	Ukraine	3,550
38	Venezuela	3,366
39	South Africa	3,123
40	Slovakia	3,078
41	Mexico	2,587
42	Yugoslavia	2,365

Rank	Country	Number of Books Published Titles
43	Croatia	2,239
44	Uzbekistan	2,080
45	Israel	2,038
46	Afghanistan	1,776
47	Slovenia	1,728
48	Belarus	1,666
49	Georgia	1,659
50	New Zealand	1,601
51	Estonia	1,557
52	Lithuania	1,524
53	Latvia	1,509
LOWER MIDDLE		
54	Chile	1,493
55	Colombia	1,481
56	Sri Lanka	1,398
57	Egypt	1,311
58	Kazakhstan	1,226
59	Bangladesh	1,209
60	Tunisia	1,165
61	Iceland	1,038
62	Nigeria	1,022
63	Bosnia & Herzegovina	966
64	Kyrgyzstan	936
65	Armenia	817
66	Jordan	790
67	Uruguay	790
68	Tajikistan	787
69	Philippines	763
70	Peru	761
71	Cuba	736
72	Ecuador	717
73	Moldova	685
74	Myanmar (Burma)	673
75	Benin	647
76	Ireland	628
77	Syria	598
78	Cyprus	534
79	Azerbaijan	530
80	Macedonia	492
81	Algeria	454
82	Turkmenistan	386
83	Qatar	372
84	Bolivia	365
85	Albania	363

Rank	Country	Number of Books Published Titles
86	Luxembourg	362
87	Ghana	338
88	Malta	283
89	Kenya	239
90	Costa Rica	230
91	Mongolia	193
92	Haiti	188
93	Kuwait	187
94	Mali	160
95	Zimbabwe	151
96	Ethiopia	147
97	Namibia	131
98	Rwanda	131
99	Tanzania	127
100	Libya	121
101	Botswana	97
102	Pakistan	70
103	Malawi	66
104	Papua New Guinea	58
105	Andorra	56
106	Mauritius	56
107	Madagascar	46
108	St. Lucia	44
109	Belize	43
110	Monaco	41
111	Burundi	37
112	Mozambique	29
113	Nicaragua	27
114	Brunei	25
115	Oman	24
116	Jamaica	23
117	Laos	19
BOTTOM 10		
118	Barbados	17
119	Bahamas	15
120	El Salvador	15
121	Gambia	15
122	Angola	14
123	Fiji	10
124	Cape Verde	9
125	Guyana	9
126	Niger	5
127	Burkina	4

Source: *UNESCO Statistical Yearbook*

264. FILM PRODUCTION

The minimum length of films classified as long films varies considerably from country to country, ranging from 1,000 meters to 3,000 meters, but the standard in most countries is closer to 2,000 meters.

Rank	Country	Long Films Produced Including Coproductions	Rank	Country	Long Films Produced Including Coproductions	Rank	Country	Long Films Produced Including Coproductions
TOP 10						42	Finland	12
1	India	910	**LOWER MIDDLE**			43	Albania	11
2	United States	345	21	Iran	52	44	Austria	11
3	France	239	22	Switzerland	51	45	Cuba	9
4	Japan	239	23	Sweden	40	46	Norway	9
5	Thailand	194	24	Poland	34	47	Venezuela	8
6	Philippines	142	25	Australia	33	48	Greece	7
7	China	130	26	Mexico	33	49	New Zealand	5
8	Italy	115	27	Yugoslavia	33	50	Romania	4
9	Korea, South	110	28	Argentina	27			
10	Pakistan	91	29	Singapore	27	**BOTTOM 10**		
			30	Belgium	26	51	Colombia	3
UPPER MIDDLE			31	Czech Republic	24	52	Mauritius	2
11	Brazil	86	32	Hungary	19	53	Peru	2
12	Myanmar (Burma)	85	33	Sri Lanka	16	54	Bolivia	1
13	Spain	82	34	Vietnam	16	55	Ecuador	1
14	Bangladesh	77	35	Bulgaria	15	56	Ethiopia	1
15	Germany	72	36	Israel	15	57	Guinea	1
16	Indonesia	64	37	Malaysia	15	58	Iceland	1
17	Turkey	63	38	Netherlands	14	59	Sudan	1
18	Egypt	59	39	Denmark	13	60	Syria	1
19	Canada	54	40	Portugal	13			
20	United Kingdom	54	41	Ukraine	13			

Source: *UNESCO Statistical Yearbook*

265. ANNUAL MOVIE ATTENDANCE

Movie attendance statistics are comparatively reliable because they are based on the number of tickets sold and almost all countries charge sales or entertainment tax on these tickets. Wherever possible these statistics include drive-ins and mobile units. Because of the rapid growth of television as a rival form of entertainment, per capita movie attendance has declined since 1970.

Rank	Country	Cinema—Annual Attendance (million)	Rank	Country	Cinema—Annual Attendance (million)	Rank	Country	Cinema—Annual Attendance (million)
TOP 10			20	Italy	88.6	42	South Africa	26.0
1	China	16,878	21	Spain	79.1	43	Bulgaria	25.7
2	India	4,297.3	22	Canada	76.3	44	Pakistan	25.3
3	United States	981.9	23	Iran	66.6			
4	Russia	750.0	24	Taiwan	64.2	**LOWER MIDDLE**		
5	Ukraine	415.8	25	Korea, South	55.3	45	Hungary	21.6
6	Mexico	351.0	26	Georgia	47.0	46	Algeria	21.0
7	Bangladesh	302.3	27	Turkmenistan	46.0	47	Poland	20.9
8	Vietnam	239.9	28	Malaysia	41.6	48	Mongolia	20.1
9	Romania	203.4	29	Colombia	41.0	49	Latvia	19.7
10	Korea, North	187.4	30	Australia	39.8	50	Argentina	18.0
			31	Sri Lanka	37.2	51	Venezuela	18.0
UPPER MIDDLE			32	Czech Republic	36.4	52	Turkey	16.5
11	Kazakhstan	150.0	33	Peru	33.0	53	Belgium	16.1
12	Japan	143.6	34	Kyrgyzstan	32.0	54	Sweden	15.6
13	Indonesia	133.2	35	Azerbaijan	31.0	55	Switzerland	15.4
14	Uzbekistan	126.0	36	Singapore	30.7	56	Netherlands	14.7
15	Germany	119.9	37	Morocco	30.2	57	Lithuania	13.9
16	France	117.5	38	Moldova	30.0	58	Slovakia	13.8
17	United Kingdom	102.0	39	Tajikistan	30.0	59	Armenia	13.4
18	Belarus	94.0	40	Cuba	29.9	60	Guyana	13.0
19	Brazil	91.3	41	Egypt	26.9	61	Sudan	13.0

Rank	Country	Cinema—Annual Attendance (million)	Rank	Country	Cinema—Annual Attendance (million)	Rank	Country	Cinema—Annual Attendance (million)
62	Ireland	11.6	79	Nigeria	4.6	96	Kuwait	0.9
63	Norway	10.7	80	Bosnia & Herzegovina	4.3	97	Bahrain	0.6
64	Austria	10.5	81	Mozambique	4.1	98	Mauritius	0.6
65	Chile	9.7	82	Ghana	3.9	99	Luxembourg	0.5
66	Portugal	9.6	83	Guinea	3.9		**BOTTOM 10**	
67	Denmark	9.2	84	Angola	3.2	100	Madagascar	0.4
68	Guatemala	7.7	85	Croatia	3.1	101	Malta	0.3
69	Estonia	7.3	86	Yugoslavia	2.9	102	Qatar	0.3
70	Albania	6.9	87	Slovenia	2.8	103	Rwanda	0.3
71	Syria	6.9	88	Brunei	2.3	104	Bermuda	0.2
72	Ecuador	6.8	89	Haiti	2.1	105	Costa Rica	0.2
73	Uruguay	6.2	90	Macedonia	2.1	106	Burundi	0.1
74	Burkina	6.0	91	Tanzania	1.8	107	Gabon	0.1
75	Finland	6.0	92	Benin	1.3	108	Monaco	0.1
76	Zimbabwe	5.6	93	Iceland	1.3	109	San Marino	0.03
77	Nicaragua	5.0	94	Laos	1.0			
78	Bolivia	4.6	95	Jordan	0.9			

Source: *UNESCO Statistical Yearbook*

266. TELEVISION SETS

Compared to radio, television made only modest gains in the developing countries, where a television set was for a long time a luxury. However, the growth of satellite communications augurs a break-through in making television a truly universal medium. Another area in which there has been considerable progress is color television. Although no separate statistics are available for color television sets, the production of black-and-white sets has been steadily decreasing in all industrially advanced countries.

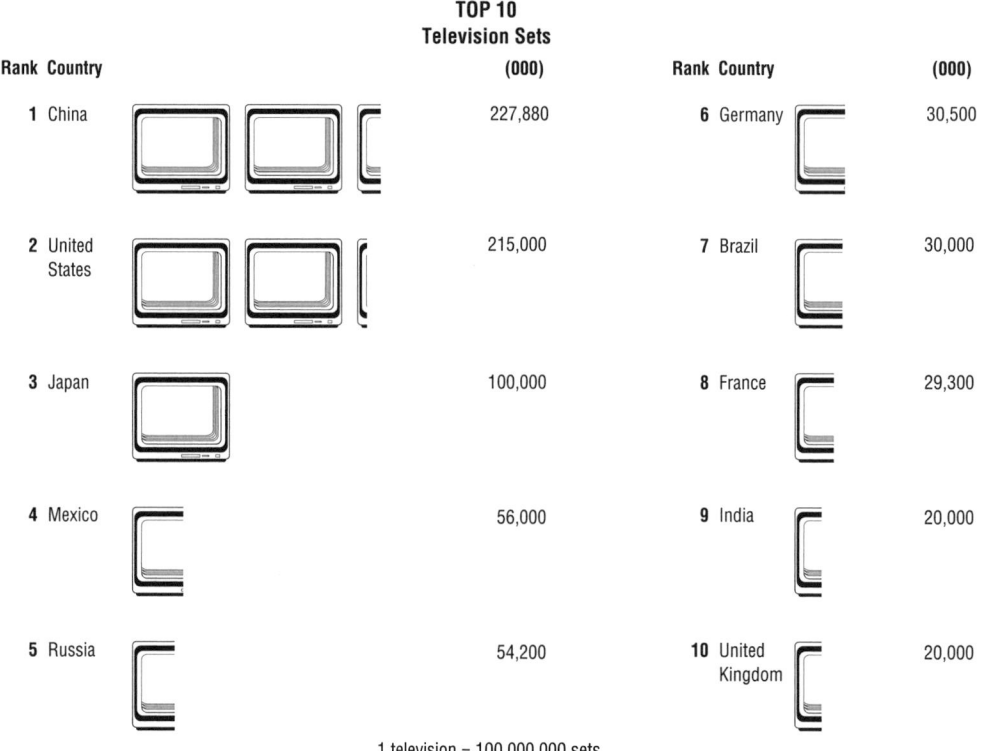

**TOP 10
Television Sets**

Rank	Country	(000)	Rank	Country	(000)
1	China	227,880	6	Germany	30,500
2	United States	215,000	7	Brazil	30,000
3	Japan	100,000	8	France	29,300
4	Mexico	56,000	9	India	20,000
5	Russia	54,200	10	United Kingdom	20,000

1 television = 100,000,000 sets

Rank	Country	Television Sets (000)
UPPER MIDDLE		
11	Canada	17,400
12	Ukraine	17,200
13	Italy	17,000
14	Spain	17,000
15	Indonesia	11,000
16	Turkey	10,530
17	Korea, South	10,403
18	Poland	10,000
19	Australia	8,000
20	Argentina	7,165
21	Iran	7,000
22	Philippines	7,000
23	Taiwan	7,000
24	Netherlands	6,500
25	Nigeria	6,100
26	Colombia	5,500
27	Egypt	5,000
28	Kazakhstan	4,795
29	Saudi Arabia	4,700
30	Hungary	4,262
31	Belgium	4,200
32	Romania	4,000
33	Sweden	3,750
34	Venezuela	3,701
35	Belarus	3,538
36	South Africa	3,445
37	Uzbekistan	3,308
38	Thailand	3,300
39	Czech Republic	3,185
40	Bulgaria	3,127
41	Austria	2,706
42	Denmark	2,700
43	Switzerland	2,545
44	Cuba	2,500
45	Vietnam	2,500
46	Greece	2,300
47	Pakistan	2,080
48	Algeria	2,000
49	Chile	2,000
50	Korea, North	2,000
51	Malaysia	2,000
52	Norway	2,000
53	Peru	2,000
54	Finland	1,900
55	Portugal	1,687
56	Yugoslavia	1,643
57	Azerbaijan	1,522
58	Israel	1,500
59	Oman	1,500
60	Lithuania	1,400
61	Slovakia	1,279
62	Moldova	1,264
63	Morocco	1,210
64	Latvia	1,200
65	Lebanon	1,100
66	New Zealand	1,100
67	Iraq	1,000
68	Ireland	1,000

Rank	Country	Television Sets (000)
69	Myanmar (Burma)	1,000
70	Ecuador	900
71	Kyrgyzstan	875
72	Tajikistan	860
73	Puerto Rico	830
74	Cote d'Ivoire	810
75	Kuwait	800
76	Croatia	750
77	Dominican Republic	728
78	Armenia	722
79	Turkmenistan	705
80	Sri Lanka	700
81	Syria	700
82	Singapore	650
83	Tunisia	650
84	Bosnia & Herzegovina	629
LOWER MIDDLE		
85	Estonia	600
86	Uruguay	600
87	El Salvador	501
88	Libya	500
89	Jamaica	484
90	Guatemala	475
91	Slovenia	445
92	Bangladesh	350
93	Paraguay	350
94	Costa Rica	340
95	Macedonia	331
96	Bahrain	270
97	Kenya	260
98	Qatar	251
99	Ghana	250
100	Jordan	250
101	Nepal	250
102	Sudan	250
103	Trinidad and Tobago	250
104	Albania	246
105	Cyprus	235
106	Nicaragua	210
107	Panama	205
108	Zambia	200
109	United Arab Emirates	170
110	Honduras	160
111	Mauritius	157
112	Togo	150
113	Zimbabwe	137
114	Malta	133
115	Madagascar	130
116	Mongolia	120
117	Uganda	115
118	Luxembourg	101
119	Afghanistan	100
120	Ethiopia	100
121	Yemen	100
122	Laos	80
123	Tanzania	80
124	Iceland	76
125	Brunei	70

Rank	Country	Television Sets (000)
126	Cambodia	70
127	Barbados	69
128	Guinea	65
129	Senegal	61
130	Bahamas	60
131	Angola	51
132	Bolivia	50
133	Lesotho	50
134	Burkina	48
135	Liberia	45
136	Suriname	43
137	Gabon	40
138	Namibia	39
139	Mozambique	35
140	Bermuda	30
141	Grenada	30
142	Antigua and Barbuda	28
143	Belize	27
144	Haiti	25
145	Niger	25
146	St. Lucia	25
147	Sierra Leone	25
148	Zaire	22
149	Sao Tome e Principe	21
150	Benin	20
151	Monaco	20
152	St. Vincent	18
153	Djibouti	17
154	Cameroon	15
155	Guyana	15
156	Botswana	14
157	Seychelles	13
158	Swaziland	13
159	Liechtenstein	11
160	Fiji	10
161	Mali	10
162	Papua New Guinea	10
163	St. Kitts and Nevis	9.5
164	Congo	8.5
165	San Marino	8.0
166	Central African Republic	7.5
167	Andorra	6.0
168	Dominica	5.2
169	Cape Verde	5.0
170	Chad	5.0
BOTTOM 10		
171	Western Samoa	5.0
172	Maldives	4.8
173	Burundi	4.5
174	Somalia	3.0
175	Tonga	3.0
176	Equatorial Guinea	2.5
177	Mauritania	1.1
178	Vanuatu	1.0
179	Bhutan	0.2
180	Comoros	0.2

Source: *UNESCO Statistical Yearbook*

267. RADIO RECEIVERS IN USE

David Lerner in *The Passing of Traditional Society: Modernizing the Middle East* has described the radio as the principal instrument of political and economic modernization in developing societies. Other scholars have drawn attention to the relation between radios per capita and mass participation and competitiveness.

Rank	Country	Radio Receivers (000)
TOP 10		
1	United States	524,200
2	China	206,000
3	Japan	110,000
4	Russia	90,000
5	United Kingdom	65,400
6	India	65,000
7	Brazil	55,000
8	France	50,000
9	Italy	43,350
10	Korea, South	42,570
UPPER MIDDLE		
11	Germany	30,000
12	Canada	26,878
13	Indonesia	26,000
14	Argentina	21,500
15	Australia	21,000
16	Mexico	21,000
17	Nigeria	18,000
18	Egypt	16,450
19	Poland	16,300
20	Ukraine	15,000
21	Netherlands	13,400
22	Iran	13,000
23	Spain	12,000
24	South Africa	11,200
25	Pakistan	10,200
26	Thailand	10,000
27	Czech Republic	9,100
28	Ethiopia	9,000
29	Turkey	8,800
30	Taiwan	8,620
31	Philippines	8,300
32	Venezuela	8,300
33	Belgium	7,640
34	Malaysia	7,460
35	Sweden	7,450
36	Vietnam	7,000
37	Hungary	6,250
38	Sudan	5,755
39	Switzerland	5,600
40	Colombia	5,400
41	Peru	5,300
42	Morocco	5,100
43	Denmark	5,000
44	Finland	4,950
45	Austria	4,710
46	Bangladesh	4,650
47	Romania	4,500
48	Chile	4,400
49	Ghana	4,300
50	Bolivia	4,250
51	Greece	4,200
52	Kazakhstan	4,188
53	Bulgaria	3,920
54	Saudi Arabia	3,800
55	Iraq	3,700
56	Azerbaijan	3,682
57	Uzbekistan	3,677
58	Cuba	3,608
59	Algeria	3,500
60	Zaire	3,480
61	New Zealand	3,350
62	Norway	3,342

Rank	Country	Radio Receivers (000)
63	Myanmar (Burma)	3,300
64	Sri Lanka	3,300
65	Ecuador	3,240
66	Belarus	3,140
67	Syria	3,000
68	Slovakia	2,895
69	Yugoslavia	2,692
70	Korea, North	2,500
71	Puerto Rico	2,480
72	Madagascar	2,300
73	Israel	2,250
74	Lebanon	2,247
75	Portugal	2,220
76	Kenya	2,200
77	Ireland	2,150
78	El Salvador	2,080
79	Croatia	2,000
80	Latvia	2,000
81	Malawi	2,000
82	Honduras	1,910
83	Uruguay	1,850
84	Uganda	1,800
LOWER MIDDLE		
85	Tunisia	1,700
86	Afghanistan	1,670
87	Cote d'Ivoire	1,600
88	Cameroon	1,500
89	Moldova	1,421
90	Lithuania	1,420
91	Chad	1,310
92	Dominican Republic	1,180
93	Kuwait	1,000
94	Libya	1,000
95	Jordan	980
96	Jamaica	955
97	Estonia	926
98	Nicaragua	925
99	Oman	900
100	Sierra Leone	900
101	Cambodia	860
102	Tajikistan	854
103	Senegal	850
104	Kyrgyzstan	825
105	Turkmenistan	823
106	Singapore	822
107	Zimbabwe	801
108	Costa Rica	760
109	Bosnia & Herzegovina	733
110	Togo	720
111	Paraguay	700
112	Yemen	665
113	Rwanda	650
114	Armenia	642
115	Nepal	625
116	Mozambique	620
117	Zambia	603
118	Slovenia	601
119	Liberia	600
120	Trinidad and Tobago	580
121	Guatemala	570
122	Tanzania	565
123	Albania	550
124	Panama	527
125	Laos	500

Rank	Country	Radio Receivers (000)
126	United Arab Emirates	490
127	Angola	450
128	Fiji	450
129	Niger	440
130	Benin	400
131	Guyana	386
132	Mauritius	380
133	Mali	350
134	Bahrain	320
135	Burundi	300
136	Mauritania	300
137	Somalia	300
138	Mongolia	286
139	Haiti	270
140	Macedonia	265
141	Suriname	262
142	Papua New Guinea	260
143	Congo	240
144	Luxembourg	240
145	Guinea	230
146	Namibia	230
147	Burkina	225
148	Barbados	224
149	Cyprus	200
150	Iceland	197
151	Central African Republic	180
152	Qatar	180
153	Gabon	155
154	Botswana	140
155	Gambia	140
156	Bahamas	134
157	Equatorial Guinea	128
158	Swaziland	117
159	Lesotho	116
160	Belize	106
161	St. Lucia	96
162	Malta	90
163	Bermuda	80
164	Antigua and Barbuda	75
165	Western Samoa	75
166	St. Vincent	73
167	Comoros	61
168	Brunei	60
169	Cape Verde	57
170	Vanuatu	55
171	Grenada	53
172	Tonga	52
173	Dominica	45
174	Guinea-Bissau	40
175	Seychelles	40
176	Solomon Islands	38
177	Djibouti	35
178	Sao Tome e Principe	31
BOTTOM 10		
179	Monaco	30
180	St. Kitts and Nevis	26
181	Maldives	25
182	Bhutan	23
183	Kiribati	15
184	San Marino	13
185	Liechtenstein	11
186	Andorra	10
187	Nauru	6.0
188	Tuvalu	3.0

Source: *UNESCO Statistical Yearbook*

268. DAILY NEWSPAPER CIRCULATION

Because the circulation of daily newspapers is in most countries certified by audit bureaus, statistics relating to the circulation of dailies are fairly reliable. (For the definition of a daily newspaper see the ranking of countries by number of daily newspapers published).

Rank	Country	Newspaper Circulation per 1,000
TOP 10		
1	Liechtenstein	700
2	Georgia	671
3	Norway	606
4	Iceland	519
5	Finland	515
6	Kazakhstan	512
7	Sweden	511
8	Czech Republic	485
9	Chile	445
10	Korea, South	407
UPPER MIDDLE		
11	Austria	400
12	Switzerland	387
13	Russia	386
14	Luxembourg	384
15	United Kingdom	383
16	Kyrgyzstan	367
17	Singapore	336
18	Denmark	332
19	Germany	331
20	Romania	322
21	Turkmenistan	319
22	Slovakia	317
23	Netherlands	311
24	Belgium	310
25	New Zealand	304
26	Monaco	296
27	Guatemala	277
28	Hungary	275
29	Australia	261
30	Bermuda	258
31	Kuwait	244
32	Israel	242
33	United States	240
34	Uruguay	240
35	Lithuania	223
36	Korea, North	221
37	Canada	215
38	Venezuela	208
39	France	205
40	Taiwan	202
41	United Arab Emirates	201
42	Latvia	193
43	Ireland	187
44	Belarus	184
45	Japan	180
46	Grenada	179
47	Lebanon	176
48	Bulgaria	164
49	Barbados	160
50	Poland	158
51	Qatar	155
52	Slovenia	154
53	Malta	150
54	Argentina	144
55	Puerto Rico	141
56	Trinidad and Tobago	138

Rank	Country	Newspaper Circulation per 1,000
57	Greece	137
58	Namibia	136
59	Bahamas	133
60	Croatia	133
61	Cuba	122
62	Malaysia	117
63	Ukraine	117
64	Mexico	116
65	Cyprus	108
66	Italy	105
67	Spain	105
68	Costa Rica	101
69	Guyana	99
70	Suriname	98
71	El Salvador	90
72	Mongolia	90
73	Panama	89
74	San Marino	87
LOWER MIDDLE		
75	Andorra	83
76	Bahrain	81
77	Brunei	74
78	Thailand	74
79	Mauritius	73
80	Tonga	72
81	Peru	71
82	Turkey	71
83	Jamaica	65
84	Colombia	63
85	Ecuador	62
86	Azerbaijan	58
87	Jordan	58
88	Brazil	55
89	Bosnia & Herzegovina	53
90	Bolivia	52
91	Yugoslavia	52
92	Albania	50
93	Philippines	49
94	Tunisia	49
95	Oman	48
96	Saudi Arabia	48
97	Portugal	47
98	Moldova	45
99	Egypt	44
100	Seychelles	44
101	Algeria	38
102	Fiji	37
103	Paraguay	37
104	Dominican Republic	35
105	Iraq	34
106	India	31
107	South Africa	31
108	Botswana	30
109	Honduras	29
110	Macedonia	27
111	Sri Lanka	27
112	Indonesia	24
113	Armenia	23

Rank	Country	Newspaper Circulation per 1,000
114	Nicaragua	23
115	Sudan	23
116	Syria	22
117	Uzbekistan	21
118	Iran	20
119	Yemen	19
120	Ghana	18
121	Zimbabwe	18
122	Gabon	16
123	Nigeria	16
124	Papua New Guinea	16
125	Libya	15
126	Swaziland	15
127	Kenya	14
128	Morocco	14
129	Liberia	13
130	Maldives	13
131	Angola	12
132	Afghanistan	11
133	Congo	8
134	Djibouti	8
135	Lesotho	8
136	Tanzania	8
137	Vietnam	8
138	Zambia	8
139	Cote d'Ivoire	7
140	Haiti	7
141	Myanmar (Burma)	7
142	Nepal	7
143	Bangladesh	6
144	Guinea-Bissau	6
145	Pakistan	6
146	Senegal	6
147	Mozambique	5
148	Cameroon	4
149	Madagascar	4
150	Mali	4
151	Uganda	4
152	Burundi	3
153	Cambodia	3
154	Equatorial Guinea	3
155	Laos	3
156	Togo	3
157	Zaire	3
158	Benin	2
159	Gambia	2
BOTTOM 10		
160	Malawi	2
161	Sierra Leone	2
162	Somalia	2
163	Central African Republic	1
164	Ethiopia	1
165	Niger	1
166	Mauritania	0.5
167	Chad	0.4
168	Burkina	0.3
169	Rwanda	0.1

Source: *UNESCO Statistical Yearbook*

269. DAILY NEWSPAPERS

A daily general-interest newspaper is defined as a publication devoted primarily to recording events of current public affairs, international affairs, politics, etc., and one that is published at least four times a week. National statistics on daily newspapers (unlike those relating to periodicals) are fairly accurate.

TOP 10
National Statisitics on Daily Newspapers

Rank	Country	Newspapers	Rank	Country	Newspapers	Rank	Country	Newspapers
1	India	2,300	4	Turkey	399	8	Mexico	292
			5	Brazil	373	9	Pakistan	274
2	United States	1,586	6	Germany	355	10	Argentina	190
			7	Russia	339			
3	Kazakhstan	456						

1 newspaper = 1,000 papers

Rank	Country	Newspapers	Rank	Country	Newspapers	Rank	Country	Newspapers
UPPER MIDDLE			51	Austria	27	90	Congo	6
11	Georgia	147	52	Nigeria	26	91	Iraq	6
12	Greece	145	53	Nepal	25	92	Mauritius	6
13	Kyrgyzstan	128	54	Portugal	25	93	San Marino	6
14	Sweden	124	55	Slovakia	21	94	Slovenia	6
15	Japan	121	56	South Africa	20	95	Uganda	6
16	Canada	106	57	Afghanistan	18	96	Algeria	5
17	United Kingdom	101	58	Lithuania	18	97	Guatemala	5
18	Taiwan	93	59	Cuba	17	98	Iceland	5
19	Ukraine	90	60	Latvia	17	99	Kenya	5
20	Netherlands	86	61	Bolivia	16	100	Luxembourg	5
21	Turkmenistan	86	62	Egypt	16	101	Moldova	5
22	Switzerland	83	63	Lebanon	16	102	Paraguay	5
23	Norway	82	64	Estonia	15	103	Sudan	5
24	Vanuatu	82	65	Morocco	14	104	Albania	4
25	Italy	78	66	Iran	13	105	Angola	4
26	France	77	67	Saudi Arabia	13	106	Costa Rica	4
27	Romania	76	68	Uzbekistan	12	107	Ethiopia	4
28	China	74	69	Dominican Republic	11	108	Ghana	4
29	Poland	72	70	Korea, North	11	109	Haiti	4
30	Australia	69	71	Syria	11	110	Honduras	4
31	Indonesia	68	72	United Arab Emirates	11	111	Jordan	4
32	Korea, South	63	73	Belarus	10	112	Libya	4
33	Peru	59	74	Singapore	10	113	Namibia	4
34	Finland	58	75	Sri Lanka	10	114	Oman	4
35	Czech Republic	55	76	Yugoslavia	10	115	Qatar	4
36	Bangladesh	51	77	Croatia	9	116	Trinidad and Tobago	4
37	Spain	48	78	Cyprus	9	117	Venezuela	4
38	Bulgaria	46	79	Kuwait	9	118	Yemen	4
39	Colombia	46	80	Tajikistan	9	119	Andorra	3
40	Chile	45				120	Bahamas	3
41	Philippines	43	**LOWER MIDDLE**			121	Bahrain	3
42	Denmark	42	81	Tunisia	9	122	Jamaica	3
43	Malaysia	39	82	Zaire	9	123	Laos	3
44	Ecuador	36	83	El Salvador	8	124	Malta	3
45	Thailand	35	84	Ireland	8	125	Mongolia	3
46	Belgium	33	85	Liberia	8	126	Nicaragua	3
47	Uruguay	32	86	Panama	8	127	Puerto Rico	3
48	Israel	31	87	Armenia	7	128	Suriname	3
49	New Zealand	31	88	Madagascar	7	129	Swaziland	3
50	Hungary	28	89	Azerbaijan	6	130	Tanzania	3

Rank	Country	Newspapers	Rank	Country	Newspapers	Rank	Country	Newspapers
131	Barbados	2	146	Benin	1	161	Guinea-Bissau	1
132	Bosnia & Herzegovina	2	147	Bermuda	1			
133	Gambia	2	148	Botswana	1	**BOTTOM 10**		
134	Guyana	2	149	Brunei	1	162	Malawi	1
135	Lesotho	2	150	Burkina	1	163	Mauritania	1
136	Liechtenstein	2	151	Burundi	1	164	Monaco	1
137	Macedonia	2	152	Cambodia	1	165	Niger	1
138	Maldives	2	153	Cameroon	1	166	Rwanda	1
139	Mali	2	154	Central African Republic	1	167	Senegal	1
140	Mozambique	2	155	Chad	1	168	Seychelles	1
141	Myanmar (Burma)	2	156	Cote d'Ivoire	1	169	Sierra Leone	1
142	Papua New Guinea	2	157	Djibouti	1	170	Somalia	1
143	Togo	2	158	Equatorial Guinea	1	171	Tonga	1
144	Zambia	2	159	Fiji	1			
145	Zimbabwe	2	160	Gabon	1			

Source: *UNESCO Statistical Yearbook*

270. PERIODICALS

Compared with other media, the world of magazines is one of great variety and profusion and one whose cultural and educational impact is much greater. There are magazines that cater to every conceivable interest and activity and to every type of religious, political and social belief. Many of the larger magazines enjoy circulations in the millions and an influence on their audience that no newspaper can match.

Rank	Country	Periodicals	Rank	Country	Periodicals	Rank	Country	Periodicals
TOP 10			38	Nepal	367	76	Cameroon	58
1	Belgium	13,706	39	Malta	359	77	Saudi Arabia	58
2	United States	11,593	40	Croatia	352	78	Barbados	52
3	Italy	10,064	41	Ukraine	321	79	Kyrgyzstan	50
4	Germany	7,831	42	Iran	318	80	Azerbaijan	49
5	Norway	7,010	43	Greece	309	81	Algeria	48
6	China	6,486	44	Denmark	285	82	Cyprus	48
7	United Kingdom	6,408	45	Pakistan	282	83	Sweden	46
8	New Zealand	5,788				84	Mongolia	45
9	Finland	5,711	**LOWER MIDDLE**			85	Peru	45
10	Taiwan	4,134	46	Dominican Republic	277	86	Bangladesh	41
			47	Egypt	266	87	Argentina	40
UPPER MIDDLE			48	Ireland	257	88	Burkina	37
11	Japan	3,918	49	Estonia	250	89	Turkmenistan	33
12	Brazil	3,782	50	Lithuania	237	90	Jordan	31
13	Switzerland	3,079	51	Qatar	190	91	Zimbabwe	28
14	Poland	2,950	52	Mexico	182	92	Tajikistan	26
15	Czech Republic	2,898	53	Latvia	170	93	Uganda	26
16	Russia	2,592	54	Sri Lanka	170	94	San Marino	18
17	France	2,672	55	Cuba	160	95	Brunei	15
18	Austria	2,524	56	Belarus	155	96	Oman	15
19	Spain	1,998	57	Albania	143	97	Rwanda	15
20	Singapore	1,786	58	Senegal	123	98	Botswana	14
21	Malaysia	1,631	59	Ghana	121	99	Malawi	14
22	Philippines	1,570	60	Indonesia	117	100	South Africa	11
23	Canada	1,400	61	Afghanistan	105	101	Chad	10
24	Romania	1,379	62	Bosnia & Herzegovina	92	102	Gambia	10
25	Turkey	1,325	63	Nigeria	92			
26	Thailand	1,293	64	Kazakhstan	88	**BOTTOM 10**		
27	Hungary	1,203	65	United Arab Emirates	80	103	Sudan	10
28	Portugal	937	66	Liechtenstein	79	104	St. Kitts and Nevis	9
29	Israel	807	67	Georgia	75	105	Panama	8
30	Bulgaria	745	68	Macedonia	74	106	Djibouti	7
31	Iceland	598	69	Kuwait	73	107	Congo	3
32	Luxembourg	508	70	Moldova	68	108	Ethiopia	3
33	Slovenia	482	71	Zaire	68	109	Guinea	3
34	Uruguay	465	72	Maldives	64	110	Monaco	3
35	Slovakia	424	73	Madagascar	63	111	Mozambique	3
36	Chile	417	74	Mauritius	62	112	Seychelles	2
37	Yugoslavia	397	75	Uzbekistan	61			

Source: *UNESCO Statistical Yearbook*

271. PERSONS PER RADIO RECEIVER

Radio is called the hot medium because, unlike television, the cool medium, it requires less attention, and listening can be combined with other activities. In many countries radio ownership has approached total saturation, with many persons owning more than one radio. Walkman radios have helped to make radios even more popular in countries lacking more refined electronic media.

Rank	Country	Persons per Radio Receivers	Rank	Country	Persons per Radio Receivers	Rank	Country	Persons per Radio Receivers
TOP 10			63	Jamaica	2.6	126	Bosnia & Herzegovina	5.9
1	Guatemala	0.5	64	Lithuania	2.6	127	Ethiopia	5.9
2	United States	0.5	65	Malaysia	2.6	128	Albania	6.1
3	Slovakia	0.7	66	Venezuela	2.6	129	Andorra	6.2
4	Bermuda	0.8	67	El Salvador	2.7	130	Madagascar	6.2
5	Antigua and Barbuda	0.9	68	Germany	2.7	131	Colombia	6.4
6	Australia	0.9	69	Honduras	2.8	132	Tajikistan	6.4
7	United Kingdom	0.9	70	Liechtenstein	2.8	133	Dominican Republic	6.6
8	Denmark	1.0	71	Mauritius	2.9	134	Cape Verde	6.7
9	Finland	1.0	72	Brazil	3.0	135	Mauritania	6.9
10	Korea, South	1.0	73	Equatorial Guinea	3.0	136	Namibia	6.9
			74	Vanuatu	3.0	137	Paraguay	6.9
UPPER MIDDLE			75	Cuba	3.1	138	Turkey	7.0
11	Monaco	1.0	76	Moldova	3.1	139	Gabon	7.3
12	Canada	1.1	77	Tuvalu	3.1	140	Indonesia	7.3
13	Czech Republic	1.1	78	Chile	3.2	141	Swaziland	7.5
14	Japan	1.1	79	Qatar	3.2	142	Gambia	7.7
15	New Zealand	1.1	80	Belarus	3.3	143	Algeria	7.8
16	Barbados	1.2	81	Slovenia	3.3	144	Mongolia	8.1
17	France	1.2	82	Spain	3.3	145	Philippines	8.2
18	Netherlands	1.2	83	Ecuador	3.5	146	Cameroon	8.6
19	Sweden	1.2	84	Ukraine	3.5	147	Comoros	8.6
20	Belgium	1.3				148	Cote d'Ivoire	8.9
21	Italy	1.3	**LOWER MIDDLE**			149	Korea, North	9.2
22	Latvia	1.3	85	Egypt	3.6	150	Laos	9.5
23	Lebanon	1.3	86	Singapore	3.6	151	Senegal	9.5
24	Norway	1.3	87	South Africa	3.6	152	Solomon Islands	9.6
25	Switzerland	1.3	88	Ghana	3.7	153	Maldives	9.8
26	Iceland	1.4	89	Yugoslavia	3.9	154	Afghanistan	10
27	St. Lucia	1.4	90	Cyprus	4.0	155	Uganda	10
28	Puerto Rico	1.5	91	Kazakhstan	4.0	156	Vietnam	10
29	St. Kitts and Nevis	1.5	92	Liberia	4.0	157	Botswana	11
30	St. Vincent	1.5	93	Jordan	4.1	158	Cambodia	11
31	Argentina	1.6	94	Malta	4.1	159	Congo	11
32	Dominica	1.6	95	Sao Tome e Principe	4.1	160	Rwanda	12
33	Hungary	1.6	96	Costa Rica	4.3	161	Zaire	12
34	Kuwait	1.6	97	Mexico	4.3	162	Benin	13
35	Russia	1.6	98	Peru	4.4	163	Kenya	13
36	Suriname	1.6	99	Portugal	4.5	164	India	14
37	Austria	1.7	100	Iran	4.6	165	Myanmar (Burma)	14
38	Bahrain	1.7	101	Saudi Arabia	4.6	166	Pakistan	14
39	Bolivia	1.7	102	Syria	4.6	167	Zimbabwe	14
40	Estonia	1.7	103	Turkmenistan	4.6	168	Zambia	15
41	Fiji	1.7	104	Brunei	4.7	169	Djibouti	16
42	Grenada	1.7	105	Chad	4.7	170	Papua New Guinea	16
43	Luxembourg	1.7	106	Nicaragua	4.7	171	Central African Republic	17
44	Nauru	1.7	107	Sudan	4.8	172	Lesotho	17
45	Uruguay	1.7	108	Panama	4.9	173	Burundi	19
46	Ireland	1.8	109	Sierra Leone	4.9	174	Yemen	19
47	Azerbaijan	1.9	110	Libya	5.0	175	Niger	20
48	Guyana	1.9	111	Romania	5.1	176	Somalia	22
49	San Marino	1.9	112	Kiribati	5.2	177	Haiti	24
50	Seychelles	1.9	113	Morocco	5.2	178	Angola	25
51	Tonga	1.9	114	Nigeria	5.2			
52	Bahamas	2.0	115	Tunisia	5.2	**BOTTOM 10**		
53	Belize	2.0	116	Iraq	5.4	179	Bangladesh	25
54	Bulgaria	2.2	117	Kyrgyzstan	5.4	180	Mali	25
55	Trinidad and Tobago	2.2	118	Macedonia	5.5	181	Guinea-Bissau	26
56	Western Samoa	2.2	119	Malawi	5.5	182	Guinea	28
57	Croatia	2.3	120	Sri Lanka	5.5	183	Mozambique	28
58	Israel	2.3	121	Armenia	5.6	184	Nepal	32
59	Oman	2.3	122	Togo	5.6	185	Bhutan	35
60	Poland	2.4	123	Uzbekistan	5.7	186	United Arab Emirates	44
61	Taiwan	2.4	124	China	5.8	187	Burkina	45
62	Greece	2.5	125	Thailand	5.8	188	Tanzania	48

Source: *UNESCO Statistical Yearbook*

272. PERSONS PER TELEVISION RECEIVER

Television is the youngest of the media, but its growth has been helped by the fact that it is the one with the most immediate visual and aural impact of any medium. But it still trails the radio in almost all countries. The cost of television sets is a limiting factor, but mass production and economies of scale have helped manufacturers to bring down the retail price to a level lower than that of 20 years ago. In almost all advanced countries television ownership has reached saturation, but in Africa and parts of Asia, it may take many more decades to reach that level. It is also noteworthy that in almost all countries, color television has displaced black and white sets common only a decade ago.

Rank	Country	Persons per Television Receiver
TOP 10		
1	United States	1.2
2	Japan	1.3
3	Oman	1.4
4	Monaco	1.5
5	Mexico	1.6
6	Slovakia	1.6
7	Canada	1.7
8	Denmark	1.9
9	Bermuda	2.0
10	France	2.0
UPPER MIDDLE		
11	Kuwait	2.0
12	Bahrain	2.1
13	Latvia	2.1
14	Australia	2.2
15	Norway	2.2
16	Antigua and Barbuda	2.3
17	Qatar	2.3
18	Spain	2.3
19	Sweden	2.3
20	Belgium	2.4
21	Hungary	2.4
22	Netherlands	2.4
23	Estonia	2.5
24	Bulgaria	2.7
25	Finland	2.7
26	Germany	2.7
27	Lebanon	2.7
28	Lithuania	2.7
29	Russia	2.7
30	Malta	2.8
31	Switzerland	2.8
32	Belarus	2.9
33	San Marino	2.9
34	United Kingdom	2.9
35	Austria	3.0
36	Liechtenstein	3.0
37	Taiwan	3.0
38	Ukraine	3.0
39	Grenada	3.1
40	Czech Republic	3.2
41	New Zealand	3.2
42	Cyprus	3.4
43	Italy	3.4
44	Iceland	3.5
45	Ireland	3.5
46	Israel	3.5
47	Kazakhstan	3.5
48	Moldova	3.5
49	Saudi Arabia	3.7
50	Barbados	3.8
51	Poland	3.9
52	Brunei	4.0
53	Luxembourg	4.0
54	St. Kitts and Nevis	4.2

Rank	Country	Persons per Television Receiver
55	Korea, South	4.3
56	Cuba	4.4
57	Puerto Rico	4.4
58	Slovenia	4.4
59	Bahamas	4.5
60	Greece	4.6
61	Azerbaijan	4.7
62	Argentina	4.8
63	Armenia	5.0
64	Trinidad and Tobago	5.0
65	Kyrgyzstan	5.1
66	China	5.2
67	Jamaica	5.2
68	Uruguay	5.2
69	Brazil	5.3
70	Turkmenistan	5.3
71	Romania	5.7
72	St. Lucia	5.7
73	Seychelles	5.7
74	Turkey	5.8
75	Venezuela	5.8
76	Laos	5.9
LOWER MIDDLE		
77	Portugal	5.9
78	Croatia	6.0
79	Macedonia	6.1
80	Sao Tome e Principe	6.1
81	St. Vincent	6.2
82	Colombia	6.3
83	Tajikistan	6.3
84	Uzbekistan	6.3
85	Yugoslavia	6.4
86	Bosnia & Herzegovina	6.9
87	Chile	7.0
88	Mauritius	7.1
89	Belize	7.6
90	Singapore	8.2
91	Iran	8.5
92	Andorra	8.6
93	Costa Rica	9.6
94	Malaysia	9.8
95	Philippines	9.8
96	Suriname	9.8
97	Libya	10
98	Dominican Republic	11
99	El Salvador	11
100	Korea, North	11
101	Peru	11
102	Egypt	12
103	South Africa	12
104	Albania	13
105	Ecuador	13
106	Panama	13
107	United Arab Emirates	13
108	Algeria	14
109	Dominica	14

Rank	Country	Persons per Television Receiver
110	Paraguay	14
111	Tunisia	14
112	Nigeria	15
113	Jordan	16
114	Indonesia	17
115	Cote d'Ivoire	18.0
116	Thailand	18
117	Mongolia	19
118	Iraq	20
119	Syria	20
120	Nicaragua	21
121	Guatemala	22
122	Morocco	22
123	Sri Lanka	26
124	Togo	27
125	Gabon	28
126	Vietnam	29
127	Western Samoa	32
128	Honduras	33
129	Tonga	33
130	Djibouti	34
131	Lesotho	40
132	Namibia	41
133	India	46
134	Myanmar (Burma)	46
135	Zambia	46
136	Guyana	49
137	Maldives	51
138	Liberia	53
139	Ghana	64
140	Cape Verde	65
141	Pakistan	66
142	Swaziland	68
143	Fiji	73
144	Nepal	79
145	Zimbabwe	80
146	Guinea	100
147	Botswana	106
148	Kenya	106
149	Sudan	109
150	Madagascar	110
151	Yemen	126
152	Senegal	132
153	Cambodia	134
154	Bolivia	144
155	Vanuatu	148
156	Equatorial Guinea	154
157	Uganda	158
158	Afghanistan	169
159	Sierra Leone	176
160	Burkina	218
161	Angola	220
162	Haiti	260
163	Benin	262
164	Congo	296
165	Bangladesh	336
166	Tanzania	341

Rank	Country	Persons per Television Receiver	Rank	Country	Persons per Television Receiver	Rank	Country	Persons per Television Receiver
167	Niger	352	**BOTTOM 10**			176	Mauritania	1,881
168	Central African Republic	409	171	Ethiopia	534	177	Zaire	1,934
169	Papua New Guinea	421	172	Cameroon	858	178	Somalia	2,270
170	Mozambique	495	173	Mali	882	179	Comoros	2,310
			174	Chad	1,050	180	Bhutan	6,180
			175	Burundi	1,289			

Source: *UNESCO Statistical Yearbook*

273. ANNUAL MOVIE ATTENDANCE PER CAPITA

When television became the premier form of information and entertainment in the 1950s, it was widely feared that it will sound the deathknell of the movie industry. For some decades, the alarm was proved right as many old gaudy movie theaters were torn down and movie attendance fell to its lowest levels since 1900. The only exception was in developing countries like India, where television had not made much headway. But in the 1980s and 1990s, movies have made a comeback even in developed countries. The industry was also helped by the insatiable demand for older movies as well as new ones on video and or television.

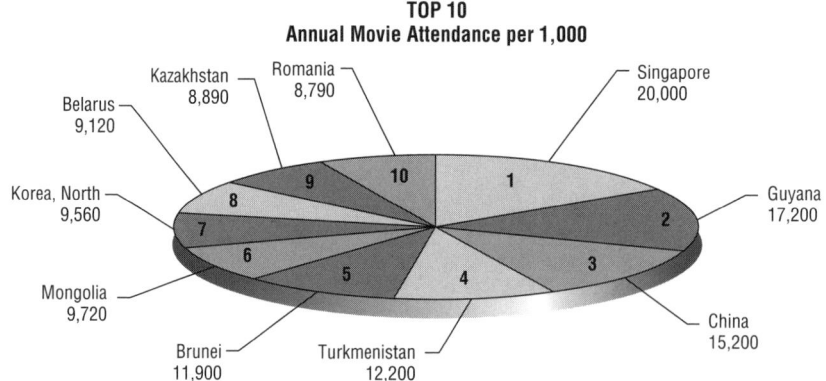

TOP 10
Annual Movie Attendance per 1,000

Kazakhstan 8,890 — Romania 8,790 — Singapore 20,000 — Belarus 9,120 — Korea, North 9,560 — Guyana 17,200 — Mongolia 9,720 — China 15,200 — Brunei 11,900 — Turkmenistan 12,200

Rank	Country	Annual Movie Attendance per 1,000	Rank	Country	Annual Movie Attendance per 1,000	Rank	Country	Annual Movie Attendance per 1,000
UPPER MIDDLE			34	Bulgaria	2,860	56	Germany	1,500
11	Georgia	8,680	35	Cuba	2,790	57	Finland	1,450
12	Uganda	8,000	36	Canada	2,750	58	Slovenia	1,440
13	Latvia	7,340	37	Slovakia	2,630	59	Austria	1,340
14	Kyrgyzstan	7,190	38	Norway	2,510	60	Luxembourg	1,330
15	Moldova	6,880	39	Malaysia	2,400	61	Korea, South	1,300
16	Uzbekistan	6,010	40	Australia	2,360	62	San Marino	1,300
17	Tajikistan	5,520	41	Sri Lanka	2,270	63	Colombia	1,290
18	Iceland	5,160	42	Switzerland	2,270	64	Morocco	1,240
19	Russia	5,040	43	Albania	2,160	65	Bahrain	1,230
20	India	5,010	44	Uruguay	2,110	66	Iran	1,200
21	Estonia	4,640	45	Spain	2,080	67	Japan	1,170
22	Mexico	4,500	46	Hungary	2,070	68	Macedonia	1,060
23	Azerbaijan	4,290	47	France	2,060	69	Bosnia & Herzegovina	1,000
24	Armenia	4,020				70	Netherlands	975
25	United States	3,890	**LOWER MIDDLE**			71	Portugal	974
26	Vietnam	3,760	48	Peru	1,910	72	Guatemala	910
27	Lithuania	3,690	49	Sweden	1,810	73	Algeria	880
28	Bermuda	3,630	50	Denmark	1,790	74	Malta	860
29	Czech Republic	3,530	51	United Kingdom	1,770	75	Guinea	780
30	Monaco	3,390	52	Nicaragua	1,750	76	Indonesia	770
31	Ireland	3,290	53	Belgium	1,630	77	Chile	740
32	Taiwan	3,200	54	Venezuela	1,590	78	Burkina	720
33	Bangladesh	3,000	55	Italy	1,550	79	Qatar	710

Rank	Country	Annual Movie Attendance per 1,000
80	Zimbabwe	690
81	Brazil	680
82	South Africa	680
83	Bolivia	650
84	Ecuador	650
85	Croatia	640
86	Sudan	600
87	Syria	590
88	Argentina	550
89	Mauritius	550
90	Poland	550

Rank	Country	Annual Movie Attendance per 1,000
91	Egypt	520
92	Kuwait	480
93	Haiti	380
94	Angola	370
95	Ghana	340
96	Benin	330
97	Mozambique	300
98	Turkey	287
99	Yugoslavia	260

Rank	Country	Annual Movie Attendance per 1,000
BOTTOM 10		
100	Pakistan	230
101	Laos	229
102	Jordan	200
103	Gabon	95
104	Costa Rica	76
105	Tanzania	72
106	Rwanda	56
107	Nigeria	51
108	Madagascar	32
109	Burundi	24

Source: *UNESCO Statistical Yearbook*

274. FIXED CINEMAS

The term *fixed cinema* refers to an indoor cinema with a permanent fixed roof as distinguished from mobile units and drive-ins. Only cinemas regularly used for showing films of 16 or 35 mm and over are included in the data.

Rank	Country	Fixed Cinemas
TOP 10		
1	United States	21,048
2	India	12,732
3	China	12,325
4	France	6,742
5	Germany	5,316
6	Italy	4,143
7	Bulgaria	3,261
8	Hungary	3,137
9	Czech Republic	2,634
10	Spain	2,234
UPPER MIDDLE		
11	Mexico	2,226
12	Japan	2,059
13	Indonesia	1,833
14	Poland	1,728
15	Brazil	1,397
16	United Kingdom	1,226
17	Korea, North	1,178
18	Sweden	1,112
19	Argentina	919
20	Yugoslavia	784
21	Bangladesh	781
22	Canada	715
23	Korea, South	673
24	Colombia	657
25	Romania	625
26	Taiwan	602
27	Thailand	577
28	Turkey	576
29	Cuba	535
30	Netherlands	445
31	Australia	444
32	Austria	444
33	Pakistan	444
34	Belgium	442
35	Venezuela	437

Rank	Country	Fixed Cinemas
36	Switzerland	431
37	Norway	426
38	Peru	425
39	Denmark	396
40	Portugal	358
41	Finland	328
LOWER MIDDLE		
42	Vietnam	322
43	Sri Lanka	313
44	Iran	294
45	Morocco	267
46	South Africa	260
47	Nigeria	240
48	Algeria	216
49	Egypt	169
50	Puerto Rico	165
51	Chile	162
52	Myanmar (Burma)	162
53	Syria	140
54	Malaysia	138
55	Nicaragua	127
56	Ireland	125
57	Uruguay	120
58	Ecuador	118
59	Guatemala	115
60	Costa Rica	104
61	Albania	103
62	Tunisia	81
63	El Salvador	79
64	Cameroon	69
65	Mozambique	60
66	Singapore	57
67	Sudan	56
68	Mongolia	51
69	Guyana	50
70	Ethiopia	46
71	Angola	44

Rank	Country	Fixed Cinemas
72	Madagascar	37
73	Mauritius	37
74	Afghanistan	34
75	Rwanda	34
76	Zimbabwe	32
77	Tanzania	30
78	Burkina	29
79	Guinea	29
80	Haiti	28
81	Oman	24
82	Iceland	19
83	Mauritania	19
84	Malta	18
85	Gabon	14
86	Kuwait	12
87	St. Lucia	8
88	Benin	7
89	Brunei	7
90	Burundi	7
91	Ghana	7
92	Maldives	7
93	Grenada	6
BOTTOM 10		
94	San Marino	6
95	Bermuda	4
96	Guinea-Bissau	4
97	Qatar	4
98	Swaziland	4
99	Dominica	3
100	Monaco	3
101	St. Kitts and Nevis	3
102	St. Vincent	2
103	Vanuatu	1

Source: *UNESCO Statistical Yearbook*

Section

XXII

THE WORLD'S CITIES

The following rankings explore the world of cities. Large cities are virtually ministates; if the ranking of the most populous cities were to be superimposed on the ranking of the most populous countries, Mexico City would rank 64th, ahead of the majority of the countries of the world. The following rankings present the highest cities, the oldest cities, the largest cities and the most populous cities by the year 2000.

It is unfortunate that neither the United Nations nor any of the other international organizations has been interested in collecting data about cities; the International Statistical Institute at The Hague, the only body that ever tried to do so, never made much progress after the 1960s. The result is that interesting and reliable statistics about cities are sparse. The inclusion of this section is an effort to highlight the importance of cities as independent entities. Because of the nature of the data, there may be some structural dissimilarities between rankings in this section and those in the sections relating to countries. For climatic factors, see the rankings on the hottest, coldest and wettest places in the chapter on geography.

275. AVERAGE URBAN GROWTH RATE, 1995–2000

Like countries, cities grow at differing rates. However, larger cities generally tend to grow at slower rates than the smaller ones, because the former have already reached sizable population levels. Following this trend curve, some cities are already showing signs of saturation. Cities can expand horizontally and vertically only so long as they are still able to provide basic amenities and services to their inhabitants. Older cities like London, built some centuries ago, will continue to decline in population for much of the 21st century. Third World cities, however, will continue to grow but their inhabitants will suffer from severe lack of jobs, water and living space.

Rank	Country	Average Annual Growth Rate 1995–2000
TOP 10		
1	Lagos, Nigeria	4.9
2	Taegu, South Korea	4.7
3	Kinshasa, Zaire	4.5
4	Dhaka, Bangladesh	4.1
5	Poona, India	4.0
6	Salvador, Brazil	4.0
7	Tehran, Iran	4.0
8	Karachi, Pakistan	3.8
9	Bangalore, India	3.6
10	Lima, Peru	3.3
UPPER MIDDLE		
11	Sao Paulo, Brazil	3.3
12	Belo Horizonte, Brazil	3.2
13	Delhi, India	3.2
14	Lahore, Pakistan	3.2
15	Monterrey, Mexico	3.2
16	Bogota, Colombia	3.1
17	Mexico City, Mexico	3.1
18	Pusan, South Korea	3.1
19	Guadalajara, Mexico	3.0
20	Istanbul, Turkey	3.0
21	Porto Alegre, Brazil	3.0
22	Ankara, Turkey	2.9
23	Ahmadabad, India	2.8
24	Baghdad, Iraq	2.8

Rank	Country	Average Annual Growth Rate 1995–2000
25	Hyderabad, India	2.8
26	Jakarta, Indonesia	2.8
27	Seoul, South Korea	2.8
28	Bangkok, Thailand	2.6
29	Casablanca, Morocco	2.6
30	Taipei, Taiwan	2.6
LOWER MIDDLE		
31	Bombay, India	2.5
32	Kanpur, India	2.5
33	Manila, Philippines	2.5
34	Chongqing, China	2.4
35	Madras, India	2.4
36	Cairo, Egypt	2.3
37	Tashkent, Uzbekistan	2.2
38	Rio de Janeiro, Brazil	2.1
39	Ho Chi Minh City, Vietnam	2.0
40	Calcutta, India	1.8
41	Dallas, Texas, United States	1.8
42	Kiev, Ukraine	1.6
43	Rangoon, Burma	1.6
44	Santiago, Chile	1.6
45	Barcelona, Spain	1.5
46	Houston, Texas, United States	1.5
47	Madrid Spain	1.4
48	Vienna, Austria	1.4
49	Lisbon, Portugal	1.3

Rank	Country	Average Annual Growth Rate 1995–2000
50	Alexandria, Egypt	1.2
51	Surabaya, Indonesia	1.2
52	Buenos Aires, Argentina	1.1
53	Miami, Florida, United States	1.1
54	Nagoya, Japan	1.1
55	Athens, Greece	1.0
56	Chengdu, China	1.0
57	Harbin, China	1.0
58	Havana, Cuba	1.0
59	Shenyang, China	1.0
60	Tianjin, China	1.0
61	Tokyo-Yokohama, Japan	1.0
62	Wuhan, China	1.0
63	Guangzhou, China	0.9
64	Shanghai, China	0.9
65	Singapore, Singapore	0.7
66	Caracas, Venezuela	0.6
67	Los Angeles, California, United States	0.6
68	Moscow, Russia	0.6
69	Bucharest, Romania	0.5
70	Montreal, Quebec, Canada	0.5
71	Naples, Italy	0.5
72	San Francisco, California, United States	0.5
73	Sydney, Australia	0.5
74	Washington, D.C., United States	0.5
75	Beijing, China	0.4
76	Hong Kong, Hong Kong	0.4

Rank	Country	Average Annual Growth Rate 1995–2000
77	Osaka-Kobe-Kyoto, Japan	0.3
78	Rome, Italy	0.3
79	Budapest, Hungary	0.2
80	Melbourne, Australia	0.2
81	Milan, Italy	0.2

Rank	Country	Average Annual Growth Rate 1995–2000
BOTTOM 10		
82	St. Petersburg, Russia	0.2
83	Chicago, Illinois, United States	0.1
84	Paris, France	0.1
85	Toronto, Ontario, Canada	0
86	Greater Berlin, Germany	(0.1)

Rank	Country	Average Annual Growth Rate 1995–2000
87	Philadelphia, Pennsylvania, United States	(0.1)
88	Essen, Germany	(0.3)
89	Birmingham, United Kingdom	(0.5)
90	Manchester, United Kingdom	(0.6)
91	London, United Kingdom	(0.7)
92	Detroit, Michigan, United States[1]	(0.9)

Source: *1993 Statistical Abstract of the United States on CD-ROM*

276. URBAN POPULATION DENSITY

The average population density at the national level is about 400, but at the urban level it is over 40,000 per square mile. The growth in density takes place in most cases without any corresponding increase in the physical size of cities. Whereas U.S. cities generally are physically larger, many Asian cities are much smaller.

Hong Kong, which has the highest density, is built on land which does not allow any room for expansion and so is Singapore. As a result, some of these cities may be forced to build more and more highrises and skyscrapers to accommodate their ever increasing populations.

Rank	Country	Area (sq mi)	Population per sq mi
TOP 10			
1	New York, New York, United States	1,274	11,482
2	Los Angeles, California, United States	1,110	9,074
3	Tokyo-Yokohama, Japan	1,089	25,290
4	London, United Kingdom	874	10,490
5	Chicago, Illinois, United States	762	8,521
6	Essen, Germany	704	10,662
7	Buenos Aires, Argentina	535	21,950
8	Mexico City, Mexico	522	41,408
9	Osaka-Kobe-Kyoto, Japan	495	28,119
10	Philadelphia, Pennsylvania, United States	471	8,429
UPPER MIDDLE			
11	Detroit, Michigan, United States	468	6,175
12	Sao Paulo, Brazil	451	42,956
13	Miami, Florida, United States	448	7,862
14	Paris, France	432	19,883
15	San Francisco, California, United States	428	9,358
16	Dallas, Texas, United States	419	6,817
17	Moscow, Russia	379	27,773
18	Manchester, United Kingdom	357	11,159
19	Washington, D.C., United States	357	7,204
20	Milan, Italy	344	13,714
21	Seoul, South Korea	342	50,684
22	Sydney, Australia	338	10,437
23	Melbourne, Australia	327	8,763
24	Houston, Texas, United States	310	7,642
25	Nagoya, Japan	307	15,990
26	Boston, Massachusetts, United States	303	8,119
27	Greater Berlin, Germany	274	11,021
28	Rio de Janeiro, Brazil	260	46,190
29	Porto Alegre, Brazil	231	13,938
30	Birmingham, United Kingdom	223	9,763
31	Calcutta, India	209	58,073
32	Karachi, Pakistan	190	43,023
LOWER MIDDLE			
33	Manila, Philippines	188	56,141
34	Istanbul, Turkey	165	42,040
35	Montreal, Quebec, Canada	164	17,881
36	Toronto, Ontario, Canada	154	20,662
37	Beijing, China	151	38,354
38	St. Petersburg, Russia	139	33,415
39	Delhi, India	138	66,976
40	Taipei, Taiwan	138	50,173
41	Budapest, Hungary	138	16,696

Rank	Country	Area (sq mi)	Population per sq mi
42	Santiago, Chile	128	42,840
43	Lima, Peru	120	58,563
44	Athens, Greece	116	31,144
45	Madras, India	115	52,156
46	Tehran, Iran	112	90,198
47	Cairo, Egypt	104	99,726
48	Bangkok, Thailand	102	59,687
49	Baghdad, Iraq	97	44,924
50	Bombay, India	95	131,051
51	Hyderabad, India	88	43,031
52	Barcelona, Spain	87	48,521
53	Bogota, Colombia	79	78,173
54	Belo Horizonte, Brazil	79	49,625
55	Guangzhou, China	79	41,952
56	Shanghai, China	78	89,739
57	Guadalajara, Mexico	78	45,192
58	Singapore, Singapore	78	35,164
59	Monterrey, Mexico	77	40,057
60	Jakarta, Indonesia	76	134,014
61	Rome, Italy	69	43,889
62	Madrid Spain	66	69,344
63	Wuhan, China	65	49,700
64	Naples, Italy	62	48,324
65	Kiev, Ukraine	62	45,751
66	Lahore, Pakistan	57	78,500
67	Kinshasa, Zaire	57	70,130
68	Lagos, Nigeria	56	151,548
69	Ankara, Turkey	55	54,551
70	Pusan, South Korea	54	95,582
71	Caracas, Venezuela	54	60,133
72	Bucharest, Romania	52	41,834
73	Bangalore, India	50	101,604
74	Tianjin, China	49	99,121
75	Rangoon, Burma	47	61,198
BOTTOM 10			
76	Surabaya, Indonesia	43	77,382
77	Shenyang, China	39	110,848
78	Casablanca, Morocco	35	89,604
79	Alexandria, Egypt	35	85,180
80	Dhaka, Bangladesh	32	144,991
81	Ahmadabad, India	32	119,555
82	Ho Chi Minh City, Vietnam	31	120,164
83	Harbin, China	30	87,506
84	Chengdu, China	25	94,610
85	Hong Kong, Hong Kong	23	250,524

Source: *1993 Statistical Abstract of the United States on CD-ROM*

277. LARGEST CITIES

Cities historically have been compact physical units. The average size of European cities is about 50 square miles. The difficulty of maintaining roads and services has worked against any expansion. It is only with the advent of cars and mass transit that it became possible for cities to grow beyond their original limits. Thus cities became the nuclei of metropolises and the term "Greater" began to be applied to the larger cities. Some cities have tended to coalesce, creating corridor cities that may cover three or more hyphenated cities. These, in turn, breed edge cities or satellite cities, terms that have displaced the former word suburb, which has now fallen into disrepute.

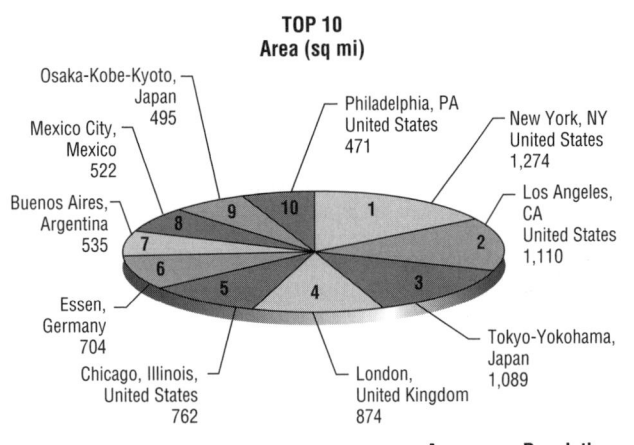

TOP 10 Area (sq mi)

Osaka-Kobe-Kyoto, Japan 495
Mexico City, Mexico 522
Buenos Aires, Argentina 535
Essen, Germany 704
Chicago, Illinois, United States 762
London, United Kingdom 874
Philadelphia, PA United States 471
New York, NY United States 1,274
Los Angeles, CA United States 1,110
Tokyo-Yokohama, Japan 1,089

TOP 10 Population per sq mi

Osaka-Kobe-Kyoto, Japan 28,119
Mexico City, Mexico 41,408
Buenos Aires, Argentina 21,950
Essen, Germany 10,662
Chicago, IL United States 8,521
London, United Kingdom 10,490
Philadelphia, PA United States 8,429
New York, NY United States 11,482
Los Angeles, CA United States 9,074
Tokyo-Yokohama, Japan 25,290

Rank	Country	Area (sq. mi)	Population per sq. mi
UPPER MIDDLE			
11	Detroit, Michigan, United States	468	6,175
12	Sao Paulo, Brazil	451	42,956
13	Miami, Florida, United States	448	7,862
14	Paris, France	432	19,883
15	San Francisco, California, United States	428	9,358
16	Dallas, Texas, United States	419	6,817
17	Moscow, Russia	379	27,773
18	Manchester, United Kingdom	357	11,159
19	Washington, D.C., United States	357	7,204
20	Milan, Italy	344	13,714
21	Seoul, South Korea	342	50,684
22	Sydney, Australia	338	10,437
23	Melbourne, Australia	327	8,763
24	Houston, Texas, United States	310	7,642
25	Nagoya, Japan	307	15,990
26	Boston, Massachusetts, United States	303	8,119
27	Greater Berlin, Germany	274	11,021
28	Rio de Janeiro, Brazil	260	46,190
29	Porto Alegre, Brazil	231	13,938
30	Birmingham, United Kingdom	223	9,763
31	Calcutta, India	209	58,073
32	Karachi, Pakistan	190	43,023
33	Manila, Philippines	188	56,141
34	Istanbul, Turkey	165	42,040
35	Montreal, Quebec, Canada	164	17,881
36	Toronto, Ontario, Canada	154	20,662
37	Beijing, China	151	38,354
LOWER MIDDLE			
38	St. Petersburg, Russia	139	33,415
39	Delhi, India	138	66,976
40	Taipei, Taiwan	138	50,173
41	Budapest, Hungary	138	16,696
42	Santiago, Chile	128	42,840
43	Lima, Peru	120	58,563
44	Athens, Greece	116	31,144
45	Madras, India	115	52,156
46	Tehran, Iran	112	90,198
47	Cairo, Egypt	104	99,726

Rank	Country	Area (sq. mi)	Population per sq. mi
48	Bangkok, Thailand	102	59,687
49	Baghdad, Iraq	97	44,924
50	Bombay, India	95	131,051
51	Hyderabad, India	88	43,031
52	Barcelona, Spain	87	48,521
53	Bogota, Colombia	79	78,173
54	Belo Horizonte, Brazil	79	49,625
55	Guangzhou, China	79	41,952
56	Shanghai, China	78	89,739
57	Guadalajara, Mexico	78	45,192
58	Singapore, Singapore	78	35,164
59	Monterrey, Mexico	77	40,057
60	Jakarta, Indonesia	76	134,014
61	Rome, Italy	69	43,889
62	Madrid Spain	66	69,344
63	Wuhan, China	65	49,700
64	Naples, Italy	62	48,324
65	Kiev, Ukraine	62	45,751
66	Lahore, Pakistan	57	78,500
67	Kinshasa, Zaire	57	70,130
68	Lagos, Nigeria	56	151,548
69	Ankara, Turkey	55	54,551
70	Pusan, South Korea	54	95,582
71	Caracas, Venezuela	54	60,133
72	Bucharest, Romania	52	41,834
73	Bangalore, India	50	101,604
74	Tianjin, China	49	99,121
75	Rangoon, Burma	47	61,198
BOTTOM 10			
76	Surabaya, Indonesia	43	77,382
77	Shenyang, China	39	110,848
78	Casablanca, Morocco	35	89,604
79	Alexandria, Egypt	35	85,180
80	Dhaka, Bangladesh	32	144,991
81	Ahmadabad, India	32	119,555
82	Ho Chi Minh City, Vietnam	31	120,614
83	Harbin, China	30	87,506
84	Chengdu, China	25	94,610
85	Hong Kong, Hong Kong	23	250,524

Source: *1993 Statistical Abstract of the United States on CD-ROM*

278. MOST POPULOUS CITIES 2000

By the year 2000, more people will be living in cities then in rural areas, thus reversing the historical dominance of rural areas in human settlements. By 2025, over two-thirds of the world's population will be urban dwellers compared with one-third as recently as 1975. Ninety percent of this growth will take place in the Third World. At the turn of the century, there were only 11 cities worldwide with over 1 million inhabitants. Now there are over 300. By 2025, according to the U.N. Habitat II Conference, there will be 570.

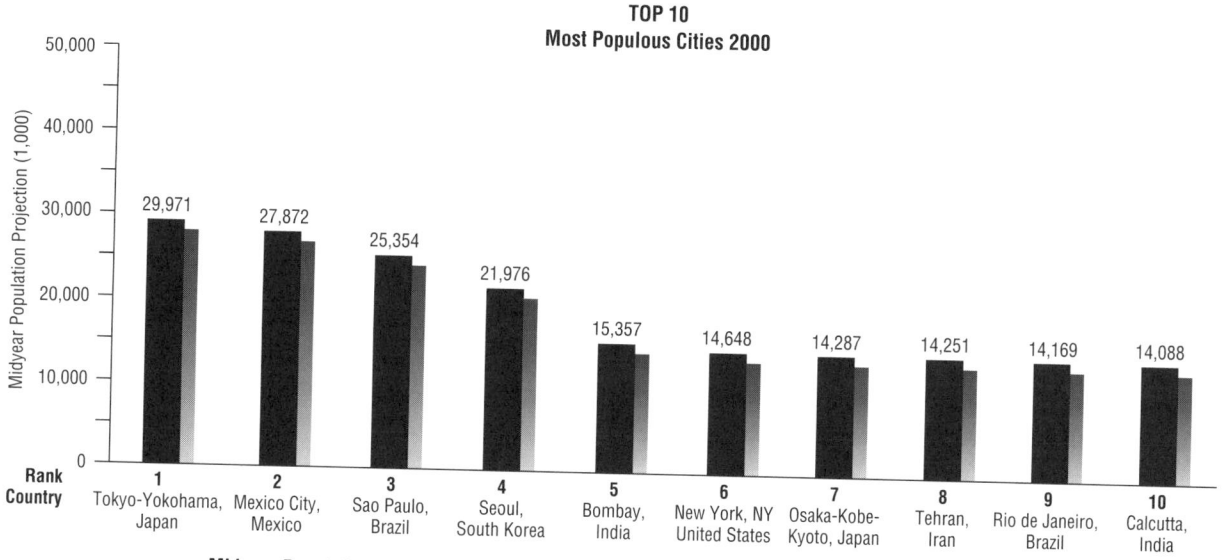

TOP 10 Most Populous Cities 2000

Rank	1	2	3	4	5	6	7	8	9	10
Population	29,971	27,872	25,354	21,976	15,357	14,648	14,287	14,251	14,169	14,088
Country	Tokyo-Yokohama, Japan	Mexico City, Mexico	Sao Paulo, Brazil	Seoul, South Korea	Bombay, India	New York, NY United States	Osaka-Kobe-Kyoto, Japan	Tehran, Iran	Rio de Janeiro, Brazil	Calcutta, India

Rank	Country	Midyear Population Projection (1,000)
UPPER MIDDLE		
11	Buenos Aires, Argentina	12,911
12	Manila, Philippines	12,846
13	Jakarta, Indonesia	12,804
14	Lagos, Nigeria	12,528
15	Cairo, Egypt	12,512
16	Delhi, India	11,849
17	Karachi, Pakistan	11,299
18	Moscow, Russia	11,121
19	Los Angeles, California, United States	10,714
20	Lima, Peru	9,241
21	Istanbul, Turkey	8,875
22	Paris, France	8,803
23	London, United Kingdom	8,574
24	Taipei, Taiwan	8,516
25	Bogota, Colombia	7,935
26	Bangkok, Thailand	7,587
27	Shanghai, China	7,540
28	Madras, India	7,384
29	Essen, Germany	7,239
30	Bangalore, India	6,764
31	Pusan, South Korea	6,700
32	Chicago, Illinois, United States	6,568
33	Dhaka, Bangladesh	6,492
34	Santiago, Chile	6,294
35	Beijing, China	5,993
36	Hong Kong, Hong Kong	5,956
37	Lahore, Pakistan	5,864
38	Kinshasa, Zaire	5,646
39	Nagoya, Japan	5,303

Rank	Country	Midyear Population Projection (1,000)
40	Tianjin, China	5,298
41	Baghdad, Iraq	5,239
42	Belo Horizonte, Brazil	5,125
LOWER MIDDLE		
43	Madrid Spain	5,104
44	Milan, Italy	4,839
45	Ahmadabad, India	4,837
46	Barcelona, Spain	4,834
47	Hyderabad, India	4,765
48	St. Petersburg, Russia	4,738
49	Shenyang, China	4,684
50	Ho Chi Minh City, Vietnam	4,481
51	Guadalajara, Mexico	4,451
52	San Francisco, California, United States	4,214
53	Porto Alegre, Brazil	4,109
54	Taegu, South Korea	4,051
55	Philadelphia, Pennsylvania, United States	3,979
56	Monterrey, Mexico	3,974
57	Miami, Florida, United States	3,894
58	A thens, Greece	3,866
59	Manchester, United Kingdom	3,827
60	Casablanca, Morocco	3,795
61	Ankara, Turkey	3,777
62	Sydney, Australia	3,708
63	Guangzhou, China	3,652
64	Poona, India	3,647
65	Surabaya, Indonesia	3,632
66	Wuhan, China	3,495
67	Caracas, Venezuela	3,435

Rank	Country	Midyear Population Projection (1,000)
68	Rangoon, Burma	3,332
69	Alexandria, Egypt	3,304
70	Toronto, Ontario, Canada	3,296
71	Salvador, Brazil	3,286
72	Dallas, Texas, United States	3,257
73	Kiev, Ukraine	3,237
74	Naples, Italy	3,134
75	Rome, Italy	3,129
76	Montreal, Quebec, Canada	3,071
77	Greater Berlin, Germany	3,006
78	Melbourne, Australia	2,968
79	Chongqing, China	2,961
80	Tashkent, Uzbekistan	2,947
81	Singapore, Singapore	2,913
82	Harbin, China	2,887
83	Detroit, Michigan, United States	2,735
84	Lisbon, Portugal	2,717
BOTTOM 10		
85	Washington, D.C., United States	2,707
86	Kanpur, India	2,673
87	Houston, Texas, United States	2,651
88	Vienna, Austria	2,647
89	Chengdu, China	2,591
90	Boston, Massachusetts, United States	2,485
91	Budapest, Hungary	2,335
92	Havana, Cuba	2,333
93	Bucharest, Romania	2,271
94	Birmingham, United Kingdom	2,078

Source: *1993 Statistical Abstract of the United States on CD-ROM*

279. URBANIZATION

Urbanization is a universal phenomenon; in some countries it has assumed alarming proportions, leading to the depletion of the rural population and the overcrowding of towns. However, urban statistics are impaired by serious limitations. The first question is at what point does a concentration of people become urban? The distinction between urban and rural areas is made in different ways in different countries. Urban status is granted to places with as few as 400 inhabitants in Albania, while in Austria the lower limit is 5,000 persons. In Bulgaria urban denotes places with urban status regardless of size, while in Israel it implies predominantly nonagricultural localities. In Sweden it is built-up areas with less than 200 meters between houses, in Peru populated centers with 100 or more occupied dwellings, in Iceland localities of 200 or more inhabitants, in Australia 250 or more dwellings of which at least 100 are occupied, in Senegal agglomerations of 15,000 or more inhabitants, in South Africa areas of more than 500 inhabitants if 100 of such inhabitants are white, in India places having a density of not less than 1,000 persons per square mile or 390 persons per square kilometer where at least three-fourths of the adult male population are employed in nonagricultural pursuits, in Yugoslavia localities of 15,000 or more inhabitants, and in Japan areas (called shis) having 50,000 or more inhabitants.

Other countries define towns not so much in terms of inhabitants but in terms of urban characteristics such as streets, plazas, water supply, sewerage systems and electric light. In still others, the distinction is based on administrative divisions with headquarters of civil divisions being gazetted as towns. The differences in definition are so bound up with historical, cultural and administrative considerations that it is difficult to discern a uniform pattern. Further, because these definitions change over time, they become inapplicable for statistical comparisons even within the same country. If the threshold of urbanization cannot be determined by size of population alone, it is more difficult to determine it on the basis of facilities of urban life. Many of the rural areas in the Untied States are relatively more modernized than the largest towns in Africa. Another potential source of error is the difficulty of estimating internal migration into the cities, which is changing the population balance in almost every country. Because of these shortcomings, the data presented in the following ranking should be used with caution and are useful only for attempting broad comparisons.

Rank	Country	Urban Population (%)	Rank	Country	Urban Population (%)	Rank	Country	Urban Population (%)
TOP 10			29	Cyprus	76.7	60	Poland	61.2
1	Bermuda	100.0	30	Canada	76.6	61	South Africa	60.3
2	Kuwait	100.0	31	New Zealand	75.9	62	Lebanon	60.1
3	Monaco	100.0	32	Brazil	75.5	63	Korea, North	59.8
4	Singapore	100.0	33	Spain	75.3	64	Switzerland	59.7
5	Belgium	96.6	34	United States	75.2	65	Jordan	59.5
6	Iceland	91.4	35	Norway	75.0	66	Brunei	59.4
7	San Marino	90.1	36	Taiwan	74.5	67	Turkey	59.0
8	United Kingdom	89.1	37	Korea, South	74.4	68	Macedonia	58.1
9	Netherlands	89.0	38	France	74.3	69	Bolivia	57.5
10	Bahrain	88.4	39	Russia	73.6	70	Iran	57.3
			40	Estonia	71.6	71	Kazakhstan	57.2
UPPER MIDDLE			41	Mexico	71.3	72	Mongolia	57.1
11	Qatar	88.0	42	Puerto Rico	71.2	73	Ireland	57.0
12	Italy	87.1	43	Latvia	71.1	74	Slovakia	56.8
13	Israel	86.9	44	Iraq	70.2	75	Georgia	55.7
14	Argentina	86.2	45	Trinidad and Tobago	69.1	76	Ecuador	55.4
15	Uruguay	86.2	46	Cuba	69.0	77	Romania	54.4
16	Luxembourg	85.9	47	Lithuania	68.0	78	Croatia	54.3
17	Australia	85.4	48	Armenia	67.8	79	Azerbaijan	53.8
18	Germany	85.3	49	Colombia	67.2	80	Panama	53.7
19	Malta	85.3	50	Bulgaria	67.1	81	Tunisia	52.8
20	Chile	85.1	51	Ukraine	66.9	82	Congo	52.0
21	Denmark	84.9	52	Andorra	66.2			
22	Sweden	84.3	53	Belarus	65.5	**LOWER MIDDLE**		
23	Venezuela	84.0	54	Peru	64.9	83	Dominican Republic	52.0
24	Djibouti	80.7	55	Austria	64.5	84	Malaysia	50.6
25	Finland	79.7	56	Libya	64.5	85	Paraguay	50.5
26	Japan	77.4	57	Bahamas	64.3	86	Jamaica	50.2
27	Saudi Arabia	77.3	58	Greece	62.5	87	Algeria	49.7
28	United Arab Emirates	76.9	59	Hungary	61.8	88	St. Kitts and Nevis	48.9

Rank	Country	Urban Population (%)	Rank	Country	Urban Population (%)	Rank	Country	Urban Population (%)
89	Slovenia	48.9	122	Albania	35.7	155	Madagascar	21.9
90	Philippines	48.6	123	Seychelles	35.5	156	Sri Lanka	21.5
91	St. Lucia	48.4	124	Nigeria	35.2	157	Gambia	21.2
92	Nicaragua	48.0	125	Kiribati	34.8	158	Haiti	20.6
93	Belize	47.5	126	Guatemala	34.3	159	Vietnam	20.1
94	Syria	47.1	127	Namibia	32.8	160	Western Samoa	20.1
95	Moldova	46.9	128	Tanzania	32.8	161	Thailand	18.7
96	Yugoslavia	46.8	129	Tajikstan	32.6	162	Laos	18.6
97	Gabon	45.7	130	Grenada	32.2	163	Vanuatu	17.7
98	Turkmenistan	45.4	131	Antigua and Barbuda	32.0	164	Bangladesh	16.4
99	Cape Verde	44.8	132	Ghana	32.0	165	Lesotho	16.0
100	Suriname	44.8	133	Sierra Leone	31.8	166	Solomon Islands	15.7
101	El Salvador	44.4	134	Indonesia	30.9	167	Niger	15.3
102	Costa Rica	43.9	135	Tonga	30.7	168	Papua New Guinea	15.2
103	Egypt	43.9	136	Guyana	30.5	169	Togo	15.2
104	Honduras	43.7	137	Chad	30.0	170	Afghanistan	15.1
105	Morocco	42.7	138	Portugal	29.7	171	Eritrea	15.1
106	Zambia	42.0	139	Pakistan	28.3	172	Angola	14.2
107	Uzbekistan	40.7	140	Equatorial Guinea	28.2	173	Guinea-Bissau	14.0
108	Sao Tome e Principe	40.5	141	China	26.4	174	Mozambique	13.2
109	Mauritius	39.3	142	Guinea	26.0	175	Burkina	11.7
110	Mauritania	39.1	143	Maldives	25.9			
111	Cote d'Ivoire	39.0	144	India	25.7	**BOTTOM 10**		
112	Liberia	38.8	145	Somalia	25.7	176	Uganda	11.3
113	Fiji	38.7	146	St. Vincent	25.4	177	Malawi	10.7
114	Senegal	38.6	147	Myanmar (Burma)	24.6	178	Oman	10.6
115	Cameroon	38.3	148	Botswana	24.0	179	Cambodia	10.3
116	Kyrgyzstan	38.2	149	Kenya	23.9	180	Yemen	10.2
117	Barbados	37.9	150	Comoros	23.6	181	Ethiopia	9.9
118	Benin	37.7	151	Zimbabwe	23.2	182	Nepal	9.6
119	Zaire	36.6	152	Swaziland	23.0	183	Burundi	6.3
120	Central African Republic	36.5	153	Sudan	22.8	184	Rwanda	5.4
121	Bosnia & Herzegovina	36.2	154	Mali	22.5	185	Bhutan	5.3
					22.0			

Source: *Demographic Yearbook*

280. CITY POPULATION

The following table ranks 94 cities in the world with populations of over one million in 1995. Except in a few cases where only the figures for the combined populations of the cities and the suburbs (variously called metropolitan areas or urban agglomerations) are available, the figures relate to the cities proper.

What is most significant about urban size is the vulnerability of larger units to disaster. At some stage, every city reaches a critical mass, making it more efficient than any rural settlement; but when it begins to grow beyond this optimal stage, it begins to slowly implode, creating massive economic problems, such as overcrowding and unemployment, and also psy-chological problems, often leading to the breakup of the family and even of the human personality. Urbanologists have called this process Calcuttaization, after the Indian city, cited as the classic case of city disintegrating as a result of overgrowth.

A further element of vulnerability is introduced in the West and in Russia, where the larger the city, the greater its vulnerability to military attack. In almost every scenario of nuclear war, the cities are destroyed first. Between implosion through over-growth and explosion as result of nuclear attack, each city has to devise an intelligent strategy for survival.

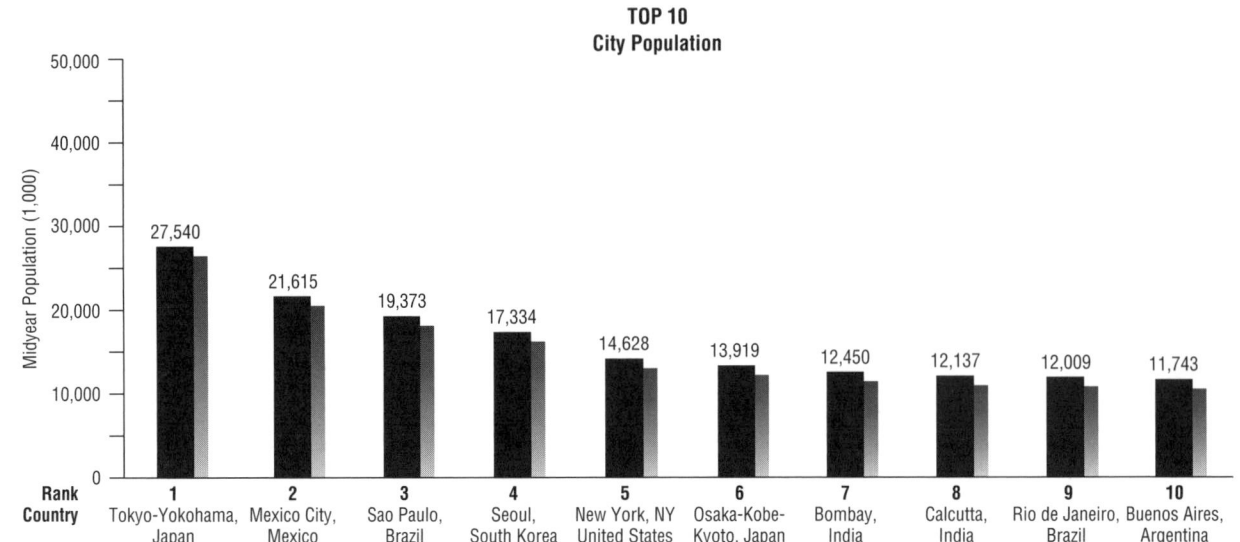

TOP 10
City Population

Rank	Country	Midyear Population (1,000)
1	Tokyo-Yokohama, Japan	27,540
2	Mexico City, Mexico	21,615
3	Sao Paulo, Brazil	19,373
4	Seoul, South Korea	17,334
5	New York, NY United States	14,628
6	Osaka-Kobe-Kyoto, Japan	13,919
7	Bombay, India	12,450
8	Calcutta, India	12,137
9	Rio de Janeiro, Brazil	12,009
10	Buenos Aires, Argentina	11,743

Rank	Country	Population (1,000)
UPPER MIDDLE		
11	Manila, Philippines	10,554
12	Moscow, Russia	10,526
13	Cairo, Egypt	10,372
14	Jakarta, Indonesia	10,185
15	Tehran, Iran	10,102
16	Los Angeles, California, United States	10,072
17	Delhi, India	9,243
18	London, United Kingdom	9,168
19	Paris, France	8,589
20	Lagos, Nigeria	8,487
21	Karachi, Pakistan	8,174
22	Essen, Germany	7,506
23	Lima, Peru	7,028
24	Shanghai, China	7,000
25	Istanbul, Turkey	6,937
26	Taipei, Taiwan	6,924
27	Chicago, Illinois, United States	6,493
28	Bogota, Colombia	6,176
29	Bangkok, Thailand	6,088
30	Madras, India	5,998
31	Beijing, China	5,791
32	Hong Kong, Hong Kong	5,762
33	Santiago, Chile	5,484
34	Pusan, South Korea	5,161
35	Bangalore, India	5,080
36	Nagoya, Japan	4,909
37	Tianjin, China	4,857
38	Milan, Italy	4,718
39	St. Petersburg, Russia	4,645

Rank	Country	Population (1,000)
40	Dhaka, Bangladesh	4,640
41	Madrid Spain	4,577
42	Lahore, Pakistan	4,475
LOWER MIDDLE		
43	Baghdad, Iraq	4,358
44	Shenyang, China	4,323
45	Barcelona, Spain	4,221
46	San Francisco, California, United States	4,005
47	Kinshasa, Zaire	3,997
48	Manchester, United Kingdom	3,984
49	Philadelphia, Pennsylvania, United States	3,970
50	Belo Horizonte, Brazil	3,920
51	Ahmadabad, India	3,826
52	Hyderabad, India	3,787
53	Ho Chi Minh City, Vietnam	3,725
54	Athens, Greece	3,613
55	Sydney, Australia	3,528
56	Guadalajara, Mexico	3,525
57	Miami, Florida, United States	3,522
58	Surabaya, Indonesia	3,327
59	Guangzhou, China	3,314
60	Caracas, Venezuela	3,247
61	Wuhan, China	3,231
62	Porto Alegre, Brazil	3,220
63	Toronto, Ontario, Canada	3,182
64	Casablanca, Morocco	3,136
65	Monterrey, Mexico	3,084
66	Rome, Italy	3,028
67	Greater Berlin, Germany	3,020

Rank	Country	Population (1,000)
68	Ankara, Turkey	3,000
69	Naples, Italy	2,996
70	Alexandria, Egypt	2,981
71	Montreal, Quebec, Canada	2,933
72	Detroit, Michigan, United States[1]	2,890
73	Rangoon, Burma	2,876
74	Melbourne, Australia	2,865
75	Dallas, Texas, United States	2,856
76	Kiev, Ukraine	2,837
77	Taegu, South Korea	2,837
78	Singapore, Singapore	2,743
79	Harbin, China	2,625
80	Poona, India	2,617
81	Washington, D.C., United States	2,572
82	Lisbon, Portugal	2,505
83	Chongqing, China	2,468
84	Tashkent, Uzbekistan	2,461
BOTTOM 10		
85	Boston, Massachusetts, United States	2,460
86	Vienna, Austria	2,392
87	Houston, Texas, United States	2,369
88	Salvador, Brazil	2,366
89	Chengdu, China	2,365
90	Budapest, Hungary	2,304
91	Kanpur, India	2,184
92	Birmingham, United Kingdom	2,177
93	Bucharest, Romania	2,175
94	Havana, Cuba	2,152

Source: *1993 Statistical Abstract of the United States on CD-ROM*

281. AGE OF CITIES

Urban settlements are older than nations; the oldest are believed to date as far back as the 16th century before Christ. Many of them were essentially riparian settlements, clustered around the great river valleys, such as the Nile, the Indus, the Yangtze and the Tigris-Euphrates. Most of them were small city-states, and modern nations may properly be considered as having developed from them. Even where a nation became large in terms of size or land area, the city remained the focus of all political and economic activities, serv-ing as the core and magnet of its social life and the showpiece of its culture. To the rest of the world, the city represented its nation, and this tradition survives in the modern usage of a city, such as Washington, Moscow or Beijing, as a synonym for its respective nations. Unlike nations, cities never truly die out; Jerusalem was virtually razed to the ground by Emperor Titus, and Dresden was bombed out, yet both have survived. Cities are thus one of the most indestructible of human institutions.

A: OLD WORLD

Rank	Country	Age of Cities (years)
TOP 10		
1	Gaziantep, Turkey	Over 5,600
2	Jerusalem, Israel	Over 5,000
3	Kirkuk, Iraq	Over 5,000
4	Zurich, Switzerland	Over 5,000
5	Konya, Turkey	Over 4,600
6	Giza, Egypt	Over 4,568
7	Sian, Shensi, China	4,200
8	Asyut, Egypt	Over 4,160
9	Luxor, Egypt	Over 4,160
10	Lisbon, Portugal	Over 4,000
UPPER MIDDLE		
11	Porto, Portugal	Over 4,000
12	Shaohing, Chekiang, China	4,000
13	Loyang, Honan, China	Over 3,900
14	Ankara, Turkey	Over 3,700
15	Changchih, Shansi, China	Over 3,600
16	Beirut, Lebanon	Over 3,500
17	Liayang, China	Over 3,500
18	Tangier, Morocco	Over 3,500
19	Tel Aviv, Israel	Over 3,470
20	Gaza, Israel	Over 3,450
21	Damascus, Syria	Over 3,400
22	Athens, Greece	Over 3,300
23	La Coruna, Spain	Over 3,200
24	Malaga, Spain	Over 3,200
25	Varanasi, India	Over 3,200
26	Pyongyang, North Korea	Over 3,120
27	Beijing, China	Over 3,100
28	Cadiz, Spain	Over 3,100
29	Hamadan, Iran	Over 3,100
30	Izmir, Turkey	Over 3,100
31	Aleppo, Syria	Over 3,000
32	Changchow, China	Over 3,000
33	Chengchow, Honan, China	Over 3,000
34	Foochow, China	Over 3,000
35	Hofei, China	Over 3,000
36	Metz, France	Over 3,000
37	Nanchung, China	Over 3,000
38	Nanning, China	Over 3,000
39	Pisa, Italy	Over 3,000
40	Rome, Italy	Over 3,000
41	Tatung, China	Over 3,000
42	Canton, China	Over 2,900
43	Toulon, France	Over 2,800
44	Syracuse, Italy	Over 2,717
45	Adana, Turkey	Over 2,700
46	Cannes, France	Over 2,700

Rank	Country	Age of Cities (years)
47	Catania, Italy	Over 2,700
48	Cordova, Spain	Over 2,700
49	Luca, Italy	Over 2,700
50	Messina, Italy	Over 2,700
51	Palermo, Italy	Over 2,700
52	Ravenna, Italy	Over 2,700
53	Reggio de Calabria, Italy	Over 2,700
54	Trebizond, Turkey	Over 2,700
55	Tripoli, Libya	Over 2,700
56	Taranto, Italy	Over 2,690
57	Istanbul, Turkey	2,641
58	Aswan, Egypt	Over 2,600
59	Bengazi, Libya	Over 2,600
60	Constanta, Rumania	Over 2,600
61	Hengyang, China	Over 2,600
62	Huelva, Spain	Over 2,600
63	Jerez de la Frontera, Spain	Over 2,600
64	Kaifeng, China	Over 2,600
65	Osaka, Japan	Over 2,600
66	Seville, Spain	Over 2,600
67	Shaoyang, China	Over 2,600
68	Suchow, China	Over 2,600
69	Terni, Italy	Over 2,600
70	Tripoli, Lebanon	Over 2,600
71	Vigo, Spain	Over 2,600
72	Yangchow, China	Over 2,600
73	Yangon, Myanmar	Over 2,580
LOWER MIDDLE		
74	Marseilles, France	Over 2,550
75	Besancon, France	Over 2,500
76	Brescia, Italy	Over 2,500
77	Bristol, England	Over 2,500
78	Colombo, Sri Lanka	Over 2,500
79	Gaya, India	Over 2,500
80	Kerch, Russia	Over 2,500
81	Kutaisi, Russia	Over 2,500
82	Mathura, India	Over 2,500
83	Monaco	Over 2,500
84	Naples, Italy	Over 2,500
85	Patna, India	Over 2,500
86	Perugia, Italy	Over 2,500
87	Samsun, Turkey	Over 2,500
88	Sialkot, Pakistan	Over 2,500
89	Soochow, China	Over 2,500
90	Stara Zagora, Bulgaria	Over 2,500
91	Tarragona, Spain	Over 2,500
92	Varna, Bulgaria	Over 2,500
93	Cagliari, Italy	Over 2,450

Rank	Country	Age of Cities (years)
94	Bergamo, Italy	Over 2,400
95	Bologna, Italy	Over 2,400
96	Genoa, Italy	Over 2,400
97	Granada, Spain	Over 2,400
98	Isfahan, Iran	Over 2,400
99	Le Mans, France	Over 2,400
100	Lerida, Spain	Over 2,400
101	Madurai, India	Over 2,400
102	Mainz, Germany	Over 2,400
103	Mantua, Italy	Over 2,400
104	Modena, Italy	Over 2,400
105	Monza, Italy	Over 2,400
106	Neuss, Germany	Over 2,400
107	Nice, France	Over 2,400
108	Omiya, Japan	Over 2,400
109	Patras, Greece	Over 2,400
110	Piraeus, Greece	Over 2,400
111	Regensburg, Germany	Over 2,400
112	Salamanca, Spain	Over 2,400
113	Siena, Italy	Over 2,400
114	Tunis, Tunisia	Over 2,400
115	Alexandria, Egypt	2,315
116	Ancona, Italy	Over 2,300
117	Arezzo, Italy	Over 2,300
118	Constantine, Algeria	Over 2,300
119	Hantan, China	Over 2,300
120	Herat, Afghanistan	Over 2,300
121	Kabul, Afghanistan	Over 2,300
122	Kweilin, China	Over 2,300
123	Milan, Italy	Over 2,300
124	Novara, Italy	Over 2,300
125	Rimini, Italy	Over 2,300
126	Samarkand, Uzbekistan	Over 2,300
127	Trent, Italy	Over 2,300
128	Turin, Italy	Over 2,300
129	Vienna, Austria	Over 2,300
130	Plovdiv, Bulgaria	Over 2,250
131	Cosenza, Italy	Over 2,225
132	Antioch, Turkey	Over 2,200
133	Padua, Italy	Over 2,200
134	Salonika, Greece	Over 2,200
135	Sfax, Tunisia	Over 2,200
136	Rheims, France	Over 2,000
137	Toulouse, France	Over 2,000
138	Cairo, Egypt	Over 1,600
139	Annaba, Algeria	Over 1,200
140	Harar, Ethiopia	Over 1,200
141	Fez, Morocco	1,175
142	Mombasa, Kenya	Over 1,100

Rank	Country	Age of Cities (years)
143	Mogadishu, Somalia	1,075
144	Algiers, Algeria	Over 980
145	Meknes, Morocco	Over 980
146	Oran, Algeria	Over 900
147	Marrakesh, Morocco	Over 900
148	Zaria, Nigeria	Over 800
149	Rabat-Sale, Morocco	Over 800
150	Timbuktu, Mali	Over 800
151	Mansurah, Egypt	Over 760
152	Kano, Nigeria	Over 700

Rank	Country	Age of Cities (years)
153	Tanta, Egypt	Over 700
154	Funchal, Madeira Islands	Over 550
155	Las Palmas, Canary Islands	Over 505
156	Ouagadougou, Burkina	Over 500

BOTTOM 10

Rank	Country	Age of Cities (years)
157	Santa Cruz de Tenerife, Canary Islands	Over 490
158	Casablanca, Morocco	Over 468
159	Maputo, Mozambique	Over 440

Rank	Country	Age of Cities (years)
160	Suez, Egypt	Over 400
161	Luanda, Angola	Over 310
162	Accra, Ghana	Over 300
163	Iwo, Nigeria	Over 300
164	Niamey, Niger	Over 300
165	Porto-Novo, Benin	Over 300
166	Zanzibar, Tanzania	Over 300

Source: Library of Congress

B: NEW WORLD

Rank	Country	Age of Cities Founding Dates
TOP 10		
1	Quito, Ecuador	1000
2	Cuzco, Peru	1100
3	Toluca, Mexico	1120
4	Jalapa, Mexico	1313
5	Mexico City	1325
6	Guanajuato, Mexico	c1400
7	Arequipa, Peru	c1425
8	Queretaro, Mexico	1440
9	Orizaba, Mexico	1457
10	Oaxaca, Mexico	1486
UPPER MIDDLE		
11	Santo Domingo, Dominican Republic	1496
12	Santiago de los Caballeros, Dominican Republic	1504
13	Santiago de Cuba	1514
14	Havana, Cuba	1519
15	Cuernavaca, Mexico	c1521
16	Managua, Nicaragua	c1521
17	San Juan, Puerto Rico	1521
18	Tepic, Mexico	1524
19	San Salvador, El Salvador	1525
20	Willemstad, Netherlands Antilles	1527
21	Camaguey, Cuba	1528
22	Merida, Mexico	c1528
23	Taxco, Mexico	1529
24	San Miguel, El Salvador	1530
25	Lima, Peru	c1532
26	Puebla, Mexico	1532
27	Cartagena, Colombia	1533
28	Culiacan, Mexico	1533
29	Pachuca de Soto, Mexico	1534
30	Trujillo, Peru	1534
31	Olinda, Brazil	1535
32	Recife, Brazil	1535
33	Vitoria, Brazil	1535
34	Cali, Colombia	1536
35	San Pedro Sula, Honduras	1536
36	Santos, Brazil	1536
37	Uruapan del Progreso, Mexico	1536
38	Asuncion, Paraguay	1537
39	Callao, Peru	1537
40	Guayaquil, Ecuador	1537
41	Bogota, Colombia	1538
42		

Rank	Country	Age of Cities Founding Dates
43	Sucre, Bolivia	1538
44	Tallahassee, Florida	1539
45	Paramaribo, Suriname	1540
46	Mazatlan, Mexico	1541
47	Morelia, Mexico	1541
48	Santiago, Chile	1541
49	Guadalajara, Mexico	1542
50	Valparaiso, Chile	1544
51	Potosi, Bolivia	1545
52	Irapuato, Mexico	1547
53	La Paz, Bolivia	1548
LOWER MIDDLE		
54	Salvador, Brazil	1549
55	Acapulco, Mexico	1550
56	Concepcion, Chile	1550
57	Ibague, Colombia	1551
58	Santo Andre, Brazil	1551
59	Barquisimeto, Venezuela	1552
60	Sao Bernardo do Campo	1552
61	Sao Paulo, Brazil	1554
62	Valencia, Venezuela	1555
63	Guarulhos, Brazil	1560
64	Netzahualcoyotl, Mexico	c1560
65	Mendoza, Argentina	1561
66	San Juan, Argentina	1562
67	Durango, Mexico	1563
68	Niteroi, Brazil	1565
69	Rio de Janeiro, Brazil	1565
70	St. Augustine, Florida	1565
71	Caracas, Venezuela	1567
72	El Valle, Venezuela	1567
73	Nova Iguacu, Brazil	1567
74	Celaya, Mexico	1570
75	Maracaibo, Venezuela	1571
76	Cordoba, Argentina	1573
77	Santa Fe, Argentina	1573
78	Cochabamba, Bolivia	1574
79	Aguascalientes, Mexico	1575
80	Saltillo, Mexico	1575
81	Leon, Mexico	1576
82	San Luis Potosi, Mexico	1576
83	Santa Ana, El Salvador	c1576
84	Tegucigalpa, Honduras	1578
85	Monterrey, Mexico	c1579

Rank	Country	Age of Cities Founding Dates
86	Buenos Aires, Argentina	1580
87	Coatzacoalcos, Mexico	1580
88	Salta, Argentina	1582
89	St. John's, New Foundland	c1583
90	Joao Pessoa, Brazil	1585
91	Vina del Mar, Chile	1586
92	Corrientes, Argentina	1588
93	San Felix De Guyana, Venezuela	1590
94	Port of Spain, Trinidad & Tobago	c1595
95	Santa Cruz, Bolivia	1595
96	Villahermosa, Mexico	1596
97	Veracruz, Mexico	1599
98	Moron, Argentina	1600
99	Quebec, Canada	1608
100	Fortaleza, Brazil	1609
101	Santa Fe, New Mexico	1609
102	Hampton, Virginia	1610
103	Sao Luis, Brazil	1612
104	Belem, Brazil	1616
105	Medellin, Colombia	1616
106	Cordoba, Mexico	1617
107	Newport News, Virginia	1621
108	Bucaramanga, Colombia	1622
109	Albany, New York	1624
110	New York, New York	1624
111	Georgetown, Guyana	1625
112	Quincy, Massachusetts	1625
113	Salem, Massachusetts	1626
114	Bridgetown, Barbados	1628
115	Barranquilla, Colombia	1629
116	Jersey City, New Jersey	c1629
117	Lynn, Massachusetts	1629
118	Boston, Massachusetts	1630
BOTTOM 10		
119	Cambridge, Massachusetts	1630
120	Somerville, Massachusetts	1630
121	Williamsburg, Virginia	1633
122	Campos, Brazil	1634
123	Trois-Rivieres, Canada	1634
124	Waltham, Massachusetts	1634
125	Hartford, Connecticut	1635
126	Providence, Rhode Island	1636
127	Springfield, Massachusetts	1636
128	Belize	1638

Source: Library of Congress

282. HIGHEST CITIES

The following ranking lists cities by their elevation. Historically, human settlements were commonly established in the plains near rivers and sea outlets. These cities—all over 3,000 ft—therefore represent exceptions, and their origins and locations were generally determined by strategic rather than trade considerations.

Rank	Country	Elevation meters	feet
TOP 10			
1	Lhasa, Tibet	3,658	12,002
2	La Paz, Bolivia	3,658	12,001
3	Le Quiaca, Argentina	3,458	11,345
4	Cusco, Peru	3,312	10,866
5	Eismitte, Greenland	3,000	9,843
6	Ipiales, Colombia	2,950	9,680
7	Potervillos, Chile	2,850	9,350
8	Sucre, Bolivia	2,848	9,344
9	Quito, Ecuador	2,811	9,222
10	Toluca, Mexico	2,680	8,793
UPPER MIDDLE			
11	Cajamarca, Peru	2,640	8,662
12	Arequipa, Peru	2,579	8,460
13	Cochabamba, Bolivia	2,557	8,390
14	Bogota, Colombia	2,546	8,355
15	Cuenca, Ecuador	2,530	8,301
16	Addis Ababa, Ethiopia	2,450	8,038
17	Asmara, Ethiopia	2,325	7,628
18	Netzahualcoyotl, Mexico	2,278	7,474
19	Sining, China	2,244	7,363
20	Sana, Yemen Arab Republic	2,242	7,360
21	Mexico City, Mexico	2,237	7,340
22	Puebla, Mexico	2,162	7,094
23	Maniazales, Colombia	2,140	7,021
24	Santa Fe, N.M.	2,118	6,950
25	Erzurum, Turkey	1,951	6,402
26	Morelia, Mexico	1,941	6,368
27	Kunming, China	1,893	6,211
28	Durango, Mexico	1,889	6,198
29	Aguascalientes, Mexico	1,888	6,195
30	Leon, Mexico	1,888	6,195
31	San Luis Potosi, Mexico	1,877	6,158
32	Cheyenne, Wyo.	1,867	6,126
33	Colorado Springs, Colo.	1,823	5,980
34	Kabul, Afghanistan	1,815	5,955
35	Hamadan, Iran	1,775	5,824
36	Johannesburg, South Africa	1,753	5,750
37	Kokiu, China	1,740	5,709
38	Windhoek, Namibia	1,728	5,669
39	Irapuato, Mexico	1,724	5,656
40	Nova Lisboa, Angola	1,700	5,577
41	Queretaro, Mexico	1,685	5,528
42	Srinagar, India	1,663	5,458
43	Nairobi, Kenya	1,662	5,453
44	Germiston, South Africa	1,661	5,450

Rank	Country	Elevation meters	feet
45	Boulder, Colorado	1,655	5,450
46	Lakewood, Colorado	1,632	5,355
47	Iringa, Tanzania	1,624	5,330
48	Albuquerque, N.M.	1,619	5,311
49	Merida, Venezuela	1,613	5,293
50	Denver, Colorado	1,609	5,280
51	Saltillo, Mexico	1,599	5,246
52	Isphahan, Iran	1,596	5,238
53	Guadalajara, Mexico	1,583	5,194
54	Casper, Wyoming	1,561	5,123
55	Siakwan, China	1,560	5,118
56	Lanchow, China	1,556	5,105
LOWER MIDDLE			
57	Leninakan, Soviet Union	1,556	5,105
58	Oaxaca, Mexico	1,550	5,086
59	Cuerna Vaca, Mexico	1,542	5,059
60	Medellin, Colombia	1,541	5,056
61	Shiraz, Iran	1,539	5,049
62	Guatemala City, Guatemala	1,480	4,855
63	Salisbury, Zimbabwe	1,472	4,831
64	Vereeniging, South Africa	1,440	4,725
65	Pueblo, Colorado	1,430	4,690
66	Jalapa, Mexico	1,427	4,682
67	Bloemfontein, South Africa	1,426	4,678
68	Pereira, Colombia	1,424	4,672
69	Kashgar, China	1,411	4,629
70	Tamanrasset, Algeria	1,400	4,593
71	Provo, Utah	1,387	4,549
72	Kasama, Zambia	1,385	4,544
73	Antananarive, Madagascar	1,372	4,500
74	Pretoria, South Africa	1,369	4,491
75	Tabriz, Iran	1,362	4,469
76	Pocatello, Idaho	1,361	4,464
77	Chihuahua, Mexico	1,350	4,429
78	Katmandu, Nepal	1,348	4,423
79	Bulawayo, Zimbabwe	1,343	4,405
80	Reno, Nevada	1,342	4,404
81	Rezaiyah, Iran	1,330	4,364
82	Cangamba, Angola	1,320	4,331
83	Kermanshah, Iran	1,320	4,331
84	Kampala, Uganda	1,312	4,304
85	Ulan Btor, Mongolia	1,307	4,287
86	Salt Lake City, Utah	1,286	4,220
87	Orizaba, Mexico	1,284	4,213
88	Lusaka, Zambia	1,277	4,191
89	Ibague, Colombia	1,249	4,098

Rank	Country	Elevation meters	feet
90	Lubumbashi, Zaire	1,230	4,035
91	Sheridan, Wyo	1,208	3,964
92	Diredawa, Ethiopia	1,200	3,937
93	Teheran, Iran	1,200	3,937
94	Kimberley, South Africa	1,197	3,927
95	El Paso, Texas	1,194	3,918
96	Salta, Argentina	1,182	3,878
97	San Jose, Costa Rica	1,146	3,760
98	Torreon, Mexico	1,130	3,708
99	Amarillo, Texas	1,123	3,685
100	Yinchwan, China	1,111	3,645
101	Ngaoundere, Cameroon	1,097	3,601
102	Guarapuava, Brazil	1,095	3,592
103	Balovale, Zambia	1,090	3,577
104	Lira, Uganda	1,085	3,560
105	Les Escaldes, Andorra	1,080	3,543
106	Calgary, Canada	1,079	3,540
107	Kayseri, Turkey	1,071	3,514
108	Kweiyang, China	1,071	3,514
109	Blantyre, Malawi	1,067	3,501
110	Huhehot, China	1,062	3,484
111	Brasilia, Brazil	1,061	3,481
112	Kandahar, Afghanistan	1,055	3,462
113	Tatung, China	1,049	3,442
114	Cali, Colombia	1,046	3,432
115	Paotow, China	1,044	3,425
116	Caracas, Venezuela	1,042	3,418
117	Yenan, China	1,036	3,400
118	Konya Turkey	1,026	3,366
119	Great Falls, Montana	1,015	3,330
120	Tegucigalpa, Honduras	1,007	3,304
121	Keetmanshoop, Namibia	1,004	3,295
BOTTOM 10			
122	Meshed, Iran	985	3,232
123	Rapid City, S.D.	985	3,232
124	Lubbock, Texas	974	3,195
125	Missoula, Mont.	972	3,190
126	Zomba, Malawi	957	3,141
127	Billings, Mont.	951	3,120
128	Curitiba, Brazil	950	3,117
129	Bucaramanga, Colombia	925	3,035
130	Herat, Afghanistan	922	3,025
131	Bangalore, India	921	3,021
132	Tepic, Mexico	915	3,002

Source: Library of Congress

Section
XXIII

CULTURE

This chapter is a mixed grab bag but its emphasis is on culture.

283. NOBEL PRIZE WINNERS

During the first century of its existence, the Nobel Prize has been acknowledged as the most prestigious and sought-after of all awards for human achievement. It is not only the ultimate accolade but also the most publicized. The following list ranks countries by the number of Nobel laureates up to 1995. Nationality is determined by domicile at the time of receipt of the award.

Rank	Country	Nobel Prize Winners
TOP 10		
1	United States	238
2	United Kingdom	87
3	Germany	70
4	France	50
5	Sweden	27
6	Switzerland	17
7	Russia	15
8	Netherlands	12
9	Denmark	11
10	Italy	10
UPPER MIDDLE		
11	Austria	9
12	Canada	9
13	Norway	8

Rank	Country	Nobel Prize Winners
14	Belgium	7
15	Japan	7
16	South Africa	5
17	Spain	5
18	Argentina	4
19	Ireland	4
20	Israel	4
21	Australia	3
22	India	3
23	Chile	2
24	Czech Republic	2
25	Egypt	2
26	Finland	2
27	Greece	2
28	Hungary	2
29	Mexico	2

Rank	Country	Nobel Prize Winners
30	Poland	2
31	Colombia	1
32	Costa Rica	1
33	Guatemala	1
BOTTOM 10		
34	Iceland	1
35	Myanmar (Burma)	1
36	Nigeria	1
37	Pakistan	1
38	Portugal	1
39	Puerto Rico	1
40	Tibet	1
41	Vietnam	1
42	West Indies	1
43	Yugoslavia	1

Source: *World Almanac*

284. MUSIC SALES

Music sales are affected by a number of factors, such as the extent and intensity of the youth culture and the amount of leisure available to adults and children. The ranking reflects only sales of legitimate music. As in the case of books, piracy has made heavy inroads into music sales worldwide. Music sales are also affected by broadcast music, and the royalties paid by broadcasting stations are not included in this ranking.

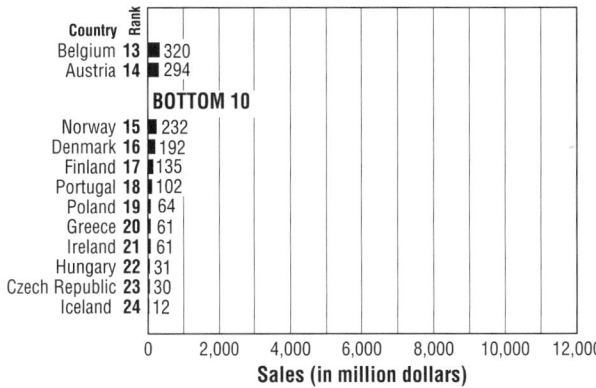

Source: "Music Is the Sound of Money." The European, 12-18 November 1993, p. 25. Primary source: International Federation of the Phonographic Industry.

285. THEATERS

Few theaters and performing arts buildings are being built today, but in the first five or six decades of this century, they were built on an unprecedented scale, and on the busiest thoroughfares of every city, some of them ornate and opulent masterpieces of architecture. The following ranking takes a look at their number in reporting countries.

Rank	Country	Performing Arts Facilities	Rank	Country	Performing Arts Facilities	Rank	Country	Performing Arts Facilities
TOP 10			19	Bulgaria	67	38	Chile	20
1	China	1,756	20	South Africa	51	39	Iran	19
2	Japan	543	21	Finland	50	40	United Arab Emirates	18
3	Canada	476	22	Cuba	49	41	Guinea-Bissau	17
4	Netherlands	422	23	Hungary	41	42	Jamaica	16
5	United Kingdom	404	24	Venezuela	39	43	Colombia	14
6	Brazil	302	25	Portugal	37	44	Ireland	14
7	Spain	301	26	Turkey	31	45	Libya	14
8	Germany	280	27	Belgium	30	46	Norway	14
9	Romania	146	28	Albania	28	47	Bolivia	13
10	Poland	144	29	Peru	28	48	Burundi	13
			30	Sweden	27	49	Maldives	11
UPPER MIDDLE						50	Mexico	11
11	Iraq	132	**LOWER MIDDLE**			51	Pakistan	11
12	Yugoslavia	123	31	Mongolia	26	52	Malaysia	10
13	Senegal	105	32	Uruguay	25	53	Costa Rica	9
14	Denmark	100	33	Switzerland	24	54	Rwanda	9
15	Australia	90	34	Nigeria	23	55	Ghana	8
16	Czech Republic	88	35	Indonesia	22	56	Algeria	7
17	Greece	88	36	Sri Lanka	22	57	Suriname	7
18	Vietnam	78	37	Tunisia	22	58	El Salvador	6

Rank	Country	Performing Arts Facilities		Rank	Country	Performing Arts Facilities		Rank	Country	Performing Arts Facilities
59	Mauritius	6		67	Angola	3		73	Luxembourg	2
60	Barbados	5		68	Bermuda	3		74	Malawi	2
61	Iceland	5		69	Ethiopia	3		75	Congo	1
62	Jordan	5		70	Fiji	3		76	Grenada	1
63	Syria	5						77	Guatemala	1
64	Chad	4		**BOTTOM 10**				78	Nicaragua	1
65	Cyprus	4		71	Guyana	3		79	St. Kitts and Nevis	1
66	Zaire	4		72	Dominican Republic	2		80	San Marino	1

Source: *World Data*

286. MUSEUMS

Museums serve as vast reservoirs of culture but in another sense they also communicate artistic values to the people. Museum attendance figures may be an imperfect index of the cultural roots of a people, but at least they indicate to some extent public awareness of the heritage of the past and the aesthetic dimension of human history.

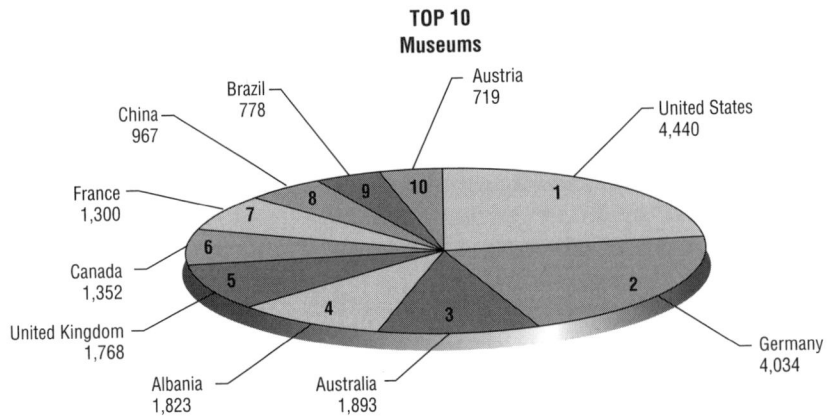

TOP 10
Museums

Austria 719
Brazil 778
China 967
France 1,300
Canada 1,352
United Kingdom 1,768
Albania 1,823
Australia 1,893
United States 4,440
Germany 4,034

Rank	Country	Museums		Rank	Country	Museums		Rank	Country	Museums
UPPER MIDDLE				31	Turkey	154		52	Chile	24
11	Switzerland	699		32	Korea, South	146		53	Puerto Rico	24
12	Japan	638		33	Indonesia	131		54	Bolivia	23
13	Netherlands	625		34	Italy	130		55	Ecuador	23
14	Hungary	571		35	New Zealand	98		56	South Africa	22
15	Yugoslavia	565		36	Mexico	93		57	Pakistan	19
16	Spain	554		37	Belarus	86		58	Cyprus	18
17	Poland	551		38	Israel	79		59	Guatemala	18
18	Greece	478		39	Philippines	76		60	Paraguay	18
19	Romania	471		40	Colombia	73		61	Korea, North	17
20	India	462		41	Venezuela	54		62	Malta	16
21	Czech Republic	422		42	Iceland	53		63	Uganda	16
22	Norway	401		43	Iran	52		64	Costa Rica	15
23	Portugal	314		44	Ireland	49		65	Bermuda	14
24	Denmark	285		45	Malaysia	43		66	Morocco	14
25	Ukraine	224		46	Tunisia	35		67	Angola	13
26	Bulgaria	223		47	Egypt	34				
27	Cuba	216		48	Syria	33		**LOWER MIDDLE**		
28	Finland	206		49	Algeria	28		68	Bangladesh	13
29	Sweden	195		50	Libya	26		69	Myanmar (Burma)	12
30	Thailand	180		51	Iraq	25		70	Nigeria	12

Rank	Country	Museums	Rank	Country	Museums	Rank	Country	Museums
71	Peru	12	97	Zambia	6	123	Mali	2
72	Singapore	12	98	Chad	5	124	Papua New Guinea	2
73	Jordan	11	99	Congo	5	125	Seychelles	2
74	Panama	11	100	Guinea	5	126	Belize	1
75	Uruguay	11	101	Liechtenstein	5	127	Bhutan	1
76	Zimbabwe	11	102	Madagascar	5	128	Cote d'Ivoire	1
77	Taiwan	10	103	Mauritius	5	129	Equatorial Guinea	1
78	Namibia	9	104	El Salvador	4	130	Ethiopia	1
79	Nicaragua	9	105	Ghana	4	131	Fiji	1
80	San Marino	9	106	Haiti	4	132	Grenada	1
81	Vietnam	9	107	Mongolia	4	133	Guinea-Bissau	1
82	Brunei	8	108	Senegal	4	134	Luxembourg	1
83	Afghanistan	7	109	Antigua and Barbuda	3			
84	Bahamas	7	110	Barbados	3	**BOTTOM 10**		
85	Central African Republic	7	111	Cambodia	3	135	Maldives	1
86	Kuwait	7	112	Malawi	3	136	St. Kitts and Nevis	1
87	Lebanon	7	113	Niger	3	137	St. Lucia	1
88	Liberia	7	114	Oman	3	138	St. Vincent	1
89	Sudan	7	115	Suriname	3	139	Saudi Arabia	1
90	Togo	7	116	United Arab Emirates	3	140	Sierra Leone	1
91	Benin	6	117	Andorra	2	141	Solomon Islands	1
92	Burkina	6	118	Bahrain	2	142	Somalia	1
93	Dominican Republic	6	119	Botswana	2	143	Swaziland	1
94	Kenya	6	120	Burundi	2	144	Vanuatu	1
95	Monaco	6	121	Cameroon	2			
96	Qatar	6	122	Guyana	2			

Source: *UNESCO Statistical Yearbook*

287. MONUMENTS AND SITES

The following list presents the protected monuments and historical sites in 39 countries. The list is compiled by the Paris-based International Council on Monuments and Sites, which has to approve the status of a historical monument as a protected site to be preserved for posterity.

Rank	Country	Monuments and Sites	Rank	Country	Monuments and Sites	Rank	Country	Monuments and Sites
TOP 10			14	Zimbabwe	166	30	Belarus	12
1	Uganda	67,941	15	Hungary	164	31	Benin	12
2	Czech Republic	45,449	16	Madagascar	155			
3	Bulgaria	40,682	17	Greece	110	**BOTTOM 10**		
4	Turkey	22,296	18	Central African Republic	82	32	Maldives	11
5	Finland	19,100	19	Nigeria	62	33	Qatar	11
6	Yugoslavia	9,719	20	Panama	57	34	Portugal	10
7	Syria	4,096	21	Romania	54	35	Austria	8
8	Iran	1,720	22	Oman	40	36	Barbados	7
9	Mali	546	23	Niger	32	37	Indonesia	6
10	Canada	368	24	Togo	30	38	San Marino	6
			25	Jordan	16	39	Brunei	4
UPPER MIDDLE			26	Kuwait	16	40	Burkina	1
11	Bangladesh	229	27	Cyprus	15	41	Burundi	1
12	Thailand	203	28	Philippines	15			
13	Italy	170	29	Norway	14			

Source: *UNESCO Statistical Yearbook*

288. NATURAL PARKS AND NATURE RESERVES

Natural Parks and Nature Reserves predate the environmental movement in many Western countries, but they gained a fresh impetus after the movement began in earnest. The data cover all types of facilities including natural parks, scientific reserves, game reserves, protected landscapes, national forests, national seashores and wetlands and other similar areas with an area of more than 4 sq mi. The data are based on information collected by the World Conservation Union, the U.N. Environmental Program and the World Wildlife Fund.

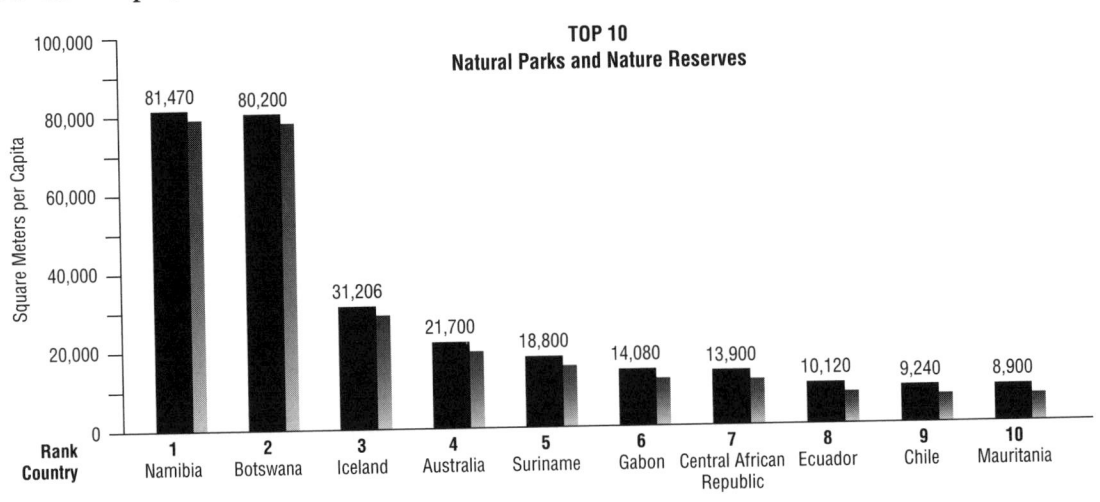

TOP 10
Natural Parks and Nature Reserves

Rank / Country	Square Meters per Capita
1 Namibia	81,470
2 Botswana	80,200
3 Iceland	31,206
4 Australia	21,700
5 Suriname	18,800
6 Gabon	14,080
7 Central African Republic	13,900
8 Ecuador	10,120
9 Chile	9,240
10 Mauritania	8,900

Rank	Country	Natural Parks and Nature Reserves (square meters per capita)
UPPER MIDDLE		
11	New Zealand	8,400
12	Zambia	7,800
13	Bolivia	6,800
14	Kiribati	6,340
15	Bhutan	6,220
16	Seychelles	5,620
17	Panama	5,590
18	Congo	5,460
19	Tanzania	5,020
20	Brunei	4,980
21	Bahamas	4,890
22	Venezuela	4,480
23	Canada	4,160
24	Saudi Arabia	4,130
25	Argentina	4,080
26	Senegal	3,070
27	Zimbabwe	3,030
28	Norway	3,000
29	Sudan	2,980
30	Paraguay	2,700
31	Zaire	2,650
32	Peru	2,520
33	Cameroon	2,500
34	Niger	2,200
35	Austria	2,060
36	Costa Rica	2,030
37	Sweden	2,010
38	Colombia	1,780
39	Luxembourg	1,720
40	Benin	1,640
41	Finland	1,630
42	South Africa	1,580
43	Cote d'Ivoire	1,530

Rank	Country	Natural Parks and Nature Reserves (square meters per capita)
44	Mongolia	1,500
45	Brazil	1,400
46	Ethiopia	1,400
47	Kenya	1,370
48	United States	1,310
49	Mozambique	1,300
50	Honduras	1,280
51	Togo	1,280
52	Czech Republic	1,270
53	Malawi	1,250
54	Mali	1,110
55	Thailand	920
56	Angola	910
57	Burkina	850
58	Dominica	830
59	Cuba	820
60	Ghana	810
61	Uganda	810
62	France	800
63	Indonesia	800
64	Dominican Republic	780
65	Uruguay	700
66	Madagascar	690
67	Belize	680
68	Russia	680
69	Iran	670
LOWER MIDDLE		
70	Mexico	660
71	Spain	650
72	Pakistan	640
73	Malaysia	630
74	Portugal	600
75	Poland	580

Rank	Country	Natural Parks and Nature Reserves (square meters per capita)
76	Somalia	570
77	Denmark	550
78	Greece	531
79	Liechtenstein	530
80	Swaziland	530
81	Antigua and Barbuda	520
82	Israel	520
83	Liberia	520
84	Nepal	520
85	Hungary	480
86	United Kingdom	450
87	Sri Lanka	440
88	Yugoslavia	440
89	Libya	380
90	Oman	380
91	Rwanda	380
92	Germany	363
93	Tonga	320
94	Sierra Leone	250
95	Italy	220
96	Burundi	210
97	Algeria	200
98	Chad	200
99	Djibouti	200
100	Guinea	190
101	Japan	190
102	Switzerland	180
103	Western Samoa	180
104	India	160
105	Guyana	150
106	Bulgaria	140
107	Gambia	140
108	Grenada	140
109	Taiwan	140

Rank	Country	Natural Parks and Nature Reserves (square meters per capita)
110	Egypt	130
111	Jordan	130
112	Korea, South	130
113	Trinidad and Tobago	130
114	Vietnam	130
115	Morocco	120
116	Nicaragua	120
117	St. Lucia	110
118	Afghanistan	100
119	Cyprus	100
120	Netherlands	100
121	Guatemala	99
122	China	90
123	Philippines	87

Rank	Country	Natural Parks and Nature Reserves (square meters per capita)
124	Belgium	85
125	Nigeria	83
126	Papua New Guinea	80
127	Fiji	73
128	Albania	70
129	Ireland	69
130	Romania	66
131	Tunisia	52
132	Solomon Islands	46
133	Turkey	44
134	El Salvador	43
135	Lesotho	40
136	Myanmar (Burma)	40
137	Mauritius	34

Rank	Country	Natural Parks and Nature Reserves (square meters per capita)
138	Korea, North	26
BOTTOM 10		
139	Cambodia	15
140	Haiti	14
141	Lebanon	12
142	Barbados	10
143	Singapore	10
144	Bangladesh	9
145	Puerto Rico	6
146	Bermuda	5
147	Jamaica	2
148	Malta	1.1

Source: *World Data*

289. PUBLIC LIBRARIES

In many countries public libraries serve as centers of continuing education for the general population, and they also perform a valuable service to the book publishing industry by selecting and storing the best books and periodicals and non-print materials and making them available to their patrons. In the electronic age, the definitions and functions of public libraries are changing, but it is difficult to conceive a more efficient mechanism for the diffusion of knowledge in whatever form. Interestingly, because libraries and reading go together, libraries play an active role in making every community more literate and book-friendly.

**TOP 10
Public Libraries**

Rank	Country	Libraries
1	Russia	33,200
2	Germany	20,448
3	Poland	10,129
4	United States	9,170
5	Czech Republic	8,398

Rank	Country	Libraries
6	Romania	7,181
7	Bulgaria	5,591
8	Hungary	4,765
9	Brazil	3,600
10	China	2,406

1 book = 10,000 Libraries

Rank	Country	Public Libraries	Rank	Country	Public Libraries	Rank	Country	Public Libraries
	UPPER MIDDLE					54	Albania	45
11	Belgium	2,351		**LOWER MIDDLE**		55	Ireland	31
12	Austria	2,081	33	Cuba	327	56	Indonesia	30
13	Spain	1,677	34	Israel	320	57	Venezuela	24
14	Norway	1,339	35	Tunisia	280	58	Benin	18
15	France	1,141	36	Chile	269	59	Panama	18
16	Japan	1,107	37	Taiwan	252	60	Syria	14
17	Canada	997	38	Denmark	250	61	Malaysia	13
18	Colombia	974	39	Iceland	234	62	Senegal	10
19	South Africa	720	40	Ecuador	210	63	Ghana	9
20	Peru	687	41	New Zealand	209	64	Solomon Islands	8
21	Sri Lanka	650	42	Turkey	206			
22	Greece	615	43	Portugal	178		**BOTTOM 10**	
23	Netherlands	593	44	Korea, South	168	65	Liechtenstein	5
24	Vietnam	568	45	United Kingdom	166	66	Ethiopia	4
25	Mexico	557	46	Cyprus	103	67	Luxembourg	3
26	Iran	507	47	Yugoslavia	102	68	Angola	2
27	Philippines	501	48	Bolivia	99	69	Bahamas	2
28	Finland	461	49	Costa Rica	81	70	Cape Verde	2
29	Sweden	381	50	Dominican Republic	68	71	Malta	2
30	Thailand	375	51	Madagascar	56	72	Andorra	1
31	Egypt	352	52	Afghanistan	55	73	Dominica	1
32	Australia	350	53	Saudi Arabia	50	74	Fiji	1

Source: *UNESCO Statistical Yearbook*

290. VCR OWNERSHIP

In most developed countries, the ownership of a VCR has become as common as ownership of television and radio sets. The ownership of VCRs reinforces the global cultural dominance of the United States, which provides most of the content of VCR programming.

Rank	Country	VCR Ownership	Rank	Country	VCR Ownership	Rank	Country	VCR Ownership
	TOP 10		8	Germany	47	14	France	35
1	Japan	79	9	Netherlands	47	15	Italy	27
2	United States	69	10	Belgium	42	16	Brazil	13
3	Australia	66						
4	United Kingdom/Ireland	64		**BOTTOM**				
5	Canada	63	11	Taiwan	38			
6	Sweden	55	12	Spain	37			
7	Switzerland	48	13	South Korea	36			

Source: "The Export of American Culture." *Public Perspective* 3, no. 4 (May/June 1992), p. 118. Primary source: Motion Picture Association of America.

291. BOTANICAL GARDENS & ZOOS

The study of the evolution of flora and fauna has taught man a great deal about his origin and behavior. As previously noted, the evolution of flora, for example, has kept man alive and helped preserve the earth's ecosystem.

Many once-important and exotic species of flora and fauna are now nearly extinct, and it is doubly important to preserve what remains of each species in botanical gardens and zoos. This table ranks nation-states by the total number of gardens and zoos, and clearly Western nations were the first to build and maintain habitats that enabled scientists to study a wide variety of species. Communist nations, however, also place value on zoos, as reflected by the fact that Beijing's zoo built a $138 million habitat with air-conditioned cages for its famous pandas, the mascot of the Asian Games held in 1990.

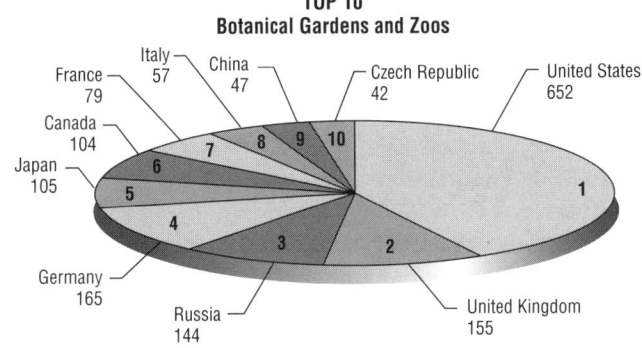

TOP 10 Botanical Gardens and Zoos

Italy 57 — China 47 — Czech Republic 42 — United States 652 — France 79 — Canada 104 — Japan 105 — Germany 165 — Russia 144 — United Kingdom 155

Rank	Country	Number of Zoos and Botanical Gardens	Rank	Country	Number of Zoos and Botanical Gardens	Rank	Country	Number of Zoos and Botanical Gardens
UPPER MIDDLE			49	Bulgaria	4	86	Uganda	2
11	India	42	50	Korea, South	4	87	United Arab Emirates	2
12	Australia	41	51	Monaco	4	88	Vietnam	2
13	Netherlands	36	52	Mozambique	4	89	Afghanistan	1
14	South Africa	35	53	Senegal	4	90	Angola	1
15	Switzerland	32	54	Singapore	4	91	Bahamas	1
16	Brazil	31	55	Sri Lanka	4	92	Bangladesh	1
17	Poland	26				93	Bermuda	1
18	Spain	22	**LOWER MIDDLE**			94	Brunei	1
19	Austria	21	56	Uruguay	4	95	Congo	1
20	Denmark	19	57	Zaire	4	96	Costa Rica	1
21	Yugoslavia	19	58	Zimbabwe	4	97	Cyprus	1
22	Sweden	18	59	Algeria	3	98	Dominica	1
23	Argentina	16	60	Ethiopia	3	99	Dominican Republic	1
24	New Zealand	15	61	Ghana	3	100	Ecuador	1
25	Hungary	14	62	Greece	3	101	El Salvador	1
26	Israel	13	63	Honduras	3	102	Fiji	1
27	Belgium	12	64	Hong Kong	3	103	Iraq	1
28	Indonesia	12	65	Iran	3	104	Kuwait	1
29	Venezuela	12	66	Madagascar	3	105	Lebanon	1
30	Mexico	11	67	Papua New Guinea	3	106	Liberia	1
31	Chile	10	68	Taiwan	3	107	Mali	1
32	Portugal	10	69	Thailand	3	108	Mauritius	1
33	Egypt	9	70	Tunisia	3	109	Namibia	1
34	Rumania	9	71	Cameroon	2	110	Nepal	1
35	Colombia	8	72	Grenada	2	111	New Caledonia	1
36	Nigeria	8	73	Guatemala	2			
37	Finland	7	74	Guyana	2	**BOTTOM 10**		
38	Norway	7	75	Iceland	2	112	Nicaragua	1
39	Turkey	7	76	Cote d'Ivoire	2	113	Paraguay	1
40	Cuba	6	77	Korea, North	2	114	Qatar	1
41	Malaysia	6	78	Libya	2	115	Sierra Leone	1
42	Pakistan	6	79	Malta	2	116	St. Vincent	1
43	Ireland	5	80	Myanmar (Burma)	2	117	Suriname	1
44	Jamaica	5	81	Netherlands Antilles	2	118	Trinidad & Tobago	1
45	Kenya	5	82	Panama	2	119	U.S. Virgin Islands	1
46	Morocco	5	83	Peru	2	120	Western Samoa	1
47	Philippines	5	84	Saudi Arabia	2	121	Zambia	1
48	Bolivia	4	85	Sudan	2			

Source: *World Data*

Section

XXIV

WOMEN

The first three editions of Rankings (1979, 1984 and 1992) had no section devoted to women. It is significant that such a section is being included in this edition. It is a direct acknowledgment of not only the importance of women in national development but also the growing body of statistical data illustrating gender inequalities.

Some rankings in the earlier editions dealt with women, but only as adjuncts to the general rankings. Thus there were separate tables dealing with female literacy and female life expectancy. But in other areas the statistical monitoring of women's progress was difficult because separate data were not collected for women at the national or global level. In many cases data on women were submerged in the general statistics, generally masking the wide disparities in the status of the two sexes. However, since the World Conference on Women in Mexico in 1975, in Copenhagen in 1980, and in Nairobi in 1985, more attention has been paid to gender issues and gender statistics are now routinely collected.

The statistics now available show that in no society do women and men enjoy equal opportunities. The degree of parity varies as also the speed in closing traditional gaps. While near equality has been achieved in many Scandinavian countries, women still are treated as chattel in Islamic countries, where the rise of fundamentalism has actually made their condition worse. They have little or no access to education, or to health, political and legal rights, three key areas of patriarchal hegemony.

Women in many developing countries fare no better. Among the world's 900 million illiterate people, women outnumber men two to one. Girls constitute the majority of the 130 million children without access to primary education. Literacy is the key to breaking the vicious cycles of poverty because it triggers advances in a number of other fields. Although half the literacy gap between men and women worldwide was closed between 1970 and 1990, the number of female illiterates actually increased during the same period.

The gender gaps in health are wider at the bottom rungs of the development ladder and narrow as societies advance. Women's special health needs suffer considerable neglect in poorer countries without proper healthcare facilities. Pregnancy complications are the single largest cause of death among Third World women in their reproductive years. Nearly half a million maternal deaths occur each year in developing countries.

Gaps in education, health and nutrition, though significant, are much narrower than the gender gaps in income and access to employment. Of the estimated 1.3 billion people living in poverty, more than 70% are female. The number of rural women living in poverty rose by over 50% in the past two decades. It has been said that now poverty has a woman's face. Women are getting poorer even in rich countries. In the United States, women constituted only 40% of the poor in 1940, but 60% in 1990. Half the female-headed households in the United States are poor. In almost every country, women have a higher rate of unemployment than men. Worldwide, the average wage for women is three-fourths that of men outside agriculture. Further, women are concentrated in low-skill and low-paying jobs, lack bargaining power, and are subject to cultural norms that segregate jobs by gender.

Women face overt legal discrimination in many countries. They have restricted rights to marry, travel, acquire nationality, manage or inherit property, get credit and seek employment. Efforts to remove or end the legal discrimination become difficult because women have little political clout. In 55 countries, the political world is essentially male-dominated, with women making up less than 5% of the national legislature. In cabinets, the percentage is only slightly higher at 6%—5% in developing countries and 8% in developed countries. Few women have been heads of state or government. Only 21 women have been elected to such high office, with 10 holding office in 1995.

292. FEMALE SHARE OF ADMINISTRATIVE AND MANAGERIAL POSITIONS AS PERCENT OF MALE

The glass ceiling is a universal phenomenon. In the workplace, the historic dominance of the male has survived many legal efforts to reduce gender disparities in not merely employment but also in advancement to the highest levels of management. In many cases, the fact that women have to combine careers with even more onerous work at home as a mother and wife, militates against such advancement. A few countries have made significant progress in making the playing field level, but in the vast majority, the numbers still lag behind the ideal.

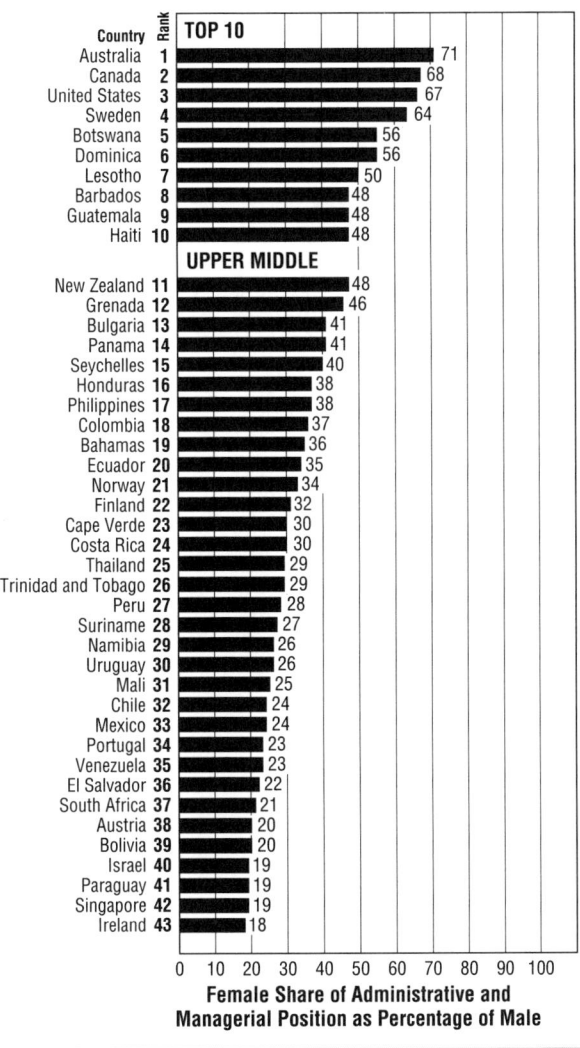

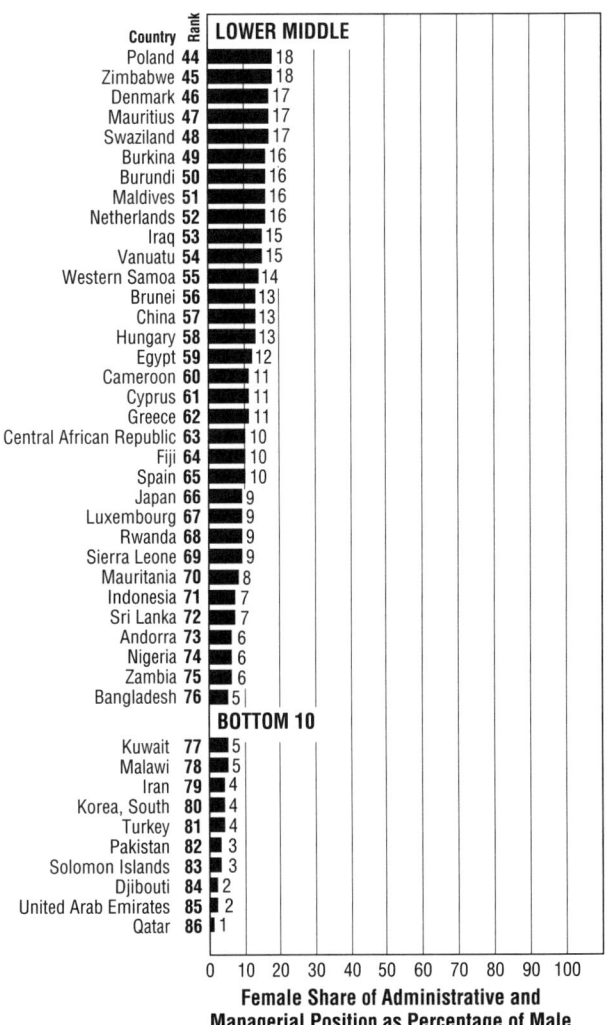

Female Share of Administrative and Managerial Position as Percentage of Male

Source: *Human Development Report*

293. SHARE OF SEATS HELD BY WOMEN IN NATIONAL LEGISLATURES

The U.N. Development Program's 1995 Report on Progress in Gender Equality found that while women throughout the world have made important gains in health and education, their progress in employment and in political arenas has been less impressive. Political power remains, as it has been always, a male preserve. In 55 countries, the political world is overwhelmingly male, with women making up less than 5% in parliament.

TOP 10
Share of Seats Held by Women in National Legislatures (%)

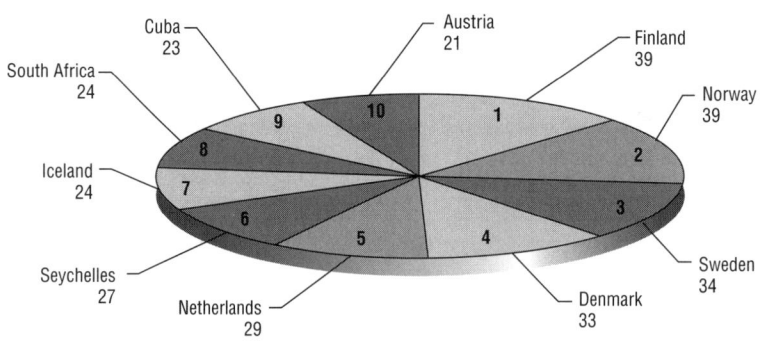

Cuba 23 — South Africa 24 — Iceland 24 — Seychelles 27 — Netherlands 29 — Austria 21 — Finland 39 — Norway 39 — Sweden 34 — Denmark 33

Rank	Country	Seats Held by Women in National Parliaments (%)	Rank	Country	Seats Held by Women in National Parliaments (%)	Rank	Country	Seats Held by Women in National Parliaments (%)
UPPER MIDDLE			48	Zimbabwe	12	84	Lithuania	7
11	China	21	49	Bahamas	11	85	Mexico	7
12	New Zealand	21	50	El Salvador	11	86	Namibia	7
13	Germany	20	51	Hungary	11	87	Panama	7
14	Guyana	20	52	Iraq	11	88	Tunisia	7
15	Korea, North	20	53	Kazakhstan	11	89	United Kingdom	7
16	Luxembourg	20	54	Philippines	11	90	Zambia	7
17	Slovakia	18	55	Sao Tome e Principe	11	91	Albania	6
18	Trinidad and Tobago	18	56	Tanzania	11	92	Benin	6
19	Vietnam	18	57	Angola	10	93	Bolivia	6
20	Canada	17	58	Bangladesh	10	94	Burkina	6
21	Rwanda	17	59	Belgium	10	95	Fiji	6
22	Uganda	17	60	Burundi	10	96	France	6
23	Chad	16	61	Czech Republic	10	97	Gabon	6
24	Mozambique	16	62	Dominican Republic	10	98	Georgia	6
25	Nicaragua	16	63	Malaysia	10	99	Greece	6
26	Switzerland	16	64	United States	10	100	Liberia	6
27	Latvia	15	65	Uzbekistan	10	101	Malawi	6
28	Spain	15	66	Colombia	9	102	Niger	6
29	Argentina	14	67	Equatorial Guinea	9	103	Paraguay	6
30	Barbados	14	68	Israel	9	104	St. Kitts and Nevis	6
31	Costa Rica	14	69	Laos	9	105	Suriname	6
32	Estonia	14	70	Peru	9	106	Venezuela	6
33	Grenada	14	71	Portugal	9	107	Botswana	5
34	St. Lucia	14	72	Belize	8	108	Brazil	5
35	Australia	13	73	Cape Verde	8	109	Cote d'Ivoire	5
36	Bulgaria	13				110	Cyprus	5
37	Dominica	13	**LOWER MIDDLE**			111	Ecuador	5
38	Guinea-Bissau	13	74	Gambia	8	112	Guatemala	5
39	Italy	13	75	Ghana	8	113	Kyrgyzstan	5
40	Poland	13	76	Honduras	8	114	Moldova	5
41	St. Vincent	13	77	Russia	8	115	Sri Lanka	5
42	Antigua and Barbuda	12	78	Swaziland	8	116	Sudan	5
43	Cameroon	12	79	Syria	8	117	Turkmenistan	5
44	Indonesia	12	80	Algeria	7	118	Uruguay	5
45	Ireland	12	81	Chile	7	119	Armenia	4
46	Jamaica	12	82	India	7	120	Belarus	4
47	Senegal	12	83	Japan	7	121	Cambodia	4

Rank	Country	Seats Held by Women in National Parliaments (%)	Rank	Country	Seats Held by Women in National Parliaments (%)	Rank	Country	Seats Held by Women in National Parliaments (%)
122	Central African Republic	4	135	Mauritius	3	**BOTTOM 10**		
123	Madagascar	4	136	Nepal	3	148	Pakistan	2
124	Maldives	4	137	Romania	3	149	Solomon Islands	2
125	Mongolia	4	138	Tajikstan	3	150	Turkey	2
126	Singapore	4	139	Afghanistan	2	151	Vanuatu	2
127	Thailand	4	140	Azerbaijan	2	152	Congo	1
128	Ukraine	4	141	Comoros	2	153	Ethiopia	1
129	Western Samoa	4	142	Egypt	2	154	Korea, South	1
130	Zaire	4	143	Lebanon	2	155	Morocco	1
131	Haiti	3	144	Lesotho	2	156	Togo	1
132	Iran	3	145	Mali	2	157	Yemen	1
133	Jordan	3	146	Malta	2			
134	Kenya	3	147	Nigeria	2			

Source: *Human Development Report*

294. FEMALE-HEADED HOUSEHOLDS

Female-headed households are becoming more common in both developed and developing countries, reflecting certain social mores. Increasing divorce and desertion rates are forcing more and more women to take over the management of households with young children. Since women earn less than men, in most countries this has led to what is described as the feminization of poverty.

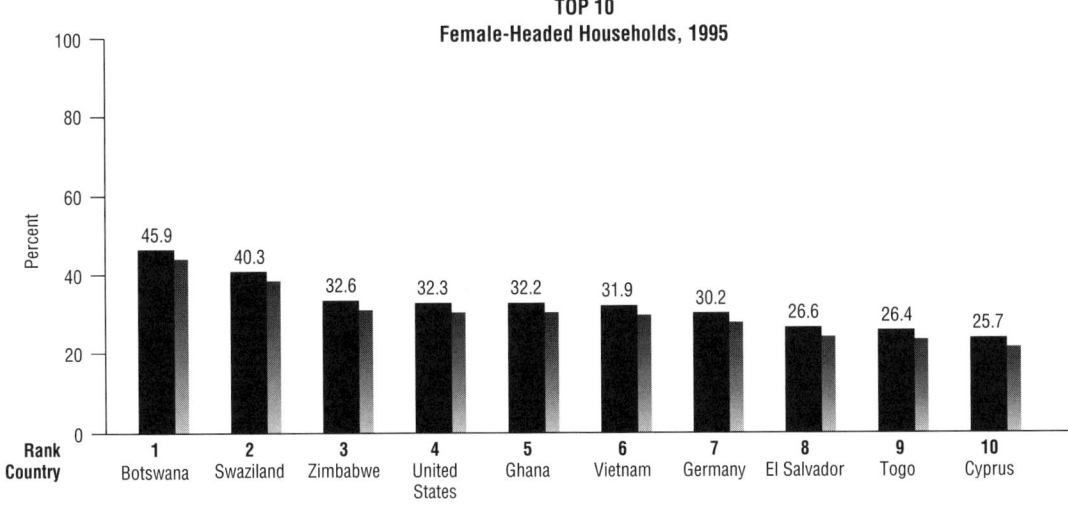

TOP 10
Female-Headed Households, 1995

Rank	Country	Female Headed Households (%)	Rank	Country	Female Headed Households (%)	Rank	Country	Female Headed Households (%)
	UPPER MIDDLE		23	Honduras	20.4	38	Estonia	15.8
11	Hong Kong	25.7	24	Brazil	20.1			
12	Czech Republic	25.6	25	Costa Rica	20.0		**BOTTOM 10**	
13	Dominican Republic	25.0	26	Liberia	19.1	39	Korea, North	15.7
14	Burundi	24.7	27	Central African Republic	18.7	40	Indonesia	13.0
15	Nicaragua	24.3	28	Tanzania	18.6	41	Western Samoa	12.5
16	Uruguay	23.0	29	Cameroon	18.5	42	Fiji	12.4
17	Colombia	22.7	30	Djibouti	18.4	43	Egypt	12.0
18	Panama	22.3	31	Morocco	17.3	44	Philippines	11.3
			32	Peru	17.3	45	Algeria	11.0
	LOWER MIDDLE		33	Japan	17.0	46	Sierra Leone	10.8
19	Kenya	22.0	34	Paraguay	17.0	47	Burkina	9.7
20	Venezuela	21.3	35	Guatemala	16.9	48	Niger	9.7
21	Chile	21.0	36	Solomon Islands	16.2			
22	Uganda	20.6	37	Zambia	16.2			

Source: *Compendium of Statistics and Indicators on the Situation of Women*

295. GENDER-RELATED DEVELOPMENT INDEX

The Gender-Related Development Index is a composite index devised by the UN Development Program. It captures gender inequalities that affect the Human Development Index (HDI). It adjusts HDI by using three variables: life expectancy (in which women have an edge), and income and educational attainment (adult literacy and combined primary, secondary and tertiary enrollment ratios) in which men have an edge. The index disaggregates data to expose areas of gender discrimination and inequality. The index also measures gender-based variations in access to basic national resources and opportunities.

Rank	Country	Gender-Related Development Index (GDI)	Rank	Country	Gender-Related Development Index (GDI)	Rank	Country	Gender-Related Development Index (GDI)
	TOP 10		29	Russia	0.822	58	Sri Lanka	0.660
1	Sweden	0.919	30	Ireland	0.813	59	Tunisia	0.641
2	Finland	0.918	31	Brunei	0.812	60	Ecuador	0.641
3	Norway	0.911	32	Uruguay	0.802	61	Qatar	0.639
4	Denmark	0.904	33	Thailand	0.798	62	Peru	0.631
5	United States	0.901	34	Spain	0.795	63	Paraguay	0.628
6	Australia	0.901	35	Luxembourg	0.790	64	Philippines	0.625
7	France	0.898	36	Trinidad and Tobago	0.786	65	Lebanon	0.622
8	Japan	0.896	37	Korea, South	0.780	66	Iran	0.611
9	Canada	0.891	38	Malaysia	0.768	67	Mongolia	0.596
10	Austria	0.882	39	Argentina	0.768	68	Indonesia	0.591
			40	Venezuela	0.765	69	Dominican Republic	0.590
	UPPER MIDDLE		41	Panama	0.765	70	Guyana	0.584
11	Barbados	0.878	42	Costa Rica	0.763	71	China	0.578
12	New Zealand	0.868	43	Chile	0.759	72	Syria	0.571
13	United Kingdom	0.862	44	Lithuania	0.750	73	Nicaragua	0.560
14	Italy	0.861	45	Turkey	0.744	74	Vietnam	0.537
15	Czech Rep.	0.858	46	Mexico	0.741	75	Libya	0.534
16	Slovakia	0.855	47	Cuba	0.726	76	El Salvador	0.533
17	Hong Kong	0.854	48	Fiji	0.722	77	Honduras	0.524
18	Belgium	0.852	49	Mauritius	0.722	78	Iraq	0.523
19	Switzerland	0.852	50	Colombia	0.720	79	Maldives	0.522
20	Netherlands	0.851	51	Kuwait	0.716	80	Bolivia	0.519
21	Estonia	0.839	52	Jamaica	0.710	81	Saudi Arabia	0.514
22	Poland	0.838	53	Brazil	0.709	82	Zimbabwe	0.512
23	Hungary	0.836	54	Suriname	0.699	83	Swaziland	0.508
24	Latvia	0.833				84	Algeria	0.508
25	Portugal	0.832		**LOWER MIDDLE**		85	Cape Verde	0.502
26	Bahamas	0.828	55	Botswana	0.696	86	Papua New Guinea	0.487
27	Greece	0.825	56	Bahrain	0.686	87	Guatemala	0.481
28	Singapore	0.822	57	United Arab Emirates	0.674	88	Kenya	0.471

Rank	Country	Gender-Related Development Index (GDI)
89	Lesotho	0.466
90	Cameroon	0.462
91	Ghana	0.460
92	Egypt	0.453
93	Morocco	0.450
94	Myanmar	0.448
95	Madagascar	0.432
96	Laos	0.405
97	Zambia	0.403
98	Comoros	0.402
99	India	0.401
100	Nigeria	0.383
101	Togo	0.380
102	Zaire	0.372
103	Pakistan	0.360

Rank	Country	Gender-Related Development Index (GDI)
104	Tanzania	0.359
105	Haiti	0.354
106	Central African Republic	0.350
107	Cote d'Ivoire	0.341
108	Bangladesh	0.334
109	Sudan	0.332
110	Uganda	0.316
111	Senegal	0.316
112	Djibouti	0.315
113	Malawi	0.315
114	Benin	0.314
115	Nepal	0.310
116	Mauritania	0.309
117	Yemen	0.307
118	Angola	0.286

Rank	Country	Gender-Related Development Index (GDI)
119	Gambia	0.277
120	Guinea-Bissau	0.276
BOTTOM 10		
121	Burundi	0.274
122	Chad	0.260
123	Mozambique	0.229
124	Ethiopia	0.217
125	Guinea	0.214
126	Burkina	0.214
127	Niger	0.196
128	Mali	0.195
129	Sierra Leone	0.195
130	Afghanistan	0.169

Source: *Human Development Report*

296. GENDER EMPOWERMENT MEASURE

Gender Empowerment Measure is a composite index devised by the UN Development Program. It concentrates on women's participation in the economic, political and professional spheres. Unlike the Gender-Related Development Index, which is concerned primarily with living standards and basic capabilities, the Gender Empowerment Measure is designed to measure women's access to power. For this purpose it combines four variables: percentage of seats in national legislatures, percentage of administrative and managerial jobs, percentage of earned income, and percentage of professional and technical workers.

Rank	Country	Gender Empowerment Measure (GEM)
TOP 10		
1	Sweden	0.757
2	Norway	0.752
3	Finland	0.722
4	Denmark	0.683
5	Canada	0.655
6	New Zealand	0.637
7	Netherlands	0.625
8	United States	0.623
9	Austria	0.610
10	Italy	0.585
UPPER MIDDLE		
11	Australia	0.568
12	Barbados	0.545
13	Luxembourg	0.542
14	Bahamas	0.533
15	Trinidad and Tobago	0.533
16	Cuba	0.524
17	Switzerland	0.513
18	Hungary	0.506
19	United Kingdom	0.483
20	Bulgaria	0.481
21	Belgium	0.479
22	Costa Rica	0.474
23	China	0.474
24	Ireland	0.469
25	Guyana	0.461
26	Spain	0.452
27	Japan	0.442
28	Philippines	0.435
29	Colombia	0.435
30	Portugal	0.435
31	France	0.433
32	Poland	0.432
33	Panama	0.430
34	Nicaragua	0.427

Rank	Country	Gender Empowerment Measure (GEM)
35	Singapore	0.424
36	Argentina	0.415
37	Dominican Republic	0.412
38	Botswana	0.407
39	Honduras	0.406
40	Chile	0.402
41	Peru	0.400
42	Mexico	0.399
43	Zimbabwe	0.398
44	El Salvador	0.397
45	Venezuela	0.391
46	Guatemala	0.390
47	Iraq	0.386
48	Cyprus	0.385
LOWER MIDDLE		
49	Malaysia	0.384
50	Korea, South	0.380
51	Cape Verde	0.379
52	Namibia	0.376
53	Ecuador	0.375
54	Thailand	0.373
55	Belize	0.369
56	Indonesia	0.362
57	Uruguay	0.361
58	Brazil	0.358
59	Swaziland	0.357
60	Romania	0.352
61	Mozambique	0.350
62	Mauritius	0.350
63	Haiti	0.349
64	Suriname	0.348
65	Bolivia	0.344
66	Paraguay	0.343
67	Greece	0.343
68	Cameroon	0.339
69	Lesotho	0.339

Rank	Country	Gender Empowerment Measure (GEM)
70	Burundi	0.337
71	Malta	0.334
72	Guinea-Bissau	0.327
73	Nepal	0.315
74	Gambia	0.315
75	Fiji	0.314
76	Ghana	0.313
77	Western Samoa	0.309
78	Maldives	0.294
79	Sri Lanka	0.288
80	Bangladesh	0.287
81	Syria	0.285
82	Burkina	0.280
83	Angola	0.278
84	Benin	0.271
85	Morocco	0.271
86	Zambia	0.271
87	Algeria	0.266
88	Senegal	0.265
89	Malawi	0.255
90	Korea, North	0.255
91	Tunisia	0.254
92	Equatorial Guinea	0.250
93	Kuwait	0.241
94	United Arab Emirates	0.239
95	Iran	0.237
96	Egypt	0.237
97	Mali	0.237
98	Turkey	0.234
99	Jordan	0.230
100	Papua New Guinea	0.228
101	India	0.226
102	Sudan	0.219
103	Lebanon	0.212
104	Congo	0.206
105	Ethiopia	0.205
106	Central African Republic	0.205

Rank	Country	Gender Empowerment Measure (GEM)	Rank	Country	Gender Empowerment Measure (GEM)	Rank	Country	Gender Empowerment Measure (GEM)
	BOTTOM 10		110	Togo	0.182	115	Djibouti	0.130
107	Zaire	0.201	111	Mauritania	0.163	116	Afghanistan	0.111
108	Nigeria	0.198	112	Cote d'Ivoire	0.157			
109	Solomon Islands	0.198	113	Comoros	0.157			
			114	Pakistan	0.153			

Source: *Human Development Report*

297. FEMALE SHARE OF EARNED INCOME

In almost all countries, women receive less remuneration than men for same or similar kind of work. Some of the wage differential is based on historic precedent and some on labor market structure. However, it is difficult to obtain firm data on wage differentials in many countries. Where such data are available, the share of earned income for women is derived by calculating their wages as a ratio of the average national wage and multiplying this ratio by their shares of the labor force. Their shares of earned income are then adjusted to their population share. Earning power is an important factor in establishing economic independence. However, there are extraneous cultural factors in the way income is distributed or controlled within a family. In some cases, women may earn but may not control the way the money is spent; in other cases, women may still control the consumption even if they do not work or earn.

TOP 10
Female Share of Earned Income (%)

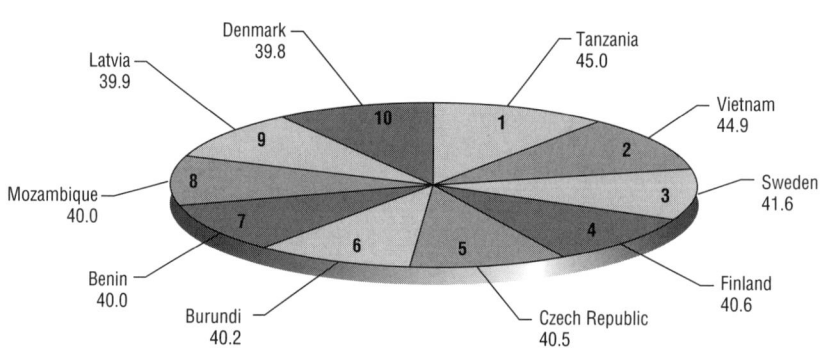

Denmark 39.8
Latvia 39.9
Tanzania 45.0
Vietnam 44.9
Mozambique 40.0
Sweden 41.6
Benin 40.0
Finland 40.6
Burundi 40.2
Czech Republic 40.5

Rank	Country	Women's Share of Earned Income (%)	Rank	Country	Women's Share of Earned Income (%)	Rank	Country	Women's Share of Earned Income (%)
	UPPER MIDDLE		29	Kenya	34.8	48	Papua New Guinea	31.2
11	Slovakia	39.7	30	Thailand	34.6	49	New Zealand	30.9
12	Niger	39.6	31	United States	34.6	50	United Kingdom	30.8
13	Estonia	39.5	32	Haiti	34.2	51	Turkey	30.2
14	Barbados	39.4	33	Austria	33.6	52	Myanmar (Burma)	30.0
15	Poland	39.3	34	Japan	33.5	53	Portugal	29.9
16	Hungary	39.1	35	Uganda	33.5	54	Ethiopia	29.4
17	Jamaica	38.6	36	Djibouti	33.4	55	Canada	29.3
18	Burkina	38.5	37	Swaziland	33.4	56	Malaysia	29.2
19	Mongolia	38.5	38	Malawi	33.3	57	Zaire	29.0
20	Russia	38.4	39	Ghana	32.7	58	Singapore	28.9
21	Lithuania	38.1	40	Gambia	32.6	59	Togo	28.9
22	Laos	37.8	41	Guinea-Bissau	32.6			
23	Norway	37.8	42	Comoros	31.9		**LOWER MIDDLE**	
24	Central African Republic	37.4	43	Madagascar	31.9	60	Botswana	28.5
25	Cameroon	36.2	44	Guinea	31.6	61	Nigeria	28.5
26	Australia	36.0	45	Angola	31.5	62	Bahamas	28.3
27	France	35.7	46	Senegal	31.3	63	Cote d'Ivoire	27.8
28	Lesotho	35.7	47	China	31.2	64	Italy	27.6

Rank	Country	Women's Share of Earned Income (%)	Rank	Country	Women's Share of Earned Income (%)	Rank	Country	Women's Share of Earned Income (%)
65	Zimbabwe	27.4	88	Mexico	22.3	111	Chad	16.5
66	Belgium	27.3	89	El Salvador	22.2	112	Morocco	16.4
67	Brunei	27.3	90	Greece	22.2	113	Paraguay	16.1
68	Cuba	27.2	91	Korea, South	22.0	114	Iran	14.9
69	Switzerland	27.1	92	Lebanon	21.8	115	Guatemala	13.8
70	Nepal	26.4	93	Guyana	21.2	116	Ecuador	13.3
71	Sierra Leone	26.2	94	Philippines	21.1	117	Dominican Republic	12.1
72	Uruguay	26.2	95	Argentina	20.9	118	Mali	11.8
73	Cape Verde	26.0	96	Colombia	20.1	119	Syria	11.3
74	Indonesia	25.3	97	Chile	19.8			
75	Zambia	25.3	98	Tunisia	19.5		**BOTTOM 10**	
76	Netherlands	25.2	99	Peru	19.4	120	Bahrain	10.1
77	Sri Lanka	25.1	100	India	19.2	121	Pakistan	10.1
78	Trinidad and Tobago	24.7	101	Costa Rica	19.0	122	Yemen	9.2
79	Suriname	24.3	102	Spain	18.6	123	Egypt	8.2
80	Nicaragua	24.2	103	Mauritania	18.5	124	Algeria	7.5
81	Ireland	23.2	104	Sudan	18.5	125	Libya	7.5
82	Luxembourg	23.1	105	Kuwait	18.4	126	Afghanistan	7.1
83	Brazil	22.9	106	Iraq	17.7	127	United Arab Emirates	6.8
84	Bangladesh	22.8	107	Maldives	17.2	128	Qatar	5.3
85	Panama	22.8	108	Bolivia	17.1	129	Saudi Arabia	3.3
86	Venezuela	22.8	109	Fiji	16.7			
87	Mauritius	22.6	110	Honduras	16.7			

Source: *Compendium of Statistics and Indicators on the Situation of Women*

Section
XXV

GLOBAL
INDEXES

Appropriately, the final chapter presents three synoptic indexes. Composite scales take the most important indicators (like Population, GNP, Literacy, Infant Mortality), and attempt to meld them into a new yardstick. Certain nations tend to do well on a few selected indicators because of some peculiarities of location or economy. But composite indexes make the playing fields level. Like the decathlons, they test a broad range of skills and achievements. By selecting indicators from demography, health, education, economy and other vital areas, they offer a more accurate assessment of national performance.

The first is the Human Development Index, devised by the United Nations Development Program, which uses development status as its criterion. Its purpose is to illustrate the gap between the developed and developing worlds. The second and third indexes are devised by Population Action International. The Human Suffering Index is a scoreboard of misery. It is a perfect illustration of "How the Other Half Lives," the title of Jacob Riis's famous book. The Status of Women Index is a sobering look at how women are faring around the world. Numbers speak louder than words, and these numbers shout.

298. HUMAN DEVELOPMENT INDEX

Human Development Index (HDI) is published annually by the United Nations Development Program. The HDI is based on three indicators: longevity, as measured by life expectancy at birth; educational attainment, as measured by a combination of adult literacy (two-thirds weight) and combined primary, secondary and tertiary enrollment ratios (one-third weight); and standard of living, as measured by real GDP per capita (Purchasing Power Parity $).

For the construction of the index, fixed minimum and maximum values have been established for each of these indicators:

- Life expectancy at birth: 25 years and 85 years
- Adult literacy: 0% and 100%
- Combined enrollment ratio: 0% and 100%
- Real GDP per capita (PPP$): PPP$100 and PPP$40,000.

Since the publication of *Human Development Report 1994,* two changes have been made in the construction of the HDI relating to variables and minimum and maximum values. First, the variable of mean years of schooling has been replaced by the combined primary, secondary and tertiary enrollment ratios, mainly because the formula for calculating mean years of schooling is complex and has enormous data requirements. Data on mean years of schooling are not provided by any UN agency or international organization. As a result, estimates must sometimes be used which are not always acceptable. The combined enrollment ratio overcomes both of these problems. It shows the stock of literacy quite easily for those under age 24, based on the work of UNESCO.

Second, the minimum value of income has been revised from PPP$200 to PPP$100. This revision was made because in the construction of the gender-related development index (GDI) for different countries, the minimum observed value of female income of PPP$100 is used as the lower goal post. It is necessary to use this fixed minimum for construction of the overall HDI to maintain consistency between the construction of the HDI and that of the GDI and to ensure comparability between the two indices. For the HDI, the revision is only marginal, and it had little effect on HDI values.

Rank	Country	Human Development Index 1995	Rank	Country	Human Development Index 1995	Rank	Country	Human Development Index 1995
HIGH HDI		**0.888**	62	Seychelles	0.810	122	Congo	0.538
1	Canada	0.950	63	Brazil	0.804	123	Cape Verde	0.536
2	USA	0.937				124	Swaziland	0.522
3	Japan	0.937	**MEDIUM HDI**		**0.632**	125	Solomon Islands	0.511
4	Netherlands	0.936	64	Kazakhstan	0.798	126	Papua New Guinea	0.508
5	Finland	0.934	65	Bulgaria	0.796	127	Cameroon	0.503
6	Iceland	0.933	66	Turkey	0.792			
7	Norway	0.932	67	Grenada	0.786	**LOW HDI**		**0.403**
8	France	0.930	68	Ecuador	0.784	128	Pakistan	0.483
9	Spain	0.930	69	Dominica	0.776	129	Ghana	0.482
10	Sweden	0.929	70	Iran	0.770	130	Kenya	0.481
11	Australia	0.927	71	Lithuania	0.769	131	Lesotho	0.473
12	Belgium	0.926	72	Cuba	0.769	132	Myanmar	0.457
13	Switzerland	0.925	73	Libyan Arab Jamahiriya	0.768	133	São Tomé and Principe	0.451
14	Austria	0.925	74	Botswna	0.763	134	India	0.439
15	Germany	0.921	75	Tunisia	0.763	135	Madagascar	0.432
16	Denmark	0.920	76	Saudi Arqbia	0.762	136	Zambia	0.425
17	New Zealand	0.919	77	Suriname	0.762	137	Yemen	0.424
18	United Kingdom	0.916	78	Syrian Arab Rep.	0.761	138	Laos	0.420
19	Ireland	0.915	79	Saint Vincent	0.761	139	Comoros	0.415
20	Italy	0.912	80	Jordan	0.758	140	Togo	0.409
21	Israel	0.907	81	Moldova, Rep. of	0.757	141	Nigeria	0.406
22	Greece	0.907	82	Albania	0.739	142	Equatorial Guinea	0.399
23	Cyprus	0.906	83	Korea, Dem. People's Rep. of	0.733	143	Zaire	0.384
24	Hong Kong	0.905	84	Saint Lucia	0.732	144	Sudan	0.379
25	Barbados	0.900	85	Algeria	0.732	145	Côte d'Ivoire	0.369
26	Bahamas	0.894	86	Turkmenistan	0.731	146	Bangladesh	0.364
27	Luxembourg	0.893	87	Paraguay	0.723	147	Tanzania	0.364
28	Costa Rica	0.883	88	Jamaica	0.721	148	Haiti	0.362
29	Belize	0.883	89	Kyrgyzstan	0.717	149	Central African Rep.	0.361
30	Argentina	0.882	90	Armenia	0.715	150	Mauritania	0.359
31	Korea, Rep. of	0.882	91	Oman	0.715	151	Nepal	0.343
32	Uruguay	0.881	92	Georgia	0.709	152	Senegal	0.340
33	Chile	0.880	93	Peru	0.709	153	Cambodia	0.337
34	Malta	0.880	94	Uzbekistan	0.706	154	Djibouti	0.336
35	Singapore	0.878	95	South Africa	0.705	155	Benin	0.332
36	Portugal	0.874	96	Dominican Rep.	0.705	156	Rwanda	0.332
37	Saint Kitts and Nevis	0.873	97	Sri Lanka	0.704	157	Malawi	0.330
38	Czech Rep.	0.872	98	Romania	0.703	158	Uganda	0.329
39	Trindad and Toabgo	0.872	99	Azerbaijan	0.696	159	Liberia	0.325
40	Slovakia	0.872	100	Philippines	0.677	160	Bhutan	0.305
41	Brunei Darussalam	0.868	101	Lebanon	0.675	161	Gambia	0.299
42	Belarus	0.866	102	Samoa (Western)	0.651	162	Chad	0.296
43	Estonia	0.862	103	Tajikistan	0.643	163	Guinea-Bissau	0.293
44	Bahrain	0.862	104	Indonesia	0.637	164	Angola	0.291
45	United Arab Emirates	0.861	105	Guyana	0.622	165	Burundi	0.286
46	Fiji	0.860	106	Iraq	0.617	166	Somalia	0.246
47	Venezuela	0.859	107	Egypt	0.613	167	Mozambique	0.246
48	Latvia	0.857	108	Namibia	0.611	168	Guinea	0.237
49	Panama	0.856	109	Nicaragua	0.611	169	Burkina Faso	0.228
50	Hungary	0.856	110	Mongolia	0.604	170	Afghanistan	0.228
51	Poland	0.855	111	China	0.594	171	Ethopia	0.227
52	Russian Federation	0.849	112	Guatemala	0.591	172	Mali	0.222
53	Mexico	0.842	113	Bolivia	0.588	173	Sierra Leone	0.221
54	Ukraine	0.842	114	Gabon	0.579	174	Niger	0.207
55	Antigua and Barbuda	0.840	115	El Salvador	0.579			
56	Qatar	0.838	116	Honduras	0.578	All developing countries		0.570
57	Colombia	0.836	117	Morocco	0.554	Least developed countries		0.337
58	Thailand	0.827	118	Maldives	0.554	Sub-Saharan Africa		0.389
59	Malaysia	0.822	119	Vanuatu	0.541	Industrial countries		0.916
60	Mauritius	0.821	120	Viet Nam	0.539	World		0.759
61	Kuwait	0.821	121	Zimbabwe	0.539			

Source: *Human Development Report*

299. HUMAN SUFFERING INDEX

The International Human Suffering Index (HSI) statistically rates living conditions in 141 countries. It was created to measure, in a single figure, differences in living conditions between countries. The presentation also allows a side-by-side comparison of rates of population increase and human suffering. Five years ago, when the first Human Suffering Index was published, 130 countries were studied. The current HSI covers 13 additional countries, and provides unified data for Germany and Yemen.

Each individual country index is compiled by adding 10 measures of human welfare related to economics, health and nutrition, education, communications and governance: (1) life expectancy, (2) daily calorie supply, (3) clean drinking water, (4) infant immunization, (5) secondary school enrollment, (6) GNP per capita, (7) rate of inflation, (8) communications technology, (9) political freedom, and (10) civil rights.

Most of the data are from official government sources. Therefore, in some cases, countries may receive an artificially high score if governments tend to overstate the extent of their social service programs, as in the case of North Korea's claim to 100 percent enrollment for secondary school.

Each of the 10 measures of well-being is ranked from 0 to 10—the most distressful being 10. For example, Afghanistan receives a rating of 10 in the Life Expectancy Index because the average life span of a baby born today is only 41 years, the shortest in the world.

The 10 measures are added together to obtain The Human Suffering Index. Those countries with low life expectancy, low gross national product per capita, poor supplies of clean drinking water, etc., scored high on the Index—a few close to 100.

Additional measures considered for the Human Suffering Index included data on pollution, unemployment, external debt, children in the work force, urban slums, income distribution, infant mortality, physicians per capita, literacy, and access to consumer goods. All had potential relevance, but each had some weakness or duplicated better measures already chosen, or covered too few countries.

Living conditions are worst in Mozambique (Mocambique). Also in the worst five are Somalia, Afghanistan, Haiti, and Sudan. Most countries with high human suffering scores have very high rates of population growth.

The most comfortable countries to live in are Denmark, the Netherlands, Belgium, Switzerland, and Canada. Virtually all the countries with low human suffering scores have low rates of population growth. Countries rated in the Human Suffering Index were grouped in the following quadrants:

Extreme Human Suffering The 27 countries with 8 percent of the world's population, or 432 million people, registered 75 or greater on the Human Suffering Index.

Of these countries, 20 are in Africa; 6 are in Asia; and 1 country —Haiti—is in the Western Hemisphere.

In the last HSI, 30 countries with 11 percent of the world's population registered in the Extreme category.

High Human Suffering The 56 countries with 65 percent of the world's population, or 3.5 billion people, registered between 50 and 74 on the Human Suffering Index.

Of these countries, 24 are in Africa; 16 are in Asia; 15 are in the Western Hemisphere and 1 is in Oceania; none are in Europe.

In the last HSI, 44 countries with 58 percent of the world's population rated High Suffering.

Moderate Human Suffering The 34 countries with 11.8 percent of the world's population, or 636 million people, recorded an index between 25 and 49, indicating moderate levels of suffering.

Of these countries, 9 are in Europe; 13 are in Asia; 8 are in the Western Hemisphere and 2 are in Oceania; Seychelles and Mauritius are the only African countries in this category.

Five years ago, 29 countries with 10 percent of the world's population registered Moderate Human Suffering.

Minimal Human Suffering The 24 countries with 14.8 percent of the world's population, or 797 million people, recorded 24 or lower on the Human Suffering Index.

Of these countries, 17 are in Europe; 2—Israel and Japan—are in Asia; 3 are in the Western Hemisphere—Canada, the United States, and Barbados; and 2 countries—Australia and New Zealand—are in Oceania.

Five years ago, 27 countries with 21 percent of the world's population scored 24 or lower on the Human Suffering Index.

Rank	Country	Life Expectancy	Daily Calorie Supply	Clean Drinking Water	Infant Immunization	Secondary School Enrollment	GNP Per Capita	Rate of Inflation	Communications Technology	Political Freedom	Civil Rights	HUMAN SUFFERING INDEX
TOP 10												
1	Mozambique	10	10	8	10	10	10	10	10	8	7	93
2	Somalia	10	5	7	10	10	10	10	10	10	10	92
3	Afghanistan	19	3	8	10	10	10	9	10	10	10	89
4	Haiti	10	7	6	9	10	9	8	10	10	10	89
5	Sudan	10	5	6	9	10	10	10	10	10	10	89
6	Zaire	10	6	7	10	10	9	10	10	8	8	88
7	Laos	10	2	7	10	10	10	9	10	8	8	87
8	Angola	10	8	7	10	10	10	10	7	6	8	86
9	Guinea	10	6	7	10	10	10	10	8	8	8	86
10	Ethiopia	10	7	9	10	10	10	4	10	7	8	85
UPPER MIDDLE												
11	Uganda	10	4	8	5	10	10	9	10	9	10	85
12	Cambodia	10	5	—	10	10	10	5	10	7	9	84
13	Sierra Leone	10	8	6	5	10	10	10	10	8	7	84
14	Chad	10	8	7	10	10	10	9	10	8	8	82
15	Guinea-Bissau	10	1	8	9	10	10	10	10	9	8	82
16	Ghana	9	4	4	9	10	10	9	10	9	8	81
17	Myanmar (Burma)	9	2	7	7	10	9	10	10	10	8	81
18	Malawi	10	4	4	5	10	10	7	10	10	9	79
19	Cameroon	10	7	6	9	10	7	9	10	9	9	77
20	Mauritania	10	4	3	10	9	1	10	10	8	10	77
21	Burundi	10	1	6	4	10	10	10	10	10	10	76
22	Liberia	9	2	5	10	—	9	9	10	8	9	76
23	Rwanda	10	6	4	9	10	10	9	10	8	9	76
24	Vietnam	5	3	6	7	10	9	10	10	9	9	76
25	Kenya	5	3	7	7	10	9	7	10	8	9	75
26	Madagascar	9	4	7	9	10	9	6	10	5	8	75
27	Yemen	10	7	6	10	10	8	10	8	7	7	75
28	Cote d'Ivoire	10	2	—	5	10	8	9	10	8	7	75
29	Bhutan	10	7	10	10	10	8	4	10	8		74
30	Burkina	10	6	3	9	10	9	0	10	8	8	73
31	Central African Republic	10	6	9	4	10	9	0	10	9	6	73
32	Tanzania	9	3	4	4	10	10	7	8	6	6	71
33	Togo	9	5	3	10	10	10	0	10	8	9	71
34	Lesotho	8	2	5	5	10	10	8	10	5	6	70
35	Mali	10	4	6	9	10	10	0	10	8	5	70
36	Niger	10	5	2	10	10	10	0	10	7	8	70
37	Nigeria	10	5	4	10	10	10	0	10	6	8	70
38	Guatemala	5	2	4	8	10	8	7	6	6	9	69
39	Nepal	10	5	5	7	10	10	3	10	6	6	69
40	Bangladesh	10	2	8	10	10	6	10	2	5	8	68
41	Bolivia	8	5	5	9	10	8	7	7	2	5	68
42	Zambia	9	5	4	5	10	10	10	10	1	5	68
43	Pakistan	8	2	4	5	10	9	6	10	5	8	67
44	Nicaragua	5	2	5	6	10		10	10	4	6	66
45	Papua New Guinea	9	3	7	7	10	8	5	10	2	5	66
46	Senegal	10	4	5	8	10	8	0	10	5	6	66
47	Swaziland	10	0	5	4	10	8	0	10	5	8	66
48	Zimbabwe	6	3	3	7	10	8	7	9	7	6	66

Rank	Country	Life Expectancy	Daily Calorie Supply	Clean Drinking Water	Infant Immunization	Secondary School Enrollment	GNP Per Capita	Rate of Inflation	Communications Technology	Political Freedom	Civil Rights	HUMAN SUFFERING INDEX
49	Iraq	4	0	1	6	10	7	9	8	10	10	65
50	Congo	10	1	6	5	10	8	0	10	7	7	64
51	El Salvador	5	2	5	7	10	7	7	9	5	7	64
52	Gambia	10	3	—	4	10	10	5	10	3	3	64
53	Indonesia	6	0	6	4	10	9	5	10	6	8	64
54	Syria	3	0	3	4	10	7	10	7	10	10	64
55	Comoros	8	5	7	1	10	9	4	10	4	5	63
56	India	8	4	2		10	9	6	10	4	8	63
57	Paraguay	3	1	4	6	10	7	9	9	5	6	63
58	Peru	4	4	4	7	7	7	10	9	4	7	63
59	Benin	10	4	5	7	10	9	0	10	2	5	62
LOWER MIDDLE												
60	Honduras	4	4	3	5	10	8	9	10	3	6	62
61	China	3	0	2	0	10	9	7	10	10	10	61
62	Guyana	4	2	4	5	8	9	9	8	5	7	61
63	Lebanon	3	0	—	8	6	8	10	6	8	6	61
64	South Africa	4	1	7	7	9	6	7	5	7	8	61
65	Egypt	8	0	3	4	8	8	5	9	6	3	59
66	Morocco	5	0	4	5	10	8	3	10	6	8	59
67	Ecuador	4	3	4	7	8	7	9	9	2	5	58
68	Sri Lanka	2	2	4	4	6	9	7	10	5	9	58
69	Botswana	4	0	—	5	10	8	6	10	0	2	57
70	Iran	4	0	3	3	10	7	6	8	7	9	56
71	Suriname	3	0	3	4	9	6	5	7	3		55
72	Algeria	4	0	3	8	6	8	9	5	7		54
73	Thailand	4	3	2	3	10						54
74	Dominican Republic	3	3	4	5	5	8	10	9	1	5	53
75	Mexico	3	0	3	6	9	7	8	6	5	7	53
76	Tunisia	4	0	3	2	10	7	3	8	5	7	53
77	Turkey	4	0	1	5	10	7	0	6	2	8	53
78	Colombia	3	1	4	4	7	9	7	5	7		51
79	Libya	3	0	—	8	7	5	7	6	10	10	51
80	Venezuela	2	1	1	8	9	5	7	6	6	3	51
81	Brazil	4	0	5	10	6	9	6	6	4		50
82	Oman	4	0	5	19	5	0	8	10	8		50
83	Philippines	4	2	2	4	5	6	10	3	6		50
84	Solomon Islands	3	4	2	6	10	8	5	10	0	1	49
85	Albania	2	3	4	0	5	7	9	—	4	8	47
86	Vanuatu	3	0	6		8	3	9	4	4		45
87	Jamaica	1	1	3	4	8	7	8	1	3		44
88	Romania	2	0	3	4	10	6	6	7	4		44
89	Saudi Arabia	5	0	1	10	4	0	5	10	9		44
90	Seychelles	2	0	4	10	5	0	4	8			44
91	Yugoslavia	2	0	2	4	6	10	4	7	9		44
92	Mongolia	4	1	3	2	8	10	—	3	4		43
93	Jordan	2	0	3	4	7	6	9	5	5		41
94	Malaysia	3	0	2	2	8	6	6	6	7		40
95	Mauritius	2	0	4	6	8	7	7	1	3		40
96	Argentina	2	0	2	6	6	10	5	1	1		39
97	Cuba	0	0	1	4	7	0	8	10	10		38
98	Panama	2	2	1	4	8	0	5	4	5		38

Rank	Country	Life Expectancy	Daily Calorie Supply	Clean Drinking Water	Infant Immunization	Secondary School Enrollment	GNP Per Capita	Rate of Inflation	Communications Technology	Political Freedom	Civil Rights	HUMAN SUFFERING INDEX
99	Chile	2	2	1	0	5	7	8	7	2	3	37
100	Korea, North	3	0	3	0	0	7	0	—	10	10	37
101	Uruguay	2	1	1	4	4	6	10	5	1	3	37
102	Costa Rica	0	0	1	1	10	7	8	5	0	2	34
103	Korea, South	2	0	2	6	3	5	5	3	3	5	34
104	United Arab Emirates	2	0	0	4	8	0	2	3	8	7	34
105	Poland	2	0	0	0	4	7	10	5	3	2	33
106	Bulgaria	2	0	0	0	4	6	10	3	2	5	32
107	Hungary	2	0	0	0	5	6	9	5	2	3	32
108	Qatar	2	0	0	4	4	3	0	2	10	7	32
109	Russia*	2	0	0	5	0	3	5	5	5	6	31
110	Bahrain	3	0	0	2	3	4	0	3	8	6	29
111	Hong Kong	0	1	0	5	5	2	5	1	5	5	29
112	Trinidad and Tobago	2	0	0	6	3	6	5	6	0	1	29
113	Kuwait	1	0	0	4	2	2	0	4	9	8	28
114	Singapore	1	1	0	4	6	2	0	1	6	7	28
115	Czech Republic	2	0	0	0	3	4	7	3	2	4	25
116	Portugal	1	0	0	0	9	5	6	3	0	1	25
117	Taiwan	1	0	1	4	1	5	1	3	4	5	25
118	Israel	0	0	0	0	4	3	7	1	2	4	21
119	Greece	0	0	0	0	1	5	8	2	1	2	19
120	United Kingdom	1	0	0	0	3	1	5	1	1	4	16
121	Italy	0	0	0	0	4	0	5	1	0	2	12
122	Barbados	0	0	0	4	1	4	0	2	0	0	11
123	Ireland	1	0	0	0	1	3	0	3	1	2	11
124	Spain	0	0	0	0	0	3	3	2	0	3	11
125	Sweden	0	3	0	0	2	0	6	0	0	0	11
126	Finland	1	3	0	0	0	0	1	1	2	0	8
127	New Zealand	1	0	0	0	2	2	1	0	0	2	8
128	France	0	0	0	0	1	0	0	1	2	3	7
129	Iceland	0	1	0	0	0	0	5	1	0	0	7
130	Japan	0	1	0	0	1	0	0	1	1	3	7
131	Luxembourg	1	0	0	0	5	0	0	1	0	0	7
BOTTOM 10												
132	Austria	1	0	0	0	4	0	0	1	0	0	6
133	Germany	1	0	0	0	1	0	0	1	0	3	6
134	United States	1	0	0	0	0	0	2	0	1	1	5
135	Australia	0	0	0	0	1	2	1	0	0	0	4
136	Norway	0	2	0	0	1	0	0	1	0	1	3
137	Canada	0	0	0	0	0	0	1	0	1	1	3
138	Switzerland	0	0	0	0	1	0	2	0	0	0	3
139	Belgium	1	0	0	0	0	0	0	1	0	0	2
140	Netherlands	0	1	0	0	0	0	0	0	0	0	2
141	Denmark	1	0	0	0	0	0	0	0	0	0	1

*Data for all indicators are for the former Soviet Union except for the Civil Rights and Political Freedom indicators, which average in separate data weighted by population size for Ukraine, Estonia, Latvia and Lithuania.

Source: Population Action International

300. STATUS OF WOMEN INDEX

The status of women varies enormously from one part of the world to another. Nowhere do women enjoy equal status with men. But in the least developed countries of Africa, the Middle East, Asia and Latin America, crushing poverty overlaid with long-standing patterns of discrimination create living conditions for women almost too harsh to imagine for women in Western industrial countries.

The world's poorest women are not merely poor. They live on the edge of subsistence. They are economically dependent and vulnerable, politically and legally powerless. As wives and mothers they are caught in a life cycle that begins with early marriage and too often ends with death in childbirth. They work longer hours and sometimes work harder than men, but their work is typically unpaid and undervalued.

Worldwide, women grow about half the world's food, but most own no land. They are one third of the official paid workforce, but are concentrated in the lowest paid occupations. They are grossly under-represented in institutions of government. If they work outside the home, most work a double day, bearing nearly total responsibility for child care and household chores, regardless of their contribution to family income.

In this study of 99 countries, representing 2.3 billion women (92 percent of the world's female population), 20 indicators measure women's well-being in five sectors: health, marriage and children, education, employment, and social equality. In each area, three indicators compare women's status from country to country, for example, the percent of girls in school. A fourth measures the relative size of the gender gap within countries, for example, the difference between male and female rates of literacy.

Original data for each of the 20 indicators, collected from standard data sets, were converted mathematically to 5 point scales, giving a maximum score for each sector of 20 and a maximum total score of 100.

Possible scores were divided into seven overall rankings, from Excellent to Extremely Poor. Although some countries received Excellent scores in one or another sector, no total country score fell in the Excellent category (scores of 90 to 100). Only seven countries had total scores of 80 or above, giving them a rank of Very Good. Sweden, with 87, scored highest. Bangladesh, with 21.5, scored lowest.

Some 51 out of 99 countries fell into the study's three bottom categories: Poor, Very Poor and Extremely Poor. Country scores for these rankings ranged from 59.5 to 21.5. The study indicates that over 60 percent of all women and girls in the world live under conditions which threaten their health, deny them choice about childbearing and limit educational attainment.

Many Islamic countries also permit polygyny, although economic factors are helping to make the practice less common. Under conservative interpretations of Islam, women generally may not initiate divorce, but men may divorce their wives almost at will and typically retain custody of children.

Like most Latin American countries, many African and Asian countries, including many moder-

ate Islamic countries, have made some attempt to modernize family law. But except where organized efforts have been made to teach women their rights and offer them legal counsel, reforms have had little impact on traditional practices. In India, for example, the official age of marriage for women was raised to 18 years in 1978 to discourage the arranged marriages of very young girls. Dowries have been specifically outlawed. But many rural Indian girls are still married at 14 or younger, and newspapers report continued incidents of bride-burning related to dowry disputes.

In a number of African countries, women's advocates are fighting an uphill battle to eliminate clitoridectomy and other more extreme genital operations on young girls, generally referred to as female circumcision. Some defenders of the practice believe, among other reasons, that it is necessary to keep women chaste and faithful. In most conservative regions, women without such operations are not considered marriageable.

In many of these same African, Asian and Middle-Eastern countries, women's inequality in marriage prevents them from exercising any independent control over when they will get pregnant or how many children they will have. They are not permitted, for instance, to use contraceptives without their husband's permission. The inability to control childbearing can increase women's vulnerability and dependence in marriage, since even in countries with child support laws, many divorced or abandoned women have little or no income from former spouses.

Government efforts to craft and enforce new equal rights provisions have improved women's status in some instances. But in most societies, ingrained inequalities and the attitudes behind them die hard.

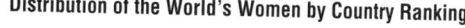

Distribution of the World's Women by Country Ranking

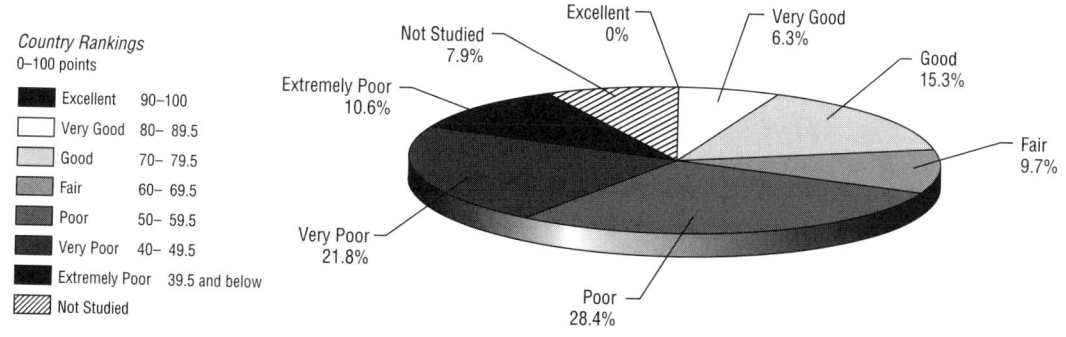

Country Rankings
0–100 points

Excellent	90–100
Very Good	80– 89.5
Good	70– 79.5
Fair	60– 69.5
Poor	50– 59.5
Very Poor	40– 49.5
Extremely Poor	39.5 and below
Not Studied	

Not Studied 7.9%
Excellent 0%
Very Good 6.3%
Good 15.3%
Extremely Poor 10.6%
Fair 9.7%
Very Poor 21.8%
Poor 28.4%

Rank	Country	Health				Marriage and Children				Education				Employment				Social Equality				Totals*		
		Infant and Child Mortality	Mortality—Childbearing Years	Life Expectancy	Female/Male, Differential Life Expectancy	Teen Marriage	Total Fertility Rate	Contraceptive Prevalence	Female/Male, Widowed, Divorced, Separated	Secondary School Teachers	Primary/Secondary School Enrollment	University Enrollment	Female/Male, Differential Literacy Rate	Self-Employment	Paid Employees	Professionals	Share of Paid Employment	Economic Equality	Political and Legal Equality	Equality in Marriage and Family	Female/Male, Societal Equality	Women's Status Subtotal	Gender Gap Subtotal	Total Score
TOP 10																								
1	Sweden	5	5	5	4	5	5	4.5	5	3.5	4.5	3.5	4	0.5	4	5	5	3.5	5	5	5	64	23	87
2	Finland	5	5	5	4	5	5	4.5	4.5	—	5	3	4	1	3.5	2	5	3.5	5	5	5	61.5	23.5	85
3	United States	5	5	5	4	4.5	5	4	5	—	5	3	4	0.5	3	2	4.5	3.5	3.5	5	4.5	60.5	22	82.5
4	Germany	5	5	4.5	3.5	5	5	4	4.5	4	4.5	3	4	0.5	4.5	—	5	3.5	3.5	5	4.5	59.5	22	82
5	Norway	5	5	5	4	5	5	5	—	5		3	4	0.5	3.5	2.5	4.5	3.5	3.5	5	4.5	59	21.5	81.5
6	Canada	5	5	5	4	5	5	4.5	3.5	5		2.5	4	0.5	3	2.5	4.5	3.5	3.5	5	4.5	58.5	21.5	80.5
7	Denmark	5	5		3.5	5	5	3.5		5		2.5	4	1	2.5	1.5	4	3.5	3.5	5	4.5	58	21.5	80
8	Australia	5	5	5	4	5	5	—	5	3.5		2.5	4	0.5	3.5	2	4.5	3.5	3.5	5	4.5	56.5	21.5	79.5
9	Bulgaria	5	5	4.5	4	4	4.5	4	4.5	4.5	4	—	4.5	1.5	2	1.5	4.5	3.5	3.5	5	4.5	56.5	21	78
10	Jamaica	5	5	5	2.5	4		3	5	5	4		1.5	3.5	1.5	4.5	3.5	3.5	5	4.5		56.5	21.5	77.5
UPPER MIDDLE																								
11	Czech Republic	5	5	4.5		4.5	4.5	4.5	4		4	1.5	4	0.5	3.5	1.5	4.5	3.5	3.5	5	4.5	55.5	21.5	77
12	Belgium	5	5			5	5	4.5	4.5	—	5	2.5	4	0.5	2.5	1	4.5	3.5	3.5	5	4.5	56.5	20.5	77
13	Hungary	5	5	4.5	4.5	4.5	5	4	4.5	5		1.5	3.5	0.5	2.5	1.5	5	3.5	3.5	5	4.5	54	23	77
14	Russia	4.5	4.5	4	5	4.5	4.5	—		5	3.5	2.5	4	0.5	4	1	3.5	3.5	3.5	5	4.5	56	20.5	76.5
15	New Zealand	5	5		3.5	5	5	4	3.5	4		2.5	4	0.5	2.5	1	3.5	3.5	3.5	5	4.5	55.5	20.5	76
16	Iceland	5	5	4	3.5	5	5	4.5		4		2	4	0.5	1	4	3.5	3.5	3.5	3.5	4	55.5	20.5	76
17	France	5	5	4.5	5	5	4.5	4	4.5		4	2	4	0.5	1	4	3.5	3.5	3.5	5	4.5	54.5	21	75.5
18	Austria	5	5	5	4.5	5	4	3.5	4	4.5		2	4	0.5	2.5	1	4.5	3.5	3.5	5	4.5	54.5	21	75.5
19	Poland	5	5	4.5		5	4	4.5	4.5		2	2.5	4	0.5	1	3.5	3.5	3.5	5	4.5		54.5	20.5	75
20	Netherlands	5	5	4		5	5	4.5	4.5	2	4.5	1.5	4	0.5	2.5	1.5	3.5	3.5	3.5	3.5	4	54.5	20	74.5
21	United Kingdom	5	5	3.5		5	5	4.5	3.5	4.5	4.5	1.5	4	0.5	1.5		3.5	3.5	3.5	3.5	4	55	19	74
22	Italy	5	5	4.5	3	5	5		2.5	4.5		1	4		1	4.5	3.5	3.5	3.5	5		54	20	74
23	Barbados	5	5	4.5	3	5		3	5		4		4	4.5	0.5	1.5	1	3.5	3.5	5	4.5	53	19	72
24	Yugoslavia	5	5	4	3.5	5	5	3		3.5		1	3.5	1.5	2	0.5	3.5	3.5	3.5	3.5		52	19.5	71.5
25	Portugal	5	5	4		4.5	4.5	3.5	4	4.5		1	3.5	1.5	2	1.5	4	3.5	3.5	2	3.5	53.5	17.5	71
26	Israel	5	5	2.5		4		4	4.5		4	2.5	4	1	2	1	3.5	3.5	3.5	2	3.5	50.5	19.5	70
27	Uruguay	4.5	5	4.5	4	4.5	4.5	—	4.5		4	2.5	3.5	1	0.5		3.5	3.5	3.5	3.5	4	52	18	70
28	Spain	5	5	3.5	4	4.5		3.5	4	3		4.5	1.5	3.5	1	0.5	3	3.5	3.5	5	4.5	52.5	17.5	70
29	Greece	5	5	3.5	4.5	4		4	4.5		3.5		1	1.5	1	3.5	3.5	3.5	3.5		51	18.5	69.5
30	Costa Rica	5	5	5	4	4	4.5		3.5		2.5	0.5	3	1	4	2	3.5	3.5		51	17.5	69.5
31	Hong Kong	5	5	3.5	4	4		3.5	4.5		2.5	2	0.5	3	3.5	5	4.5	51	18	69				
32	Cuba	5	4.5	4.5	2	3.5	3.5	5	3.5	4.5		2	3.5	1	2	3.5	3.5	3.5		50.5	18	68.5		
33	Japan	5	5	3.5		5	3.5	3.5	4		2	3.5	1	2	2	3.5	3.5	3.5	4	49.5	18.5	68		
34	Trinidad & Tobago	5	4.5	4	3		4.5	3	4.5		4.5	0.5	3.5	1	1.5	3.5	3.5	5	3	50	18	68		
35	Argentina	4.5	4.5	4.5	4	4.5	4		4.5	3.5		1	4	1	1.5	3	3.5	3.5	3.5	49	19	68		
36	Romania	5	5	4	4.5	5	4		3.5		4	2.5	3.5	0.5	1	3.5	3.5	3.5		48.5	19	67.5		
37	Panama	5	4.5	4.5	4		3.5	4	4.5		4		3.5	1.5	1	3.5	3.5	3.5	4	50	17	67		
38	Venezuela	4.5	4.5	4	3.5	4		3.5	4		4.5	3		1	0.5	3	2	3.5	4	51	16	67		
39	Taiwan	5	5	4.5		5	5	4.5			4.5	3		2	2	0.5	2	2		51	16	67		
LOWER MIDDLE																								
40	Singapore	5	5	4.5	3.5	5	5	4		3.5	4.5	1	3	0.5	2.5	1	4	3.5	2	2	3	49.5	17	66.5
41	Ireland	5	5		3.5	5	4		4	4		5	2	0.5	2	1	3.5	2	3.5	0.5	3	49	17	66
42	Philippines	4	4.5	3.5	3.5	4.5	3.5	2	4.5	—		4.5	2.5	3.5	1.5	1.5	1	2	2	3.5	3.5	45.5	16.5	62
43	Korea, South	4.5	5	4	4	5	4.5	4	2	2		4.5	1.5	3.5	1	1.5	0.5	2	2	3.5	4	44	17.5	61.5
44	Mexico	4.5	4.5	4	3.5	3.5	3.5	3	2.5	4.5		4.5	2.5	3.5	1	1	0.5	2.5	3.5	3.5	4	43.5	17.5	61
45	Ecuador	4	4.5	4	3	3.5	2.5	2.5	4.5		4	0.5	3	1	1.5	0.5	3	2	3.5	3.5		43.5	16.5	60
46	Sri Lanka	4.5	4.5	4	4	3.5	4		3	4	—		0.5	3	1	0.5	2.5	3	2	3.5		43.5	16.5	60
47	Colombia	4	4.5	3.5	4	4.5	3.5	3.5	4	3.5		4	1.5	3.5	0.5	1.5	0.5	3	2	2	0.5	1.5	43	16.5	59.5
48	Chile	5	5	4	4	4.5	2.5		4	4.5		0.5	3.5	0.5	1	2.5	3.5	2	3.5		42.5	17	59.5
49	Guyana	4.5	4.5	3.5	4	4.5	4.5	2	4.5	3.5		0.5	3.5	1	0.5	3.5	2	3.5	3.5		42.5	15.5	58
50	China	4	4.5	3.5	4	5	4.5		5	2	1	0.5	3.5	—	1	0.5	3.5	2	2	3.5		42.5	15.5	58
51	Malaysia	4.5	4.5	4	3.5	4.5	4	3	3.5	3.5	3.5	0.5	2.5	1	1.5	0.5	4	2	2	2	2	40.5	17	57.5
52	Thailand	4	4	3.5	4	4	4.5	3.5	4	4.5		3	0.5	1.5	1	0.5	4	2						

Column groups: **Health** (Infant and Child Mortality · Mortality—Childbearing Years · Life Expectancy · Female/Male, Differential Life Expectancy) | **Marriage and Children** (Teen Marriage · Total Fertility Rate · Contraceptive Prevalence · Female/Male, Widowed, Divorced, Separated · Secondary School Teachers) | **Education** (Primary/Secondary School Enrollment · University Enrollment · Female/Male, Differential Literacy Rate) | **Employment** (Self-Employment · Paid Employees · Professionals · Share of Paid Employment · Economic Equality) | **Social Equality** (Political and Legal Equality · Equality in Marriage and Family · Female/Male, Societal Equality · Women's Status Subtotal) | **Totals*** (Gender Gap Subtotal · Total Score)

Rank	Country	Infant and Child Mortality	Mortality—Childbearing Years	Life Expectancy	Female/Male, Differential Life Expectancy	Teen Marriage	Total Fertility Rate	Contraceptive Prevalence	Female/Male, Widowed, Divorced, Separated	Secondary School Teachers	Primary/Secondary School Enrollment	University Enrollment	Female/Male, Differential Literacy Rate	Self-Employment	Paid Employees	Professionals	Share of Paid Employment	Economic Equality	Political and Legal Equality	Equality in Marriage and Family	Female/Male, Societal Equality	Women's Status Subtotal	Gender Gap Subtotal	Total Score
53	Peru	3	4	3	3	4	3	2.5	4.5	3.5	4.5	1.5	2.5	2.5	—	1.5	2	2	2	3.5	3	42.5	15	57.5
54	Dominican Republic	3.5	4	3	3	4.5	3.5	3	4	—	2.5	1	3.5	—	1	0.5	3.5	2	2	3.5	3	39.5	17.5	57
55	Paraguay	4	4.5	4	3	4	2.5	2	4.5	—	3	—	3.5	1	0.5	1	2	2	3.5	3.5	3.5	41	16	57
56	El Salvador	3	4	2.5	3	4	2.5	2.5	4.5	2	3	1	3	0.5	1	1	2	2	2	3.5	4	38	17.5	55.5
57	Nicaragua	3	3	2.5	2	3.5	2	1.5	3.5	4.5	4	1	3.5	0.5	1	—	3	3.5	3.5	3.5	4	38	16.5	54.5
58	Brazil	4	4.5	3.5	3	4	3.5	3.5	4	4	4	1	3.5	1	0.5	3.5	3.5	3.5	4	3.5	3.5	38.5	16	54.5
59	Botswana	3.5	3.5	2.5	3.5	5	1.5	1.5	3.5	3	4	0.5	4	0.5	1.5	1	4	2	3.5	0.5	1.5	39.5	15	54.5
60	Turkey	3.5	4.5	3	2.5	4	3.5	3	4	2.5	3	0.5	1	0.5	0.5	0.5	4	2	3.5	2	3	35	18	53
61	South Africa	3.5	4	3	4	5	2.5	3	3.5	—	2.5	—	3.5	0.5	2	0.5	3	2	2	0.5	4	39.5	13	52.5
62	Honduras	3.5	4	3.5	2.5	3	2	2	4	3.5	3.5	1	3	0.5	1	0.5	3	2	2	0.5	1.5	37	15.5	52.5
63	Jordan	4	4.5	4	2.5	3.5	1	1.5	—	—	4.5	3	3	0.5	1	0.5	2	3.5	3.5	2	3.5	37	15	52
64	Kuwait	4.5	4.5	4.5	3	4	2	—	1.5	4	4.5	2	2.5	0.5	0.5	1	2	3.5	2	3	—	38.5	11.5	50
65	Tunisia	4.5	4.5	4	2.5	5	3	2.5	2.5	2	3	0.5	1	1	2	1.5	2	2	0.5	0.5	1	39.5	10	49.5
66	Algeria	4	4	3	3	3.5	1.5	0.5	4	2.5	3	0.5	3.5	0.5	0.5	0.5	1.5	2	3.5	2	3	38.5	10.5	49
67	Bolivia	2	3.5	2	2.5	1.5	1.5	1.5	4.5	—	3.5	—	1.5	1	1	0.5	2.5	3.5	2	2	3	33	14.5	47.5
68	Iraq	3.5	4	3	1.5	3	1.5	1	3	4	3.5	1	1.5	1	0.5	2.5	3.5	2	2	3	—	33	14	47
69	Zimbabwe	3.5	3.5	3	3	3.5	1.5	2	3.5	2	4.5	0.5	2.5	0.5	1	0.5	1.5	2	3.5	3.5	4	36.5	10.5	47
70	Indonesia	3	3.5	2.5	2.5	3	3.5	2	3	—	4	0.5	2.5	0.5	1	0.5	1.5	2	3.5	2	2	33.5	13.5	47
71	Guatemala	3.5	3.5	3	3	3	2.5	1.5	4	2.5	4	0.5	2.5	0.5	1	0.5	3	2	2	2	2	33.5	13	46.5
72	Lesotho	3.5	3.5	2.5	2.5	3	2.5	0.5	2.5	4	4.5	0.5	5	0.5	0.5	1.5	2.5	2	2	2	3	31.5	14.5	46
73	Kenya	3.5	3.5	3	3	0.5	1	1	3.5	3	4.5	0.5	5	2.5	1	0.5	1.5	2	2	3.5	3	32	13.5	45.5
74	Mozambique	1.5	1.5	1	2.5	3	1.5	—	3.5	1.5	1.5	0.5	3.5	2	1	0.5	1.5	2	2	3.5	3	32.5	12.5	45
75	India	2.5	3.5	2.5	2	2	3.5	—	4.5	2	2	0.5	1.5	2	5	0.5	3	2	2	2	2	28	16.5	44.5
76	Haiti	2.5	3	2	1.5	5	2	0.5	3.5	0.5	2	0.5	3	3.5	1	0.5	3	2	2	3.5	3	29.5	14	43.5
77	United Arab Emirates	4.5	4.5	4	3	1	1.5	—	4.5	4	1.5	3	0.5	1	0.5	4.5	2	2	2	2	—	29	14.5	43.5
78	Zambia	2.5	3	2	2.5	3	1	0.5	4	2.5	1.5	3	0.5	1	1	0.5	0.5	2.5	3.5	2	3	31.5	11.5	43
79	Cameroon	2	2	1.5	3	2	2	0.5	3.5	1.5	3	0.5	1	3	0.5	0.5	2	2	3.5	3	—	28	14	42
80	Syria	4.5	4	3.5	2	3.5	1	1.5	2.5	1.5	3.5	1	1	0.5	0.5	1	2	2	2	3.5	3.5	28	12	40
81	Tanzania	2.5	2.5	1.5	3	2.5	1	0.5	4.5	2	2.5	0.5	1	5	0.5	0.5	1	2	2	2	2	31.5	8.5	40
82	Morocco	3.5	4	3	2.5	4	3	1.5	2.5	2	2	0.5	1.5	0.5	0.5	0.5	1.5	2	2	2	2	27.5	12	39.5
83	Rwanda	2	2	1.5	2.5	4	1	0.5	4	1.5	2	0.5	1.5	2.5	0.5	0.5	1.5	0.5	2	0.5	1.5	29.5	9.5	39
84	Benin	2	2	1.5	2.5	0.5	1	0.5	4.5	—	1	0.5	0.5	2.5	0.5	—	3.5	2	2	3.5	3	26	12.5	38.5
85	Egypt	3	3.5	2.5	1.5	3.5	3	2	1.5	2.5	3	1.5	1.5	0.5	—	3.5	2	2	3.5	3.5	3.5	23.5	14.5	38
86	Nepal	2	2	1	1	1	2	1	5	0.5	1	0.5	2	5	0.5	0.5	1.5	2	2	0.5	1.5	30.5	7.5	38
87	Libya	4	4.5	3.5	3	2.5	1	—	3.5	2	—	0.5	5	0.5	0.5	1.5	2	2	2	2	2	24.5	12.5	37
88	Liberia	2.5	2.5	2	2.5	2.5	1	0.5	5	—	1.5	0.5	1.5	1.5	0.5	0.5	0.5	2	3.5	0.5	2	22.5	11.5	34

BOTTOM 10

Rank	Country	Infant and Child Mortality	Mortality—Childbearing Years	Life Expectancy	Female/Male, Differential Life Expectancy	Teen Marriage	Total Fertility Rate	Contraceptive Prevalence	Female/Male, Widowed, Divorced, Separated	Secondary School Teachers	Primary/Secondary School Enrollment	University Enrollment	Female/Male, Differential Literacy Rate	Self-Employment	Paid Employees	Professionals	Share of Paid Employment	Economic Equality	Political and Legal Equality	Equality in Marriage and Family	Female/Male, Societal Equality	Women's Status Subtotal	Gender Gap Subtotal	Total Score
89	Senegal	2.5	2.5	1.5	2.5	2	1.5	1	3.5	1	1	0.5	2	0.5	0.5	0.5	2	2	2	2	—	21	12	33
90	Malawi	2	1.5	1	2.5	1.5	1	0.5	3.5	—	2	0.5	1.5	0.5	0.5	1	2	3.5	2	3	—	20.5	11.5	32
91	Sudan	2.5	2.5	2	3	2	1.5	0.5	3.5	2	1.5	0.5	1.5	1	0.5	0.5	0.5	2	3.5	2	3	21.5	10	31.5
92	Pakistan	1.5	3	2	1.5	2.5	3	5	5	2	0.5	0.5	2	0.5	0.5	0.5	0.5	0.5	0.5	—	—	18.5	9.5	28
93	Saudi Arabia	3.5	4.5	3	2.5	—	1	1	—	3	0.5	0.5	—	0.5	0.5	0.5	0.5	0.5	0.5	0.5	0.5	23	6.5	29.5
94	Nigeria	1.5	1.5	1	2	2.5	1	0.5	—	1.5	2.5	0.5	—	0.5	—	0.5	1.5	2	2	2	—	20.5	8.5	29
95	Yemen	1.5	1.5	1	2	1.5	1.5	0.5	4	0.5	0.5	0.5	1.5	0.5	0.5	—	0.5	2	2	0.5	1.5	16.5	10	26.5
96	Mali	1.5	1	1	2	1.5	1	0.5	2.5	1	0.5	0.5	2.5	0.5	0.5	—	0.5	1	2	2	2	16	10	26
97	Afghanistan	0.5	0.5	0.5	2	1.5	1	0.5	4	2.5	0.5	0.5	2	0.5	0.5	—	1	2	2	2	2	15.5	10.5	26
98	Bangladesh	1	2.5	1.5	0.5	0.5	2	1.5	0.5	0.5	1.5	0.5	2	0.5	0.5	—	1.5	0.5	2	0.5	1	16	5.5	,21.5

Source: Population Action International

EPILOGUE

The Balance Sheet

Balance sheet of human development—developing countries

PLUS | MINUS

HEALTH

PLUS
- During 1960–92, average life expectancy increased by more than a third. By now, 30 countries have achieved a life expectancy of more than 70 years.
- Over the past three decades, the population with access to safe water almost doubled, from 36% to 70%.

MINUS
- About 17 million people die every year from infectious and parasitic diseases, such as diarrhea, malaria and tuberculosis.
- More than 90% of the 17 million HIV-infected people live in developing countries.

EDUCATION

PLUS
- Net enrollment at the primary level increased by nearly two-thirds during the past 30 years, from 48% in 1960 to 77% in 1991.

MINUS
- About 130 million children at the primary level and more than 275 million at the secondary level are out of school.

FOOD AND NUTRITION

PLUS
- Despite rapid population growth, per capita food production rose by more than 20% during the past decade.

MINUS
- Nearly 800 million people do not get enough food, and about 500 million people are chronically malnourished.

INCOME AND POVERTY

PLUS
- During the past decade, both agriculture and industry expanded at an annual rate of more than 3% in developing countries.

MINUS
- Almost a third of the population, about 1.3 billion people, live below the poverty line.

WOMEN

PLUS
- The combined primary and secondary enrollment of girls increased from 38% to 68% during the past two decades.
- During the past two decades, fertility rates declined by more than a third.

MINUS
- Maternal mortality in developing countries, at 350 per 100,000 live births, is about nine times higher than that in OECD countries.
- Women hold about 10% of parliamentary seats.

CHILDREN

PLUS
- In 1960–92, the infant mortality rate was more than halved, from 149 per thousand live births to 70.
- During the past two decades, the lives of about three million children were saved every year through the extension of basic immunization.

MINUS
- More than a third of children are malnourished and underweight.
- The under-five mortality rate, at 100 per thousand live births, is still nearly seven times higher than that in industrial countries.

ENVIRONMENT

PLUS
- Developing countries' contribution to global emissions is less than a fourth that of industrial countries, even though their population is 3.5 times larger.

MINUS
- About 200 million people are severely affected by desertification.
- Every year, some 20 million hectares of tropical forest are cleared outright or grossly degraded.

POLITICS AND CONFLICTS

PLUS
- More than two-thirds of the population in developing countries live under relatively pluralistic and democratic regimes.

MINUS
- At the end of 1993, there were more than 13 million refugees in the developing world.

Balance sheet of human development—industrial countries

PLUS	MINUS

HEALTH

• By 1992, 24 industrial countries had achieved a life expectancy of more than 75 years.	• More than 1.5 million people are infected with HIV.

EDUCATION

• The tertiary enrollment ratio more than doubled between 1960 and 1991, from 15% to 40%.	• More than a third of adults have less than an upper-secondary education.

INCOME AND POVERTY

• Between 1972 and 1992, real per capita GNP grew by 46%. • The annual rate of inflation is now less than 4%.	• The total unemployment rate is more than 8%, and the rate among youths nearly 15%. More than 35 million people are seeking jobs. • The poorest 40% of households get only 18% of total income.

WOMEN

• In science and technology at the tertiary level, the number of girls per 100 boys has more than doubled, from 25 in 1970 to 67 in 1990. • Women now make up more than 40% of the labor force and hold about 28% of administrative and managerial positions.	• Women's non-agricultural wage rate is still only three-fourths of men's. • Women hold only 12% of parliamentary seats.

SOCIAL SECURITY

• Social security expenditures account for about 16% of GDP.	• About 100 million people live below the poverty line. • More than five million people are homeless.

SOCIAL FABRIC

• There are more than five library books and one radio for every person, one TV set for every two people. One in three people reads a newspaper.	• More than a third of marriages end in divorce, and about 7% of households are headed by a single female parent. • Nearly 130,000 rapes are reported annually in the age group 15–59.

ENVIRONMENT

• Between 1965 and 1991, energy use per $100 of GDP was cut dramatically, from 168 kilograms of oil equivalent to 25 kilograms, through aggressive conservation measures and more appropriate pricing policies.	• Each year, damage to forests due to air pollution leads to economic losses of about $35 billion in Europe alone—equivalent to Hungary's GDP. • People in industrial countries constitute a little more than a fifth of the world's population but consume nearly nine times more commercial energy per capita than people in developing countries.

Balance sheet of human development—Latin America and the Caribbean

PLUS	MINUS

HEALTH

• By 1992, life expectancy had reached an average of 68 years, about 90% of the life expectancy achieved in the industrial world.	• Only 56% of the rural population have access to safe water, compared with 90% of the urban population. • Two million people in the region have been infected with HIV.

EDUCATION

• Total enrollment at the secondary and tertiary levels increased nearly eightfold, from 4 million to 31 million, between 1960 and 1991. • At the tertiary level, the net enrollment ratio increased more than fourfold, from 6% to 27%, during the past three decades.	• Less than half of grade 1 entrants reach grade 5. • At the secondary level, nearly 20 million boys and girls—and at the tertiary level, 27 million men and women—are out of school.

INCOME AND POVERTY

• During the past two decades, real GDP increased by more than 80%. • During 1989–93, of the cumulative $412 billion in private resource flows to developing countries, 30% went to Latin America. • Merchandise export grew 3% a year during 1980–92.	• About 110 million people were below the poverty line in 1990. • The Gini coefficient of land distribution is higher than 0.75. • The income share of the richest 20% of the population is 15 times the share of the poorest 20% in many countries.

WOMEN

• Women make up nearly 30% of the formal labor force. • For every 100 boys, there are 97 girls enrolled at the secondary level and 100 at the tertiary level.	• Women occupy only 10% of seats in parliaments. • More than half of those out of school at the secondary level are girls.

CHILDREN

• Between 1960 and 1992, the infant mortality rate was more than halved, from 105 per thousand live births to 45.	• In some Latin American metropolises, more than 100,000 children live on the streets.

ENVIRONMENT

• The deforestation rate has fallen in many countries, including Brazil. • Countries participating in the Summit of the Americas in 1993 expressed a commitment to sustainable development.	• Pesticide consumption per thousand people is the highest among developing regions, with adverse implications for the environment.

POLITICS AND CONFLICTS

• During 1974–93, 130 parliamentary elections were held, and since 1980, 18 countries have made the transition from a military to a democratic government. • The Esquipulas Declaration of August 1987 marked a milestone for peace and development in Central America.	• At the end of 1993, nearly 150,000 people were refugees.

Balance sheet of human development—South Asia

PLUS	MINUS

HEALTH

PLUS
- During the past three decades, life expectancy increased by 16 years, from 44 in 1960 to 20 in 1992.
- Public expenditure on health as a percentage of GDP has nearly tripled—from 0.5% in 1960 to 1.4% in 1990.

MINUS
- South Asia is the only region in the world in which, in such countries as Bangladesh, Maldives and Nepal, female life expectancy is shorter than male life expectancy.
- Nearly 60 million women are "missing"; there are fewer women per 100 men than in any other region, defying the natural sex ratio.
- About 280 million people lack access to safe water, and more than 800 million people have no access to even basic sanitation.

EDUCATION

PLUS
- The net enrollment ratio increased from 48% in 1960 to 79% in 1991 at the primary level and from 19% to 44% at the secondary level.

MINUS
- About 380 million people are still illiterate. South Asia's adult literacy rate is lower than that of any other region.
- Only half of grade 1 entrants reach grade 5.

FOOD AND NUTRITION

PLUS
- Between 1965 and 1992, daily per capita calorie intake increased from 88% to 103% of requirements.

MINUS
- About 300 million people do not have enough to eat.

INCOME AND POVERTY

PLUS
- GNP grew at an average annual rate of 5.4% during 1980–92, and per capita income at 3.0%
- During 1980–92, merchandise exports grew at an annual rate of nearly 7%.

MINUS
- South Asia is home to more than 560 million poor people, nearly half the world's poor population.
- During 1960–90, defense spending as a percentage of GDP increased by more than 40%—from 2.8% to 4% of GDP.

WOMEN

PLUS
- Of the world's ten female heads of state or government, four are in this region.
- During the past two decades, female illiteracy rates were reduced from 81% to 67%.

MINUS
- About two-thirds of adult women are illiterate.
- About 80% of pregnant women suffer from anemia—the highest rate in the world.

CHILDREN

PLUS
- The infant mortality rate declined from 164 per thousand live births to 85 between 1960 and 1992.
- About 85% of one-year-olds are immunized.

MINUS
- About 48 million children are out of primary school, and 94 million are out of secondary school.
- About a third of newborn babies are underweight.

POPULATION AND ENVIRONMENT

PLUS
- The fertility rate has declined from more than six live births per woman in the 1960s to four in 1990.
- South Asia contributes less to global emissions than any other region.

MINUS
- Every year, about 4 million hectares of land are deforested.
- For 1992–2000, the annual population growth rate has been estimated at more than 2%. That rate will result in a population of 1.5 billion in the year 2000—nearly a fourth of the world's total population.

POLITICS AND CONFLICTS

PLUS
- Since 1980, more than 20 general parliamentary elections have been held in South Asia.

MINUS
- At the end of 1993, nearly five million people were refugees.

Balance sheet of human development—Sub-Saharan Africa

PLUS

MINUS

HEALTH

- Life expectancy at birth increase from 40 to 51 years between 1960 and 1992.
- During the past decade, the share of the population with access to safe water nearly doubled, from 25% to 45%.

- There is only one doctor for every 18,000 people, compared with one per 7,000 in the developing world and one per 390 in industrial countries.
- More than ten million people have been infected by HIV. Sub-Saharan Africa presently accounts for two-thirds of those infected worldwide.

EDUCATION

- During the past two decades, adult literacy doubled, increasing from 27% to 54%.
- The net enrollment ratio at the primary level doubled, rising from 25% to 50%, and the secondary enrollment ratio almost tripled, growing from 13% to 38%, between 1960 and 1991.

- Only about half the entrants to grade 1 finish grade 5.
- More than 80 million boys and girls are still out of school at the primary and secondary levels.

INCOME AND POVERTY

- During 1980–92, five Sub-Saharan countries—Botswana, Cape Verde, Lesotho, Mauritius and Swaziland—generated an annual GDP growth rate of more than 5%.

- About 170 million people (nearly a third of the region's population) do not get enough to eat.
- During 1980–92, the annual average growth rate of per capita GDP was -0.8%
- Defense spending rose from 0.7% of GDP in 1960 to 3.0% in 1991, and during the past two decades, the debt service ratio increased from 5% to 25%.

WOMEN

- The female enrollment ratio at the secondary level increased fourfold during the past three decades—from 8% in 1960 to 32% in 1991.

- Sub-Saharan Africa has the world's highest maternal mortality rate, at 600 per 100,000 live births (compared with 10 in the industrial countries).
- There are six HIV-infected women for every four infected men.

CHILDREN

- The infant mortality rate dropped from 165 per thousand live births to 97 during the past three decades.

- About 26 million children in the region are malnourished, and more than 15% of babies are underweight.

POPULATION AND ENVIRONMENT

- Per capita emissions of carbon dioxide, at 1.04 metric tons, are the lowest in the world.
- The pesticide consumption per thousand people is about half the average consumption in the developing world.

- During the past 50 years, on average, 1.3 million hectares of productive land have turned into desert every year.
- For 1992–2000, the annual population growth rate has been estimated at 3%—the highest in the world.

POLITICS AND CONFLICTS

- The emergence of a free South Africa in 1994 is a milestone in the history of humankind.
- Since 1990, 27 multiparty presidential elections have been held—21 for the first time.
- In 31 countries, opposition parties have been legalized.

- In 1994, there were 16 governments representing a single-party system or a military regime.
- At the end of 1993, more than six million people, or more than 1% of the population, were refugees.

Balance sheet of human development—Arab States

PLUS   MINUS

HEALTH

- In 12 of the 19 countries in the region, life expectancy is more than 65 years, compared with an average of 45 years in 1960.

- Less than three-fifths of the rural population have access to safe water, and only half have access to basic sanitation facilities.

EDUCATION

- During the past two decades, adult literacy rate nearly doubled, rising from 30% in 1970 to 54% in 1992.
- The combined primary and secondary enrollment increased nearly sixfold, from 8 million to 46 million, between 1960 and 1991.

- About 80 million people are illiterate.
- Nine million children are out of primary school, and 15 million are out of secondary school.

INCOME AND POVERTY

- During 1974 and 1992, real GDP grew by nearly 40%.
- The agricultural growth rate of 4.7% a year during the past decade was the highest in the developing regions.

- About 73 million people still lived below the poverty line in 1990, and more than 10 million people were underfed.
- Defense spending increased from 5% of GDP in 1960 to 12% of GDP in 1989.

WOMEN

- Between 1970 and 1991, the gender gap in enrollment at the secondary level was reduced form 54% to 32%, and that at the tertiary level from 65% to 35%—the fastest closing of such gaps in the developing world.
- About 30% of the women enrolled at the tertiary level are in natural and applied sciences.

- Only 17% of Arab women participate in the formal labor force.
- Women hold only 4% of parliamentary seats, well below the 10% average in the developing world.

CHILDREN

- Between 1960 and 1992, the infant mortality rate declined by more than three-fifths, from 165 per thousand live births to 64.
- More than three-fourths of one-year-olds are immunized.

- At 83 per thousand live births, the under-five mortality rate is still more than five times higher than that in industrial countries.

ENVIRONMENT

- Between 1965 and 1991, energy use per $100 of GDP declined by two-thirds, from 228 kilograms of oil equivalent to 76 kilograms.

- With less than 1,000 cubic meters of water per capita available each year, about 55% of the people experience serious water scarcity.

POLITICS AND CONFLICTS

- Since 1990, three countries (Jordan, Lebanon and Morocco) have undertaken political reforms to strengthen their multiparty systems.

- At the end of 1993, more than one million people were refugees.

386

Balance sheet of human development—East Asia and South-East Asia and the Pacific

PLUS	MINUS

HEALTH

- By 1992, life expectancy in East Asia and South-East Asia and the Pacific was nearly 85% that in industrial countries. At 71 years, life expectancy in East Asia (excluding China) is only five years less than that in the industrial world.

- More than two million people have been infected with HIV.
- In South-East Asia and the Pacific, rural access to safe water at 47%, and that to basic sanitation at 38%, are only two-thirds of urban access.

EDUCATION

- During 1960–91, the tertiary enrollment ratio in South-East Asia and the Pacific quadrupled—from 4% in 1960 to 16.1% in 1991.

- In East Asia, more than 100 million boys and girls are out of school at the secondary level.

INCOME AND POVERTY

- During the 1980s, the per capita real GDP in East Asia increased more than 6% a year—a growth rate nearly three times higher than that in industrial countries.

- In East Asia, nearly 170 million people were below the poverty line in 1990.

WOMEN

- At 43%, the share of women in the labor force in East Asia is higher than that in industrial countries.
- The 19% female representation in parliaments in East Asia is 1.6 times the representation in the industrial world.

- Female enrollment at the tertiary level in East and South-East Asia is still three-fourths the male enrollment ratio.
- The maternal mortality rate in South-East Asia and the Pacific, at 295 per 100,000 live births, is more than three times higher than that in East Asia, at 92 per 100,000 live births.

CHILDREN

- Infant mortality in East Asia declined by 70% in 1960–92, from 146 per thousand live births to 42.

- More than a third of the children under five are malnourished in South-East Asia and the Pacific.

POPULATION AND ENVIRONMENT

- Between 1960 and 1992, fertility rates declined more in East and South-East Asia and the Pacific than in industrial countries.

- In East Asia (excluding China), the urban population is expected to grow to 79% of the total population in the year 2000—more than double the 36% share in 1960—leading to mounting pressure on physical facilities.

ENVIRONMENT

- In South-East Asia and the Pacific between 1965 and 1991, energy use per $100 of GDP declined by three-fourths, from 137 kilograms of oil equivalent to 37 kilograms.

- During 1981–90, more than 3 million hectares of tropical forest were lost in South-East Asia and the Pacific.
- Air pollution is a major problem in the region. In Bangkok alone, 800 motor vehicles are added each day.

POLITICS AND CONFLICTS

- Since 1980, more than 30 general elections have been held at the national level.

- At the end of 1993, more than half a million people in these regions were refugees.

Source: *Human Development Report*

APPENDIXES

APPENDIX I: SOURCES OF GLOBAL STATISTICS

Title of Publication	Name of Organization
Accident/Incident Reporting (ADREP) Annual Statistics	International Civil Aviation Organization
ACP Basic Statistics	European Community
African Socio-economic Indicators 1990-91	United Nations
African Statistical Yearbook 1988-89 Vol I, Part 1 North Africa	United Nations
African Statistical Yearbook 1988-89 Vol I, Part 2 West Africa	United Nations
African Statistical Yearbook 1988-89 Vol II, Part 3 East and Southern Africa	United Nations
African Statistical Yearbook 1988-89 Vol II, Part 4 Central Africa, Others in Africa	European Community
Agricultural Income	European Community
Agricultural Markets: Prices	European Community
Agricultural Prices: Price Indices and Absolute Prices	European Community
Agricultural Prices: Price Indices and Absolute Prices	European Community
Agriculture Statistical Yearbook	Wye College
Agrifacts: A Handbook of UK and EEC Agricultural and Food Statistics	European Community
Animal Production, Quarterly Statistics	United Nations
Annual Bulletin of Coal Statistics for Europe	United Nations
Annual Bulletin of Electric Energy Statistics for Europe	United Nations
Annual Bulletin of Gas Statistics for Europe	United Nations
Annual Bulletin of General Energy Statistics for Europe	United Nations
Annual Bulletin of Housing and Building Statistics for Europe	International Tea Committee
Annual Bulletin of Statistics	United Nations
Annual Bulletin of Steel Statistics for Europe	United Nations
Annual Bulletin of Trade in Chemical Products	United Nations
Annual Bulletin of Transport Statistics for Europe	International Energy Agency
Annual Oil Market Report	International Iron and Steel Institute
Annual Report of the International Iron and Steel Institute	International Tropical Timber Organization
Annual Review and Assessment of the World Tropical Timber Situation	Lloyds Register of Shipping
Annual Summary of Merchant Ships Completed	European Community
Areas Under Vines, Results of the Annual Surveys	Association of South-East Asian Nations Secretariat
ASEAN Selected Statistics	Association of European Airlines
Association of European Airlines Yearbook	International Monetary Fund
Balance of Payments Statistical Yearbook, Part I	International Monetary Fund
Balance of Payments Statistical Yearbook, Part 11	European Community
Balance of Payments: Geographical Breakdown	Organization for Economic Co-operation and Development
Balances of Payments of OECD Countries	Organization for Economic Co-operation and Development
Bank Profitability: Statistical Supplement—Financial Statements of Banks	Chemical Industries Association
Basic International Chemical Industry Statistics	Organization for Economic Co-operation and Development
Basic Science and Technology	Commonwealth Secretariat
Basic Statistical Data on Selected Countries	European Community
Basic Statistics of the Community	Generation Publications
The Best 'N' Most in DFS	British Petroleum Company Plc
BP Review of World Gas	British Petroleum Company Plc
BP Statistical Review of World Energy	International Dairy Federation
Bulletin-Consumption Statistics for Milk and Milk Products	Bulletin de IOIV
Bulletin de IOIV	International Labour Organization
Bulletin of Labour Statistics	World Health Organization
Bulletin of Regional Health Information	United Nations
Bulletin of Statistics on World Trade in Engineering Products	International Lead and Zinc Study Group
Bulletin of the Lead and Zinc Study Group: Lead and Zinc Statistics	International Agency for Research on Cancer
Cancer Incidence in Five Continents	Caribbean Community Secretariat
Caricom's Trade	European Community
Carriage of Goods - Inland Waterways	European Community
Carriage of Goods—Railways	European Community
Carriage of Goods—Road	Lloyds Register of Shipping
Casualty Return	European Community
Censuses of Population in the Community Countries 1981-82	International Civil Aviation Organization
Civil Aviation Statistics of the World, Doc 9180	World Meteorological Organization
Climatological Normals (CLINO) for CLIMAT and CLIMAT Ship Stations	International Energy Agency
Coal Information	E D & F Man Cocoa Limited
Cocoa Market Report	Vienna Institute for Comparative Economic Studies
Comecon Data	United Nations
Commodity Trade Statistics	European Community
Community Survey of Orchard Fruit Trees	Asian Productivity Organization
Comparative Information on Productivity Levels and Changes in APO Member Countries	United Nations
Compendium of Social Statistics and Indicators	United Nations
Compendium of Statistics and Indicators on the Situation of Women	World Tourism Organization
Compendium of Tourism Statistics	United Nations
Construction Statistics Yearbook	European Community
Consumer Price Index	European Community
Consumer Prices in the EEC	International Cotton Advisory Committee
Cotton: Review of the World Situation	

Title of Publication	Name of Organization
Cotton: World Statistics, Bulletin of the International Cotton Advisory Committee	International Cotton Advisory Committee
Country Reports, Central and Eastern Europe	European Community
Country Statements	International Textile Manufacturers Federation
Crop Production, Quarterly Statistics	European Community
Demographic Statistics	European Community
Demographic Trends in OECD Member Countries	Organization for Economic Co-operation and Development
Demographic Yearbook	United Nations
Digest of Statistics No 379, Series T—No 50, Traffic—Commercial Air Carriers	International Civil Aviation Organization
Digest of Statistics No 381, Series OFOD—No 44, On Flight Origin and Destination	International Civil Aviation Organization
Digest of Statistics No 382, Series R—No 30, Civil Aircraft on Register	International Civil Aviation Organization
Digest of Statistics No 383, Series AT—No 31, Airport Traffic	International Civil Aviation Organization
Digest of Statistics No 385, Series FP—No 44, Fleet—Personnel, Commercial Air Carriers	International Civil Aviation Organization
Digest of Statistics No 397, Series F—No 45, Financial Data, Commercial Air Carriers	International Civil Aviation Organization
Digest of Statistics No 398, Series TF—No 10, Traffic By Flight Stage	International Civil Aviation Organization
Digest of Statistics No 399, Series AF—No 9, Airport and Route Facilities, Financial Data and Summary Traffic Data	International Civil Aviation Organization
Digest of Statistics on Social Protection in Europe, Vol 1, Old Age	European Community
Digest of Statistics on Social Protection in Europe, Vol 2 Invalidity/Disability	European Community
A Digest of Trade Statistics	Caribbean Community Secretariat
Direction of Trade Statistics	International Monetary Fund
Direction of Trade Statistics Yearbook	International Monetary Fund
Distribution of Seats Between Men and Women in National Parliaments. Statistical Data from 1945 to 30 June 1991	Inter-Parliamentary Union
Earnings in Agriculture	European Community
Earnings, Industry and Services	European Community
EC Dairy Facts and Figures	Milk Marketing Board
EC External Trade Indices	European Community
Economic Accounts for Agriculture	Organization for Economic Co-operation and Development
Economic Accounts for Agriculture and Forestry	European Community
Economically Active Population 1950-2025, Vol I Asia	International Labour Organization
Economically Active Population 1950-2025, Vol II Africa	International Labour Organization
Economically Active Population 1950-2025, Vol III Latin America	International Labour Organization
Economically Active Population 1950-2025, Vol IV Northern America, Europe, Oceania and USSR	International Labour Organization
Economically Active Population 1950-2025, Vol V World	International Labour Organization
The Economies of the Arabian Gulf: A Statistical Source Book	Croom Helm Limited
ECU-EMS Information	European Community
Education at a Glance	Organization for Economic Co-operation and Development
Education in OECD Countries	Organization for Economic Co-operation and Development
EFTA Trade	European Free Trade Association
Electricity Prices	European Community
Electricity Supply in the OECD	International Energy Agency
Employment and Unemployment	European Community
Energy Balance Sheets	European Community
Energy Balances and Electricity Profiles	United Nations
Energy Balances of OECD Countries 1980-89	International Energy Agency
Energy Balances of OECD Countries 1990-91	International Energy Agency
Energy, Monthly Statistics	European Community
Energy Prices	European Community
Energy Prices and Taxes	International Energy Agency
Energy Statistics and Balances of Non-OECD Countries	International Energy Agency
Energy Statistics of OECD Countries 1980-89	International Energy Agency
Energy Statistics of OECD Countries 1989-90	International Energy Agency
Energy Statistics Yearbook	United Nations
Energy Yearly Statistics	European Community
The Environment in Europe and North America: Annotated Statistics 1992	United Nations
Environment Statistics	European Community
Euro Trends Survey	Pannell Kerr Forster
Europe in Figures	European Community
European Aluminium Statistics	European Aluminum Association
European Handbook, EEC and International Statistics	Meat and Livestock Commission
European Marketing Data and Statistics	Euromonitor
European Paper Institute Annual Statistics	European Paper Institute
European Supplies Bulletin	Sea Fish Industry Authority
Eurostatistics—Data for Short-term Economic Analysis, No 5	European Community
External Debt Statistics: The Debt and Other External Liabilities of Developing, Central and Eastern European and Certain Other Countries and Territories at end December 1988 and end December 1989	Organization for Economic Co-operation and Development
External Debt Statistics: The Debt and Other External Liabilities of Developing, CMEA and Certain Other Countries and Territories at end December 1987 and end December 1988	Organization for Economic Co-operation and Development
External Trade: Analytical Tables A-L, Imports and Exports	European Community
External Trade and Balance of Payments	European Community
External Trade Statistical Yearbook	European Community
External Trade, System of Generalized Tariff Preferences, Imports 1988, Vol I	European Community
External Trade, System of Generalized Tariff Preferences, Imports: 1988, Vol II	European Community
Facts and Figures	European Patent Office
Family Budgets: Comparative Tables, Vols I and II	European Community
Family Planning and Child Survival Programs as Assessed in 1991	The Population Council
FAO Production Yearbook	Food and Agriculture Organization
FAO Trade Yearbook	Food and Agriculture Organization
FAO Yearbook of Fishery Statistics: Catches and Landings	Food and Agriculture Organization
FAO Yearbook of Fishery Statistics: Commodities	Food and Agriculture Organization

Title of Publication	Name of Organization
Farm Structure 1985 Survey: Main Results	European Community
Farm Structure: 1985 Survey Analysis of Results. Economic Size and Other Gainful Activities	European Community
Farm Structure: 1985 Survey Analysis of Results. Regional Structure of Agricultural Production	European Community
Fatal Accident Statistics for Passenger Air Transport Services CAA Paper 83014	Civil Aviation Authority
Fearnley's Review	Fearnleys Review
Fertilizer Yearbook	Food and Agriculture Organization
Financial Market Trends	Organization for Economic Co-operation and Development
Fisheries, Yearly Statistics	European Community
Flows and Stocks of Fixed Capital: 1964-89	Organization for Economic Co-operation and Development
The Food Aid Monitor: World Food Aid Flows, Transport and Logistics	World Food Programme
Food Aid Shipments	International Wheat Council
Food Consumption Statistics	Organization for Economic Co-operation and Development
Foreign Trade by Commodities, Vols I to V, Series C	Organization for Economic Co-operation and Development
Foreign Trade Statistics for Africa, Direction of Trade Series A	United Nations
Foreign Trade Statistics of Asia and the Pacific	United Nations
Forestry Statistics	European Community
Gas Prices	European Community
General Government Accounts and Statistics	European Community
Geographical Distribution of Financial Flows to Developing Countries, Disbursements, Commitments, Economic Indicators: 1986–89	Organization for Economic Co-operation and Development
Government Finance Statistics Yearbook	International Monetary Fund
Government Financing of Research and Development	European Community
Grain Market Report	International Wheat Council
Handbook of Industrial Statistics	United Nations Industrial Development Organization
Handbook of International Trade and Development Statistics	United Nations Conference on Trade and Development
Human Development Report	United Nations
Human Settlements Basic Statistics	United Nations
IBA Quarterly Review	International Bauxite Association
Indicators of Industrial Activity	Organization for Economic Co-operation and Development
Industrial Production Quarterly Statistics	European Community
Industrial Property Statistics, Part I, Patents	World Intellectual Property Organization
Industrial Property Statistics, Part II Trademarks and Service Marks, Utility Models, Industrial Designs, Varieties of Plants, Micro-organisms	World Intellectual Property Organization
Industrial Property Statistics, Publication A (Supplement to Industrial Property) No 11	World Intellectual Property Organization
Industrial Statistics Yearbook, Vol I General Industrial Statistics	United Nations
Industrial Statistics Yearbook, Vol II Commodity Production Statistics	United Nations
Industrial Structure Statistics	Organization for Economic Co-operation and Development
Industrial Trends Monthly Statistics	European Community
Industry Statistical Yearbook	European Community
Information on Man-made Fibres	Comite International de la Rayonne et des Fibres Synthetiques
International Cocoa Organization Annual Report	International Cocoa Council Organization
International Comparisons of Energy Data	European Community
International Cotton Industry Statistics	International Textile Manufacturers Federation
International Direct Investment Statistics Yearbook	Organization for Economic Co-operation and Development
International Financial Statistics	International Monetary Fund
International Financial Statistics Yearbook	International Monetary Fund
International Historical Statistics, Africa and Asia	Macmillan Press Limited
International Historical Statistics, The Americas and Australia	Macmillan Press Limited
International Historical Statistics, Europe 1750-1988	Macmillan Press Limited
The International Markets for Meat	General Agreement on Tariffs and Trade
The International Markets for Meat. Arrangement Regarding Bovine Meat 12th Annual Report	General Agreement on Tariffs and Trade
International Molasses and Alcohol Report	F O Licht
International Narcotics Control Board—Narcotic Drugs, Estimated World Requirement Statistics for 1990	United Nations
International North Pacific Fisheries Commission Statistical Yearbook	International North Pacific Fisheries Commission
International Narcotics Control Board—Psychotropic Substances, Statistics for 1990	United Nations
International Pacific Halibut Commission, Annual Report	International Pacific Halibut Commission
International Sea-borne Trade Statistics: Yearbook 1984-85	United Nations
International Railway Statistics, Statistics of Individual Railways	International Union of Railways
International Steel Statistics Summary Tables	Iron and Steel Statistics Bureau
International Sugar and Sweetener Report	F O Licht
International Textile Machinery Shipment Statistics	International Textile Manufacturers Federation
International Trade Statistics Vol I	General Agreement on Tariffs and Trade
International Trade Statistics Vol II	General Agreement on Tariffs and Trade
International Trade Statistics Yearbook, Vol I Trade by Country	United Nations
International Trade Statistics Yearbook, Vol II Trade by Commodit	United Nations
International Whaling Statistics	International Whaling Commission
Intra-European Country to Country Traffic	Association of European Airlines
Iron and Manganese Ore Databook	Metal Bulletin Books Limited
The Iron and Steel Industry	Organization for Economic Co-operation and Development
Iron and Steel, Yearly Statistics	European Community
Joint Production of Lead and Zinc	International Lead and Zinc Study Group
Know More About Oil, World Statistics	Institute of Petroleum
Labour Force Survey, Results 1991	European Community
Labour Force Statistics	Organization for Economic Co-operation and Development
The Livestock and Meat Market	United Nations
Living Conditions in OECD Countries: Compendium of Social Indicators	Organization for Economic Co-operation and Development
Main Economic Indicators	Organization for Economic Co-operation and Development
Main Economic Indicators, Historical Statistics	Organization for Economic Co-operation and Development
Main Economic Indicators, Historical Statistics: Prices Labour and Wages 1962–91	Organization for Economic Co-operation and Development
Main Science and Technology Indicators	Organization for Economic Co-operation and Development

Title of Publication	Name of Organization
Maritime Transport	Organization for Economic Co-operation and Development
Meat Balances in OECD Countries	Organization for Economic Co-operation and Development
Medium-Term Forecast of European Scheduled Passenger Traffic	Association of European Airline
Merchant Shipbuilding Return	Lloyds Register of Shipping
Metal Bulletin's Prices and Data	Metal Bulletin Books Limited
Metals and Minerals, The Safer World of SGS	Mining Journal
Milk Quotas—their Effects on Agriculture in the European Community, Vol 1 Main Report	European Community
Milk Quotas—their Effects on Agriculture in the European Community, Vol 2 Annex	European Community
Money and Finance	European Community
Monthly Bulletin of Statistics	United Nations
Monthly Crude Iron and Steel Production	International Iron and Steel Institute
Monthly Statistical Review	Society of Motor Manufacturers and Traders Limited
Monthly Statistics of Foreign Trade, Series A	Organization for Economic Co-operation and Development
Motor Industry of Great Britain: World Automotive Statistics	Society of Motor Manufacturers and Traders Limited
National Accounts ESA Aggregates	European Community
National Accounts ESA Detailed Tables by Branch	European Community
National Accounts ESA Detailed Tables by Sector	European Community
National Accounts ESA Input-Output Tables	European Community
National Accounts Statistics: Analysis of Main Aggregates 1988–89	United Nations
National Accounts Statistics: Compendium of Income Distribution Statistics	United Nations
National Accounts Statistics: Main Aggregates and Detailed Tables Parts I and II	United Nations
National Accounts, Vol I Main Aggregates	Organization for Economic Co-operation and Development
National Accounts, Vol 11 Detailed Tables	Organization for Economic Co-operation and Development
National and International Tourism Statistics	Organization for Economic Co-operation and Development
The North Atlantic Treaty Organization 1949-89, Facts and Figures	North Atlantic Treaty Organization
Nuclear Energy Data	Organization for Economic Co-operation and Development
OECD Economic Outlook Historical Statistics	Organization for Economic Co-operation and Development
OECD Environmental Data Compendium	Organization for Economic Co-operation and Development
OECD Financial Statistics Part 1 Section 1 International Markets	Organization for Economic Co-operation and Development
OECD Financial Statistics Part 1 Section 2 Domestic Markets Interest Rates	Organization for Economic Co-operation and Development
OECD Financial Statistics Part 2 Financial Accounts of OECD Countries	Organization for Economic Co-operation and Development
OECD Financial Statistics Part 3 Non-Financial Enterprises Financial Statements	Organization for Economic Co-operation and Development
Oil and Energy Trends	Basil Blackwell Limited
Oil and Energy Trends, Annual Statistical Review	Basil Blackwell Limited
Oil and Gas Information	International Energy Agency
Oil World	Ista Mielk Gmbh
Oil World Annual	Ista Mielk Gmbh
Oil, Chemical and Combined Carriers	E A Gibson Shipbrokers Limited
OPEC Annual Statistical Bulletin	Organization of Petroleum Exporting Countries
OPEC Bulletin	Organization of Petroleum Exporting Countries
Operating Experience with Nuclear Power Stations in Member States in 1990	International Atomic Energy Agency
Operation of Nuclear Power Stations	European Community
Platinum	Johnson Matthey
Pocket Profiles	Inter-American Development Bank
Population and Vital Statistics Report	United Nations
Portrait of the Regions: Vol I Germany Benelux Denmark, Vol II France, United Kingdom, Ireland, Vol III Portugal, Spain, Italy	European Community
Price Structure of the Community Countries in 1985	European Community
Prices of Agricultural Products and Selected Inputs in Europe and North America	United Nations
The Pulp and Paper Industry	Organization for Economic Co-operation and Development
Pulp and Paper International Annual Review	Pulp and Paper International
The Purchasing Power of Working Time. An International Comparison	International Metalworkers' Federation
Purchasing Power Parities and Real Expenditures	Organization for Economic Co-operation and Development
Quarterly Bulletin of Cocoa Statistics	International Cocoa Council Organization
Quarterly Bulletin of Statistics	Food and Agriculture Organization
Quarterly Labour Force Statistics	Organization for Economic Co-operation and Development
Quarterly Market Review	International Sugar Organization
Quarterly National Accounts	Organization for Economic Co-operation and Development
Quarterly National Accounts ESA	European Community
Quarterly Oil Statistics and Energy Balances	International Energy Agency
Raw Material EC Supply	European Community
Recent Demographic Developments in Europe	Council of Europe
Reference Tables	British Paper and Board Industry Federation
Regions Statistical Yearbook	European Community
Register of Liquified Gas Carriers	E A Gibson Shipbrokers Limited
Report of the UN High Commissioner for Refugees. General Assembly Official Records: 46th Session, Supplement No 12	United Nations
Report for the Crop Year	International Wheat Council
Results of the Business Survey Carried Out Among Managements in the Community	European Community
Retail Price Indices, Statistical Bulletin of the South Pacific	South Pacific Commission
Retailing in the European Single Market 1993	European Community
Revenue Statistics of OECD Member Countries	Organization for Economic Co-operation and Development
Review of Fisheries in OECD Member Countries	Organization for Economic Co-operation and Development
Review of Maritime Transport	United Nations Conference on Trade and Development
Rubber Statistical Bulletin	International Rubber Study Group
Services: Statistics on International Transactions	Organization for Economic Co-operation and Development
Shipping Statistics	Institute of Shipping Economics and Logistics
Shipping Statistics and Economics	Drewry Shipping Consultants Limited
Shipping Statistics Yearbook	Institute of Shipping Economics and Logistics
Shipping Trade, Trends and Statistics	Drewry Shipping Consultants Limited

Title of Publication	Name of Organization
Short-term Review of International Pulp and Paper Markets	Jaakko Poyry
Silicon Carbide	Elsevier Advanced Technology
Situation de la Production Laitiere et du Controle Laitier dans les Organismes Pays Members	Federation Nationale des de Controle Laitier
Social Indicators of Development	The World Bank
A Social Portrait of Europe	European Community
Social Protection Expenditure and Receipts	European Community
South Pacific Economies	South Pacific Commission
Standardized Input-Output Tables of ECE Countries for Years Around 1975	United Nations
The State of the World's Children	United Nations Children's Fund
Statistical Appendices to AEA Yearbook	Association of European Airlines
Statistical Brief	Chamber of Shipping
Statistical Bulletin	International Commission for the Conservation of Atlantic Tunas
Statistical Bulletin	International Sugar Organization
Statistical Bulletin, Fishery Statistics for 1988	North West Atlantic Fisheries Organization
Statistical Indicators for Asia and the Pacific	United Nations
Statistical Report on Road Accidents	European Conference of Ministers of Transport
Statistical Trends in Transport	European Conference of Ministers of Transport
Statistical Yearbook for Asia and the Pacific	United Nations
Statistical Yearbook for Latin America and the Caribbean	United Nations
Statistics and Indicators on Women in Africa	United Nations
Statistics of Road Traffic Accidents in Europe	United Nations
Statistics of World Trade in Steel	United Nations
Statistics on Children in UNICEF Assisted Countries	United Nations Children's Fund
Statistics on Housing in the European Community	Ministry of Housing, Physical Planning and the Environment (Netherlands)
Steel Consumption by User Branch	European Community
The Steel Market in 1991	United Nations
Steel Market in 1991 and the Outlook for 1992	Organization for Economic Co-operation and Development
Steel Statistics of Developing Countries	International Iron and Steel Institute
Steel Statistical Yearbook	International Iron and Steel Institute
Structure and Activity of Industry: Annual Enquiry Main Results	European Community
Structure and Activity of Industry: Data by Regions	European Community
Structure and Activity of Industry: Data by Size of Enterprises	European Community
Sugar Yearbook	International Sugar Organization
Tanker Charter Record	Basil Blackwell Limited
Telecommunications: Profile of the Worldwide Telecommunications Industry	Elsevier Advanced Technology
Tourism Annual Statistics	European Community
Tourism in Europe, Trends	European Community
Tourism Policy and International Tourism in OECD Member Countries	Organization for Economic Co-operation and Development
Transport and Communications Annual Statistics	European Community
Travel and Tourism Barometer	World Tourism Organization
Trends in Developing Economies	The World Bank
Trends in the Hotel Industry	Pannell Kerr Forster
Trends in the Transport Sector	European Conference of Ministers of Transport
Tungsten Statistics	United Nations Conference on Trade and Development
UN Statistical Yearbook	United Nations
UNCTAD Commodity Yearbook	United Nations Conference on Trade and Development
UNCTAD Statistical Pocket Book	United Nations Conference on Trade and Development
Unemployment	European Community
UNHCR Activities Financed by Voluntary Funds. Report for 1990-91 and Proposed Programmes and Budget for 1992.	United Nations
Part 1: Africa	
Part 2: Asia and Oceania	
Part 3: Europe and North America	
Part 4: Latin America	
Part 5: South West Asia, North Africa and the Middle East	
Part 6: Overall Allocations	
Uranium—Resources, Production and Demand	Organization for Economic Co-operation and Development
Urea Statistics	International Fertilizer Industry Association
Western European Living Costs	Confederation of British Industry
Women and Political Power Survey carried out among the National Parliaments existing as from 31.10.91	Inter-Parliamentary Union
Wool Facts 1991-92	International Wool Secretariat
World Air Transport Statistics	International Air Transport Association
World Bulk Fleet	Fearnleys
World Bulk Trades	Fearnleys
The World Cocoa Market: An Analysis of Recent Trends and of Prospects to the Year 2000	International Cocoa Council Organization
World Crop and Livestock Statistics	Food and Agriculture Organization
World Debt Tables, Vol 1, Analysis and Summary Tables	The World Bank
World Debt Tables, Vol 2, External Finance for Developing Countries, Country Tables	The World Bank
World Energy Statistics and Balances	International Energy Agency
World Fleet Statistics	Lloyds Register of Shipping
World Footwear Markets	Satra Footwear Technology Centre
World Health Statistics Annual	World Health Organization
World Investment Directory Vol I Asia and the Pacific	United Nations
World Investment Directory Vol II Central and Eastern Europe	United Nations
The World Market for Dairy Products	General Agreement on Tariffs and Trade
World Metal Statistics	World Bureau of Metal Statistics
World Metal Statistics Quarterly Summary	World Bureau of Metal Statistics

Title of Publication	Name of Organization
World Metal Statistics Yearbook	World Bureau of Metal Statistics
World Mineral Statistics Vol 1 Metals and Energy	British Geological Survey
World Mineral Statistics Vol 2 Industrial Minerals	British Geological Survey
World Oil Trade Review of International Oil Movements	Basil Blackwell Limited
World Population Projections	The World Bank
World Population Prospects	United Nations
World Rice Statistics, 1987	International Rice Research Institute
World Road Statistics, 1986–90	World Road Federation
Worldwide Rubber Statistics	International Institute of Synthetic Rubber Producers
World Rubber Statistics Handbook	International Rubber Study Group
World Stainless Steel Statistics	World Bureau of Metal Statistics
World Statistics in Brief, United Nations Statistical Pocketbook	United Nations
World Steel in Figures	International Iron and Steel Institute
World Sugar and Sweetener Yearbook	F O Licht
World Tables	The World Bank
World Trade Stainless, High Speed and Other Alloy Steel	Iron and Steel Statistics Bureau
World Trade Steel	Iron and Steel Statistics Bureau
World Transport Data	International Road Transport Union
Worldwide Hotel Industry	Horwath International
Yearbook of Common Carrier Telecommunications Statistics	International Telecommunication Union
Yearbook of Forest Products	Food and Agriculture Organization
Yearbook of International Horticultural Statistics	International Association of Horticultural Statistics
Yearbook of Labour Statistics	International Labour Organization
Yearbook of Nordic Statistics	Nordic Council of Ministers and the Nordic Statistical Secretariat
Yearbook of Tourism Statistics, Vol 1	World Tourism Organization
Yearbook of Tourism Statistics, Vol 2	World Tourism Organization

APPENDIX II: CLASSIFICATION OF COUNTRIES

Countries in the human development aggregates

High Human Development

Antigua and Barbuda
Argentina
Australia
Austria
Bahamas
Bahrain
Barbados
Belarus
Belgium
Belize
Brazil
Brunei
Canada
Chile
Colombia
Costa Rica
Cyprus
Czech Rep.
Denmark
Estonia
Fiji
Finland
France
Germany
Greece
Hong Kong
Hungary
Iceland
Ireland
Israel
Italy
Japan
Korea, Rep. of
Kuwait
Latvia
Luxembourg
Malaysia
Malta
Mauritius
Mexico
Netherlands
New Zealand
Norway
Panama
Poland
Portugal
Qatar
Russia
Saint Kitts and Nevis
Seychelles
Singapore
Slovakia
Spain
Sweden
Switzerland
Thailand
Trinidad and Tobago
Ukraine
United Arab Emirates
United Kingdom
Uruguay
USA
Venezuela

Medium Human Development

Albania
Algeria
Armenia
Azerbaijan
Bolivia
Botswana
Bulgaria
Cameroon
Cape Verde
China
Congo
Cuba
Dominica
Dominican Rep
Ecuador
Egypt
El Salvador
Gabon
Georgia
Grenada
Guatemala
Guyana
Honduras
Indonesia
Iran
Iraq
Jamaica
Jordan
Kazakhstan
Korea, North
Kyrgyzstan
Lebanon
Libya
Lithuania
Maldives
Moldova
Mongolia
Morocco
Namibia
Nicaragua
Oman
Papua New Guinea
Paraguay
Peru
Philippines
Romania
Saint Lucia
Saint Vincent
Samoa (Western)
Saudi Arabia
Solomon Islands
South Africa
Sri Lanka
Suriname
Swaziland
Syria
Tajikistan
Tunisia
Turkey
Turkmenistan
Uzbekistan
Vanuatu
Vietnam
Zimbabwe

Low Human Development

Afghanistan
Angola
Bangladesh
Benin
Bhutan
Burkina
Burundi
Cambodia
Central African Rep.
Chad
Comoros
Cote d'Ivoire
Djibouti
Equatorial Guinea
Ethiopia
Gambia
Ghana
Guinea
Guinea-Bissau
Haiti
India
Kenya
Laos
Lesotho
Liberia
Madagascar
Malawi
Mali
Mauritania
Mozambique
Myanmar
Nepal
Niger
Nigeria
Pakistan
Rwanda
Sao Tome and Principe
Senegal
Sierra Leone
Somalia
Sudan
Tanzania
Togo
Uganda
Yemen
Zaire
Zambia

Countries in the income aggregates

High-Income
(GNP per capita above $8,625)

Australia
Austria
Bahamas
Belgium
Brunei
Canada
Cyprus
Denmark
Finland
France
Germany
Hong Kong
Iceland
Ireland
Israel
Italy
Japan
Kuwait
Luxembourg
Netherlands
New Zealand
Norway
Qatar
Singapore
Spain
Sweden
Switzerland
United Arab Emirates
United Kingdom
USA

Middle-Income
(GNP per capita $696 to $8,625)

Algeria
Angola
Antigua and Barbuda
Argentina
Armenia
Azerbaijan
Bahrain
Barbados
Belarus
Belize
Bolivia
Botswana
Brazil
Bulgaria
Cameroon
Cape Verde
Chile
Colombia
Congo
Costa Rica
Cuba
Czech Rep.
Djibouti
Dominica
Dominican Rep.
Ecuador
El Salvador
Estonia
Fiji
Gabon
Georgia
Greece
Grenada
Guatemala
Hungary
Iran
Iraq
Jamaica
Jordan
Kazakhstan
Korea, North
Korea, Rep. of
Kyrgyzstan
Latvia
Lebanon
Libya
Lithuania
Malaysia
Maldives
Malta
Mauritius
Mexico
Moldova
Morocco
Namibia
Oman
Panama
Papua New Guinea
Paraguay
Peru
Philippines
Poland
Portugal
Romania
Russia
Saint Kitts and Nevis
Saint Lucia
Saint Vincent
Samoa (Western)
Saudi Arabia
Senegal
Seychelles
Slovakia
Solomon Islands
South Africa

Suriname
Swaziland
Syria
Thailand
Trinidad and Tobago
Tunisia
Turkey
Turkmenistan
Ukraine
Uruguay
Uzbekistan
Vanuatu
Venezuela

Low-Income
(GNP per capita $695 and below)

Afghanistan
Albania
Bangladesh
Benin
Bhutan
Burkina
Burundi
Cambodia
Central African Rep.
Chad
China
Comoros
Cote d'Ivoire
Egypt
Equatorial Guinea
Ethiopia
Gambia
Ghana
Guinea
Guinea-Bissau
Guyana
Haiti
Honduras
India
Indonesia
Kenya
Laos
Lesotho
Liberia
Madagascar
Malawi
Mali
Mauritania
Mongolia
Mozambique
Myanmar
Nepal
Nicaragua
Niger
Nigeria
Pakistan
Rwanda
Sao Tome and Principe
Sierra Leone
Somalia
Sri Lanka
Sudan
Tajikistan
Tanzania
Togo
Uganda
Vietnam
Yemen
Zaire
Zambia
Zimbabwe

Countries in the major world aggregates

Least Developed Countries

Afghanistan
Angola
Bangladesh
Benin
Bhutan
Burkina
Burundi
Cambodia
Cape Verde
Central African Rep.
Chad
Comoros
Djibouti
Equatorial Guinea
Ethiopia
Gambia
Guinea
Guinea-Bissau
Haiti
Laos
Lesotho
Liberia
Madagascar
Malawi
Maldives
Mali
Mauritania
Mozambique
Myanmar
Nepal
Niger
Rwanda
Samoa (Western)
Sao Tome and Principe
Sierra Leone
Solomon Islands
Somalia
Sudan
Tanzania
Togo
Uganda
Vanuatu
Yemen
Zaire
Zambia

All Developing Countries

Afghanistan
Algeria
Angola
Antigua and Barbuda
Argentina
Bahamas
Bahrain
Bangladesh
Barbados
Belize
Benin
Bhutan
Bolivia
Botswana
Brazil
Brunei
Burkina
Burundi
Cambodia
Cameroon
Cape Verde
Central African Rep.
Chad
Chile
China
Colombia
Comoros
Congo
Costa Rica
Cote d'Ivoire
Cuba
Cyprus
Djibouti
Dominica
Dominican Rep.
Ecuador
Egypt
El Salvador
Equatorial Guinea

Ethiopia
Fiji
Gabon
Gambia
Ghana
Grenada
Guatemala
Guinea
Guinea-Bissau
Guyana
Haiti
Honduras
Hong Kong
India
Indonesia
Iran
Iraq
Jamaica
Jordan
Kenya
Korea, North
Korea, Rep. of
Kuwait
Laos
Lebanon
Lesotho
Liberia
Libya
Madagascar
Malawi
Malaysia
Maldives
Mali
Mauritania
Mauritius
Mexico
Mongolia

Morocco
Mozambique
Myanmar
Namibia
Nepal
Nicaragua
Niger
Nigeria
Oman
Pakistan
Panama
Papua New Guinea
Paraguay
Peru
Philippines
Qatar
Rwanda
Saint Kitts and Nevis
Saint Lucia
Saint Vincent
Samoa (Western)
Sao Tome and Principe
Saudi Arabia
Senegal
Seychelles
Sierra Leone
Singapore
Solomon Islands
Somalia
South Africa
Sri Lanka
Sudan
Suriname
Swaziland
Syria
Tanzania
Thailand
Togo
Trinidad and Tobago

Tunisia
Turkey
Uganda
United Arab Emirates
Uruguay
Vanuatu
Venezuela
Vietnam
Yemen
Zaire
Zambia
Zimbabwe

Industrial Countries

Albania
Armenia
Australia
Austria
Azerbaijan
Belarus
Belgium
Bulgaria
Canada
Czech Rep.
Denmark
Estonia
Finland
France
Georgia
Germany
Greece
Hungary
Iceland
Ireland
Israel
Italy
Japan
Kazakhstan
Kyrgyzstan
Latvia
Lithuania
Luxembourg
Malta
Moldova
Netherlands
New Zealand
Norway
Poland
Portugal
Romania
Russia
Slovakia
Spain
Sweden
Switzerland
Tajikistan
Turkmenistan
Ukraine
United Kingdom
USA
Uzbekistan

Countries in the regional aggregates

Sub-Saharan Africa	Arab States	Asia and the Pacific and Oceania	Latin America the Caribbean and North America	Europe	Europe
		Developing Countries			**Industrial Countries**

Sub-Saharan Africa

Angola
Benin
Botswana
Burkina
Burundi
Cameroon
Cape Verde
Central Africa Rep.
Chad
Comoros
Congo
Cote d'Ivoire
Equatorial Guinea
Ethiopia
Gabon
Gambia
Ghana
Guinea
Guinea-Bissau
Kenya
Lesotho
Liberia
Madagascar
Malawi
Mali
Mauritania
Mauritius
Mozambique
Namibia
Niger
Nigeria
Rwanda
Sao Tome and Principe
Senegal
Seychelles
Sierra Leone
South Africa
Swaziland
Tanzania
Togo
Uganda
Zaire
Zambia
Zimbabwe

Arab States

Algeria
Bahrain
Djibouti
Egypt
Iraq
Jordan
Kuwait
Lebanon
Libya
Morocco
Oman
Qatar
Saudi Arabia
Somalia
Sudan
Syria
Tunisia
United Arab Emirates
Yemen

Asia and the Pacific and Oceania

East Asia
China
Hong Kong
Korea, North
Korea, Rep. of
Mongolia

South-East Asia and the Pacific
Brunei
Cambodia
Fiji
Indonesia
Laos
Malaysia
Myanmar
Papua New Guinea
Philippines
Samoa (Western)
Singapore
Solomon Islands
Thailand
Vanuatu
Vietnam

South Asia
Afghanistan
Bangladesh
Bhutan
India
Iran
Maldives
Nepal
Pakistan
Sri Lanka

Latin America the Caribbean and North America

Latin America and the Caribbean
Antigua and Barbuda
Argentina
Bahamas
Barbados
Belize
Bolivia
Brazil
Chile
Colombia
Costa Rica
Cuba
Dominica
Dominican Rep.
Ecuador
El Salvador
Grenada
Guatemala
Guyana
Haiti
Honduras
Jamaica
Mexico
Nicaragua
Panama
Paraguay
Peru
Saint Kitts and Nevis
Saint Lucia
Saint Vincent
Suriname
Trinidad and Tobago
Uruguay
Venezuela

Europe

Southern Europe
Cyprus
Turkey

Europe

Industrial Countries

Eastern Europe and the Commonwealth of Independent States
Albania
Armenia
Azerbaijan
Belarus
Bulgaria
Czech Rep.
Estonia
Georgia
Hungary
Kazakhstan
Kyrgyastan
Latvia
Lithuania
Moldova
Poland
Romania
Russia
Slovakia
Tajikistan
Turkmenistan
Ukraine
Uzbekistan

Western and Southern Europe
Austria
Belgium
Denmark
Finland
France
Germany
Greece
Iceland
Ireland
Italy
Luxembourg
Malta
Netherlands
Norway
Portugal
Spain
Sweden
Switzerland

Industrial Countries

Australia
Israel
Japan
New Zealand

North America
Canada
USA

Other aggregates

European Union

Austria
Belgium
Denmark
Finland
France
Germany
Greece
Ireland
Italy
Luxembourg
Netherlands
Portugal
Spain
Sweden
United Kingdom

OECD

Australia
Austria
Belgium
Canada
Denmark
Finland
France
Germany
Greece
Iceland
Ireland
Italy
Japan
Luxembourg
Mexico
Netherlands
New Zealand
Norway
Portugal
Spain
Sweden
Switzerland
Turkey
United Kingdom
USA

Nordic Countries

Denmark
Finland
Iceland
Norway
Sweden

INDEX